Better Homes and Gardens®
New
GRILLING
BOOK

CHARCOAL • GAS • SMOKERS
INDOOR GRILLS • TURKEY FRYERS
ROTISSERIES

Meredith® Books
Des Moines, Iowa

Better Homes and Gardens® New Grilling Book
Editor: Jan Miller
Project Editor: Shelli McConnell
Contributing Editors: Janet Figg; Linda J. Henry; Susan Lamb Parenti; Jessica Saari; Kristi Thomas, R.D.;
   Joyce R. Trollope; Mary Williams
Recipe Developers: David Feder, R.D.; Connie Hay; Janet Pittman; Chuck Smothermon
Senior Associate Design Director: Mick Schnepf
Designers: Studio G, Brad and Sundie Ruppert; Tim Abramowitz; Diana Van Winkle
Copy Chief: Terri Fredrickson
Publishing Operations Manager: Karen Schirm
Edit and Design Production Coordinator: Mary Lee Gavin
Editorial Assistants: Cheryl Eckert, Kairee Windsor
Marketing Product Managers: Aparna Pande, Isaac Petersen, Gina Rickert, Stephen Rogers, Brent Wiersma, Tyler Woods
Book Production Managers: Pam Kvitne, Marjorie J. Schenkelberg, Rick von Holdt, Mark Weaver
Contributing Copy Editor: Kim Catanzarite
Contributing Proofreaders: Judy Friedman, Gretchen Kauffman, Donna Segal
Photographers: Blaine Moats, Jay Wilde
Food Stylists: Paige Boyle, Dianna Nolin, Charles Worthington
Prop Stylist: Sue Mitchell
Indexer: Kathleen Poole
Test Kitchen Director: Lynn Blanchard
Test Kitchen Product Supervisor: Juliana Hale
Test Kitchen Home Economists: Marilyn Cornelius; Laura Harms, R.D.; Jennifer Kalinowski, R.D.; Maryellyn Krantz;
   Jill Moberly; Colleen Weeden; Lori Wilson

Meredith® Books
Executive Director, Editorial: Gregory H. Kayko
Executive Director, Design: Matt Strelecki
Publisher and Editor in Chief: James D. Blume

Editorial Director: Linda Raglan Cunningham
Executive Director, Marketing: Jeffrey B. Myers
Executive Director, New Business Development: Todd M. Davis
Executive Director, Sales: Ken Zagor
Director, Operations: George A. Susral
Director, Production: Douglas M. Johnston
Business Director: Jim Leonard

Vice President and General Manager: Douglas J. Guendel

Better Homes and Gardens® **Magazine**
Editor in Chief: Karol DeWulf Nickell
Deputy Editor, Food and Entertaining: Nancy Hopkins

Meredith Publishing Group
President: Jack Griffin
Senior Vice President: Bob Mate

Meredith Corporation
Chairman and Chief Executive Officer: William T. Kerr
President and Chief Operating Officer: Stephen M. Lacy

In Memoriam: E.T. Meredith III (1933–2003)

Our seal assures you that every recipe in the *New Grilling Book* has been tested in the Better Homes and Gardens® Test Kitchen. This means that each recipe is practical and reliable, and meets our high standards of taste appeal. We guarantee your satisfaction with this book for as long as you own it.

All of us at Meredith® Books are dedicated to providing you with the information and ideas you need to create delicious foods. We welcome your comments and suggestions. Write to us at: Meredith Books, Cookbook Editorial Department, 1716 Locust St., Des Moines, IA 50309-3023.

If you would like to purchase any of our cooking, crafts, gardening, home improvement, or home decorating and design books, check wherever quality books are sold. Or visit us at: meredithbooks.com

TABLE OF CONTENTS

FIRE UP YOUR GRILL FOR A SERIOUS WORKOUT.

This is the go-to book for your every grilling need—a grilling universe of know-how and taste sensations published by cooks who really know their stuff. Totally updated, it's full of recipes with the power to please, kicky new flavors, tricks from the experts, timing charts, and in-depth explanations.

Are your tongs rarin' to go? Just wait until they discover taste sensations from across the country and around the globe with recipes such as Kansas City Pork Spareribs, Moroccan-Style Lamb Chops, and Dessert Burritos. And you'll find the answers to many of your questions. What's the difference between various types of molasses? Is a "mop" perfect for a steak? What sets Texas, Memphis, the Carolinas, and Kansas City barbecue apart?

You're on the first page of a glorious adventure in spicy aromas and hot diggity taste with red-hot grilling experiences dead ahead.

Easy Steak and Potato Kabobs (page 164)

Blackened Swordfish with Hominy Dirty Rice (page 326)

Bayou Rotisserie Chicken (page 286)

1

Grilling
Basics

GRILLING BASICS
SPARKING THE FLAME

Cooking over an open flame is as ancient as the cave people. Yet, over the course of its history, grilling has come to be and mean much more than just another way to get food on the table. For some it's an art form; for others, simply an excuse to gather family and friends. Equipment has become state of the art and chefs are experimenting with unusual meats and marinades.

In the pages that follow, however, grilling history has no bearing, and the debate over whether or not it's art doesn't come into play. What's important is your understanding of the simple fundamentals of grilling, as well as the latest tools and techniques from purchasing a grill to cleaning it up. *Grilling Basics* is designed to spark the flame that gets you grilling.

GRILL TALK
GETTING TO KNOW GRILLING

Cooking food over fire is stripped-down simple, and yet so sophisticated. In this section you'll get to know the basic methods of grilling foods. Understanding these techniques and their differences will give you the know-how you'll need to successfully grill just about anything.

GRILLING VS. BARBECUING

Grilling is a means of cooking food over direct heat for a short period of time. Fire up your charcoal or gas grill and place the food on the grill rack that sits above the coals or heat source. Because the cooking time is relatively brief, grilling is best suited to thin or small pieces of food such as steaks, burgers, chicken breasts, fish fillets, or vegetables. The intense heat sears the outside of the food, sealing in the juices and giving it the delicious caramelized flavor only grilling can achieve. Larger cuts of meat and poultry are grilled using the indirect method. Typically the fuel used is charcoal or gas and the temperatures climb higher than those reached when barbecuing.

Barbecuing is a slow cooking method done over a low, smoldering wood fire, using indirect heat for longer periods of time. This lower heat enables the food to cook more evenly throughout and is therefore well suited to larger items such as roasts, whole chickens, or turkeys. Cuts such as brisket and ribs also benefit from the low heat and longer cooking time, which helps break down connective tissue. Barbecue is also used to describe a backyard party at which grilled foods are served.

DIRECT VS. INDIRECT COOKING

Direct cooking requires that you place the food on the grill rack directly over the heat source, either with or without the lid closed (check manufacturer's directions). This method is best used for more tender, thinner, or smaller quick-cooking (under 30 minutes) foods such as burgers, steaks, chops, chicken pieces, and vegetables. For even cooking, turn foods only once during the cooking time.

Indirect cooking positions the food on the grill rack away from or to the side of the heat source and with the grill cover closed. Similar to the way an oven roasts, heat inside the grill reflects off the lid and other interior surfaces, cooking the food from all sides and eliminating the need to turn the food. This low, slow cooking method is ideal for large foods that take longer to cook, allowing them to cook through without burning.

Mustard Marinated Flank Steak
with Yam Fries (page 176)

TIPS FOR INDIRECT COOKING

● Place a drip pan, such as a heavy-gauge disposable aluminum pan, under the food to catch drippings that can cause flare-ups (see top photo, below).
● Add hot water to drip pans to keep drippings from burning—or use other liquids such as apple juice or beer to add flavor and moisture (see bottom photo, below).
● Resist the urge to peek. Doing so allows the heat and smoke to escape and lengthens cooking times.

TO COVER OR NOT TO COVER

That's the burning question. In general, when the lid is closed, the grill is like an oven. It reflects heat and cooks the food from all sides, thereby reducing the cooking time. With charcoal grills, it is important to keep the vents open in order to feed oxygen to the fire. Open them more to increase the temperature or partially close them to reduce the temperature. While there are no hard or fast rules, here are some general guidelines:

COVER THE GRILL

When grilling larger food items using the indirect method, allowing them to cook evenly from all sides.

To control flare-ups by reducing the supply of oxygen fueling the fire.

When smoking foods to allow the smoke to infuse the food with flavor.

UNCOVER THE GRILL

When direct cooking thinner, smaller foods with short cook times to prevent overcooking.

When monitoring foods that need careful attention, such as steaks with brushed-on sauces that could burn.

TIPS FOR MINIMIZING FLARE-UPS

● For indirect cooking, use a drip pan filled with hot water.
● Pat off excess marinades and/or oils.
● Leave a small area of the grill free of coals so you can move food to this area while the flare-ups subside.
● Keep the lid closed.

SMOKING

While grilling offers greater immediacy, smoking is something to be savored. Smoking uses low temperatures (180°F to 220°F) and much longer cooking times (up to three times as long). The low heat generates smoke as the wood chunks smolder, rather than burn, and impart that desirable outdoorsy, smoky flavor.

Smoking is done in a traditional smoker or a charcoal or gas grill that's adapted to achieve a smoky flavor in food. In both cases, the indirect cooking method is used. A water pan is placed inside the grill to add moisture. Water-soaked wood chunks, chips, and/or aromatics are distributed amongst the coals to enhance the flavor (see photo, right). With the lid on, heat and smoke envelop the food, infusing it with a deliciously complex and smoky flavor. Keep in mind, though, that not all foods can handle the assertive qualities of smoking (e.g., delicate fish). Smoke only those foods that can handle the flavor (e.g., beef, lamb, pork, poultry, oily fish, game).

TYPES OF SMOKING

Dry smoking employs indirect cooking with a low, smoldering wood fire to slowly cook foods while infusing smoke flavor.

Wet smoking, also known as water smoking, is more commonly employed and uses a pan of water to maintain moisture and tenderness.

NOW YOU'RE SMOKIN'

Don't have a traditional smoker? No worries. Here's how to turn your charcoal or gas grill into one.

For charcoal grill:

1. Soak wood chips and chunks in water for at least 1 hour; soak other aromatic twigs for 30 minutes. Drain and shake off excess water before adding to the fire.
2. Using long-handled tongs, arrange hot ash-covered coals around a foil pan that's filled with 1 inch of hot water.
3. Add presoaked chunks, chips, and/or aromatics to coals.
4. Place food on grill rack and cover.
5. Check food, temperature, and water pan once every hour.
6. Do not add additional wood during last half of smoking on a charcoal grill (or in a vertical smoker). Too much exposure to smoke imparts a bitter flavor to food.

For gas grill:

1. Soak wood chips and chunks in water for at least 1 hour; soak other aromatic twigs for 30 minutes. Drain and shake off excess water before adding to the fire.
2. If equipped with a smoker box attachment, before firing up the grill, fill water pan on smoker attachment with hot tap water. Place presoaked chunks/chips in the compartment as directed by manufacturer's instructions. If you don't have an attachment, you can use a foil pan (separate from the water pan) or a foil packet with holes punched in the bottom. Place pan on rack directly over heat source.
3. Place food on center of grill rack and cover.
4. Check food, temperature, and water pan once every hour.

TIPS FOR SMOKING SUCCESS

● Monitor temperature by adding 8 to 10 fresh briquettes. Do not add "instant-start" charcoal briquettes during the cooking process.

● Keep water pan full, replenishing as needed with hot tap water. The water helps maintain temperature and adds moisture to keep meats tender.

● Resist the temptation to peek. Heat and smoke escape each time you open the lid, sacrificing aroma and flavor.

● Add an aromatic dimension by tossing fresh leaves, stems, or herbs onto the coals. Try bay leaves, rosemary, grapevine cuttings, fruit peel, or cinnamon sticks. Generally those with higher oil content provide stronger flavor. Be sure to soak branches/stems, which otherwise burn quickly.

● Start with a small amount of wood to see how you like the flavor, then add more for more intense smoky taste. Don't overdo it, though, and don't add wood after the first half of smoking—adding wood too late in the process can impart a bitter flavor.

● Bundling wet wood chips in foil makes the wood chips last longer and prevents them from burning. Punch a few holes in the foil and place directly on the coals. Cool and discard when finished.

FOOD AND WOOD PAIRINGS

If you're just getting started, try experimenting with different foods and woods to find flavor combinations you like.

WOOD TYPE	CHARACTERISTICS	PAIR WITH
Alder	Delicate	Pork, poultry, and especially fish
Apple or cherry	Delicate, slightly sweet and fruity	Veal, pork, and poultry
Hickory	Strong and hearty, smoky	Brisket, ribs, pork chops, and game
Mesquite	Lighter, sweeter	Most meats and vegetables
Oak	Assertive but versatile	Beef, pork, and poultry
Pecan	Similar to hickory but more subtle	Pork, poultry, and fish
Seaweed	Tangy, smoky	Shellfish

Mesquite Chunks

Apple Wood Chunks

Cherry Wood Chunks

FOIL PACKETS

Aluminum foil is a handy tool when it comes to grilling. It's both an effective way to cover and keep foods warm and a great way to cook on the grill. Foil packets placed on top of the grill rack are perfect for warming tortillas, steaming vegetables, or cooking whole meals. While cooking this way doesn't produce the same char-grilled flavor you get from placing the food directly on the grill, it does help retain moisture, enhance tenderness, and make cleanup easier. Keep in mind that when cooking whole meals in the same packet, it is best to use ingredients that have similar cooking times.

HOW TO MAKE A FOIL PACKET

- Begin with a sufficient sheet of aluminum foil. (While parchment paper is a good alternative to foil when cooking in the oven, don't use parchment paper over open flames.)
- If necessary, use nonstick cooking spray to prevent food from sticking to the foil.
- Center the food on the foil sheet.
- Bring up two sides of the foil and double fold with 1-inch-wide folds, leaving enough room for the heat to circulate. Double fold the remaining two sides.
- Place the packet directly on the grill.
- When food is done cooking, use grill mitts to remove foil packet from the grill.
- Carefully open both ends of the packet to allow the steam to escape. Then open the top of the packet.

Ranch-Style Carrots and Squash (page 130)

TOOLS OF THE TRADE
CHOOSING THE RIGHT COOKING EQUIPMENT

Decisions, decisions, decisions. A wide variety of equipment and accessories makes choosing the right grill an overwhelming task. While some argue that gas grills don't generate the same naturally smoky flavor charcoal grills do, your choice really boils down to what fits best with your lifestyle and how you intend to use your grill. Here are the basic considerations.

CHARCOAL GRILLS

Fueled by charcoal, these grills have a round or square box construction with a charcoal grate that holds the coals on the bottom and a grill rack above. Most feature vents on the bottom and on the lid for controlling temperature.

Kettle grills are the most common, featuring deep rounded bowls and lids, which make them great for barbecuing and smoking as well. The grill temperature is controlled by manipulating the vents on the top and bottom. For a more portable option, consider a hibachi. Originally from Japan, these grills consist of a small rectangular or oval firebox with one or two grill racks. They're great for direct cooking small cuts of meat.

Benefits:
- More affordable than gas grills
- Can be more time-consuming than gas, but more primitive/interactive
- Achieves higher temperatures than gas

Look for:
- Vents on both top and bottom for greater temperature control
- Stainless-steel or nickel-plated cooking and charcoal grates
- Heavy-gauge bowl, tight fitting lid, and porcelain-coated finish
- Sturdy legs and construction
- Heatproof handles
- Preassembled or welded parts, which are more stable and less likely to rust

Options:
- Built-in thermometer
- Hinged grill rack for easier access to replenish with coals
- Ash catcher underneath for convenient cleaning

Tips for Using Charcoal Grills:
- Always put charcoal on top of the lower coal grate, not directly onto the bottom of the bowl.
- Allow enough time—20 to 30 minutes—for the fire to get started before cooking.
- Open top and bottom vents before lighting the charcoal and during cooking. Adjust vents to regulate heat.
- When removing the grill cover during cooking, lift it to the side rather than straight up. Otherwise, the suction may draw up ashes onto the food.
- After the grill has cooled, be sure to remove ashes that have accumulated at the bottom of the bowl or in the ash catcher to ensure proper airflow.

GAS GRILLS

A convenient alternative to charcoal, gas grills are fueled by propane tanks or a natural gas hookup. These grills feature a metal box lined with tube-shape liquid-propane burners on the bottom. The burners are topped by a heating surface of metal bars, lava rocks, or ceramic briquettes that disperse the heat from the burners throughout the grill. The smoky aroma and flavor of grilling is generated as the drippings from the food fall onto these bars or stones.

Benefits:
● Convenience: Gas grills preheat in 10 to 15 minutes
● Greater heat control with multiple burners
● Less mess with no need for charcoals or fire starters
● Burns longer: One 20-pound tank burns 12 to 14 hours, whereas charcoal needs to be replenished every time you cook

Look for:
● Solid construction made from materials such as cast aluminum, stainless steel, or porcelain-coated steel
● Stainless-steel or porcelain enamel-coated grill racks for easy cleanup and rust resistance
● Push-button ignition for easy, safe lighting
● A minimum of three burners that manipulate independently to give you greater flexibility for indirect and direct cooking and greater heat control
● A gas gauge to monitor fuel levels and built-in thermometer to monitor grill temperature
● Some lava rock systems can collect grease that may result in flare-ups

Options:
● Secondary grill racks that rest on top of the primary grill rack or are attached to the hood; these racks are good for food items that burn with direct heat (e.g., bread, tortillas); look for racks that are removable so you'll have ample room for larger cuts of meat
● Side burners to enable you to cook other dishes or heat sauces alongside the grill rather than having to cook them inside the house
● Fittings for a rotisserie or smoker box
● Extra outside shelving/work space

Tips for Using Gas Grills:
● Check the gas fitting for leaks every time you connect and disconnect by using a mixture of soap and water. Bubbles indicate a leak.
● Periodically check the tubes connecting the propane tank to the grill to ensure there are no cracks or holes.
● Preheat on high to ensure that the grill heats up thoroughly and burns off any excess residue.
● Regularly empty grease catch pan to prevent flare-ups/fires.
● Never store the liquid propane in a garage or other enclosed space. To store, detach the tank and leave outdoors.

WHAT'S A BTU?

BTU stands for British Thermal Unit, which indicates how much gas a grill can burn. For most grills, 22,000 to 50,000 BTUs is sufficient to generate enough heat—more isn't necessarily better. Well-engineered grills use fewer BTUs and cook food more efficiently, thereby minimizing fuel costs.

SMOKERS

Smoking is essentially barbecuing, which can be achieved on either a charcoal or gas grill. But if you're serious about your smoking, you might consider buying a smoker. The most common type is the **vertical water smoker.** Vertical water smokers are easy to use, compact, and affordably priced. These cylindrical-shape vessels stand from 2½ to 3½ feet high and about 18 inches in diameter. At the base of the vessel is the heat source, where the coals are fueled by charcoal, gas, or electricity. Wood chips or chunks are placed on the coals to enhance the desirable smoky flavor. Above the heat source is a water pan, which provides moisture to the smoking process. Above the water pan there are usually two levels of grill racks where food can be placed.

Look for:

● Heavy-gauge metal, usually steel, with smooth porcelain enamel inside and out to ensure its durability
● Tight-fitting lid to hold in heat and smoke
● Built-in temperature gauge to monitor the heat inside
● Access to the lower half of the vessel so you can easily add wood, water, or charcoal as needed
● Trays for catching and disposing of ashes
● Sufficient vents to help regulate heat and smoke

Not enough? If you still have a burning yen for the ultimate barbecue experience, you could invest in a **horizontal dry** or **pit smoker.** These smokers contain two chambers: one large chamber where the food is placed and a smaller offset fire chamber where the charcoal and wood chips/chunks heat the food chamber indirectly. While requiring a substantially greater investment, dry smokers offer a significantly larger area for volume cooking. It's enough to feed your neighbors and then some.

ROTISSERIE

Rotisserie cooking requires that meat or poultry is placed on a rotating spit over low or medium heat. The self-basting action encourages juices to stay in and on the meat, optimizing the tenderness and flavor of roasts, whole chickens, ribs, and other foods that benefit from long, slow cooking. Most charcoal or gas grills transform easily into a rotisserie with the proper attachment and the addition of a drip pan, as instructed by the manufacturer.

TURKEY FRYERS

Southern fried chicken just got bigger. Literally. Deep-fried turkey, an idea that originated in the South, continues to grow in popularity throughout the United States—so much so that you now can buy turkey fryer kits complete with specialized burners, stands, thermometers, and pots. The deep-fried turkey beats the traditional roasted variety on two important fronts: outer crispiness and inner juiciness. It also requires a bit of an investment, a substantial amount of

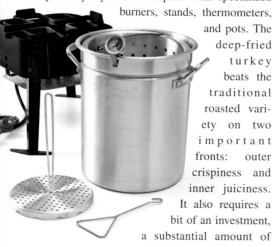

effort to set up, and (especially) close attention to safety. The chapter on turkey frying provides you with more details and recipes to make your deep-frying experience as safe as it is delicious.

INDOOR GRILLS

While nothing compares to the experience and taste of grilling in the great outdoors, indoor grills are a welcome alternative for apartment dwellers or those who prefer not to brave the elements. Most are smokeless, easy to use, easy to clean up, and relatively inexpensive compared to outdoor counterparts.

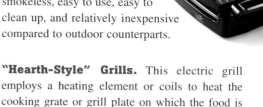

"Hearth-Style" Grills. This electric grill employs a heating element or coils to heat the cooking grate or grill plate on which the food is cooked. Simply plug it in and grill.

Contact or Clamshell Grills. The most popular being the George Foreman®, these grills feature two heated grill plates connected by a hinge that closes the plates together so food cooks simultaneously on both sides.

Stove Top Grills or Grill Pans. These are made from a variety of materials including cast iron and stainless steel. These grills of all different shapes and sizes are placed directly on the burner of your gas or electric stove. A substantial amount of heat is generated, leaving attractive grill marks, but they sometimes can generate significant amounts of smoke, so use in a well-ventilated area with a range hood running.

FUEL FOR THOUGHT
FUELS, FIRE STARTERS, AND HEAT CONTROL

After you've decided on the type of equipment that best fits your grilling needs, you need to consider the various options for fueling your fire and controlling its temperature to achieve the best results.

FUELS

Gas. The choice is simple because most gas grills run on liquid propane. Some, however, run on natural gas. For both, the gas ignites with the turn of a knob, heats quickly, and cleans up easily. The standard propane tanks hold about 20 pounds of propane, which burns for 12 to 14 hours. Today's grills come with a gas gauge, so when the tank is empty, you can trade it in for a new one at most supermarkets and hardware stores. If your home uses propane for heat, you can have your grill attached directly to the propane supply line and avoid the use of tanks altogether. To find out about natural gas hookups, contact your local utility company.

Charcoal. Three types of charcoal are available and each possesses different qualities.
● **Natural briquettes:** Made from pulverized lump charcoal held together with natural starches without the off-flavors generated by some composite briquettes.
● **Composition briquettes:** Made from burned wood and scraps, coal dust, camphor, and paraffin or petroleum binders. Use a quality brand; cheaper brands contain excessive fillers that give foods an unpleasant taste and leave heavy ashes.
● **Charwood or lump charcoal:** Formed from hardwoods, such as maple, oak, and hickory, which are burned down at very high temperatures. The fuel choice of chefs and other professional grillers, lump charcoal lights more quickly and burns cleaner and hotter than briquettes. It is additive- and petroleum-free, and it retains some natural flavor. Primary drawbacks include occasional sparking, limited availability, and higher cost than other alternatives.

Wood. The first fuel used by man, natural wood continues to be the best at delivering intense heat, longer burning, and great smoky flavor. Natural woods, such as hickory, oak, or fruit-tree wood, are available in chips and chunks.
● **Wood chips:** Readily available at most hardware stores and supermarkets, hardwood chips can add interesting flavor dimensions to your food (see "Food and Wood Pairings," page 11). The chips are presoaked in water for 30 minutes to keep them from burning too quickly, then scattered over ash-covered coals in indirect cooking. For gas grills, the chips are placed in a smoker box or foil pan positioned on the grill rack directly over the fire.
● **Wood chunks:** For even greater smoky flavor, you can build a fire entirely from wood chunks, which do not require presoaking, or in combination with charcoal briquettes. Because they take slightly longer to burn than briquettes, chunks must be lit a few minutes before the charcoal. Remember to use only dried natural hardwood, not soft woods, which cause flare-ups and result in a bitter flavor. Never use lumber or plywood, which contain toxic chemicals.

FIRE STARTERS

Starting a gas grill is as simple as turning a knob. Charcoal grills, on the other hand, are a bit more tricky. Ease and convenience are important but should not compromise the taste of the food. A variety of aids makes the process easier.

Instant-light charcoal: These briquettes light very easily. Unlike lighter fluid, which burns off relatively fast, instant-light charcoal is soaked through with a petroleum product that releases fumes throughout much of the cooking process. Charcoal added during the cooking process will impart a bitter flavor to the food.

Lighter fluid: Fluid is dispersed onto the coals and allowed to soak in for a minute or two before lighting. The fluid burns off well before you begin cooking, but many areas have outlawed its use because of resulting pollutants.

Paraffin starter: This environmentally safe, smokeless, nontoxic method for igniting your fire is easy to use too. Simply place a couple of pieces of paraffin under a mound of charcoal or in the bottom of a chimney starter and light.

Chimney starter: This is the preferred choice for the serious griller. This method uses a cylindrical steel pipe with vents in the bottom, a grate in the middle, and a heatproof handle. Charcoal or wood chunks are placed on the grate, and crumpled newspaper or paraffin starters are placed in the bottom of the cylinder. The chimney is then set on the bottom grate of the grill itself, and the newspaper or paraffin starter is lit with a long match or lighter. The cylindrical shape encourages the coals to light quickly and evenly. Once the coals are ready, lift the chimney and pour the coals directly onto the grill.

Electric starter: This metal coil heating device is placed under the charcoal briquettes, plugged in, and left to heat up and ignite the coals within minutes. Once the coals begin glowing, unplug the starter, carefully remove it, and store in a safe place to cool.

WHO FUELED THE INVENTION OF THE CHARCOAL BRIQUETTE?

In 1920, Henry Ford along with Thomas Edison invented the charcoal briquette. Better known for his impact on the American automobile industry, Ford created briquettes using wood scraps and sawdust from his car factory. Ultimately E. G. Kingsford purchased the hot invention and commercialized charcoal briquettes for the consumer market.

HEAT CONTROL

Whether you're cooking directly or indirectly, it is important to monitor the temperature of your grill to obtain the perfect doneness. Here again, gas grills offer simplicity and ease with built-in thermometers and temperature gauges to adjust the heat. When working with charcoal, there are three basic ways to manage the heat of the grill:

- **Spread the coals farther apart** to lower the heat. Or gently tap the coals with long-handled tongs to remove loose ash and pile them closer together to make the fire more intense.
- **Adjust the flow of oxygen** inside the grill by opening and closing the air vents. Open them to increase heat or partially close them to decrease the temperature.
- Some grills allow you to **adjust the height of the grill rack.** Use lower levels for searing foods and higher levels for slow cooking. For medium heat place the grate about 4 inches from the fire.

HAND CHECK

Coals are ready for grilling when they are covered with gray ash, typically after about 20 minutes. To check the temperature of the coals, use a built-in or separate flat grill thermometer. Or use the method many professional chefs use: Carefully place the palm of your hand just above the grill rack and count the number of seconds you can hold it in that position. For example, "One, I love grilling, two, I love grilling" and so on.

TIME	THERMOMETER	TEMPERATURE	VISUAL
2 seconds	400°F to 450°F	Hot (high)	Coals burning down and barely covered with gray ash.
3 seconds	375°F to 400°F	Medium-high	
4 seconds	350°F to 375°F	Medium	Coals glow through a layer of ash.
5 seconds	325°F to 350°F	Medium-low	
6 seconds	300°F to 325°F	Low	Coals are covered with a thick layer of ash.

TIME'S UP
WHEN TO TAKE IT OFF

The great taste of food hot off the grill is a reward to be savored. Knowing when to pull it off the grill is important for a great eating experience and also to ensure safety. Determining "doneness" in terms of texture, appearance, and juiciness is often a matter of personal preference. However, in terms of safety, foods are "done" when they are cooked to an internal temperature high enough to eliminate harmful microorganisms. The best way to measure internal temperature is with a food thermometer.

QUALITATIVE MEASURES

● **Steaks/chops/chicken breasts:** With lots of practice, the "poke test" provides a quick gauge for doneness. The poke test compares the tension in the fleshy part of your hand at the base of your thumb with the tension you feel as you press your index finger into the center of the cut of meat.

● **For rare:** Bring your thumb and index finger together gently.

● **For medium:** Bring your thumb and middle finger together gently.

● **For well-done:** Bring your thumb and pinky finger together.

● **Whole chicken:** Insert a skewer into the thickest part of the thigh. It's done if the juices run clear. Or wiggle the leg, which should be loose.
● **Fish:** Flesh is done when it turns opaque; breaks into large, firm flakes; and pulls away easily from any bones.

SCIENTIFIC MEASURES

The most accurate and safe way to determine doneness is to use a thermometer. To achieve an accurate reading, use the following guide to determine where to insert the thermometer:

● **Beef, lamb, pork roast:** Insert into the thickest part of the roast, avoiding the bone and fat. Remove roasts from the grill 5°F to 10°F below final desired doneness. Tent with aluminum foil. Let stand for 15 minutes. The temperature will continue to rise to reach final doneness. During standing, the meat juices redistribute and the roast becomes easier to slice.
● **Burgers, steaks, chops:** Insert horizontally into the center, away from bone and fat.
● **Whole poultry:** Gauge the temperature at part of the thigh, avoiding the bone.
● **Poultry parts:** Insert thermometer in the thickest area, avoiding the bone.

TYPES OF THERMOMETERS

Oven/grill-safe meat thermometer
● Generally used for larger items such as roasts.
● Designed to stay in the food while cooking.
● If taken out, these thermometers can take 1 to 2 minutes to register.

Instant-read thermometer
● Available in digital and dial versions.
● Measures temperatures in 15 to 20 seconds.
● Dial models are inserted 2 to 2½ inches deep (a nick on the stem indicates how deep to go) into the thickest part of the food. Insert sideways into thin foods. Most digital models have a sensor at the tip. Follow the manufacturer's instructions for correct use.
● Not designed to remain in food while cooking. Check temperature toward the end of cooking time.

Thermometer fork combination
● Utensil combines cooking fork with a food thermometer.
● Measures temperature in 2 to 10 seconds.
● Good for both thin and thick foods. Place at least ¼ inch in the thickest part of food.
● Not designed to remain in food during cooking. Check temperature toward the end of cooking time.

Disposable doneness sensors
● Designed to measure a temperature range. Relatively new to the retail market; sold as sticks or picks. This thermometer first appeared in 1965 when the turkey industry used a pop-up version.
● Designed for one-time use.
● Not designed to remain in food while cooking. Check the temperature toward the end of cooking time. If the desired temperature has not been reached, reinsert until temperature is reached.

Source: USDA FSIS

RECOMMENDED INTERNAL TEMPERATURES

FOOD	THERMOMETER
Ground Meat	
Beef, Lamb, Veal, Pork	160°F
Chicken, Turkey	165°F
Fresh Beef, Lamb, Veal	
Medium-Rare	145°F
Medium	160°F
Well-Done	170°F
Poultry	
Chicken, Turkey (whole)	180°F
Poultry breasts	170°F
Poultry thighs	180°F
Duck, Goose	180°F
Fresh Pork	
Medium	160°F
Well-Done	170°F

Source: USDA FSIS

Oven/Grill-Safe Meat
Thermometer

Instant-Read
Thermometer

Digital Instant-Read
Thermometer

PLAY IT SAFE
KEEPING YOUR FIRE AND FOOD IN CHECK

With all the excitement and activity that surround backyard barbecue, it's important to not forget these safety guidelines.

GRILL SAFETY

● Read and follow the manufacturer's instructions on how to safely light and operate your gas or charcoal grill.

● Position your grill in a well-ventilated area at least 10 feet away from trees, houses, or any combustible materials. Make sure the ground surface is level and stable. Once the grill is lit, don't move it.

● Keep children and pets a safe distance away from hot grills.

● Avoid wearing loose or highly flammable clothing.

● Use heat-resistant mitts and long-handled tools.

● Never add lighter fluid to an already lit fire.

● Keep a fire extinguisher nearby for emergencies. Do not pour water on a grease fire. Close lids and vents on a charcoal grill or turn off gas.

● Close lids and vents to extinguish flare-ups. Do not use water.

● After grilling, cover charcoal grill with the lid, close all vents, and allow coals to cool completely before cleaning or putting away your grill. For a gas grill, turn off all burners and the gas source.

● Always store propane tanks outdoors, never in a garage or enclosed space.

FOOD SAFETY

● Store raw meat, poultry, and fish separately in plastic bags and place on a tray to avoid dripping any juices onto other foods.

● Defrost meat, poultry, and fish in the refrigerator.

● Wash hands thoroughly before beginning any food preparation and after handling fresh meat, poultry, or fish.

● Remove excess fat and/or marinade from food to reduce the occurrence of flare-ups.

● Keep raw foods away from cooked foods to avoid cross contamination.

● Use clean plates and utensils with cooked food. Do not use the same plate and utensils that you used to handle raw foods.

● Sanitize cutting boards by washing with hot, soapy water, then with a solution of 2 teaspoons of household bleach and one quart of warm water. Rinse thoroughly with warm water.

● When basting, brush sauces and marinades on cooked food surfaces only. With cooked food, do not reuse leftover marinades or use a brush previously used on raw meat, poultry, or fish.

● For marinades that have been in contact with raw meat or poultry, bring to a vigorous boil for at least 1 minute before using as a baste or sauce.

● Grill foods to safe temperatures as outlined in "Time's Up" on pages 20 and 21.

● Use moderate grill heat to avoid charring meats, poultry, and fish.

● Keep hot foods hot and cold foods cold. Do not allow any cooked food to sit at room temperature for more than 2 hours.

KEEP IT CLEAN

Regular cleaning and maintenance enhance the performance and beauty of your grill for years to come. Here's how...

For Charcoal Grills:
● Clean the grill rack each time you grill. Once the coals have died and the grill rack has cooled slightly, brush off any debris using a brass wire grill brush or crumpled-up aluminum foil. For a more thorough cleaning, wash the grill rack using a mild soap and a fine steel wool pad.
● After grill has cooled, remove any ashes from bottom of the bowl or in the ash catcher to maintain proper airflow.
● When necessary, wipe the cooled inside and outside surfaces with a soft cloth and warm, soapy water. Rinse thoroughly and dry.

For Gas Grills:
● Clean the grill rack every time, either before or after you grill. To burn off any residue, turn the grill on high until the smoke subsides (about 10 to 15 minutes). Turn it off and allow to cool slightly. Then brush the grill rack with a brass wire grill brush or crumpled-up aluminum foil.
● Wipe cooled inside and outside surfaces with a soft cloth and warm, soapy water as needed. Be sure to rinse thoroughly and dry.
● When necessary, clean the bottom tray and grease catch pan, ensuring they are free from debris. Remove the cooled bottom tray from under the grill and scrape the inside with a putty knife or other straight, flat object to remove the residue. Gently wash with warm soapy water and a fine steel wool pad.
● Periodically turn over lava rocks or ceramic briquettes because they can become covered in grease and contribute to flare-ups. Replace with new ones as needed.

Note: Consult your owner's manual for any specific cleaning instructions as directed by the manufacturer.

Brass Wire Grill Brush

GRILL GADGETS
ESSENTIALS & EXTRAS

It's fun to accessorize. Gear up with a few basic tools and you'll be ready to grill in no time.

ESSENTIALS

Spatula. Good for turning foods, spatulas are available in variety of styles from basic to special purpose (e.g., fish spatula). Choose one with a long, sturdy handle and a stainless-steel blade.

Fork. Ideal for moving roasts and larger items. Avoid piercing too deeply, especially during cooking, so as not to waste the delicious juices.

Basting brush. Used for oiling the grill rack and basting foods. Choose long-handled brushes with natural bristles.

Heat-resistant gloves or long grill mitts. Protect hands and forearms from hot utensils, as well as the grill itself. Choose mitts that are heavy, well insulated, and flame-retardant.

Grill brush. Essential for cleaning the grill rack. Look for rustproof varieties, which are best for outdoor use.

Thermometer. Available in different styles, a good thermometer ensures your food is cooked properly (see "Types of Thermometers," page 21).

Flat grill thermometer. Place on grill rack and monitor the cooking temperature of the grill.

Tongs. Perfect for moving and turning without piercing foods. Spring-hinged, long-handled styles are best.

Skewers. Ideal for holding small pieces of food, skewers are available in stainless steel, wood, or bamboo. Soak disposable wood and bamboo skewers in water 30 minutes before adding foods.

Disposable foil drip pans. Easy to use and clean, these pans are perfect for indirect grilling and holding wood chips.

EXTRAS

Outdoor lighting. For outdoor grilling after dark.

Butane lighter. A good alternative to matches, this long-nose reusable lighter makes lighting fires safe and easy.

Grill baskets. Available in a variety of shapes and sizes. Some feature two grates that are hinged together (good for grilling fish, hot dogs, vegetables, and other small items that require turning). Some are more basketlike, with holes to keep food from falling through the grill rack.

Rib rack. These racks, which resemble a file holder, hold up to five racks of ribs vertically, creating more space on your grill.

Roast rack. Placed inside a disposable aluminum pan on the grill to keep the roast out of the drippings.

Chicken/poultry holder. Marketed under a variety of names, such as "beer can chicken holder," this rack enables you to roast a chicken by standing it on end.

Grill wok. The grill wok is good for stir-frying vegetables, meats, and seafood.

Grill-top pizza pan. Features holes so the flavor of the grill can infuse the pizza crust. Also used for smaller items such as shrimp, which otherwise fall through the grate.

Fireplace tools. Good for tending a charcoal fire to move coals or remove ashes.

Spatula

Fork

Basting brush

Long mitt

Grill brush

Thermometer/fork

Skewers

Grill wok

Corn basket

Rib rack

GRILLING PLANKS

Used for centuries by Native Americans in the Pacific Northwest, grilling planks are a unique way to add a delicious dimension to the meat, poultry, fish, and game that hold up to strong flavor.

● Planks of different sizes and thicknesses are available at most cookware stores or over the Internet.
● Use any untreated, aromatic hardwood you prefer. Western red cedar is the most popular, but planks also are available in maple, oak, and alder.
● Presoak the planks in water for at least 1 hour.
● Prepare grill as instructed. Medium-high (300°F) is good temperature for medium to light smoke.
● Place the soaked plank on the grill rack and close the lid. The plank will begin to smoke/crackle, at which point you can place the food on the plank. Keep a spray bottle nearby because the plank will start to flame if it becomes too hot.
● You can reuse planks if they are not exceedingly charred or cracked. Clean with warm soapy water and store in a dry place. Resoaking before the next use is optional.
● Once plank chars and blisters, dispose of it or crumble it and use as smoking chips.

READY, SET, GRILL
PUTTING IT ALL TOGETHER FROM START TO FINISH

Cooking dinner over the coals should be easy and carefree. And it is when you follow these guidelines for making sure the coals are ready to glow!

BEFORE YOU BEGIN...

● Check your fuel. Ensure you have plenty of charcoal or gas to get the job done.

● Make sure your grill rack is clean and the bottom of the grill is void of any ashes and/or debris that may interfere with airflow.

● If necessary to prevent sticking, apply nonstick cooking spray or rub cooking oil onto the cool grill rack prior to grilling.

● Preheat your grill in advance and to the right temperature. Charcoal coals should be covered with gray ash. Also do a "hand check" of the temperature. Preheat a gas grill to high. (See "Fuel for Thought," page 17.)

● Set up the grill for direct or indirect cooking (see "Get Fired Up!" below).

● Get organized. Set all of your ingredients and utensils next to your grill before you begin cooking.

● Be mindful of all grilling and food safety measures (see "Play It Safe," page 22).

GET FIRED UP!

Whether you're cooking with charcoal or gas, setting up your grill is as easy as 1, 2, 3…

FOR CHARCOAL GRILL:

1. Prepare the fire. About 25 to 30 minutes prior to cooking, remove the grill cover and open all vents. Place coals on lower charcoal grate.

● **For direct cooking method,** use enough briquettes to cover the charcoal grate completely with one layer. Then pile these briquettes into a pyramid in the center of the grate.

● **For indirect cooking method,** see "How Much Charcoal Should I Use," on page 27, to determine the number of briquettes to use.

2. Apply fire starter. Then wait 1 minute before you ignite the coals (see "Fire Starters," page 18). Wait for 25 to 30 minutes until the coals are covered with a light coating of gray ash.

3. Arrange coals accordingly:

● **For direct cooking method,** using long-handled tongs, carefully spread the coals evenly across the bottom of the grill, covering a surface area about 3 inches larger than the food you are cooking.

● **For indirect cooking method,** using long-handled tongs, carefully arrange coals to one side of the grill and place the drip pan on the other side. Or place the drip pan in the center and arrange the coals into two equal piles on each side of the pan.

4. Install grill rack. Check the cooking temperature (see "Heat Control," page 19).

FOR GAS GRILL:

1. Open the lid. Turn gas valve "on" and turn burners on high. Ignite as directed by the manufacturer, either by switch or a match. Close lid and allow grill to preheat (typically with all burners on high for 10 to 15 minutes).

2. Turn off burners directly below the food for indirect cooking method. Adjust burner controls to temperature needed for cooking.

3. Start grilling!

HOW MUCH CHARCOAL SHOULD I USE?

For direct cooking, use enough charcoal to completely cover the bottom of the grill with one layer of briquettes and add coals as needed to maintain temperature. For indirect cooking, refer to the chart below.

DIAMETER OF GRILL IN INCHES	BRIQUETTES NEEDED ON EACH SIDE TO START	BRIQUETTES TO BE ADDED TO EACH SIDE EVERY HOUR
26¾	30	9
22½	25	8
18½	16	5

Source: Weber

CHILLIN' AND GRILLIN'

Don't let cold weather or other elements keep you from grilling. Here are a few tips to keep food tasty and toasty:

● Never grill during a lightning storm or heavy rain. Windy days are bad candidates for outdoor grilling.
● Position the grill on a surface clear of any snow or ice and in an area sheltered from the wind as much as possible. Maintain a safe distance away from combustible materials.
● Ensure that you have sufficient outdoor lighting to guide your way and accurately check for doneness.
● If using charcoal, preheat your grill about 35 minutes prior to cooking to give the coals ample time to heat up.
● Prepare in advance all of the ingredients to be placed on the grill.
● Keep the vents open on charcoal grill to fuel the flame and maintain desired temperature.
● Avoid opening the grill lid too often in order to maintain the cooking temperature.
● Use heated serving platters to keep cooked food warm.

BASIC GRILL RECIPES
THE MEAT OF THE MATTER

Whether you're new to the grilling game or a highly seasoned griller, it all comes down to the basics. There's nothing fancy here, only recipes that bring out the best in burgers, steaks, chops, and kabobs.

• •

GRILLED BURGERS
Prep: 10 minutes Grill: 14 to 18 minutes Makes: 4 servings

1½ **pounds lean ground beef**
   Salt and black pepper
  4 **hamburger buns, split**
   Cheese slices, lettuce leaves, tomato slices, onion slices, and/or pickle slices (optional)

1 Lightly shape ground beef into four ¾-inch-thick patties.

2 For a charcoal grill, grill burgers on the rack of an uncovered grill directly over medium coals for 14 to 18 minutes or done (160°F), turning once halfway through grilling. (For a gas grill, preheat grill. Reduce heat to medium. Place burgers on grill rack over heat. Cover; grill as above.)

3 Remove burgers from grill. Season with salt and pepper. Serve burgers on buns. If desired, top burgers with cheese, lettuce, tomato, onion, and/or pickles.

• •

GRILLED STEAKS
Prep: 10 minutes
Grill: Medium-rare (145°F) 10 to 12 minutes; Medium (160°F) 12 to 15 minutes
Makes: 4 servings

  4 **tender beef steaks, cut 1 inch thick (Tender steaks include beef top loin [strip], tenderloin, ribeye, shoulder top blade [flat-iron], T-bone, and porterhouse.)**
   Salt and black pepper

1 Trim fat from steaks, if necessary.

2 For a charcoal grill, grill steaks on the rack of an uncovered grill directly over medium coals for 10 to 12 minutes for medium-rare (145°F) or 12 to 15 minutes for medium (160°F) doneness, turning once halfway through grilling. (For a gas grill, preheat grill. Reduce heat to medium. Place steaks on grill rack over heat. Cover; grill as above.) Remove steaks from grill. Season with salt and pepper.

GRILLED BEEF KABOBS

Prep: 10 minutes Grill: 8 minutes Makes: 4 servings

1 pound boneless beef sirloin steak, cut 1 inch thick
Cracked black pepper
Salt

1 Cut steak into 1-inch cubes. On four 6- to 8-inch metal skewers, thread an even number of beef pieces, leaving a $\frac{1}{4}$-inch space between pieces. (Loose spacing allows beef cubes to cook more quickly, and tight spacing adds to the cooking time.) Sprinkle with cracked pepper.

2 For a charcoal grill, grill kabobs on the rack of an uncovered grill directly over medium coals for 8 to 12 minutes for medium doneness (160°F), turning once halfway through grilling. (For a gas grill, preheat grill. Reduce heat to medium. Place kabobs on grill rack over heat. Cover; grill as above.) Remove kabobs from grill. Season with salt.

GRILLED PORK CHOPS

Prep: 10 minutes Grill: 11 to 13 minutes Makes: 4 servings

4 pork loin or rib chops, cut 1-inch thick (2 to 2½ pounds)
Salt and black pepper

1 Trim fat from chops. Season with salt and pepper.

2 For a charcoal grill, grill chops on the rack of an uncovered grill directly over medium coals for 11 to 13 minutes until chops are slightly pink in center and juices run clear (160°F), turning once halfway through grilling. (For a gas grill, preheat grill. Reduce heat to medium. Place chops on grill rack over heat. Cover; grill as above.) Remove chops from grill.

• •

GRILLED CHICKEN BREASTS
Prep: 10 minutes Grill: 12 to 15 minutes Makes: 4 servings

4 skinless, boneless chicken breast halves (about 1 pound)
Salt and black pepper

1 For a charcoal grill, grill chicken on the rack of an uncovered grill directly over medium coals for 12 to 15 minutes or until chicken is no longer pink (170°F), turning once halfway through grilling. (For a gas grill, preheat grill. Reduce heat to medium. Place chicken on grill rack over heat. Cover; grill as above.)

2 Remove chicken from grill. Season with salt and pepper.

• •

GRILLED CHICKEN PIECES
Prep: 10 minutes Grill: 50 minutes Makes: 4 servings

2 to 3 pounds meaty chicken pieces (breasts, thighs, and
    drumsticks)
Barbecue sauce of choice (optional)
Salt and black pepper

1 For a charcoal grill, arrange medium-hot coals around a drip pan. Test for medium heat above the pan. Place chicken pieces, bone sides up, on grill rack over drip pan. Cover and grill for 50 to 60 minutes or until chicken is no longer pink (170°F for breasts; 180°F for thighs), turning once halfway through grilling. If desired, brush with sauce during the last 15 minutes of grilling. (For a gas grill, preheat grill. Reduce heat to medium. Adjust for indirect cooking. Grill as above.)

2 Remove chicken from grill. Season with salt and pepper.

• •

GRILLED SALMON OR HALIBUT STEAKS
Prep: 10 minutes Grill: 8 minutes Makes: 4 servings

4 6-ounce fresh or frozen halibut or salmon steaks, 1 inch thick
Salt and black pepper
Lemon wedges

1 Thaw fish, if frozen. Rinse fish; pat dry with paper towels. Lightly grease or coat with nonstick cooking spray an unheated grill rack.

2 For a charcoal grill, grill fish on the greased rack of an uncovered grill directly over medium coals for 8 to 12 minutes or until fish flakes easily when tested with a fork, gently turning once halfway through grilling. (For a gas grill, preheat grill. Reduce heat to medium. Place fish on greased grill rack over heat. Cover; grill as above.)

3 Remove fish from grill. Season with salt and pepper. Serve with lemon wedges.

2

Brush-ons, Marinades & Rubs

TERIYAKI GLAZE

○Beef ○Lamb ●Pork ○Ham ●Poultry
●Fish ○Seafood

Prep: 5 minutes Cook: 10 minutes
Makes: about ¼ cup

3 tablespoons soy sauce
3 tablespoons sweet rice wine (mirin)
2 tablespoons dry white wine
1½ teaspoons sugar
1½ teaspoons honey

1 In a small saucepan stir together soy sauce, rice wine, white wine, sugar, and honey. Bring to boiling; reduce heat. Simmer, uncovered, 10 minutes or until glaze is reduced to ¼ cup.

2 To use, brush onto meat, poultry, or fish during the last 2 minutes of grilling. Discard any remaining glaze.

GINGER-ORANGE BRUSH-ON

●Beef ●Lamb ●Pork ○Ham ●Poultry
○Fish ○Seafood

Prep: 10 minutes
Makes: about ¾ cup

½ cup bottled barbecue sauce
¼ cup frozen orange juice concentrate,
thawed
2 tablespoons soy sauce
1 tablespoon grated fresh ginger

1 In a bowl stir together barbecue sauce, orange juice concentrate, soy sauce, and ginger.

2 To use, brush meat or poultry with some of the sauce during the last 15 minutes of grilling. If desired, heat any remaining sauce until bubbly and pass with meat or poultry.

LEMON-HERB BRUSH-ON

○Beef ○Lamb ●Pork ○Ham ●Poultry
●Fish ○Seafood

Prep: 5 minutes
Makes: about ⅓ cup

2 tablespoons butter or margarine
3 tablespoons lemon juice
1 teaspoon dried thyme, savory,
or sage, crushed
3 cloves garlic, minced
¼ teaspoon salt
¼ teaspoon black pepper

1 In a small saucepan melt butter; stir in lemon juice, thyme, garlic, salt, and pepper.

2 To use, brush evenly onto meat, poultry, or fish. Brush occasionally with remaining herb mixture during the first half of grilling. Discard remaining herb mixture.

SMOKIN' HOT TIP

Be careful when using barbecue sauces or other sauces that contain sugars, because they burn easily on the grill. Baste near the end of grilling as indicated in the recipe. When basting use a brush to apply an even layer of sauce to each side of the food. If desired, apply repeatedly to build a thicker glaze.

APPLE BUTTER BARBECUE SAUCE

○Beef ○Lamb ●Pork ○Ham ●Poultry
○Fish ○Seafood

Prep: 5 minutes
Makes: about 1½ cups

1 8-ounce can tomato sauce
½ cup purchased apple butter
2 tablespoons light-colored corn syrup (optional)
1 tablespoon Pickapeppa sauce or Worcestershire sauce

1 In a small saucepan stir together tomato sauce, apple butter, corn syrup (if desired), and Pickapeppa sauce. Bring mixture just to boiling; remove from heat.

2 To use, brush meat or poultry with some of the sauce during the last 10 minutes of grilling. If desired, heat any remaining sauce until bubbly, stirring occasionally. Pass with meat or poultry.

HONEY-BEER BARBECUE SAUCE

●Beef ○Lamb ●Pork ○Ham ●Poultry
○Fish ○Seafood

Prep: 25 minutes
Makes: 1½ cups

⅓ cup chopped onion (1 small)
1 clove garlic, minced
1 tablespoon cooking oil
¾ cup bottled chili sauce
½ cup beer
¼ cup honey
2 tablespoons Worcestershire sauce
1 tablespoon yellow mustard

1 In a medium saucepan cook onion and garlic in hot oil until onion is tender. Stir in chili sauce, beer, honey, Worcestershire sauce, and mustard. Bring to boiling; reduce heat. Simmer, uncovered, about 20 minutes or until desired consistency, stirring occasionally.

2 To use, brush meat or poultry with some of the sauce during the last 10 minutes of grilling. If desired, heat any remaining sauce until bubbly and pass with meat or poultry.

KANSAS CITY BARBECUE SAUCE

●Beef ○Lamb ●Pork ○Ham ●Poultry
○Fish ○Seafood

Prep: 40 minutes
Makes: about 1⅓ cups

½ cup finely chopped onion
2 cloves garlic, minced
1 tablespoon olive oil or cooking oil
¾ cup apple juice
½ of a 6-ounce can (⅓ cup) tomato paste
¼ cup cider vinegar
2 tablespoons packed brown sugar
2 tablespoons molasses
1 tablespoon paprika
1 tablespoon prepared horseradish
1 tablespoon Worcestershire sauce
1 teaspoon salt
½ teaspoon black pepper

1 In a medium saucepan cook onion and garlic in hot oil until onion is tender. Stir in apple juice, tomato paste, vinegar, brown sugar, molasses, paprika, horseradish, Worcestershire sauce, salt, and pepper. Bring to boiling; reduce heat. Simmer, uncovered, about 30 minutes or until desired consistency, stirring occasionally.

2 To use, brush meat or poultry with some of the sauce during the last 10 minutes of grilling. If desired, heat any remaining sauce until bubbly and pass with meat or poultry.

TANGY BARBECUE SAUCE

●Beef ○Lamb ●Pork ○Ham ●Poultry
○Fish ○Seafood

Prep: 20 minutes
Makes: 1½ cups

1 cup catsup
⅓ cup balsamic vinegar or cider vinegar
⅓ cup light-colored corn syrup
¼ cup finely chopped onion or thinly sliced green onions (2)
¼ teaspoon salt
Several dashes bottled hot pepper sauce

1 In a small saucepan combine catsup, vinegar, corn syrup, onion, salt, and hot pepper sauce. Bring to boiling; reduce heat. Simmer, uncovered, for 10 to 15 minutes or until desired consistency, stirring sauce occasionally.

2 To use, brush meat or poultry with some of the sauce during the last 10 minutes of grilling. If desired, heat any remaining sauce until bubbly, stirring occasionally; pass with meat or poultry.

MANGO AND PEPPER BBQ SAUCE

○Beef ○Lamb ●Pork ○Ham ●Poultry
●Fish ●Seafood

Prep: 20 minutes
Makes: about 2½ cups

- **2 cups chopped red sweet peppers (2 large)**
- **½ cup chopped onion (1 medium)**
- **2 tablespoons cooking oil**
- **2 medium mangoes, seeded, peeled, and chopped (2 cups)**
- **¼ cup packed brown sugar**
- **2 tablespoons rice vinegar**
- **½ teaspoon crushed red pepper**
- **¼ teaspoon salt**
- **2 tablespoons finely chopped green onion (1)**

1 In a large skillet cook the sweet peppers and onion in hot oil just until tender. Stir in the mangoes, brown sugar, vinegar, crushed red pepper, and salt. Bring to boiling; reduce heat. Simmer, uncovered, about 10 minutes or until mangoes are tender. Cool mixture slightly. Transfer mixture to a food processor or blender. Cover and process or blend until nearly smooth. Stir in the green onion.

2 To use sauce, brush meat, poultry, fish, or seafood with some of the sauce during the last 10 minutes of grilling. If desired, heat any remaining sauce until bubbly and pass with meat, poultry, fish, or seafood.

SPICY PEANUT SATAY SAUCE

●Beef ●Lamb ●Pork ○Ham ●Poultry
○Fish ○Seafood

Prep: 10 minutes
Makes: about 1 cup

- **½ cup creamy peanut butter**
- **¼ cup rice vinegar**
- **¼ cup soy sauce**
- **¼ cup unsweetened coconut milk**
- **2 teaspoons minced garlic**
- **1 teaspoon toasted sesame oil**
- **¼ teaspoon crushed red pepper**
- **¼ cup thinly sliced green onions (2)**
- **Chopped peanuts (optional)**

1 In a bowl stir together peanut butter, vinegar, soy sauce, coconut milk, garlic, sesame oil, and crushed red pepper. Stir in green onions.

2 To use, brush meat or poultry with sauce during the last 5 minutes of grilling. Heat remaining sauce until bubbly, stirring occasionally, and pass with meat or poultry. If desired, garnish sauce with chopped peanuts.

Spicy Peanut Satay Sauce

SMOKIN' HOT TIP

The seeds inside a chile contain most of the potent compound that gives chiles their fiery quality. Here are a few tips to help you handle the heat:

● As a general rule, the smaller the chile, the bigger its bite.

● To diminish the heat but retain all the flavor, remove the membrane and seeds from the inside of the chile.

● Use rubber gloves when cutting chiles to avoid direct contact with the oils, which can cause skin and eye irritation.

● Be careful to avoid touching your eyes or mouth when handling chiles.

● Afterwards wash your hands, the cutting board, and knives with hot, soapy water to remove any residual oils.

BERRY-JALAPEÑO BRUSH-ON

●Beef ●Lamb ●Pork ○Ham ○Poultry
○Fish ○Seafood

Prep: 10 minutes Cook: 10 minutes
Makes: about 1⅔ cups

¼ cup chopped onion
1 clove garlic, minced
1 tablespoon cooking oil
½ cup catsup
½ cup strawberry preserves or
    strawberry jam
¼ cup cider vinegar or beer
1 or 2 fresh jalapeño chile peppers,
    seeded and finely chopped (see
    tip, above)
1 tablespoon bottled steak sauce
1 teaspoon chili powder

1 In a saucepan cook onion and garlic in hot oil until tender. Stir in catsup, strawberry preserves, vinegar, jalapeño pepper(s), steak sauce, and chili powder. Bring just to boiling; reduce heat. Simmer, uncovered, about 10 minutes or until mixture thickens slightly, stirring occasionally.

2 To use, brush meat with some of the sauce during the last 10 minutes of grilling. If desired, heat any remaining sauce until bubbly and pass with meat.

SOUTHWESTERN BRUSH-ON

●Beef ●Lamb ●Pork ○Ham ●Poultry
○Fish ○Seafood

Prep: 10 minutes Cook: 25 minutes
Makes: about 2 cups

1 cup catsup
½ cup light-colored corn syrup
¼ cup white vinegar
¼ cup packed brown sugar
¼ cup finely chopped onion
2 tablespoons yellow mustard
1½ teaspoons Worcestershire sauce
2 cloves garlic, minced
½ teaspoon coarsely ground black
    pepper
½ teaspoon bottled hot pepper sauce
¼ teaspoon ground cumin or
    chili powder
⅛ teaspoon cayenne pepper

1 In a medium saucepan stir together catsup, corn syrup, vinegar, brown sugar, onion, mustard, Worcestershire sauce, garlic, black pepper, hot pepper sauce, cumin, and cayenne pepper. Bring to boiling; reduce heat. Simmer, uncovered, for 25 to 30 minutes or until thickened, stirring occasionally.

2 To use, brush meat or poultry with some of the sauce during the last 10 minutes of grilling. If desired, heat any remaining sauce and pass with meat or poultry.

BASIC MOPPIN' SAUCE

●Beef ○Lamb ●Pork ○Ham ●Poultry
○Fish ○Seafood

Prep: 15 minutes Cook: 30 minutes
Makes: 2 cups

1 cup strong coffee
1 cup catsup
1/2 cup Worcestershire sauce
1/4 cup butter or margarine
1 tablespoon sugar
1 to 2 teaspoons freshly ground
   black pepper
1/2 teaspoon salt (optional)

1 In a medium saucepan combine coffee, catsup, Worcestershire sauce, butter, sugar, pepper, and, if desired, salt. Bring to boiling, stirring occasionally; reduce heat. Simmer, uncovered, for 30 minutes, stirring frequently.

2 To use, brush meat or poultry with warm sauce during the last 10 minutes of grilling. Cover and chill any remaining sauce for up to 3 days.

TEXAS-STYLE BRUSH-ON

●Beef ●Lamb ●Pork ○Ham ●Poultry
○Fish ○Seafood

Prep: 10 minutes Cook: 10 minutes
Makes: about 1 3/4 cups

1 cup finely chopped onion (1 large)
1/2 cup honey
1/2 cup catsup
1 4-ounce can diced green chile
   peppers, drained
1 tablespoon chili powder
1 clove garlic, minced
1/2 teaspoon dry mustard

1 In a small saucepan stir together onion, honey, catsup, chile peppers, chili powder, garlic, and dry mustard. Cook and stir over low heat for 10 minutes.

2 To use, brush meat or poultry with some of the sauce during the last 10 minutes of grilling. If desired, heat any remaining sauce until bubbly and pass with meat or poultry.

BROWN SUGAR-MUSTARD BRUSH-ON

●Beef ●Lamb ●Pork ○Ham ○Poultry
○Fish ○Seafood

Prep: 10 minutes Cook: 25 minutes
Makes: about 1 2/3 cups

1 cup packed brown sugar
2/3 cup white vinegar or cider vinegar
1/2 cup chopped onion
1/3 cup spicy brown mustard or
   Dijon-style mustard
2 tablespoons honey
2 teaspoons liquid smoke
2 cloves garlic, minced
1/4 teaspoon celery seeds

1 In a medium saucepan stir together brown sugar, vinegar, onion, mustard, honey, liquid smoke, garlic, and celery seeds. Bring to boiling; reduce heat. Simmer, uncovered, for 25 to 30 minutes or until mixture is slightly thickened, stirring occasionally.

2 To use, brush meat with some of the sauce during the last 10 to 15 minutes of grilling. If desired, heat any remaining sauce until bubbly and pass with meat.

CRAN-MUSTARD BRUSH-ON

●Beef ●Lamb ●Pork ●Ham ●Poultry
○Fish ○Seafood

Prep: 10 minutes
Makes: about 1 cup

1 8-ounce can jellied cranberry sauce
2 tablespoons steak sauce
2 teaspoons packed brown sugar
2 teaspoons yellow mustard
1/2 teaspoon finely shredded lemon peel
1/4 teaspoon celery seeds

1 In a small saucepan stir together cranberry sauce, steak sauce, brown sugar, mustard, lemon peel, and celery seeds. Cook and stir until cranberry sauce melts. Remove from heat.

2 To use, brush meat or poultry with sauce during the last 15 to 30 minutes of grilling.

HONEY-PEACH SAUCE

●Beef ○Lamb ●Pork ○Ham ●Poultry
○Fish ○Seafood

Prep: 20 minutes
Makes: about 1¾ cups

4 **medium peaches**
2 **tablespoons lemon juice**
2 **tablespoons honey**
½ **teaspoon cracked black pepper**
1 **to 2 teaspoons snipped fresh thyme**
 Fresh thyme sprig (optional)

1 Peel and cut up 3 of the peaches. Place in a blender. Add lemon juice, honey, and pepper. Cover and blend until smooth. Transfer to a medium saucepan. Bring to boiling; reduce heat. Simmer, uncovered, about 15 minutes or until slightly thickened, stirring occasionally. Remove from heat. Peel and finely chop the remaining peach; stir into the sauce. Stir in thyme.

2 To use, brush meat or poultry with some of the sauce during the last 15 minutes of grilling. If desired, heat any remaining sauce until bubbly, transfer to a bowl, garnish with a sprig of thyme, if desired, and pass with meat.

CHUTNEY BRUSH-ON

●Beef ●Lamb ●Pork ●Ham ●Poultry
○Fish ○Seafood

Prep: 5 minutes
Makes: about 1½ cups

1 **cup mango chutney**
¼ **cup bottled chili sauce**
2 **tablespoons vinegar**
1 **tablespoon Worcestershire sauce**
1 **tablespoon water**
1 **teaspoon dry mustard**
½ **teaspoon onion powder**
 Several dashes bottled hot
 pepper sauce

1 Snip any large pieces of chutney. In a medium saucepan stir together chutney, chili sauce, vinegar, Worcestershire sauce, water, dry mustard, onion powder, and hot pepper sauce. Cook and stir over medium heat until heated through.

2 To use, brush meat or poultry with some of the sauce during the last 5 minutes of grilling. If desired, heat any remaining sauce until bubbly and pass with meat or poultry.

TANDOORI-STYLE BRUSH-ON

○Beef ●Lamb ○Pork ○Ham ●Poultry
○Fish ○Seafood

Prep: 10 minutes
Makes: about ¼ cup

2 **tablespoons cooking oil**
6 **cloves garlic, minced**
2 **teaspoons grated fresh ginger**
1 **tablespoon garam masala***
½ **teaspoon salt**

1 In a small bowl stir together oil, garlic, ginger, garam masala, and salt.

2 To use, brush mixture evenly onto meat or poultry. Grill according to charts.

*Note: For homemade garam masala, combine 1 teaspoon ground cumin, 1 teaspoon ground coriander, ½ teaspoon black pepper, ½ teaspoon ground cardamom, ¼ teaspoon ground cinnamon, and ¼ teaspoon ground cloves.

FOOD FOR THOUGHT
INDIAN SPICES

The flavors of India continue to gain popularity. "Masala" is an Indian term that refers to a blend of spices that is the essence of Indian cooking. "Garam," meaning "hot," is the best-known masala, which typically consists of a blend of roasted ground spices that includes peppercorns, coriander, cumin, cardamom, nutmeg, cinnamon, and turmeric. It is added toward the end of the cooking process or sprinkled on before serving.

Honey-Peach Sauce

Sage-Orange Marinade

ASIAN MARINADE

●Beef ○Lamb ●Pork ○Ham ●Poultry
●Fish ○Seafood

Prep: 10 minutes Marinate: 4 to 24 hours
Makes: about 1½ cups
(enough for 1¼ pounds of meat, poultry, or fish)

½ **cup beef broth**
⅓ **cup bottled hoisin sauce**
¼ **cup reduced-sodium soy sauce**
¼ **cup sliced green onions (2)**
3 **tablespoons dry sherry, apple juice,**
   orange juice, or pineapple juice
1 **tablespoon sugar**
4 **cloves garlic, minced**
1 **teaspoon grated fresh ginger**

1 In a small bowl stir together beef broth, hoisin sauce, soy sauce, green onions, sherry, sugar, garlic, and ginger.

2 To use, pour marinade over meat, poultry, or fish in a self-sealing plastic bag set in a shallow dish; seal bag. Or pour marinade over meat, poultry, or fish in a nonreactive container, such as a ceramic or glass bowl or dish. Turn to coat meat, poultry, or fish. Cover if in container.

3 Marinate in the refrigerator at least 4 hours or up to 24 hours, turning occasionally. Drain, discarding marinade. Grill according to charts.

SAGE-ORANGE MARINADE

○Beef ○Lamb ●Pork ○Ham ●Poultry
●Fish ○Seafood

Prep: 10 minutes Marinate: 6 to 12 hours
Makes: about ⅓ cup (enough for ¾ pound of meat)

1 **teaspoon finely shredded**
   orange peel
⅓ **cup orange juice**
2 **teaspoons olive oil or cooking oil**
¾ **teaspoon snipped fresh rosemary or**
   ¼ **teaspoon dried rosemary,**
   crushed
¾ **teaspoon snipped fresh sage or**
   ¼ **teaspoon dried sage, crushed**
1 **clove garlic, minced**
¼ **teaspoon salt**
¼ **teaspoon black pepper**

1 In a small bowl stir together orange peel, orange juice, oil, rosemary, sage, garlic, salt, and black pepper.

2 To use, pour marinade over meat, poultry, or fish in a self-sealing plastic bag set in a shallow dish; seal bag. Or pour marinade over meat, poultry, or fish in a nonreactive container, such as a ceramic or glass bowl or dish. Turn to coat meat, poultry, or fish. Cover if in container.

3 Marinate in the refrigerator at least 6 hours or up to 12 hours. Drain meat, poultry, or fish, discarding marinade. Grill according to charts.

CILANTRO-PESTO MARINADE

●Beef ●Lamb ●Pork ○Ham ○Poultry
○Fish ○Seafood

Prep: 10 minutes Marinate: 1 hour Makes: about ⅔ cup
(enough for 1½ pounds of meat)

½ **cup firmly packed fresh cilantro**
   leaves
½ **of a small red onion, cut up**
1 **teaspoon finely shredded lime peel**
2 **tablespoons lime juice**
2 **teaspoons Worcestershire sauce**
¼ **teaspoon ground cumin**
¼ **teaspoon dried oregano, crushed**

1 In a food processor or blender combine cilantro, onion, lime peel, lime juice, Worcestershire sauce, cumin, and oregano. Cover

and process or blend with a few on-off pulses just until coarsely chopped.

2 To use, pour marinade over meat in a self-sealing plastic bag set in a shallow dish; seal bag. Or pour marinade over meat in a nonreactive container, such as a ceramic or glass bowl or dish. Turn to coat meat. Cover if in container.

3 Marinate in the refrigerator for 1 hour, turning once. Drain meat, discarding marinade. Grill according to charts.

SAVORY-BALSAMIC MARINADE

●Beef ●Lamb ●Pork ○Ham ●Poultry
●Fish ○Seafood

Prep: 10 minutes Marinate: 10 minutes to 4 hours Makes: about ¼ cup (enough for 1 pound of meat, poultry, or fish)

¼ cup balsamic vinegar
1 tablespoon snipped fresh savory or
    1 teaspoon dried savory, crushed
½ teaspoon black pepper

1 In a small bowl stir together vinegar, savory, and pepper.

2 To use, pour marinade over meat, poultry, or fish in a self-sealing plastic bag set in a shallow dish; seal bag.

3 Marinate in the refrigerator at least 10 minutes or up to 4 hours, turning once. Drain meat, poultry, or fish, discarding marinade. Grill according to charts.

LEMON-GARLIC MARINADE

○Beef ○Lamb ●Pork ○Ham ○Poultry
●Fish ○Seafood

Prep: 10 minutes Marinate: 1 to 2 hours Makes: ½ cup (enough for 2 pounds of meat or fish)

¼ cup olive oil
1 teaspoon finely shredded lemon peel
¼ cup lemon juice
1 tablespoon snipped fresh tarragon
    or 1 teaspoon dried tarragon,
    crushed
2 teaspoons bottled minced garlic
½ teaspoon coarsely ground black
    pepper

1 In a small bowl combine oil, lemon peel, lemon juice, tarragon, garlic, and pepper.

2 To use, pour marinade over meat or fish in a self-sealing plastic bag set in a shallow dish; seal bag. Or pour marinade over meat, fish, or vegetables in a nonreactive container, such as a ceramic or glass bowl or dish. Turn to coat meat or fish. Cover if in container.

3 Marinate in the refrigerator for 1 to 2 hours. Drain meat or fish, reserving marinade. Grill according to charts. Brush meat or fish with marinade halfway through grilling. Discard any remaining marinade.

FOOD FOR THOUGHT MARINADES

Marinades are seasoned liquids that add flavor and also can tenderize thinner cuts of meat, poultry, and fish. Tenderizing marinades penetrate about ¼ inch into the surface of the meat and usually contain food acids (such as vinegar, wine, or salsa) or natural enzymes (such as ginger or pineapple), oil, and aromatics. The food acids and enzymes tenderize the meat or poultry. Oils protect the food from the heat of the grill. Herbs, spices, and other aromatic seasonings impart flavor.

    To enhance the flavor of tender cuts, marinate for 15 minutes to 2 hours. To tenderize less tender cuts, marinate for 4 to 24 hours. Don't overdo it. Meats and poultry that are marinated longer than 24 hours can become mushy. Be careful with fish as well: Any acidic ingredient can "cook" the fish, making it very tough.

CHIPOTLE-TOMATO MARINADE

●Beef ○Lamb ●Pork ○Ham ●Poultry
○Fish ○Seafood

Stand: 30 minutes Prep: 10 minutes Marinate: 2 to 8 hours
Makes: about 2 cups
(enough for ¾ pound of meat or poultry)

12 dried tomato halves (not oil-pack)
1 to 3 dried chipotle chile peppers
(see tip, page 36)
1 cup boiling water
1 cup dry red or white wine, or 1 cup
water plus ½ teaspoon instant
beef bouillon granules
½ cup chopped onion (1 medium)
1 tablespoon packed brown sugar
1 tablespoon lime juice or lemon juice
2 cloves garlic, quartered
¼ teaspoon black pepper

1 In a medium bowl place dried tomatoes and chipotle peppers; add boiling water. Let stand about 30 minutes or until vegetables are softened. Drain, reserving liquid.

2 Cut up tomatoes; place in a food processor or blender. Wearing disposable plastic gloves, trim stems from chile peppers; scrape out seeds. Cut up chile peppers; add to tomatoes along with ¼ cup of the reserved soaking liquid, the wine, onion, brown sugar, lime juice, garlic, and black pepper. Cover and process or blend until nearly smooth. (When necessary, stop food processor or blender and use a rubber scraper to scrape the side of bowl or container.)

3 To use, pour marinade over meat or poultry in a self-sealing plastic bag set in a shallow dish; seal bag. Or pour marinade over meat or poultry in a nonreactive container, such as a ceramic or glass bowl or dish. Turn to coat meat or poultry. Cover if in container.

4 Marinate in the refrigerator at least 2 hours or up to 8 hours. Drain meat or poultry, reserving marinade. Grill according to charts. Brush reserved marinade on meat or poultry halfway through grilling; discard any remaining marinade.

HERBED MUSTARD MARINADE

●Beef ●Lamb ○Pork ○Ham ○Poultry
○Fish ○Seafood

Prep: 10 minutes Marinate: 8 to 24 hours
Makes: about 1½ cups (enough for 4 pounds of meat)

1 8-ounce jar (1 cup) Dijon-style
mustard
¼ cup olive oil
2 tablespoons dry red wine
2 cloves garlic, minced
1 teaspoon dried rosemary, crushed
1 teaspoon dried basil, crushed
½ teaspoon dried oregano, crushed
½ teaspoon dried thyme, crushed
¼ teaspoon black pepper

1 In a small bowl stir together the mustard, oil, wine, garlic, rosemary, basil, oregano, thyme, and pepper.

2 To use, spread ½ cup of the mustard mixture evenly over meat. Cover and chill meat and reserved mustard mixture at least 8 hours or up to 24 hours. Drain meat, discarding marinade. Grill according to charts.

3 To serve, in a small saucepan heat reserved mustard mixture and pass with grilled meat.

Chipotle-Tomato Marinade

WINE-SHALLOT MARINADE

●Beef ●Lamb ●Pork ○Ham ●Poultry
●Fish ○Seafood

Prep: 10 minutes Marinate: 8 to 24 hours
Makes: about 2½ cups
(enough for 2 pounds of meat, poultry, or fish)

2 cups dry white wine
½ cup chopped onion (1 medium)
4 shallots or green onions, chopped
1 teaspoon olive oil or cooking oil
½ teaspoon cracked black pepper
½ teaspoon dried basil, crushed
¼ teaspoon dried rosemary, crushed
1 bay leaf

1 In a bowl stir together wine, onion, shallots, oil, pepper, basil, rosemary, and bay leaf.

2 To use, pour marinade over meat, poultry, or fish in a self-sealing plastic bag set in a shallow dish; seal bag. Or pour marinade over meat, poultry, or fish in a nonreactive container, such as a ceramic or glass bowl or dish. Turn to coat meat, poultry, or fish. Cover if in container.

3 Marinate in the refrigerator at least 8 hours or up to 24 hours, turning several times. Drain meat, poultry, or fish, discarding marinade. Grill according to charts.

MUSTARD-PEPPERCORN RUB

●Beef ●Lamb ●Pork ○Ham ○Poultry
○Fish ○Seafood

Prep: 10 minutes Chill: 15 minutes to 4 hours
Makes: about 3 tablespoons (enough for 3 pounds of meat)

1 tablespoon coarse-grain brown
mustard
2 teaspoons olive oil
2 teaspoons cracked black pepper
2 teaspoons snipped fresh tarragon
1 teaspoon coarse salt

1 In a small bowl stir together mustard, oil, pepper, tarragon, and salt.

2 To use, spread mixture evenly onto meat. Cover and chill at least 15 minutes or up to 4 hours. Grill according to charts.

GARLIC-FENNEL RUB

●Beef ●Lamb ●Pork ○Ham ●Poultry
○Fish ○Seafood

Prep: 5 minutes
Makes: about 4 teaspoons
(enough for 1½ pounds of meat or poultry)

1 teaspoon bottled minced garlic
1 teaspoon black pepper
½ teaspoon cayenne pepper
½ teaspoon celery seeds
½ teaspoon fennel seeds, crushed
¼ teaspoon dried thyme, crushed
¼ teaspoon ground cumin

1 In a small bowl stir together garlic, black pepper, cayenne pepper, celery seeds, fennel seeds, thyme, and cumin.

2 To use, rub mixture evenly onto meat or poultry. Grill according to charts.

SMOKIN' HOT TIP

When used properly, marinades impart wonderful flavor and texture to grilled foods. Make the most of your marinade by following these guidelines.

● Never marinate anything at room temperature. Place the food in the refrigerator when marinating.

● Turn the food occasionally to ensure the marinade distributes evenly.

● If the marinade is to be used later for basting, reserve some before it contacts any raw meat.

● If the marinade is to be served as a sauce, boil it thoroughly to destroy harmful bacteria.

● Never save or reuse marinades.

SMOKIN' HOT TIP

Fresh herbs are preferred for cooking, but dried herbs offer a convenient and easy-to-use alternative. Here are a few tips for handling herbs to give you optimal flavor:

- Store dried herbs in a dry place away from heat and use within 2 to 3 months.
- Crush dried herbs and add them early in the cooking process to bring out their full flavor.
- Dried herbs have greater concentrated flavor than fresh herbs. As a general rule, you can substitute 1 teaspoon of dried herbs or $\frac{1}{4}$ teaspoon of ground herbs for every 1 tablespoon of fresh herbs.
- Loosely wrap fresh herbs in a damp cloth or paper towels, place in plastic bags, and store in the refrigerator to keep fresh and minimize wilting.
- Snip fresh herbs with scissors or chop with a sharp knife to minimize bruising and discoloration.
- To clean fresh herbs, gently rinse with water.

FRESH HERB RUB

○Beef ○Lamb ●Pork ○Ham ●Poultry
●Fish ○Seafood

Prep: 15 minutes
Makes: about 3 tablespoons
(enough for 3 pounds meat, poultry, or fish)

1 tablespoon snipped fresh thyme or
   $\frac{3}{4}$ teaspoon dried thyme, crushed
1 tablespoon snipped fresh sage or
   $\frac{3}{4}$ teaspoon dried sage, crushed
1 tablespoon snipped fresh rosemary
   or $\frac{3}{4}$ teaspoon dried rosemary,
   crushed
2 cloves garlic, minced
1$\frac{1}{2}$ teaspoons coarsely ground black
   pepper
1 to 1$\frac{1}{2}$ teaspoons coarse salt
$\frac{1}{2}$ teaspoon crushed red pepper

1 In a small bowl stir together thyme, sage, rosemary, garlic, black pepper, salt, and crushed red pepper.

2 To use, rub mixture evenly onto meat, poultry, or fish. Grill according to charts.

TANDOORI RUB

○Beef ●Lamb ○Pork ○Ham ●Poultry
○Fish ○Seafood

Prep: 10 minutes Chill: 4 to 24 hours
Makes: about 1$\frac{1}{4}$ cups
(enough for 3 pounds of meat or poultry)

4 cloves garlic, minced
2 tablespoons grated fresh ginger
2 tablespoons curry powder
2 teaspoons ground cumin
$\frac{1}{2}$ teaspoon salt
1 8-ounce carton plain yogurt

1 In a small bowl stir together garlic, ginger, curry powder, cumin, and salt.

2 To use, wearing disposable or plastic gloves to avoid staining your hands, rub garlic mixture evenly onto meat or poultry. Spread the meat or poultry evenly with yogurt to coat. Cover and chill meat or poultry at least 4 hours or up to 24 hours. Grill according to charts.

COASTAL BLEND TEXAS RUB

●Beef ●Lamb ●Pork ○Ham ●Poultry
○Fish ○Seafood

Prep: 10 minutes Chill: 2 to 24 hours
Makes: about 1 cup
(enough for 3 pounds of meat or poultry)

4 shallots, peeled and minced
8 cloves garlic, minced
2 tablespoons packed brown sugar
2 teaspoons coarse salt
2 teaspoons cracked black pepper
**2 teaspoons coriander seeds, coarsely
    crushed**

1 In a small bowl combine shallots, garlic, brown sugar, salt, pepper, and coriander seeds.

2 To use, rub mixture evenly onto meat or poultry. Cover and chill at least 2 hours or up to 24 hours. Grill according to charts using indirect method of cooking (rub will burn over direct heat). Store unused rub in the refrigerator.

SWEET AND SPICY RUB

●Beef ○Lamb ●Pork ○Ham ●Poultry
○Fish ○Seafood

Prep: 5 minutes
Makes: about 3 tablespoons
(enough for 3 pounds of meat or poultry)

2 tablespoons butter or margarine
1 teaspoon ground cinnamon
1/2 teaspoon salt
1/2 teaspoon ground cumin
1/2 teaspoon ground turmeric
1/2 teaspoon cayenne pepper
**1/2 teaspoon freshly ground
    black pepper**
1/4 teaspoon ground cardamom
1/8 teaspoon ground cloves
1/8 teaspoon ground nutmeg
1 tablespoon sugar

1 In a small saucepan melt butter. Stir in cinnamon, salt, cumin, turmeric, cayenne pepper, black pepper, cardamom, cloves, and nutmeg. Remove from heat. Stir in sugar; cool.

2 To use, rub mixture evenly onto meat or poultry. Grill according to charts.

Kansas City Barbecue Sauce
(see page 34) and
Sweet and Spicy Rub

JAMAICAN JERK RUB

○Beef ○Lamb ●Pork ○Ham ●Poultry
○Fish ○Seafood

Prep: 10 minutes Chill: 30 minutes
Makes: about ½ cup (enough for 1 pound of meat or poultry)

½ cup coarsely chopped onion
  (1 medium)
2 tablespoons lime juice
2 cloves garlic, quartered
1 teaspoon crushed red pepper
½ teaspoon salt
¼ teaspoon ground allspice
¼ teaspoon curry powder
¼ teaspoon black pepper
⅛ teaspoon dried thyme, crushed
⅛ teaspoon ground ginger

1 In a food processor or blender combine onion, lime juice, garlic, crushed red pepper, salt, allspice, curry powder, black pepper, thyme, and ginger. Cover and process until smooth.

2 To use, rub mixture evenly onto meat or poultry. Cover and chill for 30 minutes. Grill according to charts.

FOOD FOR THOUGHT RUBS

A rub is a flavorful mixture of herbs, spices, and seasonings that is rubbed onto the surface of meat, poultry, or fish prior to grilling. Some rubs are dry, while others include liquid, such as oil, mustard, or minced garlic, to form a wet rub or paste. "Jerk" is one such popular rub that originated in Jamaica. Great on pork and chicken, jerk rub typically consists of scallions, thyme, allspice, chiles, nutmeg, cinnamon, and oil or an acidic liquid.

GINGER-ALLSPICE RUB

○Beef ○Lamb ○Pork ○Ham ●Poultry
●Fish ○Seafood

Prep: 10 minutes
Makes: about 2 teaspoons
(enough for 1 pound of poultry or fish)

1 tablespoon lime juice
1 tablespoon water
1 teaspoon paprika
½ teaspoon salt
¼ teaspoon ground ginger
¼ teaspoon ground allspice
¼ teaspoon black pepper

1 In a small bowl stir together lime juice and water; brush onto poultry or fish. In another small bowl stir together paprika, salt, ginger, allspice, and pepper.

2 To use, rub mixture onto poultry or fish. Grill according to charts.

HERBED PECAN RUB

○Beef ○Lamb ○Pork ○Ham ●Poultry
●Fish ○Seafood

Prep: 15 minutes
Makes: about 1 cup (enough for 3 pounds of poultry or fish)

½ cup broken pecans
½ cup fresh oregano leaves
½ cup fresh thyme leaves
3 cloves garlic, quartered
½ teaspoon black pepper
½ teaspoon finely shredded lemon peel
¼ teaspoon salt
¼ cup cooking oil

1 In a food processor or blender combine pecans, oregano leaves, thyme leaves, garlic, pepper, lemon peel, and salt. Cover and process with several on-off turns until a paste forms. (When necessary, stop food processor or blender and use a rubber scraper to scrape the side of bowl or container.) With the machine running, gradually add oil through feed tube or lid, processing or blending until mixture forms a paste.

2 To use, rub mixture onto poultry or fish. Grill according to charts.

3

Sauces, Salsas & More

BUTTERS
Basil Butter, 49
Blue Cheese Butter, 49
Citrus-Garlic Butter, 49
Tomato-Garlic Butter, 49

CHUTNEYS & JAMS
Blue Cheese Vidalia Onions, 52
Fresh Mango Chutney, 54
Pear-Cherry Chutney, 54
Roasted Garlic and Sweet Onion Jam, 52
Roasted Red Pepper and Apricot Chutney, 53
Tomato-Rhubarb Chutney, 52

MAYONNAISES & MUSTARDS
Curry Mayonnaise, 50
Dried Tomato Mayonnaise, 50
Herbed Mayonnaise, 51
Lime-Sage Aïoli, 51
Mango Mayonnaise, 51
Tart Apple Mustard, 51

RELISHES
Artichoke-Pepper Relish, 54
Cucumber and Zucchini Relish, 55
Curried Jicama Relish, 58
Greek Tomato Relish, 55
Grilled Corn Relish, 56
Grilled Sweet Pepper Relish, 57
Jicama-Sweet Pepper Relish, 59
Mushroom Relish, 57
Pineapple Relish, 58
Red Sweet Pepper Relish, 60
Sweet Tomato Relish, 58

SALSAS
Fresh Summer Salsa, 59
Mango Salsa, 59
Savory Strawberry Salsa, 60
Sweet Strawberry Salsa, 60

SAUCES
Bordelaise Sauce, 64
Brandy Cream Sauce, 64
Onion Chili Sauce, 60
Peach and Pear Chili Sauce, 63
Portobello Sauce, 63
Rich Brown Sauce, 63
Tangy Coconut Sauce, 64

BASIL BUTTER

●Beef ●Lamb ●Pork ○Ham ●Poultry
●Fish ○Seafood

Start to Finish: 10 minutes
Makes: ⅓ cup

⅓ cup butter, softened
1 tablespoon snipped fresh basil
¼ teaspoon black pepper
1 clove garlic, minced

1 In a small bowl stir together butter, basil, pepper, and garlic.

Nutrition Facts per tablespoon: 115 cal., 13 g total fat (8 g sat. fat), 35 mg chol., 131 mg sodium, 0 g carbo., 0 g fiber, 0 g pro. Daily Values: 10% vit. A, 1% vit. C, 1% calcium. Exchanges: 2½ Fat

BLUE CHEESE BUTTER

●Beef ○Lamb ○Pork ○Ham ○Poultry
○Fish ○Seafood

Start to Finish: 10 minutes
Makes: ½ cup

¼ cup butter, softened
¼ cup crumbled blue cheese (1 ounce)
1 tablespoon snipped fresh parsley
2 teaspoons snipped fresh basil
½ teaspoon bottled minced garlic

1 In a small bowl stir together butter, blue cheese, parsley, basil, and garlic.

Nutrition Facts per tablespoon: 69 cal., 7 g total fat (5 g sat. fat), 20 mg chol., 121 mg sodium, 0 g carbo., 0 g fiber, 1 g pro. Daily Values: 5% vit. A, 1% vit. C, 3% calcium. Exchanges: 1½ Fat

CITRUS-GARLIC BUTTER

●Beef ●Lamb ●Pork ○Ham ●Poultry
○Fish ●Seafood

Start to Finish: 10 minutes
Makes: ½ cup

½ cup butter, softened
2 tablespoons snipped fresh parsley
1 tablespoon finely shredded
**   lemon peel**
1 tablespoon finely shredded
**   orange peel**
2 cloves garlic, minced

1 In a small bowl stir together butter, parsley, lemon peel, orange peel, and garlic.

Nutrition Facts per tablespoon: 110 cal., 12 g total fat (8 g sat. fat), 32 mg chol., 125 mg sodium, 1 g carbo., 0 g fiber, 0 g pro. Daily Values: 10% vit. A, 6% vit. C, 1% calcium, 1% iron. Exchanges: 2½ Fat

TOMATO-GARLIC BUTTER

●Beef ●Lamb ○Pork ○Ham ○Poultry
○Fish ○Seafood

Start to Finish: 15 minutes Makes: ½ cup

½ cup butter, softened
1 tablespoon finely snipped dried
**   tomatoes (oil-pack), drained**
1 tablespoon chopped, pitted
**   kalamata olives**
1 tablespoon finely chopped
**   green onion**
1 clove garlic, minced

1 In a small bowl stir together butter, tomatoes, olives, green onion, and garlic.

Nutrition Facts per tablespoon: 112 cal., 12 g total fat (8 g sat. fat), 33 mg chol., 138 mg sodium, 0 g carbo., 0 g fiber, 0 g pro. Daily Values: 9% vit. A, 2% vit. C, 1% calcium, 1% iron. Exchanges: 2½ Fat

FOOD FOR THOUGHT COMPOUND BUTTERS

Also known as flavored butters, compound butters are simple ways to add flavor to grilled meats, poultry, and fish. Making this condiment is as easy as blending softened butter with your own creative combinations of herbs, spices, and other seasonings. Experiment with lime zest for zing, hot sauce for heat, or chopped garlic and thyme for an aromatic lift.

Dried Tomato Mayonnaise, Curry Mayonnaise,
Herbed Mayonnaise

DRIED TOMATO MAYONNAISE

○Beef ○Lamb ○Pork ○Ham ●Poultry
●Fish ○Seafood

Prep: 15 minutes Chill: up to 24 hours
Makes: ½ cup

Boiling water
2 tablespoons snipped dried (not oil-pack) tomatoes
⅓ cup mayonnaise or salad dressing

1 In a small bowl pour enough boiling water over the dried tomatoes to cover. Let stand about 10 minutes or until softened. Drain well. Stir tomatoes into mayonnaise. Cover and chill for up to 24 hours.

Nutrition Facts per tablespoon: 68 cal., 7 g total fat (1 g sat. fat), 3 mg chol., 67 mg sodium, 0 g carbo., 0 g fiber, 0 g pro. Daily Values: 1% vit. C. Exchanges: 1½ Fat

CURRY MAYONNAISE

○Beef ○Lamb ○Pork ○Ham ●Poultry
●Fish ○Seafood

Prep: 10 minutes Chill: up to 24 hours
Makes: ½ cup

¼ cup mayonnaise or salad dressing
¼ cup dairy sour cream
2 tablespoons frozen orange juice concentrate
¾ to 1 teaspoon curry powder
4 to 5 tablespoons fat-free milk

1 In a small bowl combine mayonnaise, sour cream, orange juice concentrate, and curry powder. Stir in enough milk to make drizzling consistency. Cover and chill for up to 24 hours.

Nutrition Facts per tablespoon: 73 cal., 7 g total fat, (2 g sat. fat), 5 mg chol., 45 mg sodium, 2 g carbo., 0 g fiber, 1 g pro. Daily Values: 2% vit. A, 11% vit. C, 2% calcium. Exchanges: 1½ Fat

---

HERBED MAYONNAISE

●Beef ●Lamb ●Pork ○Ham ●Poultry
●Fish ○Seafood

Prep: 10 minutes Chill: up to 24 hours
Makes: 1¼ cups

½ cup mayonnaise or salad dressing
½ cup dairy sour cream
3 tablespoons snipped fresh dill
2 tablespoons snipped fresh parsley
1 clove garlic, minced

1 In a food processor or blender combine mayonnaise, sour cream, dill, parsley, and garlic. Cover and process or blend until almost smooth. Transfer to a small bowl. Cover and chill for up to 24 hours.

Nutrition Facts per tablespoon: 51 cal., 5 g total fat (1 g sat. fat), 4 mg chol., 33 mg sodium, 0 g carbo., 0 g fiber, 0 g pro. Daily Values: 1% vit. A, 1% vit. C, 1% calcium. Exchanges: 1 Fat

---

MANGO MAYONNAISE

○Beef ○Lamb ●Pork ○Ham ●Poultry
●Fish ○Seafood

Prep: 10 minutes Chill: up to 24 hours
Makes: ¾ cup

½ cup finely chopped, peeled mango
¼ cup mayonnaise or light mayonnaise dressing
2 teaspoons lime juice

1 In a small bowl combine mango, mayonnaise, and lime juice. Cover; chill for up to 24 hours.

Nutrition Facts per tablespoon: 38 cal., 4 g total fat (1 g sat. fat), 2 mg chol., 25 mg sodium, 1 g carbo., 0 g fiber, 0 g pro. Daily Values: 5% vit. A, 4% vit. C. Exchanges: 1 Fat

LIME-SAGE AÏOLI

●Beef ○Lamb ●Pork ○Ham ●Poultry
○Fish ○Seafood

Prep: 15 minutes Chill: up to 24 hours
Makes: about 1 cup

¼ cup refrigerated or frozen egg product, thawed
1 tablespoon snipped fresh sage
2 teaspoons bottled minced garlic
1 teaspoon Dijon-style mustard
½ cup olive oil
1 tablespoon lime juice
⅛ teaspoon salt
⅛ teaspoon black pepper

1 In a food processor or blender combine egg product, sage, garlic, and mustard. Cover and process or blend until smooth. With machine running, add olive oil in a thin, steady stream, stopping to scrape down sides as necessary. Add lime juice, salt, and pepper. Cover and process or blend until mixture is combined and creamy. Transfer to a small bowl. Cover and chill for up to 24 hours.

Nutrition Facts per tablespoon: 127 cal., 14 g total fat (2 g sat. fat), 0 mg chol., 65 mg sodium, 1 g carbo., 0 g fiber, 1 g pro. Daily Values: 2% vit. A, 2% vit. C, 1% calcium, 1% iron. Exchanges: 3 Fat

---

TART APPLE MUSTARD

●Beef ○Lamb ●Pork ●Ham ●Poultry
○Fish ○Seafood

Prep: 5 minutes Chill: 2 to 24 hours
Makes: ⅔ cup

½ cup honey mustard
2 tablespoons shredded, unpeeled tart green apple
½ teaspoon black pepper

1 In a small bowl combine mustard, apple, and pepper. Cover and chill for 2 to 24 hours.

Nutrition Facts per tablespoon: 12 cal., 0 g total fat (0 g sat. fat), 0 mg chol., 87 mg sodium, 2 g carbo., 0 g fiber, 0 g pro. Exchanges: Free

BLUE CHEESE VIDALIA ONIONS

●Beef ○Lamb ○Pork ○Ham ○Poultry
○Fish ○Seafood

Prep: 30 minutes Grill: 25 minutes
Makes: 8 servings

**2 large Vidalia onions or other sweet
  onions, cut into ¹⁄₂-inch slices**
1 tablespoon butter or margarine
1 cup crumbled blue cheese
**¹⁄₂ of an 8-ounce package cream
  cheese, cut up**
2 teaspoons Worcestershire sauce
¹⁄₂ teaspoon black pepper
¹⁄₂ teaspoon dried dill

1 Fold a 36×18-inch piece of heavy foil in half to make an 18-inch square. Place the onion slices in the center of the foil. Dot with butter. Bring up the opposite edges of the foil and seal with a double fold. Fold the remaining edges together to completely enclose the onions, leaving space for steam to build.

2 For a charcoal grill, grill foil packet on the rack of an uncovered grill directly over medium coals for 25 to 30 minutes or until onions are just tender, turning packet once or twice. (For a gas grill, preheat grill. Reduce heat to medium. Place foil packet on grill rack over heat. Cover and grill as above.)

3 Meanwhile, in a large bowl combine the blue cheese, cream cheese, Worcestershire sauce, pepper, and dill. Use a slotted spoon to add grilled onions to the cheese mixture. Toss to coat.

Nutrition Facts per serving: 130 cal., 11 g total fat (7 g sat. fat), 30 mg chol., 273 mg sodium, 5 g carbo., 1 g fiber, 5 g pro. Daily Values: 7% vit. A, 4% vit. C, 10% calcium, 3% iron. Exchanges: ¹⁄₂ Vegetable, ¹⁄₂ High Fat Meat, 1¹⁄₂ Fat

ROASTED GARLIC AND SWEET ONION JAM

●Beef ○Lamb ●Pork ○Ham ●Poultry
○Fish ○Seafood

Prep: 15 minutes Cook: 30 minutes Roast: 45 minutes
Oven: 350°F Makes: about 1 cup

1 head garlic
1 tablespoon olive oil
**1 cup finely chopped sweet onions
  (such as Vidalia or Walla Walla)**
¹⁄₂ cup finely chopped tart green apple
¹⁄₂ cup sugar
¹⁄₂ cup balsamic vinegar

1 To roast garlic, use a sharp knife to cut off the top ¹⁄₂ inch from garlic head to expose the individual cloves. Leaving garlic head whole, remove loose, papery outer layers of skin. Place the garlic head, cut side up, in a custard cup. Drizzle with oil. Cover with foil and roast in a 350°F oven for 45 to 60 minutes or until the cloves feel soft when pressed. Let cool.

2 Gently squeeze the garlic cloves and juices into a saucepan. Stir in the onion, apple, sugar, and vinegar. Bring to boiling over medium-high heat, stirring occasionally; reduce heat. Simmer, uncovered, about 30 minutes or until onion and apple have softened and turned transparent and the mixture has thickened, stirring occasionally.

Nutrition Facts per tablespoon: 46 cal., 1 g total fat (0 g sat. fat), 0 mg chol., 1 mg sodium, 10 g carbo., 1 g fiber, 0 g pro. Daily Values: 2% vit. C, 1% calcium. Exchanges: ¹⁄₂ Other Carbo.

TOMATO-RHUBARB CHUTNEY

●Beef ○Lamb ●Pork ●Ham ●Poultry
○Fish ○Seafood

Prep: 20 minutes Cook: 30 minutes Chill: up to 1 week
Makes: about 2³⁄₄ cups

**3 medium tomatoes, peeled, seeded,
  and chopped (about 1¹⁄₂ cups)**
¹⁄₃ cup chopped onion (1 small)
**¹⁄₃ cup coarsely chopped red
  sweet pepper**
**¹⁄₃ cup dried tart red cherries, dried
  cranberries, or raisins**
¹⁄₃ cup white vinegar
¹⁄₄ cup granulated sugar
¹⁄₄ cup packed brown sugar
¹⁄₄ cup water
1 tablespoon lime juice or lemon juice

Roasted Red Pepper and Apricot Chutney

1 teaspoon grated fresh ginger or
    ¼ teaspoon ground ginger
¼ teaspoon salt
2 cloves garlic, minced
1 cup chopped fresh or frozen
    rhubarb

1 In a medium saucepan combine tomatoes, onion, sweet pepper, cherries, vinegar, granulated sugar, brown sugar, water, lime juice, ginger, salt, and garlic. Bring to boiling; reduce heat. Simmer, covered, for 25 minutes, stirring occasionally. Stir in rhubarb.

2 Simmer, covered, about 5 minutes more or until thickened (15 minutes more for frozen rhubarb). Let cool. Cover; chill for up to 1 week.

Nutrition Facts per tablespoon: 16 cal., 0 g total fat (0 g sat. fat), 0 mg chol., 15 mg sodium, 4 g carbo., 0 g fiber, 0 g pro. Daily Values: 2% vit. A, 6% vit. C. Exchanges: Free

ROASTED RED PEPPER AND APRICOT CHUTNEY

○Beef ○Lamb ●Pork ○Ham ●Poultry
○Fish ○Seafood

Prep: 25 minutes Roast: 20 minutes Cook: 20 minutes
Chill: up to 1 week Oven: 425°F Makes: about 1¾ cups

3 large red sweet peppers
1 cup finely chopped red onion
    (1 large)
⅔ cup cider vinegar

½ cup dried apricots, snipped
⅓ cup golden raisins
¼ cup granulated sugar
¼ cup packed brown sugar
1 tablespoon grated fresh ginger
1 teaspoon crushed red pepper
½ teaspoon salt
½ teaspoon dry mustard
3 cloves garlic, minced

1 To roast sweet peppers, quarter peppers lengthwise; remove stems, seeds, and membranes. Place pepper quarters, skin side up, on a foil-lined baking sheet. Roast in a 425°F oven about 20 minutes or until skins are blistered and dark. Wrap peppers in the foil. Let stand about 15 minutes or until cool enough to handle. Use a sharp knife to pull skins off gently and slowly. Discard skins. Chop peppers (you should have 1¼ cups).

2 In a medium saucepan combine roasted sweet peppers, onion, vinegar, apricots, raisins, granulated sugar, brown sugar, ginger, crushed red pepper, salt, mustard, and garlic. Bring to boiling; reduce heat. Simmer, uncovered, about 20 minutes or until slightly thickened. Let cool. (Chutney will continue to thicken as it cools.) Cover and chill for up to 1 week.

Nutrition Facts per tablespoon: 34 cal., 0 g total fat (0 g sat. fat), 0 mg chol., 43 mg sodium, 9 g carbo., 1 g fiber, 0 g pro. Daily Values: 19% vit. A, 44% vit. C, 1% calcium, 1% iron. Exchanges: ½ Other Carbo.

FRESH MANGO CHUTNEY

●Beef ○Lamb ●Pork ●Ham ●Poultry
●Fish ○Seafood

Prep: 15 minutes Cook: 10 minutes Chill: up to 1 week
Makes: about 2 cups

 1/4 **cup packed brown sugar**
 1/4 **cup finely chopped onion**
 1/4 **cup golden raisins**
 1/4 **cup cider vinegar**
 1/2 **teaspoon ground nutmeg**
 1/2 **teaspoon ground cinnamon**
 1/4 **teaspoon salt**
 1/8 **teaspoon ground cloves**
  2 **cups chopped, peeled mangoes**
     or peaches
  2 **tablespoons water**
  2 **tablespoons lemon juice or**
     lime juice

1 In a medium saucepan combine brown sugar, onion, raisins, vinegar, nutmeg, cinnamon, salt, and cloves. Bring to boiling; reduce heat. Simmer, uncovered, for 5 minutes, stirring occasionally.

2 Stir in mangoes and water. Return to boiling; reduce heat. Simmer, uncovered, about 5 minutes more or until slightly thickened, stirring frequently. Remove from heat. Stir in lemon juice. Let cool. Cover and chill for up to 1 week.

Nutrition Facts per tablespoon: 18 cal., 0 g total fat (0 g sat. fat), 0 mg chol., 18 mg sodium, 5 g carbo., 0 g fiber, 0 g pro. Daily Values: 6% vit. C. Exchanges: Free

PEAR-CHERRY CHUTNEY

●Beef ●Lamb ●Pork ○Ham ○Poultry
○Fish ○Seafood

Prep: 20 minutes Cook: 10 minutes Chill: up to 2 weeks
Makes: about 4 1/2 cups

  1 **cup dried tart red cherries**
 1/2 **cup sugar**
  2 **teaspoons finely shredded**
     lemon peel
 1/3 **cup lemon juice**
 1/2 **teaspoon ground cinnamon**
 1/2 **teaspoon ground allspice**
  5 **cups chopped, peeled firm pears**

1 In a large saucepan combine dried cherries, sugar, lemon peel, lemon juice, cinnamon, and allspice. Bring to boiling; reduce heat. Simmer, uncovered, for 5 minutes, stirring occasionally. Stir in pears. Return to boiling; reduce heat. Simmer, uncovered, about 5 minutes more or until pears are just tender. Let cool. Cover and chill for up to 2 weeks.

Nutrition Facts per tablespoon: 18 cal., 0 g total fat (0 g sat. fat), 0 mg chol., 0 mg sodium, 5 g carbo., 0 g fiber, 0 g pro. Daily Values: 2% vit. C. Exchanges: Free

ARTICHOKE-PEPPER RELISH

●Beef ●Lamb ●Pork ○Ham ○Poultry
○Fish ○Seafood

Prep: 15 minutes Chill: 2 to 24 hours
Makes: 1 3/4 cups

  1 **6 1/2-ounce jar marinated artichoke**
     hearts
  1 **7-ounce jar roasted red sweet**
     peppers, drained
 2/3 **cup jalapeño-stuffed green olives,**
     sliced
  1 **medium onion, thinly sliced and**
     separated into rings
  1 **tablespoon snipped fresh parsley**
 1/8 **teaspoon dried oregano, crushed**
 1/8 **teaspoon ground cumin**
  1 **clove garlic, minced**

1 Drain artichoke hearts, reserving marinade. Thinly slice artichoke hearts. Cut roasted sweet peppers into strips.

2 In a medium bowl combine artichokes, reserved marinade, sweet peppers, olives, onion, parsley, oregano, cumin, and garlic. Cover and chill for 2 to 24 hours, stirring occasionally.

Nutrition Facts per tablespoon: 11 cal., 1 g total fat (0 g sat. fat), 0 mg chol., 92 mg sodium, 1 g carbo., 0 g fiber, 0 g pro. Daily Values: 1% vit. A, 16% vit. C, 1% iron. Exchanges: Free

CUCUMBER AND ZUCCHINI RELISH

●Beef ○Lamb ●Pork ○Ham ○Poultry
○Fish ○Seafood

Prep: 1 hour Chill: overnight Cook: 5 minutes
Process: 10 minutes Makes: about 7 pints

2¹/₂ pounds zucchini, chopped (8 cups)
**2 pounds cucumber, seeded and
chopped (5¹/₃ cups)**
8 medium onions, chopped (4 cups)
¹/₃ cup pickling salt
4 cups sugar
2¹/₂ cups cider vinegar
**2 large red and/or green sweet
peppers, chopped (2 cups)**
**1 tablespoon finely shredded
lemon peel**
¹/₂ cup lemon juice
2 tablespoons celery seeds
1 teaspoon ground nutmeg
1 teaspoon ground cinnamon
¹/₂ teaspoon ground turmeric
¹/₂ teaspoon black pepper

1 In a very large glass or plastic bowl combine zucchini, cucumber, onions, and pickling salt. Cover and chill overnight. Drain and rinse the vegetables in a very large colander. Transfer to an 8- to 10-quart stainless-steel, enameled, or nonstick heavy kettle. Stir in sugar, vinegar, sweet peppers, lemon peel, lemon juice, celery seeds, nutmeg, cinnamon, turmeric, and black pepper. Bring to boiling; reduce heat. Simmer, uncovered, for 5 minutes.

2 Ladle the hot relish into hot, sterilized pint canning jars, leaving a ¹/₂-inch headspace. Wipe jar rims; adjust lids. Process in a boiling-water canner for 10 minutes (start timing when water returns to boil). Remove jars from canner; cool on racks.

Nutrition Facts per ¹/₄ cup: 71 cal., 0 g total fat (0 g sat. fat), 0 mg chol., 136 mg sodium, 18 g carbo., 1 g fiber, 1 g pro. Daily Values: 8% vit. A, 23% vit. C, 1% calcium, 2% iron. Exchanges: 1 Other Carbo.

GREEK TOMATO RELISH

○Beef ○Lamb ●Pork ○Ham ●Poultry
●Fish ○Seafood

Prep: 10 minutes
Makes: about 1¹/₂ cups

**3 roma tomatoes, seeded and
finely chopped**
¹/₂ cup chopped, pitted kalamata olives
**¹/₃ cup finely chopped red onion
(1 small)**
2 tablespoons olive oil
1 tablespoon snipped fresh oregano
1 tablespoon red wine vinegar
Black pepper

1 In a small bowl combine tomatoes, olives, onion, oil, oregano, and vinegar. Season to taste with pepper.

Nutrition Facts per tablespoon: 17 cal., 2 g total fat (0 g sat. fat), 0 mg chol., 32 mg sodium, 1 g carbo., 0 g fiber, 0 g pro. Daily Values: 2% vit. A, 3% vit. C. Exchanges: ¹/₂ Fat

FOOD FOR THOUGHT
RELISHES, SALSAS & CHUTNEYS

Relish and salsa are terms used to describe a condiment made with chopped fruits and/or vegetables. They can be warm or cold, sweet or savory, hot or mild. Chutneys are a type of relish made from fruit, vinegar, sugar, and spices. Best known as partners to Indian curry dishes, chutneys have broadened their horizons. With the many combinations of fruit and spices possible, they're often served with cheese and crackers.

GRILLED CORN RELISH

●Beef ○Lamb ●Pork ○Ham ●Poultry
○Fish ○Seafood

Prep: 15 minutes Grill: 25 minutes
Makes: 2 cups

- **3 tablespoons lime juice**
- **1 tablespoon cooking oil**
- **1 teaspoon bottled minced garlic**
- **2 fresh ears of corn, husked and cleaned**
- **1 teaspoon chili powder**
- **1 small avocado, halved, seeded, peeled, and cut up**
- **½ cup chopped red sweet pepper**
- **¼ cup snipped fresh cilantro**
- **¼ teaspoon salt**

1 In a medium bowl combine lime juice, oil, and garlic. Brush corn lightly with lime juice mixture. Reserve remaining juice mixture. Sprinkle corn with chili powder.

2 For a charcoal grill, grill corn on the rack of an uncovered grill directly over medium coals for 25 to 30 minutes or until tender, turning occasionally. (For a gas grill, preheat grill. Reduce heat to medium. Place corn on grill rack over heat. Cover and grill as above.)

3 Meanwhile, stir avocado, sweet pepper, cilantro, and salt into reserved lime juice mixture. Cut cooked corn kernels from cobs; stir into avocado mixture.

Nutrition Facts per tablespoon: 15 cal., 1 g total fat (0 g sat. fat), 0 mg chol., 20 mg sodium, 2 g carbo., 0 g fiber, 0 g pro. Daily Values: 5% vit. A, 10% vit. C, 1% iron. Exchanges: Free

Grilled Corn Relish

GRILLED SWEET PEPPER RELISH

○Beef ○Lamb ●Pork ○Ham ●Poultry
○Fish ○Seafood

Prep: 10 minutes Grill: 8 minutes
Makes: 4 servings

1 medium onion, thinly sliced
1 red or yellow sweet pepper,
cut into strips
1 tablespoon red wine vinegar
2 teaspoons olive oil

1 Fold a 24×18-inch piece of heavy foil in half to make a 12×18-inch rectangle. Place onion and sweet pepper in center of foil. Drizzle vinegar and oil over the onion and sweet pepper; sprinkle with ⅛ teaspoon black pepper. Bring up opposite edges of the foil and seal with a double fold. Fold remaining edges together to completely enclose vegetables, leaving space for steam to build.

2 For a charcoal grill, grill foil packet on the rack of an uncovered grill directly over medium coals for 8 minutes, turning packet once. (For a gas grill, preheat grill. Reduce heat to medium. Place foil packet on grill rack over heat. Cover and grill as above.)

Nutrition Facts per serving: 36 cal., 2 g total fat (0 g sat. fat), 0 mg chol., 1 mg sodium, 4 g carbo., 1 g fiber, 1 g pro. Daily Values: 32% vit. A, 82% vit. C, 1% calcium, 1% iron. Exchanges: Free

MUSHROOM RELISH

○Beef ○Lamb ●Pork ○Ham ●Poultry
●Fish ○Seafood

Prep: 30 minutes Cook: 8 minutes Chill: 4 to 24 hours
Makes: 2½ cups

1 cup chopped fresh button mushrooms
1 cup chopped fresh shiitake
mushrooms
1 cup chopped fresh brown mushrooms
½ cup chopped yellow and/or red
sweet pepper
4 cloves garlic, minced
1 tablespoon cooking oil
2 medium tomatoes, seeded and
coarsely chopped

¼ cup sliced green onions (2)
¼ cup rice vinegar
½ teaspoon cumin seeds, crushed
¼ teaspoon chili oil

1 In a large skillet cook mushrooms, sweet pepper, and garlic in hot oil for 8 to 10 minutes or until most of the liquid has evaporated. Transfer to a bowl; stir in tomatoes, green onions, vinegar, cumin seeds, and chili oil. Cover and chill for 4 to 24 hours. To serve, let stand at room temperature for 30 minutes. Serve with a slotted spoon.

Nutrition Facts per ¼ cup: 35 cal., 2 g total fat (0 g sat. fat), 0 mg chol., 5 mg sodium, 4 g carbo., 1 g fiber, 1 g pro. Daily Values: 4% vit. A, 42% vit. C, 1% calcium, 3% iron. Exchanges: ½ Vegetable, ½ Fat

SMOKIN' HOT TIP

Once considered food for the gods by Egyptian pharaohs, fresh mushrooms come in many shapes, sizes, colors, and textures. Mushrooms are fragile and deteriorate quickly; here are a few guidelines to maintaining their integrity:

● Buying: **When buying fresh mushrooms, choose those that are firm and intact. Avoid those that are split, dry, wrinkled, spotted, or slimy.**

● Storing: **Refrigerate fresh mushrooms for up to 1 week. To avoid rotting, provide good air circulation by placing mushrooms in a paper bag or on a tray covered with paper towels—never store them in plastic.**

● Cleaning: **Clean mushrooms just prior to use. Either wipe gently with a damp paper towel or rinse quickly with water using a soft brush, then pat dry. Don't soak mushrooms in water.**

● Preparing: **Remove or trim any tough, dry stems or edges from fresh mushrooms.**

CURRIED JICAMA RELISH

●Beef ○Lamb ●Pork ○Ham ○Poultry
○Fish ○Seafood

Prep: 20 minutes Chill: 4 to 24 hours
Makes: about 1½ cups

3 medium oranges, peeled, sectioned, and chopped
⅔ cup finely chopped red and/or green sweet pepper
½ cup finely chopped peeled jicama
2 tablespoons finely chopped red onion
2 tablespoons balsamic vinegar
1 tablespoon orange juice
1 teaspoon curry powder

1 Combine oranges, sweet pepper, jicama, onion, vinegar, orange juice, curry powder, ¼ teaspoon salt, and ¼ teaspoon black pepper. Cover and chill for 4 to 24 hours. Serve with a slotted spoon.

Nutrition Facts per tablespoon: 9 cal., 0 g total fat (0 g sat. fat), 0 mg chol., 25 mg sodium, 2 g carbo., 0 g fiber, 0 g pro. Daily Values: 3% vit. A, 18% vit. C, 1% iron. Exchanges: Free

PINEAPPLE RELISH

○Beef ○Lamb ●Pork ●Ham ○Poultry
●Fish ○Seafood

Prep: 15 minutes Chill: 2 to 24 hours
Makes: 2 cups

1 cup chopped fresh pineapple
½ cup chopped red sweet pepper
¼ cup chopped green onions (2)
3 tablespoons snipped fresh cilantro

Curried Jicama Relish

½ to 1 fresh jalapeño chile pepper, seeded and finely chopped (see tip, page 36)

1 In a medium bowl combine pineapple, sweet pepper, green onions, cilantro, and chile pepper. Cover and chill for 2 to 24 hours. To serve, let stand at room temperature for 30 minutes.

Nutrition Facts per tablespoon: 4 cal., 0 g total fat (0 g sat. fat), 0 mg chol., 1 mg sodium, 1 g carbo., 0 g fiber, 0 g pro. Daily Values: 3% vit. A, 9% vit. C. Exchanges: Free

SWEET TOMATO RELISH

●Beef ○Lamb ●Pork ●Ham ○Poultry
○Fish ○Seafood

Prep: 15 minutes Chill: 4 to 24 hours
Makes: 2½ cups

3 medium roma tomatoes, chopped
1 small zucchini, chopped
1 stalk celery, chopped
4 teaspoons lemon juice
1 tablespoon sugar
1 tablespoon finely chopped red onion
1 tablespoon strawberry balsamic vinegar or balsamic vinegar
1½ teaspoons olive oil
½ teaspoon dry mustard
½ teaspoon poppy seeds

1 In a medium bowl combine tomatoes, zucchini, and celery; set aside.

2 For dressing, in a screw-top jar combine lemon juice, sugar, onion, vinegar, oil, mustard, poppy seeds, and ½ teaspoon salt. Cover and shake well. Pour dressing over tomato mixture. Cover and chill for 4 to 24 hours. Serve with a slotted spoon.

Nutrition Facts per tablespoon: 6 cal., 0 g total fat (0 g sat. fat), 0 mg chol., 31 mg sodium, 1 g carbo., 0 g fiber, 0 g pro. Daily Values: 1% vit. A, 4% vit. C. Exchanges: Free

JICAMA-SWEET PEPPER RELISH

●Beef ○Lamb ●Pork ○Ham ○Poultry
●Fish ○Seafood

Start to Finish: 20 minutes
Makes: 1½ cups

**1 small jicama, peeled and finely
    chopped (about 1¼ cups)**
¼ cup finely chopped red sweet pepper
3 tablespoons lemon juice
2 teaspoons olive oil
**1 teaspoon snipped fresh thyme or
    ¼ teaspoon dried thyme, crushed**

1 In a medium bowl combine jicama, sweet pepper, lemon juice, oil, and thyme. Serve immediately or cover and chill for up to 24 hours.

Nutrition Facts per ¼ cup: 31 cal., 2 g total fat (0 g sat. fat), 0 mg chol., 0 mg sodium, 4 g carbo., 0 g fiber, 0 g pro. Daily Values: 7% vit. A, 37% vit. C, 2% iron. Exchanges: ½ Fat

FOOD FOR THOUGHT
JICAMA

Also known as a "Mexican potato," jicama is a root vegetable that hails from Central America and Mexico, where it is a staple item. Its ivory flesh has a mild, slightly sweet flavor and crunchy texture similar to a water chestnut. Whether eaten raw or cooked, jicama is a versatile ingredient that works well in a variety of salads, stir-fries, or side dishes. When buying jicama, look for vegetables that are heavy for their size and free of cracks or bruises. Refrigerate in a plastic bag for up to 2 weeks and peel its skin just prior to use.

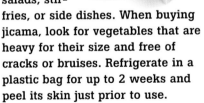

MANGO SALSA

○Beef ○Lamb ○Pork ○Ham ●Poultry
●Fish ●Seafood

Prep: 20 minutes Chill: 2 to 24 hours
Makes: 2½ cups

2 cups chopped, peeled mango
1 cup chopped red sweet pepper
¼ cup snipped fresh cilantro
2 tablespoons lime juice
⅛ teaspoon cayenne pepper

1 In a medium bowl combine mango, sweet pepper, cilantro, lime juice, and cayenne pepper. Cover and chill for 2 to 24 hours.

Nutrition Facts per ¼ cup: 27 cal., 0 g total fat (0 g sat. fat), 0 mg chol., 2 mg sodium, 7 g carbo., 1 g fiber, 0 g pro. Daily Values: 45% vit. A, 65% vit. C, 1% calcium, 1% iron. Exchanges: ½ Other Carbo.

FRESH SUMMER SALSA

●Beef ○Lamb ○Pork ○Ham ●Poultry
●Fish ○Seafood

Prep: 20 minutes Stand: 30 minutes Chill: 1 to 24 hours
Makes: about 3 cups

¼ cup finely chopped red onion
2 tablespoons white wine vinegar
**4 tomatillos, husked, rinsed, and
    finely chopped (about ¾ cup)**
**¾ cup finely chopped yellow cherry
    tomatoes**
⅔ cup finely chopped roma tomatoes
1½ teaspoons snipped fresh cilantro
**1 fresh serrano chile pepper, seeded
    and finely chopped (see tip,
    page 36)**
1 teaspoon lime juice

1 Combine onion, vinegar, and ¼ cup ice water. Let stand 30 minutes; drain well. Stir in tomatillos, cherry and roma tomatoes, cilantro, chile pepper, and lime juice. Season to taste with salt and black pepper. Cover; chill for 1 to 24 hours.

Nutrition Facts per ¼ cup: 8 cal., 0 g total fat (0 g sat. fat), 0 mg chol., 3 mg sodium, 2 g carbo., 0 g fiber, 0 g pro. Daily Values: 2% vit. A, 7% vit. C, 1% iron. Exchanges: Free

SMOKIN' HOT TIP

Roasting sweet peppers on the grill is easy. Quarter the sweet peppers lengthwise; discard seeds and membranes. Grill pepper quarters, skin sides down, directly over medium coals about 10 minutes or until blistered and dark. Wrap the pepper quarters in foil and let stand about 15 minutes or until cool enough to handle. The steam generated will loosen the skin, making it easy to peel away with a sharp knife.

RED SWEET PEPPER RELISH

●Beef ○Lamb ●Pork ●Ham ○Poultry
○Fish ○Seafood

Prep: 10 minutes Chill: up to 2 hours
Makes: ⅔ cup

**½ cup roasted red sweet peppers,
  cut into strips**
**1 tablespoon finely chopped pitted
  ripe olives**
**2 teaspoons snipped fresh thyme
  or ½ teaspoon dried thyme,
  crushed**
2 teaspoons olive oil

1 In a food processor combine sweet peppers, olives, thyme, oil, and ¼ teaspoon black pepper. Cover and process with several on-off turns until coarsely chopped. Cover; chill up to 2 hours.

Nutrition Facts per tablespoon: 10 cal., 1 g total fat (0 g sat. fat), 0 mg chol., 4 mg sodium, 1 g carbo., 0 g fiber, 0 g pro. Daily Values: 3% vit. A, 31% vit. C. Exchanges: Free

SWEET STRAWBERRY SALSA

○Beef ○Lamb ●Pork ●Ham ●Poultry
●Fish ○Seafood

Prep: 15 minutes Chill: 2 to 24 hours
Makes: about 3 cups

2 cups strawberries, coarsely chopped
1 cup coarsely chopped fresh pineapple
**½ cup coarsely chopped, peeled
  mango and/or peach**
2 tablespoons honey
1 teaspoon finely shredded lime peel
2 tablespoons lime juice
½ teaspoon grated fresh ginger
¼ teaspoon cracked black pepper

1 In a bowl combine strawberries, pineapple, mango, honey, lime peel, lime juice, ginger, and black pepper. Cover and chill for 2 to 24 hours.

Savory Strawberry Salsa: In a bowl combine 2 cups strawberries, coarsely chopped; 1 cup coarsely chopped seeded, peeled avocado; ½ cup coarsely chopped seeded cucumber; 2 tablespoons honey; 1 teaspoon finely shredded lime peel; 2 tablespoons lime juice; 1 to 2 tablespoons seeded and finely chopped fresh jalapeño chile pepper (see tip, page 36); and ¼ teaspoon coarsely cracked black pepper. Cover and chill for 2 to 24 hours. Makes about 3 cups.

Nutrition Facts per ¼ cup for both variations: 23 cal., 1 g total fat, (0 g sat. fat), 0 mg chol., 1 mg sodium, 5 g carbo., 1 g fiber, 0 g pro. Daily Values: 30% vit. C, 1% calcium, 1% iron. Exchanges: ½ Other Carbo.

ONION CHILI SAUCE

●Beef ○Lamb ●Pork ○Ham ○Poultry
○Fish ○Seafood

Prep: 20 minutes Cook: 30 minutes Chill: up to 2 weeks
Makes: about 3 cups

**1½ pounds sweet onions, halved
  lengthwise and thinly sliced
  (about 6 cups)**
1 tablespoon cooking oil
**1 medium green sweet pepper, cut
  into thin strips (1 cup)**

Sweet Strawberry Salsa

2 fresh jalapeño chile peppers, halved,
   seeded, and thinly sliced
   (see tip, page 36)
³⁄₄ cup bottled chili sauce
1 tablespoon bottled Louisiana
   hot sauce
1 tablespoon honey
¹⁄₂ teaspoon ground cinnamon
¹⁄₈ teaspoon ground cloves

1 In a large skillet cook onions, covered, in hot oil over medium heat for 20 minutes, stirring occasionally. (Reduce heat to medium-low if onions begin to brown.) Add sweet pepper and chile peppers. Cook, covered, about 5 minutes more or until sweet pepper is just tender. Stir in chili sauce, hot sauce, honey, cinnamon, cloves, ¹⁄₂ teaspoon salt, and ¹⁄₄ teaspoon black pepper. Bring to boiling; reduce heat. Simmer, uncovered, for 5 minutes. Cover and chill for up to 2 weeks.

Nutrition Facts per tablespoon: 14 cal., 0 g total fat, (0 g sat. fat), 0 mg chol., 83 mg sodium, 3 g carbo., 1 g fiber, 0 g pro. Daily Values: 1% vit. A, 6% vit. C. Exchanges: Free

Peach and Pear Chili Sauce

PEACH AND PEAR CHILI SAUCE

○Beef ○Lamb ●Pork ●Ham ●Poultry
○Fish ○Seafood

Prep: 45 minutes Cook: 2 hours Process: 15 minutes
Makes: 4 pints

4½ **pounds ripe tomatoes (14 medium)**
4 **medium pears, peeled, cored, and**
   cut into ½-inch chunks (4 cups)
4 **medium peaches, peeled, pitted, and**
   cut into ½-inch chunks (3½ cups)
3 **medium green sweet peppers,**
   chopped (2¼ cups)
4 **medium onions, chopped (2 cups)**
1 **medium red sweet pepper, chopped**
   (¾ cup)
1 to 3 **teaspoons seeded and chopped**
   fresh serrano chile peppers
   (see tip, page 36)
3 **cups sugar**
1½ **cups cider vinegar**
2 **teaspoons ground nutmeg**
1 **teaspoon whole cloves**
6 **inches stick cinnamon**

1 Peel tomatoes; remove stem ends and cores. Cut into chunks (you should have about 6¾ cups). In a 6- or 8-quart stainless-steel heavy kettle combine tomatoes, pears, peaches, green sweet peppers, onions, red sweet pepper, and chile pepper. Stir in sugar, vinegar, nutmeg, and 4 teaspoons salt.

2 For spice bag, place the cloves and cinnamon in the center of a double-thick piece of 100-percent-cotton cheesecloth. Bring corners of cloth together; tie closed with a clean string. Add spice bag to tomato mixture. Bring to boiling; reduce heat to medium. Simmer, uncovered, about 2 hours or until thick, stirring occasionally.

3 Remove spice bag and discard. Ladle hot sauce into hot, sterilized pint canning jars, leaving a ½-inch headspace. Cover and chill any extra sauce; use within 3 days. Wipe jar rims; adjust lids. Process in a boiling-water canner for 15 minutes (start timing when water returns to boil). Remove jars from canner; cool on racks.

Nutrition Facts per tablespoon: 30 cal., 0 g total fat (0 g sat. fat), 0 mg chol., 80 mg sodium, 8 g carbo., 1 g fiber, 0 g pro. Daily Values: 4% vit. A, 11% vit. C, 1% iron. Exchanges: ½ Other Carbo.

PORTOBELLO SAUCE

●Beef ●Lamb ●Pork ○Ham ●Poultry
○Fish ○Seafood

Prep: 10 minutes Cook: 5 minutes
Makes: about 1¼ cups

2 **large fresh portobello mushrooms**
8 **green onions, cut into 1-inch pieces**
1 **tablespoon butter or margarine**
⅓ **cup beef broth**
2 **tablespoons Madeira or port wine**

1 Halve and slice mushrooms. Cook and stir mushrooms and onions in butter until tender. Stir in broth and Madeira. Bring to boiling.

Nutrition Facts per ¼ cup: 53 cal., 4 g total fat (2 g sat. fat), 7 mg chol., 84 mg sodium, 4 g carbo., 1 g fiber, 2 g pro. Daily Values: 3% vit. A, 6% vit. C, 2% calcium, 4% iron. Exchanges: ½ Vegetable, 1 Fat

RICH BROWN SAUCE

●Beef ●Lamb ●Pork ○Ham ●Poultry
○Fish ○Seafood

Prep: 10 minutes Cook: 25 minutes
Makes: about 1 cup

½ **cup chopped onion (1 medium)**
½ **cup sliced carrot**
2 **tablespoons butter or margarine**
2 **teaspoons sugar**
4 **teaspoons all-purpose flour**
1½ **cups beef broth**
2 **tablespoons tomato paste**
½ **teaspoon dried thyme, crushed**
1 **bay leaf**

1 Cook onion and carrot in hot butter over medium heat until tender. Stir in sugar. Cook and stir 5 minutes. Stir in flour. Cook and stir 6 to 8 minutes more or until flour is browned. Stir in beef broth, tomato paste, thyme, bay leaf, and ⅛ teaspoon black pepper. Bring to boiling; reduce heat. Simmer, uncovered, about 10 minutes or until reduced to 1⅓ cups. Remove saucepan from heat. Strain sauce.

Nutrition Facts per tablespoon: 25 cal., 2 g total fat (1 g sat. fat), 4 mg chol., 95 mg sodium, 2 g carbo., 0 g fiber, 0 g pro. Daily Values: 21% vit. A, 2% vit. C, 1% iron. Exchanges: ½ Fat

BORDELAISE SAUCE

●Beef ●Lamb ○Pork ○Ham ○Poultry
○Fish ○Seafood

Prep: 10 minutes Cook: 15 minutes
Makes: 1 cup

- **¼ cup chopped green onions (2)**
- **2 tablespoons butter or margarine**
- **1 tablespoon all-purpose flour**
- **½ teaspoon dried thyme, crushed**
- **1 14-ounce can beef broth**
- **¼ cup dry red wine**

1 Cook green onions in hot butter until tender. Stir in flour and thyme. Stir in broth and wine. Bring to boiling, stirring occasionally; reduce heat. Boil gently, uncovered, for 15 to 20 minutes or until reduced to 1 cup.

Nutrition Facts per tablespoon: 21 cal., 2 g total fat (1 g sat. fat), 4 mg chol., 101 mg sodium, 1 g carbo., 0 g fiber, 0 g pro. Daily Values: 1% vit. A, 1% iron. Exchanges: ½ Fat

TANGY COCONUT SAUCE

○Beef ○Lamb ○Pork ○Ham ○Poultry
●Fish ●Seafood

Prep: 10 minutes Cook: 3 minutes Chill: 2 to 24 hours
Makes: ⅓ cup

- **⅓ cup coconut milk**
- **1 teaspoon cornstarch**
- **2 to 4 teaspoons wasabi paste**
- **2 teaspoons grated fresh ginger**
- **1 teaspoon lime juice**

1 Combine coconut milk and cornstarch. Cook and stir over low heat 3 to 5 minutes. Let cool.
2 Meanwhile, combine wasabi paste, ginger, and lime juice. Stir in cooled coconut milk mixture. Cover and chill for 2 to 24 hours.

Nutrition Facts per tablespoon: 33 cal., 3 g total fat (3 g sat. fat), 0 mg chol., 4 mg sodium, 2 g carbo., 0 g fiber, 0 g pro. Daily Values: 3% vit. C, 1% iron. Exchanges: ½ Fat

BRANDY CREAM SAUCE

●Beef ●Lamb ●Pork ○Ham ●Poultry
○Fish ○Seafood

Prep: 15 minutes Cook: 14 minutes
Makes: about 1 cup

- **½ cup chicken broth**
- **2 tablespoons chopped shallot**
- **⅓ cup whipping cream**
- **3 tablespoons brandy or cognac**
- **¾ cup unsalted butter, cut into small pieces and softened**
- **4 teaspoons lemon juice**

1 Combine broth and shallot. Bring to boiling; reduce heat. Simmer, covered, 2 minutes. Stir in whipping cream and brandy. Simmer, uncovered, over medium heat 12 to 14 minutes or until sauce is reduced to ½ cup. Remove from heat. Strain sauce; return to saucepan. Add butter, one piece at a time, stirring constantly with a wire whisk. Stir in lemon juice and ¼ teaspoon white pepper.

Nutrition Facts per tablespoon: 107 cal., 11 g total fat (7 g sat. fat), 31 mg chol., 35 mg sodium, 1 g carbo., 0 g fiber, 0 g pro. Daily Values: 9% vit. A, 1% vit. C, 1% calcium. Exchanges: 2 Fat

FOOD FOR THOUGHT WASABI

The wasabi plant is one of the rarest and most difficult vegetables to grow in the world. Wasabi is native to Japan but is now being cultivated in New Zealand and the western United States. Traditionally it is served as a condiment with raw fish. It generates an intense fiery sensation that dissipates quickly, while leaving a lingering sweetness. Fresh wasabi, an aboveground rootlike stem of the plant, is typically peeled to expose its green flesh, then grated. The more common and less expensive wasabi powder is made from horseradish powder and food coloring, and is mixed with water to form a paste. Prepared wasabi paste is available in a tube.

4

Beverages
& Appetizers

✪ Highlighted recipes are grilled

CRANBERRY-GINSENG TEA

A beguiling blend of flavors sets this ruby-hued beauty apart from traditional iced tea.

Prep: 15 minutes Cool: 2 hours
Makes: 5 (8-ounce) servings

2 cups water
2 green tea bags
2 ginseng tea bags
1 mint tea bag
2 cups cranberry juice, chilled
1 cup carbonated water, chilled
Ice cubes

1 Bring the 2 cups water to boiling in a medium saucepan. Remove from heat. Add green, ginseng, and mint tea bags. Cover and steep for 10 minutes. Remove and discard tea bags. Cover tea mixture and cool at room temperature for 2 hours. Transfer to a pitcher; add cranberry juice and carbonated water. Serve tea in tall glasses over ice cubes. Chill remaining tea up to 2 days.

Nutrition Facts per serving: 20 cal., 0 g total fat 0 mg chol., 5 mg sodium, 0 g carbo., 0 g fiber, 0 g pro. Daily Values: 19% vit. C. Exchanges: Free

FOOD FOR THOUGHT
GREEN TEA

Growing in popularity and availability, green tea is made from unfermented leaves that produce a yellow-green tea with a slightly astringent and bitter flavor. Green tea is among the richest sources of antioxidants, associated with the prevention of heart disease and cancer and the reduction of blood cholesterol levels. Green tea can be sipped hot or cold. A powdered form is used to flavor ice cream.

ICED GREEN TEA

Whether you drink green tea for its reputed health benefits or because you enjoy the flavor, you'll love it scented with fresh ginger and served over ice.

Prep: 25 minutes Cool: 2 hours
Makes: 12 (about 8-ounce) servings

12 cups water
¹⁄₄ cup sugar
3 inches fresh ginger, peeled and thinly sliced
12 to 16 green tea bags
12 12-inch wooden skewers (optional)
Strawberries (optional)
Key limes or limes, quartered (optional)
Orange peel strips (optional)
Ice cubes

1 In a large saucepan combine water, sugar, and ginger. Bring to boiling; reduce heat. Simmer, covered, for 5 minutes. Remove from heat. Add tea bags; cover and steep for 3 minutes. Remove and discard tea bags. Strain ginger from tea; discard ginger. Transfer tea to a 2-gallon pitcher or punch bowl. Cover and cool at least 2 hours. If desired, chill.

2 If desired, on wooden skewers alternate strawberries, lime quarters, and orange peel strips. Serve tea in tall glasses over ice cubes. Add fruit skewers (if using) to glasses as swizzle sticks.

Nutrition Facts per serving: 18 cal., 0 g total fat (0 g sat. fat), 0 mg chol., 7 mg sodium, 5 g carbo., 0 g fiber, 0 g pro. Daily Values: 15% vit. C. Exchanges: Free

HIT-THE-SPOT LEMON WATER

You'll be amazed at the refreshing burst of flavor when you soak lemons and fresh herbs in water for an hour or so. No sugar. Only pure, thirst-quenching goodness.

Prep: 15 minutes Chill: 1 to 8 hours
Makes: 6 to 8 (about 8-ounce) servings

    4 lemons, sliced
1 1/2 cups firmly packed fresh mint or
        basil leaves
    6 to 8 cups water
    Fresh mint or basil sprigs
    Ice cubes

1 Place lemon slices in a large pitcher. Carefully rub the 1 1/2 cups mint leaves between the palms of your hands to slightly bruise the leaves. Add mint to pitcher. Pour in water. Cover and chill for 1 to 8 hours.

2 Strain lemon-water mixture. Discard mint. Divide lemon slices and additional fresh mint leaves among 6 to 8 tall glasses. Add ice cubes to each glass; fill with lemon water.

Nutrition Facts per serving: 11 cal., 0 g total fat (0 g sat. fat), 0 mg chol., 8 mg sodium, 4 g carbo., 1 g fiber, 0 g pro. Daily Values: 34% vit. C, 1% calcium, 1% iron. Exchanges: Free

WATERMELON LEMONADE

Turn a summertime icon (juicy red watermelon) into a fruity thirst quencher.

Start to Finish: 10 minutes
Makes: 2 to 3 (about 6-ounce) servings

    2 cups cubed watermelon, seeded
  1/2 cup apple or white grape juice
  1/3 cup lemon or lime juice
    1 to 2 tablespoons honey
    Ice cubes

1 In a blender combine watermelon, apple juice, lemon juice, and honey. Cover and blend until smooth. Serve in tall glasses over ice cubes.

Nutrition Facts per serving: 120 cal., 1 g total fat (0 g sat. fat), 0 mg chol., 6 mg sodium, 30 g carbo., 1 g fiber, 1 g pro. Daily Values: 11% vit. A, 56% vit. C, 2% calcium, 3% iron. Exchanges: 1/2 Other Carbo., 1 1/2 Fruit

SPICED LEMON-LIME ADE

Allow at least 1 hour for the herb-spice mixture to chill. Longer chilling results in even stronger flavor.

Prep: 25 minutes Cool: 1 hour Chill: 1 to 24 hours
Makes: 8 (about 6-ounce) servings

    2 cups water
    8 6-inch fresh rosemary sprigs
    3 tablespoons whole allspice, coarsely
        cracked
1 1/4 cups sugar
  1/2 cup lemon juice
  1/2 cup lime juice
    7 cups cold water
    2 lemons and/or limes, sliced or cubed
        (optional)
    Ice cubes

1 In a medium saucepan combine the 2 cups water, rosemary, and allspice. Bring to boiling. Remove from heat. Cover; let stand for 1 hour or until cool. Remove rosemary sprigs; rinse, wrap, and chill to use later for garnishing the pitcher and glasses.

2 Strain liquid through a fine sieve, discarding solids. Stir sugar into strained liquid until dissolved. Cover and chill for 1 to 24 hours.

3 To serve, in a large pitcher combine herb-spice liquid, lemon juice, and lime juice. Stir in the 7 cups cold water. If desired, float lemon and/or lime slices and reserved rosemary sprigs in pitcher. Serve in tall glasses over ice cubes and rosemary sprigs.

Nutrition Facts per serving: 142 cal., 0 g total fat (0 g sat. fat), 0 mg chol., 10 mg sodium, 37 g carbo., 0 g fiber, 0 g pro. Daily Values: 22% vit. C, 1% calcium. Exchanges: 2 Fruit, 2 1/2 Other Carbo.

Spiced Lemon-Lime Ade

LEMONADE OR LIMEADE BASE

Summer just wouldn't be summer without this cooling classic. Keep a jar of the base in the refrigerator all season long.

Prep: 20 minutes Cool: 20 minutes Chill: up to 3 days
Makes: 8 (about 8-ounce) servings lemonade or limeade (or about 4 cups of the base)

2½ cups water
1¼ cups sugar
½ teaspoon finely shredded lemon or lime peel
1¼ cups lemon or lime juice
Ice cubes

1 For lemonade or limeade base, in a medium saucepan heat and stir water and sugar over medium heat until sugar is dissolved. Remove from heat; cool for 20 minutes. Add peel and juice to sugar mixture. Pour into a jar; cover and chill for up to 3 days.

2 For each glass of lemonade or limeade, combine equal parts base and water in ice-filled glasses; stir.

Nutrition Facts per serving: 126 cal., 0 g total fat (0 g sat. fat), 0 mg chol., 6 mg sodium, 33 g carbo., 0 g fiber, 0 g pro. Daily Values: 29% vit. C, 1% calcium. Exchanges: 2 Other Carbo.

Strawberry-Lemonade Slush: For each serving, in a blender container combine ½ cup fresh or frozen unsweetened strawberries, ⅓ cup lemonade base, and 1 tablespoon sugar. Cover and blend until smooth. With blender running, add ½ cup ice cubes, one cube at a time, through opening in lid until mixture becomes slushy. Pour into a tall glass; serve immediately.

Nutrition Facts per serving: 152 cal., 0 g total fat, (0 g sat. fat), 0 mg chol., 3 mg sodium, 39 g carbo., 2 g fiber, 1 g pro. Daily Values: 88% vit. C, 1% calcium, 2% iron. Exchanges: ½ Fruit, 2 Other Carbo.

PINK RHUBARB PUNCH

Rhubarb joins lemon in this spin on lemonade.

Prep: 20 minutes Cook: 5 minutes Chill: 4 to 24 hours
Makes: 10 (about 6-ounce) servings

6 cups fresh rhubarb, cut into ½-inch pieces, or 6 cups frozen unsweetened, sliced rhubarb (24 ounces)
3 cups water
1 cup sugar
½ of a 12-ounce can frozen pink lemonade concentrate (¾ cup), thawed
¼ cup lemon juice
1 1-liter bottle carbonated water, chilled
Crushed ice
Fresh mint leaves and/or lemon slices (optional)

1 In a large saucepan combine rhubarb and water. Bring to boiling; reduce heat. Cover and simmer for 5 minutes. Remove from heat; cool slightly. Strain mixture into a large pitcher, pressing to remove all juices. Discard pulp. Add sugar, lemonade concentrate, and lemon juice to rhubarb juice, stirring to dissolve sugar. Cover and chill for 4 to 24 hours.

2 To serve, stir in carbonated water. Serve in glasses over crushed ice. If desired, garnish with fresh mint and/or lemon slices.

Nutrition Facts per serving: 122 cal., 0 g total fat (0 g sat. fat), 0 mg chol., 7 mg sodium, 31 g carbo., 1 g fiber, 1 g pro. Daily Values: 2% vit. A, 19% vit. C, 8% calcium, 2% iron. Exchanges: 2 Other Carbo.

MOJITO FRESCO

Prep: 10 minutes Chill: 1 hour
Makes: 6 (about 5-ounce) servings

2 large limes
2 cups water
1 cup sugar
Water
Sugar
Ice cubes
¼ to ½ cup light rum
Quartered limes (optional)

1 Cut the 2 large limes into pieces. In a blender combine lime pieces, the 2 cups water, and the 1 cup sugar. Cover and blend about 30 seconds or until limes are coarsely chopped. Do not puree. Strain through a sieve into a large pitcher. Dilute mixture with 1 to 2 cups water to taste. Cover and chill for 1 to 12 hours.

2 Moisten the rims of 4 to 6 tall glasses with water; dip rims in sugar. Fill sugar-rimmed glasses with ice. Add 1 to 2 tablespoons rum to each glass. Pour chilled lime mixture over rum. If desired, add extra quartered limes.

Nutrition Facts per serving: 152 cal., 0 g total fat (0 g sat. fat), 0 mg chol., 3 mg sodium, 34 g carbo., 1 g fiber, 0 g pro. Daily Values: 11% vit. C, 1% calcium, 1% iron. Exchanges: 2½ Other Carbo.

AFTERNOON COFFEE VODKA COOLER

Save some of your morning coffee—the stronger the better—to make these afternoon creamy vodka refreshers.

Prep: 5 minutes Freeze: 4 days
Makes: 1 (about 5-ounce) serving

Ice cubes
½ cup cold brewed coffee
2 tablespoons Coffee Bean Vodka
1 tablespoon whipping cream,
half-and-half, or light cream
1 teaspoon superfine or regular
granulated sugar

1 Fill a short glass with ice. Add coffee, Coffee Bean Vodka, cream, and sugar to glass. Stir mixture gently.

Coffee Bean Vodka: Place 16 whole espresso or coffee beans on a piece of 100-percent-cotton cheesecloth and tie into a bundle with clean 100-percent-cotton string. Gently crush a few beans by tapping the tied coffee bean bundle lightly with a rolling pin. Pour a 750-milliliter bottle vodka into a plastic freezer container; add the coffee bean bundle. Cover; store in the freezer at least 4 days or up to 2 weeks. To chill longer, remove the coffee bean bundle.

Nutrition Facts per serving: 143 cal., 6 g total fat (3 g sat. fat), 21 mg chol., 8 mg sodium, 5 g carbo., 0 g fiber, 0 g pro. Daily Values: 1% calcium. Exchanges: ½ Other Carbo., 1 Fat

Espresso Martini: Fill a martini shaker with ice. Add 2 tablespoons Coffee Bean Vodka. Shake vigorously. Strain vodka into a well-chilled martini glass. Add ½ cup cold brewed coffee; stir gently. If desired, add a splash of cream or cream-based liqueur. Makes 1 (5-ounce) serving.

Nutrition Facts per serving: 127 cal., 6 g total fat (3 g sat. fat), 21 mg chol., 8 mg sodium, 1 g carbo., 0 g fiber, 0 g pro. Daily Values: 1% calcium. Exchanges: ½ Other Carbo., 1 Fat

FOOD FOR THOUGHT SUGAR

Sugar, which comes mostly from sugar cane and sugar beets, takes on different forms based on purity and degree of refinement. Below are the most common forms available.

● White sugar: **Pure and refined, white sugar is available in coarse, granulated, and superfine varieties.**

● Brown sugar: **Sugar that's refined with some impurities remaining or molasses added results in very dark to golden brown sugars. Brown sugar is generally softer and moister than white sugar.**

● Confectioner's sugar: **The finest texture of all sugars, confectioner's sugar is finely powdered and mixed with a small amount of cornstarch to prevent caking.**

GINGER PUNCH

Pineapple, orange, and lemon juices combine
with a ginger-flavor syrup for this refreshing
citrus punch.

Prep: 15 minutes Cool: 1 hour
Makes: 12 (about 6-ounce) servings

1½ **cups cold water**
  1 **cup sugar**
  3 **tablespoons grated fresh ginger**
  1 **6-ounce can frozen pineapple juice
     concentrate (³⁄4 cup), thawed**
  1 **6-ounce can frozen orange juice
     concentrate (³⁄4 cup), thawed**
 ½ **cup lemon juice**
    Ice cubes
  1 **orange, thinly sliced**
  1 **lime and/or lemon, thinly sliced**

1 In a large saucepan combine water, sugar, and
ginger. Bring just to boiling. Remove from
heat. Strain; cover and cool.

2 Meanwhile, prepare pineapple and orange
juice concentrates according to package
directions. In a large container combine pineapple
juice, orange juice, the ginger mixture, and lemon
juice. Strain the mixture into chilled, ice-filled
glasses. Garnish with orange and lime slices.

Nutrition Facts per serving: 120 cal., 0 g total fat
(0 g sat. fat), 0 mg chol., 2 mg sodium, 31 g carbo.,
1 g fiber, 1 g pro. Daily Values: 1% vit. A, 63% vit. C,
2% calcium, 1% iron. Exchanges: ½ Fruit,
1½ Other Carbo.

WHITE STRAWBERRY SANGRIA

For unbeatable flavor, select a white wine such
as Pinot Grigio or Sauvignon Blanc.

Prep: 10 minutes Chill: 1 hour
Makes: 5 or 6 (about 8-ounce) servings

  1 **750-milliliter bottle dry white wine**
 ½ **cup strawberry schnapps**
 ¼ **cup sugar**
  2 **cups sliced fresh
     strawberries**
    Ice cubes
    Whole strawberries (optional)

1 In a 2-quart pitcher stir together wine,
strawberry schnapps, and sugar until sugar
is dissolved. Add the sliced strawberries. Chill
for 1 to 4 hours. Serve in tall glasses over ice
cubes. If desired, garnish with whole strawberries.

Nutrition Facts per serving: 221 cal., 0 g total fat
(0 g sat. fat), 0 mg chol., 8 mg sodium, 22 g carbo.,
1 g fiber, 1 g pro. Daily Values: 54% vit. C, 2% calcium,
4% iron. Exchanges: 1½ Other Carbo.

ICY CRANBERRY MARGARITAS

These festive margaritas taste particularly good
with grilled poultry or pork.

Start to Finish: 10 minutes
Makes: 6 (about 4-ounce) servings

 ½ **cup frozen cranberry-raspberry juice
     concentrate, thawed**
 ½ **cup tequila**
 ¼ **cup orange liqueur**
  3 **tablespoons melon liqueur**
  5 **cups ice cubes**
    Orange wedge
    Sugar

Frozen Strawberry-Mango
Margaritas

Icy Cranberry Margaritas

1 In a blender combine juice concentrate, tequila, orange liqueur, and melon liqueur; cover and blend until combined.

2 With blender running, gradually add ice cubes, 1 at a time, through opening in lid, blending until mixture becomes slushy.

3 Rub orange wedge around rims of 6 glasses. Dip rims into a dish of sugar. Pour into margarita glasses.

Nutrition Facts per serving: 147 cal., 0 g total fat (0 g sat. fat), 0 mg chol., 2 mg sodium, 18 g carbo., 0 g fiber, 0 g pro. Daily Values: 19% vit. C. Exchanges: 1 Other Carbo.

FROZEN STRAWBERRY-MANGO MARGARITAS

For the best tropical flavor, use ripe mangoes. A ripe mango smells fruity and feels fairly firm when gently pressed. Avoid bruised, soft, or blemished fruit.

Prep: 10 minutes Freeze: 1 hour
Makes: 5 (6-ounce) servings

- 2 medium mangoes*
- 1/2 cup gold (oro) tequila
- 1/3 cup orange liqueur
- 1/4 cup lime juice
- 2 tablespoons sugar
- 2 cups frozen unsweetened whole strawberries
- 2 cups ice cubes
  - Lime wedge
  - Sugar
  - Fresh mango cubes (optional)

1 Seed, peel, and cube mangoes. Place mango cubes in a single layer in a shallow baking pan lined with plastic wrap. Cover and freeze for 1 hour. Transfer to a freezer bag or container for longer storage.

2 In a blender combine tequila, orange liqueur, lime juice, 2 tablespoons sugar, strawberries, and mango chunks. Cover and blend until smooth. With the blender running, add ice cubes, 1 at a time, through opening in lid, blending until mixture becomes slushy.

3 Pour mixture into glasses. If desired, garnish with fresh mango cubes.

***Note:** If mangoes are not available, use 2 cups frozen unsweetened peach slices and skip Step 1.

Nutrition Facts per serving: 176 cal., 0 g total fat (0 g sat. fat), 0 mg chol., 3 mg sodium, 26 g carbo., 3 g fiber, 1 g pro. Daily Values: 52% vit. A, 91% vit. C, 2% calcium, 2% iron. Exchanges: 1 Fruit, 1 Other Carbo.

SMOKIN' HOT TIP

Here's a chance to show off your creative flair by dressing up your party drinks, alcoholic or not.

⬤ Adorn sweet drinks with twists of citrus peel, fruit slices or wedges, mint leaves, chocolate shavings, whipped cream, ice cubes with fruit inside, peppermint sticks, or cinnamon sticks.

⬤ Top off savory drinks with curls, slices, or sticks of cucumber, carrot or other vegetables; julienned red peppers or green onions; or fresh herb leaves.

⬤ Moisten the rim of serving glasses and dip them in coarse salt, colored sugars, chocolate powder, or other finely crushed or powdered flavorings.

⬤ Create layers using lighter, creamier liqueurs on top of heavier, syrupy ones by pouring over the back of a spoon. For a kid-friendly layered drink, pour grenadine and orange juice in a glass. Do not stir. Finish with a splash of sparkling water.

Bloody Mary Swizzlers

LIME DAIQUIRIS

No need to dirty a measuring cup—fill the 6-ounce limeade can to measure the rum.

Start to Finish: 10 minutes
Makes: 6 (about 4-ounce) servings

1 6-ounce can frozen limeade concentrate or ¹/₂ of a 12-ounce can (³/₄ cup) frozen lemonade concentrate

²/₃ cup rum

2¹/₂ to 3 cups ice cubes

1 In a blender combine limeade concentrate and rum. Cover; blend until smooth. With blender running, add ice cubes, 1 at a time, through opening in lid until mixture becomes slushy.

Nutrition Facts per serving: 110 cal., 0 g total fat (0 g sat. fat), 0 mg chol., 0 mg sodium, 14 g carbo., 0 g fiber, 0 g pro. Daily Values: 6% vit. C. Exchanges: 1 Other Carbo.

Raspberry Daiquiris: Prepare as directed, except use half of a 6-ounce can (¹/₃ cup) frozen limeade concentrate. Add one 10-ounce package frozen red raspberries and, if desired, ¹/₃ cup sifted powdered sugar. Makes 7 (4-ounce) servings.

Nutrition Facts per serving: 88 cal., 0 g total fat (0 g sat. fat), 0 mg chol., 0 mg sodium, 10 g carbo., 1 g fiber, 0 g pro. Daily Values: 4% vit. C, 1% iron. Exchanges: ¹/₂ Other Carbo.

BLOODY MARY SWIZZLERS

Prep: 30 minutes Marinate: 12 to 24 hours
Makes: 24 skewers

24 cherry tomatoes

1 cup lemon-flavor vodka

24 almond-stuffed green olives, vermouth-marinated green olives, cocktail onions, caper berries, and/or pickled okra

3 or 4 stalks celery with tops removed, diagonally sliced into ³/₄- to 1-inch pieces (24 pieces)

1 Using a plastic or wooden pick, pierce the skins of tomatoes in several places. Place tomatoes in a self-sealing plastic bag set in a shallow dish; add vodka. Seal bag. Turn bag to coat tomatoes. Chill for 12 to 24 hours to allow flavor to penetrate.

2 Drain tomatoes; discard vodka. Thread tomatoes, olives, and celery onto cocktail picks or skewers. If desired, sprinkle with celery salt. Arrange swizzlers on a serving platter. Serve with Bloody Marys or other cocktail beverages.

Nutrition Facts per skewer: 21 cal., 1 g total fat (0 g sat. fat), 0 mg chol., 92 mg sodium, 1 g carbo., 0 g fiber, 0 g pro. Daily Values: 2% vit. A, 6% vit. C, 1% calcium, 1% iron. Exchanges: Free

STUFFED CAPRESE

Go beyond red tomatoes: Yellow are sweeter; green are a little more tart.

Start to Finish: 25 minutes
Makes: 4 servings

4 small tomatoes (3 to 4 ounces each)

¹/₄ teaspoon sea salt or salt

¹/₈ teaspoon freshly ground black pepper

3 tablespoons olive oil

3 tablespoons white wine vinegar or vinegar

¹/₂ teaspoon sugar

3 ounces fresh mozzarella, drained and cut into small chunks

¹/₄ cup slivered red onion

¹/₄ cup snipped fresh basil

1 Cut a ¹/₄-inch slice from stem end of each tomato. Using a spoon, scoop out core, seeds, and pulp, leaving up to a ¹/₂-inch shell. Discard pulp. Sprinkle tomato shells with sea salt or salt and pepper. Stand shells on a plate; set aside.

2 For dressing, in a screw-top jar combine olive oil, vinegar, and sugar. Cover and shake well. Reserve 1¹/₂ tablespoons of dressing. Spoon remaining dressing into tomato shells.

3 In a bowl combine mozzarella, red onion, basil, and reserved dressing; toss to mix. Spoon cheese mixture into tomato shells. Serve immediately or cover and chill for up to 2 hours.

Nutrition Facts per serving: 177 cal., 15 g total fat (4 g sat. fat), 16 mg chol., 187 mg sodium, 6 g carbo., 1 g fiber, 5 g pro. Daily Values: 16% vit. A, 29% vit. C, 12% calcium, 4% iron. Exchanges: ¹/₂ Other Carbo., 1 Medium-Fat Meat, 2 Fat

BACON AND CHEESE STUFFED DATES

Cambazola cheese—a cross between Camembert and Gorgonzola—tastes like a mild blue cheese.

Prep: 25 minutes Bake: 5 minutes Oven: 350°F
Makes: 24 appetizers

- **2 slices bacon, crisp-cooked, drained, and finely crumbled, or ¹⁄₄ cup chopped prosciutto (2 ounces)**
- **¹⁄₄ cup thinly sliced green onions (2)**
- **2 cloves garlic, minced**
- **¹⁄₂ cup Cambazola cheese or crumbled blue cheese (2 ounces)**
- **1 3-ounce package cream cheese, softened**
- **2 teaspoons Dijon-style mustard**
- **¹⁄₈ teaspoon black pepper**
- **24 Medjool dates (about 16 ounces unpitted)**

1 In a medium bowl stir together bacon, green onions, and garlic. Add Cambazola cheese, cream cheese, mustard, and pepper to bacon mixture. Stir to combine.

2 Using a sharp knife, make a lengthwise slit in each date. Spread dates open slightly; remove pits. Fill each date with a rounded teaspoon of the bacon mixture. Place dates, filling side up, on a baking sheet. Bake in a 350°F oven for 5 to 8 minutes or until heated through. Serve warm.

Make-ahead directions: Stuff dates, cover, and chill up to 24 hours. Uncover and bake as directed just before serving.

Nutrition Facts per appetizer: 77 cal., 2 g total fat (1 g sat. fat), 6 mg chol., 55 mg sodium, 14 g carbo., 1 g fiber, 1 g pro. Daily Values: 2% vit. A, 2% calcium, 2% iron. Exchanges: 1 Other Carbo.

SMOKY CHEESE BALL

Prep: 15 minutes Stand: 45 minutes Chill: 4 to 24 hours
Makes: 3¹⁄₂ cups

- **2 8-ounce packages cream cheese**
- **2 cups finely shredded smoked cheddar, Swiss, or Gouda cheese (8 ounces)**
- **¹⁄₂ cup butter or margarine**
- **2 tablespoons milk**
- **2 teaspoons steak sauce**
- **1 cup finely chopped toasted pistachio nuts**
- **Assorted crackers**

1 Let cream cheese, shredded cheese, and butter stand at room temperature for 30 minutes. Add milk and steak sauce; beat until fluffy. Cover and chill for 4 to 24 hours.

2 Shape mixture into a ball; roll in nuts. Let stand for 15 minutes. Serve with crackers.

Make-ahead directions: Prepare as above, except do not roll in nuts. Wrap cheese ball in moisture- and vapor-proof plastic wrap. Freeze for up to 1 month. To serve, thaw cheese ball in the refrigerator overnight. Roll in nuts. Let stand for 30 minutes at room temperature before serving.

Nutrition Facts per tablespoon spread: 73 cal., 7 g total fat (4 g sat. fat), 17 mg chol., 71 mg sodium, 1 g carbo., 0 g fiber, 2 g pro. Daily Values: 5% vit. A, 4% calcium, 1% iron. Exchanges: 1¹⁄₂ Fat

DEVILED EGGS

Deviled eggs are everything you want in a hot weather appetizer—cool, easy, and the right size to sustain you and your guests until dinner is ready. Try these internationally inspired delicacies at your next cookout.

Prep: 20 minutes Cook: 15 minutes Chill: 1 to 12 hours
Makes: 12 egg halves

- **7 hard-cooked eggs***
- **¹⁄₄ cup mayonnaise or salad dressing**
- **1 to 2 teaspoons Dijon-style mustard, balsamic herb mustard, honey mustard, or other favorite mustard**
- **¹⁄₂ teaspoon dry mustard**
- **Salt**
- **Black pepper**
- **Several leaves flat-leaf parsley or paprika (optional)**

1 Cut 6 of the eggs in half lengthwise; gently remove yolks; set whites aside. Coarsely chop the remaining egg.

2 In a self-sealing plastic bag combine egg yolks, chopped egg, mayonnaise, mustard, and dry mustard. Seal bag; gently squeeze to combine ingredients. Season to taste with salt and pepper.

3 Snip a corner of the bag. Squeeze bag, pushing egg yolk mixture through hole into egg white halves. If desired, top with fresh parsley. Cover and chill for 1 to 12 hours.

*Note: For hard-cooked eggs, place the eggs in a single layer in a large saucepan. Add enough cold water to cover 1 inch above the eggs. Bring to a full rolling boil over high heat. Reduce the heat so the water is just below simmering, then cover and cook for 15 minutes. Remove the eggs from the pan, place them in a colander, and run cold water over them until they're cool enough to handle. To peel, gently tap each egg on the counter. Roll the egg between the palms of your hands. Peel off the eggshell. Cover and chill at least 1 hour.

Nutrition Facts per egg half: 79 cal., 7 g total fat (1 g sat. fat), 127 mg chol., 99 mg sodium, 0 g carbo., 0 g fiber, 4 g pro. Daily Values: 3% vit. A, 2% calcium, 2% iron. Exchanges: ½ Medium-Fat Meat, 1 Fat

Greek-Style Deviled Eggs: Prepare Deviled Eggs as directed, except add 2 tablespoons crumbled feta cheese; 1 tablespoon finely chopped, pitted kalamata olives or other pitted ripe olives; and 2 teaspoons snipped fresh oregano to yolk mixture. If desired, season with black pepper.

Nutrition Facts per egg half: 85 cal., 7 g total fat (2 g sat. fat), 128 mg chol., 124 mg sodium, 1 g carbo., 0 g fiber, 4 g pro. Daily Values: 4% vit. A, 2% calcium, 2% iron. Exchanges: ½ Medium-Fat Meat, 1 Fat

Italian-Style Deviled Eggs: Prepare Deviled Eggs as directed, except omit mayonnaise and mustard. Add ¼ cup bottled creamy Italian salad dressing and 2 tablespoons grated Parmesan cheese to mashed yolks; mix well.

Nutrition Facts per egg half: 67 cal., 5 g total fat (1 g sat. fat), 124 mg chol., 134 mg sodium, 1 g carbo., 0 g fiber, 4 g pro. Daily Values: 3% vit. A, 2% calcium, 2% iron. Exchanges: ½ Medium-Fat Meat, ½ Fat

Mexican-Style Deviled Eggs: Prepare Deviled Eggs as directed, except omit mayonnaise and mustard. Add 3 tablespoons dairy sour cream, 1 tablespoon salsa, and ½ teaspoon ground cumin. Sprinkle eggs with snipped fresh cilantro.

Nutrition Facts per egg half: 52 cal., 4 g total fat (1 g sat. fat), 125 mg chol., 41 mg sodium, 1 g carbo., 0 g fiber, 4 g pro. Daily Values: 4% vit. A, 2% calcium, 2% iron. Exchanges: ½ Medium-Fat Meat, ½ Fat

FOOD FOR THOUGHT MUSTARD

The many types of prepared mustard on your grocer's shelves are all made from tiny mustard seeds. The seeds are ground into a powder and combined with seasonings and a liquid such as water, vinegar, or wine to make these popular condiments. Some mustards are made grainy with the addition of crushed or whole mustard seeds. You can dress up mustard by adding herbs, seasonings, or ingredients such as honey or chiles. Below are the most common types of prepared mustards.

● Yellow: Made from white and yellow seeds, sugar, vinegar, and turmeric for color, yellow mustard, also known as American-style mustard, has a smooth texture and bright yellow color.

● Dijon: Hailing from Dijon, France, this pale yellow mustard has a clean, pungent taste that ranges from mild to hot.

● English: Smooth in texture, this mustard is bright yellow in color and carries intense heat.

● German: German mustard is darker in color and strong in fragrance and taste. Sugar is added to create the sweeter Bavarian-style mustard.

● Chinese: This smooth yellow mustard is pungent and often used as a dipping sauce with Asian cooking.

SWISS CHEESE AND OLIVE SPREAD

Dry sherry lends a hint of sophistication to this creamy cheese spread.

Prep: 10 minutes Stand: 1½ hours Chill: 2 to 24 hours
Makes: 2½ cups

3 cups shredded Swiss cheese (12 ounces)
1 3-ounce package cream cheese, cubed
¼ cup dry sherry or dry white wine
3 tablespoons mayonnaise or salad dressing
1 teaspoon Worcestershire sauce
⅓ cup chopped pitted ripe olives, drained
3 tablespoons snipped fresh parsley
3 tablespoons finely chopped green onion
Toasted baguette slices or crackers

1 Place cheeses in a large mixing bowl. Let stand, covered, at room temperature for 30 minutes. Add sherry, mayonnaise, and Worcestershire sauce. Beat with an electric mixer on medium speed until combined. Stir in olives, parsley, and green onion. Transfer to a serving bowl. Cover and chill for 2 to 24 hours.

2 Let mixture stand at room temperature for 1 hour before serving. Serve spread with baguette slices.

Nutrition Facts per ¼ cup spread: 201 cal., 16 g total fat (8 g sat. fat), 43 mg chol., 182 mg sodium, 3 g carbo., 0 g fiber, 10 g pro. Daily Values: 10% vit. A, 3% vit. C, 34% calcium, 3% iron. Exchanges: 1 High-Fat Meat, 2 Fat

ONION DIP

A bag of thick potato chips sprinkled with sea salt is the perfect accompaniment for this dip.

Prep: 15 minutes Cook: 21 minutes
Makes: about 1 cup

1⅓ pounds medium onions (4), halved and coarsely chopped (2 cups)
½ teaspoon salt
2 tablespoons cooking oil
2 teaspoons snipped fresh sage
⅓ cup dairy sour cream
2 tablespoons grated Parmesan cheese
2 tablespoons finely chopped red onion
Potato chips or Armenian cracker bread (lahvosh), broken into serving-size pieces

1 In a large skillet cook the coarsely chopped onions and salt in hot oil over medium-low heat about 20 minutes or until very soft and slightly brown, stirring occasionally.

2 Stir in sage. Cook 1 minute more; remove from heat. Stir in sour cream and Parmesan cheese. Transfer to a serving bowl. Sprinkle with red onion and serve immediately with chips.

Nutrition Facts per 2 tablespoons dip: 69 cal., 6 g total fat (2 g sat. fat), 5 mg chol., 174 mg sodium, 4 g carbo., 1 g fiber, 1 g pro. Daily Values: 2% vit. A, 4% vit. C, 4% calcium, 1% iron. Exchanges: 1 Fat

THAI SPINACH DIP

Prep: 15 minutes Chill: 2 to 24 hours
Makes: about 2½ cups

1 cup chopped fresh spinach
1 8-ounce carton dairy sour cream
1 8-ounce carton plain fat-free yogurt
¼ cup snipped fresh mint
¼ cup finely chopped peanuts
¼ cup peanut butter
1 tablespoon honey
1 tablespoon soy sauce
1 to 2 teaspoons crushed red pepper
Chopped peanuts (optional)
Baby vegetables or other vegetable dippers

1 In a bowl combine spinach, sour cream, and yogurt. Stir in mint, the ¼ cup peanuts, the peanut butter, honey, soy sauce, and crushed red pepper. Cover and chill dip for 2 to 24 hours.

2 Transfer dip to serving bowl. If desired, sprinkle with chopped peanuts. Serve with vegetable dippers.

Nutrition Facts per 2 tablespoons dip: 68 cal., 6 g total fat (2 g sat. fat), 6 mg chol., 82 mg sodium, 4 g carbo., 0 g fiber, 2 g pro. Daily Values: 4% vit. A, 2% vit. C, 4% calcium, 2% iron. Exchanges: 1 Fat

DILL DIP

For colorful dippers, serve a mix of carrot or
zucchini sticks, broccoli or cauliflower florets,
radishes, and mushrooms.

Prep: 10 minutes Chill: 1 to 24 hours
Makes: about 2 cups

1 **8-ounce package cream cheese,**
   softened
1 **8-ounce carton dairy sour cream**
2 **tablespoons finely chopped green**
   onion (1)
2 **tablespoons snipped fresh dill or**
   2 teaspoons dried dill
½ **teaspoon seasoned salt or salt**
   Milk (optional)
   Assorted vegetable dippers,
   crackers, or chips

1 In a medium mixing bowl beat cream cheese,
sour cream, green onion, dill, and seasoned salt
with an electric mixer on low speed until fluffy.
Cover and chill for 1 to 24 hours. If dip thickens
after chilling, stir in 1 to 2 tablespoons milk. Serve
with vegetable dippers.

Nutrition Facts per 2 tablespoons dip: 80 cal.,
8 g total fat (4 g sat. fat), 22 mg chol., 98 mg sodium,
2 g carbo., 0 g fiber, 2 g pro. Daily Values: 6% vit. A,
2% calcium, 2% iron. Exchanges: 1½ Fat

Creamy Blue Cheese Dip: Prepare as directed,
except omit dill and seasoned salt or salt. Stir
½ cup crumbled blue cheese (2 ounces) and
⅓ cup finely chopped walnuts into the beaten
cream cheese mixture.

Nutrition Facts per 2 tablespoons dip: 110 cal.,
10 g total fat (6 g sat. fat), 24 mg chol., 100 mg sodium,
2 g carbo., 0 g dietary fiber, 2 g pro. Daily Values:
6% vit. A, 4% calcium, 2% iron. Exchanges: 2 Fat

Thai Spinach Dip

Cornmeal-Crusted Onion Rings

CORNMEAL-CRUSTED ONION RINGS

To minimize oil spatters, fry the onion rings in a pan that is taller than it is wide.

Prep: 30 minutes Cook: 3 minutes per batch Oven: 300°F
Makes: 6 appetizer servings

- **3 tablespoons honey**
- **1 teaspoon snipped fresh rosemary**
- **1 pound white onions (3 medium)**
- **1 48-ounce bottle cooking oil for deep-fat frying**
- **$1/2$ cup buttermilk**
- **1 beaten egg**
- **1 cup all-purpose flour**
- **$1/2$ cup cornmeal**
- **$1/4$ cup finely chopped pecans or peanuts**
- **$1/2$ teaspoon salt**
- **$1/4$ teaspoon freshly ground black pepper**

1 In a small saucepan heat honey and rosemary over very low heat about 3 minutes or until heated through; set aside. Cut onions into $1/2$-inch slices; separate into rings and set aside. In a deep heavy 3-quart saucepan or deep-fat fryer heat oil to 365°F.

2 Line a baking sheet with waxed paper; set aside. In a medium bowl combine buttermilk and egg. In a shallow dish combine flour, cornmeal, nuts, salt, and pepper.

3 Working in batches, dip onion rings in egg mixture, letting excess drip off into bowl. Toss rings in flour mixture until well coated; gently shake off excess. Place onion rings on prepared baking sheet. Repeat with remaining onions, egg mixture, and flour mixture.

4 With long-handled tongs, carefully add onion rings, a few at a time, to hot oil. Fry about 3 minutes, turning rings a few times, until onions are golden brown and cooked through. Drain on paper towels. Transfer to another baking sheet or shallow pan and keep warm in a 300°F oven.

5 To serve, place onion rings in a parchment paper-lined basket. Serve onion rings with honey-rosemary mixture. If desired, sprinkle with additional salt.

Nutrition Facts per serving: 385 cal., 23 g total fat (3 g sat. fat), 36 mg chol., 229 mg sodium, 41 g carbo., 3 g fiber, 6 g pro. Daily Values: 2% vit. A, 9% vit. C, 5% calcium, 10% iron. Exchanges: 1½ Starch, 1 Other Carbo., 4 Fat

HERBED MUSHROOMS

Serve these mushrooms solo as an appetizer, toss them with cooked peas for a flavorful side dish, or pile them onto a grilled burger or steak.

Prep: 15 minutes Cook: 12 minutes
Makes: 6 to 8 appetizer servings

3 shallots, peeled and cut into
    thin wedges
3 cloves garlic, minced
2 tablespoons olive oil or canola oil
1¼ pounds fresh mushrooms (such as
    maitake, oyster, white button, or
    shiitake), broken into clusters or
    sliced (about 8 cups)
¼ cup snipped fresh mixed herbs
    (such as tarragon, rosemary,
    basil, oregano, and/or parsley)
¼ teaspoon coarse salt or salt
¼ teaspoon cracked black pepper

1 In a large skillet cook shallots and garlic in hot oil over medium-high heat for 2 minutes.

2 Add maitake mushrooms. Cook, carefully stirring occasionally, for 10 to 12 minutes or until tender. If using oyster or button mushrooms, add them during the last 6 to 8 minutes. Add shiitake mushrooms during the last 4 minutes. Stir in herbs, salt, and cracked pepper.

Nutrition Facts per serving: 81 cal., 5 g total fat (1 g sat. fat), 0 mg chol., 118 mg sodium, 5 g carbo., 2 g fiber, 5 g pro. Daily Values: 3% vit. A, 2% vit. C, 1% calcium, 5% iron. Exchanges: 1 Vegetable, 1 Fat

LEMONY OVEN FRIES

The lemon added before baking yields a surprising burst of fresh flavor.

Start to Finish: 40 minutes
Makes: 10 appetizer servings

⅓ cup olive oil
1 large lemon, thinly sliced
¼ cup fresh flat-leaf parsley
1 20-ounce package frozen
    french-fried shoestring potatoes
    (about 5 cups)
Coarse sea salt
Lemon wedges

1 In a large skillet heat olive oil over medium heat. Carefully add lemon slices. Cook for 3 to 5 minutes or until lemon begins to brown; use tongs to turn lemon slices occasionally. Add parsley to the oil. Cook 20 to 30 seconds more or until parsley is crisp. Remove lemon slices and parsley with slotted spoon; drain on paper towels. Reserve the lemon-flavor oil (you should have about 3 tablespoons).

2 In a large bowl toss frozen potatoes with the 3 tablespoons reserved lemon-flavor oil until well coated. Place in a 15×10×1-inch baking pan. Bake according to package directions or until potatoes are brown and crisp, stirring occasionally.

3 To serve, toss potatoes with lemon and parsley. Sprinkle generously with sea salt. Squeeze lemon wedges over fries; serve immediately.

Nutrition Facts per serving: 126 cal., 7 g total fat (1 g sat. fat), 0 mg chol., 72 mg sodium, 14 g carbo., 1 g fiber, 2 g pro. Daily Values: 2% vit. A, 20% vit. C, 1% calcium, 4% iron. Exchanges: 1 Starch, 1 Fat

GRILLED PANZANELLA

Grilled sweet peppers and country-style bread star in this bruschettalike adaptation of the classic Italian bread salad.

Prep: 25 minutes Grill: 20 minutes Stand: 40 minutes
Makes: 8 appetizer servings

- 1 1-pound loaf country-style bread, cut into eight 1-inch slices
- 2 medium green, yellow, and/or red sweet peppers, quartered and seeded
- 2 tablespoons olive oil
- 2 large red and/or yellow tomatoes, cut up
- 1 medium cucumber, cut in half lengthwise and sliced
- ¼ cup olive oil
- ¼ cup red wine vinegar
- ½ teaspoon salt
- ½ teaspoon black pepper
- 2 tablespoons snipped fresh chives

1 Brush bread and sweet peppers with the 2 tablespoons olive oil. For a charcoal grill, place bread and sweet peppers on the rack of an uncovered grill directly over medium coals. Grill bread slices for 2 to 4 minutes or until toasted, turning once halfway through grilling; set aside. Grill sweet peppers for 20 minutes, turning once halfway through grilling. (For a gas grill, preheat grill. Reduce heat to medium. Place bread and sweet peppers on grill rack over heat. Cover; grill as above.) Wrap sweet peppers in foil; let stand for 10 minutes.

2 Peel sweet peppers and cut into 1-inch pieces. In a large bowl toss together sweet pepper pieces, tomatoes, and cucumber.

3 In a small bowl combine the ¼ cup olive oil, the red wine vinegar, salt, and black pepper. Drizzle half of the oil mixture over the vegetable mixture. Toss to coat. Let stand at room temperature for 30 minutes. Arrange bread slices on a serving platter. Top with vegetable mixture and chives. Pass remaining oil mixture.

Nutrition Facts per serving: 266 cal., 12 g total fat (2 g sat. fat), 0 mg chol., 482 mg sodium, 34 g carbo., 3 g fiber, 6 g pro. Daily Values: 12% vit. A, 63% vit. C, 6% calcium, 12% iron. Exchanges: ½ Vegetable, 2 Starch, 2 Fat

SMOKED SALSA

Add this spunky salsa to the menu when you're smoking the main course.

Prep: 30 minutes Soak: 1 hour Grill: 15 minutes
Makes: about 3 cups

- 2 cups hickory wood chips
- 3 large cloves garlic
- 2 large fresh jalapeño chile peppers, halved lengthwise and seeded (see tip, page 36)
- 1 tablespoon cooking oil
- 2 teaspoons chili oil
- 8 roma tomatoes
- 1 medium onion, cut into ¾-inch slices
- ½ cup coarsely chopped, peeled jicama
- ¼ cup snipped fresh cilantro
- 1 tablespoon lime juice
- ½ teaspoon salt
  Tortilla chips

1 At least 1 hour before grilling, soak wood chips in enough water to cover.

2 On a metal skewer thread garlic cloves and jalapeño pepper halves. In a small bowl stir together cooking oil and chili oil. Brush garlic, jalapeño peppers, tomatoes, and onion lightly with the oil mixture.

3 Drain wood chips. For a charcoal grill, arrange medium-hot coals around a drip pan. Test for medium heat above the pan. Sprinkle drained wood chips over coals. Place tomatoes, onion slices, and the skewers on grill rack over drip pan. Cover; grill about 15 minutes or until vegetables are almost tender, turning once halfway through grilling. (For a gas grill, preheat grill. Reduce heat to medium. Adjust heat for indirect cooking. Add wood chips according to manufacturer's directions. Grill as above.) Cool vegetables slightly.

4 Remove garlic and jalapeño peppers from skewers. Transfer vegetables, half at a time, to a food processor. Coarsely chop the vegetables with several on-off turns. Transfer to a medium bowl. Stir in jicama, cilantro, lime juice, and salt. Serve with tortilla chips.

Black Bean Smoked Salsa: Prepare salsa as above, except omit jicama. Stir ½ cup canned black beans, rinsed and drained, into the chopped vegetable mixture.

Nutrition Facts per ¼ cup salsa: 37 cal., 2 g total fat (0 g sat. fat), 0 mg chol., 103 mg sodium, 4 g carbo., 1 g fiber, 1 g pro. Daily Values: 9% vit. A, 26% vit. C, 1% calcium, 2% iron. Exchanges: ½ Fat

VEGETABLE FAJITAS WITH HOT PEPPER CREAM SAUCES

Prep: 30 minutes Grill: 12 minutes
Makes: 10 fajitas

- ⅔ **cup dairy sour cream**
- 2 **tablespoons snipped fresh cilantro**
- 1 **to 2 teaspoons finely chopped canned chipotle peppers in adobo sauce**
- 2 **tablespoons finely chopped fresh poblano chile pepper (see tip, page 36)**
- 1 **medium sweet onion, cut into ½-inch slices**
- 1 **medium green sweet pepper**
- 1 **medium red sweet pepper**
- 1 **medium yellow sweet pepper**
- 2 **tablespoons olive oil**
- ½ **to 1 teaspoon Mexican seasoning**
- 1 **Japanese eggplant, halved lengthwise**
- 10 **4- to 5-inch flour tortillas**
- ¼ **teaspoon salt**
- ½ **cup bottled chunky salsa**
  Lime wedges (optional)

1 For chipotle cream, in a small bowl combine half of the sour cream, half of the cilantro, and the chipotle peppers; cover and chill.

2 For poblano cream, in a small bowl combine remaining sour cream, remaining cilantro, and the poblano pepper; cover and chill.

3 To hold onion slices together during grilling, soak short wooden skewers in water for 20 minutes. Insert skewers into onion slices from the sides to the centers. Halve sweet peppers lengthwise; discard stems, membranes, and seeds. In a small bowl combine olive oil and Mexican seasoning; lightly brush cut sides of onion, sweet peppers, and eggplant with oil mixture. (Or place

vegetables in a heavy, large self-sealing plastic bag; add oil mixture. Seal bag; shake bag to coat.)

4 For a charcoal grill, grill vegetables on the rack of an uncovered grill directly over medium coals until tender, turning occasionally. Allow 8 to 12 minutes for sweet peppers and eggplant and 12 to 14 minutes for onion. (For a gas grill, preheat grill. Reduce heat to medium. Place vegetables on the grill rack over heat. Cover; grill as above.) Remove vegetables from grill; cool until easy to handle.

5 Meanwhile, wrap tortillas in foil. Place tortillas on grill rack directly over medium heat. Grill tortillas 8 minutes or until heated through.

6 Remove skewers from onion slices; separate into rings. Cut sweet peppers into bite-size pieces; cut eggplant into ½-inch slices. Place all vegetables in a large serving bowl; toss lightly with salt. Serve vegetables in warm tortillas with chipotle cream, poblano cream, salsa, and if desired, lime wedges.

Nutrition Facts per fajita: 122 cal., 7 g total fat (2 g sat. fat), 6 mg chol., 161 mg sodium, 14 g carbo., 2 g fiber, 2 g pro. Daily Values: 22% vit. A, 118% vit. C, 4% calcium, 5% iron. Exchanges: ½ Vegetable, 1 Starch, 1 Fat

FOOD FOR THOUGHT SALT

A staple in every kitchen, salt is sourced from salt mines, the sea, or salt lakes. Here are the various types.

● Table Salt: **Used for both cooking and as a condiment, this refined, fine-grain product has been treated to ensure that it flows freely. It also comes as iodized with iodine added to help prevent enlargement of the thyroid gland due to iodine deficiency.**

● Kosher Salt: **A coarse-grain salt free of additives, its texture and flavor is preferred among many chefs.**

● Sea Salt: **Derived from evaporated sea water, sea salt has a fresh, distinct flavor that varies depending on its source.**

● Pickling Salt: **This additive-free, fine-grain salt is used to make brines that stay clear and cloudless.**

GRILLED POTATO SLICES

Another time, skip the capers and garnish these appetizers with a fresh herb such as basil, oregano, or dill.

Prep: 30 minutes Grill: 15 minutes
Makes: about 20 appetizers

- **4 medium russet potatoes (about 1 1/3 pounds)**
- **2 tablespoons olive oil**
  Coarse salt
  Cracked black pepper
- **1/2 cup crème fraîche**
- **3 tablespoons dried tomatoes (oil-packed), drained and snipped**
- **2 tablespoons drained capers**

1 Scrub potatoes. Cut potatoes into 1/2-inch slices. Brush slices on both sides generously with oil. Sprinkle with salt and pepper.

2 For a charcoal grill, grill potato slices on the rack of an uncovered grill directly over medium coals for 15 to 20 minutes or until tender and brown, turning occasionally. (For a gas grill, preheat grill. Reduce heat to medium. Place potato slices on grill rack over heat. Cover; grill as above.) Remove potato slices from grill.

3 To serve, top warm or room temperature potato slices with crème fraîche, snipped tomatoes, and capers.

Nutrition Facts per appetizer: 70 cal., 5 g total fat (2 g sat. fat), 11 mg chol., 60 mg sodium, 6 g carbo., 1 g fiber, 1 g pro. Daily Values: 10% vit. C, 2% calcium, 3% iron. Exchanges: 1/2 Starch, 1 Fat

WALNUT, ONION, AND PROSCIUTTO BRUSCHETTA

Mild, sweet onions are at their best in spring and early summer. Look for Vidalia, Walla Walla, Maui, Texas Spring Sweet, Imperial Sweet, or Carzalia Sweet onions.

Prep: 25 minutes Grill: 10 minutes
Makes: 8 bruschetta

- **Short wooden skewers or toothpicks**
- **1 medium sweet onion, cut into 3/4-inch slices**
- **1 tablespoon olive oil**
- **1/4 cup walnuts, toasted and chopped**
- **2 ounces prosciutto, chopped**
- **3 tablespoons bottled balsamic vinaigrette**
- **1/2 cup finely shredded smoked provolone or smoked Gouda cheese (2 ounces)**
- **8 1/2-inch slices crusty country bread**
- **2 tablespoons snipped fresh oregano or 2 teaspoons snipped fresh thyme**

1 To hold onion slices together during grilling, use short wooden skewers or toothpicks that have been soaked in water for 20 minutes. Insert skewers into onion slices from the sides to the centers. Brush onion slices lightly with olive oil.

2 For a charcoal grill, grill onion slices on the rack of an uncovered grill directly over medium coals for 10 to 12 minutes or until tender, turning once halfway through grilling. Grill bread slices on grill rack directly over coals for 1 to 2 minutes or until toasted (do not turn). (For a gas grill, preheat grill. Reduce heat to medium. Place onion directly over heat. Cover; grill as above.) Remove onions from grill and place on cutting board; cool slightly. Remove and discard skewers. Coarsely chop onion.

3 In a bowl combine walnuts and prosciutto. Add onion and balsamic vinaigrette; toss to coat. Spoon mixture evenly onto toasted side of bread slices; sprinkle with cheese. Place slices on grill, topping side up. Cover; grill about 2 minutes or just until heated through and bottoms are toasted. Sprinkle with fresh herbs before serving.

Nutrition Facts per bruschetta: 214 cal., 10 g total fat (2 g sat. fat), 10 mg chol., 547 mg sodium, 24 g carbo., 1 g fiber, 8 g pro. Daily Values: 1% vit. A, 2% vit. C, 11% calcium, 9% iron. Exchanges: 1 Starch, 1/2 Other Carbo., 1/2 High-Fat Meat, 1 Fat

Walnut, Onion, and Prosciutto Bruschetta

POTATO SKINS

Make two or more of the toppings and let guests
choose what they want to pile onto these
grilled potato halves.

Prep: 30 minutes Grill: 55 minutes
Makes: 12 potato skins

**6 6-ounce baking potatoes (such as
     russet or long white)**
**2 tablespoons olive oil
     Salt
     Black pepper**
1 recipe desired potato topping

1 Scrub potatoes; cut each potato in half lengthwise. Brush cut surfaces with oil and sprinkle
with salt and pepper.

2 For a charcoal grill, arrange medium-hot coals
around edge of grill; test for medium heat
above center of grill. Place potatoes, cut sides up,
on grill rack in the center of the grill. Cover; grill
for 50 to 60 minutes or until tender. (For a gas
grill, preheat grill. Reduce heat to medium. Adjust
heat for indirect cooking. Grill as above.)

3 Carefully scoop out the insides of each potato
half, leaving a $1/2$-inch shell. Brush the insides
of the potato shells with any remaining oil. Fill
with desired topping. Return potatoes to grill
filled sides up. Grill for 5 to 7 minutes more or
until heated through.

O'Brien Topping: Combine $3/4$ cup packaged
shredded cabbage with carrot; 3 ounces thinly
sliced cooked corned beef, shredded; and
2 tablespoons bottled creamy garlic salad
dressing. Divide among potato shells. Sprinkle
with 1 cup shredded Swiss cheese (4 ounces).

Nutrition Facts per potato skin: 123 cal., 7 g fat
(3 g sat. fat), 16 mg chol., 234 mg sodium, 5 g carbo.,
1 g dietary fiber, 5 g pro. Daily Values: 2% vit. A,
13% vit. C., 10% calcium, 5% iron. Exchanges: ½ Starch,
1 Fat

Spicy Topping: In a medium skillet cook
6 ounces crumbled chorizo sausage and $1/2$ cup
chopped onion until onion is tender; drain off fat.
Stir in $1/4$ cup salsa. Divide among potato shells.
Sprinkle with 1 cup shredded Monterey Jack
cheese (4 ounces). Serve with additional salsa.

Nutrition Facts per potato skin: 159 cal., 11 g fat
(4 g sat. fat), 21 mg chol., 338 mg sodium, 9 g carbo.,
1 g dietary fiber, 7 g pro. Daily Values: 2% vit. A,
18% vit. C., 8% calcium, 8% iron. Exchanges: ½ Starch,
1 High-Fat Meat

All-American Topping: In a large skillet cook
6 slices bacon until crisp; remove from skillet and
crumble. Combine crumbled bacon; 10 cherry
tomatoes, quartered; $1/3$ cup thinly sliced green
onions; and 2 tablespoons bottled ranch salad
dressing. Divide among potato shells. Sprinkle
with 1 cup shredded cheddar or American cheese
(4 ounces).

Nutrition Facts per potato skin: 134 cal., 9 g fat
(3 g sat. fat), 14 mg chol., 246 mg sodium, 9 g carbo.,
1 g dietary fiber, 5 g pro. Daily Values: 4% vit. A, 22%
vit. C., 8% calcium, 7% iron. Exchanges: ½ Starch,
½ High-Fat Meat, 1 Fat

Caramelized Onion Topping: In a large
skillet cook 3 slices peppered bacon until crisp;
remove from skillet, reserving 1 tablespoon
drippings in skillet. Crumble bacon and set aside.
Add 1 thinly sliced large onion to skillet; cook
until tender. Stir in 1 tablespoon brown sugar.
Cook and stir until onion is golden. Remove from
heat and stir in the bacon. Divide among potato
shells. Sprinkle with 1 cup shredded smoked
cheddar or smoked Gouda cheese (4 ounces).

Nutrition Facts per potato skin: 126 cal., 8 g fat
(3 g sat. fat), 13 mg chol., 193 mg sodium, 11 g carbo.,
1 g dietary fiber, 4 g pro. Daily Values: 2% vit. A,
18% vit. C., 8% calcium, 8% iron. Exchanges: ½ Starch,
½ High-Fat Meat, 1 Fat

HOT RIBEYE BITES

Prep: 15 minutes Grill: 11 minutes
Makes: about 24 appetizers

¼ cup jalapeño pepper jelly
2 tablespoons Kansas City steak
   seasoning
2 boneless beef ribeye steaks, cut
   1 inch thick (about 1¼ pounds),
   or 1 boneless beef top
   sirloin steak
24 pickled baby banana chile peppers,
   jalapeño chile peppers, other
   mild baby chile peppers, and/or
   cornichons

1 For glaze, in a small saucepan stir together pepper jelly and steak seasoning. Cook and stir over low heat for 1 to 2 minutes or until jelly is melted. Set aside.

2 For a charcoal grill, grill the steaks on grill rack of an uncovered grill directly over medium coals to desired doneness, turning steaks once halfway through grilling and brushing with glaze during the last 5 minutes. For ribeye steaks, allow 11 to 15 minutes for medium rare (145°F) or 14 to 18 minutes for medium (160°F). Or for top sirloin, allow 14 to 18 minutes for medium rare or 18 to 22 minutes for medium. (For a gas grill, preheat grill. Reduce heat to medium. Place steaks on grill rack over heat. Cover; grill as above.)

Hot Ribeye Bites

3 Cut steak into 1-inch cubes. Top each cube with a pickled pepper. Serve immediately.

Nutrition Facts per appetizer: 47 cal., 1 g total fat (1 g sat. fat), 11 mg chol., 179 mg sodium, 3 g carbo., 0 g fiber, 5 g pro. Daily Values: 4% vit. C, 1% calcium, 3% iron. Exchanges: 1 Very Lean Meat

FLANK STEAK SKEWERS

A tangy yogurt marinade transforms flank steak into juicy, tender morsels with an exotic flair.

Prep: 30 minutes Marinate: 2 hours Grill: 10 minutes
Makes: 12 appetizers

    1 **pound beef flank steak**
    1 **8-ounce carton plain yogurt**
  1/4 **cup bottled chili sauce**
    1 **tablespoon snipped fresh cilantro**
    2 **teaspoons grated fresh ginger**
    2 **cloves garlic, minced**
  1/2 **teaspoon salt**
  1/2 **teaspoon ground coriander**
  1/8 **teaspoon black pepper**
   12 **8- to 10-inch wooden skewers**

1 Thinly slice beef across the grain into thin strips. Place beef in a self-sealing plastic bag set in a shallow dish. For marinade, in a small bowl stir together the yogurt, chili sauce, cilantro, ginger, garlic, salt, coriander, and pepper. Pour over beef. Seal bag; turn bag several times to coat meat. Marinate in the refrigerator for 2 to 6 hours, turning bag occasionally.

2 At least 1 hour before grilling, soak wooden skewers in water; drain. Remove meat from marinade, discarding marinade. Thread beef, accordion-style, onto the skewers.

3 For a charcoal grill, grill beef skewers on the rack of an uncovered grill directly over medium coals for 10 to 12 minutes or until desired doneness, turning once halfway through grilling. (For a gas grill, preheat grill. Reduce heat to medium. Place skewers on the grill rack over the heat. Cover; grill as above.)

Nutrition Facts per appetizer: 77 cal., 3 g total fat (1 g sat. fat), 16 mg chol., 197 mg sodium, 3 g carbo., 0 g fiber, 9 g pro. Daily Values: 1% vit. A, 2% vit. C, 4% calcium, 4% iron. Exchanges: 1½ Lean Meat

GRILLED STUFFED PORTOBELLOS

Wedges of sausage-stuffed portobellos make hefty appetizers that are sure to appeal to mushroom lovers.

Prep: 30 minutes Grill: 10 minutes
Makes: 16 appetizers

    5 **portobello mushrooms (4 to**
       5 inches in diameter)
    8 **ounces bulk pork sausage**
    2 **tablespoons finely chopped shallots**
    1 **clove garlic, minced**
  1/3 **cup fine dry bread crumbs**
    2 **tablespoons snipped fresh sage or**
       1/2 teaspoon ground sage
    1 **tablespoon dry sherry**
  1/4 **teaspoon black pepper**
  1/4 **cup finely shredded Parmesan**
       cheese
       Snipped fresh sage (optional)

1 Wash mushrooms; remove and discard stems and gills. Chop 1 mushroom cap (should have ¾ cup). In a large skillet cook chopped mushroom, sausage, shallots, and garlic over medium heat until sausage is brown. Remove from heat. If necessary, drain all but 2 tablespoons of fat from skillet. Stir in bread crumbs, the 2 tablespoons sage, sherry, and pepper. Spoon sausage mixture into the 4 remaining mushroom caps.

2 For a charcoal grill, grill mushrooms on the rack of a covered grill directly over medium coals for 10 to 15 minutes or until mushrooms are tender. (For a gas grill, preheat grill. Reduce heat to medium. Place mushrooms on grill rack over heat. Grill as above.)

3 Sprinkle mushrooms with cheese and, if desired, additional fresh sage. To serve, cut each stuffed mushroom into quarters. Serve warm.

Nutrition Facts per appetizer: 137 cal., 10 g total fat (4 g sat. fat), 19 mg chol., 301 mg sodium, 4 g carbo., 0 g fiber, 8 g pro. Daily Values: 1% vit. A, 1% vit. C, 12% calcium, 4% iron. Exchanges: 1 Vegetable, 1 High-Fat Meat, ½ Fat

CANADIAN BACON PIZZA

This fast-grilling appetizer puts all of the sizzle and smoke you love into one of the world's most popular treats. Purchased Italian bread shells make the recipe a snap to prepare.

Prep: 20 minutes Grill: 5 minutes
Makes: 8 appetizer servings

1 6-ounce jar marinated artichoke
  hearts, quartered
2 6-inch Italian bread shells (Boboli)
1 cup shredded fontina or mozzarella
  cheese (4 ounces)
6 slices Canadian-style bacon, cut into
  strips (about 5 ounces)
3 roma tomatoes, sliced
1/4 cup crumbled feta cheese (1 ounce)
1/4 cup thinly sliced green onions (2)
1 tablespoon snipped fresh oregano
  or basil

1 Drain artichoke hearts, reserving marinade. Brush the bread shells with some of the reserved marinade (discard any remaining marinade). Sprinkle half of the fontina cheese over shells. In a large bowl toss together the artichoke hearts, bacon, tomatoes, feta cheese, green onions, and oregano; divide among shells. Sprinkle with remaining fontina cheese. Transfer the bread shells to a pizza grill pan or a large piece of double-thickness heavy foil.

2 For a charcoal grill, place the pan or foil on the grill rack directly over medium coals. Cover; grill for 5 to 8 minutes or until cheese is melted and pizza is heated through. (For a gas grill, preheat grill. Reduce heat to medium. Place the pan or foil on grill rack over heat. Grill as above.)

Nutrition Facts per serving: 270 cal., 12 g total fat (4 g sat. fat), 32 mg chol., 794 mg sodium, 29 g carbo., 1 g fiber, 15 g pro. Daily Values: 8% vit. A, 20% vit. C, 17% calcium, 9% iron. Exchanges: 1½ Vegetable, 1½ Starch, 1½ Medium-Fat Meat

CURRIED PORK BITES

A quick dunk in a cool yogurt sauce tempers these robustly flavored curried pork cubes. Use purchased garam masala or make your own using the recipe on page 38.

Prep: 25 minutes Chill: 1 to 24 hours Grill: 12 minutes
Makes: 6 appetizer servings

2 tablespoons garam masala or
  curry powder
2 tablespoons finely chopped green
  onion (1)
2 cloves garlic, minced
1 tablespoon grated fresh ginger
1 tablespoon cooking oil
1/8 teaspoon crushed red pepper
1 pound pork tenderloin, cut into
  1- to 1½-inch cubes
1/2 cup plain yogurt
2 tablespoons snipped fresh cilantro

1 In a medium bowl combine garam masala, green onion, garlic, ginger, oil, and crushed red pepper. Stir in pork, working spice mixture into meat with fingers. Thread the meat onto metal skewers, leaving a 1/4-inch space between each piece; cover and chill for 1 to 24 hours.

2 For a charcoal grill, grill pork skewers on the lightly greased rack of an uncovered grill directly over medium coals for 12 to 15 minutes or until juices run clear, turning once halfway through grilling. (For a gas grill, preheat grill. Reduce heat to medium. Place pork skewers on lightly oiled grill rack over heat. Cover; grill as above.) Meanwhile, in a small serving bowl stir together yogurt and cilantro. Cover and chill.

3 To serve, use a fork to remove grilled pork cubes from skewers. Arrange the pork cubes on a tray around yogurt mixture. Serve pork with cocktail picks.

Nutrition Facts per serving (about 3 pieces): 134 cal., 5 g total fat (1 g sat. fat), 50 mg chol., 52 mg sodium, 3 g carbo., 0 g fiber, 17 g pro. Daily Values: 3% vit. A, 4% vit. C, 6% calcium, 9% iron. Exchanges: 2½ Very Lean Meat, 1 Fat

Chicken and Kiwi Tacos

CHICKEN AND KIWI TACOS

If you prefer to make your own taco shells, heat
¹/₂ inch of cooking oil in a large, heavy skillet.
Cook six 5-inch tortillas, one at a time, in hot oil
just until golden. Remove from hot oil with tongs.
Fold over a rolling pin lined with paper towels or
wire tortilla rack placed over a plate lined with
paper towels. Let cool until firm.

Prep: 25 minutes Grill: 6 minutes
Makes: 12 mini tacos

¹/₂ **teaspoon ground cumin**
¹/₄ **teaspoon salt**
¹/₈ **to** ¹/₄ **teaspoon crushed red pepper**
 8 **ounces skinless, boneless chicken
   breast halves**
 1 **teaspoon cooking oil**
12 **purchased mini taco shells**
 1 **cup shredded romaine lettuce**
¹/₂ **cup shredded Monterey Jack cheese
   or Monterey Jack cheese with
   jalapeño peppers (2 ounces)**
 3 **kiwifruits, peeled and chopped**
 1 **small tomato, chopped**
 1 **tablespoon lime or lemon juice**

1 In a small bowl combine cumin, salt, and
crushed red pepper. Brush chicken breasts with
the cooking oil. Rub chicken breasts with cumin
mixture. Place each breast half between 2 pieces
of plastic wrap; gently pound with a meat mallet
to ¹/₂-inch thickness.

2 For a charcoal grill, grill chicken on the
lightly oiled rack of an uncovered grill directly over medium coals for 6 to 8 minutes or until
tender and no longer pink, turning once halfway
through grilling. (For a gas grill, preheat grill.
Reduce heat to medium. Place chicken on lightly
oiled grill rack over heat. Cover; grill as above.)
Remove chicken; set aside until cool enough to
handle. Meanwhile, heat taco shells according to
the package directions.

3 Cut chicken into thin strips and arrange in taco
shells. Top with lettuce and cheese. In a small
bowl toss together kiwifruits, tomato, and lime
juice. Sprinkle on tacos.

Nutrition Facts per taco: 81 cal., 3 g total fat
(1 g sat. fat), 15 mg chol., 104 mg sodium, 6 g carbo.,
1 g fiber, 6 g pro. Daily Values: 10% vit. A, 36% vit. C,
5% calcium, 2% iron. Exchanges: ¹/₂ Starch, ¹/₂ Very Lean
Meat, ¹/₂ Fat

PORK AND CHICKEN
BBQ STICKS

Chipotle peppers lend a smoky, spicy flavor to this honey-sweetened barbecue sauce. Keep the sauce in mind anytime you grill chicken or pork chops.

Prep: 20 minutes Chill: 15 minutes Grill: 12 minutes
Makes: 16 appetizers

12 ounces pork tenderloin
12 ounces skinless, boneless
    chicken thighs
16 6-inch wooden skewers
    Salt
    Black pepper
1 recipe Chipotle Barbecue Sauce

1 Trim fat from pork. Cut pork into 1-inch cubes. Cut chicken into 1-inch pieces. Thread 3 pork pieces onto 8 of the skewers, leaving ¼ inch between pieces. Thread 3 chicken pieces on each of the remaining 8 skewers, leaving ¼ inch between pieces. Place skewers on a tray.

2 Sprinkle salt and pepper evenly over pork and chicken. Cover; chill 15 minutes to 2 hours.

3 For a charcoal grill, grill pork kabobs on the greased rack of an uncovered grill directly over medium coals for 12 to 14 minutes or until pork is slightly pink in center and juices run clear, brushing generously with the Chipotle Barbecue Sauce halfway through grilling. Grill chicken kabobs on the rack of an uncovered grill directly over medium coals for 12 to 14 minutes or until chicken is tender and no longer pink, brushing generously with the remaining sauce halfway through grilling. (For a gas grill, preheat grill. Reduce heat to medium. Place kabobs on greased grill rack over heat. Cover; grill as above.)

Chipotle Barbecue Sauce: In small saucepan combine ½ cup bottled barbecue sauce, 1 tablespoon chopped canned chipotle peppers in adobo sauce, 2 cloves minced garlic, and 1 tablespoon honey. Bring to boiling; reduce heat. Boil gently, uncovered, for 5 minutes or until slightly thickened. Set aside to cool slightly.

Nutrition Facts per appetizer: 63 cal., 2 g total fat (0 g sat. fat), 31 mg chol., 116 mg sodium, 2 g carbo., 0 g fiber, 9 g pro. Daily Values: 2% vit. A, 2% vit. C, 1% calcium, 3% iron. Exchanges: 1½ Very Lean Meat

QUESADILLA APPETIZER
SANDWICH BOARD

Make one or all three quesadilla fillings for a change from the traditional cheese. Any one of the three versions—all with different types of cheese—will intrigue your guests.

Start to Finish: 30 minutes
Makes: 6 appetizer servings

6 7-inch flour tortillas
1 tablespoon cooking oil
1 recipe desired Quesadilla Filling

1 Brush 1 side of each tortilla with some of the cooking oil. Place 3 tortillas, oiled side down, on a large baking sheet or tray. Fill with desired filling. Top with remaining tortillas oiled side up.

2 For a charcoal grill, grill quesadillas on rack of an uncovered grill directly over medium coals about 2 minutes or until cheese begins to melt and tortillas start to brown, turning once halfway through grilling. (For a gas grill, preheat grill. Reduce heat to medium. Place quesadillas on grill rack over heat. Cover; grill as above.)

3 To serve, carefully cut each quesadilla into 4 wedges.

Veggie Quesadilla Filling: In a small bowl combine ½ cup shredded carrot, ½ cup finely chopped broccoli, and ¼ cup thinly sliced green onions. Spread 3 of the tortillas evenly with 3 tablespoons dried tomato-flavor mayonnaise. Layer with ½ cup shredded smoked Gouda or provolone cheese (2 ounces), the carrot mixture, and another ½ cup shredded smoked Gouda or provolone cheese (2 ounces). Top with remaining 3 tortillas. Continue as directed above.

Nutrition Facts per serving: 198 cal., 12 g total fat (5 g sat. fat), 20 mg chol., 472 mg sodium, 18 g carbo., 1 g dietary fiber, 6 g pro. Daily Values: 59% vit, A, 14% vit. C, 16% calcium, 6% iron. Exchanges: ½ Vegetable, 1 Starch, ½ High-Fat Meat, 1½ Fat

Club Quesadilla Filling: In a small bowl combine 2 ounces thinly sliced cooked ham, shredded; 2 ounces thinly sliced cooked turkey, shredded; 3 slices bacon, crisp-cooked and crumbled; and 2 tablespoons dried tomatoes (oil-pack). Spread 3 tortillas evenly with 2 tablespoons creamy Dijon-style mustard blend. Layer with

½ cup shredded cheddar cheese (2 ounces), the meat mixture, and another ½ cup shredded cheddar cheese (2 ounces). Top with remaining 3 tortillas. Continue as directed on page 90.

Nutrition Facts per serving: 258 cal., 16 g total fat (6 g sat. fat), 36 mg chol., 508 mg sodium, 17 g carbo., 1 g dietary fiber, 12 g pro. Daily Values: 5% vit, A, 4% vit. C, 17% calcium, 8% iron. Exchanges: 1 Starch, 1½ Medium-Fat Meat, 1½ Fat

Grilled Cheese Quesadilla Filling: In a small bowl combine 1¼ cups shredded cheddar, American, Swiss, mozzarella, and/or provolone cheese (5 ounces); ¼ cup crumbled blue or feta cheese (1 ounce); and ¼ cup thinly sliced green onions. Spread 3 tortillas evenly with 3 tablespoons purchased French onion dip. Top with cheese mixture. Top with the remaining 3 tortillas. Continue as directed on page 90.

Nutrition Facts per serving: 237 cal., 15 g total fat (8 g sat. fat), 28 mg chol., 391 mg sodium, 16 g carbo., 1 g dietary fiber, 9 g pro. Daily Values: 6% vit. A, 1% vit. C, 23% calcium, 7% iron. Exchanges: 1 Starch, 1 High-Fat Meat, 1½ Fat

SMOKY WINGS WITH DOUBLE DIPPERS

Prep: 30 minutes Grill: 25 minutes
Makes: 8 appetizer servings

2 cups mesquite, hickory, or fruit wood chips
2 pounds chicken wings and/or wing drumettes
1 tablespoon sugar
1 tablespoon finely shredded lime peel
1 teaspoon celery seeds
1 recipe Spicy Pesto Ranch Dipper
1 recipe Black Pepper-Blue Cheese Dipper
    Assorted fresh vegetables such as carrots and celery sticks (optional)

1 At least 1 hour before grilling, soak wood chips in enough water to cover. If desired, cut off and discard wing tips from chicken wings. Sprinkle wings with salt and pepper. In a large bowl toss together wings, sugar, lime peel, and celery seeds. If desired, cover and marinate in the refrigerator for 1 hour.

2 Drain wood chips. For a charcoal grill, arrange medium-hot coals around a drip pan. Test for medium heat above pan. Sprinkle drained wood chips over coals. Pour 1 inch of water into drip pan. Place chicken wings on lightly greased grill rack over drip pan. Cover; grill until chicken is tender and juices run clear. Allow 25 to 30 minutes for drumettes or 35 to 40 minutes for wings. (For a gas grill, preheat grill. Reduce heat to medium. Adjust heat for indirect cooking. Add wood chips according to manufacturer's directions. Grill as above.)

3 Serve with Spicy Pesto Ranch Dipper or Black Pepper-Blue Cheese Dipper. If desired, serve wings with assorted fresh vegetables.

Spicy Pesto Ranch Dipper: In a small bowl stir together ¼ cup mayonnaise or salad dressing, ¼ cup purchased basil pesto, 3 tablespoons bottled ranch salad dressing, and ⅛ to ¼ teaspoon cayenne pepper. Cover and chill until needed.

Black Pepper-Blue Cheese Dipper: In a small bowl stir together ¼ cup mayonnaise or salad dressing, ¼ cup crumbled blue cheese (1 ounce), 3 tablespoons buttermilk, and ¼ to ½ teaspoon black pepper. Cover; chill until needed.

Nutrition Facts per serving: 338 cal., 30 g total fat (5 g sat. fat), 62 mg chol., 352 mg sodium, 4 g carbo., 0 g fiber, 13 g pro. Daily Values: 2% vit. A, 2% vit. C, 4% calcium, 4% iron. Exchanges: 2 Lean Meat, 5 Fat

Smoky Wings with Double Dippers

CHICKEN AND VEGETABLE MINI PIZZAS

Prep: 15 minutes Marinate: 1 to 6 hours Bake: 12 minutes
Grill: 14 minutes Oven: 425°F
Makes: 12 mini pizzas

**12 ounces skinless, boneless chicken
    breast halves**
**2 small zucchini, halved lengthwise
    (5 to 6 ounces each)**
**1 medium red onion, cut into
    1/2-inch slices**
**1 8-ounce bottle Italian salad dressing
    or vinaigrette salad dressing**
1 16-ounce package hot roll mix
**1 4 1/2-ounce can chopped pitted ripe
    olives, well drained**
1/2 cup shredded Parmesan cheese
**10 small yellow pear-shape tomatoes
    or grape tomatoes, halved or
    quartered**
2 cups shredded mozzarella cheese

1 Place chicken, zucchini, and red onion in a
self-sealing plastic bag set in a shallow dish.
Pour 1/2 cup of the salad dressing over chicken and
vegetables; seal bag. Marinate in the refrigerator
for 1 to 6 hours, turning bag occasionally.

2 Meanwhile, for crusts, prepare hot roll mix
according to package directions for pizza
dough, adding olives and Parmesan cheese to the
flour mixture.

3 Grease 2 large baking sheets; set aside. Divide
dough into 12 balls. On a lightly floured
surface, pat each ball into a 4-inch circle. Place
circles 2 inches apart on prepared baking sheets.
Bake in a 425°F oven about 12 minutes or until
crusts are light brown. Cool on wire racks.

4 Drain chicken and vegetables, discarding
marinade. For a charcoal grill, grill chicken,
zucchini, and onion on rack of uncovered grill
directly over medium coals for 12 to 15 minutes or
until chicken is tender and no longer pink (170°F)
and vegetables are crisp-tender, turning once
halfway through grilling. (For a gas grill, preheat
grill. Reduce heat to medium. Place chicken,
zucchini, and onion on grill rack over heat. Cover;
grill as above.) Transfer chicken and vegetables to
a cutting board; cut into bite-size pieces.

5 Top crusts with chicken, vegetables, tomatoes.
Drizzle with remaining dressing. Top with
cheese. Place on the rack of the grill directly over
low to medium heat. Cover; grill 2 to 3 minutes
more or until cheese is melted. Serve warm.

Nutrition Facts per mini pizza: 441 cal., 22 g total
fat (7 g sat. fat), 60 mg chol., 972 mg sodium,
35 g carbo., 1 g fiber, 26 g pro. Daily Values: 8% vit. A,
7% vit. C, 42% calcium, 11% iron. Exchanges:
1 Vegetable, 2 Starch, 2 1/2 Lean Meat, 2 1/2 Fat

CALYPSO SHRIMP SKEWERS

Prep: 30 minutes Grill: 8 minutes
Makes: about 30 appetizers

30 6-inch wooden skewers
1/3 cup honey
1 teaspoon grated fresh ginger
2/3 cup shredded coconut
2/3 cup finely chopped peanuts
**1 pound large shrimp, peeled and
    deveined (about 30)**
**1 3-ounce package very thinly sliced
    prosciutto, cut into 7×1/2-inch strips**
1 7-ounce container crème fraîche
**1 teaspoon finely shredded lime peel
    Lime juice**

1 Soak skewers in water for 30 minutes. In a bowl
combine honey and ginger; set aside. In a shallow dish combine coconut and peanuts; set aside.

2 Drain skewers. Thread shrimp lengthwise onto
skewers beginning at tail end until they are
straight. Brush each shrimp with honey mixture,
coating completely, then roll in coconut mixture.
Wrap a strip of prosciutto around each shrimp.

3 For a charcoal grill, arrange medium-hot coals
around a drip pan. Test for medium heat above
pan. Place shrimp on grill rack over pan. Cover; grill
for 8 to 10 minutes or until shrimp turn opaque. (For
a gas grill, preheat grill. Reduce heat to medium.
Adjust heat for indirect cooking. Grill as above.)

4 In a small bowl stir together crème fraîche,
lime peel, and enough lime juice to make
desired consistency. Serve with shrimp.

Nutrition Facts per appetizer: 70 cal., 5 g total fat
(2 g sat. fat), 22 mg chol., 108 mg sodium, 4 g carbo.,
0 g fiber, 4 g pro. Daily Values: 1% vit. C, 1% calcium,
2% iron. Exchanges: 1/2 Other Carbo., 1/2 Very Lean
Meat, 1/2 Fat

Calypso Shrimp Skewers

SMOKIN' HOT TIP

Rice papers, made from rice flour, salt, and water, are translucent, brittle sheets that are perfect for making fresh spring rolls filled with your favorite meats, shellfish, and/or vegetables. Soften each sheet, one at a time, by soaking in warm water for a few seconds, then fill with your choice of ingredients and serve with a variety of dipping sauces. Rice paper wrappers are sold in Asian markets, gourmet stores, and many supermarkets.

MAHI MAHI SPRING ROLLS

Light and refreshing, spring rolls are tasty beginnings to a backyard meal. This version features a filling of grilled fish, coconut, and napa cabbage.

Prep: 40 minutes Grill: 4 minutes per $\frac{1}{2}$-inch thickness
Makes: 12 appetizers

12 ounces fresh or frozen mahi mahi, monkfish, or red snapper fillets
2 teaspoons sesame oil
1 teaspoon cooking oil
12 8-inch rice papers
1 recipe Hoisin Dipping Sauce
1½ cups shredded napa or green cabbage
⅔ cup shredded carrot
⅓ cup shredded coconut
¼ cup thinly sliced green onions (2)

1 Thaw fish, if frozen. Rinse fish; pat dry with paper towels. In a small bowl combine sesame and cooking oils. Brush oil mixture onto both sides of fish fillets. Place fish in a well-greased grill basket. For a charcoal grill, place grill basket on the rack of an uncovered grill directly over medium coals. Grill 4 to 6 minutes per ½-inch thickness of fish or until fish flakes easily when tested with a fork, turning once halfway through grilling. (For a gas grill, preheat grill. Reduce heat to medium. Place fish fillets in well greased grill basket over heat. Cover; grill as above.) Set fish aside to cool slightly.

2 Pour 1 cup warm water into a pie plate. Carefully dip rice papers into water, one at a time. Place papers, not touching, on clean dry kitchen towels. Let rice papers soften for a few minutes until pliable.

3 For filling, prepare Hoisin Dipping Sauce. Gently flake fish; place in a large bowl. Add 6 tablespoons of the Hoisin Dipping Sauce. Gently fold in the cabbage, carrot, coconut, and green onions.

4 Spoon about ⅓ cup of the fish filling onto a softened rice paper, just below center of paper. Tightly roll rice paper up from bottom around filling, tucking in opposite sides as you roll. Repeat with remaining papers and fish filling, covering rolls as you make them to prevent drying. Serve with remaining Hoisin Dipping Sauce.

Hoisin Dipping Sauce: In a bowl combine ½ cup hoisin sauce, 3 tablespoons unsweetened pineapple juice, 1 tablespoon rice vinegar, and ⅛ teaspoon cayenne pepper.

Nutrition Facts per appetizer: 120 cal., 3 g total fat (1 g sat. fat), 21 mg chol., 160 mg sodium, 16 g carbo., 1 g fiber, 7 g pro. Daily Values: 42% vit. A, 7% vit. C, 2% calcium, 4% iron. Exchanges: 1 Starch, ½ Very Lean Meat, ½ Fat

5

Salads
& Side Dishes

✪ Highlighted recipes are grilled

DIRECT GRILLING VEGETABLES

Before grilling, rinse, trim, cut up, and precook vegetables as directed below. To precook vegetables, bring a small amount of water to boiling in a saucepan; add desired vegetables and simmer, covered, for the time specified in the chart. Drain well. Generously brush vegetables with olive oil, butter, or margarine before grilling to prevent vegetables from sticking to the grill rack. Place vegetables on a piece of heavy foil or directly on grill rack. (If grilling vegetables directly on grill rack, lay them perpendicular to rack wires so they won't fall into the coals.) For a charcoal grill, place vegetables directly over medium coals. Grill, uncovered, for the time given below or until crisp-tender, turning occasionally. For a gas grill, preheat grill. Reduce heat to medium. Place vegetables on grill rack directly over heat. Cover the grill. Monitor grilling closely so vegetables don't char.

VEGETABLE	PREPARATION	PRECOOKING TIME	APPROXIMATE DIRECT-GRILLING TIME
Asparagus	Snap off and discard tough bases of stems. Precook, then tie asparagus in bundles with strips of cooked green onion tops.	3 minutes	3 to 5 minutes
Baby carrots, fresh	Cut off carrot tops. Wash and peel carrots.	3 to 5 minutes	3 to 5 minutes
Corn on the cob	Peel back corn husks but do not remove. Remove corn silks. Rinse corn; pat dry. Fold husks back around cobs. Tie husk tops with 100-percent-cotton kitchen string.	Do not precook.	25 to 30 minutes
Eggplant	Cut off top and bottom ends; cut crosswise into 1-inch slices.	Do not precook.	8 minutes
Fennel	Snip off feathery leaves; cut off stems.	10 minutes; then cut into 6 to 8 wedges	8 minutes
Leeks	Cut off green tops; trim bulb roots and remove 1 or 2 layers of white skin.	10 minutes or until almost tender; halve lengthwise	5 minutes
New potatoes	Halve potatoes.	10 minutes or until almost tender	10 to 12 minutes
Potatoes	Scrub potatoes; prick with a fork. Wrap individually in a double thickness of foil.	Do not precook.	1 to 2 hours
Sweet peppers	Remove stems. Halve peppers lengthwise; remove seeds and membranes. Cut into 1-inch-wide strips.	Do not precook.	8 to 10 minutes
Tomatoes	Remove cores; cut in half crosswise.	Do not precook.	5 minutes
Zucchini or yellow summer squash	Wash; cut off ends. Quarter lengthwise.	Do not precook.	5 to 6 minutes

SUMMER BEEF SALAD

Look for edamame (green soybeans) in the frozen food section of your supermarket or in health food stores.

Prep: 35 minutes Chill: 1 to 4 hours Grill: 14 minutes
Makes: 4 main-dish servings

- 3 tablespoons balsamic vinegar
- 3 tablespoons cider vinegar
- 1 tablespoon brown sugar
- 1/2 teaspoon ground cumin
- 2 cloves garlic, minced
- 1 1/2 cups cooked edamame
- 1 1/2 cups cooked fresh corn
- 1/2 cup chopped red sweet pepper
- 1/3 cup thinly sliced green onions
- 12 ounces beef top sirloin steak, cut 1 inch thick
  Salt
  Black pepper
- 4 cups torn mixed salad greens
- 2 tablespoons snipped fresh cilantro
- 2 tomatoes, cored and cut into wedges

1 In a medium bowl combine vinegars, brown sugar, cumin, and garlic. Stir to dissolve sugar. Add edamame, corn, sweet pepper, and green onions to vinegar mixture; toss to coat. Cover and chill for 1 to 4 hours, stirring once.

2 Trim fat from steak. Lightly sprinkle both sides of steak with salt and black pepper. For a charcoal grill, grill steak on the rack of an uncovered grill directly over medium coals until desired doneness, turning once halfway through grilling. Allow 14 to 18 minutes for medium-rare (145°F) and 18 to 22 minutes for medium (160°F). (For gas grill, preheat grill. Reduce heat to medium. Place meat on grill rack over heat. Cover; grill as above.)

3 Cut meat into bite-size strips; stir into vegetable mixture. Add salad greens and cilantro; toss lightly to mix. Transfer salad to a large platter. Garnish with tomato wedges.

Nutrition Facts per serving: 313 cal., 8 g total fat (2 g sat. fat), 40 mg chol., 221 mg sodium, 34 g carbo., 6 g fiber, 30 g pro. Daily Values: 41% vit. A, 109% vit. C, 15% calcium, 26% iron. Exchanges: 2 Vegetable, 1 1/2 Starch, 3 Lean Meat

BEEF WITH MIXED TOMATO SALAD

Prep: 35 minutes Grill: 14 minutes Cool: 30 minutes
Chill: 4 to 24 hours Marinate: 2 hours
Makes: 4 main-dish servings

- 12 ounces beef top sirloin steak, cut 1 inch thick
  Salt
  Black pepper
- 1 9-ounce package frozen artichoke hearts, cooked and drained
- 1 recipe Basil and Green Onion Dressing
- 1 10-ounce package torn mixed salad greens (about 8 cups)
- 2 medium red and/or golden tomatoes, cut into wedges
- 1 cup assorted cherry tomatoes, such as grape, pear, and yellow
- 2 tablespoons shredded fresh basil (optional)
- 1/2 cup crumbled feta cheese (2 ounces)
- 1/3 cup pitted kalamata olives

1 Trim fat from steaks. Lightly sprinkle both sides of steak with salt and pepper. For a charcoal grill, grill steaks on the rack of an uncovered grill directly over medium coals until desired doneness, turning once halfway through grilling. Allow 14 to 18 minutes for medium-rare (145°F) or 18 to 22 minutes for medium (160°F). (For a gas grill, preheat grill. Reduce heat to medium. Place meat on grill rack over heat. Cover; grill as above.) Transfer meat to a cutting board. Cool for 30 minutes.

2 Thinly slice meat and place in a self-sealing plastic bag set in a shallow dish; seal bag and chill for 4 to 24 hours. About 2 hours before serving add artichoke hearts and 1/3 cup of the Basil and Green Onion Dressing to beef in bag; seal bag. Marinate in refrigerator for 2 hours. Drain and discard marinade.

3 Place salad greens on 4 plates. Arrange tomatoes, artichoke hearts, and beef strips on greens. Stir shredded basil (if using) into remaining dressing; drizzle dressing over salads. Top with feta cheese and olives.

Summer Beef Salad

Basil and Green Onion Dressing: In a screw-top jar combine ⅓ cup salad oil; ⅓ cup red wine vinegar; 2 tablespoons thinly sliced green onion (1); 1½ teaspoons dried basil, crushed; 1 teaspoon Dijon-style mustard; 1 clove garlic, minced; ⅛ teaspoon salt; and ⅛ teaspoon black pepper. Cover and shake well.

Nutrition Facts per serving: 371 cal., 25 g total fat (6 g sat. fat), 68 mg chol., 586 mg sodium, 14 g carbo., 7 g fiber, 24 g pro. Daily Values: 22% vit. A, 47% vit. C, 16% calcium, 20% iron. Exchanges: 3 Vegetable, 2½ Lean Meat, 3½ Fat

FOOD FOR THOUGHT
EDAMAME

Pronounced ed-uh-MAH-may, these edible Japanese soybeans consist of pods filled with two to three beans each that are great for snacks or as an ingredient in salads or other dishes. Prepared fresh, the pods are boiled in salted water about 10 minutes, and the bright green beans are popped out of the pods to be eaten. Edamame is also available frozen, having already been steamed. To prepare, cook the beans in boiling water for 2 to 3 minutes, refresh them in cold water, and serve.

GRILLED STEAK, MANGO, AND PEAR SALAD

Prep: 20 minutes Grill: 11 minutes Chill: 4 to 6 hours
Makes: 4 main-dish servings

**12 ounces boneless beef top loin steak,
   cut 1 inch thick**
2 tablespoons olive oil or cooking oil
½ teaspoon salt
¼ teaspoon black pepper
**1 10-ounce package torn mixed
   salad greens (about 8 cups)**
**2 medium mangoes, seeded, peeled,
   and chopped**
**1 medium pear, peeled, cored,
   and chopped**
**1 recipe Blue Cheese Dressing
   Cracked black pepper**

1 Rub steak with the oil; sprinkle both sides with salt and the ¼ teaspoon pepper.

2 For a charcoal grill, grill steak on the rack of an uncovered grill directly over medium coals until desired doneness, turning once halfway through grilling. Allow 11 to 15 minutes for medium-rare (145°F) and 14 to 18 minutes for medium (160°F). (For a gas grill, preheat grill. Reduce heat to medium. Place steaks on grill rack over heat. Cover; grill as above.)

3 To serve, thinly slice steak. Arrange greens on a platter; top with meat, mangoes, and pear. Stir Blue Cheese Dressing; pour some of the dressing over salad. Sprinkle with cracked pepper. Pass remaining dressing.

Blue Cheese Dressing: Stir together ½ cup light mayonnaise or salad dressing; 2 tablespoons dairy sour cream; 1½ teaspoons snipped fresh parsley; ¾ teaspoon lemon juice; ¾ teaspoon Worcestershire sauce; 1 clove garlic, minced; dash black pepper; and dash bottled hot pepper sauce. Gently stir in ¼ cup crumbled blue cheese (1 ounce). Cover and chill for 4 to 6 hours.

Nutrition Facts per serving: 456 cal., 30 g total fat (10 g sat. fat), 73 mg chol., 632 mg sodium, 30 g carbo., 4 g fiber, 19 g pro. Daily Values: 88% vit. A, 58% vit. C, 8% calcium, 12% iron. Exchanges: 1½ Vegetable, 1½ Fruit, 2½ Lean Meat, 4½ Fat

SMOKIN' HOT TIP

To remove the large, flat mango pit, use a sharp knife to cut along both sides of the pit, creating two separate sections of flesh. Take one of the sections and make a series of cuts crosswise down through the skin to the flesh. Using both hands press up on the skin side of the section, inverting it to expose the cubes of flesh, and release them from the skin using the knife. Repeat with the other section.

GRILLED STEAK HOUSE SALAD

This hearty salad features the classic steak house duo, grilled steak and blue cheese. Toasted walnuts and a Honey-Lemon Dressing provide the unexpected.

Prep: 45 minutes Marinate: 8 to 24 hours Grill: 17 minutes
Makes: 8 main-dish servings

1 1½-pound beef flank steak
2 tablespoons soy sauce
2 tablespoons toasted sesame oil
1 tablespoon grated fresh ginger
**2 teaspoons finely shredded
   lemon peel**
2 cloves garlic, minced
**½ teaspoon coarsely ground
   black pepper**
**1 large Vidalia or other sweet onion,
   cut into ½-inch slices**
1 tablespoon cooking oil
**2 hearts of romaine lettuce, torn
   (about 8 cups)**
1 5-ounce package arugula
1 recipe Honey-Lemon Dressing
1 cup chopped walnuts, toasted
**½ cup crumbled Gorgonzola cheese,
   crumbled (2 ounces)**

1 Trim fat from steak. Score steak on both sides by making shallow cuts at 1-inch intervals in a diamond pattern. Place steak in a self-sealing plastic bag set in a shallow dish.

2 For marinade, combine the soy sauce, sesame oil, ginger, lemon peel, garlic, and pepper. Pour over steak; seal bag. Marinate in refrigerator for 8 to 24 hours, turning bag occasionally.

3 Drain steak, discarding marinade. Brush onion slices with cooking oil. For a charcoal grill, grill steak and onion slices on the rack of an uncovered grill directly over medium coals until steak is desired doneness, turning once halfway through grilling. Allow 17 to 21 minutes for medium (160° F). Remove onion slices when they are tender and slightly charred. (For a gas grill, preheat grill. Reduce heat to medium. Place steak and onion slices on grill rack over heat. Cover; grill as above.) Transfer steak and onion slices to a cutting board; cool slightly. Thinly slice the steak diagonally across the grain.

4 In an extra large bowl toss together the romaine lettuce and arugula. Drizzle with half of the Honey-Lemon Dressing; toss to coat. Add the steak, grilled onion, walnuts, and remaining dressing. Toss to mix. Divide among 8 salad plates. Sprinkle with Gorgonzola cheese.

Honey-Lemon Dressing: In a bowl whisk together ¾ cup olive oil, ¼ cup white balsamic vinegar, 3 tablespoons lemon juice, 2 tablespoons finely chopped shallots, 1 tablespoon honey, 1 tablespoon Dijon-style mustard, ½ teaspoon black pepper, and ¼ teaspoon salt.

Nutrition Facts per serving: 482 cal., 39 g total fat (8 g sat. fat), 39 mg chol., 502 mg sodium, 11 g carbo., 2 g fiber, 24 g pro. Daily Values: 39% vit. A, 35% vit. C, 11% calcium, 16% iron. Exchanges: 2 Vegetable, 3 Lean Meat, 6 Fat

ASIAN SALAD WITH BEEF

The enticing noodle salads of Vietnamese cuisine inspired this beefy pasta salad. If you prefer, use linguine or spaghetti in place of the fusilli.

Prep: 25 minutes Marinate: 30 minutes Grill: 17 minutes
Makes: 6 main-dish servings

1 1¼- to 1½-pound beef flank steak
½ cup red wine vinegar
3 tablespoons sugar
3 tablespoons cooking oil
1 tablespoon toasted sesame oil
1 tablespoon fish sauce or soy sauce
4 cloves garlic, minced
2 teaspoons grated fresh ginger
½ teaspoon salt
½ teaspoon crushed red pepper
12 ounces dried fusilli
2 medium carrots, thinly bias-sliced
1 medium red or yellow sweet pepper, cut into squares or thin strips
⅓ cup snipped fresh mint or cilantro

1 Trim fat from steak. Score steak on both sides by making shallow cuts at 1-inch intervals in a diamond pattern. Place steak in a self-sealing plastic bag set in a shallow dish.

2 For marinade, in a screw-top jar combine vinegar, sugar, cooking oil, sesame oil, fish sauce, garlic, ginger, salt, and crushed red pepper; cover and shake well. Pour ⅓ cup of the marinade over steak; seal bag. Marinate in the refrigerator for 30 minutes or up to 8 hours, turning bag occasionally. Cover and chill the remaining marinade until needed.

3 In a Dutch oven cook pasta in lightly salted boiling water for 10 to 15 minutes or until tender but still firm, adding carrots to pasta the last 1 minute of cooking. Drain pasta and carrots in colander. Rinse with cold water; drain well. Transfer to a large bowl; drizzle with the reserved marinade. Add sweet pepper and mint; toss gently to coat. Set aside.

4 Drain steak, discarding the marinade. For a charcoal grill, grill steak on the rack of an uncovered grill directly over medium coals until desired doneness, turning once halfway through grilling. Allow 17 to 21 minutes for medium (160°F). (For a gas grill, preheat grill. Reduce heat to medium. Place steak on grill rack over heat. Cover; grill as above.)

5 To serve, thinly slice the steak diagonally across the grain. Add to pasta mixture; toss gently to coat.

Nutrition Facts per serving: 474 cal., 16 g total fat (4 g sat. fat), 45 mg chol., 311 mg sodium, 56 g carbo., 3 g fiber, 26 g pro. Daily Values: 68% vit. A, 41% vit. C, 2% calcium, 34% iron. Exchanges: 1 Vegetable, 3½ Starch, 2 Lean Meat, 1½ Fat

PORK WITH DRIED CHERRY DRESSING

Before adding the cherries to the dressing, set aside 2 teaspoons of the oil and vinegar mixture to brush on the chops as they finish grilling.

Start to Finish: 30 minutes
Makes: 4 main-dish servings

1 recipe Dried Cherry Dressing
12 ounces boneless pork loin chops,
  cut ³/₄ inch thick
  Salt
  Black pepper
4 cups packaged mixed baby greens
  or other salad greens
1 ripe avocado, seeded, peeled,
  and sliced

1 Prepare Dried Cherry Dressing; set aside. Trim fat from chops. Lightly sprinkle both sides of meat with salt and pepper.

2 For a charcoal grill, grill chops on the rack of an uncovered grill directly over medium coals for 7 to 9 minutes or until done (160°F), turning once halfway through grilling. Brush with the 2 teaspoons reserved dressing just before removing chops from the grill. (For gas grill, preheat grill. Reduce heat to medium. Place meat on grill rack over heat. Cover; grill as above.)

3 Thinly slice pork chops. Divide greens among 4 dinner plates. Arrange avocado and meat on top of the greens. Spoon Dried Cherry Dressing over salads.

Dried Cherry Dressing: In a screw-top jar combine 3 tablespoons balsamic vinegar, 2 tablespoons salad oil, 1 teaspoon Dijon-style mustard, 1 teaspoon snipped fresh thyme, 1 teaspoon snipped fresh rosemary, and ¹/₈ teaspoon black pepper. Cover; shake well. Remove 2 teaspoons of the dressing for brushing on meat and set aside. Stir ¹/₄ cup chopped tart red dried cherries into remaining dressing.

Nutrition Facts per serving: 310 cal., 19 g total fat (4 g sat. fat), 46 mg chol., 221 mg sodium, 14 g carbo., 3 g fiber, 20 g pro. Daily Values: 9% vit. A, 10% vit. C, 2% calcium, 8% iron. Exchanges: 1½ Vegetable, ½ Fruit, 2½ Very Lean Meat, 3½ Fat

ITALIAN SAUSAGE AND ARUGULA SALAD

Choose hot or sweet Italian sausage for this speedy supper salad. Cook the sausage over indirect heat to prevent fat from dripping into hot coals and causing flare-ups.

Start to Finish: 30 minutes
Makes: 4 main-dish servings

1 pound hot or sweet Italian
  sausage links
6 cups arugula
1 15¹/₂-ounce can cannellini beans,
  rinsed and drained
1 7-ounce jar roasted red sweet
  peppers, drained and coarsely
  chopped
1 tablespoon capers, drained
¹/₄ cup bottled balsamic vinaigrette
¹/₃ cup finely shredded Parmesan
  cheese

1 Using a fork, prick each sausage link several times. For a charcoal grill, arrange medium-hot coals around a drip pan. Test for medium heat above the pan. Place sausage on grill rack over drip pan. Cover; grill about 20 minutes or until juices run clear (170°F). (For a gas grill, preheat grill. Reduce heat to medium. Adjust for indirect cooking. Grill as above.)

2 Divide arugula among 4 salad plates. Cut sausage links into ¹/₂-inch slices; arrange sausage over arugula. Top with beans, peppers, and capers. Drizzle with vinaigrette. Sprinkle with Parmesan cheese.

Nutrition Facts per serving: 477 cal., 32 g total fat (12 g sat. fat), 81 mg chol., 1,146 mg sodium, 20 g carbo., 6 g fiber, 26 g pro. Daily Values: 15% vit. A, 158% vit. C, 17% calcium, 16% iron. Exchanges: 1 Vegetable, 1 Starch, 3 High-Fat Meat, 1½ Fat

Italian Sausage and Arugula Salad

FOOD FOR THOUGHT SALAD GREENS

Once upon a time iceberg lettuce was the basis for salads. But today the colorful and flavorful variety of lettuces and leafy vegetables is more sought after. Mesclun is simply a mixture of small, young salad greens. The following is a general flavor guide to help you toss together your own blend.

Mild	Peppery	Bitter
Boston/Butterhead	Arugula	Belgian Endive
Iceberg	Watercress	Curly Endive/Frisée
Leaf		Escarole
Mâche/Lamb's Leaf		Radicchio
Romaine		

PORK WITH FENNEL AND APPLE

Crushed fennel seeds provide a crusty coating for pork tenderloin. Use a mortar and pestle to crush the fennel seeds and a mandoline or food processor to cut the fennel bulb and apple.

Prep: 20 minutes Grill: 25 minutes
Makes: 4 main-dish servings

- 1 **1-pound pork tenderloin**
- 1 **tablespoon fennel seeds, crushed**
  Black pepper
- 1 **medium fennel bulb, cored and very thinly sliced (2 cups)**
- 1 **red apple, cored and very thinly sliced**
  Lettuce leaves
- 1 **recipe Fennel Seed Dressing**

1 Trim fat from meat. Rub pork with fennel seeds and pepper. For a charcoal grill, grill tenderloin on the rack of an uncovered grill directly over medium coals for 25 to 30 minutes or until an instant-read thermometer inserted in center registers 160°F, turning occasionally to brown evenly. (For gas grill, preheat grill. Reduce heat to medium. Place meat on grill rack over heat. Cover; grill as above.)

2 Thinly slice tenderloin. Arrange fennel and apple slices on lettuce-lined plates. Top with pork. Drizzle with Fennel Seed Dressing.

Fennel Seed Dressing: In a screw-top jar combine ¼ cup cider vinegar; 3 tablespoons salad oil; 1 teaspoon fennel seeds, crushed; 1 teaspoon snipped fresh sage leaves; 1 teaspoon Dijon-style mustard; and ⅛ teaspoon black pepper. Cover and shake well. Chill for up to 3 days. Shake before serving.

Nutrition Facts per serving: 271 cal., 14 g total fat (3 g sat. fat), 73 mg chol., 109 mg sodium, 11 g carbo., 3 g fiber, 25 g pro. Daily Values: 4% vit. A, 18% vit. C, 7% calcium, 14% iron. Exchanges: 2 Vegetable, 3 Very Lean Meat, 2½ Fat

PORK AND CITRUS SALAD

Chewy bulgur, crisp jicama, and tangy bits of orange provide a lively backdrop to grilled pork.

Prep: 25 minutes Stand: 1 hour Chill: 4 to 24 hours
Grill: 7 minutes Makes: 4 main-dish servings

- ¾ **cup bulgur**
- ⅓ **cup thinly sliced green onions**
- 1½ **cups boiling water**
- ½ **cup olive oil or salad oil**
- 1 **tablespoon finely shredded orange peel**
- ½ **cup orange juice**
- 1 **teaspoon snipped fresh thyme**
- ½ **teaspoon salt**
- ¼ **teaspoon black pepper**
- 12 **ounces boneless pork loin chops, cut ¾ inch thick**
  Salt
  Black pepper
- 3 **medium oranges, peeled and sectioned (2 cups)**
- ½ **cup chopped, peeled jicama**

1 In a large bowl combine bulgur and green onion. Pour boiling water over bulgur mixture. Cover; let stand for 1 hour.

2 Meanwhile, for dressing, in a screw-top jar combine the oil, orange peel, orange juice, thyme, the ½ teaspoon salt, and the ¼ teaspoon pepper. Cover and shake well.

3 Drain bulgur mixture in a fine-mesh sieve, using the back of a spoon to squeeze out excess water. Transfer bulgur mixture to a bowl. Pour the dressing over the bulgur mixture. Toss gently to coat. Cover and chill for 4 to 24 hours.

4 Trim fat from chops. Lightly sprinkle both sides of meat with salt and pepper. For a charcoal grill, grill chops on the rack of an uncovered grill directly over medium coals for 7 to 9 minutes

FOOD FOR THOUGHT FENNEL

Florence Fennel, also called finochio, resembles celery but has a large, white bulbous base and green feathery fronds extending from its stalks. Its sweet, mild anise or licorice flavor becomes even mellower when cooked. Fennel can be shaved paper thin and added to a salad or baked, sautéed, or grilled during which its taste and texture become more tender. Its feathery fronds can be trimmed and used as an herb or garnish.

or until done (160°F), turning once halfway through grilling. (For gas grill, preheat grill. Reduce heat to medium. Place chops on grill rack over heat. Cover; grill as above.)

5 Cut pork into bite-size pieces. Add pork, orange sections, and jicama to bulgur mixture. Toss gently to mix.

Nutrition Facts per serving: 503 cal., 32 g total fat (5 g sat. fat), 46 mg chol., 479 mg sodium, 32 g carbo., 6 g fiber, 23 g pro. Daily Values: 4% vit. A, 79% vit. C, 5% calcium, 10% iron. Exchanges: 1 Fruit, 1 Starch, 3 Lean Meat, 4½ Fat

THAI CHICKEN SALAD

Make the dressing ahead and chill it for up to 2 days to allow the flavors to mingle.

Prep: 30 minutes Marinate: 2 to 24 hours Grill: 12 minutes
Makes: 4 main-dish servings

  2 tablespoons rice vinegar
  1 tablespoon reduced-sodium
    soy sauce
  1 teaspoon toasted sesame oil
  ¼ teaspoon grated fresh ginger
  ⅛ teaspoon ground white pepper
  4 medium skinless, boneless chicken
    breast halves
  2 cups pea pods, trimmed and
    strings removed
  1 10-ounce package torn mixed salad
    greens (about 8 cups)
  1 recipe Peanut-Sesame Vinaigrette
    Toasted sesame seeds (optional)

1 For marinade, in a small bowl combine rice vinegar, soy sauce, sesame oil, ginger, and white pepper. Place chicken in a self-sealing plastic bag set in a shallow dish. Pour marinade over chicken; seal bag. Marinate in refrigerator for 2 to 24 hours, turning bag occasionally.

2 Drain chicken, discarding marinade. For a charcoal grill, grill chicken on the rack of an uncovered grill directly over medium coals for 12 to 15 minutes or until tender and no longer pink (170°F), turning once halfway through grilling. (For a gas grill, preheat grill. Reduce heat to medium. Place chicken on grill rack over heat. Cover; grill as above.)

FOOD FOR THOUGHT
THE BIRTH OF BRIQUETTES

For thousands of years, humans have been cooking with charcoal, originally made of wood naturally transformed into carbon by slow burning in pits. Only after World War II did charcoal briquettes become the most common backyard fuel for outdoor cooking, thanks to Henry Ford. While trying to find uses for the wood remnants from his auto plant, he developed charcoal and installed automatic briquetting equipment to supply foundries and businesses with the fuel. Charles Kingsford later bought out Ford's charcoal-making business.

3 Meanwhile, in a saucepan cook pea pods in a small amount of boiling water for 1 to 2 minutes or until crisp-tender; drain.

4 To serve, diagonally cut chicken into thin slices. Arrange greens on a serving platter or 4 dinner plates. Top with sliced chicken and pea pods. Stir Peanut-Sesame Vinaigrette; drizzle over salad. If desired, sprinkle with sesame seeds.

Peanut-Sesame Vinaigrette: In a bowl whisk ¼ cup salad oil into 2 tablespoons peanut butter. Stir in 3 tablespoons rice vinegar, 1 tablespoon reduced-sodium soy sauce, 1 teaspoon brown sugar, ½ teaspoon toasted sesame oil, and ¼ to ½ teaspoon crushed red pepper.

Nutrition Facts per serving: 407 cal., 23 g total fat (4 g sat. fat), 82 mg chol., 419 mg sodium, 9 g carbo., 3 g fiber, 38 g pro. Daily Values: 11% vit. A, 14% vit. C, 7% calcium, 13% iron. Exchanges: 2 Vegetable, 5 Very Lean Meat, 4 Fat

Adobo Turkey Taco Salad

SMOKIN' HOT TIP

A tortilla bowl is a fun way to serve salads and side dishes.

● Coat a small, oven-safe bowl or 16-ounce individual casserole with nonstick cooking spray.

● Lightly coat one side of a 9- or 10-inch flour tortilla with a small amount of water or nonstick cooking spray. Press the tortilla, coated side up, into the prepared bowl or casserole. Place a ball of foil into each cupped tortilla.

● Bake in a 350°F oven for 15 to 20 minutes or until light brown. Remove the foil and cool.

● Once cooled, remove the bowl-shape tortilla from the dish and fill with your favorite salad or side dish.

SPICY BUFFALO CHICKEN SALAD

Set aside a tablespoon or two of the blue cheese to adorn this colorful melange of ingredients.

Prep: 20 minutes Marinate: 3 to 4 hours Grill: 12 minutes
Makes: 4 main-dish servings

- 1 pound skinless, boneless chicken breast halves
- 2 tablespoons olive oil
- 1 tablespoon bottled hot pepper sauce or Louisiana hot sauce
- 1 tablespoon cider vinegar
- 2 cups shredded savoy or green cabbage
- 1 cup packaged julienned carrots
- 1 cup thinly sliced celery (2 stalks)
- 1/2 cup crumbled blue cheese (2 ounces)
- 1/3 cup bottled blue cheese salad dressing
- 1/2 teaspoon bottled hot pepper sauce or Louisiana hot sauce

1 Place chicken in a self-sealing plastic bag set in a shallow dish. For marinade, in a small bowl combine olive oil, the 1 tablespoon bottled hot pepper sauce, and the vinegar. Pour over chicken; seal bag. Marinate in refrigerator for 3 to 4 hours.

2 Drain chicken, reserving marinade. For a charcoal grill, grill chicken on the rack of an uncovered grill directly over medium coals for 12 to 15 minutes or until chicken is tender and no longer pink (170°F), turning once and brushing with reserved marinade during first 8 minutes of grilling. (For gas grill, preheat grill. Reduce heat to medium. Place chicken on grill rack over heat. Cover; grill as above.) Transfer chicken to a cutting board; cool slightly. Using two forks, shred meat into bite-size pieces.

3 In a bowl combine cabbage, carrots, celery, and three-fourths of the blue cheese. In a small bowl combine salad dressing and the 1/2 teaspoon hot pepper sauce; add to cabbage mixture and toss to coat. Serve shredded chicken on top of cabbage mixture. Sprinkle with remaining blue cheese.

Nutrition Facts per serving: 367 cal., 23 g total fat (6 g sat. fat), 80 mg chol., 563 mg sodium, 8 g carbo., 3 g fiber, 32 g pro. Daily Values: 88% vit. A, 24% vit. C, 14% calcium, 7% iron. Exchanges: 1½ Vegetable, 4 Very Lean Meat, 4 Fat

ADOBO TURKEY TACO SALAD

Prep: 40 minutes Marinate: 1 to 24 hours Grill: 25 minutes
Makes: 6 main-dish servings

- 1/4 cup sauce from canned chipotle peppers in adobo sauce
- 3 tablespoons honey
- 1 tablespoon lime juice
- 1 cup purchased black bean and corn salsa
- 1/2 cup Mexican crema or sour cream
- 1 1/2 pounds turkey breast tenderloins
- 1 4.3-ounce package Spanish rice mix
- 6 cups spring mix salad greens or 6 cups shredded lettuce
- 6 baked crisp salad shells
- 1/2 cup crumbled queso blanco or queso fresco or shredded farmer cheese (2 ounces)
- 2 limes, cut into wedges

1 In a bowl combine adobo sauce, honey, and lime juice. For dressing, remove 2 tablespoons adobo mixture; place in a bowl. Stir in salsa and crema. Cover and chill until ready to serve.

2 Place turkey in a self-sealing plastic bag set in a shallow dish. Add remaining adobo sauce mixture to turkey; seal bag. Marinate in refrigerator for 1 to 24 hours, turning bag occasionally.

3 Prepare Spanish rice mix according to package directions; set aside.

4 Drain turkey, discarding marinade. For a charcoal grill, arrange medium-hot coals around a drip pan. Test for medium heat above the pan. Place turkey on grill rack over drip pan. Cover; grill for 25 to 30 minutes or until turkey is tender and no longer pink (170°F). (For a gas grill, preheat grill. Reduce heat to medium. Adjust for indirect cooking. Grill as above.) Transfer turkey to a cutting board; cool slightly. Slice turkey diagonally into thin strips.

5 To assemble, divide greens among salad shells. Top with rice and turkey. Sprinkle with cheese and serve with lime wedges. Serve with dressing.

Nutrition Facts per serving: 491 cal., 17 g total fat (5 g sat. fat), 78 mg chol., 889 mg sodium, 50 g carbo., 4 g fiber, 35 g pro. Daily Values: 13% vit. A, 24% vit. C, 8% calcium, 17% iron. Exchanges: 1 Vegetable, 3 Starch, 3½ Very Lean Meat, 2½ Fat

CHICKEN SALAD WITH GOAT CHEESE AND PINE NUTS

Look for steak seasoning in the spice section of your supermarket. Several varieties are available; use them to impart zesty flavors to chicken and pork as well as beef.

Prep: 20 minutes Grill: 12 minutes Stand: 1 hour
Makes: 4 main-dish servings

    4 medium skinless, boneless chicken
        breast halves
        Montreal or Kansas City steak
        seasoning
    8 cups mesclun, spring salad greens,
        or torn spinach
    ³⁄₄ cup seedless red grapes, halved
    ¹⁄₃ cup crumbled goat cheese
    ¹⁄₄ cup pine nuts, toasted
    1 recipe Dill Vinaigrette

1 Sprinkle chicken breast halves lightly with steak seasoning.

2 For a charcoal grill, grill chicken on the rack of an uncovered grill directly over medium coals for 12 to 15 minutes or until tender and no longer pink (170°F), turning once halfway through grilling. (For a gas grill, preheat grill. Reduce heat to medium. Place chicken on the grill rack over heat. Cover; grill as above.) Transfer chicken to a cutting board; cool slightly.

3 Arrange salad greens on 4 plates; top with grapes, goat cheese, and pine nuts. Slice each chicken breast; arrange 1 sliced breast on each salad. Shake Dill Vinaigrette; drizzle over salads.

Dill Vinaigrette: In a screw-top jar combine ¹⁄₄ cup grape seed oil or olive oil; 3 tablespoons balsamic vinegar; 1 tablespoon dried dill; 1 large clove garlic, minced; ¹⁄₄ teaspoon black pepper; and ¹⁄₄ teaspoon dried oregano, crushed. Cover and shake well; let stand for 1 hour.

Nutrition Facts per serving: 400 cal., 23 g total fat (4 g sat. fat), 86 mg chol., 167 mg sodium, 12 g carbo., 2 g fiber, 38 g pro. Daily Values: 22% vit. A, 21% vit. C, 9% calcium, 18% iron. Exchanges: 1 Vegetable, ½ Fruit, 5 Very Lean Meat, 4 Fat

CHICKEN AND WILD RICE SALAD

Start to Finish: 30 minutes
Makes: 4 main-dish servings

    1 recipe Thyme Vinaigrette
    12 ounces skinless, boneless chicken
        breast halves or thighs
    1 cup frozen loose-pack French-cut
        green beans
    2 cups cooked brown and wild rice
        blend, chilled
    1 14-ounce can artichoke hearts,
        drained and quartered
    1 cup shredded red cabbage
    ¹⁄₂ cup shredded carrot (1 medium)
    2 tablespoons sliced green onion (1)
        Lettuce leaves (optional)

1 Prepare Thyme Vinaigrette. Brush chicken with 2 tablespoons of the vinaigrette; set aside the remaining vinaigrette until ready to serve.

2 For a charcoal grill, grill chicken on the rack of an uncovered grill directly over medium coals for 12 to 15 minutes or until chicken is tender and no longer pink (170°F), turning once halfway through grilling. (For a gas grill, preheat grill to medium. Reduce heat. Place chicken on the grill rack over heat. Cover; grill as above.) Transfer chicken to a cutting board; cool slightly. Cut chicken into bite-size strips.

3 Meanwhile, rinse green beans with cool water for 30 seconds; drain. In a large bowl toss together beans, cooked rice, artichoke hearts, cabbage, carrot, and green onion. Pour remaining vinaigrette over rice mixture; toss gently to coat.

4 If desired, arrange lettuce leaves on 4 dinner plates. Top with the rice mixture and chicken.

Thyme Vinaigrette: In a screw-top jar combine ¹⁄₄ cup white wine vinegar; 2 tablespoons olive oil; 2 tablespoons water; 1 tablespoon grated Parmesan cheese; 2 teaspoons snipped fresh thyme; 1 clove garlic, minced; ¹⁄₄ teaspoon salt; and ¹⁄₄ teaspoon black pepper. Cover; shake well.

Nutrition Facts per serving: 305 cal., 8 g total fat (1 g sat. fat), 50 mg chol., 541 mg sodium, 29 g carbo., 6 g fiber, 26 g pro. Daily Values: 92% vit. A, 27% vit. C, 9% calcium, 20% iron. Exchanges: 1 Vegetable, 1½ Starch, 3 Very Lean Meat, 1 Fat

GLAZED DUCK WITH THREE-ONION SALAD

Sweet, tangy raspberries pair deliciously with the rich, succulent flavor of duck. Nestle slices of raspberry-glazed duck in a bed of mild napa cabbage, drizzle with raspberry dressing, and garnish with plump fresh raspberries for an elegant patio meal.

Prep: 30 minutes Grill: 10 minutes
Makes: 4 main-dish servings

1 **recipe Raspberry Dressing**
2 **tablespoons seedless raspberry preserves**
1 **tablespoon olive oil**
4 **skinless, boneless duck breasts (about 1 pound)**
 Salt
 Black pepper
4 **cups shredded napa cabbage**
½ **cup thinly sliced sweet onion, such as Vadalia (1 medium)**
½ **cup thinly sliced red onion (1 medium)**
½ **cup sliced green onions (4)**
1 **cup fresh raspberries**

1 For glaze, in a saucepan combine 2 tablespoons of the Raspberry Dressing and the preserves. Bring just to boiling; reduce heat and stir until preserves are melted.

2 Brush oil over both sides of duck breasts. Sprinkle with salt and pepper.

3 For a charcoal grill, grill duck on the rack of an uncovered grill directly over medium coals for 10 to 12 minutes or until tender and an instant-read thermometer inserted in breasts registers 155°F, turning once halfway through grilling and brushing occasionally with the glaze during last 5 minutes of grilling. (For gas grill, preheat grill. Reduce heat to medium. Place duck on grill rack over heat. Cover; grill as above.) Transfer duck to a cutting board. Cover with foil; let stand while preparing salad.

4 Meanwhile, for salad, in a large bowl combine napa cabbage, sweet onion, red onion, and green onions. Add remaining Raspberry Dressing and toss to coat. Divide among 4 plates. Slice each duck breast and arrange 1 sliced breast on each salad. Garnish with raspberries.

Raspberry Dressing: In screw-top jar combine ¼ cup olive oil, ¼ cup red raspberry vinegar, 1 tablespoon finely chopped shallots, 1 tablespoon honey, ¼ teaspoon salt, and ¼ teaspoon black pepper. Cover; shake well.

Nutrition Facts per serving: 381 cal., 20 g total fat (3 g sat. fat), 142 mg chol., 409 mg sodium, 23 g carbo., 5 g fiber, 29 g pro. Daily Values: 22% vit. A, 61% vit. C, 10% calcium, 30% iron. Exchanges: 1½ Vegetable, 1 Other Carbo., 3½ Very Lean Meat, 3½ Fat

SMOKIN' HOT TIP

Toasting seeds and nuts increases their richness. Here are two easy ways, both of which require a close eye to avoid burning.

● Oven Method: **Arrange shelled nuts or seeds in an even layer in a shallow baking pan. Bake in a 350°F oven for 5 to 10 minutes, stirring occasionally, or until the nuts become fragrant and turn light brown. Remove and transfer to another pan or dish to cool.**

● Stove Top Method: **Cook shelled nuts or seeds in a skillet over moderate heat about 5 minutes, stirring frequently, until the nuts/seeds become fragrant and are lightly browned. Cool by transferring to a different pan or dish.**

MARINATED SHRIMP AND PASTA SALAD

A bed of pasta and mixed greens keeps this shrimp salad colorful and refreshing.

Prep: 25 minutes Marinate: 1 hour Grill: 6 minutes
Makes: 4 main-dish servings

1 pound fresh or frozen large shrimp
½ cup olive oil
⅓ cup red wine vinegar
2 tablespoons capers, drained
1 tablespoon anchovy paste
3 cloves garlic, minced
1 medium red sweet pepper,
    quartered lengthwise and seeded
8 ounces dried rotini or penne pasta
8 cups torn mixed salad greens

1 Thaw shrimp, if frozen. Peel and devein shrimp. Rinse shrimp; pat dry with paper towels. Place shrimp in a medium bowl.

2 For marinade, in a screw-top jar combine olive oil, vinegar, capers, anchovy paste, and garlic. Cover; shake well. Reserve ½ cup of the marinade for salad dressing. Pour remaining marinade over shrimp. Cover; marinate in refrigerator for 1 hour, stirring occasionally. Drain shrimp, discarding marinade. Thread shrimp on 4 long metal skewers, leaving a ¼-inch space between each piece.

3 For a charcoal grill, grill kabobs and sweet pepper quarters, cut sides up, on the greased rack of an uncovered grill directly over medium coals for 6 to 10 minutes or until shrimp are opaque and sweet pepper begins to char, turning kabobs once halfway through grilling. (For a gas grill, preheat grill. Reduce heat to medium. Place kabobs and peppers on greased grill rack over heat. Cover; grill as above.) Cool sweet pepper slightly and coarsely chop.

4 Meanwhile, cook pasta according to package directions; drain. Rinse with cold water; drain again. In a large salad bowl combine cooked pasta, greens, and grilled pepper. Add the reserved salad dressing; toss gently to coat. Remove shrimp from skewers; arrange on pasta mixture.

Nutrition Facts per serving: 486 cal., 21 g total fat (3 g sat. fat), 131 mg chol., 226 mg sodium, 48 g carbo., 4 g fiber, 27 g pro. Daily Values: 44% vit. A, 105% vit. C, 8% calcium, 24% iron. Exchanges: 2 Vegetable, 2½ Starch, 2½ Very Lean Meat, 3½ Fat

LEMON SHRIMP WITH FATTOUSH

Toss grilled shrimp and crisp garden veggies with toasted pita bread to make this Middle Eastern bread salad. Serve the salad right away before the bread soaks up all the dressing.

Prep: 30 minutes Marinate: 1 hour Grill: 10 minutes
Stand: 20 minutes Makes: 4 to 6 main-dish servings

1 pound fresh or frozen large shrimp
3 tablespoons olive oil
1 teaspoon lemon-pepper seasoning
2 large pita bread rounds
2 yellow sweet peppers, quartered
    lengthwise and seeded
1 cup chopped tomatoes (2 medium)
½ cup chopped English cucumber or
    cucumber
¼ cup sliced radishes
¼ cup sliced green onions (2)
¼ cup bottled red wine vinaigrette
Salt
Black pepper

1 Thaw shrimp, if frozen. Peel and devein shrimp. Rinse shrimp; pat dry with paper towels. Place shrimp in a medium bowl. For marinade, in a small bowl stir together 2 tablespoons of the olive oil and the lemon-pepper seasoning. Pour marinade over shrimp in bowl; toss to coat. Cover and marinate in the refrigerator for 1 hour, stirring occasionally. Thread shrimp onto 4 long metal skewers, leaving a ¼-inch space between each piece.

2 Lightly brush pita bread and sweet peppers with the remaining 1 tablespoon olive oil.

3 For a charcoal grill, grill sweet peppers, cut sides up, on the rack of an uncovered grill directly over medium-hot coals about 10 minutes or until pepper skins are blistered and dark. Remove peppers from grill. Wrap peppers in foil and let stand for 20 minutes. Meanwhile, grill shrimp for 6 to 8 minutes or until shrimp are opaque. Grill pita bread for 2 to 4 minutes or until lightly toasted, turning once halfway through grilling. (For a gas grill, preheat grill. Reduce heat to medium-hot. Place peppers, cut sides up, and then shrimp and bread on grill rack over heat. Cover; grill as above.)

4 Remove and discard skins from peppers. Coarsely chop peppers. Cut pita bread into 1-inch pieces. Remove shrimp from skewers. In a large bowl combine grilled peppers, bread, and shrimp. Stir in tomatoes, cucumber, radishes, and green onions. Drizzle with vinaigrette. Toss gently to coat. Season to taste with salt and black pepper. Serve immediately.

Nutrition Facts per serving: 374 cal., 19 g total fat (3 g sat. fat), 129 mg chol., 1,002 mg sodium, 28 g carbo., 2 g fiber, 22 g pro. Daily Values: 14% vit. A, 264% vit. C, 9% calcium, 20% iron. Exchanges: 2½ Vegetable, 1 Starch, 2 Very Lean Meat, 3½ Fat

FOOD FOR THOUGHT
FATTOUSH

Fattoush, which means moist or wet bread in Arabic, is a salad enjoyed throughout the Middle East, particularly during Ramadan. Traditionally it consists of lettuce leaves, cucumber, tomato, onion, parsley, mint, sumac (a dark red, tart spice powder), toasted pita bread, and a dressing of lemon juice, olive oil, and garlic.

Lemon Shrimp with Fattoush

SALMON CAESAR SALAD

Prep: 25 minutes Grill: 8 minutes
Makes: 4 main-dish servings

1 **pound fresh or frozen skinless**
   salmon fillets
1 **tablespoon olive oil**
1 **teaspoon finely shredded lemon peel**
1 **tablespoon lemon juice**
¼ **teaspoon black pepper**
1 **pound asparagus spears, trimmed**
2 **cups sliced hearts of romaine**
   lettuce
2 **cups torn curly endive**
½ **of a medium cucumber, thinly sliced**
½ **cup bottled Caesar salad dressing**
   Thin slices baguette-style French
   bread, toasted (optional)

1 Thaw fish, if frozen. Rinse fish; pat dry with paper towels. In a small bowl combine olive oil, lemon peel, lemon juice, and pepper. Brush salmon steaks with lemon mixture.

2 In a covered large skillet cook the asparagus in a small amount of boiling water for 3 minutes; drain. Place asparagus in a grill wok.

3 For a charcoal grill, grill fish on greased rack of an uncovered grill directly over medium coals for 8 to 12 minutes or until fish flakes easily when tested with a fork, gently turning halfway through grilling. Place grill wok on grill immediately after turning salmon; grill for 3 to 5 minutes or until asparagus is tender and beginning to brown, turning once halfway through grilling. (For gas grill, preheat grill. Reduce heat to medium. Place fish then grill wok with asparagus on grill rack over heat. Cover; grill as above.)

4 In a large bowl combine romaine, endive, and cucumber. Divide romaine mixture among 4 salad plates. Using a fork, flake salmon into pieces. Arrange salmon and asparagus on salad. Drizzle with Caesar dressing. If desired, serve with toasted baguette slices.

Nutrition Facts per serving: 351 cal., 25 g total fat (4 g sat. fat), 59 mg chol., 418 mg sodium, 5 g carbo., 3 g fiber, 26 g pro. Daily Values: 31% vit. A, 48% vit. C, 6% calcium, 11% iron. Exchanges: 1 Vegetable, 3½ Lean Meat, 3 Fat

GRILLED TUNA SALAD NIÇOISE

Peeling a strip of skin from each potato is the traditional way to prepare this classic salad. It also prevents the potato skins from splitting during cooking.

Prep: 30 minutes Marinate: 30 minutes Grill: 8 minutes
Makes: 4 main-dish servings

1 **pound fresh or frozen tuna steaks,**
   cut 1 inch thick
1 **recipe Caper Vinaigrette**
8 **tiny new potatoes**
8 **ounces green beans, trimmed**
2 **small heads Boston or Bibb (butter-**
   head) lettuce, rinsed and cored
8 **cherry or grape tomatoes, halved**
½ **cup thinly sliced red onion**
   (1 medium)
2 **hard-cooked eggs, sliced**
¼ **cup niçoise olives**
1 **2-ounce can anchovy fillets**
   (optional)

1 Thaw fish, if frozen. Rinse fish; pat dry with paper towels. Set fish aside. Prepare Caper Vinaigrette and remove ⅓ cup to use as marinade. Cover remaining vinaigrette and set aside.

2 Place fish in a shallow dish; drizzle with the ⅓ cup vinaigrette. Cover and marinate in the refrigerator for 30 minutes, turning once.

3 Meanwhile, peel a strip around the center of each potato. Place potatoes in a large saucepan; cover with water. Bring to boiling over high heat; reduce heat. Simmer, covered, for 15 minutes. Add green beans; simmer, covered, about 5 minutes more or until potatoes and beans are tender. Drain. Rinse with cold water; drain again. Set aside.

4 Drain fish, reserving marinade. For a charcoal grill, grill fish on greased rack of an uncovered grill directly over medium coals for 8 to 12 minutes or until fish flakes easily when tested with a fork, carefully turning and brushing with marinade halfway through grilling. (For a gas grill, preheat grill. Reduce heat to medium. Place fish on greased grill rack over heat. Cover; grill as above.) Discard any remaining marinade.

5 Using 2 forks, flake the tuna into pieces. Line 4 plates with lettuce. Arrange fish, potatoes, green beans, tomatoes, onion, eggs, and olives on lettuce. If desired, crisscross 2 anchovy fillets over the top of each salad. Drizzle with the remaining Caper Vinaigrette.

Caper Vinaigrette: In a screw-top jar combine ½ cup olive oil, ⅓ cup tarragon or white wine vinegar, 2 tablespoons drained capers, 2 teaspoons sugar, 2 teaspoons Dijon-style mustard, ½ teaspoon salt, and ½ teaspoon black pepper. Cover and shake well.

Nutrition Facts per serving: 605 cal., 40 g total fat (6 g sat. fat), 149 mg chol., 693 mg sodium, 28 g carbo., 6 g fiber, 34 g pro. Daily Values: 74% vit. A, 56% vit. C, 10% calcium, 23% iron. Exchanges: 1½ Vegetable, 1½ Starch, 4 Very Lean Meat, 7 Fat

GRILLED VEGETABLE AND MOZZARELLA ENSALADA

Some of the vinaigrette that remains on the veggies may cause flare-ups during grilling. Start the pepper quarters cut sides down to keep the oil from pooling on the inside.

Prep: 35 minutes Marinate: 30 minutes Grill: 7 minutes
Makes: 4 side-dish servings

- **4 medium roma tomatoes, halved lengthwise**
- **2 small zucchini, halved lengthwise**
- **1 medium yellow sweet pepper, seeded and quartered**
- **1 medium red onion, cut into wedges**
- **1 recipe Pear-Infused Balsamic Vinaigrette**
- **8 slices baguette-style French bread, cut ½ inch thick**
- **1 tablespoon olive oil**
- **1 10-ounce package Italian blend salad greens (romaine and radicchio) (8 cups)**
- **¼ cup snipped fresh basil**
- **4 ounces fresh mozzarella, cut into chunks (1 cup)**

1 Place tomatoes, zucchini, sweet pepper, and onion in self-sealing plastic bag in shallow dish. Pour Pear-Infused Balsamic Vinaigrette over vegetables; seal bag. Marinate at room temperature for 30 minutes, turning bag occasionally.

2 Drain vegetables, reserving vinaigrette. For a charcoal grill, grill vegetables on the rack of an uncovered grill directly over medium coals. Grill sweet pepper and onion for 7 to 10 minutes or until crisp-tender, turning once. Grill zucchini for 5 to 7 minutes or until crisp-tender, turning once. Grill tomatoes, skin sides down, about 5 minutes or until tomatoes soften and skins begin to char. (For a gas grill, preheat grill. Reduce heat to medium. Place vegetables on grill rack over medium heat. Cover; grill as above.) Transfer vegetables to a cutting board; cool slightly.

3 Brush baguette slices lightly with oil. Grill about 2 minutes or until light brown and crisp, turning once.

4 In an extra large bowl combine salad greens and basil. Add reserved vinaigrette; toss to coat. Arrange greens on a large platter. Cut zucchini and sweet peppers into bite-size pieces. Arrange vegetables and mozzarella cheese on top of greens. Serve with grilled baguette slices.

Pear-Infused Balsamic Vinaigrette: In a screw-top jar combine ¼ cup pear-infused white balsamic vinegar or other vinegar, 3 tablespoons extra virgin olive oil, 1 tablespoon brown sugar, ½ teaspoon salt, and ½ teaspoon black pepper. Cover and shake well.

Nutrition Facts per serving: 422 cal., 22 g total fat (6 g sat. fat), 22 mg chol., 720 mg sodium, 46 g carbo., 5 g fiber, 12 g pro. Daily Values: 24% vit. A, 157% vit. C, 22% calcium, 15% iron. Exchanges: 3 Vegetable, 1 Starch, 1 Other Carbo., 1 Medium-Fat Meat, 3 Fat

Grilled Vegetable and Mozzarella Ensalada

FRUIT SALAD BOWL

A colorful combination of peaches, berries, and honeydew served in cantaloupe halves makes an attractive and refreshing side dish.

Start to Finish: 30 minutes
Makes: 6 to 8 side-dish servings

4 cups sliced fresh peaches, nectarines, plums, and/or apricots
1 to 2 cups assorted fresh berries, such as raspberries, blackberries, blueberries, and/or halved strawberries
1 to 2 cups 1-inch chunks honeydew or cantaloupe melon
1 to 2 tablespoons fresh lemon juice
1 to 2 tablespoons sugar (optional)
3 or 4 small cantaloupes, halved (optional)

1 In a large bowl combine desired fruit. Toss gently just until fruits are mixed. Sprinkle with the lemon juice. If desired, sprinkle with sugar to taste; toss gently until sugar is dissolved. If desired, serve in cantaloupe halves.

Nutrition Facts per serving: 67 cal., 0 g total fat (0 g sat. fat), 0 mg chol., 3 mg sodium, 17 g carbo., 3 g fiber, 1 g pro. Daily Values: 13% vit. A, 49% vit. C, 1% calcium, 1% iron. Exchanges: 1 Fruit

24-HOUR VEGETABLE SALAD

Layer salad greens, vegetables, and cheese in a clear glass bowl and top with a peppery, orange-scented yogurt dressing to create a colorful side salad.

Prep: 25 minutes Chill: 2 to 24 hours
Makes: 8 side-dish servings

1 medium carrot
5 cups torn mixed salad greens
1 cup sliced fresh mushrooms
1 medium cucumber, halved, seeded, and cut into $1/4$-inch slices ($1 3/4$ cups)
$1/2$ cup sliced radishes
$1/2$ cup mayonnaise or salad dressing
$1/4$ cup plain low-fat yogurt
1 teaspoon finely shredded orange peel
$1/2$ to $3/4$ teaspoon crushed red pepper
$1/8$ to $1/4$ teaspoon black pepper
$1/4$ cup sliced green onions (2)
$1/4$ cup coarsely chopped pitted kalamata olives
$1/4$ cup crumbled feta cheese (1 ounce)

1 Peel carrot. Using the vegetable peeler, carefully cut carrot lengthwise into long, paper-thin ribbons. Set aside.

FOOD FOR THOUGHT CANTALOUPE

Cantaloupes are perfectly ripe when they have a thick, yellow-green netted rind and pale yellow-orange flesh that's juicy and sweet. To pick the perfect cantaloupe, find one that is heavy for its size (which means it's juicy) and that has a sweet aroma. A ripe melon will give slightly, then spring back when pressed on the stem end. Avoid those that are very soft, have a pronounced yellow color, or a moldy smell—indications of being overripe. Store cantaloupes ripe from the vine in the refrigerator. Leave underripe cantaloupes on the kitchen counter to develop their flavor and aroma.

2 In a clear 2½- to 3-quart straight-side bowl or soufflé dish layer greens, carrot ribbons, mushrooms, cucumber, and sliced radishes.

3 For dressing, in a small bowl stir together mayonnaise, yogurt, orange peel, crushed red pepper, and black pepper. Spread dressing over salad, sealing to edge of bowl. Cover tightly with plastic wrap. Chill for 2 to 24 hours.

4 To serve, sprinkle with green onions, olives, and feta cheese. Just before serving, toss to coat vegetables with dressing.

Nutrition Facts per serving: 140 cal., 13 g total fat (2 g sat. fat), 10 mg chol., 188 mg sodium, 4 g carbo., 1 g fiber, 2 g pro. Daily Values: 47% vit. A, 10% vit. C, 5% calcium, 3% iron. Exchanges: 1 Vegetable, 2½ Fat

MARINATED CUCUMBERS

On your next trip to the farmer's market, bring home a cucumber to make this much-loved summertime staple.

Prep: 15 minutes Chill: 4 hours to 5 days
Makes: 6 side-dish servings

- **¼ cup vinegar or lemon juice**
- **1 to 2 tablespoons sugar**
- **½ teaspoon salt**
- **¼ teaspoon celery seeds**
- **1 large cucumber, halved lengthwise and thinly sliced (3 cups)**
- **1 small onion, thinly sliced (⅓ cup)**

1 For marinade, in a covered container combine vinegar, sugar, salt, and celery seeds. Add cucumber and onion; toss to coat. Cover and chill at least 4 hours or up to 5 days; stir occasionally. Stir before serving.

Nutrition Facts per serving: 20 cal., 0 g total fat (0 g sat. fat), 0 mg chol., 195 mg sodium, 5 g carbo., 1 g fiber, 0 g pro. Daily Values: 2% vit. A, 6% vit. C, 1% calcium, 1% iron. Exchanges: 1 Vegetable

Creamy Cucumbers: Prepare recipe as above, except omit marinade ingredients (vinegar, sugar, salt, and celery seeds). In a medium bowl stir together ½ cup dairy sour cream or plain yogurt, 1 tablespoon vinegar, 1 teaspoon sugar, ½ teaspoon salt, ¼ teaspoon dried dill, and a dash black pepper. Add cucumber and onion; toss to coat. Cover and chill for 4 to 24 hours, stirring often. Stir before serving.

Nutrition Facts per serving: 48 cal., 3 g total fat (2 g sat. fat), 7 mg chol., 204 mg sodium, 4 g carbo., 1 g fiber, 1 g pro. Daily Values: 5% vit. A, 6% vit. C, 3% calcium, 1% iron. Exchanges: 1 Vegetable, ½ Fat

SOUTHWESTERN-STYLE THREE-BEAN SALAD

Cilantro, cumin, and lime juice put a new spin on the traditional three-bean salad.

Prep: 20 minutes Chill: 3 to 24 hours
Makes: 8 side-dish servings

- **1 15-ounce can garbanzo beans (chickpeas), rinsed and drained**
- **1 15-ounce can black beans, rinsed and drained**
- **1 15-ounce can red kidney beans, rinsed and drained**
- **1 cup thinly sliced celery (2 stalks)**
- **¾ cup chopped red onion**
- **1 recipe Cilantro-Lime Dressing**

1 In a large bowl stir together the garbanzo beans, black beans, red kidney beans, celery, and onion.

2 Pour Cilantro-Lime Dressing over bean mixture; toss to coat. Cover and chill for 3 to 24 hours, stirring occasionally. Serve salad with a slotted spoon.

Cilantro-Lime Dressing: In a screw-top jar combine ¼ cup salad oil; ¼ cup vinegar; 1 garlic clove, minced; 2 tablespoons snipped fresh cilantro; ½ teaspoon chili powder; ½ teaspoon ground cumin; and ¼ teaspoon salt. Cover and shake well.

Nutrition Facts per serving: 202 cal., 8 g total fat (1 g sat. fat), 0 mg chol., 562 mg sodium, 27 g carbo., 9 g fiber, 9 g pro. Daily Values: 3% vit. A, 9% vit. C, 7% calcium, 11% iron. Exchanges: ½ Vegetable, 1½ Starch, ½ Very Lean Meat, 1 Fat

From top:
Sweet Corn, Red Pepper, and Cheese Salad
Greek Pasta Salad
Sesame Noodle Slaw (page 118)

SWEET CORN, RED PEPPER, AND CHEESE SALAD

When corn on the cob is out of season, you can use frozen instead of fresh. Cook the frozen ears of corn briefly and then chill.

Start to Finish: 40 minutes
Makes: 12 side-dish servings

8 ears sweet corn
²⁄₃ cup finely chopped red sweet pepper
8 ounces Manchego, Teleme, or Monterey Jack cheese with jalapeño peppers, cut into ¹⁄₄-inch cubes
1 recipe Sherry Vinaigrette
2 tablespoons snipped fresh flat-leaf parsley
Salt or kosher salt
Black pepper

1 Remove husks from corn. Scrub ears with a vegetable brush to remove silks; rinse. Using a sharp knife, cut kernels from cobs; scrape cobs with knife to release juices. In a large bowl combine corn and juices, sweet pepper, and cheese. Add Sherry Vinaigrette; stir to coat. Stir in parsley. Season to taste with salt and black pepper. Serve immediately.

Sherry Vinaigrette: In a medium bowl combine 3 tablespoons sherry wine vinegar, 2 teaspoons Dijon-style mustard, and ¹⁄₂ teaspoon kosher salt; whisk until smooth. Gradually add ²⁄₃ cup olive oil, whisking constantly until dressing thickens slightly. Season to taste with black pepper. Cover and chill for up to 3 days.

Nutrition Facts per serving: 233 cal., 18 g total fat (5 g sat. fat), 17 mg chol., 209 mg sodium, 12 g carbo., 2 g fiber, 7 g pro. Daily Values: 17% vit. A, 35% vit. C, 14% calcium, 3% iron. Exchanges: 1 Starch, ¹⁄₂ High-Fat Meat, 2 Fat

GREEK PASTA SALAD

The fresh herbs, oils, and olives that characterize Greek cuisine complement pasta in this sprightly salad. Add a flourish of feta cheese, and any grilled steak you serve with it will be smitten.

Prep: 35 minutes Chill: 2 to 24 hours
Makes: 12 to 16 side-dish servings

12 ounces dried mostaccioli (about 4 cups)
8 roma tomatoes, chopped
1 medium cucumber, halved lengthwise and sliced
¹⁄₂ cup sliced green onions (4)
¹⁄₃ cup sliced pitted ripe olives
1 recipe Lemon-Herb Dressing
1 cup crumbled feta cheese (4 ounces)
Fresh oregano sprigs (optional)

1 In a large saucepan cook the mostaccioli according to package directions; drain. Rinse with cold water; drain again.

2 In a large bowl toss together the cooked mostaccioli, tomatoes, cucumber, green onions, and olives. Drizzle Lemon-Herb Dressing over pasta mixture; toss gently to coat.

3 Cover and chill for 2 to 24 hours. Add feta cheese. Toss before serving. If desired, garnish with fresh oregano.

Lemon-Herb Dressing: In a screw-top jar combine ¹⁄₂ cup olive oil or salad oil; ¹⁄₂ cup lemon juice; 2 tablespoons anchovy paste (if desired); 2 tablespoons snipped fresh basil or 2 teaspoons dried basil, crushed; 2 teaspoons snipped fresh oregano or 2 teaspoons dried oregano, crushed; 4 to 6 cloves garlic, minced; ¹⁄₄ teaspoon salt; and ¹⁄₄ teaspoon black pepper. Cover and shake well.

Nutrition Facts per serving: 234 cal., 12 g total fat (3 g sat. fat), 8 mg chol., 193 mg sodium, 27 g carbo., 2 g fiber, 6 g pro. Daily Values: 10% vit. A, 30% vit. C, 68% calcium, 1% iron. Exchanges: 1 Vegetable, 1¹⁄₂ Starch, 2 Fat

SESAME NOODLE SLAW

The Oriental noodles are crunchy when you first make this cabbage salad. If you prefer softer noodles, chill the salad to give them time to absorb some of the soy-vinegar dressing (see photo, page 116).

Start to Finish: 20 minutes Bake: 10 minutes Oven: 300°F
Makes: 8 side-dish servings

- ½ cup slivered almonds
- 2 tablespoons sesame seeds
- ⅓ cup salad oil
- 3 tablespoons vinegar
- 2 tablespoons reduced-sodium soy sauce
- 1 3-ounce package chicken-flavor ramen noodles
- 1 tablespoon sugar
- ¼ teaspoon black pepper
- ½ of a medium head cabbage, cored and shredded (about 6 cups)
- ⅓ to ½ cup thinly sliced green onions (3 or 4)

1 Spread almonds and sesame seeds in a shallow baking pan. Bake in 300°F oven about 10 minutes or until toasted, stirring once; cool.

2 Meanwhile, for dressing, in a screw-top jar combine oil, vinegar, soy sauce, seasoning packet from noodles, sugar, and black pepper. Cover and shake well.

3 In a large bowl layer cabbage, green onions, almonds, and sesame seeds. Break noodles into small pieces. Sprinkle onto salad.

4 Add dressing; toss gently to coat. Cover and chill in the refrigerator for up to 1 hour.

Nutrition Facts per serving: 211 cal., 16 g total fat (3 g sat. fat), 0 mg chol., 360 mg sodium, 14 g carbo., 3 g fiber, 4 g pro. Daily Values: 3% vit. A, 30% vit. C, 6% calcium, 6% iron. Exchanges: 1 Vegetable, ½ Starch, 3 Fat

PESTO MACARONI SALAD

Torn basil leaves lend a fresh-from-the-garden air to this pesto-dressed pasta salad.

Start to Finish: 30 minutes
Makes: 14 side-dish servings

- 3 cups dried elbow macaroni
- 5 ounces fresh green beans, trimmed and cut into 1-inch pieces (about 1 cup)
- 1 pound small fresh mozzarella balls, drained and sliced
- 1 7-ounce container refrigerated basil pesto
- ½ cup fresh basil leaves, torn
- ½ teaspoon salt

1 Cook macaroni according to directions on package; drain. Rinse with cold water; drain again. In a saucepan cook green beans, covered, in a small amount of boiling salted water for 10 to 15 minutes or until crisp-tender; drain. Rinse with cold water; drain again.

2 In a large bowl combine macaroni, green beans, mozzarella, and pesto. Stir in basil and salt. Serve salad immediately or cover and chill for up to 2 hours.

Nutrition Facts per serving: 249 cal., 14 g total fat (4 g sat. fat), 26 mg chol., 255 mg sodium, 20 g carbo., 1 g fiber, 11 g pro. Daily Values: 8% vit. A, 3% vit. C, 18% calcium, 5% iron. Exchanges: 1½ Starch, 1 High-Fat Meat, 1 Fat

SUMMER TOMATO SALAD

This salad with an accent of tarragon offers the perfect opportunity to experiment with different colors and types of tomatoes. Let the selection at the farmer's market (or in your own garden) be your guide.

Start to Finish: 30 minutes
Makes: 6 side-dish servings

3 cups mesclun or torn romaine lettuce
2 medium red tomatoes, cut into wedges or sliced
2 medium yellow or heirloom green tomatoes, cut into wedges
1 cup red or yellow cherry tomatoes, halved if desired
1 small red onion, cut into very thin slices
¼ teaspoon coarse salt
¼ teaspoon black pepper
1 recipe Tarragon Vinaigrette

1 Divide the greens among 6 salad plates. Arrange the tomatoes on the greens. Top with onion slices. Sprinkle with salt and pepper. Drizzle with desired amount of Tarragon Vinaigrette. Store any remaining dressing, covered, in the refrigerator for up to 1 week.

Tarragon Vinaigrette: In a small bowl whisk together ½ cup olive oil, ¼ cup red or white wine vinegar, 1 tablespoon finely snipped fresh tarragon, 1 tablespoon finely snipped fresh chives, and ¼ teaspoon Dijon-style mustard.

Nutrition Facts per serving: 192 cal., 19 g total fat (3 g sat. fat), 0 mg chol., 109 mg sodium, 7 g carbo., 2 g fiber, 2 g pro. Daily Values: 14% vit. A, 37% vit. C, 3% calcium, 5% iron. Exchanges: 1½ Vegetable, 4 Fat

FOOD FOR THOUGHT TOMATOES

Summer is peak season for tomatoes, which come in all shapes, sizes, and colors. While all tomatoes taste similar, their levels of sweetness and acidity depend on the exact variety, growing conditions, and when they are harvested. Here are some of the most common varieties:

● Beefsteak: These large, deep red, juicy tomatoes peak in late summer. They are the most commonly marketed and are perfect for salads, sandwiches, and cooking.

● Plum or Roma: Relatively small and oblong in shape, plum tomatoes are meatier. Their higher flesh-to-seed ratio makes them less watery and, therefore, good for making sauces and purees.

● Pear and Grape: These bite-size tomatoes resemble the shapes their names suggest. Available in red and yellow varieties, they are sweet and tasty fresh or sautéed.

● Cherry: Available in red or yellow, these small round tomatoes grow in clusters and make beautiful, fresh additions to salads or roasted accompaniments to grilled steak.

● Yellow or Orange: These tomatoes tend to be sweeter and less acidic than their red or green counterparts.

What is an Heirloom Tomato? Heirloom tomatoes are not a variety per se, but a term used to describe tomatoes or other vegetables cultivated from seeds that have been passed down from one generation to the next (or that date back at least 50 years). In an age where produce is grown to meet certain size or shipping specifications, heirloom vegetables are grown to achieve superior flavor and tenderness. Heirloom tomatoes grow in green, pink, yellow, and striped varieties, with Brandywine being the most common. Look for heirlooms at specialty produce or farmers' markets.

GRILLED POTATO SALAD

If you like the tangy sweetness of German-style potato salad, you'll love this grilled version. A maple-mustard vinaigrette dresses potatoes, crumbled bacon, and hard-cooked eggs.

Prep: 25 minutes Grill: 50 minutes
Makes: 8 to 10 side-dish servings

6 medium Yukon gold potatoes
    (about 2 pounds)
1 tablespoon olive oil
1/3 cup white balsamic vinegar
1/3 cup olive oil
1 tablespoon snipped fresh sage
1 tablespoon Dijon-style mustard
1 teaspoon pure maple syrup
1 clove garlic, minced
1/4 teaspoon salt
1/8 teaspoon black pepper
2 cups fresh baby spinach
4 slices bacon, crisp-cooked, drained,
    and crumbled
2 hard-cooked eggs, coarsely chopped
1/4 cup finely chopped red onion

1 Scrub potatoes thoroughly with a brush; pat dry. Prick potatoes with a fork. Rub potatoes with the 1 tablespoon olive oil.

2 For a charcoal grill, arrange medium-hot coals around edge of grill. Test for medium heat above center of grill. Place potatoes on grill rack over center of grill. Cover; grill for 50 to 60 minutes or until potatoes are tender. (For a gas grill, preheat grill. Reduce heat to medium. Adjust for indirect cooking. Grill as above.)

3 Meanwhile, for vinaigrette, in a screw-top jar combine vinegar, the 1/3 cup olive oil, the sage, mustard, maple syrup, garlic, salt, and pepper. Cover and shake well. Set aside.

4 When potatoes are done, remove from grill and cool slightly. Coarsely chop potatoes. Transfer potatoes to an extra large bowl. Stir in spinach, bacon, eggs, and red onion. Gently stir in vinaigrette until combined.

Nutrition Facts per serving: 221 cal., 14 g total fat (3 g sat. fat), 56 mg chol., 209 mg sodium, 19 g carbo., 2 g fiber, 5 g pro. Daily Values: 12% vit. A, 27% vit. C, 3% calcium, 10% iron. Exchanges: 1½ Starch, 2½ Fat

CHUNKY MUSTARD POTATO SALAD

Prep: 35 minutes Chill: 6 to 24 hours
Makes: 12 side-dish servings

2 20-ounce packages refrigerated
    new potato wedges
1/4 teaspoon salt
1/2 cup coarsely chopped dill pickles
1/4 cup Dijon-style mustard
1/4 cup chopped, roasted red
    sweet pepper
1 cup chopped celery (2 stalks)
1/2 cup sliced green onions (4)
1/3 cup chopped radishes
4 hard-cooked eggs, peeled and
    coarsely chopped
1/2 teaspoon salt
1/4 teaspoon black pepper
3/4 cup mayonnaise or salad dressing

1 Place potatoes in a large saucepan. Add enough water to cover the potatoes. Add the 1/4 teaspoon salt. Bring to boiling; reduce heat. Cover and simmer for 5 minutes. Drain potatoes well; cool for 10 minutes.

2 In a very large serving bowl combine warm potatoes, pickles, mustard, and roasted pepper; stir gently. Cover and chill for 2 hours. Add celery, green onions, radishes, eggs, the 1/2 teaspoon salt, and black pepper. Add mayonnaise and mix gently. Cover and chill for 4 to 24 hours.

Nutrition Facts per serving: 194 cal., 13 g total fat (2 g sat. fat), 76 mg chol., 521 mg sodium, 13 g carbo., 3 g fiber, 5 g pro. Daily Values: 3% vit. A, 22% vit. C, 2% calcium, 4% iron. Exchanges: 1 Starch, 2½ Fat

Grilled Potato Salad

SMOKIN' HOT TIP

To hard-cook eggs, place eggs in a single layer in a saucepan and fill with enough cold water just to cover the eggs. Place the pan on the stove and bring to a rapid boil over high heat. Remove from heat. Cover and let stand for 15 minutes. Run cold water over the eggs and place them in ice water until cool enough to handle; drain. Peel eggs and use as needed.

ASPARAGUS IN DILL BUTTER

To prevent flare-ups, grill the buttery asparagus spears in a disposable foil pan. The pan prevents the butter from dripping into the fire.

Prep: 10 minutes Grill: 7 minutes
Makes: 4 to 6 side-dish servings

1 pound asparagus spears, trimmed
2 tablespoons butter, melted
1 tablespoon snipped fresh dill or
    1 teaspoon dried dill
1 clove garlic, minced
¼ teaspoon cracked black pepper
    Finely shredded Parmesan cheese

1 Place asparagus in a large disposable foil pan. Drizzle with butter and sprinkle with dill, garlic, and pepper. Toss to mix.

2 For a charcoal grill, place the asparagus in foil pan on the rack of an uncovered grill directly over medium coals. Grill for 7 to 10 minutes or until asparagus is crisp-tender, stirring occasionally. (For a gas grill, preheat grill. Reduce heat to medium. Place foil pan on grill rack over heat. Cover; grill as above.)

3 To serve, transfer asparagus to a serving dish. Sprinkle with Parmesan cheese.

Nutrition Facts per serving: 83 cal., 7 g total fat (4 g sat. fat), 18 mg chol., 96 mg sodium, 2 g carbo., 1 g fiber, 3 g pro. Daily Values: 6% vit. A, 27% vit. C, 4% calcium, 3% iron. Exchanges: ½ Vegetable, 1½ Fat

SMOKIN' HOT TIP

Wood and metal skewers fulfill their purpose when making kabobs. But if you want to infuse extra flavor and flair, you can use rosemary sprigs. Strip the sprig of its leaves, leaving just a leafy top inch. Soak sprigs in cold water, skewer meat or vegetables onto the sprig, then grill. The sprigs enhance flavor and make for a unique presentation. To make skewering easier, use a metal skewer first to make a small hole in the meat or vegetables.

ROSEMARY BABY BEETS AND PEARS

Prep: 25 minutes Cook: 15 minutes
Marinate: 4 to 8 hours Grill: 10 minutes
Makes: 4 to 6 side-dish servings

1 pound trimmed red and/or golden
    baby beets or medium beets
2 tablespoons snipped fresh rosemary
    or 2 teaspoons dried rosemary,
    crushed
2 teaspoons finely shredded
    orange peel
¼ cup orange juice
¼ cup cooking oil
2 tablespoons white balsamic vinegar
¼ teaspoon salt
⅛ teaspoon ground white pepper
    Large rosemary twigs or metal
    skewers
2 medium pears, cut into wedges
    Blue or Brie cheese, crumbled
    (optional)

1 Scrub beets. In a medium saucepan cook beets and 1 tablespoon of the fresh rosemary or 1 teaspoon of the dried rosemary, covered, in a small amount of lightly salted boiling water for 15 to 18 minutes (30 minutes for medium beets) or just until tender. Drain and cool slightly. Peel or slip skins off beets.

2 Place beets in a self-sealing plastic bag set in a shallow dish. In a bowl whisk together orange peel, orange juice, remaining snipped or dried rosemary, oil, vinegar, salt, and white pepper. Pour over beets; seal bag. Marinate in the refrigerator for 4 to 8 hours, turning bag occasionally.

3 Drain beets, reserving marinade. On rosemary twigs or metal skewers, alternately thread beets and pear wedges. Brush with some of the reserved marinade.

4 For a charcoal grill, grill kabobs on the rack of an uncovered grill directly over medium coals for 10 to 12 minutes or until heated through, turning once and brushing with reserved marinade halfway through grilling. (For a gas grill, preheat grill. Reduce heat to medium. Place kabobs on grill rack over heat. Cover; grill as above.) Discard any remaining marinade.

Rosemary Baby Beets and Pears

5 To serve, if desired, remove beets and pears from skewers; top each serving with cheese.

Nutrition Facts per serving: 168 cal., 7 g total fat (1 g sat. fat), 0 mg chol., 158 mg sodium, 26 g carbo., 4 g fiber, 2 g pro. Daily Values: 2% vit. A, 20% vit. C, 3% calcium, 7% iron. Exchanges: 1 Vegetable, 1 Fruit, ½ Other Carbo., 1½ Fat

ALOHA KABOBS

Prep: 30 minutes Grill: 6 minutes
Makes: 10 side-dish servings

10 8-inch wooden skewers
1 fresh pineapple, peeled, cored, and cut into 1-inch pieces (about 3 cups)
20 red or white pearl onions, peeled
2 yellow and/or red sweet peppers, cut into 1-inch pieces
20 sugar snap peas
¼ cup purchased teriyaki or Szechwan glaze

1 Soak the wooden skewers in water for 30 minutes. Drain. Alternately thread pineapple, onions, peppers, and peas onto skewers, leaving a ¼-inch space between pieces.

2 For a charcoal grill, grill kabobs on the rack of an uncovered grill directly over medium coals for 6 to 8 minutes or just until onions are tender and pineapple is heated through, turning once halfway through grilling and brushing frequently with glaze. (For a gas grill, preheat grill. Reduce to medium heat. Place kabobs on grill rack over heat. Cover; grill as above).

Nutrition Facts per serving: 59 cal., 0 g total fat (0 g sat. fat), 0 mg chol., 250 mg sodium, 13 g carbo., 2 g fiber, 2 g pro. Daily Values: 10% vit. A, 134% vit. C, 3% calcium, 3% iron. Exchanges: 1 Vegetable, ½ Fruit

CONFETTI GRILLED CORN SOUP

Prep: 30 minutes Grill: 15 minutes Stand: 10 minutes
Cook: 10 minutes Makes: 4 side-dish servings

- **4 fresh ears corn, husked and cleaned**
- **1 medium yellow sweet pepper, quartered lengthwise and seeded**
- **1 fresh Anaheim chile pepper, quartered lengthwise and seeded (see tip, page 36)**
- **1 tablespoon cooking oil**
- **1 14-ounce can chicken broth**
- **1 teaspoon Mexican seasoning**
- **½ cup half-and-half or light cream**
- **1 roma tomato, seeded and finely chopped**
- **2 tablespoons thinly sliced green onion (1)**

1 Brush corn, sweet pepper, and Anaheim pepper with oil. For a charcoal grill, grill corn and peppers, cut sides up, on the rack of an uncovered grill directly over medium coals until corn is crisp-tender and pepper skins are charred, turning corn occasionally. Allow 15 to 20 minutes for corn, 10 to 15 minutes for sweet pepper, and 8 to 10 minutes for Anaheim pepper. (For a gas grill, preheat grill. Reduce heat to medium. Place corn and peppers on rack over heat. Cover; grill as above.)

2 Wrap peppers tightly in foil. Let stand for 10 minutes. Using a paring knife, gently remove skins from peppers; discard skins. Cut corn kernels from cobs. In a food processor or blender place half of the corn and half of the grilled peppers. Add chicken broth; cover and process or blend until smooth.

3 Pour pepper mixture into a medium saucepan. Chop remaining peppers. Add chopped peppers, remaining corn, and Mexican seasoning to saucepan. Bring to boiling, stirring frequently. Stir in half-and-half; heat through (do not boil). Season to taste with salt and black pepper. Ladle soup into bowls. Sprinkle with tomato and onion.

Nutrition Facts per serving: 182 cal., 9 g total fat (3 g sat. fat), 11 mg chol., 664 mg sodium, 24 g carbo., 3 g fiber, 6 g pro. Daily Values: 37% vit. A, 185% vit. C, 4% calcium, 6% iron. Exchanges: ½ Vegetable, 1½ Starch, 1½ Fat

MEXICALI VEGETABLE KABOBS

Prep: 30 minutes Grill: 15 minutes
Makes: 6 side-dish servings

- **4 fresh ears corn, husked, cleaned, and cut into 2-inch pieces**
- **2 medium zucchini and/or yellow summer squash, cut into 1-inch slices**
- **1 red onion, cut into wedges**

Mexicali Vegetable Kabobs

⅓ **cup butter or margarine, melted**
1 teaspoon chili powder
½ **teaspoon ground cumin**
¼ **teaspoon garlic powder**
¼ **teaspoon dried oregano, crushed**

1 On six 12-inch skewers alternately thread the corn, zucchini, and onion wedges. In a small bowl combine butter, chili powder, cumin, garlic powder, and oregano. Brush over vegetables.

2 For a charcoal grill, grill kabobs on the rack of an uncovered grill directly over medium coals for 15 to 18 minutes or until vegetables are tender and brown, turning and brushing occasionally with butter mixture. (For a gas grill, preheat grill. Reduce heat to medium. Place kabobs on grill rack over heat. Cover; grill as above.)

Nutrition Facts per serving: 160 cal., 12 g total fat (7 g sat. fat), 29 mg chol., 124 mg sodium, 14 g carbo., 3 g fiber, 3 g pro. Daily Values: 18% vit. A, 16% vit. C, 2% calcium, 4% iron. Exchanges: ½ Vegetable, 1 Starch, 2 Fat

---

BUTTERY GRILLED CORN ON THE COB

Grilling ears of corn ensures moist, tender kernels. Choose one of the flavored butters to bring new excitement to this summertime treat.

Prep: 20 minutes Grill: 25 minutes
Makes: 6 side-dish servings

6 fresh ears sweet corn with husks*
1 recipe Crazy Cajun Butter, Pesto Butter, Ginger and Garlic Butter, Chipotle Butter, or Nutty Butter

1 Carefully peel back corn husks but do not remove. Remove and discard the silk. Gently rinse the corn. Pat dry. Spread about 1 tablespoon flavored butter over each ear of corn. Carefully fold husks back around ears. Tie husk tops with 100-percent-cotton kitchen string to secure.

2 For a charcoal grill, grill corn on the rack of a covered grill directly over medium coals for 25 to 30 minutes or until kernels are tender, turning and rearranging ears using long-handle tongs 3 times. (For a gas grill, preheat grill. Reduce heat to medium. Place corn on grill rack over heat. Cover; grill as above.)

3 To serve, remove string from corn. Peel back husks. If desired, serve with additional flavored butter. Store any remaining flavored butters in tightly covered containers in refrigerator for up to 3 days.

*Note: If husks have been removed from corn, wrap each ear in a piece of heavy aluminum foil.

Crazy Cajun Butter: In a small mixing bowl combine ⅔ cup softened butter, 1 teaspoon garlic salt, ¼ teaspoon black pepper, ¼ teaspoon cayenne pepper, ⅛ teaspoon ground ginger, ⅛ teaspoon ground cinnamon, and ⅛ teaspoon ground cloves. Beat with an electric mixer on low speed until combined.

Pesto Butter: In a small mixing bowl combine ½ cup softened butter and ¼ cup purchased basil or dried tomato pesto. Beat with an electric mixer on low speed until combined.

Ginger and Garlic Butter: In a small mixing bowl combine ⅔ cup softened butter; 2 cloves garlic, minced; 1 teaspoon seasoned salt; and ½ teaspoon ground ginger. Beat with an electric mixer on low speed until combined.

Chipotle Butter: Coarsely chop 1 or 2 chipotle chiles in adobo sauce. In a small mixing bowl combine chopped chipotle peppers; ⅔ cup softened butter; 1 clove garlic, minced; and ½ teaspoon salt. Beat with an electric mixer on low speed until combined.

Nutty Butter: In a small mixing bowl combine ½ cup softened butter, ¼ cup very finely chopped peanuts or pecans, 1 tablespoon honey, ½ teaspoon garlic salt, and several dashes bottled hot pepper sauce. Beat with an electric mixer on low speed until combined.

Nutrition Facts per serving for all butters: 271 cal., 23 g total fat (14 g sat. fat), 59 mg chol., 395 mg sodium, 17 g carbo., 3 g fiber, 3 g pro. Daily Values: 22% vit. A, 9% vit. C, 1% calcium, 3% iron. Exchanges: 1 Starch 4½ Fat

NEW POTATOES GRUYÈRE

Be sure to use a double thickness of foil to make the packet; it helps to keep the ultra rich cheese sauce from scorching.

Prep: 20 minutes Grill: 20 minutes
Makes: 6 side-dish servings

1 1/2 **pounds tiny new potatoes, quartered**
  2 **small onions, cut into 8 wedges each**
  2 **tablespoons olive oil**
  2 **cloves garlic, minced**
 1/4 **teaspoon dried marjoram, crushed**
 1/4 **teaspoon salt**
 1/8 **teaspoon black pepper**
 1/8 **teaspoon ground nutmeg**
 3/4 **cup half-and-half or light cream**
 1/2 **cup shredded Gruyère cheese (2 ounces)**
  4 **teaspoons all-purpose flour**
  2 **tablespoons fine dry bread crumbs**
  2 **tablespoons finely chopped walnuts**
  2 **teaspoons olive oil**

1 In a large saucepan cook potatoes and onion wedges in lightly salted boiling water for 5 minutes; drain. Return to pan.

2 Meanwhile, for sauce, in a small saucepan heat the 2 tablespoons olive oil over medium heat. Add garlic, marjoram, salt, pepper, and nutmeg. Cook and stir for 30 seconds. Add half-and-half. Bring mixture just to a simmer (watch closely and do not allow the mixture to foam). Combine Gruyère cheese and flour; gradually add to simmering mixture, stirring after each addition until melted. Stir sauce into potato mixture.

3 Tear off a 44×18-inch piece of heavy-duty foil; fold in half to make a 22×18-inch rectangle. Place potato mixture in center of foil. Bring up two opposite edges of foil and seal with a double fold. Fold remaining edges together to completely enclose potatoes, leaving space for steam to build.

4 For a charcoal grill, grill the foil packet on rack of uncovered grill directly over medium coals about 20 minutes or until potatoes and onions are tender, turning packet over once halfway through grilling. (For a gas grill, preheat

FOOD FOR THOUGHT POTATOES

Whether red, white, or purple, baked, fried, or mashed, Americans love potatoes, and they eat about 50 pounds per person each year. While new varieties are continually being developed and discovered, here are some favorites.

● Red: Round in shape, these potatoes have a thin, smooth light pink to dark red skin and a crisp, white, waxy flesh. They're best suited to boiling or steaming.

● Russet: Russets are also known as Idaho potatoes or baking potatoes. They are oblong in shape with russet brown skin. Their mealy texture makes them good for frying, baking, and boiling for mashed potatoes.

● White: Also called Chef's potatoes, this variety has a thin, tender skin and waxy yellow or white flesh. Yukon gold is one particularly well-known variety that has a delicate pale yellow skin with shallow pink eyes. Its golden flesh is silky, rich, and buttery, and withstands most cooking methods well.

● New: These small, immature potatoes are harvested before their sugars are able to convert to starch, making them waxier and moister than their mature counterparts. They are available in all varieties and colors.

● Heirloom: Like other heirloom vegetables, these potatoes come in many varieties unique in appearance and flavor. Two popular heirlooms are fingerlings, which are small, long, and finger-shape, and purple potatoes, which have a purple skin and bluish white flesh.

grill. Reduce heat to medium. Place foil packet on grill rack over heat. Cover; grill as at left.)

5 Meanwhile, in a small bowl combine bread crumbs, walnuts, and the 2 teaspoons olive oil. To serve, carefully open packet and sprinkle with crumb mixture.

Nutrition Facts per serving: 231 cal., 14 g total fat (5 g sat. fat), 21 mg chol., 192 mg sodium, 20 g carbo., 2 g fiber, 7 g pro. Daily Values: 5% vit. A, 24% vit. C, 15% calcium, 9% iron. Exchanges: 1½ Starch, ½ High-Fat Meat, 1½ Fat

HONEY-SAGE VEGETABLE KABOBS

Serve these honey-glazed veggie kabobs on skewers or remove them from the skewers and pass in a serving bowl.

Prep: 25 minutes Grill: 6 minutes
Makes: 4 side-dish servings

- **1** tablespoon honey
- **1** tablespoon balsamic vinegar
- **2** teaspoons Dijon-style mustard
- **2** teaspoons snipped fresh sage or
    1 teaspoon dried sage, crushed
- **16** baby carrots or 4 medium carrots, peeled and cut into 2-inch pieces
- **8** tiny new potatoes or 2 medium red or Yukon gold potatoes, quartered
- **8** pearl onions, peeled, or 1 small onion, cut into small wedges

1 In a small bowl stir together honey, vinegar, mustard, and sage; set aside.

2 In a large saucepan combine carrots and potatoes; add enough water to cover. Bring to boiling over high heat. Add onions. Simmer, covered, for 3 to 5 minutes or until potatoes, carrots, and onions are slightly tender. Drain vegetables; let stand until cool enough to handle.

3 Onto 4 metal skewers, alternately thread carrots, potatoes, and onions, leaving a ¼-inch space between each piece.

4 For a charcoal grill, grill kabobs on the rack of an uncovered grill directly over medium coals for 6 to 8 minutes or until potatoes are tender, turning once halfway through grilling and brushing frequently with honey-sage mixture. (For a gas grill, preheat grill. Reduce to medium heat. Place kabobs on grill rack over heat. Cover; grill as above.)

Nutrition Facts per serving: 108 cal., 0 g total fat (0 g sat. fat), 0 mg chol., 77 mg sodium, 24 g carbo., 2 g fiber, 2 g pro. Daily Values: 29% vit. C, 2% calcium, 7% iron. Exchanges: 1 Vegetable, 1 Starch

TOMATO-STUFFED SWEET PEPPERS WITH FETA

Here's a fabulous way to enjoy a bumper crop of sweet peppers and juicy tomatoes. These tomato-filled peppers are as delicious as they are simple.

Prep: 15 minutes Grill: 10 minutes
Makes: 6 side-dish servings

- **3** large yellow or red sweet peppers
- **3** medium tomatoes, peeled and quartered, or 12 cherry tomatoes, halved
- **1** tablespoon olive oil
- **¼** teaspoon garlic salt
- **¼** teaspoon black pepper
- **¼** cup crumbled feta cheese (1 ounce)
- **2** tablespoons small fresh basil leaves or thinly sliced basil leaves

1 Cut peppers, including stems, in half. Remove and discard seeds and membranes.

2 For a charcoal grill, arrange peppers, cut sides down, on the rack of an uncovered grill directly over medium-hot coals. Grill for 4 minutes; turn peppers cut sides up. Divide tomatoes among pepper halves; brush with olive oil and sprinkle with garlic salt and pepper. Grill for 4 minutes more. Sprinkle tomatoes with feta cheese; grill about 2 minutes more or until cheese is softened. (For a gas grill, preheat grill. Reduce heat to medium-high. Arrange peppers on the grill rack over heat. Cover; grill as above.)

3 Remove peppers from grill; sprinkle with basil leaves. Serve at once.

Nutrition Facts per serving: 79 cal., 4 g total fat (1 g sat. fat), 4 mg chol., 100 mg sodium, 11 g carbo., 2 g fiber, 2 g pro. Daily Values: 15% vit. A, 399% vit. C. Exchanges: 2 Vegetable, ½ Fat

RANCH-STYLE CARROTS AND SQUASH

Ranch salad dressing makes an easy, tasty sauce for this mixed-veggie packet.

Prep: 20 minutes Grill: 20 minutes
Makes: 4 side-dish servings

2½ **cups packaged peeled baby carrots (about 14 ounces)**
2 **cups baby sunburst squash, green baby pattypan squash, or**
1 **medium zucchini or yellow summer squash, cut into ½-inch slices**
1 **cup grape tomatoes**
½ **cup bottled ranch salad dressing**
2 **teaspoons all-purpose flour**
1 **teaspoon finely shredded lemon peel**
¼ **cup fine dry bread crumbs**
¼ **cup finely chopped walnuts, toasted**
2 **tablespoons finely shredded Parmesan cheese**
1 **tablespoon olive oil**

1 In a saucepan cook carrots in a small amount of boiling salted water for 5 minutes; drain.

2 Cut any large baby squash in half. In a large bowl combine drained carrots, squash, and tomatoes. In a small bowl combine salad dressing, flour, and lemon peel; stir into vegetable mixture. Tear off a 36×18-inch piece of heavy-duty foil; fold in half to make an 18-inch square. Place vegetables in the center of foil. Bring up opposite edges of foil and seal with a double fold. Fold remaining edges together to completely enclose vegetables, leaving space for steam to build.

3 For a charcoal grill, grill the foil packet on rack of uncovered grill directly over medium coals for 20 to 25 minutes or until carrots are tender, turning packet once halfway through grilling. (For a gas grill, preheat grill. Reduce heat to medium. Place foil packet on grill rack over heat. Cover; grill as above.)

4 Meanwhile, in another small bowl combine bread crumbs, walnuts, Parmesan cheese, and oil. Carefully open packet (mixture may appear slightly curdled). Sprinkle with crumb mixture.

Nutrition Facts per serving: 384 cal., 30 g total fat (6 g sat. fat), 17 mg chol., 736 mg sodium, 21 g carbo., 2 g fiber, 10 g pro. Daily Values: 12% vit. A, 38% vit. C, 26% calcium, 6% iron. Exchanges: 1½ Vegetable, 1 Other Carbo., ½ High-Fat Meat, 5 Fat

Ranch-Style Carrots and Squash

GRILLED VEGETABLE PLATTER

The vibrant colors of grilled vegetables combine in this visually alluring dish. Pass a beautifully arranged platter around the table as either a side dish or first course.

Prep: 25 minutes Grill: 30 minutes
Makes: 8 to 10 side-dish servings

 1 pound yellow baby pattypan squash
   (about 3 cups)
 2 medium yellow, orange, and/or red
   sweet peppers, seeded and cut
   into strips or squares
 12 ounces fresh green beans,
   trimmed (3 cups)
 15 baby carrots with tops, trimmed
 10 cherry sweet peppers
 2 tablespoons olive oil or cooking oil
 1/2 teaspoon salt
 1/4 teaspoon black pepper
 2 teaspoons finely shredded
   lemon peel
 2 teaspoons lemon juice
 2 cloves garlic, minced
   Nonstick cooking spray

1 In an extra large bowl combine squash, sweet peppers, green beans, carrots, cherry sweet peppers, oil, salt, and black pepper; toss to coat. In a small bowl combine lemon peel, lemon juice, and garlic; set aside.

2 Lightly coat unheated grill wok with nonstick cooking spray. For a charcoal grill, preheat grill wok on the rack of an uncovered grill directly over medium coals for 15 seconds. Place the vegetables in the wok. Grill for 30 to 35 minutes or just until vegetables are tender and light brown, stirring occasionally. (For a gas grill, preheat grill. Reduce heat to medium. Preheat grill wok on grill rack over heat for 15 seconds. Add vegetable mixture. Cover; grill as above.)

3 Return cooked vegetables to the extra-large bowl. Add the lemon mixture; toss to coat. To serve, arrange vegetables on a large platter.

Nutrition Facts per serving: 75 cal., 4 g total fat (1 g sat. fat), 0 mg chol., 289 mg sodium, 10 g carbo., 3 g fiber, 2 g pro. Daily Values: 9% vit. A, 188% vit. C, 4% calcium, 5% iron. Exchanges: 2 Vegetable, 1/2 Fat

GRILLED VEGETABLE COUSCOUS

Lime and garlic, chipotle pepper, roasted tomato, and cilantro salsas are a few variations to try.

Prep: 15 minutes Grill: 15 minutes
Makes: 4 to 6 side-dish servings

 2 medium yellow summer squash
   and/or zucchini, cut into
   1-inch pieces
 2 medium red, yellow, and/or green
   sweet peppers, cut into
   1-inch pieces
 1 medium red onion, cut into wedges
 1 tablespoon olive oil
 1/4 teaspoon ground cumin
   Nonstick cooking spray
 1/2 cup grape tomatoes
 1 cup bottled lime and garlic salsa
   or other salsa
 1/4 teaspoon salt
 1/4 teaspoon black pepper
 3 cups hot cooked couscous or
   brown rice
   Bottled lime and garlic salsa or
   other salsa (optional)

1 In a large bowl combine squash, sweet peppers, and onion. In a small bowl combine oil and cumin. Add oil mixture to vegetables; toss to coat.

2 Lightly coat unheated grill wok with nonstick cooking spray. For a charcoal grill, preheat grill wok on rack of an uncovered grill directly over medium coals for 15 seconds. Place the vegetable mixture in the wok. Grill for 15 to 20 minutes or until vegetables are tender and charred, stirring occasionally. Add tomatoes the last 5 minutes of grilling. (For a gas grill, preheat grill. Reduce heat to medium. Preheat grill wok on grill rack over heat for 15 seconds. Place vegetable mixture in wok. Cover; grill as above.)

3 Transfer vegetables to a large bowl. Stir the 1 cup salsa, salt, and black pepper into vegetables; serve over couscous. If desired, pass additional salsa.

Nutrition Facts per serving: 219 cal., 4 g total fat (1 g sat. fat), 0 mg chol., 331 mg sodium, 40 g carbo., 6 g fiber, 7 g pro. Daily Values: 75% vit. A, 194% vit. C, 5% calcium, 9% iron. Exchanges: 2 Vegetable, 2 Starch, 1/2 Fat

FIRE-ROASTED ACORN SQUASH

Falling leaves and chilly evenings set the stage for winter squash. Instead of the usual glaze of brown sugar and butter, try basting rings of squash with tarragon butter. They're delicious served with pork and a dry white wine.

Prep: 10 minutes Grill: 45 minutes
Makes: 4 side-dish servings

    1 tablespoon olive oil
  1/2 teaspoon salt
  1/4 teaspoon black pepper
    2 small acorn squash, cut crosswise
        into 1-inch rings and seeded
    2 tablespoons butter or margarine,
        melted
    2 teaspoons snipped fresh tarragon
        or 1/2 teaspoon dried tarragon,
        crushed

1 In a small bowl combine oil, salt, and pepper; brush over squash rings. In another small bowl stir together melted butter and tarragon; set aside.

2 For a charcoal grill, arrange medium-hot coals around a drip pan. Test for medium heat above the pan. Place squash rings on grill rack over drip pan. Cover; grill about 45 minutes or until squash is tender, turning squash occasionally and brushing with butter mixture after 30 minutes of grilling. (For a gas grill, preheat grill. Reduce heat to medium. Adjust for indirect cooking. Grill as above.)

Nutrition Facts per serving: 153 cal., 10 g total fat (4 g sat. fat), 16 mg chol., 358 mg sodium, 18 g carbo., 3 g fiber, 1 g pro. Daily Values: 16% vit. A, 27% vit. C, 6% calcium, 7% iron. Exchanges: 1 Starch, 2 Fat

ALMOST STUFFED ZUCCHINI

As its name implies, this dish mixes together the same ingredients used to make stuffed zucchini. Here a nutty corn bread stuffing and chunks of zucchini are grilled in a foil packet.

Prep: 30 minutes Grill: 20 minutes
Makes: 8 side-dish servings

    2 cups mushrooms, thinly sliced
    1 medium onion, cut into very
        thin wedges
    1 clove garlic, minced
    3 tablespoons butter or margarine
    1 teaspoon snipped fresh thyme or
        1/4 teaspoon dried thyme, crushed
 2 1/2 cups corn bread stuffing mix
  1/2 cup water
  1/4 cup walnuts or pecans, toasted
        and chopped
    2 pounds zucchini and/or yellow
        summer squash, cut into
        1/2-inch pieces
    2 tablespoons olive oil
  1/4 teaspoon salt
  1/8 teaspoon black pepper
      Nonstick cooking spray

1 In a large skillet cook mushrooms, onion, and garlic in hot butter until onion is tender. Stir in thyme; cook for 30 seconds more. Remove skillet from heat; stir in stuffing mix, water, and walnuts (mixture will be dry). In a large bowl combine zucchini, olive oil, salt, and black pepper, tossing to coat zucchini. Add the stuffing mixture and toss to combine.

FOOD FOR THOUGHT SQUASH

Members of the gourd family, squash fall into two categories that are determined by peak season and type of skin.

● Winter squash, including acorn, butternut, Hubbard, pumpkin, and spaghetti, have a thick outer skin and center cavity of seeds, both of which are removed before or after cooking. The flesh is dense, sweet, and intensely flavored.

● Summer squash has a thinner, more tender skin and edible interior seeds. You can eat most raw or with minimal cooking. Although available year-round, their peak season is April through September. Pattypan, crookneck, and zucchini are summer squash.

2 Fold a 36×18-inch piece of heavy-duty foil in half to make an 18-inch square. Coat one side of the foil with nonstick cooking spray. Mound zucchini mixture in a 12×7-inch rectangle. Bring up two opposite edges of foil and seal with a double fold. Fold remaining edges together to completely enclose the mixture, leaving space for steam to build.

3 For a charcoal grill, grill foil packet on the rack of an uncovered grill directly over medium coals about 20 minutes or until squash is crisp-tender, turning packet over twice. (For a gas grill, preheat grill. Reduce heat to medium. Place foil packet on grill rack over heat. Cover; grill as above.)

Nutrition Facts per serving: 224 cal., 12 g total fat (4 g sat. fat), 12 mg chol., 424 mg sodium, 26 g carbo., 2 g fiber, 6 g pro. Daily Values: 11% vit. A, 15% vit. C, 3% calcium, 9% iron. Exchanges: 1 Vegetable, 1½ Starch, 2 Fat

---

PEANUT-SAUCED GRILLED RICE CAKES

Firmly pack the warm rice into the cake pan and chill it thoroughly. This way the rice cakes keep their shape during grilling.

Prep: 30 minutes Chill: 2 to 24 hours Grill: 13 minutes
Makes: 8 side-dish servings

   3 cups water
   1 teaspoon salt
1½ cups uncooked long grain white rice
     Nonstick cooking spray
   ⅓ cup reduced-sodium soy sauce
   2 tablespoons brown sugar
   ½ cup chunky peanut butter
   3 tablespoons water
   2 tablespoons toasted sesame oil
   2 tablespoons sliced green onion (1)

1 In a medium saucepan bring the 3 cups of water and salt to boiling. Stir in rice and return water to boiling; reduce heat. Simmer, covered, about 15 minutes or until all liquid is absorbed and rice is tender. Remove from heat; remove lid and let rice cool for 10 minutes. Do not stir.

2 Line an 8-inch square or 9-inch round cake pan with foil, extending foil edges slightly beyond the edge of the pan. Coat foil lightly with nonstick cooking spray. Spread warm rice into prepared pan, packing it down with the back of a large metal spoon coated with cooking spray. Cover surface of rice with plastic wrap. Firmly press rice with bottom of a saucepan or your hand to form a compact "cake." Chill for 2 to 24 hours.

3 Remove and discard plastic wrap. Invert rice cake onto a cutting board. Remove and discard foil. Cut rice cake into 8 rectangles or wedges.

4 For sauce, in a medium bowl combine soy sauce and brown sugar; stir until sugar is dissolved. Whisk in peanut butter, the 3 tablespoons water, and sesame oil until well combined.

5 For a charcoal grill, grill rice cakes on the greased rack of an uncovered grill directly over medium coals for 8 to 10 minutes or until grill marks appear on bottoms of cakes. Carefully turn rice cakes. Spread tops with some of the sauce. Grill about 5 minutes more or until cakes are heated through. (For a gas grill, preheat grill. Reduce heat to medium. Place cakes on a greased grill rack over heat. Cover; grill as above.)

6 Transfer rice cakes to a serving platter. Sprinkle with onion. Pass remaining sauce.

Nutrition Facts per serving: 276 cal., 12 g total fat (2 g sat. fat), 0 mg chol., 461 mg sodium, 36 g carbo., 2 g fiber, 7 g pro. Daily Values: 1% vit. A, 1% vit. C, 3% calcium, 11% iron. Exchanges: 2 Starch, ½ Other Carbo., 1 High-Fat Meat

Peanut-Sauced Grilled Rice Cakes

GRILLED PARMESAN BREADSTICKS

These buttery breadsticks disappear quickly. You might want to keep the ingredients for a second batch on hand.

Prep: 10 minutes Grill: 2 minutes
Makes: 8 breadsticks

- **½ cup grated Parmesan cheese (2 ounces)**
- **1¼ teaspoons dried Italian seasoning, crushed**
- **¼ teaspoon crushed red pepper**
- **8 purchased soft breadsticks**
- **3 tablespoons butter, melted**

1 In a shallow dish stir together the Parmesan cheese, Italian seasoning, and crushed red pepper. Brush breadsticks with butter. Roll each breadstick in the cheese mixture to coat.

2 For a charcoal grill, grill breadsticks on the rack of an uncovered grill directly over medium coals for 2 to 3 minutes or until golden, turning to brown evenly. (For a gas grill, preheat grill. Reduce heat to medium. Place breadsticks on grill rack over heat. Grill as above.) Serve warm.

Grilled Greek Breadsticks: Prepare as above, except use grated Romano cheese in place of the Parmesan, use Mediterranean seasoning in place of the Italian seasoning, omit the crushed red pepper, and add ½ teaspoon finely shredded lemon peel to the cheese mixture.

Nutrition Facts per breadstick: 194 cal., 7 g total fat (4 g sat. fat), 16 mg chol., 430 mg sodium, 25 g carbo., 1 g fiber, 7 g pro. Daily Values: 4% vit. A, 15% calcium, 11% iron. Exchanges: 1½ Starch, ½ Lean Meat, 1 Fat

Grilled Parmesan Breadsticks

DILL BATTER BREAD

This speedy yeast bread rises just once and requires no kneading or shaping.

Prep: 15 minutes Rise: 50 minutes Bake: 25 minutes
Oven: 375°F Makes: 1 loaf (8 servings)

2 cups all-purpose flour
1 package active dry yeast
$\frac{1}{2}$ cup water
$\frac{1}{2}$ cup cream-style cottage cheese
1 tablespoon sugar
1 tablespoon dillseeds or
**   caraway seeds**
1 tablespoon butter or margarine
1 teaspoon dried minced onion
1 teaspoon salt
1 beaten egg
$\frac{1}{2}$ cup toasted wheat germ

1 Grease a 9×1½-inch round baking pan or a 1-quart casserole; set aside. In a large mixing bowl stir together 1 cup of the flour and the yeast; set aside.

2 In a medium saucepan heat and stir water, cottage cheese, sugar, dillseeds, butter, dried onion, and salt just until warm (120°F to 130°F) and butter almost melts. Add cottage cheese mixture to flour mixture; add egg. Beat with an electric mixer on low to medium speed for 30 seconds, scraping sides of bowl constantly. Beat on high speed for 3 minutes. Using a wooden spoon, stir in the wheat germ and the remaining flour (batter will be stiff).

3 Spoon batter into prepared pan or casserole, spreading to edges. Cover; let rise in a warm place until double in size (50 to 60 minutes).

4 Bake in a 375° oven for 25 to 30 minutes or until golden. Immediately remove from pan or casserole. Serve warm or cool on a wire rack.

Nutrition Facts per serving: 185 cal., 4 g total fat (2 g sat. fat), 33 mg chol., 369 mg sodium, 30 g carbo., 2 g fiber, 8 g pro. Daily Values: 3% vit. A, 1% vit. C, 3% calcium, 13% iron. Exchanges: 2 Starch, ½ Fat

MARINATED BABY CARROTS WITH PISTACHIOS

Cardamom has a floral aroma and sweet flavor. Since it loses its flavor soon after it is ground, purchase cardamom in small amounts and store no more than two months.

Prep: 10 minutes Cook: 7 minutes Chill: 4 to 24 hours
Makes: 4 to 6 side-dish servings

1$\frac{1}{4}$ pounds baby carrots with tops
**   or 1 pound carrots**
2 tablespoons lemon juice
$\frac{1}{4}$ teaspoon salt
$\frac{1}{4}$ teaspoon black pepper
$\frac{1}{8}$ teaspoon crushed cardamom seeds
**   or ground cardamom**
1 tablespoon olive oil
$\frac{1}{4}$ cup coarsely chopped, shelled
**   unsalted pistachios**

1 Peel carrots. If present, trim green stems from baby carrots so just ½ to 1 inch remains. Cut long carrots in half lengthwise; halve crosswise.

2 Place a steamer basket in a large saucepan. Add water to just below basket. Bring to boiling. Add carrots to basket. Cover and steam for 7 to 9 minutes or until tender.

3 In a small bowl combine lemon juice, salt, pepper, and cardamom; whisk in oil. Transfer to a shallow bowl. Add carrots; toss to coat. Cover and chill for 4 to 24 hours. To serve, place carrots in a serving bowl. Sprinkle with pistachios.

Nutrition Facts per serving: 133 cal., 8 g total fat (1 g sat. fat), 0 mg chol., 188 mg sodium, 15 g carbo., 1 g fiber, 3 g pro. Daily Values: 1% vit. A, 25% vit. C, 4% calcium, 2% iron. Exchanges: 3 Vegetable, 1½ Fat

FARM-STYLE GREEN BEANS

Try this recipe in the summer when fresh green beans and homegrown tomatoes are at their peak. You'll see why people say it's one of the best ways to prepare green beans.

Prep: 20 minutes Cook: 10 minutes
Makes: 8 side-dish servings

4 thick slices bacon, cut up
2 medium onions, sliced
3 medium tomatoes, peeled, seeded,
   and chopped (2 cups)
½ teaspoon salt
1 pound green beans, washed,
   trimmed, and cut up (4 cups)

1 In a large skillet cook bacon until crisp. Remove bacon, reserving 3 tablespoons drippings. Drain bacon and set aside. Cook the onions in the reserved drippings over medium heat until onions are tender. Add the tomatoes and salt; cook, uncovered, for 5 minutes more or until most of the liquid is absorbed.

2 Meanwhile, in a medium saucepan cook the beans in a small amount of boiling salted water for 10 to 15 minutes or until crisp-tender; drain. Transfer beans to a serving bowl. Top beans with the tomato mixture and bacon pieces.

Nutrition Facts per serving: 86 cal., 5 g total fat (2 g sat. fat), 6 mg chol., 217 mg sodium, 8 g carbo., 3 g fiber, 3 g pro. Daily Values: 13% vit. A, 29% vit. C, 3% calcium, 5% iron. Exchanges: 1½ Vegetable, 1 Fat

ORZO AND CORN-OFF-THE-COB

For less cleanup, cook the corn and orzo in the same pot. Orzo is a quick-cooking pasta that resembles large grains of rice. Feel free to substitute other small types of pasta such as acini di pepe.

Prep: 30 minutes Cook: 8 minutes
Makes: 6 to 8 side-dish servings

4 fresh ears sweet corn
1¼ cups orzo (rosamarina)
1 cup kalamata olives, pitted
   and halved
¾ cup chopped red sweet pepper
   (1 medium)
¼ cup thinly sliced green onions (2)
¼ cup finely snipped fresh basil
¼ cup finely snipped fresh parsley
¼ cup olive oil
2 tablespoons white wine vinegar
¼ teaspoon salt
¼ teaspoon black pepper

1 Using a sharp knife, cut corn kernels off cob (should yield about 2 cups). Set aside. Bring a large pot of lightly salted water to boiling. Add orzo and cook, stirring occasionally, for 8 to 9 minutes or just until tender, adding corn the last 3 minutes of cooking. Drain well and place in a large serving bowl.

2 Add the olives, sweet pepper, and green onions; toss well. Add the basil, parsley, oil, vinegar, salt, and black pepper. Toss gently to combine. Serve at room temperature.

Nutrition Facts per serving: 308 cal., 13 g total fat (1 g sat. fat), 0 mg chol., 361 mg sodium, 42 g carbo., 4 g fiber, 7 g pro. Daily Values: 30% vit. A, 75% vit. C, 2% calcium, 12% iron. Exchanges: 1½ Vegetable, 2 Starch, 2½ Fat

BAKED BEAN QUINTET

Prep: 10 minutes Bake: 1 hour Oven: 375°F
Makes: 12 to 16 side-dish servings

6 slices bacon, cut up
1 cup chopped onion (1 large)
1 clove garlic, minced
1 16-ounce can lima beans, rinsed
   and drained
1 16-ounce can pork and beans in
   tomato sauce
1 15½-ounce can red kidney beans,
   rinsed and drained
1 15-ounce can garbanzo beans
   (chickpeas), rinsed and drained
1 15-ounce can butter beans, drained
¾ cup catsup
½ cup molasses
¼ cup packed brown sugar
1 tablespoon prepared mustard
1 tablespoon Worcestershire sauce
   Crumbled, cooked bacon (optional)

1 In a skillet cook the cut-up bacon, the onion, and garlic until bacon is crisp and onion is tender; drain. In a large bowl combine onion mixture, lima beans, pork and beans, kidney beans, garbanzo beans, butter beans, catsup, molasses, brown sugar, mustard, and Worcestershire sauce. Transfer bean mixture to a 3-quart casserole.

2 Bake, covered, in a 375°F oven for 1 hour. If desired, top with additional cooked bacon.

Slow cooker directions: Prepare bean mixture as at left. Transfer to 3½- or 4-quart slow cooker. Cover and cook on low-heat setting for 10 to 12 hours or on high-heat setting for 4 to 5 hours.

Nutrition Facts per serving: 245 cal., 3 g total fat (1 g sat. fat), 5 mg chol., 882 mg sodium, 47 g carbo., 9 g fiber, 10 g pro. Daily Values: 5% vit. A, 13% vit. C, 10% calcium, 22% iron. Exchanges: 2 Starch, 1 Other Carbo., ½ Very Lean Meat

Baked Bean Quintet

ZUCCHINI-OLIVE COUSCOUS

Start to Finish: 30 minutes
Makes: 8 side-dish servings

2 cloves garlic, minced
1 tablespoon olive oil
3 cups chicken broth
1 cup pimiento-stuffed green olives,
    pitted green olives, and/or pitted
    ripe olives, cut up
3 medium zucchini, halved lengthwise
    and thinly sliced (about 3³/₄ cups)
1 10-ounce package quick-cooking
    couscous
2 teaspoons finely shredded
    lemon peel
¹/₄ teaspoon black pepper
¹/₂ cup sliced green onions (4)
2 tablespoons snipped fresh parsley
    Thin strips of lemon peel (optional)
    Lemon wedges

1 In a large saucepan cook garlic in hot oil for 1 minute, stirring frequently. Add broth and olives; bring to boiling. Stir in zucchini, couscous, shredded lemon peel, and pepper. Cover; remove saucepan from heat. Let stand for 5 minutes.

2 To serve, gently stir green onions and parsley into couscous mixture. If desired, garnish with strips of lemon peel. Serve with lemon wedges.

Nutrition Facts per serving: 190 cal., 5 g total fat (1 g sat. fat), 0 mg chol., 762 mg sodium, 31 g carbo., 3 g fiber, 6 g pro. Daily Values: 7% vit. A, 18% vit. C, 4% calcium, 6% iron. Exchanges: ¹/₂ Vegetable, 2 Starch, ¹/₂ Fat

SQUASH, PEAR, AND ONION AU GRATIN

Prep: 25 minutes Bake: 1 hour Oven: 350°F
Makes: 6 side-dish servings

1¹/₂ pounds acorn, buttercup, or
    turban squash
1 large onion, sliced and separated
    into rings (1 cup)
1 tablespoon butter or margarine
1 medium pear, peeled and
    thinly sliced (1 cup)
    Salt
3 tablespoons fine dry bread crumbs
3 slices bacon, crisp-cooked, drained,
    and crumbled
2 tablespoons chopped walnuts
1 tablespoon grated Romano cheese
1 tablespoon butter or margarine,
    melted
2 tablespoons snipped fresh
    parsley (optional)

1 Slice squash in half lengthwise. Remove and discard seeds. If desired, remove peel. Cut crosswise into ¹/₂-inch slices. Set aside.

2 In a large skillet cook onion in 1 tablespoon hot butter for 5 to 10 minutes or until tender.

3 Arrange half of the squash slices in the bottom of an 8×8×2-inch baking dish. Top with half of the pear slices. Repeat layers. Sprinkle lightly with salt. Cover with the cooked onions. Bake, covered, in a 350°F oven about 45 minutes or until vegetables are nearly tender.

FOOD FOR THOUGHT OLIVES

The two basic categories of olives are green and black.

● Green Olives: These olives are harvested once they have reached their mature size but before they change color. These "young" fruits are more dense than black olives, are treated and cured to reduce bitterness, and have a slightly sharper flavor. One of the most common types is the Spanish olive, which is typically pitted and stuffed with pimientos.

● Black Olives: These olives are harvested when fully ripe and may appear reddish black, deep violet, or greenish black. Some are firm, smooth, and glossy, while others are shriveled from aging on the tree or having been treated with salt.

4 Meanwhile, for topping, in a small bowl toss together bread crumbs, bacon, walnuts, Romano cheese, and the 1 tablespoon melted butter; sprinkle over vegetables. Bake, uncovered, about 15 minutes more or until squash is tender. If desired, sprinkle with parsley.

Nutrition Facts per serving: 153 cal., 8 g total fat (3 g sat. fat), 14 mg chol., 270 mg sodium, 20 g carbo., 1 g fiber, 3 g pro. Daily Values: 146% vit. A, 35% vit. C, 7% calcium, 6% iron. Exchanges: 1½ Starch, 1 Fat

GO-WITH-ANYTHING TOMATO SAUTÉ

This quick-to-fix medley of warm grape tomatoes, shallots, thyme, and fresh mozzarella cheese is terrific over pasta or wilted greens, but don't be afraid to serve it on its own.

Prep: 12 minutes Cook: 3 minutes
Makes: 4 side-dish servings

2½ **cups whole red grape or yellow teardrop tomatoes and/or cherry tomatoes**
  Nonstick olive oil cooking spray
¼ **cup finely chopped shallots**
1 **clove garlic, minced**
1 **teaspoon snipped fresh lemon-thyme or thyme**
¼ **teaspoon salt**
¼ **teaspoon black pepper**
4 **ounces fresh mozzarella, cut into ½-inch cubes (1 cup)**

1 Halve about 1½ cups of the tomatoes; set aside. Lightly coat a 10-inch nonstick skillet with nonstick cooking spray. Add shallots, garlic, and thyme. Cook and stir over medium heat for 2 to 3 minutes or until shallots are tender.

2 Add all of the tomatoes, the salt, and pepper. Cook and stir for 1 to 2 minutes or until tomatoes are just warmed. Remove from heat. Stir in mozzarella cheese.

Nutrition Facts per serving: 107 cal., 5 g total fat (3 g sat. fat), 16 mg chol., 289 mg sodium, 9 g carbo., 1 g fiber, 8 g pro. Daily Values: 14% vit. A, 43% vit. C, 19% calcium, 5% iron. Exchanges: 1 Vegetable, 1 Medium-Fat Meat, 3½ Fat

HASH BROWNS

Better than store-bought, this combination of potatoes, onion, and optional jalapeño pepper is cooked until crispy and golden brown.

Prep: 15 minutes Cook: 25 minutes
Makes: 4 side-dish servings

¼ **teaspoon salt**
4 **to 5 small russet, white, or red potatoes (1 pound)**
¼ **cup finely chopped onion**
1 **small fresh jalapeño chile pepper or banana pepper, seeded, and cut into thin strips (see tip, page 36) (optional)**
¼ **teaspoon salt**
⅛ **teaspoon coarsely ground black pepper (optional)**
3 **tablespoons butter, cooking oil, or margarine**

1 Fill a medium saucepan one-third full of water; add ¼ teaspoon salt. Coarsely chop unpeeled potatoes by slicing lengthwise into strips, then cutting crosswise. Place potatoes in saucepan. Bring to boiling over high heat; reduce heat. Cook, uncovered, for 5 minutes. Remove from heat; drain well.

2 In a medium bowl combine potatoes, onion, pepper strips (if desired), ¼ teaspoon salt, and, if desired, black pepper.

3 In a large nonstick skillet melt butter. Add potato mixture and cook over medium heat about 20 minutes or until potatoes are soft and browned, turning occasionally.

Nutrition Facts per serving: 159 cal., 8 g total fat (8 g sat. fat), 21 mg chol., 280 mg sodium, 19 g carbo., 3 g fiber, 3 g pro. Daily Values: 6% vit. A, 27% vit. C, 2% calcium, 5% iron. Exchanges: 1 Starch, 1½ Fat

CHEESY GARLIC POTATO GRATIN

Medium-starch potatoes such as Yukon gold and Finnish yellow contain more moisture than high-starch potatoes such as russets. They're good choices for gratins and casseroles because they retain their shape after cooking.

Prep: 15 minutes Bake: 1¼ hours Oven: 350°F
Makes: 6 to 8 side-dish servings

1½ pounds Yukon gold or other yellow potatoes, thinly sliced (about 5 cups)
⅓ cup sliced green onions
1½ cups shredded Swiss cheese (6 ounces)
4 cloves garlic, minced
1 teaspoon salt
¼ teaspoon black pepper
1 cup whipping cream

1 Grease a 2-quart square baking dish. Layer half of the sliced potatoes and half of the green onions in the dish. Sprinkle with half of the Swiss cheese, garlic, salt, and pepper. Repeat layers. Pour whipping cream over top.

2 Bake, covered, in a 350°F oven for 1 hour. Uncover; bake for 15 to 20 minutes more or until potatoes are tender and top is golden brown.

Nutrition Facts per serving: 365 cal., 23 g total fat (14 g sat. fat), 80 mg chol., 454 mg sodium, 30 g carbo., 1 g fiber, 12 g pro. Daily Values: 25% vit. A, 31% vit. C, 26% calcium, 10% iron. Exchanges: 1½ Starch, ½ Other Carbo., 1 High-Fat Meat, 2½ Fat

Cheesy Garlic Potato Gratin

6

Beef, Veal
& Lamb

DIRECT GRILLING BEEF, VEAL & LAMB

For a charcoal grill, place meat on grill rack directly over medium coals. Grill, uncovered, for the time given below or to desired doneness, turning once halfway through grilling. For a gas grill, preheat grill. Reduce heat to medium. Place meat on grill rack over heat. Cover the grill. Test for doneness using a meat thermometer.

CUT	THICKNESS/ WEIGHT	GRILLING TEMPERATURE	APPROXIMATE DIRECT-GRILLING TIME	DONENESS
BEEF				
Boneless steak (beef top loin [strip], ribeye, shoulder top blade [flat-iron], tenderloin)	1 inch	Medium	10 to 12 minutes	145°F medium-rare
			12 to 15 minutes	160°F medium
	1½ inches	Medium	15 to 19 minutes	145°F medium-rare
			18 to 23 minutes	160°F medium
Boneless top sirloin steak	1 inch	Medium	14 to 18 minutes	145°F medium-rare
			18 to 22 minutes	160°F medium
	1½ inches	Medium	20 to 24 minutes	145°F medium-rare
			24 to 28 minutes	160°F medium
Boneless tri-tip steak (bottom sirloin)	¾ inch	Medium	9 to 11 minutes	145°F medium-rare
			11 to 13 minutes	160°F medium
	1 inch	Medium	13 to 15 minutes	145°F medium-rare
			15 to 17 minutes	160°F medium
Flank steak	1¼ to 1¾ pounds	Medium	17 to 21 minutes	160°F medium
Steak with bone (porterhouse, rib, T-bone)	1 inch	Medium	10 to 13 minutes	145°F medium-rare
			12 to 15 minutes	160°F medium
	1½ inches	Medium	18 to 21 minutes	145°F medium-rare
			22 to 25 minutes	160°F medium
GROUND MEAT				
Patties (beef, lamb, or veal)	½ inch	Medium	10 to 13 minutes	160°F medium
	¾ inch	Medium	14 to 18 minutes	160°F medium
KABOBS				
Beef, lamb, or veal	1-inch cubes	Medium	8 to 12 minutes	160°F medium
	1½-inch cubes	Medium	12 to 14 minutes	160°F medium
LAMB				
Chop (loin or rib)	1 inch	Medium	12 to 14 minutes	145°F medium-rare
			15 to 17 minutes	160°F medium
Chop (sirloin)	¾ to 1 inch	Medium	14 to 17 minutes	160°F medium
VEAL				
Chop (loin or rib)	1 inch	Medium	12 to 15 minutes	160°F medium

All cooking times are based on meat removed directly from refrigerator.

INDIRECT GRILLING BEEF, VEAL & LAMB

For a charcoal grill, arrange medium-hot coals around a drip pan. Test for medium heat above pan, unless chart says otherwise. Place meat, fat side up, on grill rack over drip pan. Cover and grill for the time given below or to desired temperature, adding more charcoal to maintain heat as necessary. For a gas grill, preheat grill. Reduce heat to medium. Adjust heat for indirect cooking.

To test for doneness, insert a meat thermometer, using an instant-read thermometer to test smaller portions. Thermometer should register the "final grilling temperature." Remove meat from grill. For larger cuts, such as roasts, cover with foil and let stand 15 minutes before slicing. The meat's temperature will rise 10°F during the time it stands. Thinner cuts, such as steaks, do not have to stand.

CUT	THICKNESS/ WEIGHT	APPROXIMATE INDIRECT-GRILLING TIME	FINAL GRILLING TEMPERATURE (when to remove from grill)	FINAL DONENESS TEMPERATURE (after 15 minutes standing)
BEEF				
Boneless top sirloin steak	1 inch	22 to 26 minutes	145°F medium-rare	No standing time
		26 to 30 minutes	160°F medium	No standing time
	1½ inches	32 to 36 minutes	145°F medium-rare	No standing time
		36 to 40 minutes	160°F medium	No standing time
Boneless tri-tip roast (bottom sirloin)	1½ to 2 pounds	35 to 40 minutes	135°F	145°F medium-rare
		40 to 45 minutes	150°F	160°F medium
Flank steak	1¼ to 1¾ pounds	23 to 28 minutes	160°F medium	No standing time
Ribeye roast (medium-low heat)	4 to 6 pounds	1¼ to 1¾ hours	135°F	145°F medium-rare
		1½ to 2¼ hours	150°F	160°F medium
Rib roast (chine bone removed) (medium-low heat)	4 to 6 pounds	2 to 2¾ hours	135°F	145°F medium-rare
		2½ to 3¼ hours	150°F	160°F medium
Steak (porterhouse, rib, ribeye, shoulder blade [flat-iron], T-bone, tenderloin, top loin [strip])	1 inch	16 to 20 minutes	145°F medium-rare	No standing time
		20 to 24 minutes	160°F medium	No standing time
	1½ inches	22 to 25 minutes	145°F medium-rare	No standing time
		25 to 28 minutes	160°F medium	No standing time
Tenderloin roast (medium-high heat)	2 to 3 pounds	¾ to 1 hour	135°F	145°F medium-rare
	4 to 5 pounds	1 to 1¼ hours	135°F	145°F medium-rare

CUT	THICKNESS/ WEIGHT	APPROXIMATE INDIRECT-GRILLING TIME	FINAL GRILLING TEMPERATURE (when to remove from grill)	FINAL DONENESS TEMPERATURE (after 15 minutes standing)
LAMB				
Boneless leg roast (medium-low heat)	3 to 4 pounds	1½ to 2¼ hours	135°F	145°F medium-rare
		1¾ to 2½ hours	150°F	160°F medium
	4 to 6 pounds	1¾ to 2½ hours	135°F	145°F medium-rare
		2 to 2¾ hours	150°F	160°F medium
Boneless sirloin roast (medium-low heat)	1½ to 2 pounds	1 to 1¼ hours	135°F	145°F medium-rare
		1¼ to 1½ hours	150°F	160°F medium
Chop (loin or rib)	1 inch	16 to 18 minutes	145°F medium-rare	No standing time
	1 inch	18 to 20 minutes	160°F medium	No standing time
Leg of lamb (with bone) (medium-low heat)	5 to 7 pounds	1¾ to 2¼ hours	135°F	145°F medium-rare
		2¼ to 2¾ hours	150°F	160°F medium
VEAL				
Chop (loin or rib)	1 inch	19 to 23 minutes	160°F medium	No standing time
GROUND MEAT				
Patties (beef, lamb, or veal)	½ inch	15 to 18 minutes	160°F medium	No standing time
	¾ inch	20 to 24 minutes	160°F medium	No standing time

All cooking times are based on meat removed directly from refrigerator.

TEXAS CHEESEBURGERS

Texas-big in both size and flavor, these cheese-topped burgers say howdy with poblano peppers and chili powder.

Prep: 30 minutes Chill: 1 hour Grill: 14 minutes
Makes: 4 servings

$\frac{1}{4}$ **cup finely chopped onion**
 2 large fresh poblano chile peppers, roasted* and chopped (see tip, page 36)
 2 tablespoons chili powder
 1 teaspoon salt
$\frac{1}{2}$ **teaspoon black pepper**
$1\frac{1}{2}$ **pounds lean ground beef**
 3 ounces Monterey Jack cheese with jalapeño peppers or Monterey Jack cheese, shredded ($\frac{3}{4}$ cup)
 4 large hamburger buns, split and toasted
 Assorted condiments

1 In a large bowl combine onion, poblano peppers, chili powder, salt, and black pepper. Add ground meat; mix well. Shape mixture into four $\frac{3}{4}$-inch-thick patties. Place on a tray; cover and chill for 1 to 2 hours.

2 For a charcoal grill, grill patties on the rack of an uncovered grill directly over medium coals for 14 to 18 minutes or until done (160°F), turning once. Top burgers with shredded cheese during the last 1 minute of grilling. (For a gas grill, preheat grill. Reduce heat to medium. Place patties on grill rack over heat. Cover; grill as above.) Serve burgers on buns with condiments.

*Note: To roast poblano peppers, halve peppers lengthwise. Remove seeds and membranes. Roast peppers, cut sides down, on a foil-lined baking sheet in a 425°F oven about 20 minutes or until skins are dark. Wrap in foil; let stand 20 minutes. Pull skins off gently and slowly.

Nutrition Facts per serving: 552 cal., 30 g total fat (12 g sat. fat), 120 mg chol., 1,008 mg sodium, 30 g carbo., 3 g fiber, 39 g pro. Daily Values: 37% vit. A, 212% vit. C, 15% calcium, 36% iron. Exchanges: 2 Starch, 1 High-Fat Meat, 4 Medium-Fat Meat

BURGERS WITH MUSHROOM-VERMOUTH TOPPER

An elegant mushroom and wine sauce takes these burgers from simple to simply spectacular.

Prep: 30 minutes Grill: 14 minutes
Makes: 6 servings

$\frac{1}{2}$ **cup finely chopped sweet onion (1 medium)**
$\frac{1}{4}$ **cup fine dry bread crumbs**
 1 beaten egg
$\frac{1}{2}$ **teaspoon salt**
$\frac{1}{4}$ **teaspoon black pepper**
 2 pounds lean ground beef
 6 hamburger buns, split and toasted*
 1 recipe Mushroom-Vermouth Topper

1 In a large bowl combine onion, bread crumbs, egg, salt, and pepper. Add ground beef; mix well. Shape mixture into six $\frac{3}{4}$-inch-thick patties.

2 For a charcoal grill, grill patties on the rack of an uncovered grill directly over medium coals for 14 to 18 minutes or until done (160°F), turning once halfway through grilling. (For a gas grill, preheat grill. Reduce heat to medium. Place patties on grill rack over heat. Cover; grill as above.)

3 Serve burgers on buns with Mushroom-Vermouth Topper.

*Note: To toast buns, brush cut sides of buns lightly with olive oil or butter. Grill, cut sides down, directly over medium coals for 30 seconds to 1 minute or until just toasted.

Mushroom-Vermouth Topper: In a large skillet melt $\frac{1}{4}$ cup butter. Add 3 cups quartered small mushrooms, $\frac{1}{2}$ cup thinly sliced shallots, $\frac{1}{2}$ teaspoon salt, and $\frac{1}{4}$ to $\frac{1}{2}$ teaspoon black pepper; cook over medium heat until mushrooms are tender. Stir in 1 tablespoon all-purpose flour; cook and stir 1 minute more. Remove skillet from heat. Carefully add $\frac{2}{3}$ cup dry vermouth. Return skillet to heat. Cook and stir until thickened and bubbly; cook and stir 1 minute more. Serve immediately.

Nutrition Facts per serving: 525 cal., 27 g total fat (12 g sat. fat), 153 mg chol., 869 mg sodium, 30 g carbo., 2 g fiber, 34 g pro. Daily Values: 10% vit. A, 3% vit. C, 9% calcium, 28% iron. Exchanges: $\frac{1}{2}$ Vegetable, 2 Starch, 4 Medium-Fat Meat, 1 Fat

LATINO BARBECUE BURGERS

The zesty south-of-the-border-style catsup
is as great on steak as it is on these
mushroom-stuffed burgers.

Prep: 35 minutes Grill: 24 minutes
Makes: 4 servings

 2 tablespoons olive oil
 1 tablespoon butter or margarine
 8 ounces fresh mushrooms, sliced
 ¼ teaspoon kosher or coarse salt
 **¼ teaspoon coarsely ground black
     pepper**
 **1 tablespoon sherry wine vinegar
     or red wine vinegar**
 2 pounds lean ground beef
 ½ cup Latino Catsup
 4 large buns, split

1 In a large skillet heat oil and butter over medium-high heat. Add mushrooms, salt, and pepper. Cook about 3 minutes or until mushrooms are just tender. Add vinegar. Cook and stir mushroom mixture about 2 minutes or until most of the liquid has evaporated. Set aside.

2 Shape beef into eight thin 4-inch patties. Press one-fourth of the mushroom mixture into the center of 4 of the patties. Top with remaining patties; press edges to seal.

3 For a charcoal grill, grill patties on the rack of an uncovered grill directly over medium coals for 12 minutes; turn. Brush burgers with ¼ cup of the Latino Catsup. Grill for 12 to 14 minutes more or until done (160°F). (For a gas grill, preheat grill. Reduce heat to medium. Place patties on grill rack over heat. Cover; grill as above.) If desired, toast buns on grill. Serve burgers on buns with Latino Catsup.

Latino Catsup: In a food processor combine 1 cup chopped green onions; ¼ to ½ cup chipotle peppers in adobo sauce; 1 fresh jalapeño chile pepper, chopped (see tip, page 36); 2 cloves garlic, minced; 1 tablespoon snipped fresh oregano; and ½ teaspoon salt. Cover; process until combined. Add 1 cup catsup, ¼ cup red wine vinegar, and 2 tablespoons olive oil; process until smooth.

Nutrition Facts per serving: 726 cal., 47 g total fat (16 g sat. fat), 159 mg chol., 666 mg sodium, 27 g carbo., 2 g fiber, 47 g pro. Daily Values: 5% vit. A, 3% vit. C, 4% calcium, 32% iron. Exchanges: 1 Vegetable, 1½ Starch, 6 Medium-Fat Meat, 3 Fat

SMOKIN' HOT TIP

● At the store, choose packages of ground beef that are not damaged and feel cold to the touch.

● Buy ground beef that's bright red in color with no excessive juices. Vacuum-packed ground beef appears burgundy in color but changes to red once opened and exposed to oxygen. The lack of oxygen is also the reason the center of ground beef may look different from the outside surface.

● Refrigerate and use within 2 days or freeze for up to 4 months.

● Thaw packages of ground beef in the refrigerator, never at room temperature.

● The color of cooked ground beef varies and is therefore not a good indicator of doneness. Cook burgers to 160°F (medium). Insert a thermometer sideways into the burger to measure the temperature.

● When handling and cooking ground beef, be sure to avoid cross contamination by using a clean plate for serving up cooked burgers and washing your hands and any cooking utensils and surfaces well with hot soapy water.

Burgers with Onion Jam

BURGERS WITH ONION JAM

Prepare the Onion Jam for the burgers a day or two in advance; cover and chill until needed.

Prep: 10 minutes Grill: 18 minutes
Makes: 6 servings

2 pounds lean ground beef
1 recipe Onion Jam
4 ounces goat cheese (chèvre)
1 teaspoon salt
½ teaspoon crushed red pepper
12 slices grilled Texas toast
    Goat cheese (chèvre) (optional)

1 In a large bowl combine ground beef, half of the Onion Jam, the goat cheese, salt, and crushed red pepper. Shape mixture into six 1-inch-thick patties.

2 For a charcoal grill, grill patties on the rack of an uncovered grill directly over medium coals for 18 to 23 minutes or until done (160°F), turning once halfway through grilling. (For a gas grill, preheat grill. Reduce heat to medium. Place patties on grill rack over heat. Cover; grill as above.)

3 Serve on Texas toast with Onion Jam and, if desired, additional goat cheese.

Onion Jam: In a large skillet heat 2 tablespoons cooking oil over medium heat. Add 2 large yellow onions, thinly sliced, and 2 large red onions, thinly sliced; cook and stir for 5 minutes. Stir in 2 cups chopped green onions; cook for 25 to 30 minutes or until browned, stirring occasionally. Add ½ cup balsamic vinegar and ¼ cup packed brown sugar; reduce heat. Simmer for 10 to 12 minutes or until most of the liquid has evaporated. Remove from heat. Cover and chill for up to 1 week.

Nutrition Facts per serving: 597 cal., 29 g total fat (11 g sat. fat), 104 mg chol., 1,047 mg sodium, 44 g carbo., 3 g fiber, 37 g pro. Daily Values: 3% vit. A, 16% vit. C, 14% calcium, 29% iron. Exchanges: 1 Vegetable, 2 Starch, ½ Other Carbo., 4 Medium-Fat Meat, 1½ Fat

OPEN-FACE SPANISH BURGERS

The mix of lively ingredients packed inside these burgers will have you shouting "olé!"

Prep: 15 minutes Grill: 14 minutes
Makes: 4 servings

- **1 beaten egg**
- **³⁄₄ cup quick-cooking rolled oats**
- **¹⁄₂ cup sliced pimiento-stuffed green olives**
- **¹⁄₄ cup snipped fresh parsley**
- **¹⁄₄ cup tomato paste**
- **¹⁄₄ teaspoon black pepper**
- **1 pound lean ground beef**
- **¹⁄₄ cup jalapeño pepper jelly or apple jelly, melted**
- **1 medium tomato, chopped**
- **¹⁄₃ cup chunky salsa**
- **¹⁄₄ cup chopped, seeded cucumber**
- **2 tablespoons sliced pimiento-stuffed green olives (optional)**
- **2 cups mixed salad greens**
- **8 thin slices bread, toasted (optional)**

1 In a large bowl combine egg, rolled oats, the ½ cup olives, the parsley, tomato paste, and pepper. Add ground beef; mix well. Shape meat mixture into four 4×2½-inch oval patties.

2 For a charcoal grill, grill patties on the rack of an uncovered grill directly over medium coals for 14 to 18 minutes or until done (160°F), turning once and brushing once with melted jelly halfway through grilling. (For a gas grill, preheat grill. Reduce heat to medium. Place patties on grill rack over heat. Cover; grill as above.) Discard any remaining melted jelly.

3 Meanwhile, for relish, in a small bowl combine tomato, salsa, cucumber, and, if desired, the 2 tablespoons olives.

4 To serve, divide the salad greens and, if desired, toasted bread slices among 4 dinner plates. Top with the patties and relish.

Nutrition Facts per serving: 395 cal., 19 g total fat (6 g sat. fat), 124 mg chol., 524 mg sodium, 30 g carbo., 3 g fiber, 27 g pro. Daily Values: 15% vit. A, 32% vit. C, 5% calcium, 23% iron. Exchanges: 1 Vegetable, ½ Starch, 1 Other Carbo., 3½ Medium-Fat Meat

JERK BURGERS WITH PINEAPPLE SALSA

For a more authentic island flavor, substitute eight ounces fresh pineapple, grilled and finely chopped (1 cup), for the canned pineapple.

Prep: 20 minutes Cook: 5 minutes Grill: 10 minutes
Makes: 4 servings

- **¹⁄₄ cup finely chopped onion**
- **¹⁄₄ cup finely chopped red sweet pepper**
- **¹⁄₄ cup finely chopped green sweet pepper or 1 to 2 fresh jalapeño chile peppers, finely chopped (see tip, page 36)**
- **1 teaspoon grated fresh ginger**
- **2 teaspoons cooking oil**
- **1 8-ounce can crushed pineapple in juice, drained**
- **¹⁄₄ cup apple jelly**
- **1 tablespoon lime juice**
- **Dash salt**
- **1 pound lean ground beef**
- **¹⁄₃ cup bottled jerk sauce**
- **4 ounces Monterey Jack cheese, shredded (optional)**
- **4 hamburger buns, split and toasted**

1 For pineapple salsa, cook onion, sweet peppers, and ginger in hot oil in a medium saucepan over medium heat for 3 minutes. Add drained pineapple, apple jelly, lime juice, and salt; cook for 2 minutes more or until jelly melts. Cover and chill until ready to serve.

2 In a bowl combine beef and ¼ cup of the jerk sauce. Shape into four ½-inch-thick patties. For a charcoal grill, grill patties on the rack of an uncovered grill directly over medium coals for 10 to 13 minutes or until done (160°F), turning once and brushing with remaining jerk sauce. (For a gas grill, preheat grill. Reduce heat to medium. Place patties on grill rack over heat. Cover; grill as above.) Place cheese, if using, on roll bottoms. Top with burgers, pineapple salsa, and roll tops.

Nutrition Facts per serving: 493 cal., 19 g total fat (6 g sat. fat), 71 mg chol., 396 mg sodium, 55 g carbo., 3 g fiber, 26 g pro. Daily Values: 15% vit. A, 57% vit. C, 9% calcium, 22% iron. Exchanges: ½ Fruit, 2 Starch, 1 Other Carbo., 3 Medium-Fat Meat, ½ Fat

CHIMICHURRI BURGERS WITH GRILLED PLANTAINS

A traditional South American condiment that's terrific with beef, chimichurri brings to mind the heat of a volcano.

Prep: 30 minutes Grill: 18 minutes Makes: 6 servings

  2 **pounds lean ground beef**
¼ **teaspoon salt**
¼ **teaspoon cayenne pepper**
  1 **recipe Chimichurri**
  6 **hamburger rolls, split and toasted**
    Sliced tomatoes and onions
  1 **recipe Grilled Plantains (optional)**

1 In a large bowl combine ground beef, salt, and cayenne pepper. Shape mixture into twelve 3½-inch patties. Spoon about 1 tablespoon of Chimichurri into the center of 6 of the patties. Top with remaining patties; press edges to seal.

2 For a charcoal grill, grill patties on the rack of an uncovered grill directly over medium coals for 18 to 22 minutes or until done (160°F), turning once halfway through grilling. (For a gas grill, preheat grill. Reduce heat to medium. Place patties on rack over heat. Cover; grill as above.)

3 Brush rolls with some of the Chimichurri. Top with burgers, remaining sauce, tomatoes, and onions. If desired, serve with Grilled Plantains.

FOOD FOR THOUGHT
CHIMICHURRI

Popular in Argentinean cuisine, the basic chimichurri sauce features a blend of oil, vinegar, parsley, garlic, onion, salt, black pepper, and cayenne pepper. It is commonly used as a marinade for grilled meats, poultry, or seafood. It also is an accompaniment to top sandwiches and salads.

Chimichurri: In a blender combine 1 cup lightly packed fresh cilantro leaves, 1 cup lightly packed fresh Italian parsley leaves, 2 tablespoons white wine vinegar, 1 tablespoon ground cumin, 1 teaspoon crushed red pepper, and ¼ teaspoon salt. Cover; with blender running on low speed, slowly add ¼ cup olive oil or salad oil.

Nutrition Facts per serving: 650 cal., 44 g total fat (13 g sat. fat), 162 mg chol., 563 mg sodium, 28 g carbo., 2 g fiber, 33 g pro. Daily Values: 34% vit. A, 31% vit. C, 6% calcium, 30% iron. Exchanges: 2 Starch 4 Medium-Fat Meat, 4 Fat

Grilled Plantains: Bias-cut 3 peeled plantains into ½-inch slices. Lightly brush with peanut or cooking oil. Grill directly over medium coals about 8 minutes or until centers are just soft, turning once halfway through grilling. Drain on paper towels. Serve warm.

SURF AND TURF BURGERS WITH SPICY MAYO

A surprising combination of shrimp with ground beef makes up these plump patties. Prepare the spicy mayo up to several days ahead of time, cover, and chill until you're ready to serve.

Prep: 30 minutes Grill: 18 minutes Chill: 1 hour
Makes: 4 servings

1½ **pounds lean ground beef**
  4 **ounces peeled and cooked baby**
    shrimp, chopped
  2 **tablespoons snipped fresh dill**
½ **teaspoon sea salt**
  4 **large onion or sesame kaiser**
    rolls, split
  1 **recipe Spicy Mayo**
    Lettuce (optional)
    Sliced tomatoes (optional)
    Sweet pickle slices (optional)

1 In a large bowl combine ground beef, shrimp, dill, sea salt, and ¼ teaspoon black pepper; mix well. Shape mixture into four 1-inch-thick patties.

2 For a charcoal grill, grill patties on the rack of an uncovered grill directly over medium coals for 18 to 23 minutes or until done (160°F), turning once halfway through grilling. (For a gas grill, preheat grill. Reduce heat to medium. Place patties on grill rack over heat. Cover; grill as above.)

3 Serve burgers on rolls with Spicy Mayo and, if desired, lettuce, tomatoes, and pickle slices.

Spicy Mayo: In a large skillet cook 1 large onion, finely chopped, in 1 tablespoon hot olive oil over medium-high heat for 7 minutes or until browned, stirring occasionally. Reduce heat to medium. Add 1 small shallot, minced, and 1 teaspoon purchased red curry paste; cook and stir for 2 minutes more. Transfer mixture to a bowl; cover and chill. Stir $\frac{1}{2}$ cup mayonnaise or salad dressing into chilled mixture. Cover and chill for 1 hour or until ready to serve.

Nutrition Facts per serving: 498 cal., 32 g total fat (6 g sat. fat), 93 mg chol., 867 mg sodium, 30 g carbo., 1 g fiber, 21 g pro. Daily Values: 3% vit. A, 10% vit. C, 3% calcium, 17% iron. Exchanges: 2½ Starch, ½ Medium-Fat Meat, 6½ Fat

SMOKIN' HOT TIP

Juicy grilled burgers are easy to achieve when you follow these tips.

● **Choose ground beef that is not too lean. Whether using chuck or sirloin, 15 to 20 percent fat is ideal to maintain moisture and flavor.**

● **Use a measuring cup or shape ground beef into a log and cut into patties to achieve a consistent portion size for even cooking.**

● **When forming patties, don't overhandle the ground beef. A few pats are all that is needed.**

● **Once on the grill, do not press down on the burgers with a spatula. Doing so releases valuable juices needed to keep burgers moist and tender.**

SASSY MEAT LOAF

If you've never grilled meat loaf, give it a try. More moist than oven-cooked, this version features a mixture of beef and pork.

Prep: 30 minutes Grill: 1 hour
Makes: 6 to 8 servings

$1\frac{1}{4}$ **cups soft bread crumbs**
$\frac{1}{4}$ **cup milk**
1 slightly beaten egg
1 cup shredded taco cheese
$\frac{1}{2}$ **cup shredded carrot**
$\frac{1}{4}$ **cup bottled steak sauce**
1 to 2 tablespoons prepared horseradish
$\frac{1}{2}$ **teaspoon seasoned salt**
$\frac{1}{2}$ **teaspoon black pepper**
1 pound ground beef
8 ounces ground pork

1 In a large bowl combine bread crumbs, milk, and egg. Add cheese, carrot, 2 tablespoons of the steak sauce, the horseradish, seasoned salt, and pepper. Add ground meats; mix well.

2 Shape meat loaf into an 8×4-inch loaf. Fold a 24×18-inch piece of heavy foil in half crosswise. Trim to 12-inches square. Cut several large slits in the foil. Place meat on foil.

3 For a charcoal grill, arrange medium coals around a drip pan. Test for medium-low heat above pan. Place foil with meat loaf on grill rack over drip pan. Cover; grill for 60 to 70 minutes or until meat is no longer pink (160°F), brushing with remaining 2 tablespoons steak sauce during the last 5 minutes of grilling. (For a gas grill, preheat grill. Reduce heat to medium-low. Adjust for indirect cooking. Grill as above.)

4 Carefully remove meat loaf from grill. Cover with foil; let stand 15 minutes before slicing.

Nutrition Facts per serving: 305 cal., 13 g total fat (9 g sat. fat), 117 mg chol., 534 mg sodium, 8 g carbo., 2 g fiber, 22 g pro. Daily Values: 64% vit. A, 6% vit. C, 14% calcium, 12% iron. Exchanges: ½ Other Carbo, 3 Medium-Fat Meat, 2½ Fat

BACON-WRAPPED BEEF AND VEGETABLE BURGERS

Prep: 30 minutes Grill: 20 minutes
Makes: 5 servings

1 **pound lean ground beef**
1/4 **teaspoon lemon-pepper seasoning**
1/4 **cup grated Parmesan cheese**
1 **4-ounce can mushroom stems and pieces, drained and chopped**
3 **tablespoons finely chopped pimiento-stuffed olives**
2 **tablespoons finely chopped onion**
2 **tablespoons finely chopped green sweet pepper**
10 **slices bacon, partially cooked**

1 On waxed paper pat ground beef into a 12×7½-inch rectangle. Sprinkle with lemon-pepper seasoning and ⅛ teaspoon salt. Top with Parmesan cheese. Combine mushrooms, olives, onion, and sweet pepper; sprinkle evenly over meat. Lightly press into meat.

2 Starting from a short side, carefully roll meat into a spiral. Cut into five 1½-inch slices. Wrap the edge of each slice with two strips of partially cooked bacon, overlapping as needed and securing ends with wooden toothpicks.

3 For a charcoal grill, grill meat on the rack of an uncovered grill directly over medium coals about 20 minutes or until meat is done (160°F), turning once halfway through grilling. (For a gas grill, preheat grill. Reduce heat to medium. Place patties on grill rack over heat. Cover; grill as above.) If desired, serve with cherry tomatoes.

Nutrition Facts per serving: 271 cal., 18 g total fat (7 g sat. fat), 74 mg chol., 672 mg sodium, 2 g carbo., 1 g fiber, 23 g pro. Daily Values: 2% vit. A, 7% vit. C, 7% calcium, 12% iron. Exchanges: 3 Medium-Fat Meat, ½ High-Fat Meat

Bacon-Wrapped Beef and Vegetable Burgers

MOROCCAN RIB ROAST

You can prepare this recipe using leg of lamb instead of a beef rib roast, if you wish. For a 3- to 4-pound leg of lamb, grill for 2 to 3 hours or until a meat thermometer registers 150°F for medium doneness.

Prep: 15 minutes Grill: 2 hours Stand: 15 minutes
Makes: 8 to 10 servings

1 **4- to 5-pound beef rib roast**
2 **tablespoons coriander seeds, crushed**
2 **tablespoons finely shredded lemon peel**
1 **tablespoon olive oil**
1 **teaspoon whole cumin seeds, crushed**
½ **to 1 teaspoon crushed red pepper**
½ **teaspoon coarse salt**
8 **cloves garlic, peeled and cut into slivers**

1 Trim fat from meat. For rub, in a small bowl stir together coriander seeds, lemon peel, olive oil, cumin, crushed red pepper, and salt. Sprinkle over surface of meat; rub in with your fingers.

2 Cut ½-inch-wide slits randomly into top and sides of roast. Insert garlic slivers deep into slits. If desired, cover and chill for up to 24 hours. Insert a meat thermometer into center of meat.

3 For a charcoal grill, arrange medium coals around a drip pan. Test for medium-low heat above pan. Place roast, bone side down, on grill rack over drip pan. Cover; grill until thermometer registers desired doneness. Allow 2 to 2½ hours for medium-rare (135°F) or 2¼ to 2¾ hours for medium doneness (150°F). (For a gas grill, preheat grill. Reduce heat to medium-low. Adjust for indirect cooking. Grill as above, except place meat on rack in roasting pan.)

4 Remove meat from grill. Cover with foil; let stand for 15 minutes before slicing. (The meat temperature will rise 10°F during standing.)

Nutrition Facts per serving: 228 cal., 11 g total fat (4 g sat. fat), 68 mg chol., 196 mg sodium, 2 g carbo., 1 g fiber, 29 g pro. Daily Values: 5% vit. C, 3% calcium, 16% iron. Exchanges: 4 Lean Meat

PEPPERED RIB ROAST

A robust pepper-and-herb rub clings to the meat throughout grilling.

Prep: 10 minutes Grill: 2 hours Stand: 15 minutes
Makes: 10 to 12 servings

1 6-pound beef rib roast
**4 teaspoons coarsely ground
      black pepper**
2 tablespoons finely chopped shallots
1 teaspoon coarse salt
1 teaspoon dried basil, crushed
1 teaspoon dried thyme, crushed
1 tablespoon olive oil

1 Trim fat from meat. For rub, combine pepper, shallots, salt, basil, and thyme. Brush meat with oil. Rub pepper mixture over surface of roast with fingers. Insert a meat thermometer into center of meat without touching bone.

2 For a charcoal grill, arrange medium coals around drip pan. Test for medium-low heat above pan. Place roast, bone side down, on grill rack over drip pan. Cover; grill until meat thermometer registers desired doneness. Allow 2 to 2¾ hours for medium-rare (135°F) or 2½ to 3¼ hours for medium doneness (150°F). (For a gas grill, preheat grill. Reduce heat to medium-low. Adjust for indirect cooking. Grill as above, except place meat on a rack in a roasting pan.)

3 Remove meat from grill. Cover with foil and let stand for 15 minutes before slicing. (The meat's temperature will rise 10°F during standing.)

Nutrition Facts per serving: 310 cal., 18 g total fat (7 g sat. fat), 100 mg chol., 305 mg sodium, 1 g carbo., 0 g fiber, 34 g pro. Daily Values: 2% vit. A, 2% vit. C, 1% calcium, 23% iron. Exchanges: 5 Lean Meat, ½ Fat

RIBEYES WITH CHIPOTLE BUTTER

Prep: 20 minutes Grill: 10 minutes
Makes: 4 servings

2 teaspoons ground cumin
1 teaspoon paprika
½ teaspoon salt
½ teaspoon ground white pepper
1 tablespoon olive oil
**¼ teaspoon adobo sauce (from canned
      chipotle pepper in adobo sauce)**
4 beef ribeye steaks, cut 1 inch thick
1 recipe Chipotle Butter

1 In a small bowl stir together cumin, paprika, salt, and pepper. Stir in oil and adobo sauce until a paste forms. Spread mixture over both sides of steaks.

2 For a charcoal grill, grill steaks on the rack of an uncovered grill directly over medium coals until desired doneness, turning once halfway through grilling. Allow 10 to 12 minutes for medium-rare (145°F) or 12 to 15 minutes for medium doneness (160°F). (For a gas grill, preheat grill. Reduce heat to medium. Place steaks on grill rack over heat. Cover; grill as above.) Serve with Chipotle Butter.

Chipotle Butter: In a small bowl combine ¼ cup butter, softened; 1 tablespoon finely chopped shallots; 2 teaspoons snipped fresh basil or thyme; 1½ teaspoons lime juice; and 1 teaspoon finely chopped chipotle pepper in adobo sauce. Stir until combined; set aside.

Nutrition Facts per serving: 416 cal., 27 g total fat (12 g sat. fat), 118 mg chol., 519 mg sodium, 2 g carbo., 1 g fiber, 40 g pro. Daily Values: 17% vit. A, 4% vit. C, 3% calcium, 19% iron. Exchanges: 6 Lean Meat, 2 Fat

FOOD FOR THOUGHT BEEF RIB ROAST

A rib roast is cut from the sixth through twelfth ribs along the upper section of the back of the animal. The "small end" is closest to the loin and therefore relatively lean, tender, and flavorful. The "large end" is closer to the chuck primal, making it slightly less tender. This roast is featured as "prime rib" on most restaurant menus or also may be called a standing rib roast.

ROASTED GARLIC STEAK

Roasting the garlic with herbs results in a delicious, mild garlic flavor that brings out the best in beef.

Prep: 15 minutes Grill: 30 minutes
Makes: 6 servings

1 or 2 whole garlic bulb(s)
3 to 4 teaspoons snipped fresh basil
    or 1 teaspoon dried basil, crushed
1 tablespoon snipped fresh rosemary
    or 1 teaspoon dried rosemary,
    crushed
2 tablespoons olive oil or cooking oil
1½ pounds beef ribeye steaks or
    boneless sirloin steak, cut
    1 inch thick
1 to 2 teaspoons cracked black
    pepper
½ teaspoon salt

1 With a sharp knife, cut off the top ½ inch from each garlic bulb to expose the ends of the individual cloves. Leaving garlic bulb(s) whole, remove any loose, papery outer layers.

2 Fold a 20×18-inch piece of heavy foil in half crosswise. Trim into a 10-inch square. Place garlic bulb(s), cut sides up, in center of foil square. Sprinkle garlic with basil and rosemary and drizzle with oil. Bring up opposite edges of foil and seal with a double fold. Fold remaining edges together to completely enclose garlic, leaving space for steam to build.

3 For a charcoal grill, grill garlic on the rack of an uncovered grill directly over medium coals about 30 minutes or until garlic feels soft when packet is squeezed, turning garlic occasionally.

4 Meanwhile, trim fat from steaks. Sprinkle pepper and salt evenly over both sides of steaks; rub in with your fingers. While garlic is grilling, add steaks to grill. Grill to desired doneness, turning once halfway through grilling. For ribeye steaks, allow 10 to 12 minutes for medium-rare (145°F) and 12 to 15 minutes for medium doneness (160°F). For sirloin steak, allow 14 to 18 minutes for medium-rare (145°F) and 18 to 22 minutes for medium doneness (160°F). (For a gas grill, preheat grill. Reduce heat to medium. Place garlic, then steaks on grill rack over heat. Cover; grill as above.)

5 To serve, cut steaks into 6 serving-size pieces. Remove garlic from foil, reserving oil mixture. Squeeze garlic pulp from each clove onto steaks. Mash pulp slightly with a fork; spread over steaks. Drizzle with reserved oil mixture.

Nutrition Facts per serving: 189 cal., 9 g total fat (2 g sat. fat), 52 mg chol., 139 mg sodium, 4 g carbo., 0 g fiber, 22 g pro. Daily Values: 1% vit. A, 6% vit. C, 3% calcium, 14% iron. Exchanges: 3 Lean Meat, ½ Fat

RIBEYES WITH AVOCADO SAUCE

Ribeye is one of the most tender and flavorful steaks you can buy. Its partner, the rib steak, is basically the same cut with the addition of a large, curved bone on the side. Both steaks taste great grilled.

Prep: 25 minutes Chill: 30 minutes Grill: 15 minutes
Makes: 4 to 6 servings

2 12-ounce beef ribeye steaks or
    boneless top loin steaks,
    cut 1¼ to 1½ inches thick
1 tablespoon packed brown sugar
1 teaspoon chili powder
½ teaspoon garlic salt
½ teaspoon black pepper
8 ounces fresh tomatillos, husked
    and quartered (6 medium)
¼ cup water
2 ounces cream cheese
1 avocado, halved, seeded, peeled,
    and cut up
¼ cup sliced green onions (2)
1 medium red onion, cut into
    ½-inch slices
1 teaspoon cooking oil

1 Trim fat from steaks. For rub, in a small bowl combine brown sugar, chili powder, garlic salt, and pepper. Sprinkle rub evenly over both sides of the steaks; rub in with your fingers. Cover and chill for 30 minutes.

2 Meanwhile, for sauce, in a small saucepan bring tomatillos and water to boiling; reduce heat. Cover and simmer for 5 to 7 minutes or until tomatillos are soft. Drain. Stir in cream cheese until melted; cool mixture slightly. In a food processor or blender combine tomatillo mixture, avocado, sliced green onions, and ½ teaspoon salt; cover and process or blend until smooth. Transfer sauce to a serving bowl.

3 For a charcoal grill, grill steaks on rack of an uncovered grill directly over medium coals until desired doneness, turning once halfway through grilling. Allow 15 to 19 minutes for medium-rare (145°F) or 18 to 23 minutes for medium doneness (160°F). Brush the onion slices lightly with oil. Grill directly over medium heat about 5 minutes, turning occasionally. (For a gas grill, preheat grill. Reduce heat to medium. Place steaks, then onion slices on grill rack over heat. Cover; grill as at left.)

4 To serve, slice steaks. Serve with sauce and grilled onions.

Nutrition Facts per serving: 425 cal., 24 g total fat (8 g sat. fat), 96 mg chol., 556 mg sodium, 13 g carbo., 4 g fiber, 40 g pro. Daily Values: 11% vit. A, 19% vit. C, 4% calcium, 21% iron. Exchanges: ½ Vegetable, ½ Other Carbo., 5½ Lean Meat, 1½ Fat

Ribeyes with Avocado Sauce

COUNTRY FRENCH RIBEYES

Prep: 5 minutes Grill: 10 minutes
Makes: 4 servings

4 beef ribeye steaks, cut 1 inch thick
5 green onions
2 teaspoons dried lavender, crushed
2 teaspoons dried thyme, crushed
1 teaspoon coarsely ground black pepper
1/2 teaspoon freshly ground rock sea salt or coarse salt
1 tablespoon olive oil
4 to 8 roma tomatoes
1 recipe Steak Fries (optional)

1 Trim fat from steaks. Finely chop 1 green onion; set remaining onions aside. For rub, in a small bowl combine chopped onion, lavender, thyme, pepper, and sea salt. Sprinkle over both sides of steaks; rub in with your fingers. Brush steaks with half of the olive oil. Brush tomatoes and remaining green onions with remaining oil.

2 For a charcoal grill, grill steaks on the rack of an uncovered grill directly over medium coals until desired doneness, turning once halfway through grilling. Allow 10 to 12 minutes for medium-rare (145°F) or 12 to 15 minutes for medium doneness (160°F). Grill tomatoes and onions for 8 to 10 minutes or until slightly charred, turning several times. (For a gas grill, preheat grill. Reduce heat to medium. Place steaks, tomatoes, and onions on grill rack over heat. Cover; grill as above.) Serve steaks with vegetables and, if desired, Steak Fries.

Nutrition Facts per serving: 433 cal., 18 g total fat (5 g sat. fat), 94 mg chol., 422 mg sodium, 18 g carbo., 3 g fiber, 46 g pro. Daily Values: 19% vit. A, 5% vit. C, 48% calcium, 29% iron. Exchanges: 1 Starch, 6 Lean Meat

Steak Fries: Cut 2 medium potatoes into 1/4-inch wedges. Toss wedges with 2 teaspoons olive oil. Add seasoned salt to taste. Fold a 36×18-inch piece of heavy foil in half to make an 18-inch square. Arrange potatoes evenly in center of square. Bring up opposite edges of foil. Seal with a double fold. Fold remaining edges together to completely enclose potatoes, leaving space for steam to build. Grill packet on grill rack directly over medium coals about 25 minutes or until tender.

RIBEYE STEAKS WITH SWEET ONION RELISH

Prep: 25 minutes Grill: 10 minutes
Makes: 4 servings

4 beef ribeye steaks, cut 1 inch thick
1 teaspoon coarse salt
3/4 teaspoon cracked black pepper
1/2 teaspoon mustard seed, coarsely ground
1 Vidalia or other sweet onion, halved and thinly sliced
1 clove garlic, minced
1 tablespoon olive oil
1/4 cup chopped red sweet pepper
1 fresh jalapeño chile pepper, seeded and finely chopped (see tip, page 36)
2 tablespoons balsamic vinegar
1 teaspoon packed brown sugar
1/2 teaspoon dried sage, crushed

1 Trim fat from steaks. For rub, combine salt, pepper, and mustard seed; divide in half. Sprinkle half of the rub onto one side of each steak; rub in with your fingers. Set aside.

2 In a large skillet cook onion and garlic in hot olive oil over medium heat about 5 minutes or until tender. Add sweet pepper and jalapeño pepper; cook and stir 1 minute more. Add balsamic vinegar, brown sugar, sage, and remaining rub; cook and stir 1 minute more. Cover; keep warm.

3 For a charcoal grill, grill steaks on the rack of an uncovered grill directly over medium coals until desired doneness, turning once halfway through grilling. Allow 10 to 12 minutes for medium-rare (145°F) and 12 to 15 minutes for medium doneness (160°F). (For a gas grill, preheat grill. Reduce heat to medium. Place steaks on grill rack over heat. Cover; grill as above.) Serve steaks with onion mixture.

Nutrition Facts per serving: 320 cal., 14 g total fat (4 g sat. fat), 81 mg chol., 575 mg sodium, 8 g carbo., 1 g fiber, 38 g pro. Daily Values: 11% vit. A, 38% vit. C, 3% calcium, 18% iron. Exchanges: 1/2 Other Carbo., 51/2 Lean Meat

FOOD FOR THOUGHT
SWEET ONIONS

Sweet onions have the same onion flavor as regular onions, but they are much more mild and sweet. They contain lower levels of the sulfur compounds which cause tears and must contain a minimum of 6% sugar to qualify as sweet. Sweets are picked in the spring and early summer, cured for a short time, and sent directly to market, making them exceptionally fresh compared to regular onions, which are stored for year-round availability. Sweet onions have a slightly flattened shape and have thinner, lighter skins. The more common varieties are listed here:

● Vidalia: **The grandparent of American sweet onions. Available April to June.**

● SpringSweet and 1015 SuperSweet: **Developed by Texas A&M University, these are the first spring onions on the market. Available March to June.**

● Walla Walla: **Grown in Southeast Washington and Northeast Oregon, this onion came to the United States via a French soldier who picked it up in Italy in the late 1800s. Available June to August.**

● Sweet Imperial: **This is the Californian version of the Vidalia. Available April to June.**

● Maui: **These famous Hawaiian onions are grown in volcanic soil. Available April to December.**

● Cippolini: **Featured in Italian Kabobs with Herbed Orzo, page 163, this trendy Italian newcomer has a small flat shape with a sweet, mild flavor that is great for grilling and making kabobs.**

RIBEYE STEAKS WITH HOT-AS-HECK SAUCE

You like spicy? Here's spicy. Sizzling ribeye steaks fire up your palate with a hot and smoky chipotle pepper sauce.

Prep: 10 minutes Cook: 20 minutes Grill: 10 minutes
Makes: 4 servings

- ⅓ **cup sugar**
- ½ **cup finely chopped onion**
- 2 **cloves garlic, minced**
- 1½ **cups light beer or water**
- 1 **6-ounce can tomato paste**
- ¼ **cup Worcestershire sauce**
- ¼ **cup vinegar**
- 1 **to 2 tablespoons bottled habanero hot pepper sauce**
- 1 **tablespoon chopped canned chipotle peppers in adobo sauce**
- 4 **beef ribeye steaks or sirloin strip steaks, cut 1 inch thick**

1 For sauce, in a medium saucepan cook sugar over medium-high heat until it begins to melt, shaking the pan occasionally (do not stir). Reduce heat to low; add onion and garlic. Cook and stir for 5 minutes more or until mixture is golden brown. In a small skillet bring beer just to boiling. Carefully and gradually add boiling beer to sugar mixture, stirring constantly. Whisk in tomato paste, Worcestershire sauce, vinegar, habanero sauce, and chipotle peppers. Bring to boiling; reduce heat. Simmer, uncovered, for 15 to 20 minutes or to desired consistency. Set aside.

2 For a charcoal grill, grill steaks on the rack of an uncovered grill directly over medium coals until desired doneness, turning once and brushing with some of the sauce during the last few minutes of grilling. Allow 10 to 12 minutes for medium-rare (145°F) or 12 to 15 minutes for medium doneness (160°F). (For a gas grill, preheat grill. Reduce heat to medium. Place steaks on grill rack over heat. Cover; grill as above.)

3 Pass remaining sauce with steaks. Cover and chill any remaining sauce for up to 1 week.

Nutrition Facts per serving: 572 cal., 18 g total fat (7 g sat. fat), 134 mg chol., 532 mg sodium, 31 g carbo., 2 g fiber, 65 g pro. Daily Values: 2% vit. A, 19% vit. C, 5% calcium, 38% iron. Exchanges: 2 Other Carbo., 9 Very Lean Meat, 3 Fat

FIVE-SPICE TRI-TIP ROAST
WITH DAIKON RELISH

Five-spice powder, often used in Asian cooking, is slightly sweet and mildly spicy. Find it at Asian markets and in the spice section at supermarkets.

Prep: 10 minutes Chill: 2 to 4 hours Grill: 35 minutes
Stand: 15 minutes Makes: 6 servings

1 1½- to 2-pound boneless beef
    tri-tip roast (bottom sirloin)
1 tablespoon toasted sesame oil
2 teaspoons five-spice powder
1 recipe Daikon Relish

1 Trim fat from meat. In a small bowl combine sesame oil, five-spice powder, and ½ teaspoon salt. Rub oil mixture over meat with your fingers. Place meat in a self-sealing plastic bag; seal bag. Chill in refrigerator for 2 to 4 hours.

2 For a charcoal grill, arrange medium-hot coals around a drip pan. Test for medium heat above the pan. Place roast on grill rack over drip pan. Cover; grill until desired doneness. Allow 35 to 40 minutes for medium-rare (135°F) or 40 to 45 minutes for medium doneness (150°F). (For a gas grill, preheat grill. Reduce heat to medium. Adjust for indirect cooking. Grill as above, except place meat on a rack in a roasting pan.) Remove meat from grill. Cover with foil and let stand for 15 minutes before slicing. (Meat temperature will rise 10°F during standing.) Serve slices topped with Daikon Relish.

Daikon Relish: Finely chop 8 ounces peeled daikon radish or jicama (you should have about 1¾ cups). In a medium bowl combine chopped daikon, ⅓ cup seasoned rice vinegar, 1 teaspoon crushed red pepper, and ½ teaspoon toasted sesame oil.

Nutrition Facts per serving: 196 cal., 8 g total fat (2 g sat. fat), 54 mg chol., 267 mg sodium, 3 g carbo., 1 g fiber, 26 g pro. Daily Values: 2% vit. A, 15% vit. C, 3% calcium, 16% iron. Exchanges: 4 Very Lean Meat, 1 Fat

RASPBERRY-SESAME
TRI-TIP ROAST

Raspberry vinaigrette salad dressing does double duty as both marinade for the beef and dressing for the crisp slaw.

Prep: 25 minutes Marinate: 2 to 4 hours Grill: 35 minutes
Stand: 15 minutes Makes: 6 servings

1 1½- to 2-pound boneless beef
    tri-tip roast (bottom sirloin)
1¼ cups bottled raspberry vinaigrette
    salad dressing
¼ cup sesame seeds, toasted
3 cups shredded romaine lettuce
1 cup thinly sliced Belgian endive
½ of a small red onion, very
    thinly sliced

1 Trim fat from meat. Place meat in a self-sealing plastic bag set in a shallow dish. Pour 1 cup of the salad dressing over meat; seal bag. Marinate in the refrigerator for 2 to 4 hours, turning bag occasionally. Drain meat, discarding marinade. Coat meat with sesame seeds (some seeds will fall off during handling and grilling).

2 For a charcoal grill, arrange medium coals around a drip pan. Test for medium heat above pan. Place roast on lightly oiled grill rack over drip pan. Cover; grill until desired doneness. Allow 35 to 40 minutes for medium-rare (135°F) or 40 to 45 minutes for medium doneness (150°F). (For gas grill, preheat grill. Reduce heat to medium. Adjust for indirect grilling. Grill as above, except place meat on a rack in a roasting pan.)

3 Remove meat from grill. Cover with foil and let stand for 15 minutes before slicing. (The meat's temperature will rise 10°F during standing.)

4 Meanwhile, for slaw, in a medium bowl combine romaine, endive, and onion. Toss with remaining salad dressing. Cover and chill until ready to serve. Slice meat and serve with slaw.

Nutrition Facts per serving: 297 cal., 15 g total fat (2 g sat. fat), 54 mg chol., 616 mg sodium, 11 g carbo., 1 g fiber, 27 g pro. Daily Values: 15% vit. A, 14% vit. C, 2% calcium, 17% iron. Exchanges: 1 Vegetable, ½ Other Carbo., 3½ Lean Meat, 1 Fat

TRI-TIP ROAST WITH JAMBALAYA RICE

The tri-tip beef roast, appropriately named after its triangular shape, usually weighs about 2 pounds and is ideal for grilling or braising. If you can't find a beef roast labeled "tri-tip" in your supermarket, look instead for a sirloin roast or sirloin steak that is cut 1½ to 2 inches thick.

Prep: 25 minutes Grill: 35 minutes Stand: 15 minutes
Makes: 6 servings

¼ **cup soy sauce**
2 **tablespoons finely chopped onion**
2 **tablespoons granulated sugar**
2 **tablespoons packed brown sugar**
2 **tablespoons lemon juice**
1 **tablespoon vinegar**
½ **teaspoon chili powder**
1 **1½- to 2-pound boneless beef**
   tri-tip roast (bottom sirloin)
1 **recipe Jambalaya Rice**

1 For sauce, stir together soy sauce, onion, granulated sugar, brown sugar, lemon juice, vinegar, and chili powder; set aside.

2 For a charcoal grill, arrange medium-hot coals around a drip pan. Test for medium heat above pan. Place roast on grill rack over drip pan. Cover; grill until desired doneness. Allow 35 to 40 minutes for medium-rare (135°F) or 40 to 45 minutes for medium doneness (150°F). Brush meat often with sauce during last 10 minutes of grilling. (For a gas grill, preheat grill. Reduce heat to medium. Adjust for indirect cooking. Grill as above, except place meat on rack in roasting pan.)

3 Remove meat from grill. Cover with foil and let stand for 15 minutes before slicing. (Meat temperature will rise 10°F during standing.) Slice meat and serve with Jambalaya Rice.

Jambalaya Rice: In a large saucepan cook 4 ounces bulk hot Italian sausage until lightly browned. Add 1 cup chopped celery, ¾ cup chopped red sweet pepper, ¾ cup chopped yellow sweet pepper, ⅓ cup chopped onion, and 1 clove garlic, minced. Cook and stir for 5 minutes. Add ¾ cup long grain rice, ¼ teaspoon cayenne pepper, and ¼ teaspoon paprika; cook and stir 2 minutes more. Add one 10½-ounce can condensed cream of mushroom or cream of chicken soup and 1¼ cups water. Bring just to boiling; reduce heat. Cover and simmer for 15 to 20 minutes or until rice is tender, stirring occasionally.

Nutrition Facts per serving: 408 cal., 14 g total fat (5 g sat. fat), 67 mg chol., 1156 mg sodium, 36 g carbo., 2 g fiber, 32 g pro. Daily Values: 17% vit. A, 102% vit. C, 5% calcium, 22% iron. Exchanges: 2 Starch, 3½ Lean Meat

FOOD FOR THOUGHT BEEF TRI-TIP ROAST

California's best kept secret, tri-tip, gained popularity as part of the Santa Maria community's traditional barbecue. This unique roast comes from the bottom sirloin and is triangular in shape, thus its name "tri-tip" or "triangle roast." Used whole as a roast or cut into steaks, the tri-tip roast offers the same great taste as top sirloin. It is tender and therefore doesn't require marinating before cooking. However, it is ideal for use with rubs as it holds the flavor well, especially when grilled, barbecued, or roasted.

ITALIAN KABOBS WITH HERBED ORZO

Because of their petite size, cipollini onions are time-consuming to peel. Drop them into boiling water for 30 seconds, and the peel will be easier to remove.

Prep: 50 minutes Marinate: 6 to 24 hours Grill: 12 minutes
Makes: 4 servings

> **2** tablespoons olive oil
> **12** cipollini onions, peeled and ends trimmed
> **12** medium fresh cremini mushrooms
> **1** large red sweet pepper, cut into 12 pieces
> **1½** pounds boneless beef sirloin steak, cut into 1½-inch cubes
> **1** 8-ounce bottle Italian vinaigrette salad dressing (about 1 cup)
> **1** recipe Herbed Orzo

1 In a large skillet heat oil over medium heat. Arrange onions in an even layer in hot oil; cook 2 to 3 minutes on each side or until browned and just tender, turning once (do not stir). Reduce heat; add mushrooms. Cook, covered, 3 to 5 minutes or until mushrooms are almost tender. Transfer onions and mushrooms to a dish; set aside until cool.

2 Place onions, mushrooms, sweet pepper, and beef in a self-sealing plastic bag set in a shallow dish. Pour salad dressing over mixture; seal bag. Marinate in the refrigerator for 6 to 24 hours, turning bag occasionally. On four 12- to 14-inch metal skewers, alternately thread beef and vegetables, leaving a ¼-inch space between pieces. Transfer remaining marinade to a saucepan; bring to boiling. Set aside.

3 For a charcoal grill, grill kabobs on the rack of an uncovered grill directly over medium coals for 12 to 14 minutes for medium doneness (160°F), turning occasionally and brushing with some of the remaining marinade during the last 2 minutes of grilling. (For a gas grill, preheat grill. Reduce heat to medium. Place kabobs on grill rack over heat. Cover; grill as above.) Serve with Herbed Orzo. Pass hot marinade.

Herbed Orzo: Prepare 1 cup orzo (rosamarina) according to package directions; drain. Stir in 2 tablespoons olive oil and 1 tablespoon snipped fresh herb, such as oregano, marjoram, and/or thyme. Season to taste with salt and black pepper. If desired, top with freshly grated Parmigiano-Reggiano cheese.

Nutrition Facts per serving: 803 cal., 48 g total fat (8 g sat. fat), 80 mg chol., 836 mg sodium, 49 g carbo., 4 g fiber, 45 g pro. Daily Values: 44% vit. A, 128% vit. C, 7% calcium, 33% iron. Exchanges: 1½ Vegetable, 2 Starch, 1 Other Carbo., 5 Lean Meat, 6 Fat

BLT STEAK

A loaf of crusty bread and a bottle of red wine complete this bistro-style dinner.

Start to Finish: 30 minutes
Makes: 4 servings

> **2** boneless beef top loin steaks, cut 1¼ inches thick
> **2** slices bacon
> **½** cup bottled balsamic vinaigrette salad dressing
> **8** slices red and/or yellow tomato
> **2** cups mixed baby salad greens

1 Trim fat from steaks. For a charcoal grill, grill steaks on the rack of an uncovered grill directly over medium coals until desired doneness, turning once halfway through grilling. Allow 13 to 17 minutes for medium-rare (145°F) or 17 to 21 minutes for medium doneness (160°F). (For a gas grill, preheat grill. Reduce heat to medium. Place steaks on grill rack over heat. Cover; grill as above.)

2 Meanwhile, in a large skillet cook bacon over medium heat until crisp. Remove bacon and drain on paper towels. Crumble bacon and set aside. Drain fat, reserving 1 tablespoon drippings in skillet. Add the salad dressing to the skillet. Cook and stir over high heat about 1 minute, scraping up browned bits. Remove from heat.

3 To serve, halve the steaks. Place a piece of steak on each of four dinner plates. Top each steak with 2 tomato slices, some cooked bacon, some mixed greens, and a splash of the hot dressing from the skillet.

Nutrition Facts per serving: 556 cal., 42 g total fat (14 g sat. fat), 122 mg chol., 636 mg sodium, 5 g carbo., 1 g fiber, 38 g pro. Daily Values: 6% vit. A, 12% vit. C, 2% calcium, 17% iron. Exchanges: 1 Vegetable, 3 Lean Meat, 2 Fat

EASY STEAK AND POTATO KABOBS

This is the perfect kabob for the meat-and-potato lover. The marinade, based on bottled salad dressing, is deliciously easy.

Prep: 20 minutes Marinate: 4 to 6 hours Grill: 8 minutes
Makes: 4 servings

1 boneless beef sirloin steak,
   cut 1 inch thick
¼ cup bottled red wine vinegar and oil
   salad dressing
2 tablespoons snipped fresh thyme or
   2 teaspoons dried thyme, crushed
2 tablespoons Worcestershire sauce
¼ teaspoon garlic powder
2 medium green and/or yellow sweet
   peppers, cut into 1-inch squares
1 medium red onion, cut into wedges
½ of a 20-ounce package refrigerated
   potato wedges (about 32 wedges)

1 Trim fat from steak. Cut steak into 1-inch cubes. Place steak cubes in a self-sealing plastic bag set in a shallow dish. For marinade, in a bowl combine the salad dressing, thyme, Worcestershire sauce, and garlic powder. Pour over steak; seal bag. Marinate in the refrigerator for 4 to 6 hours, turning bag occasionally.

2 Drain steak, reserving marinade. On eight 10-inch metal skewers, alternately thread steak, sweet peppers, onion, and potato wedges, leaving a ¼-inch space between pieces.

3 For a charcoal grill, grill kabobs on the rack of an uncovered grill directly over medium coals for 8 to 12 minutes for medium doneness (160°F), turning once and brushing occasionally with reserved marinade up to the last 5 minutes of grilling. (For a gas grill, preheat grill. Reduce heat to medium. Place kabobs on grill rack over heat. Cover; grill as above.) Discard remaining marinade.

Nutrition Facts per serving: 230 cal., 5 g total fat (2 g sat. fat), 69 mg chol., 230 mg sodium, 17 g carbo., 4 g fiber, 27 g pro. Daily Values: 8% vit. A, 85% vit. C, 2% calcium, 24% iron. Exchanges: ½ Vegetable, 1 Starch, 3½ Very Lean Meat, ½ Fat

Easy Steak and Potato Kabobs

CURRIED STEAK WITH MANGO-CUCUMBER RELISH

An oil seasoned with red pepper and curry lends just the right amount of heat to tender steaks. The mint-infused relish is a cool contrast.

Prep: 35 minutes Grill: 10 minutes
Makes: 4 servings

1 tablespoon cooking oil
1 teaspoon curry powder
¼ teaspoon salt
¼ teaspoon crushed red pepper
4 boneless beef top loin steaks,
**   cut 1 inch thick**
1 recipe Mango-Cucumber Relish

1 In a small bowl stir together oil, curry powder, salt, and crushed red pepper; set aside. Trim fat from steaks.

2 For a charcoal grill, grill steaks on the rack of an uncovered grill directly over medium coals until desired doneness, brushing with oil mixture halfway through grilling. Turn steaks and brush lightly again with oil mixture. Allow 10 to 12 minutes for medium-rare (145°F) or 12 to 15 minutes for medium doneness (160°F). (For a gas grill, preheat grill. Reduce heat to medium. Place steaks on grill rack over heat. Cover; grill as above.) Serve with Mango-Cucumber Relish.

Mango-Cucumber Relish: In a bowl combine 1¼ cups coarsely chopped, seeded cucumber; ¾ cup chopped mango; ⅓ cup chopped red onion; ⅓ cup chopped red or green sweet pepper; ⅓ cup chopped, peeled jicama; 2 tablespoons snipped fresh mint or parsley; 2 tablespoons seasoned rice vinegar; ½ teaspoon curry powder; ⅛ teaspoon salt; and ⅛ teaspoon crushed red pepper. Cover and chill up to 8 hours.

Nutrition Facts per serving: 391 cal., 14 g total fat (4 g sat. fat), 155 mg chol., 348 mg sodium, 9 g carbo., 1 g fiber, 55 g pro. Daily Values: 32% vit. A, 60% vit. C, 3% calcium, 41% iron. Exchanges: ½ Vegetable, ½ Other Carbo., 8 Very Lean Meat, 2 Fat

ONION-STUFFED STEAK

Serve these boldly flavored steaks with grill-roasted potatoes and a big salad. It's the kind of hearty meal that never goes out of style.

Prep: 20 minutes Grill: 10 minutes
Makes: 4 servings

4 boneless beef top loin steaks,
**   cut 1 inch thick**
1½ cups chopped onion
4 cloves garlic, minced
¼ cup butter or margarine
¼ teaspoon celery salt
¼ teaspoon black pepper
¼ cup dry red wine
2 tablespoons soy sauce
8 ounces fresh mushrooms, quartered
¼ cup butter or margarine

1 Cut a horizontal pocket in each steak, cutting almost to, but not through, the other side; set steaks aside.

2 In a large skillet cook onion and garlic in ¼ cup butter until onion is tender. Stir in celery salt and pepper. Stuff pockets with onion mixture; skewer closed. Mix wine and soy sauce; brush on steaks.

3 For a charcoal grill, grill steaks on the rack of an uncovered grill directly over medium coals until desired doneness, turning once halfway through grilling. Allow 10 to 12 minutes for medium-rare (145°F) or 12 to 15 minutes for medium doneness (160°F). (For a gas grill, preheat grill. Reduce heat to medium. Place steaks on grill rack over heat. Cover; grill as above.)

4 Meanwhile, in a large skillet cook mushrooms in remaining ¼ cup butter until tender. Serve steaks with mushrooms.

Nutrition Facts per serving: 511 cal., 34 g total fat (18 g sat. fat), 165 mg chol., 898 mg sodium, 8 g carbo., 2 g fiber, 41 g pro. Daily Values: 18% vit. A, 7% vit. C, 4% calcium, 20% iron. Exchanges: 1 Vegetable, 5½ Lean Meat, 3½ Fat

Southwestern
Steak Hero

SOUTHWESTERN STEAK HERO

Herbed crème fraîche cools the heat generated
by the peppery rub.

Prep: 20 minutes Chill: 4 to 8 hours Grill: 14 minutes
Makes: 4 servings

- 1 1-pound boneless beef sirloin steak,
  cut 1 inch thick
- 3 tablespoons olive oil
- 1 tablespoon chili powder
- 1 tablespoon paprika
- 1 teaspoon ground cumin
- 1 teaspoon garlic powder
- 1 teaspoon dried oregano, crushed
- ½ teaspoon salt
- ½ teaspoon black pepper
- ½ teaspoon cayenne pepper
- 4 hoagie buns, split
   Sweet-hot mustard (optional)
- 1 recipe Cilantro Crème Fraîche
   Prepared pico de gallo or bottled
   salsa (optional)

1 Trim fat from steak. For rub, in a small bowl combine oil, chili powder, paprika, cumin, garlic powder, oregano, salt, black pepper, and cayenne pepper. Sprinkle evenly over both sides of steak; rub in with your fingers. Place steak in a self-sealing plastic bag; seal bag. Chill in the refrigerator for 4 to 8 hours.

2 For a charcoal grill, grill steak on the rack of an uncovered grill directly over medium coals until desired doneness, turning once halfway through grilling. Allow 14 to 18 minutes for medium-rare (145°F) and 18 to 22 minutes for medium doneness (160°F). (For a gas grill, preheat grill. Reduce heat to medium. Place steak on the grill rack over heat. Cover; grill as above.) Remove steak from grill. Add buns, cut sides down, to grill. Grill for 1 to 2 minutes or until lightly toasted.

3 To serve, thinly slice steak. If desired, spread toasted buns with mustard. Top with steak slices, Cilantro Crème Fraîche, and, if desired, pico de gallo.

Cilantro Crème Fraîche: In a bowl combine ½ of a 7-ounce container (about ½ cup) crème fraîche and 3 tablespoons snipped fresh cilantro.

Nutrition Facts per serving: 589 cal., 27 g total fat (8 g sat. fat), 91 mg chol., 882 mg sodium, 54 g carbo., 4 g fiber, 33 g pro. Daily Values: 34% vit. A, 5% vit. C, 13% calcium, 32% iron. Exchanges: 3½ Starch, 3 Lean Meat, 3 Fat

FIRESTARTER STRIP STEAK WITH LIME AND SWEET ONION SALSA

One habanero pepper is plenty hot for the average palate, but if you're from the school of "the hotter, the better," use two.

Prep: 20 minutes Grill: 10 minutes
Makes: 4 servings

4 boneless beef top loin strip steaks, cut 1 inch thick
1 fresh habanero chile pepper, seeded and finely chopped (see tip, page 36)
1 tablespoon ground sage
1 recipe Lime and Sweet Onion Salsa

1 Trim fat from steaks. For rub, combine habanero pepper, sage, and ½ teaspoon salt. Sprinkle over both sides of steaks; rub in with your fingers. If desired, cover and chill for up to 24 hours.

2 For a charcoal grill, grill steaks on the rack of an uncovered grill directly over medium coals until desired doneness, turning once halfway through grilling. Allow 10 to 12 minutes for medium-rare (145°F) and 12 to 15 minutes for medium doneness (160°F). (For a gas grill, preheat grill. Reduce heat to medium. Place steaks on grill rack over heat. Cover; grill as above.) Serve with Lime and Sweet Onion Salsa.

Lime and Sweet Onion Salsa: Peel and section 2 large limes; chop lime segments. Combine the chopped lime, ½ cup finely chopped sweet onion, 3 tablespoons snipped fresh cilantro, ½ teaspoon sugar, and ¼ teaspoon salt. Cover and chill until ready to serve.

Nutrition Facts per serving: 431 cal., 17 g total fat (6 g sat. fat), 166 mg chol., 581 mg sodium, 4 g carbo., 1 g fiber, 62 g pro. Daily Values: 6% vit. A, 18% vit. C, 3% calcium, 29% iron. Exchanges: 9 Very Lean Meat, 2½ Fat

BEEF STEAKS WITH GORGONZOLA BUTTER

Gorgonzola butter is awesome on steak and also delicious on fresh green beans. Make an extra recipe of the butter to freeze for later use. It will keep in the freezer up to 1 month.

Prep: 15 minutes Grill: 11 minutes
Makes: 8 servings

2 tablespoons crumbled Gorgonzola cheese or blue cheese
2 tablespoons soft-style cream cheese with onion and garlic
1 to 2 tablespoons butter, softened
1 tablespoon chopped pine nuts or walnuts, toasted
4 boneless beef top loin steaks, cut 1 inch thick
Salt (optional)

1 For butter, in a bowl stir together Gorgonzola, cream cheese, butter, and nuts. Shape into a 1-inch-diameter log. Wrap in plastic wrap. Chill until firm. Trim fat from steaks.

2 For a charcoal grill, grill steaks on the rack of an uncovered grill directly over medium coals until desired doneness, turning once halfway through grilling. Allow 10 to 12 minutes for medium-rare (145°F) or 12 to 15 minutes for medium doneness (160°F).(For a gas grill, preheat grill. Reduce heat to medium. Place steaks on grill rack over heat. Cover; grill as above.)

3 If desired, season grilled steaks with salt. To serve, cut butter into 8 slices. Place 2 slices of butter on each steak; serve immediately.

Nutrition Facts per serving: 268 cal., 19 g total fat (8 g sat. fat), 82 mg chol., 110 mg sodium, 0 g carbo., 0 g fiber, 23 g pro. Daily Values: 3% vit. A, 2% calcium, 11% iron. Exchanges: 3 Lean Meat, 2 Fat

FOOD FOR THOUGHT STRIP STEAK

Technically called a beef top loin steak, the strip steak comes from the beef short loin. This is where you'll find most steak-house steaks, such as T-bone, porterhouse, and tenderloin steaks. Depending on where you are in the country, you may find beef top loin (strip) steaks under any one of the following names.

- Strip Loin
- New York Strip
- Ambassador Steak
- Boneless Club Steak
- Kansas City Steak

FLAT-IRON STEAK WITH AVOCADO BUTTER

Second only to beef tenderloin in tenderness, flat-iron steaks are the more affordable choice.

Prep: 25 minutes Grill: 7 minutes
Makes: 6 servings

6 beef shoulder top blade (flat-iron) steaks or boneless ribeye (Delmonico) steaks, cut ³/₄ inch thick
1 tablespoon olive oil
1 tablespoon herbes de Provence, crushed
¹/₂ teaspoon salt
¹/₂ teaspoon freshly ground black pepper
1 recipe Avocado Butter

1 Trim fat from steaks. Brush steaks with the olive oil. For rub, in a small bowl stir together herbes de Provence, salt, and pepper. Sprinkle evenly over both sides of steaks; rub in with your fingers. If desired, cover and chill for up to 24 hours.

2 For a charcoal grill, grill steaks on the rack of an uncovered grill directly over medium coals until desired doneness, turning once halfway through grilling. Allow 7 to 9 minutes for medium-rare (145°F) and 10 to 12 minutes for medium doneness (160°F). (For a gas grill, preheat grill. Reduce heat to medium. Place steaks on grill rack over heat. Cover; grill as above.) Serve with Avocado Butter.

Avocado Butter: Seed, peel, and chop 1 ripe avocado. In a medium bowl combine the chopped avocado, ¹/₄ cup softened butter, 3 tablespoons lime juice, 2 tablespoons snipped fresh chervil or parsley, 1 tablespoon snipped fresh tarragon, ¹/₄ teaspoon salt, and, if desired, ¹/₈ teaspoon cayenne pepper. Using a fork, gently mash the ingredients together until thoroughly combined (if desired, leave somewhat chunky). Spoon into a small bowl; chill until almost firm.

Nutrition Facts per serving: 387 cal., 27 g total fat (10 g sat. fat), 111 mg chol., 492 mg sodium, 3 g carbo., 2 g fiber, 34 g pro. Daily Values: 12% vit. A, 10% vit. C, 5% calcium, 23% iron. Exchanges: 5 Lean Meat, 2¹/₂ Fat

FLAT-IRON STEAK WITH BALSAMIC TOMATOES

Prep: 10 minutes Chill: 2 to 24 hours Grill: 7 minutes
Makes: 6 servings

1 recipe Balsamic Tomatoes
1 tablespoon dried marjoram, crushed
¹/₂ teaspoon garlic salt
¹/₂ teaspoon freshly ground black pepper
4 beef shoulder top blade (flat-iron) steaks, cut ³/₄ inch thick
Arugula (optional)

1 Prepare Balsamic Tomatoes. For rub, in a small bowl combine marjoram, garlic salt, and pepper. Sprinkle rub evenly over both sides of steaks; rub in with your fingers. If desired, cover and chill for 2 to 24 hours.

2 For a charcoal grill, grill steaks on the rack of an uncovered grill directly over medium coals until desired doneness, turning once halfway through grilling. Allow 7 to 9 minutes for medium-rare (145°F) or 10 to 12 minutes for medium doneness (160°F). (For a gas grill, preheat grill. Reduce heat to medium. Place steaks on grill rack over heat. Cover; grill as above.)

3 Serve steaks with Balsamic Tomatoes and, if desired, arugula. If desired, drizzle with marinade from Balsamic Tomatoes.

Balsamic Tomatoes: Remove cores from 2 ripe medium tomatoes. Trim off ends. Cut tomatoes crosswise into ³/₄-inch slices. Arrange slices in a shallow dish; sprinkle lightly with salt and pepper. Pour ¹/₃ cup balsamic vinegar over tomatoes. Drizzle with 3 tablespoons olive oil. Cover and chill for 2 to 24 hours, turning occasionally. Remove tomatoes, reserving marinade. For a charcoal grill, grill tomatoes on the rack of an uncovered grill directly over medium coals about 4 minutes or until lightly charred and slightly soft, turning once. (For a gas grill, preheat grill. Reduce heat to medium. Place tomatoes on grill rack over heat. Cover; grill as above.)

Nutrition Facts per serving: 277 cal., 16 g total fat (4 g sat. fat), 69 mg chol., 273 mg sodium, 6 g carbo., 1 g fiber, 26 g pro. Daily Values: 6% vit. A, 14% vit. C, 4% calcium, 18% iron. Exchanges: ¹/₂ Other Carbo., 4 Lean Meat, 1 Fat

**Flat-Iron Steak with
Balsamic Tomatoes**

FOOD FOR THOUGHT FLAT-IRON STEAK

Although it comes from the chuck, which is generally considered a less tender part of the animal, the flat-iron steak is one of the most tender cuts of beef available. Marketed to consumers as "beef shoulder top blade steak (flat-iron)," this cut is well marbled (for wonderful flavor) and generally less expensive than other, more popular steaks. Flat-iron steaks don't require marinating and are great for grilling. The flat-iron is equally good cut into strips and skewered or used in stir-fries.

Porterhouse Steak with Chipotle Potato Hash

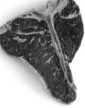

FOOD FOR THOUGHT T-BONE VS. PORTERHOUSE

A T-bone steak features a bone in the shape of a "T," with part of the tenderloin on one side and part of the top loin (or strip) on the other.

A porterhouse is the same as a T-bone steak except its portion of the tenderloin is larger. One way to remember the difference: If the tenderloin is smaller than a golf ball, it's a T-bone; if the tenderloin is larger than a golf ball, it's a porterhouse.

PORTERHOUSE STEAK WITH CHIPOTLE POTATO HASH

Prep: 30 minutes Cook: 9 minutes Grill: 15 minutes
Makes: 2 to 3 servings

1 1½-pound beef porterhouse steak,
   cut 1½ inches thick
¼ teaspoon ground chipotle chile
   pepper
⅛ teaspoon garlic salt
⅛ teaspoon black pepper
1 medium russet potato, peeled and
   finely chopped (1¼ cups)
¼ cup finely chopped sweet onion
1 tablespoon olive oil or cooking oil
1 teaspoon chili powder
½ teaspoon dried marjoram or
   dried oregano, crushed
¼ teaspoon salt
⅓ cup tomato juice
1 tablespoon snipped fresh cilantro

1 Trim fat from steak. For rub, in a bowl combine
⅛ teaspoon of the ground chipotle pepper, the
garlic salt, and black pepper. Sprinkle evenly over
both sides of steak; rub in with your fingers.

2 For a charcoal grill, grill steak on the rack of
an uncovered grill directly over medium coals
until desired doneness, turning once. Allow 15 to
19 minutes for medium-rare (145°F) or 18 to
23 minutes for medium (160°F). (For a gas grill,
preheat grill. Reduce heat to medium. Place steak
on grill rack over heat. Cover; grill as above.)

3 Meanwhile, in a large skillet cook and stir
potato and onion in hot oil over medium heat
for 7 minutes or until tender. Stir in remaining
ground chipotle pepper, chili powder, marjoram,
and salt. Cook and stir for 1 minute. Remove from
heat. Add tomato juice; return to heat and bring to
boiling. Reduce heat; simmer, uncovered, about
1 minute or until most of the liquid evaporates.
Stir in cilantro. Spoon mixture over steak.

Nutrition Facts per serving: 497 cal., 24 g total fat
(7 g sat. fat), 134 mg chol., 626 mg sodium, 21 g carbo.,
2 g fiber, 48 g pro. Daily Values: 17% vit. A, 39% vit. C,
4% calcium, 36% iron. Exchanges: ½ Vegetable, 1 Starch,
6 Lean Meat, 1 Fat

GARLIC AND PEPPER T-BONES WITH GRILLED CORN RELISH

Prep: 25 minutes Grill: 10 minutes
Makes: 4 servings

4 beef T-bone steaks, cut 1 inch thick
6 cloves garlic, crushed
1 teaspoon coarsely ground black
   pepper
½ teaspoon salt
1 recipe Grilled Corn Relish

1 Trim fat from steaks. For rub, in a small bowl
combine garlic, pepper, and salt. Sprinkle over
both sides of steaks; rub in with your fingers.

2 For a charcoal grill, grill steaks on the rack of
an uncovered grill directly over medium coals
until desired doneness, turning once halfway
through grilling. Allow 10 to 12 minutes for
medium-rare (145°F) or 12 to 15 minutes for
medium doneness (160°F.) (For a gas grill,
preheat grill. Reduce heat to medium. Place steak
on grill rack over heat. Cover; grill as above.)
Serve with Grilled Corn Relish.

Grilled Corn Relish: In a small bowl combine
3 tablespoons lime juice, 1 tablespoon olive oil,
and 1 teaspoon chili powder. Remove husks and
silks from 2 ears fresh sweet corn. Brush corn
lightly with some of the lime juice mixture. For a
charcoal grill, grill corn on the rack of an
uncovered grill directly over medium-hot coals for
10 to 20 minutes or until tender and slightly
charred, turning occasionally. (For a gas grill,
preheat grill. Reduce heat to medium-high. Place
corn on grill rack over heat. Cover and grill as
above.) Set corn aside until cool enough to handle.

Cut corn kernels from cobs. Combine corn
kernels; 2 tomatillos, finely chopped; 1 small
sweet pepper, chopped; ¼ cup snipped fresh
cilantro; 3 tablespoons finely chopped red onion;
¼ teaspoon salt; ¼ teaspoon cayenne pepper; and
the remaining lime juice mixture.

Nutrition Facts per serving: 491 cal., 22 g total fat
(7 g sat. fat), 142 mg chol., 583 mg sodium, 16 g carbo.,
2 g fiber, 57 g pro. Daily Values: 33% vit. A, 74% vit. C,
4% calcium, 37% iron. Exchanges: ½ Vegetable, 1 Starch,
7½ Lean Meat

CHILLED THAI TENDERLOIN AND PASTA WITH BASIL

A tied tenderloin keeps its shape during cooking. It's not hard to tie a roast, but if you don't want to tackle the task yourself, ask your butcher to do it.

Prep: 30 minutes Grill: 45 minutes Stand: 15 minutes
Chill: 8 hours Makes: 10 servings

- **1 3-pound center cut beef tenderloin roast**
- **Freshly ground black pepper**
- **½ cup purchased Thai peanut sauce**
- **3 cups packed purple basil sprigs (do not remove leaves from stems)**
- **2 pounds angel hair pasta, cooked according to package directions**
- **1½ cups purchased Thai peanut sauce**
- **2 cups sliced fennel**
- **1 cup slivered fresh purple or green basil**
- **2 tablespoons olive oil**

1 Butcher-tie the beef tenderloin.* Season roast with pepper. Spread the ½ cup peanut sauce over the roast until coated. Tuck the basil sprigs under the string "cage," covering as much of the meat as possible. Insert a meat thermometer into thickest part of roast.

2 For a charcoal grill, arrange hot coals around a drip pan. Test for medium-high heat above the pan. Place roast on grill rack over drip pan. Cover; grill for 45 minutes to 1 hour or until thermometer registers 135°F for medium-rare. (For a gas grill, preheat grill. Reduce heat to medium-high. Adjust for indirect cooking. Grill as above, except place roast on rack in a roasting pan.) Remove meat from grill. Cover with foil and let stand for 15 minutes. (The meat's temperature will rise 10°F during standing.) Place meat in a food storage container; cover and store in refrigerator for up to 2 days until ready to serve.

3 In a very large bowl, toss cooked pasta with the 1½ cups peanut sauce and the fennel. Add slivered basil. Cover and chill until ready to serve.

4 To serve, toss pasta mixture with olive oil; arrange on a serving platter. Remove tenderloin from refrigerator. Cut string and remove basil sprigs; discard basil. Cut tenderloin into ¼-inch slices; serve with pasta.

*Note: To butcher-tie the tenderloin, place roast on a cutting board. Using an 8-foot piece of kitchen string, slide the string under roast crosswise about 2 inches from one end. Pull string up and around the top, and make a knot, keeping one end of the string short. Do not cut the long end of the string. Using the long end, pull string toward the other end of roast. About 2 inches from first tie, hold string and loop under roast, bring it up and around, insert long end of string under top string to secure; pull to tighten the loop. Repeat, making a loop about every 2 inches until the end of the tenderloin. Bring string around to the underside of the roast and back to the starting point at the top side of the tenderloin; knot it around the initial loop. Cut the string.

Nutrition Facts per serving: 670 cal., 19 g total fat (5 g sat. fat), 62 mg chol., 828 mg sodium, 83 g carbo., 7 g fiber, 37 g pro. Daily Values: 13% vit. A, 9% vit. C, 6% calcium, 33% iron. Exchanges: 4 Starch, 1½ Other Carbo., 3½ Lean Meat, 1 Fat

FOOD FOR THOUGHT BASIL

Native to India and a member of the mint family, this typically green, aromatic leaf imparts a distinct flavor that's reminiscent of licorice and cloves. Basil is available dried as a seasoning but is at its best when used fresh to make pesto, salads, or to enliven sauces (add at the end of the cooking process to maintain its fragrant aroma). Although sweet basil is the most common, there are about 60 other varieties that grow in shades of green, red, and purple. Some, such as sweet basil, have large silky leaves; others are known for their more ornamental leaves, such as "ruffle" basil. Because each variety has its own flavor nuances—for instance, lemon basil and cinnamon basil—it's a flavorful herb to experiment with.

THREE-PEPPER BEEF TENDERLOIN ROAST

Fork-tender beef tenderloin seasoned with a trio of peppers is the kind of meal that makes guests feel you've gone the extra mile for them.

Prep: 15 minutes Grill: 1 hour Stand: 15 minutes
Makes: 9 or 10 servings

1 3- to 3½-pound center cut beef
    tenderloin roast
1 teaspoon salt
1 teaspoon dried oregano, crushed
1 teaspoon dried thyme, crushed
1 teaspoon paprika
½ teaspoon garlic powder
½ teaspoon onion powder
½ teaspoon ground white pepper
½ teaspoon freshly ground
    black pepper
¼ teaspoon cayenne pepper

1 For rub, in a small bowl combine salt, oregano, thyme, paprika, garlic powder, onion powder, white pepper, black pepper, and cayenne pepper. Sprinkle evenly over roast; rub in with your fingers. Insert a meat thermometer into thickest part of roast.

2 For a charcoal grill, arrange hot coals around a drip pan. Test for medium-high heat above the pan. Place roast on grill rack over drip pan. Cover; grill for 1 to 1¼ hours or until meat thermometer registers 135°F for medium-rare. (For a gas grill, preheat grill. Reduce heat to medium-high. Adjust for indirect cooking. Grill as above, except place roast on a rack in a roasting pan.)

3 Remove meat from grill. Cover with foil and let stand for 15 minutes before slicing. (Meat temperature will rise 10°F during standing.)

Nutrition Facts per serving: 253 cal., 13 g total fat (5 g sat. fat), 93 mg chol., 328 mg sodium, 1 g carbo., 0 g fiber, 32 g pro. Daily Values: 3% vit. A, 2% calcium, 24% iron. Exchanges: 4½ Lean Meat

BEEF STEAKS WITH CHUNKY VEGETABLE RELISH

Prep: 30 minutes Grill: 15 minutes
Makes: 4 servings

4 beef tenderloin steaks, cut 1 inch
    thick
    Kosher salt
    Coarsely ground black pepper
8 ounces fresh mushrooms
1 medium onion, cut into ½-inch slices
    Olive oil
4 roma tomatoes, halved lengthwise
3 tablespoons snipped fresh basil
2 tablespoons bottled minced garlic
2 tablespoons olive oil
1 teaspoon kosher salt
1 teaspoon coarsely ground
    black pepper

1 Trim fat from steaks. Season steaks with salt and pepper. For the vegetable relish, cut large mushrooms into halves or quarters and thread onto metal skewers. Brush mushrooms and onion slices lightly with olive oil.

2 For a charcoal grill, grill steaks, mushrooms, onion, and tomatoes on the rack of an uncovered grill directly over medium coals until desired doneness, turning once halfway through grilling. Allow 10 to 12 minutes for medium-rare (145°F) or 12 to 15 minutes for medium doneness (160°F). Grill mushrooms, onion, and tomatoes until tender, turning once halfway through grilling. Allow 10 minutes for mushrooms, 15 minutes for onion, and 7 minutes for tomatoes. (For a gas grill, preheat grill. Reduce heat to medium. Place steaks and vegetables on grill rack over heat. Cover; grill as above.) Remove vegetables and steaks from grill as they are done.

3 Cut onion and tomatoes into 1-inch pieces. Remove mushrooms from skewers. In a medium bowl stir together basil, garlic, the 2 tablespoons olive oil, 1 teaspoon kosher salt, and 1 teaspoon pepper; stir in grilled vegetables. To serve, spoon warm relish over steaks.

Nutrition Facts per serving: 329 cal., 18 g total fat (5 g sat. fat), 87 mg chol., 617 mg sodium, 9 g carbo., 2 g fiber, 33 g pro. Daily Values: 4% vit. A, 25% vit. C, 4% calcium, 26% iron. Exchanges: 1 Vegetable, 4½ Lean Meat, 1 Fat

BEEF TENDERLOIN WITH MEDITERRANEAN RELISH

Prep: 25 minutes Grill: 1 hour Stand: 15 minutes
Makes: 10 servings

- 2 **teaspoons dried oregano, crushed**
- 2 **teaspoons cracked black pepper**
- 1½ **teaspoons finely shredded lemon peel**
- 3 **cloves garlic, minced**
- 1 **3- to 4-pound center cut beef tenderloin roast**
- 2 **Japanese eggplants, halved lengthwise**
- 2 **red or yellow sweet peppers, halved lengthwise and seeded**
- 1 **sweet onion (such as Walla Walla or Vidalia), cut into ½-inch slices**
- 2 **tablespoons olive oil**
- 2 **roma tomatoes, chopped**
- 2 **tablespoons chopped, pitted kalamata olives**
- 2 **tablespoons snipped fresh basil**
- 1 **tablespoon balsamic vinegar**
- ¼ **to ½ teaspoon salt**
- ⅛ **teaspoon black pepper**

1 For rub, combine oregano, cracked pepper, lemon peel, and 2 cloves of the garlic. Sprinkle evenly over roast; rub in with your fingers. Insert a meat thermometer into thickest part of meat.

2 For a charcoal grill, arrange hot coals around a drip pan. Test for medium-high heat above pan. Place roast on grill rack over drip pan. Cover; grill for 1 to 1¼ hours or until a meat thermometer registers 135°F for medium-rare. Brush eggplants, sweet peppers, and onion slices with olive oil. Arrange vegetables on edges of grill rack directly over coals during the last 10 to 12 minutes of grilling or until vegetables are tender, turning once. (For a gas grill, preheat grill. Reduce heat to medium-high. Adjust for indirect cooking. Grill as above, except place roast on a rack in a roasting pan.) Remove meat and vegetables from grill. Cover meat with foil; let stand 15 minutes. (Meat temperature will rise 10°F during standing.)

3 Meanwhile, for relish, coarsely chop grilled vegetables. Combine vegetables, tomatoes, olives, basil, the remaining garlic, the vinegar, salt, and black pepper. Serve beef with relish.

Nutrition Facts per serving: 240 cal., 12 g total fat (4 g sat. fat), 77 mg chol., 133 mg sodium, 6 g carbo., 2 g fiber, 27 g pro. Daily Values: 12% vit. A, 49% vit. C, 1% calcium, 25% iron. Exchanges: 1 Vegetable, 3½ Lean Meat

SMOKIN' HOT TIP

Here are a few guidelines to make choosing the perfect cut of beef easier.

● Cuts with "loin" and "rib" in the name are more tender than those called "chuck," "round," or "flank."

● The three grades of beef are USDA Prime, USDA Choice, and USDA Select. Grade is determined primarily by the amount of marbling and the age of the animal. The higher the grade, typically the more tender, juicy, and flavorful the meat. Prime beef is the highest grade and more commonly found on restaurant menus, while Choice and Select are available in the supermarket.

● In general choose cuts that are bright red and firm to the touch. Keep in mind that beef in vacuum-sealed packages may appear burgundy in color but will change to red upon exposure to oxygen.

● Choose packages that are undamaged and contain little or no excess liquid.

● Select packages that are cool to the touch and always check the "sell by" date.

STUFFED TENDERLOIN PLATTER

These big, juicy steaks are naturally lean, so grill them only to medium doneness for best flavor and maximum juiciness.

Prep: 30 minutes Grill: 10 minutes
Makes: 6 servings

- **6 beef tenderloin steaks, cut 1 inch thick**
  Salt and black pepper
- **1 12-ounce jar roasted red sweet peppers, drained**
- **6 to 12 fresh basil leaves**
- **⅓ cup bottled red wine vinaigrette or Italian salad dressing**
- **6 small zucchini and/or yellow summer squash, halved lengthwise**
- **3 cloves garlic, quartered**
- **1 green onion, cut up**
- **1 tablespoon snipped fresh basil or oregano or ½ teaspoon dried basil or oregano, crushed**

1 Sprinkle steaks lightly with salt and black pepper. Cut a 2-inch-wide pocket in the side of each steak, cutting almost to, but not through, the other side. Cut six 2×1-inch pieces roasted red pepper; set remaining peppers aside. Place a red pepper piece and 1 or 2 basil leaves in the pocket of each steak. Brush 3 tablespoons of the vinaigrette on steak and squash.

2 For a charcoal grill, grill steaks on the rack of an uncovered grill directly over medium coals until desired doneness. turning once. Allow 10 to 12 minutes for medium-rare (145°F) or 12 to 15 minutes for medium doneness (160°F). Allow 7 to 9 minutes for squash, turning once. (For a gas grill, preheat grill. Reduce heat to medium. Place steaks, then squash on grill rack over heat. Cover; grill as above.)

3 Meanwhile, for relish, in a food processor combine remaining sweet peppers, garlic, green onion, and basil. Process until finely chopped. Stir in remaining vinaigrette. Serve steak with squash and relish.

Nutrition Facts per serving: 415 cal., 23 g total fat (7 g sat. fat), 122 mg chol., 259 mg sodium, 6 g carbo., 2 g fiber, 43 g pro. Daily Values: 9% vit. A, 130% vit. C, 4% calcium, 34% iron. Exchanges: 1 Vegetable, 6 Lean Meat, 1 Fat

Stuffed Tenderloin
Platter

PEPPER STEAK WITH HORSERADISH SAUCE

Taking a minute to score the meat on both sides makes it more tender. Cut the cooked meat diagonally across the grain into thin slices.

Prep: 20 minutes Grill: 17 minutes
Makes: 4 to 6 servings

- 1/2 cup mayonnaise or salad dressing
- 2 tablespoons vinegar
- 1 to 2 tablespoons prepared horseradish
- 1 tablespoon snipped fresh parsley
- 1 1- to 1 1/2-pound beef flank steak
- 2 teaspoons cracked black pepper

1 For sauce, in a small bowl stir together the mayonnaise, vinegar, horseradish, and parsley. Cover and chill sauce until needed.

2 Trim fat from steak. Score both sides of steak in a diamond pattern by making shallow diagonal cuts at 1-inch intervals. Sprinkle both sides of steak with cracked black pepper, gently pressing into surface.

3 For a charcoal grill, grill steak on the rack of an uncovered grill directly over medium coals for 17 to 21 minutes for medium doneness (160°F), turning once halfway through grilling. (For a gas grill, preheat grill. Reduce heat to medium. Place steak on grill rack over heat. Cover; grill as above.)

4 To serve, thinly slice steak diagonally across the grain. Serve meat with sauce.

Nutrition Facts per serving: 301 cal., 21 g total fat (7 g sat. fat), 68 mg chol., 253 mg sodium, 6 g carbo., 0 g fiber, 23 g pro. Daily Values: 1% vit. A, 2% vit. C, 1% calcium, 14% iron. Exchanges: 3½ Lean Meat, 2 Fat

SESAME BEEF

The flank steak marinates in a classic combination of soy sauce, toasted sesame oil, garlic, and dry sherry. Flecks of crushed red pepper keep it interesting.

Prep: 30 minutes Marinate: 4 to 24 hours Grill: 17 minutes
Makes: 4 servings

- 1 12-ounce beef flank steak
- 2 tablespoons soy sauce
- 2 tablespoons toasted sesame oil
- 1 green onion, sliced
- 2 cloves garlic, minced
- 1 1/2 teaspoons sugar
- 1 1/2 teaspoons dry sherry (optional)
- 1/2 teaspoon sesame seeds
- 1/2 teaspoon crushed red pepper
- 4 ounces fresh pea pods, trimmed and halved diagonally crosswise (about 3/4 cup)
- Hot cooked rice (optional)

1 Trim fat from steak. Score both sides of steak in a diamond pattern, making shallow diagonal cuts at 1-inch intervals. Place steak in a self-sealing plastic bag set in a shallow dish. For marinade, combine soy sauce, toasted sesame oil, green onion, garlic, sugar, sherry (if using), sesame seeds, and crushed red pepper. Pour over steak; seal bag. Marinate in the refrigerator for 4 to 24 hours, turning bag occasionally. Drain steak, discarding marinade.

2 For a charcoal grill, grill steak on the rack of an uncovered grill directly over medium coals for 17 to 21 minutes for medium doneness (160°F), turning once halfway through grilling. (For a gas grill, preheat grill. Reduce heat to medium. Place steak on grill rack over heat. Cover; grill as above.)

3 Meanwhile, in a covered small saucepan cook pea pods in a small amount of boiling water for 2 to 4 minutes or until crisp-tender; drain.

4 To serve, thinly slice steak diagonally across the grain. Serve with pea pods and, if desired, hot cooked rice.

Nutrition Facts per serving: 182 cal., 10 g total fat (3 g sat. fat), 34 mg chol., 277 mg sodium, 2 g carbo., 0 g fiber, 20 g pro. Daily Values: 2% vit. A, 3% vit. C, 2% calcium, 9% iron. Exchanges: 3 Lean Meat

GOLDEN TEQUILA FAJITAS

Prep: 20 minutes Marinate: 2 to 4 hours Grill: 17 minutes
Makes: 6 servings

1 1¼- to 1½-pound beef flank steak
¼ cup olive oil
⅓ cup lemon juice
¼ cup golden tequila
¼ cup sliced green onions (2)
4 cloves garlic, minced
2 small fresh jalapeño chile peppers,
   seeded and finely chopped
   (see tip, page 36)
2 tablespoons snipped fresh cilantro
½ teaspoon salt
1 medium sweet onion
2 medium red and/or green
   sweet peppers
1 tablespoon olive oil
2 tablespoons golden tequila
2 limes, cut into wedges
6 9- to 10-inch flour tortillas
1 large tomato, chopped
1 large avocado, halved, seeded,
   peeled, and chopped

1 Trim fat from steak. Score both sides of steak in a diamond pattern, making shallow diagonal cuts at 1-inch intervals. For marinade, in a small bowl combine the ¼ cup olive oil, the lemon juice, the ¼ cup tequila, green onions, garlic, jalapeño peppers, cilantro, and the ½ teaspoon salt. Place steak in a self-sealing plastic bag set in a shallow dish. Pour marinade over steak; seal bag. Marinate in refrigerator for 2 to 4 hours, turning bag occasionally.

2 Soak several wooden skewers in water for 1 hour. Cut onion into thick slices. Secure slices by inserting wooden skewers into the sides of onion slices through to the center. Remove stems from sweet peppers. Quarter peppers lengthwise; remove seeds and membranes. Brush onion slices and sweet pepper quarters with 1 tablespoon olive oil; set aside. Drain steak; discard marinade. Sprinkle steak with salt and black pepper.

3 For a charcoal grill, grill steak on the rack of an uncovered grill directly over medium coals for 17 to 21 minutes for medium doneness (160°F), turning once halfway through grilling. (For a gas grill, preheat grill. Reduce heat to medium. Place steak on grill rack over heat. Cover; grill as above.) Add onion slices and sweet pepper quarters to grill the last 8 to 10 minutes of cooking time; grill until tender, turning once.

4 Transfer steak to a cutting surface; drizzle immediately with the 2 tablespoons tequila. Squeeze 1 or 2 of the lime wedges over steak. Cover with foil; let stand 5 minutes. Wrap tortillas tightly in foil. Heat on grill rack about 10 minutes or until heated through, turning once. Remove skewers from onion slices. Break onion slices into rings; thinly slice sweet pepper quarters.

5 To serve, thinly slice meat diagonally across the grain. Serve on tortillas with onion, sweet pepper, tomato, avocado, and remaining lime wedges. If desired, top with bottled salsa, dairy sour cream, and fresh cilantro sprigs.

Nutrition Facts per serving: 414 cal., 20 g total fat (5 g sat. fat), 38 mg chol., 382 mg sodium, 32 g carbo., 4 g fiber, 25 g pro. Daily Values: 49% vit. A, 144% vit. C, 7% calcium, 21% iron. Exchanges: ½ Vegetable, 2 Starch, 2½ Lean Meat, 2½ Fat

FOOD FOR THOUGHT FAJITAS

A favorite in restaurants and backyard barbecues, this popular menu item has humble beginnings. In the late 1930s, Mexican ranch hands in southwest Texas were often given skirt steak or other lower-end cuts as compensation for their work. The meat was typically marinated in lime juice, cooked over an open flame, and served in tortillas. The beltlike shape of skirt steak lends itself to the name "fajita," which is Spanish for "little belt" or "sash." Today fajitas are served up much the same way—with skirt steak or other cuts of beef such as flank steak, top round steak, and even chicken or portobello mushrooms.

Tunisian Beef Pinwheels

TUNISIAN BEEF PINWHEELS

Prep: 30 minutes Grill: 40 minutes Stand: 10 minutes
Makes: 4 servings

- $^1/_3$ **cup finely chopped onion (1 small)**
- **6 cloves garlic, minced**
- $1^1/_2$ **teaspoons cumin seeds, crushed**
- $^1/_2$ **teaspoon crushed red pepper**
- **1 tablespoon olive oil**
- $^2/_3$ **cup golden raisins, chopped**
- $^1/_3$ **cup dry white wine**
- $^1/_2$ **teaspoon salt**
- $1^1/_2$ **teaspoons snipped fresh mint (optional)**
- **1 $1^1/_4$- to $1^1/_2$-pound beef flank steak**

1 Soak 24 inches of 100-percent-cotton string or 8 wooden toothpicks in water 30 minutes; drain.

2 Meanwhile, for stuffing, in a large skillet cook and stir onion, garlic, cumin, and crushed red pepper in hot oil over medium heat until tender. Stir in raisins, wine, and salt. Bring to boiling; reduce heat. Simmer, uncovered, about 10 minutes or until most of the liquid evaporates, stirring occasionally. Remove from heat. If desired, stir in snipped mint, set aside.

3 Trim fat from steak. Score both sides of steak in a diamond pattern, making shallow diagonal cuts at 1-inch intervals. Place steak between 2 pieces of plastic wrap. Working from the center to the edges use the flat side of a meat mallet to pound steak to about ½-inch thickness (about a 12×8-inch rectangle). Remove plastic wrap. Spread raisin mixture on steak to within 1 inch of edges. Starting from a long side, roll up. Tie roll with string or secure opening with wooden toothpicks.

4 For a charcoal grill, arrange medium-hot coals around a drip pan. Test for medium heat above pan. Place the steak roll on grill rack over drip pan. Cover; grill for 40 to 45 minutes or until an instant-read thermometer inserted in center of roll registers 150°F. (For a gas grill, preheat grill. Reduce heat to medium. Adjust for indirect cooking. Grill as above.)

5 Remove steak roll from grill. Cover with foil; let stand for 10 minutes. (Meat temperature will rise 10°F during standing.) Remove string. Cut steak roll crosswise into 1-inch slices.

Nutrition Facts per serving: 361 cal., 13 g total fat (5 g sat. fat), 57 mg chol., 373 mg sodium, 25 g carbo., 2 g fiber, 33 g pro. Daily Values: 1% vit. A, 5% vit. C, 4% calcium, 19% iron. Exchanges: 1½ Fruit, 5 Lean Meat

---

SPICY GRILLED BRISKET

Treat a fresh beef brisket to an easy salt-and-pepper rub before a long, slow cooktime. Cut thin slices and serve with the spicy-sweet sauce.

Prep: 25 minutes Grill: 3 hours Stand: 10 minutes
Makes: 15 servings

- **4 to 6 cups mesquite wood chips**
- **1 4- to 5-pound fresh beef brisket**
- **1 tablespoon cooking oil**
- **2 tablespoons paprika**
- **1 tablespoon coarse salt**
- **1 tablespoon black pepper**
- **1 teaspoon cayenne pepper**
- **1 teaspoon dried thyme, crushed**
- **1 recipe Sweet-Hot Barbecue Sauce
  or 3 cups bottled barbecue sauce**

1 At least 1 hour before grilling, soak wood chips in enough water to cover.

2 Trim fat from meat. Brush meat with oil. Stir together paprika, salt, black pepper, cayenne pepper, and thyme. Sprinkle mixture evenly over both sides of meat; rub in with your fingers. Drain wood chips.

3 For a charcoal grill, arrange medium-low coals around a drip pan. Test for low heat above pan. Sprinkle some of the drained wood chips over the coals. Place brisket on grill rack over drip pan. Cover; grill for 3 to 3¾ hours or until meat is tender. Add more wood chips about every 30 minutes and add more coals as necessary. (For a gas grill, preheat grill. Reduce heat to low. Adjust for indirect cooking. Add wood chips according to manufacturer's directions. Grill as above, except place meat on a rack in a roasting pan.)

4 Meanwhile, prepare Sweet-Hot Barbecue Sauce or warm bottled barbecue sauce in a saucepan over low heat. Let meat stand for 10 minutes. To serve, slice meat thinly across the grain. Serve with sauce.

Sweet-Hot Barbecue Sauce: In a large saucepan cook ½ cup chopped onion; 6 fresh jalapeño chile peppers, seeded and chopped (see tip, page 36); and 2 cloves garlic, minced, in 1 tablespoon hot cooking oil until onion is tender. Stir in 2 cups catsup, ¼ cup packed brown sugar, ¼ cup white wine vinegar, ¼ cup orange juice, 3 tablespoons Worcestershire sauce, and 1 teaspoon dry mustard. Bring to boiling; reduce heat. Simmer, uncovered, for 10 to 15 minutes or to desired consistency.

Nutrition Facts per serving: 253 cal., 9 g total fat (2 g sat. fat), 71 mg chol., 956 mg sodium, 15 g carbo., 1 g fiber, 27 g pro. Daily Values: 19% vit. A, 19% vit. C, 3% calcium, 18% iron. Exchanges: 1 Other Carbo., 3½ Lean Meat

FOOD FOR THOUGHT BEEF BRISKET

Cut from the breast section of the animal, brisket is a very flavorful cut of beef but it can be tough. It benefits from such slow cooking methods as smoking and braising, and it is often used to make pot roast and corned beef. Brisket is sometimes divided into two cuts. The "first cut" or "flat half" contains less fat than the "point half" and is more expensive.

K.C.-STYLE BEEF RIBS

Prep: 25 minutes Marinate: 4 to 24 hours Grill: 1¼ hours
Makes: 6 to 8 servings

½ cup cider vinegar
3 tablespoons sugar
2 teaspoons dry mustard
2 cups pineapple juice
½ cup Worcestershire sauce
⅓ cup chopped onion (1 small)
2 tablespoons cooking oil
2½ to 3 pounds boneless beef chuck
    short ribs
4 teaspoons paprika
1½ teaspoons sugar
1 teaspoon garlic powder
4 cups hickory or oak wood chips

1 For marinade, bring vinegar to boiling. Remove from heat. Stir in 3 tablespoons sugar, mustard, and ⅛ teaspoon salt, stirring until sugar dissolves. Stir in pineapple juice, Worcestershire sauce, onion, and oil. Cool to room temperature.

2 Trim fat from ribs. Cut ribs into serving-size pieces. Place ribs in self-sealing plastic bag set in a shallow dish. Pour marinade over ribs; seal bag. Marinate in refrigerator 4 to 24 hours, turning bag occasionally. For rub, combine paprika, the 1½ teaspoons sugar, garlic powder, ½ teaspoon black pepper, and ¼ teaspoon salt; set aside.

3 At least 1 hour before grilling, soak wood chips in enough water to cover. Drain ribs; discard marinade; pat ribs dry. Generously sprinkle rub over both sides of ribs; rub in with your fingers. Drain wood chips.

4 For a charcoal grill, arrange medium-hot coals around a drip pan. Test for medium heat above pan. Sprinkle one-fourth of the wood chips over the coals. Place ribs on grill rack over drip pan. Cover; grill 1¼ to 1½ hours or until tender. Add more wood chips every 15 minutes and add more coals as necessary. (For a gas grill, preheat grill. Reduce heat to medium. Adjust for indirect cooking. Add wood chips following manufacturer directions. Grill as above, except place ribs, fat sides up, in a roasting pan.)

Nutrition Facts per serving: 394 cal., 20 g total fat (8 g sat. fat), 110 mg chol., 356 mg sodium, 14 g carbo., 1 g fiber, 37 g pro. Daily Values: 15% vit. A, 10% vit. C, 3% calcium, 30% iron. Exchanges: 1 Other Carbo., 5 Lean Meat, 1 Fat

LEMON-PEPPER BARBECUE RIBS

Prep: 30 minutes Cook: 1½ hours Cool: 30 minutes
Marinate: 4 to 24 hours Grill: 15 minutes Makes: 6 servings

3 to 4 pounds beef chuck short ribs
½ cup cooking oil
½ cup dry white wine
½ cup lemon juice
⅓ cup snipped fresh flat-leaf parsley
1 to 1½ teaspoons freshly ground
    black pepper
1 recipe Molasses Barbecue Sauce or
    1½ cups bottled barbecue sauce

1 Trim fat from ribs. Place ribs in a 4- to 6-quart Dutch oven with enough water to cover. Bring to boiling; reduce heat. Simmer, covered, about 1½ hours or until tender. Drain; cool 30 minutes.

2 Place ribs in a large self-sealing plastic bag set in a shallow dish. For marinade, in a medium bowl combine oil, wine, lemon juice, parsley, and pepper. Pour marinade over ribs; seal bag. Marinate in the refrigerator for 4 to 24 hours, turning bag occasionally. Drain ribs, discarding marinade. Sprinkle ribs with salt.

3 For a charcoal grill, place medium-hot coals around a drip pan. Test for medium heat above pan. Place ribs, bone sides down, on the grill rack over drip pan. Cover; grill for 15 minutes, brushing frequently with Molasses Barbecue Sauce during the last 15 minutes of grilling. (For a gas grill, preheat grill. Reduce heat to medium. Adjust for indirect cooking. Grill as above.)

4 Heat any remaining barbecue sauce until bubbly; serve with ribs.

Molasses Barbecue Sauce: In a medium bowl combine 1 cup catsup, ¼ cup dark molasses, ¼ cup water, ½ teaspoon finely shredded lemon peel, 1 tablespoon lemon juice, 2 teaspoons Worcestershire sauce, ½ teaspoon black pepper, and ⅛ teaspoon salt. If desired, stir in 2 tablespoons port wine. Cover and chill until needed.

Nutrition Facts per serving: 292 cal., 14 g total fat (4 g sat. fat), 44 mg chol., 611 mg sodium, 22 g carbo., 1 g fiber, 19 g pro. Daily Values: 9% vit. A, 18% vit. C, 5% calcium, 16% iron. Exchanges: 1½ Other Carbo., 3 Medium-Fat Meat

LONE STAR BBQ RIBS

The flavor of the beer comes through the marinade, so be sure to use one of your favorites. Be careful: Although the sauce might not seem hot at first, it'll sneak up on you!

Prep: 25 minutes Marinate: 4 to 24 hours Cook: 1 hour
Grill: 10 minutes Makes: 4 to 5 servings

4 to 5 pounds beef back ribs
3 12-ounce bottles or cans bock beer
   or dark beer
2 cups water
2 bay leaves
4 medium onions, sliced (2 cups)
¼ cup butter or margarine
¼ cup packed brown sugar
2 cups catsup
½ cup canned chipotle peppers in
   adobo sauce
¼ cup Worcestershire sauce
¼ cup lemon juice
¼ cup bottled hoisin sauce
¼ cup balsamic vinegar

1 Trim fat from ribs. Cut ribs into 2 portions. Place ribs in a 4-quart stainless-steel Dutch oven or a very large bowl. Pour beer over ribs. Cover and marinate in refrigerator 4 to 24 hours.

2 If necessary, transfer ribs and beer to a Dutch oven. Add the water and bay leaves. Bring to boiling; reduce heat. Simmer, covered, for 1 hour.

3 Meanwhile, in a large saucepan cook onions in butter over medium heat about 12 minutes or until tender. Stir in brown sugar; cook for 2 minutes more. Remove half of the onion mixture; set aside. For sauce, stir catsup, chipotle peppers in adobo sauce, Worcestershire sauce, lemon juice, hoisin sauce, and vinegar into remaining onion mixture. Bring to boiling; reduce heat to medium-low. Simmer, uncovered, for 40 minutes, stirring occasionally. Remove from heat. Cool slightly. Transfer half of the catsup mixture to a food processor or blender. Process or blend until smooth. Strain through a fine-mesh strainer, discarding solids. Repeat with remaining catsup mixture. Set sauce aside. Drain ribs, discarding liquid and bay leaves. Brush ribs with some of the sauce.

4 For a charcoal grill, grill ribs, bone sides down, on the rack of an uncovered grill directly over medium coals about 10 minutes or until browned. (For a gas grill, preheat grill. Reduce heat to medium. Place ribs on grill rack over heat. Cover; grill as above.)

5 To serve, reheat remaining sauce until bubbly. Serve ribs with warm sauce and reserved onion mixture.

Nutrition Facts per serving: 719 cal., 21 g total fat (10 g sat. fat), 185 mg chol., 2,324 mg sodium, 72 g carbo., 5 g fiber, 58 g pro. Daily Values: 40% vit. A, 51% vit. C, 8% calcium, 52% iron. Exchanges: ½ Vegetable, 4½ Other Carbo., 8 Very Lean Meat, 3 Fat

FOOD FOR THOUGHT RIBS

Barbecued ribs are the ultimate crowd-pleasers at neighborhood backyard barbecues. To keep it interesting, serve several varieties and pair them with your favorite marinades and rubs.

● Beef Back Ribs: **Cut from the sixth to twelfth ribs of the tender rib section of the animal, these ribs are cooked using dry or moist heat cookery methods or a combination of both. With a dry heat method, the meat remains on the long bones and tends to be chewier, while a moist method produces meat that is incredibly tender and falls off the bone.**

● Beef Short Ribs: **These meaty ribs are from the chuck or plate. They benefit from a moist or combination dry/moist cooking method.**

Apricot-Habanero Shortribs

SMOKIN' HOT TIP

For fork-tender ribs that fall off the bone, braise them before grilling. Braising involves simmering meats in liquid that just covers the surface of the meat in a covered pot at a low temperature for a long period of time. You can braise the meat either on the stove top or in the oven. This cooking method has a tenderizing effect; it melts the connective tissue. Braise ribs to "fork-tender," not until they fall apart. In other words, to the point where a fork inserts into the thickest part of the rib without resistance. Once cooked, drain and finish the ribs off on the grill to achieve that delicious smoky flavor.

APRICOT-HABANERO SHORTRIBS

Habanero peppers and their near-identical cousins Scotch bonnets are some of the hottest peppers grown. Those who have tender palates may opt to substitute jalapeño or sweet peppers.

Prep: 20 minutes Cook: 1½ hours Grill: 15 minutes
Makes: 6 servings

3 pounds beef chuck short ribs
¼ cup chopped onion
3 cloves garlic, minced
1 tablespoon cooking oil
½ cup catsup
½ cup apricot preserves
¼ cup cider vinegar
1 fresh habanero or Scotch bonnet chile pepper, seeded, if desired, and finely chopped (see tip, page 36)
1 tablespoon bottled steak sauce
1 teaspoon chili powder
½ teaspoon ground cumin
¼ teaspoon salt

1 Trim fat from ribs. Place the ribs in a 4- to 6-quart Dutch oven with enough water to cover. Bring to boiling; reduce heat. Simmer, covered, about 1½ hours or until tender. Drain.

2 For sauce, in a small saucepan cook onion and garlic in hot oil until tender. Stir in catsup, preserves, vinegar, pepper, steak sauce, and chili powder. Bring to boiling; reduce heat. Simmer, uncovered, about 10 minutes or until mixture thickens slightly, stirring occasionally. Set aside.

3 For rub, in a small bowl stir together cumin and salt. Sprinkle mixture evenly over both sides of ribs; rub in with your fingers.

4 For a charcoal grill, arrange medium-hot coals around a drip pan. Test for medium heat above the pan. Place ribs, bone sides down, on lightly oiled grill rack directly over drip pan. Cover; grill about 15 minutes or until ribs are tender, brushing occasionally with sauce. (For a gas grill, preheat grill. Reduce heat to medium. Adjust grill for indirect cooking. Grill as above.) Heat remaining sauce until bubbly; pass with ribs.

Nutrition Facts per serving: 284 cal., 11 g total fat (4 g sat. fat), 44 mg chol., 444 mg sodium, 26 g carbo., 1 g fiber, 19 g pro. Daily Values: 8% vit. A, 15% vit. C, 3% calcium, 12% iron. Exchanges: 1½ Other Carbo., 2½ Medium-Fat Meat

OLD-WORLD VEAL BURGERS

Rye bread takes the place of the traditional buns and Swiss cheese ousts American. Top each burger with your choice of mustard.

Prep: 30 minutes Grill: 14 minutes
Makes: 4 servings

1 beaten egg
2 tablespoons beer or water
¾ cup soft rye bread crumbs (1 slice)
1 clove garlic, minced
½ teaspoon caraway seeds
½ teaspoon dried marjoram, crushed
¼ teaspoon salt
¼ teaspoon black pepper
1 pound ground veal
4 slices rye bread
4 slices Swiss cheese (4 ounces)
3 tablespoons German-style mustard, creamy Dijon-style mustard blend, or stone-ground mustard

1 In a large bowl combine egg and beer. Stir in bread crumbs, garlic, caraway, marjoram, salt, and pepper. Add ground veal; mix well. Shape mixture into four ¾-inch-thick patties.

2 For a charcoal grill, grill patties on the rack of an uncovered grill directly over medium coals for 14 to 18 minutes or until done (160°F), turning once halfway through grilling. (For a gas grill, preheat grill. Reduce heat to medium. Place the patties on grill rack over heat. Cover; grill as above.) When burgers are nearly done, place rye bread slices on grill rack with burgers. Grill for 1 to 2 minutes or until bottoms are lightly browned; turn bread slices and top each with a cheese slice. Grill for 1 to 2 minutes more or until bottoms are lightly browned and cheese is melted.

3 Place burgers on top of cheese on rye slices. Top with mustard.

Nutrition Facts per serving: 423 cal., 20 g total fat (9 g sat. fat), 172 mg chol., 735 mg sodium, 24 g carbo., 2 g fiber, 35 g pro. Daily Values: 7% vit. A, 1% vit. C, 33% calcium, 14% iron. Exchanges: 1½ Starch, 4½ Lean Meat, 1 Fat

Veal Chops with Eggplant Relish

VEAL CHOPS WITH EGGPLANT RELISH

The Mediterranean-style relish conveniently cooks in a foil packet alongside the chops. Because it needs more time to cook, give it a head start.

Prep: 25 minutes Grill: 20 minutes
Makes: 6 servings

- **2 cups Japanese eggplant cut into ½-inch cubes (6 ounces)**
- **2 roma tomatoes, chopped (¾ cup)**
- **¼ cup chopped onion**
- **¼ cup chopped celery**
- **2 teaspoons dried Italian seasoning, crushed**
- **2 tablespoons olive oil**
- **6 veal loin chops, cut 1 inch thick**
- **2 cloves garlic, minced**
- **½ teaspoon salt**
- **½ teaspoon black pepper**
- **2 teaspoons olive oil**
- **1 tablespoon red wine vinegar**
- **1 tablespoon tomato paste**
- **1 teaspoon sugar**
- **¼ cup sliced pitted kalamata olives**
- **1 tablespoon pine nuts**
- **1 tablespoon snipped fresh parsley**
- **1 tablespoon drained capers**

1 For relish, combine eggplant, tomatoes, onion, celery, ½ teaspoon of the Italian seasoning, and 2 tablespoons olive oil; toss to coat. Fold a 36×18-inch piece of heavy foil in half to make an 18-inch square. Place vegetables in center of foil. Bring up opposite edges of foil; seal with a double fold. Fold remaining edges together to enclose vegetables, leaving space for steam to build.

2 Trim fat from chops. For rub, in a small bowl combine remaining 1½ teaspoons Italian seasoning, the garlic, salt, and pepper. Stir in 2 teaspoons olive oil. Spoon mixture over both sides of chops; rub in with your fingers.

3 For a charcoal grill, grill foil packet on the rack of an uncovered grill directly over medium coals for 20 to 25 minutes or until tender, turning occasionally. Grill chops on the rack next to packet for 12 to 15 minutes for medium doneness (160°F), turning once halfway through grilling. (For a gas grill, preheat grill. Reduce heat to medium. Place foil packet, then chops on grill rack over heat. Cover; grill as above.)

4 Meanwhile, combine vinegar, tomato paste, and sugar. Stir in olives, nuts, parsley, and capers. Remove packet from grill; carefully open, allowing steam to escape. Transfer vegetables to a serving bowl; stir in olive mixture. Serve with chops.

Nutrition Facts per serving: 320 cal., 14 g total fat (3 g sat. fat), 157 mg chol., 452 mg sodium, 6 g carbo., 2 g fiber, 41 g pro. Daily Values: 4% vit. A, 12% vit. C, 5% calcium, 12% iron. Exchanges: ½ Vegetable, 6 Very Lean Meat, 2 Fat

FOOD FOR THOUGHT JAPANESE EGGPLANT

The Japanese eggplant is merely a small version of the common eggplant. It has the same taste, texture, and cooking qualities but is longer and more slender. Choose fruits that have a glossy purplish black skin. Those that appear brown in color are overripe and will be tough and/or bitter. It's best to store the eggplant in the refrigerator produce drawer for up to 1 week. With its tender skin and flesh, grilled Japanese eggplant takes on the smoky flavor particularly well.

VEAL CHOPS STUFFED WITH MUSHROOMS

Prep: 30 minutes Cook: 7 minutes Grill: 12 minutes
Makes: 6 servings

- **8 ounces fresh mushrooms, finely chopped**
- **2 tablespoons shallots, finely chopped**
- **1 tablespoon butter or margarine**
- **2 tablespoons dried tart cherries, chopped**
- **1 tablespoon dry sherry**
- **¼ teaspoon salt**
- **⅛ teaspoon black pepper**
- **6 veal loin chops, cut 1 inch thick**
- **1 tablespoon cooking oil**

1 For stuffing, in a large skillet cook mushrooms and shallots in butter for 5 minutes or until most of liquid evaporates, stirring frequently. Stir in cherries, sherry, salt, and pepper. Cook for 2 or 3 minutes more or until all the liquid evaporates. Cool slightly.

2 Trim fat from chops. Make a pocket in each chop by cutting horizontally from the fat side almost to the bone. Divide stuffing evenly among pockets. Secure with wooden toothpicks. Brush chops with oil; sprinkle lightly with additional salt and pepper.

3 For a charcoal grill, grill chops on the rack of an uncovered grill directly over medium coals for 12 to 15 minutes for medium doneness (160°F), turning once halfway through grilling. (For a gas grill, preheat grill. Reduce heat to medium. Place chops on grill rack over heat. Cover; grill as above.) Remove toothpicks.

Nutrition Facts per serving: 265 cal., 11 g total fat (3 g sat. fat), 146 mg chol., 352 mg sodium, 4 g carbo., 0 g fiber, 37 g pro. Daily Values: 2% vit. A, 3% calcium, 8% iron. Exchanges: ½ Vegetable, 5 Very Lean Meat, 2 Fat

VEAL CHOPS WITH GINGER BUTTER

The chunky butter has plenty of potential. Toss it with grilled vegetables, spread it over toasted bread, or serve over grilled fish or chicken.

Prep: 15 minutes Grill: 12 minutes
Makes: 4 servings

- **¼ cup butter, softened**
- **2 tablespoons chopped crystallized ginger**
- **1 tablespoon chopped shallot**
- **1 tablespoon snipped fresh tarragon**
- **4 veal loin chops, cut 1 inch thick**
- **Salt and black pepper**

1 For butter mixture, in a small bowl combine butter, ginger, shallot, and tarragon; set aside.

2 Trim fat from chops; sprinkle with salt and pepper. For a charcoal grill, grill chops on the rack of an uncovered grill directly over medium coals for 12 to 15 minutes for medium doneness (160°F), turning once halfway through grilling. (For a gas grill, preheat grill. Reduce heat to medium. Place chops on grill rack over heat. Cover; grill as above.)

3 To serve, top each chop with 1 tablespoon butter mixture.

Nutrition Facts per serving: 251 cal., 16 g total fat (9 g sat. fat), 123 mg chol., 358 mg sodium, 3 g carbo., 0 g fiber, 23 g pro. Daily Values: 10% vit. A, 2% calcium, 5% iron. Exchanges: 3½ Very Lean Meat, 3 Fat

VEAL CHOPS WITH CREAMY VIDALIA SAUCE

Keep an eye on sweet onions when you cook them. Because they contain more sugar than ordinary onions, they cook—and burn—faster than you might expect.

Prep: 35 minutes Grill: 12 minutes
Makes: 6 servings

**6 veal rib chops or loin chops,
    cut 1 inch thick**
1½ teaspoons onion salt
**2 cups finely chopped Vidalia onions
    or other sweet onion**
2 tablespoons butter
2 tablespoons all-purpose flour
½ teaspoon salt
   Dash ground white pepper
1 cup milk
½ cup whipping cream
1 recipe Parsnip Mashed Potatoes

1 Trim fat from chops. Sprinkle onion salt over both sides of chops; rub in with your fingers.

2 For a charcoal grill, grill chops on the rack of an uncovered grill directly over medium coals for 12 to 15 minutes for medium doneness (160°F), turning once halfway through grilling. (For a gas grill, preheat grill. Reduce heat to medium. Place chops on grill rack over heat. Cover; grill as above.) Remove chops from grill.

3 Meanwhile, for sauce, in a medium saucepan cook onion in butter, covered, over medium-low heat for 10 to 15 minutes or until onion is very tender but not brown, stirring occasionally. Stir in flour, salt, and pepper. Stir in milk. Cook and stir over medium heat until thickened and bubbly. Cook and stir 1 minute more. Stir in whipping cream; heat through. Serve with chops and Parsnip Mashed Potatoes.

Parsnip Mashed Potatoes: Peel and quarter 3 medium potatoes. Peel and quarter 3 parsnips. Cook potatoes and parsnips, covered, in enough lightly salted boiling water to cover for 20 to 25 minutes or until tender; drain. In a medium mixing bowl mash with a potato masher or beat with an electric mixer on low speed. Add 2 tablespoons butter. Gradually beat in 2 to 4 tablespoons milk to make light and fluffy. Season to taste with salt and black pepper. If desired, sprinkle with snipped fresh chives.

Nutrition Facts per serving: 467 cal., 22 g total fat (12 g sat. fat), 163 mg chol., 924 mg sodium, 37 g carbo., 1 g fiber, 32 g pro. Daily Values: 14% vit. A, 40% vit. C, 13% calcium, 13% iron. Exchanges: ½ Vegetable, 1 Starch, 1 Other Carbo., 3½ Lean Meat, 2 Fat

VEAL CHOPS WITH APPLES

Americans love apples baked, stewed, or whirled into applesauce. Here they're sliced into thick pieces and grilled alongside veal chops that have been jazzed up with white wine and sage.

Prep: 10 minutes Marinate: 6 to 24 hours Grill: 10 minutes
Makes: 4 servings

**4 boneless veal top loin chops,
    cut ¾ inch thick**
½ cup dry white wine
2 tablespoons cooking oil
2 teaspoons dried sage, crushed
½ teaspoon salt
½ teaspoon black pepper
2 medium tart cooking apples

1 Trim fat from chops. Place the chops in a self-sealing plastic bag set in a shallow dish. For marinade, in a small bowl combine wine, oil, sage, salt, and pepper. Pour over chops; seal bag. Marinate in the refrigerator for 6 to 24 hours, turning bag occasionally.

2 Drain chops, reserving marinade. Just before grilling, core the apples. Cut apples crosswise into 1-inch slices.

3 For a charcoal grill, grill chops and apple slices on the rack of an uncovered grill directly over medium coals for 10 to 12 minutes for medium doneness (160°F), turning and brushing once with marinade halfway through grilling. (For a gas grill, preheat grill. Reduce heat to medium. Place chops and apple slices on grill rack over heat. Cover; grill as above.) Serve chops with apple slices.

Nutrition Facts per serving: 271 cal., 13 g total fat (3 g sat. fat), 95 mg chol., 354 mg sodium, 9 g carbo., 1 g fiber, 24 g pro. Daily Values: 5% vit. C, 2% calcium, 7% iron. Exchanges: ½ Fruit, 3½ Lean Meat, 1 Fat

Veal Chops with Creamy Vidalia Sauce

Veal Rolls
Stuffed with Herb Cheese

VEAL ROLLS STUFFED WITH HERB CHEESE

Precooking the beans ensures that they'll be crisp-tender when the meat is done.

Prep: 25 minutes Grill: 20 minutes
Makes: 4 servings

1 pound boneless veal leg top
  round steak
4 ounces haricots vert or tiny young
  green beans
4 tablespoons semisoft cheese with
  garlic and herb
4 slices prosciutto (about 2½ ounces)
2 tablespoons butter or
  margarine, melted

1 Trim fat from meat. Cut into 4 serving-size pieces. Place meat between 2 pieces of plastic wrap. Working from center to edges, use the flat side of a meat mallet to pound meat to ¼-inch thickness. Remove plastic wrap.

2 Trim beans and cook, covered, in lightly salted boiling water for 4 minutes. Drain.

3 Spread each veal piece with cheese. Top with a slice of prosciutto and one-fourth of the beans (trim beans and fold prosciutto if necessary to fit). Fold in sides; roll up meat. Seal edges with wooden toothpicks or small metal skewers. Brush meat rolls with melted butter.

4 For a charcoal grill, arrange medium-hot coals around a drip pan. Test for medium heat above the pan. Place meat rolls on grill rack over pan. Cover; grill for 20 to 24 minutes for medium doneness (160°F), turning once. (For a gas grill, preheat grill. Reduce heat to medium. Adjust for indirect cooking. Grill as above.)

5 Remove toothpicks or skewers from meat rolls. Place rolls on serving platter.

Nutrition Facts per serving: 245 cal., 12 g total fat (7 g sat. fat), 117 mg chol., 641 mg sodium, 2 g carbo., 1 g fiber, 30 g pro. Daily Values: 8% vit. A, 6% vit. C, 2% calcium, 7% iron. Exchanges: ½ Vegetable, 4 Very Lean Meat, 2 Fat

VEAL KABOBS WITH ROMESCO SAUCE

Originally from the Catalan region of Spain, the classic romesco sauce features ground tomatoes and red sweet peppers and is an accompaniment for all grilled meats or fish.

Prep: 30 minutes Grill: 12 minutes
Makes: 4 servings

1 pound boneless veal
1 medium yellow, green, or red sweet
  pepper, cut into 1½-inch pieces
1 medium zucchini, cut into
  ¾-inch slices
1 medium yellow summer squash,
  cut into ¾-inch slices
3 tablespoons olive oil
2 tablespoons snipped fresh
  oregano or 1½ teaspoons dried
  oregano, crushed
1 teaspoon bottled hot pepper sauce
1 cup finely chopped roasted red
  sweet peppers
1 cup bottled spicy pasta sauce
1 clove garlic, minced
2 cups hot cooked orzo (rosamarina)

1 Trim fat from meat. Cut meat into 1¼-inch pieces. On four 10- to 12-inch metal skewers, alternately thread meat, sweet pepper, zucchini, and yellow squash, leaving a ¼-inch space between pieces. In a small bowl combine olive oil, oregano, and hot pepper sauce. Set aside half the oil mixture. Brush kabobs with the remaining oil mixture.

2 For a charcoal grill, grill kabobs on the rack of an uncovered grill directly over medium coals for 12 to 15 minutes for medium doneness (160°F), turning once halfway through grilling. (For a gas grill, preheat grill. Reduce heat to medium. Place kabobs on grill rack over heat. Cover; grill as above.)

3 For sauce, in a small saucepan combine roasted red sweet peppers, pasta sauce, and garlic. Bring to boiling; remove from heat. Keep warm. Toss reserved oil mixture with cooked orzo. To serve, arrange kabobs on orzo; top with sauce.

Nutrition Facts per serving: 346 cal., 17 g total fat (3 g sat. fat), 71 mg chol., 377 mg sodium, 26 g carbo., 4 g fiber, 21 g pro. Daily Values: 28% vit. A, 214% vit. C, 3% calcium, 17% iron. Exchanges: 2 Vegetable, 1 Starch, 2 Lean Meat, 2 Fat

VEAL STEAK WITH EASY ORANGE PESTO

Repeating the basil-garlic flavor of the marinade, the simple, two-ingredient pesto further enhances veal.

Prep: 20 minutes Marinate: 4 to 24 hours Grill: 8 minutes
Makes: 4 servings

1 pound boneless veal leg top round steak
¼ cup white wine vinegar
2 tablespoons snipped fresh basil
2 tablespoons olive oil
1 clove garlic, minced
1 recipe Easy Orange Pesto

1 Trim fat from meat. Cut into 4 serving-size pieces. Place meat in a self-sealing plastic bag set in a shallow dish. For marinade, in a small bowl combine vinegar, basil, oil, garlic, ½ teaspoon salt, and ¼ teaspoon black pepper. Pour over meat; seal bag. Marinate in refrigerator for 4 to 24 hours, turning the bag occasionally. Drain the meat, discarding marinade.

2 For a charcoal grill, grill meat on the rack of an uncovered grill directly over medium coals until desired doneness, turning once halfway through grilling. Allow 8 to 10 minutes for medium-rare (145°F) or 10 to 14 minutes for medium doneness (160°F). (For a gas grill, preheat grill. Reduce heat to medium. Place meat on grill rack over heat. Cover; grill as above.)

3 To serve, thinly slice steak across the grain. Serve with Easy Orange Pesto.

Easy Orange Pesto: In a small bowl combine ¼ cup purchased basil pesto and ½ teaspoon finely shredded orange peel. Let pesto stand for 10 minutes before serving.

Nutrition Facts per serving: 253 cal., 14 g total fat (1 g sat. fat), 91 mg chol., 271 mg sodium, 3 g carbo., 0 g fiber, 26 g pro. Daily Values: 1% vit. C, 1% calcium, 5% iron. Exchanges: 4 Very Lean Meat, 2½ Fat

STUFFED LAMB BURGERS

In every hot and spicy bite, the feta cheese melts in your mouth. Curry powder spikes the mayonnaise topping.

Prep: 15 minutes Grill: 14 minutes
Makes: 4 servings

2 tablespoons finely chopped onion
1 tablespoon dry red wine
1 teaspoon dried oregano, crushed
¼ teaspoon salt
⅛ teaspoon black pepper
1 pound ground lamb
2 ounces feta cheese, cut into 4 pieces
4 whole wheat hamburger buns, split and toasted
1 recipe Curried Mayonnaise
**   Fresh mesclun greens**

1 In a medium bowl combine onion, red wine, oregano, salt, and pepper. Add ground meat; mix well. Shape into eight 4-inch patties. Place feta on 4 of the patties; cover with remaining patties; press edges to seal.

SMOKIN' HOT TIP

Generally attributed to Northern Italy, pesto sauce is traditionally made using basil, garlic, olive oil, Parmesan cheese, and pine nuts. It's mixed together using a mortar and pestle or a food processor. Today it has taken on new forms using different blends of herbs, nuts, and other ingredients, such as those found in Veal Steak with Easy Orange Pesto, above. You can create your own variations by substituting parsley, cilantro, or arugula or by using peanuts, almonds, or walnuts. Or take the traditional basil blend and add a little interest by incorporating chopped sun-dried tomatoes or jalapeños. Regardless of the combination, pesto is an easy, versatile way to give sandwiches, pastas, pizzas, chicken, and fish new personality.

2 For a charcoal grill, grill patties on the rack of an uncovered grill directly over medium coals for 14 to 18 minutes or until done (160°F), turning once halfway through grilling. (For gas grill, preheat grill. Reduce heat to medium. Place patties on grill rack over heat. Cover; grill as above.) Remove from grill.

3 Spread bottoms of buns with Curried Mayonnaise. Top with lamb patties, mesclun greens, and bun tops.

Curried Mayonnaise: In a small bowl combine ⅓ cup mayonnaise or salad dressing, ½ teaspoon curry powder, and 2 tablespoons golden raisins.

Nutrition Facts per serving: 253 cal., 14 g total fat (1 g sat. fat), 91 mg chol., 271 mg sodium, 3 g carbo., 0 g fiber, 26 g pro. Daily Values: 1% vit. C, 1% calcium, 5% iron. Exchanges: 1½ Starch, 3½ Medium-Fat Meat, 4½ Fat

FOOD FOR THOUGHT KEFTA

A street-vendor favorite in Morocco and throughout the Middle East, kefta are ground lamb meatballs generously seasoned with herbs and spices. For authentic kefta, the meat is shaped into logs around skewers and served with refreshing cucumber-and-yogurt sauce. If you like, serve kefta with pita bread or rice.

LAMB KEFTA
Prep: 25 minutes Grill: 10 minutes
Makes: 4 servings

- ⅓ **cup finely chopped onion (1 small)**
- ½ **cup soft bread crumbs**
- 4 **cloves garlic, minced**
- 2 **tablespoons snipped fresh parsley**
- 1 **tablespoon snipped fresh cilantro**
- 2 **teaspoons snipped fresh oregano**
- 2 **teaspoons snipped fresh mint**
- ½ **teaspoon salt**
- ½ **teaspoon ground cumin**
- ½ **teaspoon ground cinnamon**
- ¼ **teaspoon crushed red pepper (optional)**
- 2 **beaten eggs**
- 1½ **pounds ground lamb**
- ½ **of a small cucumber, peeled and seeded**
- ¾ **cup plain yogurt**
  Salt and black pepper (optional)

1 In a large bowl combine onion, bread crumbs, garlic, parsley, cilantro, oregano, mint, the ½ teaspoon salt, cumin, cinnamon, crushed red pepper (if desired), and eggs. Add lamb; mix well. Divide mixture into 8 portions; shape each around a metal skewer, forming a 6-inch log.

2 For a charcoal grill, grill skewers on the rack of an uncovered grill directly over medium coals for 10 to 12 minutes or until done (160°F), turning once. (For a gas grill, preheat grill. Reduce heat to medium. Place skewers on grill rack over heat. Cover; grill as above.)

3 For cucumber sauce, in a small bowl, stir together cucumber and yogurt. If desired, season to taste with salt and pepper. Serve lamb skewers with cucumber sauce.

Nutrition Facts per serving: 397 cal., 26 g total fat (10 g sat. fat), 220 mg chol., 451 mg sodium, 6 g carbo., 1 g fiber, 33 g pro. Daily Values: 7% vit. A, 9% vit. C, 6% calcium, 17% iron. Exchanges: ½ Other Carbo., 4½ Medium-Fat Meat, ½ Fat

LEMONY LAMB AND LENTILS

Before you fire up the grill, cook the lentil mixture in a saucepan and keep it warm while the lamb chops grill.

Prep: 35 minutes Marinate: 2 to 3 hours Cook: 25 minutes
Grill: 12 minutes Makes: 4 servings

8 lamb loin chops, cut 1 inch thick
3 tablespoons olive oil
2 tablespoons lemon juice
2 teaspoons paprika
½ teaspoon sugar
1 clove garlic, minced
½ teaspoon salt
¼ teaspoon dry mustard
1 14-ounce can beef broth
1 cup lentils, rinsed and drained
¾ cup chopped red sweet pepper
    (1 medium)
2 teaspoons finely shredded lemon peel
2 tablespoons lemon juice
2 cloves garlic, minced
½ cup thinly sliced green onions (4)
¼ cup snipped fresh cilantro
    Crumbled feta cheese (optional)
    Lemon wedges (optional)

1 Trim fat from chops. Place the chops in a self-sealing plastic bag set in a shallow dish. For marinade, in a small bowl combine oil, 2 table-spoons lemon juice, paprika, sugar, garlic, salt, and dry mustard; whisk until well combined. Remove 2 tablespoons of the marinade; set aside. Pour remaining marinade over chops; seal bag. Marinate in refrigerator 2 to 3 hours, turning bag occasionally. Drain chops, discarding marinade.

2 In a medium saucepan combine beef broth, lentils, sweet pepper, lemon peel, 2 table-spoons lemon juice, and garlic. Bring to boiling; reduce heat. Simmer, covered, for 25 to 30 minutes or until lentils are tender, stirring occasionally. Remove from heat. Add reserved marinade, green onions, and cilantro; stir to combine. Cover and keep warm.

3 Meanwhile, for a charcoal grill, grill chops on rack of uncovered grill directly over medium coals until desired doneness, turning once halfway through grilling. Allow 12 to 14 minutes for medium-rare (145°F); 15 to 17 minutes for medium doneness (160°F). (For a gas grill, preheat grill.

Reduce heat to medium. Place chops on grill rack over heat. Cover; grill as at left.)

4 Serve chops with lentil mixture. If desired, sprinkle lentils with the feta cheese and serve with lemon wedges.

Nutrition Facts per serving: 391 cal., 11 g total fat (3 g sat. fat), 80 mg chol., 514 mg sodium, 33 g carbo., 16 g fiber, 41 g pro. Daily Values: 41% vit. A, 98% vit. C, 6% calcium, 40% iron. Exchanges: ½ Vegetable, 2 Starch, 5 Very Lean Meat, 1 Fat

MUSTARD-ROSEMARY GRILLED LAMB

The thick mustard mixture coats the chops just like a marinade. To develop the best flavor, chill the coated chops for 2 to 3 hours.

Prep: 20 minutes Chill: 2 to 3 hours Grill: 12 minutes
Makes: 4 servings

8 lamb rib or loin chops, cut
    1 inch thick
¼ cup stone-ground mustard
¼ cup thinly sliced green onions (2)
2 tablespoons dry white wine
1 tablespoon balsamic vinegar
    or rice vinegar
3 cloves garlic, minced
1 teaspoon snipped fresh rosemary
1 teaspoon honey

1 Trim fat from chops. In a small bowl stir together mustard, green onions, wine, vinegar, garlic, rosemary, honey, ½ teaspoon salt, and ½ teaspoon black pepper. Spread mixture evenly over both sides of chops. Place chops on a large plate and cover loosely with plastic wrap. Chill for 2 to 3 hours.

2 For a charcoal grill, grill chops on the rack of an uncovered grill directly over medium coals until desired doneness, turning once halfway through grilling. Allow 12 to 14 minutes for medium-rare (145°F) and 15 to 17 minutes for medium doneness (160°F). (For a gas grill, preheat grill. Reduce heat to medium. Place chops on grill rack over heat. Cover; grill as above.)

Nutrition Facts per serving: 194 cal., 9 g total fat (3 g sat. fat), 64 mg chol., 557 mg sodium, 4 g carbo., 0 g fiber, 21 g pro. Daily Values: 1% vit. A, 4% vit. C, 4% calcium, 12% iron. Exchanges: ½ Other Carbo., 3 Lean Meat

Lemony Lamb and Lentils

Lamb Chops and Beans with Chile Butter

LAMB CHOPS AND BEANS WITH CHILE BUTTER

Lamb chops slathered with spicy butter and accompanied by a side of Southwestern bean relish are the perfect choice for a casual backyard get-together. Chili Butter enhances other meats and poultry too.

Prep: 25 minutes Chill: 1 hour Grill: 12 minutes
Makes: 4 servings

8 lamb loin chops, cut 1 inch thick
   Salt and black pepper
1 15-ounce can cannellini or pinto beans, rinsed and drained
½ cup chopped celery
¼ cup chopped green onions (2)
1 recipe Chile Butter
1 tablespoon lime juice
   Lime wedges (optional)

1 Trim fat from chops. Sprinkle chops lightly with salt and pepper. For a charcoal grill, grill chops on the rack of an uncovered grill directly over medium coals until desired doneness, turning once halfway through grilling. Allow 12 to 14 minutes for medium-rare (145°F) and 15 to 17 minutes for medium doneness (160°F). (For a gas grill, preheat grill. Reduce heat to medium. Place the chops on grill rack over heat. Cover; grill as above.)

2 Meanwhile, in a medium saucepan combine beans, celery, green onions, and 2 tablespoons of the Chile Butter; heat through. Stir in lime juice. Top each lamb chop with a slice of Chile Butter and serve with bean mixture. If desired, garnish with lime wedges.

Chile Butter: In a small bowl stir together ½ cup softened butter; ¼ cup finely snipped fresh cilantro; 2 fresh jalapeño chile peppers, seeded and finely chopped (see tip, page 36); 1 clove garlic, minced; and 1 teaspoon chili powder. Place on waxed paper; form into a log. Wrap well; chill for 1 hour or overnight. Store in refrigerator for up to 2 weeks or freeze for up to 1 month.

Nutrition Facts per serving: 478 cal., 32 g total fat (18 g sat. fat), 156 mg chol., 661 mg sodium, 17 g carbo., 6 g fiber, 36 g pro. Daily Values: 30% vit. A, 15% vit. C, 7% calcium, 23% iron. Exchanges: ½ Vegetable, 1 Starch, 4½ Lean Meat, 3 Fat

LAMB CHOPS WITH SPICED ONION RELISH

Toward the end of the cooking time, watch the savory-sweet onion mixture closely to be sure it doesn't burn.

Prep: 35 minutes Marinate: 4 to 24 hours Grill: 12 minutes
Makes: 4 servings

- **8 lamb loin chops, cut 1 inch thick**
- **1 cup dry red wine**
- **2 tablespoons cooking oil**
- **2 tablespoons honey**
- **8 whole cloves**
- **6 inches stick cinnamon, broken**
- **2 teaspoons grated fresh ginger**
- **1/2 teaspoon salt**
- **2 large red onions, thinly sliced and separated into rings**
- **1 tablespoon cooking oil**
  Salt and black pepper

1 Trim fat from chops. Place the chops in a self-sealing plastic bag set in a shallow dish. For marinade, in a small bowl stir together wine, the 2 tablespoons oil, the honey, cloves, cinnamon, ginger, and salt. Pour marinade over chops; seal bag. Marinate in the refrigerator for 4 to 24 hours, turning bag occasionally. Drain chops, reserving marinade. Strain marinade; discard cloves and cinnamon. Sprinkle chops with salt and pepper.

2 For a charcoal grill, grill chops on the rack of an uncovered grill directly over medium coals until desired doneness, turning once halfway through grilling. Allow 12 to 14 minutes for medium-rare (145°F) and 15 to 17 minutes for medium doneness (160°F). (For a gas grill, preheat grill. Reduce heat to medium. Place chops on grill rack over heat. Cover; grill as above.)

3 Meanwhile, in a large skillet cook onions in the 1 tablespoon oil over medium heat about 8 minutes or until tender, stirring occasionally. Carefully add reserved marinade to skillet. Bring to boiling; reduce heat. Simmer, uncovered, for 6 to 8 minutes or until most of the liquid is absorbed. Serve onion mixture with chops.

Nutrition Facts per serving: 407 cal., 19 g total fat (4 g sat. fat), 100 mg chol., 533 mg sodium, 15 g carbo., 1 g fiber, 33 g pro. Daily Values: 5% vit. C, 4% calcium, 20% iron. Exchanges: 1½ Vegetable, ½ Other Carbo., 4 Lean Meat, 2½ Fat

ISLAND GLAZED LAMB CHOPS

Baste these thick chops with a dark, sweet-tangy glaze during the last 5 minutes of grilling, just long enough to impart flavor without charring.

Prep: 15 minutes Cook: 15 minutes Grill: 12 minutes
Makes: 4 servings

- **1 cup catsup**
- **1/3 cup molasses**
- **1/3 cup cider vinegar**
- **1/3 cup dark rum**
- **2 tablespoons yellow mustard**
- **1 tablespoon Worcestershire sauce**
  Several dashes bottled hot pepper sauce
- **8 lamb loin chops, cut 1 inch thick**
  Salt and black pepper

1 For the sauce, in a small saucepan combine catsup, molasses, vinegar, rum, mustard, Worcestershire sauce, and hot pepper sauce. Bring to boiling; reduce heat. Simmer, uncovered, for 15 to 20 minutes or until desired consistency, stirring sauce occasionally.

2 Trim fat from chops. Sprinkle with salt and pepper. For a charcoal grill, grill chops on the rack of an uncovered grill directly over medium coals until desired doneness, turning once halfway through grilling and brushing with sauce during final 5 minutes of grilling. Allow 12 to 14 minutes for medium-rare (145°F) and 15 to 17 minutes for medium doneness (160°F). (For a gas grill, preheat grill. Reduce heat to medium. Place chops on grill rack over heat. Cover; grill as above.) Reheat and pass remaining sauce.

Nutrition Facts per serving: 387 cal., 8 g total fat (3 g sat. fat), 90 mg chol., 1,070 mg sodium, 38 g carbo., 1 g fiber, 30 g pro. Daily Values: 12% vit. A, 15% vit. C, 9% calcium, 26% iron. Exchanges: 2½ Other Carbo., 3½ Lean Meat

LAMB CHOPS WITH MASHED CELERIAC

Celeriac flavors creamy mashed potatoes with gentle hints of celery and parsley, making it the perfect accompaniment to these rosemary- and lemon-scented lamb chops.

Prep: 25 minutes Marinate: 1 to 4 hours Grill: 12 minutes
Makes: 4 servings

8 lamb loin chops, cut 1 inch thick
Salt and black pepper
3 tablespoons sherry vinegar or white wine vinegar
3 tablespoons olive oil
1 tablespoon snipped fresh rosemary or 1/2 teaspoon dried rosemary, crushed
2 cloves garlic, minced
1 teaspoon finely shredded lemon peel
3 medium potatoes, peeled and quartered (1 pound)
8 ounces celeriac (celery root), peeled and cut into 1-inch cubes
1 to 2 teaspoons olive oil (optional)
1/4 teaspoon salt
1/8 teaspoon black pepper
1/4 to 1/2 cup milk or chicken broth, warmed

1 Trim fat from chops. Sprinkle chops with salt and pepper. Place chops in a self-sealing plastic bag set in a shallow dish. For marinade, in a small bowl combine vinegar, the 3 tablespoons oil, the rosemary, garlic, and lemon peel. Pour over chops; seal bag. Marinate in the refrigerator for 1 to 4 hours, turning bag occasionally.

2 In a medium covered saucepan cook potatoes and celeriac in lightly salted boiling water for 15 to 20 minutes or until vegetables are tender; drain. Use a ricer or potato masher to mash vegetables. Stir in 1 to 2 teaspoons oil (if desired), salt, and pepper. Stir in enough of the milk to make the vegetables light and fluffy. Cover and keep warm.

3 Drain chops, discarding marinade. For a charcoal grill, grill meat on the rack of an uncovered grill directly over medium coals until desired doneness, turning once halfway through grilling. Allow 12 to 14 minutes for medium-rare (145°F) and 15 to 17 minutes for medium doneness (160°F). (For a gas grill, preheat grill. Reduce heat to medium. Place meat on grill rack over heat. Cover; grill as above.) Serve chops with mashed vegetables.

Nutrition Facts per serving: 429 cal., 20 g total fat (5 g sat. fat), 84 mg chol., 254 mg sodium, 23 g carbo., 3 g fiber, 29 g pro. Daily Values: 1% vit. A, 31% vit. C, 7% calcium, 20% iron. Exchanges: 1½ Starch, 4 Lean Meat, 2 Fat

FOOD FOR THOUGHT CELERIAC

Celeriac, also called celery root, is a variety of celery grown specifically for its root. At its peak in September through May, this round bulbous root has a thick, rough, knobby skin and a crisp white flesh with a strong celery and parsley flavor. Once the skin is removed, place celeriac in water with some lemon juice to prevent discoloration. To serve, thinly slice raw celeriac and use it in salads, or cook and use celeriac similarly to potatoes in purees or gratins.

CURRIED LAMB CHOPS AND POTATOES

Lemon juice, garlic, and curry powder coat lamb chops and skewered new potatoes with enticing flavor.

Prep: 25 minutes Marinate: 4 to 24 hours Grill: 12 minutes
Makes: 4 servings

- ⅓ **cup cooking oil**
- ⅓ **cup lemon juice**
- 1 **tablespoon honey**
- 2 **cloves garlic, minced**
- 2 **teaspoons curry powder**
- 1 **teaspoon salt**
- ¼ **teaspoon black pepper**
- 12 **ounces tiny new potatoes**
- 8 **lamb loin chops, cut 1 inch thick**

1 For the marinade, in a small bowl whisk together oil, lemon juice, honey, garlic, curry powder, salt, and pepper. Set aside.

2 In a medium saucepan cook potatoes in enough water to cover for 15 to 20 minutes or until tender; drain. Halve potatoes and place in a self-sealing plastic bag set in a shallow dish. Pour ½ cup marinade over potatoes; seal bag. Toss gently to mix. Marinate in the refrigerator for 4 to 24 hours, turning bag occasionally.

3 Meanwhile, trim fat from meat. Place chops in a self-sealing plastic bag set in a shallow dish. Pour remaining ¼ cup marinade over lamb chops; seal bag. Marinate in the refrigerator for 4 to 24 hours, turning bag occasionally.

4 Drain chops, discarding marinade. Drain potatoes, discarding marinade. On 4 long metal skewers, thread potatoes, leaving a ¼-inch space between pieces.

5 For a charcoal grill, grill chops and potato skewers on rack of uncovered grill directly over medium coals until desired doneness and potatoes are tender, turning meat once halfway through grilling. Allow 12 to 14 minutes for medium-rare (145°F), 15 to 17 minutes for medium doneness (160°F). Turn potatoes as needed until browned. (For a gas grill, preheat grill. Reduce heat to medium. Place chops and potato skewers on grill rack over heat. Cover; grill as above.)

Nutrition Facts per serving: 288 cal., 11 g total fat (3 g sat. fat), 90 mg chol., 202 mg sodium, 16 g carbo., 1 g fiber, 31 g pro. Daily Values: 25% vit. C, 3% calcium, 21% iron. Exchanges: 1 Starch, 4 Lean Meat

Curried Lamb Chops and Potatoes

LAMB CHOPS WITH TAPENADE

For a feast that takes diners to the Mediterranean, top chops with tapenade, a traditional condiment in southern France, and serve with focaccia, the Italian flatbread, if you like.

Prep: 25 minutes Grill: 12 minutes
Makes: 4 servings

8 lamb loin chops, cut 1 inch thick
1 tablespoon olive oil
¹⁄₂ teaspoon dried Italian seasoning,
   crushed
¹⁄₄ teaspoon black pepper
1 recipe Tapenade
4 3-inch squares focaccia bread or
   8 slices sourdough bread,
   toasted (optional)

1 Trim fat from the chops. For the rub, in a bowl combine olive oil, Italian seasoning, and pepper. Evenly spoon rub over chops; rub in with your fingers.

2 For a charcoal grill, grill chops on the rack of an uncovered grill directly over medium coals until desired doneness, turning once halfway through grilling. Allow 12 to 14 minutes for medium-rare (145°F) and 15 to 17 minutes for medium doneness (160°F). (For a gas grill, preheat grill. Reduce heat to medium. Place chops on grill rack over heat. Cover; grill as above.)

3 Spoon Tapenade on chops. If desired, serve with toasted focaccia bread.

Tapenade: In a blender or food processor combine ¹⁄₂ cup chopped roasted red sweet pepper; ¹⁄₂ cup thinly sliced pimiento-stuffed green olives; 1 tablespoon olive oil; 1 tablespoon capers, drained; 1 tablespoon red wine vinegar; ¹⁄₂ teaspoon dried Italian seasoning, crushed; 1 clove garlic, minced; and ¹⁄₄ teaspoon black pepper. Cover and blend or process with several on/off turns until finely chopped. Set aside.

Nutrition Facts per serving: 452 cal., 20 g total fat (4 g sat. fat), 116 mg chol., 772 mg sodium, 27 g carbo., 2 g fiber, 41 g pro. Daily Values: 2% vit. A, 89% vit. C, 14% calcium, 24% iron. Exchanges: ¹⁄₂ Vegetable, 1¹⁄₂ Starch, 5 Lean Meat, 1 Fat

Lamb Chops with Tapenade

LAMB WITH APPLE-MINT VINAIGRETTE

The delightfully minty marinade in this lamb recipe replaces ho-hum mint jelly.

Prep: 20 minutes Marinate: 4 to 24 hours Grill: 11 minutes
Makes: 4 servings

- **1 lamb leg center slice, cut ³/₄ inch thick**
- **³/₄ cup apple juice**
- **¹/₂ cup snipped fresh mint**
- **¹/₄ cup olive oil**
- **3 tablespoons lime juice**
- **2 shallots, finely chopped**
- **¹/₂ teaspoon salt**
- **¹/₂ teaspoon black pepper**

1 Trim fat from meat. Place the meat in a self-sealing plastic bag set in a shallow dish. For marinade, in a small bowl combine apple juice, mint, olive oil, lime juice, shallots, salt, and pepper. Pour half of the marinade over meat; seal bag. Marinate in refrigerator for 4 to 24 hours, turning occasionally. Cover and chill remaining marinade. Drain meat; discard marinade.

2 For a charcoal grill, grill meat on the rack of an uncovered grill directly over medium coals until desired doneness, turning meat once halfway through grilling. Allow 11 to 12 minutes for medium-rare (145°F) and 13 to 14 minutes for medium doneness (160°F). (For a gas grill, preheat grill. Reduce heat to medium. Place meat on grill rack over heat. Cover; grill as above.) Serve with reserved marinade.

Nutrition Facts per serving: 255 cal., 15 g total fat (4 g sat. fat), 72 mg chol., 248 mg sodium, 5 g carbo., 0 g fiber, 24 g pro. Daily Values: 1% vit. A, 12% vit. C, 2% calcium, 20% iron. Exchanges: ½ Other Carbo., 3½ Lean Meat, 1 Fat

INDIAN-SPICED LAMB KABOBS

Indian cooks favor fragrant turmeric and often blend it into curry powder for extra flavor and color. It tastes especially good with lamb.

Prep: 15 minutes Marinate: 4 to 6 hours Grill: 12 minutes
Makes: 4 to 6 servings

- **2 pounds boneless leg of lamb, cut into 1¹/₂-inch cubes**
- **¹/₃ cup olive oil**
- **¹/₄ cup sherry vinegar**
- **¹/₄ cup snipped fresh oregano**
- **1 teaspoon ground cumin**
- **1 teaspoon paprika**
- **¹/₂ teaspoon salt**
- **¹/₂ teaspoon ground turmeric**
- **2 oranges**

1 Trim fat from meat. Place meat in a self-sealing plastic bag set in a shallow dish. For marinade, in a small bowl combine olive oil, vinegar, 1 tablespoon of the oregano, cumin, paprika, salt, and turmeric. Pour over meat; seal bag. Marinate in the refrigerator for 4 to 6 hours, turning bag occasionally. Meanwhile, cut the oranges into ¹/₂-inch slices; quarter slices.

2 On long metal skewers, alternately thread meat and orange pieces, leaving a ¹/₄-inch space between pieces.

3 For a charcoal grill, grill kabobs on the rack of an uncovered grill directly over medium coals for 12 to 14 minutes or until meat is slightly pink in the center (145°F), turning and brushing once with marinade halfway through grilling. (For a gas grill, preheat grill. Reduce heat to medium. Place kabobs on grill rack over heat. Cover; grill as above.)

4 To serve, remove meat and orange pieces from skewers; sprinkle with the remaining 3 tablespoons oregano.

Nutrition Facts per serving: 475 cal., 26 g total fat (5 g sat. fat), 144 mg chol., 398 mg sodium, 9 g carbo., 2 g fiber, 47 g pro. Daily Values: 8% vit. A, 60% vit. C, 6% calcium, 26% iron. Exchanges: ½ Fruit, 7 Lean Meat, 1 Fat

LAMB KABOBS WITH MUSTARD MARINADE

Prep: 20 minutes Marinate: 2 to 6 hours Grill: 12 minutes
Makes: 4 servings

12 ounces lean boneless leg of lamb
¼ cup Dijon-style mustard
 3 tablespoons lemon juice
 1 green onion, finely chopped
 2 teaspoons snipped fresh thyme or
     ½ teaspoon dried thyme, crushed
16 tiny new potatoes, halved
     (about 1¼ pounds)
 1 small red onion, cut into wedges
 1 red, yellow, or green sweet pepper,
     cut into 1½-inch squares
     Hot cooked orzo (rosamarina)
     (optional)

1 Trim fat from meat. Cut meat in 1-inch cubes. Place meat in self-sealing plastic bag set in a shallow dish. For marinade, combine mustard, lemon juice, green onion, and thyme. Pour half the marinade over meat; seal bag. Marinate in refrigerator for 2 to 6 hours; turn occasionally. Cover and chill remaining marinade.

2 Place a steamer basket in a large saucepan. Add water to just below the bottom of the steamer basket. Bring to boiling. Add potatoes. Steam, covered, for 10 to 12 minutes or just until potatoes are tender. Remove steamer basket from saucepan; cool potatoes for 5 minutes. Break each onion wedge into 2 or 3 layers. Drain meat, discarding marinade. On eight 6- to 8-inch metal skewers, alternately thread meat, potatoes, onion, and sweet pepper, leaving a ¼-inch space between pieces.

3 For a charcoal grill, grill kabobs on the rack of an uncovered grill directly over medium coals for 12 to 14 minutes or until meat is slightly pink in the center (145°F), turning and brushing occasionally with reserved marinade up to the last 5 minutes of grilling. (For a gas grill, preheat grill. Reduce heat to medium. Place kabobs on grill rack over heat. Cover; grill as above.) If desired, serve kabobs with orzo.

Nutrition Facts per serving: 249 cal., 4 g total fat (1 g sat. fat), 56 mg chol., 413 mg sodium, 32 g carbo., 3 g fiber, 24 g pro. Daily Values: 18% vit. A, 125% vit. C, 6% calcium, 23% iron. Exchanges: 1 Vegetable, 1½ Starch, 2 Lean Meat

GYROS WITH TZATZIKI

Tzatziki, a traditional Greek yogurt and cucumber sauce, is the ideal accompaniment to grilled lamb. Serve a generous spoonful in each lamb-filled pita bread.

Prep: 25 minutes Marinate: 4 to 24 hours Grill: 1½ hours
Stand: 15 minutes Makes: 8 servings

 1 3- to 4-pound boneless leg of lamb,
     rolled and tied
½ cup olive oil
 3 tablespoons lemon juice
 6 cloves garlic, minced
¼ cup snipped fresh oregano
¼ cup snipped fresh mint
 1 teaspoon salt
¼ teaspoon black pepper
 8 pita bread rounds
 1 recipe Tzatziki
     Sliced tomatoes (optional)
     Shredded lettuce (optional)

1 Untie roast and trim fat from meat. Place lamb in a self-sealing plastic bag set in a shallow dish. For marinade, in a small bowl stir together olive oil, lemon juice, garlic, oregano, mint, salt, and pepper. Pour over meat; seal bag. Marinate in the refrigerator for 4 to 24 hours, turning bag occasionally. Drain meat, reserving marinade. Retie meat with 100-percent-cotton kitchen string. Insert a meat thermometer into the center of meat.

2 For a charcoal grill, arrange medium coals around a drip pan. Test for medium-low heat above pan. Place roast on grill rack over drip pan. Cover; grill until meat thermometer registers desired doneness. Allow 1½ to 2¼ hours for medium-rare (135°F) or 1¾ to 2½ hours for medium doneness (150°F). Brush occasionally with marinade during first 1½ hours of grilling. (For a gas grill, preheat grill. Reduce heat to medium-low. Adjust for indirect cooking. Grill as above, except place roast on rack in roasting pan.)

3 Remove meat from grill. Cover with foil and let stand for 15 minutes before slicing. (Meat temperature will rise 10°F during standing.) To serve, remove strings and thinly slice meat. Serve in pita bread with Tzatziki and, if desired, tomatoes and lettuce.

Tzatziki: In a medium bowl combine one 8-ounce carton plain yogurt; 1 cup shredded, seeded cucumber; 1 tablespoon lemon juice; 1 tablespoon olive oil; 1 tablespoon snipped fresh mint; 1 clove garlic, minced; and ¼ teaspoon salt. Cover and chill for up to 4 hours.

Nutrition Facts per serving: 531 cal., 23 g total fat (5 g sat. fat), 110 mg chol., 784 mg sodium, 38 g carbo., 2 g fiber, 42 g pro. Daily Values: 2% vit. A, 14% vit. C, 13% calcium, 30% iron. Exchanges: 2½ Starch, 5 Lean Meat, 1 Fat

GREEK LAMB PLATTER

Today's boneless legs of lamb are tender, deliciously mild, and easy to prepare. Consider young spring lamb from Australia and New Zealand. It costs a little more, but its mellow flavor is a global favorite.

Prep: 20 minutes Marinate: 8 to 24 hours Grill: 8 minutes
Makes: 6 servings

1½ **to 2 pounds boneless leg of lamb**
  1 **tablespoon finely shredded lemon peel**
  ⅔ **cup lemon juice**
  6 **tablespoons olive oil**
  ⅓ **cup snipped fresh oregano**
  ½ **teaspoon salt**
  ⅛ **teaspoon black pepper**
  ½ **cup snipped fresh parsley**
  2 **ounces crumbled feta cheese (½ cup)**
  ¼ **cup pitted, sliced kalamata olives**
      or other ripe olives
  ¼ **teaspoon ground cinnamon**
  ¼ **teaspoon black pepper**
  2 **pounds roma tomatoes**

1 Trim fat from meat. Cut lamb across the grain into ½- to ¾-inch slices. Place lamb in a large self-sealing plastic bag set in a shallow dish. For marinade, in a small bowl stir together lemon peel, ⅓ cup of the lemon juice, 4 tablespoons of the oil, the oregano, salt, and the ⅛ teaspoon pepper. Pour marinade over meat; seal bag. Marinate in refrigerator 8 to 24 hours; turning occasionally.

2 In a large bowl combine the remaining lemon juice, 1 tablespoon of the remaining oil, the parsley, feta cheese, olives, cinnamon, and the ¼ teaspoon pepper; set aside. Drain lamb; discard marinade. Brush tomatoes with the remaining 1 tablespoon oil.

3 For a charcoal grill, grill lamb and tomatoes on rack of uncovered grill directly over medium coals until meat is desired doneness and tomatoes are slightly charred, turning once halfway through grilling. Allow about 8 minutes for medium-rare (145°F), about 10 minutes for medium doneness (160°F). (For a gas grill, preheat grill. Reduce heat to medium. Place meat and tomatoes on grill rack over heat. Cover; grill as above.)

4 Transfer tomatoes to a cutting board; cool slightly; slice. Toss the tomatoes with the feta cheese mixture. Serve lamb with tomato mixture.

Nutrition Facts per serving: 256 cal., 14 g total fat (4 g sat. fat), 66 mg chol., 493 mg sodium, 11 g carbo., 0 g fiber, 22 g pro. Daily Values: 15% vit. A, 80% vit. C, 6% calcium, 18% iron. Exchanges: 2 Vegetable, 2½ Lean Meat, 1½ Fat

Greek Lamb Platter

DIRECT GRILLING PORK

For a charcoal grill, place meat on grill rack directly over medium coals. Grill, uncovered, for the time given below or to desired doneness, turning once halfway through grilling. For a gas grill, preheat grill. Reduce heat to medium. Place meat on grill rack over heat. Cover the grill. Test for doneness using a meat thermometer.

CUT	THICKNESS/ WEIGHT	GRILLING TEMPERATURE	APPROXIMATE DIRECT-GRILLING TIME	DONENESS
Chop with bone (loin or rib)	¾ to 1 inch 1¼ to 1½ inches	Medium Medium	11 to 13 minutes 16 to 20 minutes	160°F medium 160°F medium
Chop (boneless top loin)	¾ to 1 inch 1¼ to 1½ inches	Medium Medium	7 to 9 minutes 14 to 18 minutes	160°F medium 160°F medium
Ground pork patties	½ inch ¾ inch	Medium Medium	10 to 13 minutes 14 to 18 minutes	160°F medium 160°F medium
Ham, cooked (slice)	1 inch	Medium	14 to 18 minutes	140°F medium
Kabobs	1-inch cubes 1½-inch cubes	Medium Medium	12 to 15 minutes 18 to 20 minutes	160°F medium 160°F medium
Sausages, cooked (frankfurters, smoked bratwurst, etc.)		Medium	3 to 7 minutes	Heated through

INDIRECT GRILLING PORK

For a charcoal grill, arrange medium-hot coals around a drip pan. Test for medium heat above pan, unless chart says otherwise. Place meat, fat side up, on grill rack over drip pan. Cover and grill for the time given below or to desired temperature, adding more charcoal to maintain heat as necessary. For a gas grill, preheat grill. Reduce heat to medium. Adjust heat for indirect cooking. Test for doneness using a meat thermometer. Thermometer should register the "final grilling temperature." Remove meat from grill. For larger cuts, such as roasts, cover with foil and let stand 15 minutes before slicing. The meat's temperature will rise 5°F to 10°F during the time it stands.

CUT	THICKNESS/ WEIGHT	APPROXIMATE INDIRECT-GRILLING TIME	FINAL GRILLING TEMPERATURE (when to remove from grill)	FINAL DONENESS TEMPERATURE (after 15 minutes standing)
Boneless top loin roast (medium-low heat)	2 to 3 pounds (single loin) 3 to 5 pounds (double loin, tied)	1 to 1½ hours 1½ to 2¼ hours	150°F 150°F	160°F medium 160°F medium
Chop (boneless top loin)	¾ to 1 inch 1¼ to 1½ inches	20 to 24 minutes 30 to 35 minutes	160°F medium 160°F medium	No standing time No standing time
Chop (loin or rib)	¾ to 1 inch 1¼ to 1½ inches	22 to 25 minutes 35 to 40 minutes	160°F medium 160°F medium	No standing time No standing time
Country-style ribs		1½ to 2 hours	Tender	No standing time
Loin back ribs or spareribs		1½ to 1¾ hours	Tender	No standing time
Sausages, uncooked (bratwurst, Polish or Italian sausage links, etc.)	about 4 per pound	20 to 30 minutes	160°F medium	No standing time
Smoked shoulder picnic (with bone), cooked (medium-low heat)	4 to 6 pounds	1½ to 2¼ hours	140°F	No standing time
Tenderloin (medium-high heat)	¾ to 1 pound	30 to 35 minutes	155°F	160°F medium

All cooking times are based on meat removed directly from refrigerator.

Spiced Pork Burgers with Mango Mayonnaise

SPICED PORK BURGERS WITH MANGO MAYONNAISE

The versatile burger does it again: Try this one featuring ginger, curry powder, allspice, and a refreshing fruit-and-mayonnaise topping.

Prep: 25 minutes Grill: 14 minutes
Makes: 6 servings

- **2 tablespoons dry white wine or water**
- **2 tablespoons fine dry bread crumbs**
- **1 to 2 tablespoons bottled hot pepper sauce**
- **3 to 4 teaspoons grated fresh ginger**
- **3 to 4 teaspoons curry powder**
- **¹⁄₂ teaspoon ground allspice**
- **4 cloves garlic, minced**
- **1¹⁄₂ pounds ground pork**
- **6 ¹⁄₄-inch-thick slices sweet onion (such as Vidalia or Maui)**
- **6 hamburger buns, split and toasted**
- **1 bunch stemmed watercress**
- **1 recipe Mango Mayonnaise**

1 In a medium bowl combine wine, bread crumbs, hot pepper sauce, ginger, curry powder, ¹⁄₂ teaspoon salt, allspice, and garlic. Add ground pork; mix well. Shape pork mixture into six ³⁄₄-inch-thick patties.

2 For a charcoal grill, grill patties and onion slices on the rack of an uncovered grill directly over medium coals for 14 to 18 minutes or until meat is done (160°F), turning pork and onion slices once halfway through grilling. (For a gas grill, preheat grill. Reduce heat to medium. Place patties and onion slices on grill rack over heat. Cover; grill as above.)

3 Serve burgers on buns with grilled onion slices, watercress, and Mango Mayonnaise.

Nutrition Facts per serving: 357 cal., 18 g total fat (5 g sat. fat), 60 mg chol., 578 mg sodium, 29 g carbo., 2 g fiber, 19 g pro. Daily Values: 4% vit. A, 12% vit. C, 9% calcium, 16% iron. Exchanges: 2 Starch, 2 Medium-Fat Meat, 1¹⁄₂ Fat

PORK BURGERS WITH TANGY-SWEET BARBECUE SAUCE

Sausage seasoning is a ready-mixed blend of salt, sage, and other herbs. Look for it in the herb and spice aisle of your supermarket.

Prep: 10 minutes Grill: 14 minutes
Makes: 4 servings

1 pound ground pork
1 teaspoon sausage seasoning
1 recipe Tangy-Sweet Barbecue
   Sauce
8 slices Texas toast, toasted
4 lettuce leaves
4 tomato slices
4 onion slices

1 In a medium bowl combine ground pork and sausage seasoning. Shape pork mixture into four ¾-inch-thick patties.

2 For a charcoal grill, grill patties on the rack of an uncovered grill directly over medium coals for 14 to 18 minutes or until meat is done (160°F), turning once and brushing with Tangy-Sweet Barbecue Sauce halfway through grilling. (For a gas grill, preheat grill. Reduce heat to medium. Place patties on grill rack over heat. Cover; grill as above.)

3 Serve burgers on Texas toast with lettuce, tomato, and onion. If desired, spoon any remaining sauce over burgers.

Tangy-Sweet Barbecue Sauce: In a medium saucepan combine 1 cup catsup, ½ cup packed brown sugar, ⅓ cup granulated sugar, 3 tablespoons cooking oil, 2 tablespoons vinegar, 1 tablespoon honey, and 2 teaspoons Worcestershire sauce. Cook and stir catsup mixture over medium heat until sugars dissolve and sauce is heated through. (Sauce can be covered and chilled for up to 1 week.)

Nutrition Facts per serving: 613 cal., 20 g total fat (5 g sat. fat), 53 mg chol., 1,144 mg sodium, 91 g carbo., 3 g fiber, 20 g pro. Daily Values: 20% vit. A, 23% vit. C, 10% calcium, 21% iron. Exchanges: ½ Vegetable, 3 Starch, 3 Other Carbo., 2 Medium-Fat Meat, 1 Fat

PORK SKEWERS WITH CHERRY-PINEAPPLE GLAZE

Serve these shiny pork meatballs over hot cooked rice to soak up the sweet glaze.

Prep: 30 minutes Grill: 12 minutes
Makes: 6 servings

1 slightly beaten egg
⅓ cup finely chopped water chestnuts
¼ cup fine dry bread crumbs
2 teaspoons grated fresh ginger
½ teaspoon garlic salt
¼ teaspoon black pepper
1 pound ground pork
1 large red, yellow, or green sweet
   pepper, cut into 1-inch pieces
1 recipe Cherry-Pineapple Glaze

1 In a medium bowl combine egg, water chestnuts, bread crumbs, ginger, garlic salt, and pepper. Add ground pork; mix well. Shape pork mixture into thirty 1¼- to 1½-inch meatballs.

2 Onto 6 long metal skewers, alternately thread meatballs and sweet pepper pieces, leaving a ¼-inch space between pieces.

3 For a charcoal grill, arrange medium-hot coals around a drip pan. Test for medium heat above pan. Place skewers on greased grill rack over pan. Cover; grill for 12 to 15 minutes or until meatballs are no longer pink and juices run clear. Brush with some of the Cherry-Pineapple Glaze. Immediately remove skewers from grill. (For a gas grill, preheat grill. Reduce heat to medium. Adjust for indirect cooking. Grill as above.) Serve skewers with remaining glaze.

Cherry-Pineapple Glaze: Place ⅔ cup cherry preserves in a small saucepan; snip any large pieces. Stir in ¼ cup pineapple juice, 1 tablespoon lemon juice, and ¼ teaspoon ground cardamom. Bring to boiling; reduce heat. Simmer, uncovered, for 15 minutes. Cool about 10 minutes (glaze will thicken as it cools).

Nutrition Facts per serving: 230 cal., 7 g total fat (3 g sat. fat), 71 mg chol., 220 mg sodium, 31 g carbo., 1 g fiber, 11 g pro. Daily Values: 31% vit. A, 91% vit. C, 3% calcium, 7% iron. Exchanges: 2 Other Carbo., 2 Medium-Fat Meat

JALAPEÑO SAUSAGES

This is homemade sausage done the easy way. A delicious mix of spices and a tortilla wrapping give it authentic Southwestern flair.

Prep: 15 minutes Chill: 6 to 24 hours Grill: 20 minutes
Makes: 4 servings

  4 ounces fresh jalapeño chile peppers,
    seeded and finely chopped (see
    tip, page 36), or one 4-ounce can
    jalapeño chile peppers, drained
    and chopped
  2 tablespoons snipped fresh cilantro
  2 tablespoons beer or water
  1 teaspoon cumin seeds, crushed
  ½ teaspoon salt
  ¼ teaspoon black pepper
  ⅛ teaspoon cayenne pepper
  1 clove garlic, minced
  1 pound ground pork
  4 8-inch whole wheat flour tortillas
    or 4 frankfurter buns, split
    and toasted

1 In a medium bowl combine jalapeño peppers, cilantro, beer, cumin seeds, salt, black pepper, cayenne pepper, and garlic. Add ground pork; mix well. Divide pork mixture into 4 equal portions. Shape each portion into a 6-inch-long log. Cover and chill for 6 to 24 hours or until firm.

2 Stack tortillas and wrap in foil; set tortillas aside. For a charcoal grill, arrange medium-hot coals around a drip pan. Test for medium heat above pan. Place meat on grill rack over drip pan. Cover; grill for 15 minutes, turning occasionally. Add tortillas to grill directly over coals. Cover; grill for 5 to 10 minutes more or until meat is done (160°F) and tortillas are heated through, turning tortillas once halfway through grilling. (For a gas grill, preheat grill. Reduce heat to medium. Adjust for indirect cooking. Grill as above.) Serve sausages in warm tortillas.

Nutrition Facts per serving: 288 cal., 11 g total fat (4 g sat. fat), 53 mg chol., 716 mg sodium, 28 g carbo., 3 g fiber, 19 g pro. Daily Values: 8% vit. A, 19% vit. C, 4% calcium, 4% iron. Exchanges: 2 Starch, 2 Medium-Fat Meat

HOMEMADE PORK SAUSAGE LINKS

Nestle these skewered and grilled pork logs in a hot dog bun and wrap your hands around this meal.

Prep: 15 minutes Grill: 14 minutes
Makes: 4 servings

  3 tablespoons finely snipped
    fresh basil
  1 teaspoon sugar
  1 teaspoon fennel seeds
  1 teaspoon crushed red pepper
  ¾ teaspoon salt
  ½ teaspoon black pepper
  1 clove garlic, minced
  1½ pounds ground pork
  4 frankfurter buns, split and toasted

1 In a large bowl combine basil, sugar, fennel seeds, red pepper, salt, black pepper, and garlic. Add ground pork; mix well. Divide pork mixture into 4 equal portions. Shape each portion around a flat-sided metal skewer to form a 6-inch-long log.

2 For a charcoal grill, grill meat on the rack of an uncovered grill directly over medium coals for 14 to 18 minutes or until done (160°F), turning once halfway through grilling. (For a gas grill, preheat grill. Reduce heat to medium. Place meat on grill rack over heat. Cover; grill as above.)

3 To serve, use the tines of a fork to remove the meat from skewers. Serve in toasted buns.

Nutrition Facts per serving: 210 cal., 12 g total fat (5 g sat. fat), 79 mg chol., 469 mg sodium, 2 g carbo., 0 g fiber, 21 g pro. Daily Values: 3% vit. A, 1% vit. C, 1% calcium, 10% iron. Exchanges: 3 Medium-Fat Meat

ASIAN-APRICOT GLAZED CHOPS

Handle this very spicy Oriental chili-garlic sauce
the same way you would hot pepper sauce:
A little goes a long way.

Prep: 15 minutes Grill: 11 minutes
Makes: 4 servings

- **¹/₃ cup apricot preserves**
- **1 tablespoon Oriental chili-garlic sauce**
- **2 teaspoons soy sauce**
- **¹/₄ teaspoon ground ginger**
- **4 boneless pork sirloin chops,
  cut ³/₄ inch thick**
- **Salt**
- **Black pepper**

1 For glaze, place apricot preserves in a small bowl; snip any large pieces of fruit. Stir in chili-garlic sauce, soy sauce, and ginger. Set glaze aside. Sprinkle both sides of pork chops with salt and pepper.

2 For a charcoal grill, grill chops on the rack of an uncovered grill directly over medium coals for 11 to 13 minutes or until chops are slightly pink in the centers and juices run clear (160°F), turning once halfway through grilling and brushing with glaze during the last 2 to 3 minutes of grilling. (For a gas grill, preheat grill. Reduce heat to medium. Place chops on grill rack over heat. Cover; grill as above.)

Nutrition Facts per serving: 317 cal., 9 g total fat (3 g sat. fat), 106 mg chol., 515 mg sodium, 20 g carbo., 0 g fiber, 36 g pro. Daily Values: 3% vit. A, 6% vit. C, 3% calcium, 10% iron. Exchanges: 1½ Other Carbo., 5 Very Lean Meat, 1 Fat

FOOD FOR THOUGHT CHILES

Over 200 varieties of chiles available today offer a great range in color, heat, and taste. Whether you use fresh or dried varieties, chiles add a flavorful dimension to sauces, marinades, and rubs. Here is an overview of the more common types which you can find in most grocery stores and Hispanic and Asian markets.

● Anaheim: **Grown in New Mexico and California, the Anaheim is easy to find in supermarkets, either fresh or canned. It is moderate in heat. When ripened to red and dried, it's used to make decorative hangings.**

● Poblano: **Typically dark green in color, poblanos have a rich but slightly bitter flavor with varying levels of heat. Poblanos are commonly used to make the classic dish called chile rellenos. They are often roasted to sweeten their flavor.**

● Ancho: **A dried poblano chile, the ancho is dark purple in color with a deep, complex flavor and subdued heat.**

● Jalapeño: **Used commonly in salsas, jalapeños are fresh, grassy, slightly sweet, and range from medium to medium hot.**

● Chipotle: **A jalapeño that has been dried and smoked to derive an earthy, sweet flavor. Chipotles are very hot and are often sold marinated and canned in a vinegary tomato sauce called "adobo."**

● Serrano: **Green or red when ripe, serranos have a grassy flavor and are used to add sharp heat to salsas and sauces.**

● Habanero: **Ranging from light green to orange when ripe, habaneros have the highest heat of all the chiles, but the heat dissipates relatively quickly.**

● Thai: **These small chiles pack a fiery heat that lingers. They are popular in Southeast Asian dishes and come in green, red, and yellow.**

APPLE BUTTER CHOPS

A zesty steak seasoning combines with sweet apple butter to give your taste buds a reason to smile.

Prep: 10 minutes Grill: 11 minutes
Makes: 4 servings

- **4 pork rib chops, cut ³/₄ inch thick**
- **¹/₂ teaspoon Kansas City or Montreal steak seasoning**
- **¹/₂ cup bottled chili sauce**
- **¹/₄ cup apple butter**
- **¹/₂ teaspoon apple pie spice, pumpkin pie spice, or ground cinnamon**
- **2 medium zucchini or yellow summer squash, halved lengthwise**

1 Trim fat from chops. Sprinkle both sides of chops lightly with steak seasoning. For sauce, in a small bowl stir together chili sauce, apple butter, and apple pie spice. Set sauce aside.

2 For a charcoal grill, grill chops and zucchini on the rack of an uncovered grill directly over medium coals for 11 to 13 minutes or until chops are slightly pink in the centers and juices run clear (160°F) and zucchini is tender, turning once halfway through grilling and brushing chops and zucchini with sauce during the last 5 minutes of grilling. (For a gas grill, preheat grill. Reduce heat to medium. Place chops and zucchini on grill rack over heat. Cover; grill as above.)

Nutrition Facts per serving: 378 cal., 9 g total fat (3 g sat. fat), 110 mg chol., 622 mg sodium, 33 g carbo., 4 g fiber, 39 g pro. Daily Values: 10% vit. A, 20% vit. C, 5% calcium, 12% iron. Exchanges: 1 Vegetable, 2 Other Carbo., 5 Very Lean Meat, 1 Fat

LEMON-AND-HERB RUBBED PORK CHOPS

The rub is just moist enough to cover the chops easily. The recipe makes exactly the right amount for four thick chops.

Prep: 15 minutes Grill: 35 minutes
Makes: 4 servings

- **1¹/₂ teaspoons finely shredded lemon peel**
- **1 teaspoon dried rosemary, crushed**
- **¹/₂ teaspoon salt**
- **¹/₂ teaspoon dried sage, crushed**
- **¹/₂ teaspoon black pepper**

- **8 cloves garlic, minced**
- **4 pork loin chops, cut 1¹/₄ inches thick**

1 For rub, in a small bowl combine lemon peel, rosemary, salt, sage, pepper, and garlic. Trim fat from chops. Sprinkle rub evenly over both sides of chops; rub in with your fingers.

2 For a charcoal grill, arrange medium-hot coals around a drip pan. Test for medium heat above pan. Place chops on grill rack over pan. Cover; grill for 35 to 40 minutes or until chops are slightly pink in centers and juices run clear (160°F), turning once halfway through grilling. (For a gas grill, preheat. Reduce heat to medium. Adjust for indirect cooking. Grill as above.)

Nutrition Facts per serving: 292 cal., 10 g total fat (4 g sat. fat), 105 mg chol., 371 mg sodium, 3 g carbo., 1 g fiber, 43 g pro. Daily Values: 1% vit. A, 6% vit. C, 5% calcium, 8% iron. Exchanges: 6 Very Lean Meat, 1¹/₂ Fat

DOUBLE PEANUT-CRUSTED CHOPS

Keep the grill cover handy for this one. The Better Homes and Gardens₀ Test Kitchen recommends that you cover the grill after adding the peanut "crust" so it gets slightly crispy.

Prep: 15 minutes Grill: 11 minutes
Makes: 4 servings

- **¹/₃ cup creamy peanut butter**
- **¹/₃ cup pineapple juice**
- **2 tablespoons finely chopped green onion (1)**
- **1 tablespoon soy sauce**
- **1 tablespoon honey**
- **1 teaspoon grated fresh ginger or ¹/₄ teaspoon ground ginger**
- **¹/₂ teaspoon dry mustard**
- **Several dashes bottled hot pepper sauce**
- **¹/₃ cup finely chopped honey-roasted peanuts**
- **2 tablespoons fine dry bread crumbs**
- **1 tablespoon toasted sesame seeds**
- **4 boneless pork sirloin chops, cut ³/₄ inch thick**
- **4 ounces Chinese egg noodles or dried angel hair pasta**

1 For peanut sauce, in a small saucepan heat peanut butter until melted; gradually whisk in pineapple juice, green onion, soy sauce, honey, ginger, mustard, and hot pepper sauce. Set aside 2 tablespoons of the peanut sauce. Keep remaining peanut sauce warm. For crust, in a small bowl combine peanuts, bread crumbs, and sesame seeds; set aside.

2 For a charcoal grill, grill chops on the rack of an uncovered grill directly over medium coals for 6 minutes. Turn chops; brush with the reserved 2 tablespoons peanut sauce. Sprinkle chops with crust mixture. With the back of a metal spatula, press crust mixture onto chops. Cover; grill for 5 to 7 minutes more or until chops are slightly pink in the centers and juices run clear (160°F). (For a gas grill, preheat grill. Reduce heat to medium. Place chops on grill rack over heat. Cover; grill as above.)

3 Meanwhile, cook noodles according to package directions; drain. Toss noodles with remaining warm peanut sauce. Serve with chops.

Nutrition Facts per serving: 510 cal., 23 g total fat (5 g sat. fat), 89 mg chol., 518 mg sodium, 39 g carbo., 6 g fiber, 42 g pro. Daily Values: 2% vit. A, 7% vit. C, 8% calcium, 20% iron. Exchanges: 1 Starch, 1½ Other Carbo., 5½ Lean Meat, 1 Fat

Mushroom-Stuffed Pork Chops

MUSHROOM-STUFFED PORK CHOPS

The only thing better than a grilled pork chop is a grilled stuffed pork chop.

Prep: 25 minutes Grill: 35 minutes
Makes: 4 servings

¹/₂ **cup coarsely chopped fresh mushrooms (such as button, chanterelle, or shiitake)**
¹/₄ **cup chopped onion**
 1 **tablespoon butter or margarine**
 1 **teaspoon grated fresh ginger**
¹/₄ **teaspoon salt**
¹/₄ **teaspoon black pepper**
 1 **cup coarsely chopped fresh spinach**
¹/₄ **cup soft bread crumbs**
 4 **pork loin chops or pork rib chops, cut 1¹/₄ inches thick**
¹/₄ **cup ginger jelly or preserves or orange marmalade**

1 For stuffing, in a small saucepan cook mushrooms and onion in hot butter until onion is tender. Remove saucepan from heat; stir in ginger, salt, and pepper. Add spinach and bread crumbs, tossing gently until combined.

2 Trim fat from chops. Make a pocket in each chop by cutting horizontally from the fat side almost to the bone. Spoon one-fourth of the stuffing into each pocket. Secure openings with wooden toothpicks. Sprinkle chops with additional salt and pepper.

3 For a charcoal grill, arrange medium-hot coals around a drip pan. Test for medium heat above pan. Place chops on grill rack over pan. Cover; grill for 35 to 40 minutes or until chops are slightly pink in center and juices run clear (160°F), turning once, brushing occasionally with ginger jelly during the last 5 minutes of grilling. (For a gas grill, preheat. Reduce heat to medium. Adjust for indirect cooking. Grill as above.)

Nutrition Facts per serving: 375 cal., 14 g total fat (5 g sat. fat), 114 mg chol., 268 mg sodium, 16 g carbo., 1 g fiber, 43 g pro. Daily Values: 16% vit. A, 6% vit. C, 6% calcium, 10% iron. Exchanges: ¹/₂ Vegetable, 1 Other Carbo., 6 Very Lean Meat, 2 Fat

GINGER-LEMON PORK CHOPS WITH SOY RICE

Start cooking the rice just before putting the chops on the grill.

Prep: 20 minutes Marinate: 4 to 24 hours Grill: 11 minutes
Makes: 4 servings

4 pork top loin chops, cut 1 inch thick
½ cup soy sauce
¼ cup water
1 tablespoon grated fresh ginger
1 teaspoon finely shredded lemon peel
1 tablespoon lemon juice
1 recipe Soy Rice

1 Trim fat from chops. Place chops in a self-sealing plastic bag set in a shallow dish. For marinade, in a small bowl stir together soy sauce, water, ginger, lemon peel, and lemon juice. Pour over chops; seal bag. Marinate in refrigerator for 4 to 24 hours, turning bag occasionally. Drain chops, discarding marinade.

2 For a charcoal grill, grill chops on the rack of an uncovered grill directly over medium coals for 11 to 13 minutes or until chops are slightly pink in center and juices run clear (160°F), turning once halfway through grilling. (For a gas grill, preheat grill. Reduce heat to medium. Place meat on grill rack over heat. Cover; grill as above.) Serve chops with Soy Rice.

Soy Rice: In a medium saucepan stir together 2 cups water, 1 cup uncooked long grain rice, 2 tablespoons soy sauce, 2 teaspoons grated fresh ginger, and ½ teaspoon toasted sesame oil. Bring to boiling; reduce heat. Simmer, covered, for 18 to 20 minutes or until rice is tender and liquid is absorbed. Stir in ¼ cup sliced green onions.

Nutrition Facts per serving: 412 cal., 11 g total fat (4 g sat. fat), 88 mg chol., 1,138 mg sodium, 38 g carbo., 1 g fiber, 35 g pro. Daily Values: 1% vit. A, 5% vit. C, 4% calcium, 18% iron. Exchanges: 2½ Starch, 4 Very Lean Meat, 1½ Fat

GRAPE-GLAZED CHOPS

A short ingredient list delivers pork chops that are long on flavor.

Prep: 5 minutes Cook: 20 minutes Grill: 14 minutes
Makes: 4 servings

½ cup grape juice
½ cup grape jelly
½ cup bottled barbecue sauce
2 tablespoons red wine vinegar
Dash ground cinnamon
4 boneless pork top loin chops, cut 1¼ inches thick
Salt
Black pepper

1 For glaze, in a small saucepan combine grape juice, jelly, barbecue sauce, vinegar, and cinnamon. Bring to boiling; reduce heat. Boil gently, uncovered, for 20 to 30 minutes or until reduced to about ¾ cup and thickened to glazing consistency. Set glaze aside.

2 Trim fat from chops. Sprinkle both sides of chops with salt and pepper. For a charcoal grill, grill chops on the rack of an uncovered grill directly over medium coals for 14 to 18 minutes or until chops are slightly pink in center and juices run clear (160°F), turning once halfway through grilling and brushing with some of the glaze during the last 10 minutes of grilling. (For a gas grill, preheat grill. Reduce heat to medium. Place meat on grill rack over heat. Cover; grill as above.) Spoon remaining glaze over chops.

Nutrition Facts per serving: 567 cal., 17 g total fat (6 g sat. fat), 154 mg chol., 526 mg sodium, 36 g carbo., 1 g fiber, 63 g pro. Daily Values: 6% vit. A, 5% vit. C, 2% calcium, 12% iron. Exchanges: 2½ Other Carbo., 9 Very Lean Meat, 2 Fat

GRILLED PORK CHOPS WITH HONEY-ORANGE GLAZE

To save time, use 1 tablespoon of bottled minced garlic instead of peeling and mincing six cloves.

Prep: 20 minutes Marinate: 2 hours Grill: 30 minutes
Makes: 6 servings

**6 boneless pork loin chops, cut
        1 to 1¼ inches thick
2 tablespoons honey
1 tablespoon finely shredded orange peel
¼ cup orange juice
2 tablespoons soy sauce
2 tablespoons Dijon-style mustard
2 tablespoons grated fresh ginger
6 cloves garlic, minced
1 recipe Honey-Orange Glaze**

1 Drain chops, discarding marinade. Trim fat from chops. Place chops in a self-sealing plastic bag set in a shallow dish. For marinade, in a small bowl stir together honey, orange peel, orange juice, soy sauce, mustard, ginger, and garlic. Pour over chops; seal bag. Marinate in refrigerator for 2 hours, turning bag occasionally. Drain chops, discarding marinade.

2 For a charcoal grill, arrange medium-hot coals around a drip pan. Test for medium heat above pan. Place chops on grill rack over pan. Cover; grill for 30 to 35 minutes or until chops are slightly pink in centers and juices run clear (160°F), turning once halfway through grilling and brushing with Honey-Orange Glaze during the last 5 minutes of grilling. (For a gas grill, preheat. Reduce heat to medium. Adjust for indirect cooking. Grill as above).

Honey-Orange Glaze: In a 2-quart saucepan combine ⅓ cup honey, ¼ cup orange juice, 2 tablespoons soy sauce, and 4 teaspoons ground ginger. Bring to boiling; reduce heat. Boil gently, uncovered, about 5 minutes or until sauce is reduced by half (slightly less than ½ cup), stirring frequently. (Watch carefully; mixture will bubble.)

Nutrition Facts per serving: 372 cal., 11 g total fat (4 g sat. fat), 103 mg chol., 552 mg sodium, 23 g carbo., 0 g fiber, 43 g pro. Daily Values: 1% vit. A, 15% vit. C, 2% calcium, 8% iron. Exchanges: 1½ Other Carbo., 6 Very Lean Meat, 1½ Fat

PORK CHOP AND POTATO DINNER

Prep: 30 minutes Grill: 30 minutes Makes: 4 servings

**8 tiny new potatoes, halved
1 medium red onion, thinly sliced and
        separated into rings
4 boneless pork loin chops, cut
        ¾ inch thick
1 medium red sweet pepper, cut into
        thin bite-size strips
2 medium carrots or 1 medium
        rutabaga, peeled and cut into thin
        bite-size strips
½ cup reduced-sodium chicken broth
½ teaspoon dry mustard
¼ teaspoon dried thyme, crushed**

1 Divide potatoes among 4 pieces of 18×12-inch heavy foil. Top each with a few of the onion rings. Trim fat from chops. Sprinkle with salt and pepper. Lay chops on top of onion rings. Top each chop with a few of the remaining onion rings, the sweet pepper strips, and carrot strips.

2 In a bowl combine chicken broth, mustard, and thyme. Drizzle 2 tablespoons of the broth

SMOKIN' HOT TIP

The secret to getting the most juice from citrus fruit is first to roll the fruit on a hard surface, pressing firmly but gently with the palm of your hand. Doing so encourages the pulp to release the juices. Select fruit that is heavy for its size. When zesting fruit use the fine edge of a box grater or use a microplane zester, making sure to avoid the white pith, which is bitter. The following outlines how much juice and peel you can expect to get:

● A medium orange yields about ¼ to ⅓ cup juice and 1 to 2 tablespoons finely shredded peel.

● A medium lemon or lime yields about 2 to 3 tablespoons juice and ½ to 1 tablespoon finely shredded peel.

mixture over each pork chop. Bring up two opposite edges of foil and seal with a double fold. Fold remaining edges together to completely enclose the pork chops and vegetables, leaving space for steam to build.

3 For a charcoal grill, grill foil packets on the rack of an uncovered grill directly over medium coals for 30 to 35 minutes or until chops are slightly pink in centers and juices run clear (160°F) and vegetables are tender, turning packets twice. (For a gas grill, preheat grill. Reduce heat to medium. Place foil packets on grill rack over heat. Cover; grill as above.)

Nutrition Facts per serving: 281 cal., 7 g total fat (2 g sat. fat), 62 mg chol., 283 mg sodium, 24 g carbo., 4 g fiber, 29 g pro. Daily Values: 91% vit. A, 119% vit. C, 3% calcium, 12% iron. Exchanges: 1 Vegetable, 1½ Starch, 3 Very Lean Meat, 1 Fat

PORK AND APPLE SANDWICHES WITH HONEY-PECAN GLAZE

Prep: 25 minutes Grill: 10 minutes Makes: 4 servings

  2 tenderized butterflied pork chops, halved, or 4 tenderized boneless pork loin slices (1¼ pounds total)
  1 large tart apple, cored and cut crosswise into 4 rings
  1 recipe Honey-Pecan Glaze
  4 1-ounce slices provolone cheese
⅓ cup dairy sour cream
⅓ cup mayonnaise or salad dressing
  2 teaspoons prepared horseradish
  4 kaiser rolls, split and toasted

1 Sprinkle pork with salt and pepper. For a charcoal grill, grill pork and apple rings on the rack of an uncovered grill directly over medium coals for 10 to 12 minutes or until pork juices run clear and apples are just tender, turning once halfway through grilling and brushing with Honey-Pecan Glaze during the last 3 minutes of grilling. Top pork with provolone cheese the last minute of grilling. (For a gas grill, preheat grill. Reduce heat to medium. Place pork and apple rings on grill rack over heat. Cover; grill as above.)

2 Meanwhile, in a small bowl combine sour cream, mayonnaise, and horseradish; spread on cut sides of toasted rolls. Place a pork slice and an apple slice on roll bottoms; add roll tops.

Honey-Pecan Glaze: In a small saucepan combine ¼ cup honey; ¼ cup chopped pecans, toasted; 2 tablespoons butter or margarine; and ½ teaspoon finely shredded lemon peel. Heat and stir until butter is melted.

Nutrition Facts per serving: 822 cal., 46 g total fat (16 g sat. fat), 126 mg chol., 936 mg sodium, 55 g carbo., 3 g fiber, 46 g pro. Daily Values: 12% vit. A, 6% vit. C, 32% calcium, 18% iron. Exchanges: ½ Fruit, 3 Starch, 5 Medium-Fat Meat, 4 Fat

BEER-BRINED BUTTERFLY CHOPS

This recipe calls for stout—a strong, dark beer with bittersweet undertones.

Prep: 15 minutes Marinate: 8 to 24 hours Grill: 30 minutes
Makes: 4 servings

  4 pork loin butterflied chops, cut 1¼ to 1½ inches thick
1¾ cups water
1¾ cups stout (dark beer)
  3 tablespoons coarse salt
  2 tablespoons mild-flavored molasses
  2 teaspoons coarsely cracked black pepper
  4 cloves garlic, minced

1 Trim fat from chops. Place chops in a self-sealing plastic bag set in a shallow dish. For beer brine, combine water, stout, salt, and molasses; stir until salt dissolves. Pour over chops; seal bag. Marinate in refrigerator for 8 to 24 hours, turning bag occasionally.

2 Drain chops, discarding beer brine. Pat chops dry. In a small bowl combine pepper and garlic. Sprinkle pepper mixture evenly over both sides of chops; rub in with your fingers.

3 For a charcoal grill, arrange medium-hot coals around a drip pan. Test for medium heat above pan. Place chops on grill rack over pan. Cover; grill for 30 to 35 minutes or until chops are slightly pink in centers and juices run clear (160°F), turning once halfway through grilling. (For a gas grill, preheat. Reduce heat to medium. Adjust for indirect cooking. Grill as above.)

Nutrition Facts per serving: 345 cal., 12 g total fat (4 g sat. fat), 123 mg chol., 702 mg sodium, 3 g carbo., 0 g fiber, 50 g pro. Daily Values: 3% vit. C, 5% calcium, 10% iron. Exchanges: 7 Very Lean Meat, 2 Fat

CHOPS IN SMOKY CHILE MARINADE

The indispensable ingredient in this marinade is smoky chipotle chile peppers. Canned chipotles are packed in a piquant sauce made from chiles, herbs, and vinegar.

Prep: 20 minutes Marinate: 4 hours Grill: 7 minutes
Makes: 4 servings

4 pork loin butterfly chops, cut
 ³/₄ inch thick
3 tablespoons olive oil
¹/₂ teaspoon finely shredded lime peel
2 tablespoons lime juice
2 tablespoons finely chopped canned
 chipotle peppers in adobo sauce
1¹/₂ teaspoons dried oregano, crushed
1 teaspoon salt
3 cloves garlic, minced

1 Trim fat from chops. Place chops in a self-sealing plastic bag set in a shallow dish. For marinade, in a small bowl combine olive oil, lime peel, lime juice, chipotle peppers, oregano, salt, and garlic. Pour over chops; seal bag. Marinate in refrigerator for 4 hours, turning bag occasionally. Drain chops, discarding marinade.

2 For a charcoal grill, grill chops on the rack of an uncovered grill directly over medium coals for 7 to 9 minutes or until slightly pink in the centers and juices run clear (160°F), turning once halfway through grilling. (For a gas grill, preheat grill. Reduce heat to medium. Place chops on grill rack over heat. Cover; grill as above.)

Nutrition Facts per serving: 433 cal., 23 g total fat (6 g sat. fat), 123 mg chol., 709 mg sodium, 2 g carbo., 0 g fiber, 50 g pro. Daily Values: 2% vit. A, 7% vit. C, 1% calcium, 9% iron. Exchanges: 7 Very Lean Meat, 4 Fat

JAMAICAN PORK SKEWERS WITH MELON

Straight off the island grill, these pork kabobs flaunt the spice of Jamaican jerk seasoning and the sweetness of ripe melons and honey.

Prep: 15 minutes Grill: 18 minutes
Makes: 4 servings

1¹/₂ pounds pork tenderloin
2 small red onions, quartered
 lengthwise
2 tablespoons roasted peanut oil or
 peanut oil
4 teaspoons Jamaican jerk seasoning
¹/₄ of a small honeydew melon, cut into
 2-inch cubes
¹/₂ of a small cantaloupe, cut into
 2-inch cubes
1 tablespoon honey

1 Trim fat from pork. Cut pork into 1¹/₂-inch cubes. In a medium bowl toss pork cubes and onions with oil and jerk seasoning until coated.

2 On eight 12-inch metal skewers, alternately thread pork, onion, honeydew, and cantaloupe pieces, leaving a ¹/₄-inch space between pieces.

3 For a charcoal grill, grill skewers on greased grill rack of an uncovered grill directly over medium coals for 18 to 20 minutes or until pork is no longer pink and juices run clear, turning once halfway through grilling. (For a gas grill, preheat grill. Reduce heat to medium. Place skewers on grill rack over heat. Cover; grill as above.) Remove skewers from grill; brush with honey.

Nutrition Facts per serving: 321 cal., 12 g total fat (3 g sat. fat), 110 mg chol., 379 mg sodium, 16 g carbo., 1 g fiber, 37 g pro. Daily Values: 39% vit. A, 66% vit. C, 2% calcium, 13% iron. Exchanges: ¹/₂ Vegetable, 1 Fruit, 5 Very Lean Meat, 2 Fat

SMOKIN' HOT TIP

Skewers are the perfect solution for cooking small pieces of meat and vegetables on the grill. Here are a few tips for success:

● Cut pieces of food into uniform sizes to ensure even cooking.

● Clean metal skewers well and rub with oil to keep foods from sticking to them.

● Soak wooden skewers in water for 30 minutes before you thread the food on the skewers to prevent the skewers from burning during grilling.

● Insert two skewers parallel to each other when cooking larger pieces to allow for easier maneuvering and to stabilize the food.

Chops in Smoky Chile Marinade

ASIAN PORK SKEWERS WITH SOBA NOODLES

Prep: 40 minutes Cook: 20 minutes Grill: 12 minutes
Makes: 4 servings

- 1 **cup orange marmalade**
- ¼ **cup soy sauce**
- 2 **tablespoons finely chopped shallots**
- 2 **tablespoons dry sherry**
- 1 **tablespoon grated fresh ginger**
- 4 **cloves garlic, minced**
- 12 **ounces pork tenderloin**
- 16 **fresh shiitake mushrooms, stems removed (about 5 ounces)**
- 2 **plums, pitted and cut into wedges**
- 3 **green onions, cut into 2-inch pieces**
- 8 **ounces hot cooked soba or udon noodles**

1 For sauce, in a saucepan combine marmalade, soy sauce, shallots, sherry, ginger, and garlic. Bring to boiling. Boil gently, uncovered, over medium-high heat for 20 to 25 minutes or until reduced to 1 cup. Reserve ⅔ cup of sauce.

2 Trim fat from pork; cut pork into 1-inch cubes. On eight 8-inch metal skewers, alternately thread pork cubes and mushrooms, leaving a ¼-inch space between pieces. On four 8-inch metal skewers, alternately thread plum wedges and green onions, leaving a ¼-inch space between pieces. Brush plum wedges and green onions with some of the remaining ⅓ cup sauce.

3 For a charcoal grill, grill pork skewers on the rack of an uncovered grill directly over medium coals for 12 to 15 minutes or until pork is no longer pink and juices run clear, turning and brushing with sauce once halfway through grilling. Add plum and green onion skewers the last 5 minutes of grilling, turning once. (For a gas grill, preheat grill. Reduce heat to medium. Place skewers on grill rack over heat. Cover; grill as above.)

4 Toss reserved sauce with hot cooked noodles. Serve skewers over noodles.

Nutrition Facts per serving: 586 cal., 4 g total fat (1 g sat. fat), 55 mg chol., 1,233 mg sodium, 115 g carbo., 5 g fiber, 30 g pro. Daily Values: 8% vit. A, 27% vit. C, 7% calcium, 15% iron. Exchanges: ½ Vegetable, 2 Starch, 5½ Other Carbo., 3 Very Lean Meat

FOOD FOR THOUGHT
JAPANESE NOODLES

Served throughout the day, noodles are staples in Asian cuisine. They are easy to cook and their different flavors and textures make them versatile ingredients for soups, salads, stir-fries, and side dishes. The following are the more common varieties that have gained popularity in American kitchens:

● Soba Noodles: **These hearty brownish noodles are made from buckwheat and are about as thick as spaghetti. High in protein and fiber, they are served cold with dipping sauce or hot in soups.**

● Ramen Noodles: **A college student favorite, these Chinese-style noodles made from egg, wheat flour, and water are recognized on store shelves as "instant" ramen noodles. They are usually served with meat and vegetables in broth.**

● Udon Noodles: **Udon noodles are thick, soft, creamy, and white. Made from wheat flour, egg, and water, these noodles are round, square, or flat in shape. They are usually boiled in soup broth and are interchangeable with soba noodles.**

● Somen Noodles: **These delicate, fine white noodles are made from wheat dough with a small amount of sesame seed or cottonseed oil. Traditionally they are cooked lightly in boiling water and served cold with dipping sauce but also can be served warm in broth.**

PROSCIUTTO PORK KABOBS

To hold the prosciutto in place on the skewers, thread the skewers through the pork cubes in the spot where the prosciutto strips meet.

Prep: 20 minutes Grill: 18 minutes
Makes: 4 servings

- ¼ cup garlic-flavored olive oil
- 2 tablespoons lemon juice
- ¼ teaspoon crushed red pepper
- 1 pound pork tenderloin
- 3 to 4 ounces thinly sliced prosciutto
- 8 ounces fresh mushrooms, stems removed
- 2 small zucchini and/or yellow summer squash, cut into ¾-inch-thick slices
- 2 tablespoons finely shredded Parmesan or Romano cheese

1 In a small bowl combine oil, lemon juice, and crushed red pepper; set aside.

2 Trim fat from pork. Cut pork into 1½-inch cubes. Cut prosciutto into 1½-inch-wide strips. Wrap a strip of prosciutto around each pork cube. On 4 long metal skewers, alternately thread pork cubes, mushrooms, and zucchini, leaving a ¼-inch space between pieces.

3 For a charcoal grill, grill kabobs on the greased grill rack of an uncovered grill directly over medium coals for 18 to 20 minutes or until pork is no longer pink and juices run clear, turning once halfway through grilling and brushing with the oil mixture during the last 4 minutes of grilling. (For a gas grill, preheat grill. Reduce heat to medium. Place kabobs on grill rack over heat. Cover; grill as above.)

4 Just before serving, sprinkle kabobs with Parmesan cheese.

Nutrition Facts per serving: 354 cal., 23 g total fat (3 g sat. fat), 75 mg chol., 468 mg sodium, 5 g carbo., 1 g fiber, 32 g pro. Daily Values: 5% vit. A, 18% vit. C, 5% calcium, 13% iron. Exchanges: 1 Vegetable, 4 Lean Meat, 3 Fat

MALAYSIAN PORK AND NOODLES

Malaysian food reflects Chinese, Indonesian, and Indian influences, a most interesting mix.

Prep: 20 minutes Marinate: 30 to 60 minutes Grill: 12 minutes
Makes: 4 servings

- 1 pound pork tenderloin
- ¼ cup Brazil nuts or whole almonds
- ¼ cup light soy sauce
- 3 tablespoons lemon juice
- 1 tablespoon olive oil
- 1 tablespoon ground coriander
- 1 tablespoon brown sugar
- ¾ teaspoon black pepper
- 1 clove garlic, minced
- 8 ounces thin noodles
- 1 tablespoon butter or margarine, softened
- 2 tablespoons toasted sesame seeds

1 Trim fat from pork. Cut pork into 1-inch cubes. Place pork cubes in a self-sealing plastic bag set in a shallow dish. For marinade, in a food processor combine nuts, soy sauce, lemon juice, oil, coriander, brown sugar, ½ teaspoon of the pepper, and garlic. Cover and process until combined. Pour marinade over pork; seal bag. Marinate in refrigerator for 30 to 60 minutes, turning bag occasionally.

2 Drain pork, discarding marinade. On 4 long metal skewers, thread pork cubes, leaving a ¼-inch space between pieces.

3 For a charcoal grill, grill kabobs on the rack of an uncovered grill directly over medium coals for 12 to 15 minutes or until pork is no longer pink and juices run clear, turning once halfway through grilling. (For a gas grill, preheat grill. Reduce heat to medium. Place kabobs on grill rack over heat. Cover; grill as above.)

4 Meanwhile, cook noodles according to package directions; drain. Return noodles to hot saucepan. Toss noodles with the remaining ¼ teaspoon pepper, butter, and sesame seeds. Serve kabobs over noodles.

Nutrition Facts per serving: 490 cal., 19 g total fat (5 g sat. fat), 135 mg chol., 363 mg sodium, 46 g carbo., 3 g fiber, 35 g pro. Daily Values: 3% vit. A, 7% vit. C, 6% calcium, 23% iron. Exchanges: 2½ Starch, ½ Other Carbo., 4 Lean Meat, 1 Fat

Grilled Pork with Melon-Tomato Tumble

GRILLED PORK WITH MELON-TOMATO TUMBLE

Although the colorful pear-shape tomatoes make a stunning statement here, chopped plum tomatoes work well too.

Prep: 20 minutes Grill: 30 minutes Stand: 10 minutes
Makes: 4 servings

3 tablespoons olive oil
3 tablespoons white wine vinegar
¼ teaspoon salt
⅛ teaspoon black pepper
1 1-pound pork tenderloin
½ of a small cantaloupe
½ of a small honeydew melon
1 cup yellow, red, and/or orange pear-shape tomatoes, halved or quartered
1 small red onion, halved and thinly sliced
⅓ cup fresh mint leaves

1 In a small bowl whisk together oil, vinegar, salt, and pepper. Brush 1 tablespoon of the oil mixture over the tenderloin. Reserve remaining oil mixture to use in the tumble.

2 For a charcoal grill, arrange hot coals around a drip pan. Test for medium-high heat above pan. Place meat on grill rack over pan. Cover; grill for 30 to 35 minutes or until a meat thermometer registers 155°F. Remove meat from grill. Cover with foil and let stand 10 minutes. (The meat's temperature will rise 5°F during standing.)

3 Meanwhile, for tumble, cut either the cantaloupe or honeydew melon half into bite-size pieces. Cut the remaining melon half into four wedges. In a medium bowl combine the melon pieces, tomatoes, onion, and mint. Add the reserved oil mixture; toss to coat.

4 Slice pork diagonally. Serve with the tumble spooned over the melon wedges.

Nutrition Facts per serving: 292 cal., 14 g total fat (3 g sat. fat), 73 mg chol., 211 mg sodium, 15 g carbo., 2 g fiber, 26 g pro. Daily Values: 88% vit. A, 122% vit. C, 3% calcium, 19% iron. Exchanges: ½ Vegetable, 1 Fruit, 3½ Lean Meat, ½ Fat

PORK SATAY WITH TAHINI-COCONUT DIPPING SAUCE

Here's an exotic dish that draws its worldly flavor from tahini, coconut, and curry.

Prep: 40 minutes Marinate: 2 to 3 hours Grill: 10 minutes
Makes: 6 servings

1½ **pounds pork tenderloin**
¼ **cup coconut milk**
2 **tablespoons lime juice**
1 **tablespoon brown sugar**
1 **tablespoon curry powder**
1 **recipe Tahini-Coconut Dipping Sauce**

1 Trim fat from pork. Cut pork into ¾-inch cubes. Place pork cubes in a self-sealing plastic bag set in a shallow dish. For marinade, in a medium bowl stir together coconut milk, lime juice, brown sugar, and curry powder. Pour over pork; seal bag. Marinate in refrigerator for 2 to 3 hours, turning bag occasionally.

2 Drain pork, discarding marinade. On 6 long metal skewers, thread pork cubes, leaving a ¼-inch space between pieces.

3 For a charcoal grill, grill kabobs on the rack of an uncovered grill directly over medium coals for 10 to 12 minutes or until pork is no longer pink and juices run clear, turning occasionally. (For a gas grill, preheat grill. Reduce heat to medium. Place kabobs on grill rack over heat. Cover; grill as above.) Serve with Tahini-Coconut Dipping Sauce.

Tahini-Coconut Dipping Sauce: In a small saucepan heat 1½ teaspoons cooking oil over medium heat until hot. Add 1 tablespoon red chili paste and ⅛ teaspoon crushed red pepper; reduce heat to low. Cook and stir about 1 minute or until fragrant. Stir in ¾ cup coconut milk, ¼ cup tahini (sesame seed paste), 4 teaspoons orange juice, 2 teaspoons brown sugar, and 1½ teaspoons fish sauce. Bring just to simmering. Simmer gently, uncovered, 5 minutes or until combined and thickened, stirring frequently. Serve warm.

Nutrition Facts per serving: 283 cal., 15 g total fat (7 g sat. fat), 81 mg chol., 223 mg sodium, 9 g carbo., 1 g fiber, 28 g pro. Daily Values: 6% vit. C, 2% calcium, 16% iron. Exchanges: ½ Other Carbo., 4 Lean Meat, ½ Fat

FOOD FOR THOUGHT ASIAN PANTRY

Many of the ingredients used in Asian cooking are easy to find in Asian markets or the Oriental section at the supermarket. Here are a few basics you'll use in several recipes in this book:

● Chinese Five-Spice Powder: **A powder made from a blend of ground cloves, fennel seed, star anise, cinnamon, and Szechwan pepper.**

● Coconut Milk: **The result of soaking coconut meat in water. Coconut milk infuses mild flavor and enhances the richness of curries, soups, and sauces. It has a thinner consistency and is less sweet and imposing than coconut cream.**

● Fish Sauce: **This thin, dark brown liquid made from salted, fermented fish has a strong, pungent flavor and aroma that dissipates when cooked. It's used both as a condiment and flavoring in Southeast Asian cooking.**

● Red Curry Paste: **Curry pastes come in many varieties, but red curry paste is one of the most basic used in Thai cookery. Containing red chiles, galangal, lemongrass, kaffir lime zest, coriander root, salt, shrimp paste, shallots, and garlic, it is used to make curries and partners especially well with seafood.**

● Toasted Sesame Oil: **Extracted from sesame seeds, this oil has a rich, nutty flavor. Unflavored sesame oil is also available.**

GRILLED PORK TENDERLOIN SANDWICHES

Rubbed with seasonings, topped with spicy Italian ham, and served on focaccia, this tenderloin sandwich touts an Italian twist!

Prep: 20 minutes Grill: 6 minutes
Makes: 6 servings

1 pound pork tenderloin
1 tablespoon olive oil
1/2 teaspoon ground sage
1/4 teaspoon salt
1/4 teaspoon black pepper
6 thin slices coppacola, salami, prosciutto, or cooked ham (about 1/2 ounce each)
2 6- to 8-inch focaccia bread loaves
1/2 to 2/3 cup dried tomato-flavored light mayonnaise dressing
6 romaine leaves

1 Trim fat from pork. Cut pork crosswise into six equal pieces. Place each piece of pork between 2 pieces of plastic wrap. Use the flat side of a meat mallet to lightly pound each pork piece to 1/4-inch thickness.

2 Brush both sides of pork with olive oil. In a small bowl combine sage, salt, and pepper. Sprinkle both sides of pork with sage mixture; rub in with your fingers. Place one slice of coppacola on each pounded pork piece, folding as necessary so the coppacola doesn't extend over the pork. Weave a skewer through each piece of pork to hold the pork and coppacola together.

3 For a charcoal grill, grill pork on the rack of an uncovered grill directly over medium coals for 6 to 8 minutes or until pork is slightly pink in the center, turning once. (For a gas grill, preheat grill. Reduce heat to medium. Place pork on grill rack over heat. Cover; grill as above.)

4 To serve, cut each focaccia loaf into three wedges; halve wedges horizontally. Spread cut sides of each wedge with mayonnaise dressing. Line bottom wedges with a romaine leaf; top with grilled pork. If desired, add tomato, onion, and olives. Add bread tops.

Nutrition Facts per serving: 272 cal., 14 g total fat (4 g sat. fat), 72 mg chol., 736 mg sodium, 14 g carbo., 1 g fiber, 23 g pro. Daily Values: 1% vit. A, 2% vit. C, 2% calcium, 8% iron. Exchanges: 1 Starch, 3 Lean Meat, Fat

PORK STUFFED WITH ORANGE AND THYME

Prep: 40 minutes Chill: 1 to 8 hours Grill: 30 minutes
Stand: 10 minutes Makes: 6 to 8 servings

2 12- to 16-ounce pork tenderloins
1/4 cup finely chopped onion
3 tablespoons finely shredded orange peel
2 tablespoons snipped fresh thyme
2 tablespoons olive oil
4 teaspoons coarsely cracked black pepper
1 teaspoon kosher salt
1 recipe Orange-Thyme Sauce

1 Trim fat from pork. Split each tenderloin lengthwise, cutting from one side almost to, but not through, the other side. Spread meat open. In a small bowl combine onion, orange peel, and thyme; divide between tenderloins, spreading onto cut sides of each tenderloin. Fold each tenderloin back together. Tie with 100-percent-cotton string at 1-inch intervals. Brush tenderloins with oil. In a small bowl combine pepper and salt. Sprinkle evenly over each tenderloin; rub in with your fingers. Cover; chill tenderloins for 1 to 8 hours.

2 For a charcoal grill, arrange hot coals around a drip pan. Test for medium-high heat above pan. Place meat on grill rack over pan. Cover; grill for 30 to 35 minutes or until a meat thermometer registers 155°F. (For a gas grill, preheat grill. Reduce heat to medium-high. Adjust for indirect cooking. Grill as above, except place pork on a rack in a roasting pan.) Remove pork from grill. Cover pork with foil and let stand 10 minutes before slicing. (The meat's temperature will rise 5°F during standing.)

3 To serve, slice pork diagonally; serve with Orange-Thyme Sauce.

Orange-Thyme Sauce: In a small saucepan combine 1/2 cup orange juice, 2 tablespoons coarse-grain brown mustard, 2 tablespoons olive oil, and 1 tablespoon snipped fresh thyme. Cook and stir over medium heat until heated through.

Nutrition Facts per serving: 236 cal., 13 g total fat (2 g sat. fat), 73 mg chol., 445 mg sodium, 5 g carbo., 1 g fiber, 25 g pro. Daily Values: 2% vit. A, 30% vit. C, 3% calcium, 12% iron. Exchanges: 1/2 Other Carbo., 3 1/2 Lean Meat, 1/2 Fat

MAPLE-PLUM PORK PLATTER

For ease, halve and pit the plums, then
reassemble them on the skewers.

Prep: 30 minutes Grill: 18 minutes
Makes: 4 to 6 servings

1½ **pounds pork tenderloin**
12 **slices packaged ready-to-serve
        cooked bacon**
3 **large fresh button mushrooms**
3 **large fresh shiitake mushrooms**
3 **fresh ears of corn, cut crosswise
        into 1-inch pieces**
1 **large onion, cut into wedges**
12 **plums**
    Cooking oil
12 **ounces fresh asparagus spears,
        trimmed**
½ **cup pure maple syrup**
2 **tablespoons finely chopped shallot**
1 **tablespoon butter or margarine**
2 **teaspoons finely shredded
        orange peel**
½ **cup orange juice**
2 to 4 **tablespoons cider or white
        wine vinegar**
⅛ **teaspoon cayenne pepper**
    Dash black pepper
    Fresh rosemary sprigs (optional)

1 Trim fat from pork. Cut pork crosswise into twelve 1½-inch-thick slices. Wrap one slice of bacon around each piece of tenderloin; thread onto metal skewers. Thread mushrooms onto a second set of metal skewers. Thread corn pieces and onion wedges onto a third set of metal skewers. Pit 8 plums; thread onto a fourth set of metal skewers. Brush skewers with cooking oil.

2 For a charcoal grill, grill pork skewers and corn and onion skewers on the rack of an uncovered grill directly over medium coals for 18 to 20 minutes or until a meat thermometer registers 160°F. Halfway through grilling, turn skewers and add mushroom skewers to grill rack. During the last 5 minutes of grilling, add plum skewers and asparagus spears to grill rack, turning once. Brush all skewers with ¼ cup of the maple syrup. Immediately remove skewers from grill.

(For a gas grill, preheat grill. Reduce heat to medium. Place skewers on grill rack over heat. Cover; grill as above.)

3 Meanwhile, for sauce, pit and quarter the remaining 4 plums. In a medium saucepan cook and stir shallot in hot butter for 1 minute. Add pitted plums, orange peel, orange juice, vinegar, cayenne pepper, and black pepper. Bring to boiling; reduce heat. Boil gently, uncovered, for 8 to 10 minutes or until thickened. Stir in the remaining ¼ cup maple syrup; heat through.

4 To serve, arrange the asparagus spears on a large platter. Top with pork, plum, and vegetable kabobs. Serve with sauce. If desired, garnish with rosemary.

Nutrition Facts per serving: 775 cal., 20 g total fat (7 g sat. fat), 133 mg chol., 384 mg sodium, 108 g carbo., 10 g fiber, 48 g pro. Daily Values: 44% vit. A, 141% vit. C, 9% calcium, 25% iron. Exchanges: 2 Vegetable, 2 Fruit, 1 Starch, 4 Other Carbo., 6 Lean Meat

FOOD FOR THOUGHT
TRY A LITTLE TENDERNESS

Asparagus is at its peak from February to June; the earliest stalks are the most tender. The flesh of larger stalks, on the other hand, is tough and woody, but don't let that discourage you from enjoying their flavor.

Begin by snapping off the base of each stalk, which will have a natural breaking point, or trim with a knife. Then, using a vegetable peeler, expose the tender inner flesh by peeling away the tough outer skin.

PLANK-SMOKED PORK TENDERLOIN

Always soak the plank before putting it on the grill and watch the heat source carefully to avoid a fire.

Prep: 30 minutes Grill: 30 minutes
Makes: 6 servings

1 12×6×¾-inch cedar or alder plank
2 12-ounce pork tenderloins
2 tablespoons Dijon-style mustard
   Salt
   Black pepper
2 tablespoons snipped fresh sage
2 tablespoons snipped fresh thyme
1 tablespoon snipped fresh rosemary
1 recipe Apple-Cherry Salad

1 At least 1 hour before grilling, soak plank in enough water to cover. Weigh plank down to keep it submerged during soaking.

2 Trim fat from pork. Brush tenderloins with mustard; sprinkle generously with salt and pepper. In a small bowl combine sage, thyme, and rosemary. Sprinkle herb mixture evenly over each tenderloin; rub in with your fingers. Drain plank.

3 For a charcoal grill, place plank on the rack of an uncovered grill directly over medium coals about 5 minutes or until plank begins to crackle and smoke. Place tenderloins on plank. Cover; grill for 30 to 35 minutes or until a meat thermometer registers 160°F. (For a gas grill, preheat grill. Reduce heat to medium. Place tenderloins on plank over heat. Cover; grill as above.) Serve with Apple-Cherry Salad.

Apple-Cherry Salad: In a medium bowl combine 2 Granny Smith apples, chopped; ¼ cup coarsely chopped walnuts, toasted; 1 ounce crumbled blue cheese; 2 tablespoons snipped dried tart red cherries; 2 tablespoons Calvados or applejack; and 1 tablespoon extra virgin olive oil. Just before serving, stir in 3 slices bacon, cooked, drained, and crumbled.

Nutrition Facts per serving: 280 cal., 12 g total fat (3 g sat. fat), 80 mg chol., 345 mg sodium, 10 g carbo., 2 g fiber, 27 g pro. Daily Values: 3% vit. A, 8% vit. C, 5% calcium, 9% iron. Exchanges: ½ Fruit, 4 Very Lean Meat, 2 Fat

FOOD FOR THOUGHT APPLES

With so many varieties available, it's difficult to know which apples are best for your recipe. Here are the characteristics of some of the more common varieties:

● Golden Delicious: Sweet, semifirm flesh with a golden freckled skin. Good all-purpose apple. Peak season is September to May.

● Granny Smith: Tart, firm, and very crisp flesh with bright green skin. Good all-purpose apple. Available year-round.

● Jonathan: Tart, soft flesh with bright red, green-tinged skin. Good for eating fresh, pies, and sauces. Available September to April.

● McIntosh: Tart, slightly spicy, soft flesh with red skin that has a yellowish green blush. Good for eating fresh, sauces, and cider. Available September to May.

● Red Delicious: Sweet, crisp, semifirm flesh with deep red skin. Good for eating fresh. Available year-round.

● Rome Beauty: Sweet, mildly tart, firm flesh with bright red skin. Good for baking and sautéing. Available October to June.

Plank-Smoked Pork Tenderloin

GRILLED PORK TENDERLOIN WITH BLACKBERRY SAUCE

Prep: 30 minutes Marinate: 2 to 4 hours Cook: 8 minutes
Grill: 30 minutes Stand: 10 minutes Makes: 4 servings

- 1 1-pound pork tenderloin
- 1/4 cup olive oil
- 1/3 cup dry white wine
- 3 tablespoons balsamic vinegar
- 2 tablespoons Dijon-style mustard
- 1 teaspoon snipped fresh rosemary
- 1/2 teaspoon soy sauce
- 1/4 teaspoon black pepper
  Dash cayenne pepper
- 2 cloves garlic, minced
- 1/4 cup seedless blackberry jam
- 1 teaspoon finely shredded lemon peel

1 Trim fat from pork. Place pork in a self-sealing plastic bag set in a shallow dish. For marinade, in a small bowl combine olive oil, wine, vinegar, mustard, rosemary, soy sauce, black pepper, cayenne pepper, and garlic. Pour marinade over meat; seal bag. Marinate in refrigerator for 2 to 4 hours, turning bag occasionally. Drain meat, reserving marinade.

2 For a charcoal grill, arrange hot coals around a drip pan. Test for medium-high heat above pan. Place meat on grill rack over pan. Cover; grill for 30 to 35 minutes or until a meat thermometer registers 155°F. (For a gas grill, preheat grill. Reduce heat to medium-high. Adjust for indirect cooking. Grill as above, except place pork on a rack in a roasting pan.) Remove pork from grill. Cover pork with foil and let stand 10 minutes before slicing. (The meat's temperature will rise 5°F during standing.)

3 Meanwhile, for sauce, in a small saucepan bring the reserved marinade to boiling; reduce heat. Simmer, uncovered, for 8 to 10 minutes or until reduced by about half. Strain mixture through a sieve. Return strained mixture to saucepan. Stir in jam and lemon peel; heat through. Slice pork diagonally; serve with sauce.

Nutrition Facts per serving: 347 cal., 17 g total fat (3 g sat. fat), 73 mg chol., 266 mg sodium, 18 g carbo., 0 g fiber, 24 g pro. Daily Values: 6% vit. C, 2% calcium, 10% iron. Exchanges: 1 Other Carbo., 3½ Very Lean Meat, 3½ Fat

PORK IN PITA POCKETS

Fans of the gyro, a Greek specialty, will love this yogurt-and-cucumber-sauced pork sandwich.

Prep: 25 minutes Marinate: 6 to 24 hours Grill: 12 minutes
Makes: 8 to 10 servings

- 2 pounds lean boneless pork
- 1/4 cup cooking oil
- 1/4 cup chopped onion
- 3 tablespoons lemon juice
- 1 tablespoon finely snipped fresh parsley
- 1/2 teaspoon dried marjoram, crushed
- 1 clove garlic, minced
- 4 to 5 large pita bread rounds, halved crosswise
- 1 recipe Yogurt-Cucumber Sauce

1 Trim fat from pork. Cut pork into 1-inch cubes. Place cubes in a self-sealing plastic bag set in a shallow dish. For marinade, in a bowl combine oil, onion, lemon juice, parsley, marjoram, garlic, ½ teaspoon salt, and ⅛ teaspoon black pepper. Pour over pork; seal bag. Marinate in refrigerator for 6 to 24 hours, turning bag occasionally.

2 Drain pork, discarding marinade. On 8 to 10 long metal skewers, thread pork cubes, leaving a ¼-inch space between pieces.

3 For a charcoal grill, grill kabobs on the rack of an uncovered grill directly over medium coals for 12 to 15 minutes or until pork is no longer pink and juices run clear, turning once halfway through grilling. (For a gas grill, preheat grill. Reduce heat to medium. Place kabobs on grill rack over heat. Cover; grill as above.)

4 Serve pork cubes in pita bread. Top each with some of the Yogurt-Cucumber Sauce. If desired, top each with tomato and lettuce.

Yogurt-Cucumber Sauce: In a medium bowl stir together one 8-ounce carton plain yogurt, ½ cup finely chopped cucumber, 1 tablespoon chopped onion, 1 tablespoon snipped fresh parsley, 1 teaspoon lemon juice, and ⅛ teaspoon garlic salt. Cover and chill up to 24 hours.

Nutrition Facts per serving: 303 cal., 11 g total fat (3 g sat. fat), 64 mg chol., 310 mg sodium, 20 g carbo., 1 g fiber, 29 g pro. Daily Values: 2% vit. A, 6% vit. C, 9% calcium, 10% iron. Exchanges: 1 Starch, 4 Very Lean Meat, 2 Fat

PORK AND SWEET PEPPER KABOBS

When assembling these skewers, wear plastic or rubber gloves to protect your hands from the oils in the chipotle peppers.

Prep: 20 minutes Marinate: 4 to 6 hours Grill: 12 minutes
Makes: 4 servings

- 12 ounces lean boneless pork
- 2 medium red sweet peppers, cut into 1-inch pieces
- 1 medium red onion, cut into 1-inch pieces
- 1 8-ounce carton plain low-fat yogurt
- 3 green onions, thinly sliced
- 2 chipotle peppers in adobo sauce, finely chopped
- 2 tablespoons snipped fresh parsley
- 1 tablespoon grated fresh ginger
- 1 teaspoon sugar
- 1 teaspoon ground coriander
- 1/4 teaspoon salt
- 1/8 teaspoon black pepper
- 2 cloves garlic, minced

1 Trim fat from pork. Cut pork into 1-inch cubes. Place pork cubes, sweet pepper, and onion in a self-sealing plastic bag set in a shallow dish.

2 For marinade, in a small bowl stir together yogurt, green onions, chipotle peppers, parsley, ginger, sugar, coriander, salt, black pepper, and garlic. Pour over pork and vegetables; seal bag. Marinate in refrigerator for 4 to 6 hours, turning bag occasionally.

3 Drain pork and vegetables; discard marinade. On eight 6- to 8-inch metal skewers, alternately thread pork cubes, sweet pepper, and onion, leaving a 1/4-inch space between pieces.

4 For a charcoal grill, grill kabobs on the rack of an uncovered grill directly over medium coals for 12 to 15 minutes or until pork is no longer pink and juices run clear, turning once halfway through grilling. (For a gas grill, preheat grill. Reduce heat to medium. Place kabobs on grill rack over heat. Cover; grill as above.) If desired, serve with rice.

Nutrition Facts per serving: 184 cal., 3 g total fat (1 g sat. fat), 53 mg chol., 298 mg sodium, 14 g carbo., 2 g fiber, 24 g pro. Daily Values: 68% vit. A, 173% vit. C, 13% calcium, 10% iron. Exchanges: 1½ Vegetable, ½ Milk, 2½ Very Lean Meat

PAPAYA PORK KABOBS

Prep: 45 minutes Marinate: 4 to 6 hours Grill: 18 minutes
Makes: 4 servings

- 1½ pounds lean boneless pork
- 3 medium papayas
- 1 cup orange juice
- 1/2 teaspoon ground allspice
- 1/2 teaspoon salt
- 1/2 teaspoon ground ginger
- 1/2 teaspoon black pepper
- 1/2 of a medium red sweet pepper, cut into 1-inch pieces
- 2 small star fruit, cut into 1-inch slices
- 2 cups hot cooked rice

1 Trim fat from pork. Cut pork into 1½-inch cubes. Place pork cubes in a self-sealing plastic bag set in a shallow dish; set aside.

2 Peel and seed the 3 papayas. Cut one of the papayas into 1½-inch pieces; cover and chill until ready to assemble kabobs. Cut up the remaining 2 papayas.

3 For marinade, place the 2 cut-up papayas in a blender or food processor. Add orange juice, allspice, salt, ginger, and pepper. Cover and blend or process until smooth. Divide marinade in half. Pour half of the marinade over pork cubes in bag; seal bag. Marinate pork in refrigerator for 4 to 6 hours, turning bag occasionally. Cover and chill remaining marinade.

4 Remove pork cubes, discarding marinade. Onto 4 long metal skewers, alternately thread pork cubes, papaya, sweet pepper, and star fruit, leaving a 1/4-inch space between pieces.

5 For a charcoal grill, grill kabobs on the greased rack of an uncovered grill directly over medium coals for 18 to 20 minutes or until pork is no longer pink and juices run clear, turning once halfway through grilling. (For a gas grill, preheat grill. Reduce heat to medium. Place kabobs on grill rack over heat. Cover; grill as above.)

6 Transfer reserved marinade to a small saucepan; heat through. Serve kabobs over rice with warm marinade.

Nutrition Facts per serving: 509 cal., 8 g total fat (3 g sat. fat), 106 mg chol., 409 mg sodium, 63 g carbo., 6 g fiber, 41 g pro. Daily Values: 17% vit. A, 330% vit. C, 11% calcium, 17% iron. Exchanges: 2½ Fruit, 1½ Starch, ½ Other Carbo., 5 Very Lean Meat, 1 Fat

Papaya Pork Kabobs

FOOD FOR THOUGHT PAPAYAS

Delicious when fresh, pureed, juiced, or used in salsas or chutneys, the papaya's juicy yellowish orange flesh has a mild melonlike flavor with varying levels of sweetness. Its texture resembles that of cantaloupe but is a bit softer. The center of the fruit is filled with tiny black seeds that taste peppery, making them a unique garnish when used whole or ground and used like pepper. Choose a papaya that has a golden yellow skin that gives slightly when pressed with your fingertips. To ripen papayas, place them in a brown paper bag and store them at room temperature.

Caribbean Pork with Three-Pepper Salsa

CARIBBEAN PORK WITH THREE-PEPPER SALSA

A prismatic salsa accompanies citrus-marinated pork roast for picture-perfect presentation.

Prep: 25 minutes Marinate: 6 to 8 hours Grill: 1 hour
Stand: 15 minutes Makes: 6 to 8 servings

1 cup orange juice
2 teaspoons finely shredded lime peel
1/4 cup lime juice
1/4 cup cooking oil
1/2 cup chopped green onions (4)
2 tablespoons soy sauce

1 tablespoon grated fresh ginger
2 fresh serrano chile peppers, seeded and finely chopped (see tip, page 36)
2 cloves garlic, minced
1 2- to 2½-pound boneless pork top loin roast (single loin)
1 medium green sweet pepper, quartered lengthwise
1 medium yellow or orange sweet pepper, quartered lengthwise
1/2 cup cherry tomatoes, quartered
2 tablespoons snipped fresh cilantro

1 For marinade, in a small bowl combine orange juice, lime peel, lime juice, oil, ¼ cup of the green onions, soy sauce, ginger, chile peppers, and garlic. Reserve 2 tablespoons of the marinade for the salsa; cover and chill until needed.

2 Trim fat from pork. Place the pork in a self-sealing plastic bag set in a shallow dish. Pour remaining marinade over pork in bag; seal bag. Marinate pork in the refrigerator for 6 to 8 hours, turning the bag occasionally. Drain pork, discarding the marinade.

3 For a charcoal grill, arrange medium coals around a drip pan. Test for medium-low heat above pan. Place meat on grill rack over drip pan. Cover; grill for 1 to 1½ hours or until a meat thermometer registers 150°F. Place sweet peppers, skin sides down, on grill rack directly over the coals. Grill about 10 minutes or until skin is charred. Wrap pepper quarters in foil. Let stand until cool enough to handle. Use a sharp knife to gently and slowly peel off the skin. Discard skin. Chop peppers. (For a gas grill, preheat grill. Reduce heat to medium-low. Adjust for indirect cooking. Grill as above, except place meat on a rack in a roasting pan.)

4 Remove meat from grill. Cover meat with foil and let stand for 15 minutes before slicing. (The meat's temperature will rise 10°F during standing.)

5 Meanwhile, for salsa, in a medium bowl combine the reserved marinade, chopped grilled sweet peppers, the remaining ¼ cup green onions, cherry tomatoes, and cilantro. Serve salsa with pork.

Nutrition Facts per serving: 297 cal., 14 g total fat (4 g sat. fat), 82 mg chol., 212 mg sodium, 7 g carbo., 1 g fiber, 34 g pro. Daily Values: 9% vit. A, 153% vit. C, 2% calcium, 9% iron. Exchanges: ½ Vegetable, 5 Very Lean Meat, 2 Fat

TOP LOIN ROAST WITH ARTICHOKE RELISH

Prep: 30 minutes Marinate: 4 to 24 hours Grill: 1 hour
Stand: 15 minutes Makes: 6 to 8 servings

1 6½-ounce jar marinated artichoke hearts
1 2- to 2½-pound boneless pork top loin roast (single loin)
¼ cup lemon juice
1 teaspoon salt
1 teaspoon black pepper
4 cloves garlic, minced
1½ cups finely chopped tomatoes
½ cup chopped roasted red sweet peppers
¼ cup finely chopped pimiento-stuffed green olives
2 tablespoons snipped fresh basil

1 Drain artichoke hearts, reserving marinade. Cover and chill artichoke hearts until needed.

2 Trim fat from meat. Place meat in self-sealing plastic bag set in a shallow dish. For marinade, in a small bowl combine reserved artichoke marinade, lemon juice, salt, pepper, and garlic. Pour over meat; seal bag. Marinate in refrigerator for 4 to 24 hours, turning bag occasionally.

3 For relish, chop chilled artichoke hearts. In a small bowl combine chopped artichoke hearts, tomatoes, sweet peppers, olives, and basil. Let stand at room temperature while grilling pork.

4 Drain meat, discarding marinade. For a charcoal grill, arrange medium coals around a drip pan. Test for medium-low heat above pan. Place meat on grill rack over drip pan. Cover; grill for 1 to 1½ hours or until a meat thermometer registers 150°F. (For a gas grill, preheat grill. Reduce heat to medium-low. Adjust for indirect cooking. Grill as above, except place meat on a rack in a roasting pan.)

5 Remove meat from grill. Cover with foil and let stand for 15 minutes before slicing. (The meat's temperature will rise 10°F during standing.) Serve with artichoke relish.

Nutrition Facts per serving: 266 cal., 11 g total fat (3 g sat. fat), 82 mg chol., 467 mg sodium, 7 g carbo., 1 g fiber, 35 g pro. Daily Values: 7% vit. A, 88% vit. C, 5% calcium, 10% iron. Exchanges: ½ Vegetable, 5 Very Lean Meat, 2 Fat

FENNEL AND CORN BREAD STUFFED PORK

A honey mustard and bourbon glaze makes this company-special pork roast glisten.

Prep: 40 minutes Grill: 2 hours Stand: 15 minutes
Makes: 6 servings

1⅓ cups chopped fennel
⅓ cup chopped onion (1 small)
¼ cup butter or margarine
1½ cups corn bread stuffing mix
½ teaspoon fennel seeds, crushed
¼ cup pure maple syrup
2 tablespoons bourbon
1 tablespoon honey mustard
1 4- to 4½-pound pork loin center rib roast, backbone loosened (6 ribs)

1 For stuffing, in a large skillet cook fennel and onion in 3 tablespoons of the hot butter until just tender. Stir in stuffing mix, ⅓ cup water, and fennel seeds; set stuffing aside. For glaze, in a small saucepan combine maple syrup, bourbon, honey mustard, and the remaining 1 tablespoon butter. Cook and stir just until butter is melted.

2 Trim fat from roast. Place roast, rib side down, on a work surface. Cut six pockets in roast from meaty side over rib bones. Spoon stuffing into pockets. Sprinkle roast with salt and black pepper. Insert a meat thermometer into center of meat without touching bone.

3 For a charcoal grill, arrange medium coals around a drip pan. Test for medium-low heat above pan. Place meat, bone side down, on grill rack over pan. Cover loosely with foil. Cover; grill for 2 to 2¾ hours or until thermometer registers 150°F, removing foil and brushing occasionally with glaze the last 25 minutes of grilling. (For a gas grill, preheat grill. Reduce heat to medium-low. Adjust for indirect cooking. Grill as above, except place meat, bone side down, in a roasting pan.)

4 Remove meat from grill. Cover with foil; let stand 15 minutes before slicing. (The meat's temperature will rise 10°F during standing.)

Nutrition Facts per serving: 662 cal., 27 g total fat (11 g sat. fat), 187 mg chol., 558 mg sodium, 28 g carbo., 4 g fiber, 69 g pro. Daily Values: 6% vit. A, 5% vit. C, 4% calcium, 18% iron. Exchanges: ½ Starch, 1½ Other Carbo., 10 Very Lean Meat, 4 Fat

RHUBARB-GLAZED PORK ROAST

Prep: 15 minutes Cook: 30 minutes
Grill: 1¼ hours Stand: 15 minutes
Makes: 4 servings

2 cups fresh or frozen sliced rhubarb (12 ounces)
1 6-ounce can (⅔ cup) frozen apple juice concentrate
  Several drops red food coloring (optional)
2 tablespoons honey
1 3- to 4-pound pork loin center rib roast, backbone loosened (4 ribs)

1 For glaze, in a saucepan combine rhubarb, apple juice concentrate, and, if desired, red food coloring. Bring to boiling; reduce heat. Simmer, covered, for 15 to 20 minutes or until rhubarb is very tender. Strain mixture into a small bowl, pressing out liquid with the back of a spoon; discard pulp. Return rhubarb liquid to saucepan. Bring to boiling; reduce heat. Simmer, uncovered, about 15 minutes or until reduced to ½ cup. Remove saucepan from heat; stir in honey. Set aside ¼ cup of the glaze.

2 Meanwhile, trim fat from meat. Insert a meat thermometer into center of meat without touching bone.

3 For a charcoal grill, arrange medium coals around a drip pan. Test for medium-low heat above pan. Place meat, bone side down, on grill rack over pan. Cover; grill for 1¼ to 2 hours or until thermometer registers 150°F, brushing occasionally with reserved glaze the last 15 minutes of grilling. (For a gas grill, preheat grill. Reduce heat to medium-low. Adjust for indirect cooking. Grill as above, except place meat, bone side down, in a roasting pan.)

4 Remove meat from grill. Cover with foil; let stand 15 minutes before slicing. (The meat temperature will rise 10°F during standing.)

5 Cook and stir remaining glaze over medium-low heat until heated through; pass with meat.

Nutrition Facts per serving: 510 cal., 16 g total fat (6 g sat. fat), 145 mg chol., 109 mg sodium, 28 g carbo., 1 g fiber, 59 g pro. Daily Values: 1% vit. A, 11% vit. C, 7% calcium, 14% iron. Exchanges: 2 Other Carbo., 8 Very Lean Meat, 2½ Fat

BARBECUED PORK SANDWICHES

Let this slow-cooking pork roast take its time on the grill—it needs all afternoon to reach fall-off-the-bone tenderness.

Prep: 40 minutes Grill: 4 hours Stand: 30 minutes
Makes: 8 to 10 servings

- 1 4¹⁄₂- to 5-pound boneless pork
  shoulder roast
- ¹⁄₂ teaspoon salt
- ¹⁄₂ teaspoon black pepper
- ¹⁄₄ teaspoon celery seeds
- ¹⁄₈ teaspoon onion powder
- ¹⁄₈ teaspoon garlic powder
- ¹⁄₈ teaspoon ground cloves
  Dash cayenne pepper
- 1 8-ounce can tomato sauce
- 1 cup catsup
- 1 cup chopped onion (1 large)
- ¹⁄₂ cup chopped green sweet pepper
- ¹⁄₄ cup vinegar
- 2 tablespoons brown sugar
- 2 tablespoons Worcestershire sauce
- 1 tablespoon yellow mustard
- 2 teaspoons chili powder
- 2 cloves garlic, minced
- 8 to 10 French-style rolls, split
  and toasted

1 Trim fat from meat. In a small bowl combine salt, black pepper, celery seeds, onion powder, garlic powder, cloves, and cayenne pepper. Sprinkle mixture evenly over all sides of meat; rub in with your fingers.

2 For a charcoal grill, arrange medium-hot coals around a drip pan. Test for medium heat above pan. Place meat on grill rack over drip pan. Cover; grill about 4 hours or until meat is very tender, adding more coals as necessary. (For a gas grill, preheat grill. Reduce heat to medium. Adjust for indirect cooking. Grill as above, except place meat on a rack in a roasting pan.) Remove meat from grill. Cover with foil and let stand 30 minutes.

3 Meanwhile, for sauce, in a large saucepan combine tomato sauce, catsup, onion, sweet pepper, vinegar, brown sugar, Worcestershire sauce, mustard, chili powder, and garlic. Bring mixture to boiling; reduce heat. Simmer, covered, for 15 minutes.

4 Shred pork with 2 forks. Stir shredded pork into sauce; heat through. To serve, spoon pork onto toasted rolls.

Nutrition Facts per serving: 553 cal., 20 g total fat (7 g sat. fat), 172 mg chol., 1,074 mg sodium, 35 g carbo., 3 g fiber, 54 g pro. Daily Values: 13% vit. A, 28% vit. C, 12% calcium, 29% iron. Exchanges: 2¹⁄₂ Starch, 6¹⁄₂ Lean Meat

FOOD FOR THOUGHT PULLED PORK

In the old South, pork was traditionally preferred over beef, simply because raising pork required minimal effort. Wealthy colonists enjoyed tender cuts from the rib and loin, while poorer colonists could only afford less tender cuts, such as pork shoulder and pork butt. These cuts benefited from pit smoking, which both preserved and tenderized the meat. Today the same slow-cooking method is used to make pulled pork, which has become popular well beyond its southern roots. The meat is smoked, pulled off the bones, shredded by hand, and served on sandwiches with barbecue sauce.

CHIPOTLE PORK WRAPS

Prep: 40 minutes Grill: 4 hours Stand: 30 minutes
Makes: 8 to 10 servings

- 1 4- to 5-pound boneless pork shoulder roast
- 2 teaspoons ground chipotle chile powder
- 1 teaspoon kosher salt
- ½ teaspoon black pepper
- 2 medium red onions, cut into ½-inch slices
- 1 tablespoon olive oil
- 8 to 10 eight-inch flour tortillas, warmed
- 1 recipe Chipotle Mayonnaise or 1 cup chipotle-flavor light mayonnaise dressing
- 2 cups shredded Monterey Jack cheese (8 ounces)

1 Trim fat from meat. In a bowl stir together chile powder, salt, and pepper. Evenly sprinkle mixture over all sides of meat; rub in with fingers.

2 For a charcoal grill, arrange medium-hot coals around a drip pan. Test for medium heat above pan. Place meat on grill rack over drip pan. Cover; grill about 4 hours or until meat is very tender, adding more coals as necessary. Brush onion slices lightly with oil; place on grill rack directly over coals the last 20 minutes of grilling, turning once. (For a gas grill, preheat grill. Reduce heat to medium. Adjust for indirect cooking. Grill as above, except place meat on a rack in a roasting pan.) Remove meat from grill. Cover with foil and let stand for 30 minutes.

3 Shred pork with 2 forks. Spread some of the Chipotle Mayonnaise on one side of each tortilla. Top each tortilla with meat, grilled onion slices, and cheese. Tightly roll up each tortilla.

Chipotle Mayonnaise: In a small bowl stir together 1 cup mayonnaise or salad dressing and 2 to 3 canned chipotle peppers in adobo sauce, drained and finely chopped. Cover and chill until serving time or up to 1 week.

Nutrition Facts per serving: 653 cal., 44 g total fat (12 g sat. fat), 133 mg chol., 1,159 mg sodium, 25 g carbo., 1 g fiber, 38 g pro. Daily Values: 12% vit. A, 7% vit. C, 28% calcium, 20% iron. Exchanges: 1½ Starch, 5 Medium-Fat Meat, 3½ Fat

MAHOGANY-GLAZED PORK AND SLAW

Hoisin sauce—a sweet, pungent condiment—is responsible for the mahogany color.

Prep: 15 minutes Grill: 12 minutes
Makes: 4 servings

- ⅓ cup hoisin sauce
- 2 tablespoons cider vinegar
- ½ teaspoon toasted sesame oil
- ¼ teaspoon black pepper
- 2 cloves garlic, minced
- 3 cups packaged shredded broccoli (broccoli slaw mix)
- 2 pork shoulder blade steaks, cut ¾ inch thick

1 In a small bowl combine hoisin sauce, vinegar, sesame oil, pepper, and garlic. Toss half the hoisin sauce mixture with shredded broccoli. Cover; chill until ready to serve. Reserve remaining hoisin sauce mixture.

2 For a charcoal grill, grill pork steaks on the rack of an uncovered grill directly over medium coals for 12 to 14 minutes or until steaks are slightly pink in the centers and juices run clear (160°F), turning once and brushing occasionally with reserved hoisin sauce mixture during the last 2 to 3 minutes of grilling. (For a gas grill, preheat grill. Reduce heat to medium. Place steaks on grill rack over heat. Cover; grill as above.) Serve pork steaks with slaw.

Nutrition Facts per serving: 414 cal., 18 g total fat (6 g sat. fat), 153 mg chol., 486 mg sodium, 14 g carbo., 3 g fiber, 47 g pro. Daily Values: 21% vit. A, 106% vit. C, 9% calcium, 21% iron. Exchanges: 1 Vegetable, ½ Other Carbo., 6½ Lean Meat

PEPPER-JELLY PORK STEAKS

Prep: 15 minutes Marinate: 8 to 24 hours Grill: 12 minutes
Makes: 6 servings

- 6 12-ounce pork shoulder steaks, cut ¾ inch thick
- ½ teaspoon garlic salt
- 1¾ cups red jalapeño jelly
- 1 cup apple juice
- 1 cup cider vinegar
- ⅓ cup very finely chopped onion
- 2 tablespoons cider vinegar

1 Trim fat from steaks. Sprinkle garlic salt evenly over both sides; rub in with fingers. Place pork steaks in a self-sealing plastic bag set in a shallow dish. For marinade, in a bowl combine 1 cup of the jelly, apple juice, the 1 cup cider vinegar, and onion. Pour over meat; seal bag. Marinate in refrigerator for 8 to 24 hours, turning bag occasionally.

2 For glaze, in a saucepan stir together remaining ¾ cup jelly and 2 tablespoons cider vinegar; heat and stir until jelly is melted.

3 Drain steaks, discarding the marinade. For a charcoal grill, grill steaks on the rack of an uncovered grill directly over medium coals for 12 to 14 minutes or until steaks are slightly pink in the center and juices run clear (160°F), turning steaks once and brushing occasionally with half of the glaze during the last 5 minutes of grilling. (For a gas grill, preheat grill. Reduce heat to medium. Place the steaks on grill rack over heat. Cover; grill as above.)

4 To serve, bring remaining glaze to boiling. Pass with pork steaks.

Nutrition Facts per serving: 488 cal., 16 g total fat (6 g sat. fat), 151 mg chol., 220 mg sodium, 38 g carbo., 1 g fiber, 44 g pro. Daily Values: 4% vit. C, 5% calcium, 17% iron. Exchanges: 2½ Other Carbo., 6 Lean Meat,

2 For sauce, in a large bowl combine wine, pineapple juice, honey, vinegar, soy sauce, mustard, bourbon, and hot pepper sauce.

3 Place rib portions, bone sides down, in a large roasting pan. Pour sauce over ribs. For a charcoal grill, arrange medium-hot coals around the edge of the grill. Test for medium heat. Place uncovered roasting pan on grill rack in center of grill. Cover; grill for 1½ to 1¾ hours or until ribs are tender, spooning sauce over ribs every 20 to 25 minutes. (For a gas grill, preheat grill. Reduce heat to medium. Adjust for indirect cooking, except do not use a drip pan. Place uncovered roasting pan on grill rack directly over where drip pan would be. Grill as above.)

Chuck Wagon Rub: In a small bowl combine 1 tablespoon black pepper, 2 teaspoons kosher salt or sea salt, 2 teaspoons chili powder, 1 teaspoon sugar, 1 teaspoon onion powder, 1 teaspoon garlic powder, 1 teaspoon dried parsley, and 1 teaspoon dried oregano, crushed.

Nutrition Facts per serving: 731 cal., 21 g total fat (7 g sat. fat), 135 mg chol., 3,106 mg sodium, 52 g carbo., 2 g fiber, 68 g pro. Daily Values: 13% vit. A, 18% vit. C, 10% calcium, 27% iron. Exchanges: 3½ Other Carbo., 10 Very Lean Meat, 3½ Fat

CHUCK WAGON BABY BACK RIBS

To keep the roasting pan from blackening, wrap the outside with heavy foil.

Prep: 20 minutes Grill: 1½ hours
Makes: 4 to 5 servings

 4 to 5 pounds pork loin back ribs or meaty pork spareribs
 1 recipe Chuck Wagon Rub
 1 cup dry red wine
 1 cup pineapple juice
 ½ cup honey
 ½ cup cider vinegar
 ½ cup soy sauce
 ¼ cup yellow mustard
 2 tablespoons bourbon
 1 teaspoon bottled hot pepper sauce

1 Trim fat from ribs. Sprinkle Chuck Wagon Rub evenly over both sides of ribs; rub in with your fingers. If desired, cut ribs into 2- to 3-rib portions.

Chuck Wagon Baby Back Ribs

KANSAS CITY PORK SPARERIBS

Prep: 10 minutes Grill: 1½ hours
Makes: 4 servings

- **2 cups hickory, oak, or apple wood chips**
- **4 pounds meaty pork spareribs or pork loin back ribs**
- **1 tablespoon brown sugar**
- **1 tablespoon garlic pepper**
- **1 tablespoon paprika**
- **1½ teaspoons chili powder**
- **1 teaspoon salt**
- **½ teaspoon celery seeds**
- **¼ cup cider vinegar**
- **1 recipe Kansas City Barbecue Sauce**

1 At least 1 hour before grilling, soak wood chips in enough water to cover. Trim fat from ribs. For rub, in a small bowl combine brown sugar, garlic pepper, paprika, chili powder, salt, and celery seeds. Brush ribs with vinegar. Sprinkle the rub evenly over both sides of ribs; rub in with your fingers.

2 Drain wood chips. For a charcoal grill, arrange medium-hot coals around a drip pan. Test for medium heat above pan. Sprinkle wood chips over coals. Place ribs, bone sides down, on grill rack over drip pan. (Or place ribs in a rib rack; place on grill rack.) Cover; grill for 1½ to 1¾ hours or until ribs are tender. (For a gas grill, preheat grill. Reduce heat to medium. Adjust for indirect cooking. Grill as above, except place the ribs in a roasting pan. Add wood chips according to manufacturer directions.) Serve ribs with Kansas City Barbecue Sauce.

Kansas City Barbecue Sauce: In a medium saucepan cook ½ cup finely chopped onion and 2 cloves garlic, minced, in 1 tablespoon hot olive oil until onion is tender. Stir in ¾ cup apple juice, ½ of a 6-ounce can (⅓ cup) tomato paste, ¼ cup cider vinegar, 2 tablespoons brown sugar, 2 tablespoons mild-flavor molasses, 1 tablespoon paprika, 1 tablespoon prepared horseradish, 1 tablespoon Worcestershire sauce, 1 teaspoon salt, and ½ teaspoon black pepper. Bring mixture to boiling; reduce heat. Simmer, uncovered, about 30 minutes or until sauce is desired consistency, stirring occasionally.

Nutrition Facts per serving: 688 cal., 42 g total fat (14 g sat. fat), 176 mg chol., 1,470 mg sodium, 34 g carbo., 2 g fiber, 46 g pro. Daily Values: 28% vit. A, 38% vit. C, 8% calcium, 34% iron. Exchanges: 2 Other Carbo., 6½ Medium-Fat Meat, 2 Fat

TENNESSEE PORK RIBS

Prep: 20 minutes Chill: 6 to 24 hours Grill: 1½ hours
Makes: 4 to 5 servings

- **4 to 5 pounds pork loin back ribs or meaty pork spareribs**
- **1 tablespoon paprika**
- **1 tablespoon brown sugar**
- **1 teaspoon black pepper**
- **1 teaspoon ground cumin**
- **1 teaspoon dry mustard**
- **½ teaspoon garlic powder**
- **½ teaspoon cayenne pepper**
- **¼ teaspoon celery seeds**
- **1½ cups hickory wood chips**
- **½ cup cider vinegar**
- **2 tablespoons yellow mustard**
- **¼ teaspoon salt**

1 Trim fat from ribs. For rub, in a small bowl combine paprika, brown sugar, black pepper, cumin, dry mustard, garlic powder, cayenne pepper, and celery seeds. Sprinkle rub evenly over both sides of ribs; rub in with your fingers. Cover and chill for 6 to 24 hours.

2 At least 1 hour before grilling, soak wood chips in enough water to cover. Meanwhile, in a bowl combine vinegar, yellow mustard, and salt. Drain wood chips.

3 For a charcoal grill, arrange medium-hot coals around a drip pan. Test for medium heat above pan. Sprinkle drained wood chips over coals. Place ribs, bone sides down, on grill rack over drip pan. (Or place ribs in a rib rack; place on grill rack.) Cover; grill for 1½ to 1¾ hours or until ribs are tender, brushing with mustard mixture three times during the last 30 minutes of grilling. (For a gas grill, preheat grill. Reduce heat to medium. Adjust for indirect cooking. Grill as above, except place ribs in a roasting pan. Add wood chips according to manufacturer's directions.)

Nutrition Facts per serving: 485 cal., 21 g total fat (7 g sat. fat), 135 mg chol., 336 mg sodium, 8 g carbo., 1 g fiber, 63 g pro. Daily Values: 23% vit. A, 4% vit. C, 5% calcium, 18% iron. Exchanges: ½ Other Carbo., 9 Very Lean Meat, 3 Fat

EAST-WEST RIBS

This recipe offers another angle on East meets West. The hoisin, ginger, and especially the sesame flavors shine through.

Prep: 25 minutes Marinate: 6 to 24 hours Grill: 1½ hours
Makes: 4 servings

**4 pounds pork loin back ribs or meaty
    pork spareribs**
1 recipe Hoisin-Ginger Glaze
2 cups hickory or apple wood chips

1 Trim fat from ribs. Place ribs in a self-sealing plastic bag set in a shallow dish. Cover and chill ½ cup of the Hoisin-Ginger Glaze. Pour remaining glaze over ribs; seal bag. Marinate ribs in the refrigerator for 6 to 24 hours, turning the bag occasionally.

2 At least 1 hour before grilling, soak wood chips in enough water to cover. Drain ribs, discarding marinade. Drain wood chips.

3 For a charcoal grill, arrange medium-hot coals around a drip pan. Test for medium heat above pan. Sprinkle drained wood chips over coals. Place ribs, bone sides down, on grill rack over drip pan. (Or place ribs in a rib rack; place on grill rack.) Cover; grill for 1½ to 1¾ hours or until ribs are tender. Brush occasionally with the ½ cup reserved glaze during the last 15 minutes of grilling. (For a gas grill, preheat grill. Reduce heat to medium. Adjust for indirect cooking. Grill as above, except place ribs in a roasting pan. Add wood chips according to manufacturer's directions.)

Hoisin-Ginger Glaze: In a medium bowl combine ½ cup hoisin sauce, ¼ cup bottled plum sauce, ¼ cup reduced-sodium soy sauce, 2 tablespoons dry sherry, 2 tablespoons toasted sesame oil, 2 tablespoons honey, 1 tablespoon grated fresh ginger, ½ teaspoon freshly ground black pepper, and 5 cloves garlic, minced.

Nutrition Facts per serving: 657 cal., 28 g total fat (8 g sat. fat), 135 mg chol., 1,179 mg sodium, 28 g carbo., 0 g fiber, 65 g pro. Daily Values: 7% vit. A, 5% vit. C, 8% calcium, 14% iron. Exchanges: 2 Other Carbo., 9 Very Lean Meat, 5 Fat

East-West Ribs

CHINESE-STYLE RIBS

Prep: 25 minutes Chill: 6 to 24 hours Grill: 1½ hours
Makes: 4 to 5 servings

**4 pounds pork loin back ribs or
meaty pork spareribs**
2 tablespoons granulated sugar
½ teaspoon salt
¼ teaspoon paprika
¼ teaspoon ground turmeric
¼ teaspoon celery seeds
¼ teaspoon dry mustard
¼ cup catsup
¼ cup soy sauce
2 tablespoons brown sugar
2 tablespoons water
**1 teaspoon grated fresh ginger or
1 teaspoon ground ginger**
2 cups alder or oak wood chips

1 Trim fat from ribs. For rub, in a small bowl combine granulated sugar, salt, paprika, turmeric, celery seeds, and dry mustard. Sprinkle rub evenly over both sides of ribs; rub in with your fingers. Cover and chill for 6 to 24 hours.

2 For sauce, in a small bowl combine catsup, soy sauce, brown sugar, water, and ginger. Cover and chill for 6 to 24 hours.

3 At least 1 hour before grilling, soak the wood chips in enough water to cover. Drain wood chips.

4 For a charcoal grill, arrange medium-hot coals around a drip pan. Test for medium heat above pan. Sprinkle drained wood chips over coals. Place ribs, bone sides down, on grill rack over drip pan. (Or place ribs in a rib rack; place on grill rack.) Cover; grill for 1½ to 1¾ hours or until ribs are tender, brushing once with the sauce during the last 15 minutes of grilling. (For a gas grill, preheat grill. Reduce heat to medium. Adjust for indirect cooking. Grill as above, except place ribs in a roasting pan. Add wood chips according to manufacturer directions.) Before serving, brush ribs with any remaining sauce.

Nutrition Facts per serving: 527 cal., 20 g total fat (7 g sat. fat), 135 mg chol., 1,484 mg sodium, 17 g carbo., 0 g fiber, 65 g pro. Daily Values: 5% vit. A, 6% vit. C, 5% calcium, 15% iron. Exchanges: 1 Other Carbo., 9 Very Lean Meat, 3 Fat

COUNTRY RIBS WITH DRIED PLUM BARBECUE SAUCE

Looking for a good wine to serve with your ribs?
California Zinfandel is a superb match.

Prep: 20 minutes Cook: 5 minutes Grill: 1½ hours
Makes: 6 servings

2 tablespoons cooking oil
1 cup finely chopped onion (1 large)
1 15-ounce can tomato puree
**1½ cups cut-up pitted dried plums
(prunes)**
⅔ cup water
½ cup packed brown sugar
⅓ cup Dijon-style mustard
¼ cup lemon juice
¼ cup Worcestershire sauce
4 teaspoons bottled hot pepper sauce
½ teaspoon ground allspice
½ teaspoon ground ginger
Salt
Black pepper
4 pounds pork country-style ribs

1 For sauce, in a medium saucepan heat oil over medium heat. Add onion; cook and stir about 10 minutes or until tender. Add tomato puree, dried plums, water, brown sugar, mustard, lemon juice, Worcestershire sauce, hot pepper sauce, allspice, and ginger. Bring plum mixture to boiling; reduce heat. Simmer gently, uncovered, for 5 to 10 minutes or until sauce thickens. Season to taste with salt and pepper. Trim fat from ribs.

2 For a charcoal grill, arrange medium-hot coals around a drip pan. Test for medium heat above pan. Place ribs, bone sides down, on grill rack over pan. (Or place ribs in a rib rack; place on grill rack.) Cover; grill for 1½ to 2 hours or until ribs are tender, brushing occasionally with sauce during the last 10 minutes of grilling. (For a gas grill, preheat grill. Reduce heat to medium. Adjust for indirect cooking. Grill as above, except place ribs in a roasting pan.) Pass any remaining sauce with ribs.

Nutrition Facts per serving: 537 cal., 18 g total fat (5 g sat. fat), 107 mg chol., 610 mg sodium, 59 g carbo., 4 g fiber, 37 g pro. Daily Values: 19% vit. A, 31% vit. C, 10% calcium, 26% iron. Exchanges: 1 Fruit, 3 Other Carbo., 5 Lean Meat, ½ Fat

GLAZED COUNTRY RIBS

To prevent this rich, tart-sweet sauce from scorching before the ribs are done, brush it on only during the last 10 minutes of grilling.

Prep: 15 minutes Cook: 10 minutes Grill: 1½ hours
Makes: 4 servings

- **1 cup catsup**
- **½ cup water**
- **¼ cup finely chopped onion**
- **¼ cup cider vinegar or wine vinegar**
- **¼ cup mild-flavored molasses**
- **2 tablespoons Worcestershire sauce**
- **2 teaspoons chili powder**
- **2 cloves garlic, minced**
- **2½ to 3 pounds pork country-style ribs**

1 For sauce, in a medium saucepan combine catsup, water, onion, vinegar, molasses, Worcestershire sauce, chili powder, and garlic. Bring to boiling; reduce heat. Simmer, uncovered, for 10 to 15 minutes or to desired consistency, stirring often. Trim fat from ribs.

2 For a charcoal grill, arrange medium-hot coals around a drip pan. Test for medium heat above pan. Place ribs, bone sides down, on grill rack over pan. (Or place ribs in a rib rack; place on grill rack.) Cover; grill for 1½ to 2 hours or until ribs are tender. Brush occasionally with sauce during last 10 minutes of grilling. (For a gas grill, preheat grill. Reduce heat to medium. Adjust for indirect cooking. Grill as above, except place ribs in a roasting pan.) Pass remaining sauce with ribs.

Nutrition Facts per serving: 431 cal., 18 g total fat (6 g sat. fat), 112 mg chol., 852 mg sodium, 34 g carbo., 1 g fiber, 33 g pro. Daily Values: 22% vit. A, 21% vit. C, 11% calcium, 20% iron. Exchanges: 2 Other Carbo., 4 Medium-Fat Meat

TEXAS RIB SANDWICHES WITH COLESLAW

Coleslaw is a must-have accompaniment to these barbecued sandwiches. Spoon some slaw onto the bun or serve it on the side.

Prep: 10 minutes Grill: 1½ hours
Makes: 6 servings

- **2 pounds boneless pork country-style ribs**
- **¾ cup bottled or homemade barbecue sauce**
- **6 crusty dinner rolls or hamburger buns, split and toasted**
-    **Bottled hot pepper sauce (optional)**
- **1 cup prepared coleslaw**

1 Trim fat from ribs. For a charcoal grill, arrange medium-hot coals around a drip pan. Test for medium heat above pan. Place ribs on grill rack over pan. (Or place ribs in a rib rack; place on grill rack.) Cover; grill for 1½ to 2 hours or until ribs are tender, brushing occasionally with barbecue sauce during the last 10 minutes of grilling. (For a gas grill, preheat grill. Reduce heat to medium. Adjust for indirect cooking. Grill as above, except place ribs in a roasting pan.) Remove ribs from grill and brush with the remaining sauce. Cut ribs into serving-size pieces.

2 To serve, top toasted roll bottoms with rib pieces and, if desired, sprinkle with hot pepper sauce. Spoon coleslaw on top of ribs; add roll tops.

Nutrition Facts per serving: 464 cal., 22 g total fat (7 g sat. fat), 89 mg chol., 635 mg sodium, 37 g carbo., 1 g fiber, 28 g pro. Daily Values: 4% vit. A, 15% vit. C, 6% calcium, 21% iron. Exchanges: 2 Starch, ½ Other Carbo., 3 Medium-Fat Meat, 1 Fat

Ham Steak Sandwiches with Apricot-Cherry Chutney

HAM STEAK SANDWICHES WITH APRICOT-CHERRY CHUTNEY

Lose the bun, if you like, and simply serve the sweet chutney over grilled ham steak.

Prep: 15 minutes Cook: 10 minutes
Grill: 14 minutes Stand: 15 minutes
Makes: 8 to 10 servings

- **1 cup dried apricots, coarsely snipped**
- **1 cup dried tart red cherries**
- **¹/₂ cup golden raisins**
- **³/₄ cup apricot preserves**
- **¹/₃ cup thinly sliced green onions**
- **¹/₄ cup white wine vinegar**
- **2 cloves garlic, minced**
- **1 2-pound cooked center-cut ham slice, cut ¹/₂ inch thick**
- **8 to 10 large potato rolls or hamburger buns, split and toasted**
- **8 ounces thinly sliced Havarti cheese**

1 For chutney, in a medium bowl stir together apricots, cherries, and raisins. Add enough boiling water to cover; let stand 15 minutes. Drain. In a medium saucepan stir together drained fruit, apricot preserves, green onions, vinegar, and garlic. Bring to boiling; reduce heat. Simmer, uncovered, for 10 to 15 minutes or until thickened. Set chutney aside.

2 Trim fat from ham. For a charcoal grill, grill ham on the rack of an uncovered grill directly over medium coals for 14 to 18 minutes or until heated through (140°F). (For a gas grill, preheat grill. Reduce heat to medium. Place ham on grill rack over heat. Cover; grill as above.)

3 To serve, cut ham into thin strips. Serve on toasted rolls topped with cheese and chutney.

Nutrition Facts per serving: 672 cal., 26 g total fat (4 g sat. fat), 100 mg chol., 1,956 mg sodium, 77 g carbo., 4 g fiber, 33 g pro. Daily Values: 12% vit. A, 6% vit. C, 24% calcium, 20% iron. Exchanges: 1 Fruit, 3 Starch, 1 Other Carbo., 3 Medium-Fat Meat, 2 Fat

GRILLED PEPPERED HAM STEAK AND PASTA

Store mixed peppercorns in a cool,
dark place for about a year.

Prep: 15 minutes Grill: 14 minutes
Makes: 4 to 6 servings

- 1 **1-pound cooked center-cut ham slice, cut ¹/₂ inch thick**
- 1 **tablespoon dried whole mixed peppercorns, crushed**
- 12 **ounces dried penne**
- 2 **cups fresh sugar snap peas, trimmed**
- ¹/₂ **cup chopped onion (1 medium)**
- 1 **tablespoon olive oil**
- ³/₄ **cup milk**
- 1 **5-ounce container semi-soft cheese with garlic and herb**

1 Trim fat from ham. Sprinkle crushed peppercorns over both sides of the ham; rub in with your fingers.

2 For a charcoal grill, grill ham on the rack of an uncovered grill directly over medium coals for 14 to 18 minutes or until heated through (140°F). (For a gas grill, preheat grill. Reduce heat to medium. Place ham on grill rack over heat. Cover; grill as above.)

3 Meanwhile, cook pasta according to package directions, adding sugar snap peas the last 1 minute of cooking. Drain; return pasta and peas to saucepan. Cover and keep warm.

4 For sauce, in a medium saucepan cook onion in hot oil over medium-high heat until tender. Stir in milk and cheese until smooth. Add sauce to pasta mixture, tossing to coat. Cut grilled ham into bite-size pieces; toss with pasta mixture.

Nutrition Facts per serving: 762 cal., 29 g total fat (11 g sat. fat), 100 mg chol., 1,733 mg sodium, 83 g carbo., 5 g fiber, 36 g pro. Daily Values: 2% vit. A, 34% vit. C, 17% calcium, 29% iron. Exchanges: ¹/₂ Vegetable, 4 Starch, 1¹/₂ Other Carbo., 3 Medium-Fat Meat, 2 Fat

CANADIAN BACON AND PINEAPPLE PIZZA

If you notice that one side of the pizza is getting
browner than the other, give it a turn.

Prep: 20 minutes Grill: 15 minutes
Makes: 4 servings

- 1 **8-ounce can pizza sauce**
- 1 **14-ounce Italian bread shell (Boboli)**
- 1 **3¹/₂-ounce package Canadian-style bacon (pizza-style)**
- 1 **small green sweet pepper, cut crosswise into thin rings**
- 1¹/₂ **cups chopped fresh pineapple**
- 1 **cup finely shredded mozzarella cheese**
- 2 **tablespoons grated Parmesan cheese**

1 Spread pizza sauce over bread shell. Top with Canadian-style bacon, sweet pepper rings, and pineapple. Sprinkle with mozzarella cheese and Parmesan cheese.

2 For a charcoal grill, arrange medium-hot coals around the edge of grill. Test for medium heat above center of grill. Place assembled pizza on grill rack over center of grill. Cover; grill for 15 to 20 minutes or until cheese is melted and bottom of bread shell is crisp. (For a gas grill, preheat grill. Reduce heat to medium. Adjust for indirect cooking. Grill as above.) Use spatulas to remove pizza from grill.

Nutrition Facts per serving: 454 cal., 14 g total fat (4 g sat. fat), 35 mg chol., 1,310 mg sodium, 57 g carbo., 3 g fiber, 26 g pro. Daily Values: 6% vit. A, 47% vit. C, 33% calcium, 16% iron. Exchanges: ¹/₂ Vegetable, ¹/₂ Fruit, 3 Starch, 2 Medium-Fat Meat, ¹/₂ Fat

Grilled Italian Panini

GRILLED ITALIAN PANINI

Prep: 20 minutes Grill: 8 minutes
Makes: 4 servings

1 16-ounce loaf unsliced ciabatta or
    Italian bread
6 ounces thinly sliced provolone cheese
¼ cup mayonnaise or salad dressing
1 tablespoon purchased basil pesto
4 ounces thinly sliced coppacola or
    cooked ham
4 ounces thinly sliced salami
1 recipe Red Onion Relish
1 cup arugula
1 tablespoon olive oil

1 Carefully trim off and discard top crust of the
  bread to make a flat surface. Turn bread over;
trim off and discard bottom crust. Cut remaining
bread horizontally into two ½-inch-thick slices.
Brush one side of each bread slice with oil.

2 Place half of the provolone cheese on the
  unoiled side of one slice of bread. In a small
bowl stir together mayonnaise and pesto; spread
over cheese. Layer with coppacola, salami, Red
Onion Relish, arugula, and remaining cheese. Top
with the other slice of bread, oiled side up.

3 For a charcoal grill, place panini on greased
  grill rack of uncovered grill directly over
medium coals. Put a 13×9×2-inch baking pan on
panini; weigh down with several baking potatoes.
Grill about 5 minutes or until lightly browned.
Use hot pads to remove baking pan. Carefully turn
panini. Replace baking pan on panini; grill
3 minutes more or until cheese is melted. (For gas
grill, preheat. Reduce heat to medium. Place
panini on grill rack. Cover; grill as above.)

Red Onion Relish: Combine 1 medium red
onion, halved and thinly sliced (1 cup);
2 tablespoons olive oil; 1 tablespoon red wine
vinegar; and 1 teaspoon snipped fresh oregano.
Season to taste with salt and black pepper. Cover;
let stand at room temperature for up to 2 hours.

Nutrition Facts per serving: 840 cal., 51 g total fat
(15 g sat. fat), 77 mg chol., 2,118 mg sodium,
62 g carbo., 4 g fiber, 33 g pro. Daily Values:
9% vit. A, 4% vit. C, 42% calcium, 24% iron.
Exchanges: ½ Vegetable, 4 Starch, 1 Lean Meat,
2 High-Fat Meat, 6 Fat

FIRECRACKER FOOT-LONGS

Prep: 10 minutes Marinate: 2 to 24 hours Grill: 3 minutes
Makes: 4 servings

4 foot-long or bun-length frankfurters
1 5-ounce bottle hot pepper sauce
⅓ cup finely chopped red onion
1 teaspoon dried oregano, crushed
4 frankfurter buns, split and toasted

1 Place frankfurters in a self-sealing plastic bag
  set in a shallow dish. For marinade, in a small
bowl combine hot pepper sauce, onion, and
oregano. Pour marinade over frankfurters; seal
bag. Marinate in refrigerator for 2 to 24 hours,
turning bag occasionally. Drain frankfurters,
reserving marinade.

2 For a charcoal grill, grill frankfurters on
  the rack of an uncovered grill directly over
medium coals for 3 to 7 minutes or until heated
through, turning once. (For a gas grill, preheat
grill. Reduce heat to medium. Place frankfurters
on grill rack over heat. Cover; grill as above.)

3 Meanwhile, in a small saucepan bring reserved
  marinade to boiling. Serve frankfurters in
toasted buns; top with marinade.

Nutrition Facts per serving: 477 cal., 34 g total fat
(13 g sat. fat), 57 mg chol., 2,420 mg sodium,
25 g carbo., 4 g fiber, 18 g pro. Daily Values: 4% vit. A,
45% vit. C, 8% calcium, 17% iron. Exchanges: 1½ Starch,
2 High-Fat Meat, 3½ Fat

FOOD FOR THOUGHT CIABATTA

**Based on its shape, ciabatta derives
its name from the Italian word for
"slipper." Ciabatta has a high liquid
content and is subject to a long
rising period, which both contribute
to the bread's light, porous texture.
The crust is crunchy and dusted with
flour, giving it a rustic appearance.**

SAUCY HOT DOGS

Prep: 10 minutes Grill: 3 minutes
Makes: 4 servings

⅓ cup catsup
¼ cup chopped pickled peppers
2 tablespoons pickle relish
2 tablespoons chopped onion
¼ teaspoon poppy seeds
4 jumbo frankfurters
4 frankfurter buns, split and toasted

1 For sauce, in a small bowl combine catsup, pickled peppers, relish, onion, and poppy seeds.

2 For a charcoal grill, grill frankfurters on rack of an uncovered grill directly over medium coals for 3 to 7 minutes or until heated through, turning and brushing once with sauce halfway through grilling. (For a gas grill, preheat grill. Reduce heat to medium. Place frankfurters on grill rack over heat. Cover; grill as above.)

3 Serve frankfurters in toasted buns; top with remaining sauce.

Nutrition Facts per serving: 528 cal., 35 g total fat (13 g sat. fat), 58 mg chol., 2,052 mg sodium, 35 g carbo., 0 g fiber, 17 g pro. Daily Values: 52% vit. A, 68% vit. C, 6% calcium, 19% iron. Exchanges: 2 Starch, ½ Other Carbo., 2 High-Fat Meat, 3 Fat

FOOD FOR THOUGHT HOT DOGS

Hot dogs are a popular choice for backyard barbecues and beyond. Here are a few facts about one of America's most beloved foods:

● On average, Americans eat 70 hot dogs each year.
● Mustard is the most popular condiment; catsup is second.
● Americans typically consume 7 billion hot dogs between Memorial Day and Labor Day.
● July is National Hot Dog Month.
● Annually, Americans eat enough hot dogs in major league ball parks to reach from Dodger Stadium to Yankee Stadium.

BRATS WITH JALAPEÑO-GREEN APPLE KRAUT

Prep: 10 minutes Cook: 20 minutes Grill: 3 minutes
Makes: 6 servings

6 uncooked bratwurst
3 cups apple juice or apple cider
⅓ cup apple jelly
1 8-ounce can sauerkraut, drained
1 tart green apple, cored and cut into thin bite-size pieces
2 to 3 fresh jalapeño chile peppers, seeded and cut in thin strips (see tip, page 36)
6 bratwurst or hot dog buns, split and toasted

1 Use the tines of a fork to pierce the skin of each bratwurst several times. In a Dutch oven combine bratwurst and apple juice. Bring to boiling; reduce heat. Simmer, covered, about 20 minutes or until bratwurst are no longer pink and juices run clear (160°F); drain.

2 Meanwhile, in a saucepan melt apple jelly over low heat. In a bowl combine 2 tablespoons of the melted jelly, sauerkraut, apple, and chile peppers. Set aside remaining melted jelly.

3 Fold a 30×18-inch piece of heavy foil in half to make a 15×18-inch rectangle. Mound sauerkraut mixture in center of foil. Bring up two opposite edges of foil; seal with a double-fold. Fold remaining edges together to completely enclose sauerkraut mixture, leaving space for steam to build.

4 For a charcoal grill, grill bratwurst and foil packet on the rack of an uncovered grill directly over medium coals for 3 to 7 minutes or until bratwurst are browned, turning both once halfway through grilling and brushing bratwurst with the reserved melted jelly during the last 2 minutes of grilling. (For a gas grill, preheat grill. Reduce heat to medium. Place bratwurst and foil packet on grill rack over heat. Grill as above.)

5 Serve bratwurst in toasted buns; top with sauerkraut mixture.

Nutrition Facts per serving: 737 cal., 48 g total fat (21 g sat. fat), 101 mg chol., 2,014 mg sodium, 42 g carbo., 3 g fiber, 34 g pro. Daily Values: 2% vit. A, 17% vit. C, 9% calcium, 23% iron. Exchanges: 2 Starch, 1 Other Carbo., 3½ High-Fat Meat, 3 Fat

Bratwurst with Kickin' Cranberry Catsup

BRATWURST WITH KICKIN' CRANBERRY CATSUP

To keep this recipe quick and easy, rely on your supermarket's deli for the coleslaw.

Prep: 20 minutes **Grill:** 3 minutes
Makes: 6 servings

- **6 cooked, smoked bratwurst**
- **6 hoagie buns, split and toasted**
- **1 recipe Kickin' Cranberry Catsup**
- **1 cup prepared vinaigrette-style coleslaw**

1 For a charcoal grill, grill bratwurst on the rack of an uncovered grill directly over medium coals for 3 to 7 minutes or until bratwurst are browned and heated through, turning once halfway through grilling. (For a gas grill, preheat grill. Reduce heat to medium. Place bratwurst on grill rack over heat. Cover; grill as above.)

2 To serve, top toasted buns with coleslaw, a bratwurst, and Kickin' Cranberry Catsup.

Kickin' Cranberry Catsup: Coarsely chop ¼ cup dried cranberries; place in a small bowl. Add enough boiling water to cover; let stand 5 minutes. Drain cranberries. Stir in ⅓ cup catsup, 2 teaspoons prepared horseradish, and several dashes bottled hot pepper sauce.

Nutrition Facts per serving: 705 cal., 33 g total fat (10 g sat. fat), 52 mg chol., 1,550 mg sodium, 84 g carbo., 5 g fiber, 21 g pro. Daily Values: 5% vit. A, 21% vit. C, 11% calcium, 28% iron. Exchanges: 4 Starch, 1½ Other Carbo., 1½ High-Fat Meat, 3½ Fat

BACKYARD BRATS

The unique blend of sauerkraut sets these sausage sandwiches apart from the traditional.

Prep: 20 minutes Grill: 20 minutes
Makes: 6 servings

- ½ **cup chopped green sweet pepper**
- ⅓ **cup chopped onion (1 small)**
- 1 **tablespoon butter or margarine**
- 2 **tablespoons brown sugar**
- 1 **teaspoon yellow mustard**
- ½ **teaspoon caraway seeds**
- 1 **cup drained sauerkraut**
- 6 **uncooked bratwurst**
- 6 **hoagie buns, split and toasted**

1 In a small skillet cook sweet pepper and onion in hot butter about 5 minutes or until tender. Stir in brown sugar, mustard, and caraway seeds. Add the sauerkraut; toss to combine.

2 Tear off a 36×18-inch piece of heavy foil; fold in half to make an 18-inch square. Mound the sauerkraut mixture in center of foil. Bring up two opposite edges of foil and seal with a double fold. Fold remaining edges together to completely enclose the sauerkraut mixture, leaving space for steam to build. Use the tines of a fork to pierce the skin of each bratwurst several times.

3 For a charcoal grill, arrange medium-hot coals around a drip pan. Test for medium heat above pan. Place bratwurst and foil packet on grill rack over drip pan. Cover; grill for 20 to 30 minutes or until bratwurst are no longer pink and juices run clear (160°F), turning once halfway through grilling. (For a gas grill, preheat grill. Reduce heat to medium. Adjust for indirect cooking. Cover; grill as above.)

4 Serve bratwurst in toasted buns; top with sauerkraut mixture.

Nutrition Facts per serving: 763 cal., 39 g total fat (13 g sat. fat), 62 mg chol., 1,648 mg sodium, 80 g carbo., 5 g fiber, 23 g pro. Daily Values: 28% vit. C, 16% calcium, 32% iron. Exchanges: 4 Starch, 1½ Other Carbo., 1½ High-Fat Meat, 5 Fat

PORK SAUSAGES WITH GRAPE RELISH

Prep: 20 minutes Grill: 20 minutes
Makes: 6 servings

- 1¾ **cups chopped fennel**
- 1½ **cups red and/or green seedless grapes, halved**
- 1 **to 2 tablespoons white balsamic vinegar**
- 1 **tablespoon cooking oil**
- ⅛ **teaspoon salt**
- ⅛ **teaspoon crushed red pepper**
- 6 **4- to 6-ounce uncooked spicy pork sausage links**
- ¼ **cup snipped fresh parsley**

1 For grape relish, in a medium bowl combine fennel, grapes, vinegar, oil, salt, and red pepper. Set relish aside.

2 Fold a 36×18-inch piece of heavy foil in half to make an 18-inch square. Mound the grape relish in center of foil. Bring up two opposite edges of foil; seal with a double-fold. Fold remaining edges together to completely enclose the grape relish, leaving space for steam to build.

3 For a charcoal grill, arrange medium-hot coals around a drip pan. Test for medium heat above pan. Place sausage links and foil packet on grill rack over drip pan. Cover; grill for 20 to 30 minutes or until sausage juices run clear (160°F), turning once halfway through grilling. (For a gas grill, preheat. Reduce heat to medium. Adjust for indirect cooking. Cover; grill as above.)

4 To serve, arrange sausage links on a serving platter; spoon grape relish over sausage; sprinkle with parsley.

Nutrition Facts per serving: 383 cal., 28 g total fat (11 g sat. fat), 77 mg chol., 680 mg sodium, 9 g carbo., 4 g fiber, 17 g pro. Daily Values: 3% vit. A, 18% vit. C, 3% calcium, 6% iron. Exchanges: ½ Other Carbo., 2½ High-Fat Meat, 2 Fat

Grilled Roasted Garlic and Sausage Pizzas

GRILLED ROASTED GARLIC AND SAUSAGE PIZZAS

Have all your pizza toppers ready to go so you can quickly layer them on the partially cooked crusts.

Prep: 25 minutes Grill: 38 minutes
Makes: 4 to 6 servings

- 2 **heads garlic**
  Olive oil
- 1 **package active dry yeast**
- 1 **cup warm water (105°F to 115°F)**
- 2 **tablespoons cornmeal**
- 1 **teaspoon olive oil**
- 1/2 **teaspoon salt**
  Dash sugar
- 2 1/2 to 2 3/4 **cups all-purpose flour**
  Cornmeal
- 1 **pound bulk Italian sausage**
- 2 **cups sliced fresh mushrooms**
- 1 **8-ounce can pizza sauce**
- 1 **medium green sweet pepper, cut into thin bite-size strips**
- 2 **roma tomatoes, sliced and quartered**
- 2 **cups shredded provolone cheese (8 ounces)**

1 To roast garlic, use a sharp knife to cut off the top 1/2-inch from each garlic head to expose individual cloves. Leaving garlic heads whole, remove loose papery outer layers. Place garlic heads, cut sides up, in center of a 10-inch square of heavy foil. Brush sides and tops of garlic heads with olive oil. Bring up two opposite edges of foil; seal with a double-fold. Fold remaining edges together to completely enclose the garlic, leaving space for steam to build.

2 For a charcoal grill, grill foil packet on rack of an uncovered grill directly over medium coals about 35 minutes or until garlic feels soft when packet is squeezed, turning packet occasionally. (For a gas grill, preheat grill. Reduce heat to medium. Place foil packet on grill rack over heat. Cover; grill as above.) Remove packet from grill; let cool. Squeeze roasted garlic cloves from the skins, leaving cloves intact. Discard skins.

3 Meanwhile, for crust, in a large bowl dissolve yeast in warm water. Let stand 5 minutes. Stir in the 2 tablespoons cornmeal, the 1 teaspoon olive oil, salt, and sugar. Using a wooden spoon, stir in as much of the flour as you can.

4 Turn out dough onto a lightly floured surface. Knead in enough of the remaining flour to make a moderately stiff dough that is smooth and elastic (about 6 minutes total). Shape dough into two balls. Cover; let rest 10 minutes. Line two baking sheets with waxed paper; sprinkle each with additional cornmeal. Roll each dough portion into a 10-inch circle. Transfer each circle to a prepared baking sheet. Cover dough; set aside.

5 In a large skillet cook sausage and mushrooms until no pink remains; drain well and set aside.

6 For a charcoal grill, use the waxed paper to carefully invert each dough circle onto the rack of an uncovered grill directly over medium coals; remove waxed paper. Grill for 1 to 2 minutes or until dough is puffed in some places, starting to become firm, and bottom is lightly browned. Remove crusts from grill; turn crusts browned sides up. Spread browned side of each crust with half of the sauce; top with half of the sausage mixture, half of the roasted garlic cloves, half of the sweet pepper strips, half of the tomato slices, and half of the cheese,. Return crusts to grill. Cover; grill about 2 minutes more or until cheese is melted and bottom crust is browned and crisp. (For a gas grill, preheat grill. Reduce heat to medium. Place dough circles on grill rack over heat. Cover; grill as above.)

Nutrition Facts per serving: 946 cal., 46 g total fat (21 g sat. fat), 115 mg chol., 1,654 mg sodium, 81 g carbo., 5 g fiber, 44 g pro. Daily Values: 19% vit. A, 59% vit. C, 49% calcium, 35% iron. Exchanges: 1 Vegetable, 4 Starch, 1 Other Carbo., 4 High-Fat Meat, 2 1/2 Fat

KIELBASA WITH MAPLE-MUSTARD GLAZE

Prep: 15 minutes Grill: 3 minutes Makes: 6 servings

6 **cooked kielbasa or cooked, smoked**
    Polish sausage
1 **recipe Maple-Mustard Glaze**
6 **frankfurter buns, split and toasted**

1 For a charcoal grill, grill kielbasa on the rack of an uncovered grill directly over medium coals for 3 to 7 minutes or until kielbasa is browned and heated through, turning and brushing once with Maple-Mustard Glaze halfway through grilling. (For a gas grill, preheat grill. Reduce heat to medium. Place kielbasa on grill rack over heat. Cover; grill as above.) Serve kielbasa in toasted buns. If desired, pass any remaining glaze.

Maple-Mustard Glaze: In a small saucepan combine $1/3$ cup pure maple syrup, $1/4$ cup dry white wine, 3 tablespoons Dijon-style mustard, and 1 tablespoon butter or margarine. Bring to boiling; reduce heat. Boil gently, uncovered, about 3 minutes or until slightly thickened.

Nutrition Facts per serving: 455 cal., 27 g total fat (12 g sat. fat), 39 mg chol., 1,049 mg sodium, 36 g carbo., 1 g fiber, 13 g pro. Daily Values: 2% vit. A, 3% vit. C, 7% calcium, 12% iron. Exchanges: 2 Starch, $1/2$ Other Carbo., 1 High-Fat Meat, 4 Fat

ANDOUILLE SAUSAGE KABOBS WITH CREOLE SAUCE

Prep: 20 minutes Grill: 20 minutes Makes: 4 servings

1 **pound uncooked andouille sausage**
    or uncooked Italian sausage links,
    cut into 24 pieces
2 **medium green and/or yellow sweet**
    peppers, cut into 48 pieces
2 **cups hot cooked rice**
1 **recipe Creole Sauce**

1 On 4 long metal skewers, alternately thread sausage pieces and sweet pepper pieces, leaving $1/4$-inch space between pieces.

2 For a charcoal grill, arrange medium-hot coals around a drip pan. Test for medium heat above pan. Place kabobs on grill rack over drip pan. Cover; grill for 20 to 30 minutes or until sausage is

no longer pink and juices run clear (160°F), turning occasionally. (For a gas grill, preheat grill. Reduce heat to medium. Adjust for indirect cooking. Grill as above.) Serve over rice with Creole Sauce.

Creole Sauce: In a medium saucepan cook $1/2$ cup chopped onion; $1/2$ cup chopped celery; and 2 cloves garlic, minced, in 1 tablespoon cooking oil until tender. Stir in one $14 1/2$-ounce can undrained diced tomatoes; $1/2$ cup bottled chili sauce; $1/4$ teaspoon dried thyme, crushed; and $1/8$ teaspoon cayenne pepper. Bring to boiling; reduce heat. Simmer, uncovered, about 10 minutes or until desired consistency, stirring occasionally. Just before serving, stir in 2 tablespoons snipped fresh parsley.

Nutrition Facts per serving: 539 cal., 29 g total fat (11 g sat. fat), 77 mg chol., 1,208 mg sodium, 40 g carbo., 4 g fiber, 20 g pro. Daily Values: 11% vit. A, 77% vit. C, 9% calcium, 17% iron. Exchanges: $1 1/2$ Vegetable, $1 1/2$ Starch, $1/2$ Other Carbo., 2 High-Fat Meat, 4 Fat

FOOD FOR THOUGHT SAUSAGE

Sausages today are made from all kinds of meat, including pork, beef, veal, and game. Each sausage is a unique blend of meat and/or spices:

● Fresh: Sausages made from fresh ingredients that haven't been cooked or cured must be cooked. These can include bratwurst (a German sausage), kielbasa (Polish sausage), Italian sausage, and chorizo (Mexican sausage).

● Smoked and Cooked: Cured and/or smoked, these fully cooked sausages are ready to eat. Frankfurters and andouille, a spicy sausage used in Cajun cooking, are examples. Bratwurst and kielbasa are also available fully cooked and/or smoked.

● Dried or Hard: These sausages are made with cured meats that are air-dried in a controlled environment. Distinctive in flavor and ready to eat, these sausages may or may not be smoked. Salami and pepperoni fall into this category.

Chicken & Turkey

DIRECT GRILLING POULTRY

If desired, remove skin from poultry. For a charcoal grill, place poultry on grill rack, bone side up, directly over medium coals. Grill, uncovered, for the time given below or until the proper temperature is reached and meat is no longer pink, turning once halfway through grilling. For a gas grill, preheat grill. Reduce heat to medium. Place poultry on grill rack, bone side down, over heat. Cover and grill.

Test for doneness using a meat thermometer (use an instant-read thermometer to test smaller portions). Thermometer should register 180°F, except in breast meat where thermometer should register 170°F. Poultry should be tender and no longer pink. If desired, during last 5 to 10 minutes of grilling, brush often with a sauce.

TYPE OF BIRD	WEIGHT	GRILLING TEMPERATURE	APPROXIMATE DIRECT-GRILLING TIME	DONENESS
CHICKEN				
Chicken, broiler-fryer, half or quarters	1½- to 1¾-pound half or 12- to 14-ounce quarters	Medium	40 to 50 minutes	180°F
Chicken breast half, skinned and boned	4 to 5 ounces	Medium	12 to 15 minutes	170°F
Chicken thigh, skinned and boned	4 to 5 ounces	Medium	12 to 15 minutes	180°F
Meaty chicken pieces (breast halves, thighs, and drumsticks)	2½ to 3 pounds total	Medium	35 to 45 minutes	180°F
TURKEY				
Turkey tenderloin	8 to 10 ounces (¾ to 1 inch thick)	Medium	16 to 20 minutes	170°F

All cooking times are based on poultry removed directly from refrigerator.

INDIRECT GRILLING POULTRY

If desired, remove skin from poultry. Rinse whole birds; pat dry. For a charcoal grill, arrange medium-hot coals around a drip pan. Test for medium heat above the pan. Place unstuffed poultry, breast side up, on grill rack over drip pan. Cover and grill for the time given below or until the proper temperature is reached and meat is no longer pink, adding more charcoal to maintain heat as necessary. For large poultry cuts and whole birds, we suggest placing the poultry on a rack in a roasting pan and omitting the drip pan. For a gas grill, preheat grill. Reduce heat to medium. Adjust heat for indirect cooking.

Test for doneness using a meat thermometer (use an instant-read thermometer to test smaller portions). For whole birds, insert thermometer into the center of the inside thigh muscle, not touching bone. Thermometer should register 180°F, except in breast meat where thermometer should register 170°F. Poultry should be tender and no longer pink. (Note: Birds vary in size and shape. Use these times as general guides.)

TYPE OF BIRD	WEIGHT	GRILLING TEMPERATURE	APPROXIMATE INDIRECT-GRILLING TIME	DONENESS
CHICKEN				
Chicken, whole	2½ to 3 pounds 3½ to 4 pounds 4½ to 5 pounds	Medium Medium Medium	1 to 1¼ hours 1¼ to 1¾ hours 1¾ to 2 hours	180°F 180°F 180°F
Chicken breast half, skinned and boned	4 to 5 ounces	Medium	15 to 18 minutes	170°F
Chicken, broiler-fryer, half	1½ to 1¾ pounds	Medium	1 to 1¼ hours	180°F
Chicken, broiler-fryer, quarters	12 to 14 ounces each	Medium	50 to 60 minutes	180°F
Chicken thigh, skinned and boned	4 to 5 ounces	Medium	15 to 18 minutes	180°F
Meaty chicken pieces (breast halves, thighs, and drumsticks)	2½ to 3 pounds total	Medium	50 to 60 minutes	180°F
Cornish game hen, whole	1¼ to 1½ pounds	Medium	50 to 60 minutes	180°F
TURKEY				
Turkey, whole	6 to 8 pounds 8 to 12 pounds 12 to 16 pounds	Medium Medium Medium	1¾ to 2¼ hours 2½ to 3½ hours 3 to 4 hours	180°F 180°F 180°F
Turkey breast, half	2 to 2½ pounds	Medium	1¼ to 2 hours	170°F
Turkey breast, whole	4 to 6 pounds 6 to 8 pounds	Medium Medium	1¾ to 2¼ hours 2½ to 3½ hours	170°F 170°F
Turkey drumstick	½ to 1 pound	Medium	¾ to 1¼ hours	180°F
Turkey tenderloin	8 to 10 ounces (¾ to 1 inch thick)	Medium	25 to 30 minutes	170°F
Turkey thigh	1 to 1½ pounds	Medium	50 to 60 minutes	180°F

All cooking times are based on poultry removed directly from refrigerator.

TANDOORI CHICKEN BURGERS

Most prepackaged ground chicken consists of both light and dark meat and sometimes some of the skin. If you prefer all lean chicken breast, ask the butcher to coarsely grind it for you.

Prep: 15 minutes Grill: 14 minutes
Makes: 4 servings

- ¼ **cup fine dry bread crumbs**
- 2 **teaspoons garam masala or curry powder**
- ¼ **teaspoon salt**
- ¼ **teaspoon cayenne pepper**
- 1 **pound uncooked ground chicken**
- 2 **tablespoons plain yogurt**
- 4 **seeded hamburger buns or kaiser rolls, split and toasted**
- 1 **recipe Minty Cucumbers**
  Kale or lettuce

1 In a large bowl combine bread crumbs, garam masala, salt, and cayenne pepper. Add ground chicken and yogurt; mix well. Shape chicken mixture into four ¾-inch-thick patties.

2 For a charcoal grill, grill patties on the rack of an uncovered grill directly over medium coals for 14 to 18 minutes or until no longer pink (170°F), turning once halfway through grilling. (For a gas grill, preheat grill. Reduce heat to medium. Place patties on grill rack over heat. Cover; grill as above.)

3 Serve burgers on toasted buns with Minty Cucumbers and kale.

Minty Cucumbers: Combine 1 cup thinly sliced cucumber, ½ cup thinly sliced red onion, ¼ cup snipped fresh mint, 1 tablespoon bottled balsamic vinaigrette, and ¼ teaspoon salt.

Nutrition Facts per serving: 383 cal., 13 g total fat (1 g sat. fat), 0 mg chol., 841 mg sodium, 37 g carbo., 2 g fiber, 27 g pro. Daily Values: 2% vit. A, 10% vit. C, 12% calcium, 25% iron. Exchanges: ½ Vegetable, 2 Starch, 3 Lean Meat, 1 Fat

BISTRO BURGERS

Enjoy elegant restaurant fare at home. These chicken-and-pork patties go gourmet when teamed with nutty Brie cheese and slightly bitter radicchio.

Prep: 20 minutes Chill: 30 minutes Grill: 17 minutes
Makes: 6 servings

- 2 **tablespoons dry white wine or water**
- ¼ **teaspoon salt**
- ¼ **teaspoon black pepper**
- 12 **ounces uncooked ground chicken**
- 12 **ounces ground pork**
- 2 **tablespoons creamy Dijon-style mustard blend**
- 1 **tablespoon snipped fresh chives**
- 1 to 2 **cloves garlic, minced**
- 1 **4½-ounce round Brie cheese, rind removed and cut into 12 slices**
- 6 **slices French bread, toasted, or 3 bagels, halved and toasted**
- 6 **tomato slices**
  Radicchio or leaf lettuce

1 In a large bowl combine wine, salt, and pepper. Add ground chicken and pork; mix well. Shape meat mixture into six ¾-inch-thick patties. Cover and chill for 30 minutes.

2 Meanwhile, for sauce, stir together mustard blend, chives, and garlic; set aside.

3 For a charcoal grill, grill patties on the rack of an uncovered grill directly over medium coals for 14 to 18 minutes or until no longer pink (170°F), turning once halfway through grilling. Top each burger with 2 slices of the cheese. Grill, uncovered, about 3 minutes more or until cheese begins to melt. (For a gas grill, preheat grill. Reduce heat to medium. Place patties on grill rack over heat. Cover; grill as above.)

4 To serve, spread sauce on one side of each toasted bread slice. Add tomato slices, radicchio, and burgers.

Nutrition Facts per serving: 297 cal., 15 g total fat (7 g sat. fat), 69 mg chol., 551 mg sodium, 16 g carbo., 1 g fiber, 22 g pro. Daily Values: 7% vit. A, 12% vit. C, 6% calcium, 13% iron. Exchanges: 1 Starch, 3 Lean Meat, 1 Fat

BASIL-CHICKEN BURGERS

Prep: 15 minutes Grill: 10 minutes
Makes: 4 servings

1 pound uncooked ground chicken
¼ cup snipped fresh basil
¼ cup fine dry bread crumbs
4 teaspoons Worcestershire sauce
⅛ teaspoon salt
⅛ teaspoon black pepper
8 slices French bread, toasted, or
4 kaiser rolls or hamburger buns,
split and toasted
Desired toppers, such as lettuce
leaves, sliced tomato, or sliced
onion (optional)

1 In a large bowl combine ground chicken, basil, bread crumbs, Worcestershire sauce, salt, and pepper. Shape chicken mixture into four ½-inch-thick patties. (The mixture may be sticky. If necessary, wet hands to shape patties.)

2 For a charcoal grill, grill patties on the rack of an uncovered grill directly over medium coals for 10 to 13 minutes or until no longer pink (170°F), turning once halfway through grilling. (For a gas grill, preheat grill. Reduce heat to medium. Place patties on grill rack over heat. Cover; grill as above.)

3 Serve the burgers on toasted bread with desired toppers.

Nutrition Facts per serving: 389 cal., 17 g total fat (0 g sat. fat), 0 mg chol., 692 mg sodium, 32 g carbo., 2 g fiber, 25 g pro. Daily Values: 3% vit. A, 1% vit. C, 8% calcium, 18% iron. Exchanges: 2 Starch, 3 Medium-Fat Meat

Chicken Wraps with Spanish Rice

CHICKEN WRAPS WITH SPANISH RICE

Prep: 25 minutes Marinate: 30 minutes Grill: 12 minutes
Makes: 4 servings

8 ounces skinless, boneless chicken
breast halves
2 tablespoons olive oil
2 tablespoons lime juice
½ teaspoon ground cumin
½ teaspoon dried oregano, crushed
1 recipe Spanish Rice
4 7- to 8-inch spinach- or tomato
flavored or whole-wheat flour
tortillas
1 avocado, seeded, peeled, and sliced
2 tablespoons snipped fresh cilantro

1 Place chicken in a self-sealing plastic bag set in a shallow dish. For marinade, in a small bowl combine oil, lime juice, cumin, oregano, and ¼ teaspoon salt. Pour over chicken; seal bag. Marinate in the refrigerator for 30 minutes, turning bag occasionally. Drain chicken, discarding marinade. Meanwhile, prepare Spanish Rice.

2 For a charcoal grill, grill chicken on the rack of an uncovered grill directly over medium coals for 12 to 15 minutes or until chicken is no longer pink (170°), turning once halfway through grilling. Place tortillas on the grill rack directly over medium coals the last 1 to 2 minutes of grilling or until heated through, turning once. (For a gas grill, preheat grill. Reduce heat to medium. Place chicken and tortillas on grill rack over heat. Cover; grill as above.)

3 Spread some of the hot Spanish Rice on each tortilla. Top with avocado slices and cilantro. Chop chicken and arrange on top of vegetables. Fold in sides of tortillas and roll up. If desired, serve with salsa, sour cream, and lime wedges.

Spanish Rice: In a saucepan combine 1 cup chicken broth, ¾ cup mild chunky salsa, and ⅔ cup long grain rice. Bring to boiling; reduce heat. Simmer, covered, about 20 minutes or until the rice is tender and most of liquid is absorbed.

Nutrition Facts per serving: 388 cal., 15 g total fat (3 g sat. fat), 33 mg chol., 658 mg sodium, 45 g carbo., 3 g fiber, 19 g pro. Daily Values: 11% vit. A, 16% vit. C, 7% calcium, 19% iron. Exchanges: 3 Starch, 1½ Very Lean Meat, 2½ Fat

MARGARITA KABOBS

Tequila helps blend the flavors of the brush-on, but you can omit it if you wish.

Prep: 30 minutes Grill: 10 minutes
Makes: 6 servings

1¼ **pounds skinless, boneless chicken breast halves or thighs**
 1 **large red or green sweet pepper, cut into bite-size pieces**
 1 **medium red onion, cut into wedges**
 1 **cup orange marmalade**
⅓ **cup lime juice**
¼ **cup tequila (optional)**
 2 **tablespoons snipped fresh cilantro**
 2 **tablespoons cooking oil**
 1 **teaspoon bottled minced garlic (2 cloves)**
 6 **½-inch slices peeled fresh pineapple**

1 Cut chicken into 1-inch pieces. On long metal skewers, alternately thread chicken, sweet pepper, and onion, leaving a ¼-inch space between pieces.

2 For sauce, in a small saucepan stir together marmalade, lime juice, tequila (if desired), cilantro, oil, and garlic. Cook and stir just until marmalade melts.

3 For a charcoal grill, grill kabobs on the rack of an uncovered grill directly over medium coals for 10 to 12 minutes or until chicken is no longer pink (170°F), turning once halfway through grilling. After 5 minutes of grilling, add pineapple to grill rack. Turn pineapple once and brush pineapple and chicken once with sauce during the last 3 minutes of grilling. (For a gas grill, preheat grill. Reduce heat to medium. Place kabobs and pineapple on grill rack over heat. Cover; grill as above.)

4 To serve, reheat sauce until bubbly; pass with kabobs and pineapple.

Nutrition Facts per serving: 347 cal., 6 g total fat (1 g sat. fat), 55 mg chol., 88 mg sodium, 52 g carbo., 2 g fiber, 23 g pro. Daily Values: 22% vit. A, 129% vit. C, 5% calcium, 6% iron. Exchanges: 3½ Other Carbo., 3 Very Lean Meat, 1 Fat

SOUTHWESTERN FAJITAS

To warm the tortillas, wrap them in foil and grill alongside the chicken for 10 minutes, turning the packet often.

Prep: 30 minutes Marinate: 1 hour Grill: 12 minutes
Makes: 6 servings

 6 **skinless, boneless chicken breast halves**
½ **cup lime juice**
 2 **teaspoons bottled minced garlic**
 1 **teaspoon crushed red pepper**
¾ **teaspoon salt**
12 **6- to 8-inch flour tortillas, warmed**
 1 **recipe Salsa Cruda**
 1 **recipe Guacamole**

1 Place chicken in a self-sealing plastic bag set in a shallow dish. For marinade, in a small bowl combine lime juice, garlic, and crushed red pepper. Pour over chicken; seal bag. Marinate in the refrigerator for 1 hour, turning the bag occasionally. Drain chicken, discarding marinade. Sprinkle chicken with salt.

2 For a charcoal grill, grill chicken on the rack of an uncovered grill directly over medium coals for 12 to 15 minutes or until chicken is no longer pink (170°F), turning once halfway through grilling. (For a gas grill, preheat grill. Reduce heat to medium. Place chicken on grill rack over heat. Cover; grill as above.) Slice chicken. Serve with warmed tortillas, Salsa Cruda, and Guacamole.

Salsa Cruda: In a medium bowl combine 6 roma tomatoes, diced (3 cups); ½ cup finely chopped red onion; ¼ cup snipped fresh cilantro; 2 medium fresh jalapeño chile peppers, finely chopped (see tip, page 36); and 1 teaspoon salt.

Guacamole: In a medium bowl use a potato masher or fork to mash 2 ripe avocados, peeled and seeded. Stir in ¼ cup finely chopped red onion, 2 tablespoons lime juice, and ¼ teaspoon bottled hot pepper sauce.

Nutrition Facts per serving: 475 cal., 16 g total fat (3 g sat. fat), 88 mg chol., 1,034 mg sodium, 41 g carbo., 7 g fiber, 41 g pro. Daily Values: 22% vit. A, 40% vit. C, 11% calcium, 21% iron. Exchanges: 2 Starch, 1 Vegetable, 4½ Very Lean Meat, 2 Fat

GRILLED CHICKEN AND VEGETABLE SOUP

Classic chicken soup gets a makeover with grilled chicken and vegetables.

Prep: 20 minutes Grill: 32 minutes
Makes: 8 servings

2 **medium carrots, sliced**
1 **large red, green, or yellow sweet**
   pepper, cut into bite-size pieces
1 **medium zucchini, cut into bite-size**
   pieces
1/3 **cup coarsely chopped onion (1 small)**
2 **tablespoons olive oil**
1/2 **teaspoon black pepper**
1/4 **teaspoon salt**
2 **cloves garlic, minced**
8 **ounces skinless, boneless chicken**
   breast halves or thighs
2 **14-ounce cans reduced-sodium**
   chicken broth
2 **cups water**
1 **cup dried radiatore, cavatelli, or**
   farfalle (bow ties) pasta
2 **tablespoons snipped fresh basil,**
   cilantro, or parsley

1 In a small saucepan cook carrots in a small amount of boiling water for 2 minutes; drain. In a large bowl combine cooked carrots, sweet pepper, zucchini, and onion. In a small bowl combine oil, black pepper, salt, and garlic. Drizzle oil mixture over the vegetables; toss lightly to coat.

2 For a charcoal grill, preheat a lightly greased grill wok over medium coals for 15 seconds. Spoon vegetable mixture into wok or onto a large piece of heavy foil. Place wok or foil on the rack of an uncovered grill directly over medium coals. Grill about 20 minutes or until lightly charred, stirring often. Remove wok or foil from grill; set aside. Grill chicken on the grill rack directly over medium coals for 12 to 15 minutes or until chicken is no longer pink (170°F for breasts; 180°F for thighs), turning once halfway through grilling. (For a gas grill, preheat grill. Reduce heat to medium. Place wok and chicken on grill rack over heat. Cover and grill as above.) Cool chicken slightly; cut into bite-size pieces.

3 Meanwhile, in a 4-quart Dutch oven combine broth and the water; bring to boiling. Add pasta; cook according to package directions. Do not drain. Stir in grilled vegetables, grilled chicken, and basil. Heat through.

Nutrition Facts per serving: 268 cal., 10 g total fat (2 g sat. fat), 58 mg chol., 734 mg sodium, 24 g carbo., 3 g fiber, 19 g pro. Daily Values: 198% vit. A, 114% vit. C, 5% calcium, 11% iron. Exchanges: 1/2 Vegetable, 1 1/2 Starch, 2 Very Lean Meat, 1 1/2 Fat

ZESTY CURRY-LIME CHICKEN KABOBS

To easily snip cilantro or other fresh herbs, place the herb in a small bowl and use kitchen shears to snip it.

Prep: 20 minutes Marinate: 4 to 24 hours Grill: 15 minutes
Makes: 4 servings

1 **pound skinless, boneless chicken**
   breast halves, cut into 1 1/2-inch
   pieces
1/2 **cup plain yogurt**
1/4 **cup snipped fresh cilantro**
1 **teaspoon finely shredded lime peel**
2 **tablespoons lime juice**
2 **tablespoons olive oil or cooking oil**
1 **tablespoon honey**
1 **tablespoon Dijon-style mustard**
2 **cloves garlic, minced**
1/2 **teaspoon curry powder**
1/4 **teaspoon salt**
1/4 **teaspoon black pepper**
2 **medium green and/or red sweet**
   peppers, cut into 1-inch pieces
1 **medium zucchini, cut into**
   1/2-inch slices
8 **cherry tomatoes**

1 Place chicken in a self-sealing plastic bag set in a shallow dish. For marinade, in a small bowl stir together yogurt, cilantro, lime peel, lime juice, oil, honey, mustard, garlic, curry powder, salt, and black pepper. Pour over chicken; seal bag. Marinate in the refrigerator for 4 to 24 hours, turning bag occasionally. Drain chicken, reserving the marinade.

2 On 8 long metal skewers, alternately thread chicken, sweet peppers, and zucchini, leaving a ¼-inch space between pieces. Brush vegetables with the reserved marinade. Discard any remaining marinade.

3 For a charcoal grill, arrange medium-hot coals around a drip pan. Test for medium heat above the pan. Place kabobs on grill rack over drip pan. Cover; grill for 15 to 18 minutes or until chicken is no longer pink (170°F). Place a cherry tomato on the end of each skewer for the last 1 minute of grilling. (For a gas grill, preheat grill. Reduce heat to medium. Adjust for indirect cooking. Grill as above.)

Nutrition Facts per serving: 205 cal., 6 g total fat (1 g sat. fat), 67 mg chol., 200 mg sodium, 10 g carbo., 2 g fiber, 29 g pro. Daily Values: 13% vit. A, 91% vit. C, 6% calcium, 8% iron. Exchanges: 1 Vegetable, ½ Other Carbo., 4 Very Lean Meat, ½ Fat

---

GREEK-STYLE CHICKEN SKEWERS WITH VEGETABLES

Haloumi is a white sheep's milk cheese from Cyprus usually found packed in brine.

Prep: 35 minutes Marinate: 2 to 4 hours Grill: 10 minutes
Makes: 4 servings

12 ounces skinless, boneless chicken breast halves, cut into 1-inch pieces
½ of a small eggplant, peeled and cut into 1-inch pieces (2 cups)
1 large zucchini, cut into 1-inch pieces (1½ cups)
¼ cup olive oil
2 teaspoons finely shredded lemon peel
¼ cup lemon juice
2 tablespoons snipped fresh oregano
1 tablespoon honey
3 cloves garlic, minced
Nonstick cooking spray
1 cup cherry tomatoes
8 ounces haloumi cheese, cut into four ¼-inch slices (optional)
1 recipe Cool Yogurt Dip

1 Place chicken, eggplant, and zucchini in a self-sealing plastic bag set in a large bowl. For marinade, combine oil, lemon peel, lemon juice, oregano, honey, garlic, ½ teaspoon salt, and ¼ teaspoon black pepper. If using cheese, remove 1 tablespoon marinade to a small bowl; cover and set aside. Pour remaining marinade over chicken and vegetables; seal bag. Marinate in refrigerator for 2 to 4 hours, turning bag occasionally. Drain chicken and vegetables, discarding marinade.

2 On four 8- to 10-inch or two 12-inch metal skewers, thread chicken, leaving a ¼-inch space between pieces. Lightly coat an unheated grill wok with cooking spray.

3 For a charcoal grill, preheat the grill wok on the rack of an uncovered grill directly over medium coals for 15 seconds. Add eggplant, zucchini, and tomatoes to heated grill wok. Place chicken skewers on the rack next to the grill wok directly over medium coals. Grill vegetables and chicken for 10 to 14 minutes or until vegetables are tender and chicken is no longer pink (170°F), turning chicken and stirring vegetables occasionally. If using cheese, brush both sides of cheese slices with the reserved marinade. Place cheese slices on grill rack the last 2 minutes of grilling; turn once. (For a gas grill, preheat grill, reduce heat to medium. Place vegetables, chicken, and, if desired, cheese on grill rack over heat. Cover; grill as above.) Serve with Cool Yogurt Dip.

Cool Yogurt Dip: Stir together one 8-ounce container plain yogurt; ⅔ cup finely chopped, seeded cucumber; 2 tablespoons snipped fresh mint; 1 clove garlic, minced; and ⅛ teaspoon salt.

Nutrition Facts per serving: 233 cal., 9 g total fat (2 g sat. fat), 53 mg chol., 313 mg sodium, 14 g carbo., 3 g fiber, 24 g pro. Daily Values: 11% vit. A, 33% vit. C, 14% calcium, 9% iron. Exchanges: 1½ Vegetable, ½ Other Carbo., 3 Very Lean Meat, 1 Fat

CHICKEN AND SAUSAGE KABOBS

Prep: 25 minutes Marinate: 2 to 8 hours
Grill: 12 minutes Makes: 6 servings

**4 medium skinless, boneless chicken
breast halves**
2 tablespoons olive oil
**2 tablespoons finely chopped green
onion (1)**
1 tablespoon lime juice
**1 tablespoon snipped fresh flat-leaf
parsley**
1 tablespoon snipped fresh oregano
1 clove garlic, minced
**8 ounces apple-flavored smoked
chicken sausage or smoked
sausage, halved lengthwise and
cut into 3/4-inch pieces**
1 recipe Herbed Dipping Sauce

1 Cut chicken into long strips about 1/2 inch thick. Place chicken in a self-sealing plastic bag set in a shallow dish. For marinade, in a small bowl combine oil, green onion, lime juice, parsley, oregano, and garlic. Pour marinade over chicken; seal bag. Marinate in the refrigerator for 2 to 8 hours, turning bag occasionally. Drain chicken, discarding marinade.

2 On 6 long skewers, thread chicken and sausage, leaving a 1/4-inch space between pieces.

3 For a charcoal grill, grill kabobs on the rack of an uncovered grill directly over medium coals for 12 to 14 minutes or until chicken is no longer pink (170°F), turning to brown evenly. (For a gas grill, preheat grill. Reduce heat to medium. Place kabobs on grill rack over heat. Cover; grill as above.) Serve with Herbed Dipping Sauce.

Herbed Dipping Sauce: In a small bowl combine 1/4 cup dairy sour cream; 1/4 cup mayonnaise; 2 tablespoons finely chopped green onion or chives; 1 tablespoon lime juice; 1 clove garlic, minced; 1 tablespoon snipped fresh flat-leaf parsley; and 1 tablespoon snipped fresh oregano.

Nutrition Facts per serving: 262 cal., 18 g total fat (4 g sat. fat), 61 mg chol., 347 mg sodium, 1 g carbo., 0 g fiber, 23 g pro. Daily Values: 3% vit. A, 8% vit. C, 3% calcium, 5% iron. Exchanges: 3½ Lean Meat, 1½ Fat

CACCIATORE-STYLE CHICKEN KABOBS

Prep: 30 minutes Marinate: 2 to 8 hours Grill: 12 minutes
Makes: 4 servings

**1 pound skinless, boneless chicken
breast halves**
1/2 cup bottled Italian salad dressing
**1 medium red sweet pepper, cut into
1-inch pieces**
**1 10-ounce package frozen artichoke
hearts, cooked according to
package directions**
8 medium mushrooms
1 16-ounce jar pasta sauce
8 ounces dried linguine
**Shredded fresh Parmesan cheese
(optional)**

1 Cut chicken into 1-inch pieces. Place chicken in a self-sealing plastic bag set in a shallow dish. Pour Italian dressing over chicken; seal bag. Marinate in the refrigerator for 2 to 8 hours; turn bag occasionally. Drain chicken; reserve marinade.

2 On 4 medium skewers, alternately thread chicken, sweet pepper, and half of the artichoke hearts, leaving a 1/4-inch space between pieces. Place 2 mushrooms on the end of each skewer. Brush kabobs with reserved marinade.

3 For a charcoal grill, grill kabobs on the rack of an uncovered grill directly over medium coals for 10 to 12 minutes or until chicken is no longer pink (170°F), turning once halfway through grilling. Brush with 1/4 cup of the pasta sauce during the last 5 minutes of grilling. (For a gas grill, preheat grill. Reduce heat to medium. Place kabobs on grill rack over heat. Cover; grill as above.)

4 Meanwhile, cook pasta according to package directions; drain. Heat remaining pasta sauce and remaining artichoke hearts until heated through. Spoon over linguine. Top with kabobs. If desired, sprinkle with Parmesan cheese.

Nutrition Facts per serving: 720 cal., 28 g total fat (9 g sat. fat), 90 mg chol., 1,443 mg sodium, 69 g carbo., 9 g fiber, 51 g pro. Daily Values: 41% vit. A, 118% vit. C, 51% calcium, 25% iron. Exchanges: 1 Vegetable, 3 Starch, 1½ Other Carbo., 5½ Very Lean Meat, 3½ Fat

GRILLED CHICKEN FETTUCCINE

Pesto and a rich, creamy sauce turn grilled chicken strips into an elegant entrée.

Prep: 20 minutes Grill: 12 minutes
Makes: 6 servings

1 cup whipping cream
¹⁄₃ cup butter or margarine
³⁄₄ cup grated Parmesan cheese
4 skinless, boneless chicken
    breast halves
12 ounces dried fettuccine
¹⁄₄ cup purchased pesto
1 cup cherry tomatoes, halved
    Dash black pepper
    Toasted pine nuts (optional)
    Snipped fresh basil (optional)

1 In a small saucepan heat whipping cream and butter until butter melts. Gradually add Parmesan cheese, stirring until combined. Cover and keep warm over low heat.

2 For a charcoal grill, grill chicken on the rack of an uncovered grill directly over medium coals for 12 to 15 minutes or until chicken is no longer pink (170°F), turning once halfway through grilling. (For a gas grill, preheat grill. Reduce heat to medium. Place chicken on grill rack over heat. Cover; grill as above.)

3 Meanwhile, cook pasta according to package directions. Drain and keep warm.

4 Cut chicken into bite-size pieces. In a medium bowl toss chicken with 1 tablespoon of the pesto. Add remaining pesto and Parmesan mixture to the hot cooked fettuccine. Add tomatoes. Toss to coat. Arrange fettuccine on a serving platter; sprinkle with pepper. Top with grilled chicken. If desired, sprinkle with pine nuts and/or basil.

Nutrition Facts per serving: 673 cal., 38 g total fat (17 g sat. fat), 148 mg chol., 389 mg sodium, 47 g carbo., 2 g fiber, 36 g pro. Daily Values: 25% vit. A, 7% vit. C, 16% calcium, 14% iron. Exchanges: 3 Starch, 4 Very Lean Meat, 6½ Fat

Grilled Chicken Fettuccine

SPICY MOROCCAN-GLAZED CHICKEN

Yogurt combined with hot pepper sauce and a host of other seasonings gives chicken a deliciously exotic flair.

Prep: 10 minutes Marinate: 4 to 8 hours Grill: 12 minutes
Makes: 4 servings

   **4 skinless, boneless chicken
     breast halves**
¹⁄₂ cup plain yogurt
¹⁄₃ cup lime juice
   2 tablespoons olive oil
   2 tablespoons honey
   **1 teaspoon bottled minced garlic
     (2 cloves)**
   1 teaspoon bottled hot pepper sauce
¹⁄₂ teaspoon ground turmeric
¹⁄₂ teaspoon ground cardamom
¹⁄₂ teaspoon ground allspice
¹⁄₂ teaspoon ground cumin
¹⁄₄ teaspoon salt
¹⁄₄ teaspoon ground white pepper

1 Place chicken in a self-sealing plastic bag set in a shallow dish. For marinade, in a small bowl combine yogurt, lime juice, oil, honey, garlic, hot pepper sauce, turmeric, cardamom, allspice, cumin, salt, and white pepper. Pour marinade over chicken; seal bag. Marinate in the refrigerator for 4 to 8 hours, turning bag occasionally. Drain chicken, reserving marinade.

2 For a charcoal grill, grill chicken on the rack of an uncovered grill directly over medium coals for 12 to 15 minutes or until chicken is no longer pink (170°F), turning once halfway through grilling and brushing often with reserved marinade during the first 5 minutes of grilling. (For a gas grill, preheat grill. Reduce heat to medium. Place chicken on grill rack over heat. Cover; grill as above.) Discard any remaining marinade.

Nutrition Facts per serving: 222 cal., 6 g total fat (1 g sat. fat), 83 mg chol., 165 mg sodium, 7 g carbo., 0 g fiber, 34 g pro. Daily Values: 1% vit. A, 6% vit. C, 5% calcium, 6% iron. Exchanges: ½ Other Carbo., 5 Very Lean Meat, ½ Fat

CHICKEN FAJITAS WITH JICAMA RELISH

The relish takes a traditional fajita of chicken, peppers, and onion to an interesting new level.

Prep: 45 minutes Marinate: 1 to 24 hours Grill: 12 minutes
Makes: 8 servings

   **4 skinless, boneless chicken
     breast halves**
¹⁄₂ cup bottled Italian salad dressing
¹⁄₂ teaspoon chili powder
¹⁄₂ teaspoon ground cumin
   **2 small red, green, and/or yellow
     sweet peppers, quartered
     lengthwise and seeded**
   **1 small red onion, cut into ¹⁄₂-inch
     slices**
   8 10-inch flour tortillas, warmed*
   1 recipe Jicama Relish
   1 16-ounce jar salsa

1 Place chicken in a self-sealing plastic bag set in a shallow dish. For marinade, combine Italian dressing, chili powder, and cumin. Pour over chicken; seal bag. Marinate in the refrigerator for 1 to 24 hours, turning bag occasionally. Drain chicken, reserving marinade. Brush marinade over sweet peppers and red onion.

2 For a charcoal grill, grill chicken, peppers, and onion on rack of uncovered grill directly over medium coals until chicken is no longer pink (170°F) and vegetables are crisp-tender, turning once halfway through grilling. Allow 12 to 15 minutes for chicken; 8 to 10 minutes for vegetables. (For a gas grill, preheat grill. Reduce heat to medium. Place chicken and vegetables on grill rack over heat. Cover; grill as above.)

3 Remove chicken and vegetables from grill; carefully slice into thin bite-size strips. Spoon chicken and vegetable mixture onto warmed tortillas. Top with Jicama Relish and salsa; roll up.

Jicama Relish: In a bowl combine one 15-ounce can black beans, rinsed and drained; 1 cup chopped, peeled jicama; 1 large tomato, chopped; 1 medium avocado, halved, seeded, peeled, and chopped; and ¹⁄₂ cup snipped fresh cilantro.

*Note: To warm tortillas, wrap tortillas tightly in foil. Place on edge of grill rack and heat for 10 minutes, turning once.

Nutrition Facts per serving: 396 cal., 16 g total fat (3 g sat. fat), 41 mg chol., 720 mg sodium, 42 g carbo., 6 g fiber, 25 g pro. Daily Values: 38% vit. A, 91% vit. C, 11% calcium, 22% iron. Exchanges: ½ Vegetable, 2½ Starch, 2½ Very Lean Meat, 2½ Fat

CHICKEN BREASTS WITH FIRECRACKER BARBECUE SAUCE

To prevent burning, brush on sweet sauces only during the last few minutes of grilling.

Prep: 25 minutes Grill: 12 minutes
Makes: 6 servings

¼ **cup chipotle peppers in adobo sauce**
   Nonstick cooking spray
⅓ **cup finely chopped onion (1 small)**
3 **cloves garlic, minced**
1 **cup catsup**
3 **tablespoons white wine vinegar**
3 **tablespoons full-flavored molasses**
   or sorghum
1 **tablespoon Worcestershire sauce**
6 **skinless, boneless chicken**
   breast halves

1 For sauce, remove any stems from chipotle peppers. Place peppers and adobo sauce in a blender. Cover and blend until smooth. Set aside.

2 Lightly coat an unheated medium saucepan with nonstick cooking spray. Cook onion and garlic in saucepan until tender. Stir in chipotle pepper mixture, catsup, vinegar, molasses, and Worcestershire sauce. Bring to boiling; reduce heat. Simmer, uncovered, about 10 minutes or until sauce is slightly thickened.

3 For a charcoal grill, grill chicken on the rack of an uncovered grill directly over medium coals for 12 to 15 minutes or until chicken is no longer pink (170°F), turning once halfway through grilling and brushing with sauce during the last 5 minutes of grilling. (For a gas grill, preheat grill. Reduce heat to medium. Place chicken on grill rack over heat. Cover; grill as above.) Bring the remaining sauce to boiling; pass sauce with chicken.

Nutrition Facts per serving: 207 cal., 2 g total fat (0 g sat. fat), 66 mg chol., 612 mg sodium, 20 g carbo., 1 g fiber, 27 g pro. Daily Values: 11% vit. A, 14% vit. C, 5% calcium, 10% iron. Exchanges: 1½ Other Carbo., 3½ Very Lean Meat

FOOD FOR THOUGHT FREE-RANGE AND ORGANIC CHICKENS

Free-range and organic chickens are more readily available than they were in the past. Many consumers favor the fuller flavor and texture over mass-marketed varieties, but the basic differences are as follows:

● Unlike conventional chickens, free-range chickens are allowed access to the outdoors to roam, often feeding on natural grasses and/or seeds. Many free-range chickens also are organic.

● Organic chickens are fed an organic diet, raised without the use of hormones or antibiotics, processed without preservatives, and are often free-range as well. The USDA has established federal guidelines that must be followed in order to earn the USDA organic seal.

● Both varieties cost more than conventional chickens due to the greater investment companies must make to raise and process the chickens according to the required specifications.

Double Cherry-Chicken Roll-Ups

DOUBLE CHERRY-CHICKEN ROLL-UPS

Prep: 30 minutes Grill: 20 minutes
Makes: 4 servings

- ½ of an 8-ounce container mascarpone cheese or ½ of an 8-ounce tub (about ½ cup) cream cheese
- ⅓ cup snipped dried tart red cherries
- 3 tablespoons thinly sliced green onions
- 4 skinless, boneless chicken breast halves
- 1 tablespoon brown sugar
- ½ teaspoon salt
- ¼ teaspoon black pepper
- 1 recipe Cherry-Orange Sauce

1 For filling, combine mascarpone cheese, dried cherries, and green onions. Set aside.

2 Place a chicken breast half between 2 pieces of plastic wrap. Using the flat side of a meat mallet, pound chicken lightly into a rectangle about ¼ inch thick. Remove plastic wrap. Repeat with remaining chicken pieces. Spread filling evenly over chicken pieces to within ½ inch of edges. Fold in sides of each chicken piece; roll up from a short end. Secure with wooden toothpicks. For rub, combine brown sugar, salt, and pepper. Sprinkle over chicken; rub in with your fingers.

3 For a charcoal grill, arrange medium-hot coals around a drip pan. Test for medium heat above the pan. Place chicken on grill rack over drip pan. Cover; grill for 20 to 25 minutes or until chicken is no longer pink (170°F). (For a gas grill, preheat grill. Reduce heat to medium. Adjust for indirect cooking. Grill as above.) Serve with Cherry-Orange Sauce.

Cherry-Orange Sauce: Finely shred enough peel from 1 orange to equal 1 teaspoon. Set aside. Peel and section the orange over a bowl to catch the juices. Add enough additional orange juice to equal ¼ cup. In a small saucepan combine ½ cup cherry preserves and the orange juice; heat and stir until melted. Remove from heat. Coarsely chop the orange sections; add to preserves mixture along with the 1 teaspoon peel.

Nutrition Facts per serving: 459 cal., 15 g total fat (8 g sat. fat), 118 mg chol., 400 mg sodium, 45 g carbo., 2 g fiber, 40 g pro. Daily Values: 3% vit. A, 38% vit. C, 4% calcium, 8% iron. Exchanges: 3 Other Carbo., 5½ Very Lean Meat, 2 Fat

CHICKEN AND PROSCIUTTO ROLL-UPS

This pretty dish takes the Italian technique called "braciola"—a method of wrapping thin slices of meat around savories such as Italian ham, cheese, and herbs—and applies it to chicken.

Prep: 20 minutes Grill: 15 minutes
Makes: 4 servings

1/4 cup dry white wine
2 teaspoons snipped fresh thyme or
    1/2 teaspoon dried thyme, crushed
4 skinless, boneless chicken
    breast halves
4 thin slices prosciutto (about 1 ounce
    total), trimmed of fat
2 ounces fontina cheese, thinly sliced
1/2 of a 7-ounce jar roasted red sweet
    peppers, cut into thin strips
    (about 1/2 cup)
    Fresh thyme (optional)

1 For sauce, in a small bowl combine wine and thyme. Set aside.

2 Place a chicken breast half between 2 pieces of plastic wrap. Using the flat side of a meat mallet, pound chicken lightly into a rectangle about 1/8 inch thick. Remove plastic wrap. Repeat with remaining chicken pieces.

3 Place a slice of prosciutto and one-fourth of the fontina cheese slices on each chicken piece. Arrange one-fourth of the roasted pepper strips on cheese near bottom edge of chicken. Fold in sides of each chicken piece; roll up from a short end, pressing edges to seal. Secure with wooden toothpicks, if necessary.

4 For a charcoal grill, arrange medium-hot coals around a drip pan. Test for medium heat above the pan. Place chicken on grill rack over drip pan. Brush with sauce. Cover; grill for 25 to 30 minutes or until chicken is no longer pink (170°F). (For a gas grill, preheat grill. Reduce heat to medium. Adjust for indirect cooking. Grill as above.) If desired, garnish with additional fresh thyme.

Nutrition Facts per serving: 214 cal., 9 g total fat (4 g sat. fat), 76 mg chol., 294 mg sodium, 2 g carbo., 0 g fiber, 27 g pro. Daily Values: 14% vit. A, 85% vit. C, 7% calcium, 7% iron. Exchanges: 4 Very Lean Meat, 1 1/2 Fat

PINEAPPLE-LEMON CHICKEN

Be warned—this saucy chicken is finger-lickin' messy and oh so good.

Prep: 30 minutes Marinate: 2 to 24 hours Grill: 50 minutes
Makes: 4 servings

4 chicken breast halves
1 20-ounce can crushed pineapple
    (juice pack)
1 small lemon, very thinly sliced
1/3 cup catsup
1/3 cup honey
1 tablespoon Worcestershire sauce
1 teaspoon bottled minced garlic
    (2 cloves)
1 teaspoon salt
1/4 teaspoon dried rosemary, crushed
1 teaspoon cornstarch
    Hot cooked rice

1 Place chicken in a self-sealing plastic bag set in a shallow dish. Drain pineapple, reserving 1/4 cup juice. For marinade, in a medium bowl combine pineapple, reserved pineapple juice, lemon slices, catsup, honey, Worcestershire sauce, garlic, salt, and rosemary. Pour marinade over chicken; seal bag. Marinate in the refrigerator for 2 to 24 hours. Drain chicken, reserving marinade.

2 For charcoal grill, arrange medium-hot coals around drip pan. Test for medium heat above pan. Place chicken breasts, bone sides up, on grill rack over drip pan. Brush with some reserved marinade. Cover; grill 50 to 60 minutes or until chicken is no longer pink (170°F); turn once halfway through grilling and brush with reserved marinade during last 10 minutes of grilling. (For a gas grill, preheat grill. Reduce heat to medium. Adjust for indirect cooking. Grill as above.)

3 In a medium saucepan combine remaining reserved marinade and the cornstarch. Cook and stir over medium heat until thickened and bubbly. Cook for 2 minutes more. To serve, spoon sauce over chicken and rice.

Nutrition Facts per serving: 618 cal., 21 g total fat (6 g sat. fat), 135 mg chol., 848 mg sodium, 62 g carbo., 2 g fiber, 44 g pro. Daily Values: 6% vit. A, 31% vit. C, 6% calcium, 17% iron. Exchanges: 1 Fruit, 1 1/2 Starch, 1 1/2 Other Carbo., 5 1/2 Lean Meat, 1 Fat

MARINATED ITALIAN CHICKEN

Italian seasoning and garlic provide all the herbs necessary for this Mediterranean chicken.

Prep: 15 minutes Marinate: 8 to 24 hours Grill: 50 minutes
Makes: 4 to 6 servings

4 to 6 chicken breast halves
1½ cups dry white wine
½ cup olive oil
1 tablespoon dried Italian seasoning, crushed
2 teaspoons bottled minced garlic
Fresh herb sprigs

1 If desired, remove skin from chicken. Place chicken in a self-sealing plastic bag set in a shallow dish. For marinade, in a medium bowl stir together wine, oil, Italian seasoning, and garlic. Pour marinade over chicken; seal bag. Marinate in the refrigerator for 8 to 24 hours, turning bag occasionally. Drain chicken, reserving marinade.

2 For a charcoal grill, arrange medium-hot coals around a drip pan. Test for medium heat above pan. Place chicken breasts, bone sides up, on grill rack over drip pan. Cover; grill for 50 to 60 minutes or until chicken is no longer pink (170°F), turning once and brushing with reserved marinade halfway through grilling. (For a gas grill, preheat grill. Reduce heat to medium. Adjust for indirect cooking. Grill as above.) Discard any remaining marinade. Garnish with herb sprigs.

Nutrition Facts per serving: 462 cal., 29 g total fat (7 g sat. fat), 135 mg chol., 108 mg sodium, 1 g carbo., 0 g fiber, 41 g pro. Daily Values: 3% vit. A, 1% vit. C, 3% calcium, 10% iron. Exchanges: 6 Lean Meat, 2 Fat

ASIAN CHICKEN

This can't-miss grilled chicken gets its captivating flavor from an Asian-accented marinade, which includes hoisin sauce, ginger, and five-spice powder.

Prep: 15 minutes Marinate: 1 to 2 hours Grill: 50 minutes
Makes: 4 servings

4 chicken breast halves
1 cup dry red wine
¼ cup bottled hoisin sauce
¼ cup chopped onion
1 tablespoon soy sauce
1 teaspoon bottled minced garlic
½ teaspoon grated fresh ginger
½ teaspoon five-spice powder
¼ teaspoon crushed red pepper

1 Place chicken in a self-sealing plastic bag set in a shallow dish. For marinade, combine wine, hoisin sauce, onion, soy sauce, garlic, ginger, five-spice powder, and crushed red pepper. Pour over chicken; seal bag. Marinate in the refrigerator for 1 to 2 hours, turning bag occasionally. Drain chicken, reserving marinade.

2 For a charcoal grill, arrange medium-hot coals around a drip pan. Test for medium heat above the pan. Place chicken, bone sides up, on grill rack over drip pan. Cover; grill for 50 to 60 minutes or until chicken is no longer pink (170°F), turning once halfway through grilling. (For a gas grill, preheat grill. Reduce heat to medium. Adjust for indirect cooking. Grill as above.)

3 Meanwhile, place reserved marinade in a small saucepan. Bring to boiling; reduce heat. Simmer, uncovered, for 10 minutes. Strain, if desired. Drizzle hot marinade over chicken.

Nutrition Facts per serving: 449 cal., 21 g total fat (6 g sat. fat), 135 mg chol., 548 mg sodium, 8 g carbo., 0 g fiber, 43 g pro. Daily Values: 6% vit. A, 2% vit. C, 5% calcium, 12% iron. Exchanges: ½ Other Carbo., 6 Lean Meat, ½ Fat

CHICKEN STUFFED WITH SPINACH AND SWEET PEPPERS

Use a small sharp, pointed knife to cut the pockets into the chicken breasts before marinating them, when the breasts are easier to handle.

Prep: 30 minutes Marinate: 2 to 4 hours Grill: 45 minutes
Makes: 6 servings

6 chicken breast halves
¼ cup honey mustard
2 tablespoons mayonnaise or salad dressing
1 tablespoon olive oil
1 tablespoon red wine vinegar
1 teaspoon dried oregano, crushed
1 teaspoon dried basil, crushed
1 teaspoon dried rosemary, crushed
1 cup finely shredded mozzarella cheese (4 ounces)

Chicken Stuffed with Spinach and Sweet Peppers

1 cup chopped fresh spinach

¹/₂ cup finely chopped red sweet pepper

¹/₄ teaspoon black pepper

3 cloves garlic, minced

Grilled asparagus (optional)

Roma tomatoes, cut up (optional)

1 Using a sharp knife, make a horizontal pocket in each chicken breast half by cutting from one side almost to, but not through, the other side. Place chicken in a self-sealing plastic bag set in a shallow dish. For marinade, in a small bowl stir together mustard, mayonnaise, oil, vinegar, oregano, basil, and rosemary. Pour marinade over chicken; seal bag. Marinate in the refrigerator for 2 to 4 hours, turning bag occasionally.

2 Meanwhile, for stuffing, in a medium bowl combine mozzarella cheese, spinach, sweet pepper, black pepper, and garlic. Drain chicken, discarding marinade. Spoon stuffing into pockets in chicken breast halves. Fasten pockets with wooden toothpicks, if necessary.

3 For charcoal grill, arrange medium-hot coals around drip pan. Test for medium heat above pan. Place chicken breasts, bone sides up, on grill over drip pan. Cover; grill for 45 to 55 minutes or until chicken is no longer pink (170°F), turning once halfway through grilling. (For a gas grill, preheat grill. Reduce heat to medium. Adjust for indirect cooking. Grill as above.) If desired, serve with asparagus and tomatoes.

Nutrition Facts per serving: 297 cal., 11 g total fat (3 g sat. fat), 103 mg chol., 282 mg sodium, 5 g carbo., 1 g fiber, 41 g pro. Daily Values: 25% vit. A, 45% vit. C, 16% calcium, 9% iron. Exchanges: 6 Very Lean Meat, 2 Fat

TEXAS-STYLE BARBECUED CHICKEN LEGS

Prep: 15 minutes Grill: 35 minutes
Makes: 6 servings

$^1/_2$ **cup finely chopped onion (1 medium)**
2 cloves garlic, minced
1 teaspoon chili powder
$^1/_4$ **teaspoon ground sage**
1 tablespoon butter or margarine
$^1/_2$ **cup catsup**
2 tablespoons water
2 tablespoons vinegar
1 tablespoon sugar
1 tablespoon lemon juice
1 tablespoon Worcestershire sauce
$^1/_2$ **teaspoon salt**
$^1/_2$ **teaspoon bottled hot pepper sauce**
$^1/_4$ **teaspoon cracked black pepper**
6 whole chicken legs
   (thigh-drumstick pieces)

1 For sauce, in a small saucepan cook onion, garlic, chili powder, and sage in hot butter until onion is tender. Stir in catsup, water, vinegar, sugar, lemon juice, Worcestershire sauce, salt, hot pepper sauce, and black pepper. Bring to boiling; reduce heat. Simmer, uncovered, for 5 minutes, stirring occasionally. Remove from heat.

2 For a charcoal grill, arrange medium-hot coals around a drip pan. Test for medium heat above the pan. Place chicken legs, bone sides up, on grill rack over drip pan. Cover; grill for 50 to 60 minutes or until chicken is no longer pink (180°F), turning once halfway through grilling and brushing with sauce during the last 10 minutes of grilling. (For a gas grill, preheat grill. Reduce heat to medium. Adjust for indirect cooking. Grill as above.)

3 To serve, reheat any remaining sauce until bubbly; pass with the chicken.

Nutrition Facts per serving: 276 cal., 15 g total fat (4 g sat. fat), 86 mg chol., 596 mg sodium, 11 g carbo., 1 g fiber, 25 g pro. Daily Values: 10% vit. A, 16% vit. C, 2% calcium, 11% iron. Exchanges: ½ Other Carbo., 3½ Lean Meat, ½ Fat

MAPLE-SAUCED CHICKEN

For a barbecue sauce that's simple to make, dress up catsup with maple-flavored syrup and zesty spices.

Prep: 20 minutes Grill: 50 minutes
Makes: 6 servings

$^3/_4$ **cup catsup**
$^1/_3$ **cup maple-flavored syrup**
2 tablespoons cider vinegar
1 tablespoon bottled steak sauce
1 tablespoon yellow mustard or
   Dijon-style mustard
1 teaspoon ground cinnamon
$^1/_4$ **teaspoon ground allspice**
$^1/_4$ **teaspoon black pepper**
$^1/_8$ **teaspoon ground cloves**
   Several dashes bottled hot pepper
   sauce
6 whole chicken legs
   (thigh-drumstick pieces)

1 For sauce, in a small saucepan stir together catsup, maple syrup, vinegar, steak sauce, mustard, cinnamon, allspice, pepper, cloves, and hot pepper sauce. Bring to boiling; reduce heat. Simmer, uncovered, for 15 minutes.

2 For a charcoal grill, arrange medium-hot coals around a drip pan. Test for medium heat above the pan. Place chicken legs, bone sides up, on grill rack over drip pan. Cover; grill for 50 to 60 minutes or until chicken is no longer pink (180°F), turning once halfway through grilling and brushing with sauce twice during the last 10 minutes of grilling. (For a gas grill, preheat grill. Reduce heat to medium. Adjust for indirect cooking. Grill as above.)

3 To serve, reheat any remaining sauce until bubbly; pass with the chicken.

Nutrition Facts per serving: 387 cal., 20 g total fat (5 g sat. fat), 138 mg chol., 525 mg sodium, 21 g carbo., 1 g fiber, 31 g pro. Daily Values: 10% vit. A, 14% vit. C, 4% calcium, 12% iron. Exchanges: 1½ Other Carbo., 4½ Lean Meat, 1½ Fat

SMOKIN' DRUMSTICKS

Jalapeño jelly provides sweetness and heat. To tip the balance toward more heat, use red jelly.

Prep: 15 minutes Grill: 50 minutes
Makes: 5 servings

2 cups mesquite wood chips
2¹⁄₂ to 3 pounds chicken drumsticks
   Salt and black pepper
¹⁄₂ cup jalapeño jelly
1 recipe Dipping Sauce

1 At least 1 hour before grilling, soak wood chips in water. If desired, remove skin from drumsticks. Sprinkle drumsticks with salt and pepper.

2 For a charcoal grill, arrange medium-hot coals around a drip pan. Test for medium heat above the pan. Drain wood chips and add to coals. Place drumsticks on grill rack over drip pan. Cover; grill for 50 to 60 minutes or until chicken is no longer pink (180°F). Meanwhile, in a small saucepan, heat jelly until melted. Brush drumsticks with jelly occasionally during last 10 minutes of grilling. (For a gas grill, preheat grill. Reduce heat to medium. Adjust for indirect cooking. Grill as above.)

Dipping Sauce: In a small bowl combine one 8-ounce container dairy sour cream, 2 tablespoons snipped fresh cilantro, ¹⁄₂ teaspoon finely shredded lime peel, 2 tablespoons lime juice, and ¹⁄₈ teaspoon salt. Cover; chill until ready to serve.

Nutrition Facts per serving: 488 cal., 29 g total fat (11 g sat. fat), 157 mg chol., 313 mg sodium, 24 g carbo., 0 g fiber, 32 g pro. Daily Values: 13% vit. A, 11% vit. C, 7% calcium, 9% iron. Exchanges: 1¹⁄₂ Other Carbo., 4¹⁄₂ Medium-Fat Meat, 1¹⁄₂ Fat

CHICKEN DRUMSTICKS EXTRAORDINAIRE

Prep: 15 minutes Grill: 50 minutes
Makes: 4 servings

1 cup lightly packed fresh basil leaves
¹⁄₂ cup broken pecans
¹⁄₄ cup olive oil
2 cloves garlic, minced
¹⁄₄ teaspoon salt
¹⁄₄ teaspoon black pepper
8 chicken drumsticks

1 In a blender or small food processor combine basil, pecans, oil, garlic, salt, and pepper. Cover and blend or process until almost smooth, scraping down sides as needed. Divide mixture in half; chill half of the mixture.

2 If desired, remove skin from chicken. Brush chicken with unchilled basil mixture; discard remainder of the basil mixture used as brush-on.

3 For a charcoal grill, arrange medium-hot coals around a drip pan. Test for medium heat above the pan. Place chicken on grill rack over drip pan. Cover; grill for 50 to 60 minutes or until chicken is no longer pink (180°F), turning once halfway through grilling and brushing with the chilled basil mixture during the last 5 minutes of grilling. (For a gas grill, preheat grill. Reduce heat to medium. Adjust for indirect cooking. Grill as above.)

Nutrition Facts per serving: 453 cal., 36 g total fat (6 g sat. fat), 118 mg chol., 268 mg sodium, 3 g carbo., 2 g fiber, 30 g pro. Daily Values: 14% vit. A, 11% vit. C, 5% calcium, 13% iron. Exchanges: 4 Medium-Fat Meat, 3 Fat

SMOKIN' HOT TIP

For chicken that's grilled to perfection, follow these tips.

● Bone-in and skin-on chicken pieces grill best over indirect medium heat. This allows even cooking and minimizes flare-ups.

● Leave the skin on chicken pieces. The skin holds a great deal of flavor and helps retain the moistness of the meat. Remove it after grilling, if you like.

● If you're grilling skinless poultry, take care not to overcook it. Turn it with tongs, not a fork. A marinade or basting sauce will help keep the chicken moist.

● Cook whole chickens, thighs, legs, and drumsticks to an internal temperature of 180°F and chicken breasts to 170°F or until no longer pink.

MANGO-LIME-SAUCED CHICKEN THIGHS

With the tang of tropical fruit and a hint of pepper, the mango sauce enlivens chicken with complementary flavors.

Prep: 30 minutes Grill: 50 minutes
Makes: 4 servings

- 8 **chicken thighs**
- 1/2 **teaspoon salt**
- 1/4 **teaspoon ground nutmeg**
- 1/8 **teaspoon cayenne pepper**
- 1 **large mango, peeled, pitted, and cubed (about 1 1/4 cups)**
- 2 **tablespoons brown sugar**
- 1 **teaspoon finely shredded lime peel**
- 1 **tablespoon lime juice**
- 2 **teaspoons Worcestershire sauce**
- 1/8 **teaspoon cayenne pepper**
  Mango wedges, lime slices, and/or sweet cherries (optional)

1 If desired, remove skin from chicken. For rub, in a bowl combine salt, nutmeg, and 1/8 teaspoon cayenne pepper. Sprinkle over chicken pieces; rub in with your fingers.

2 In a blender or food processor combine mango, brown sugar, lime peel, lime juice, Worcestershire sauce, and 1/8 teaspoon cayenne pepper. Blend or process until smooth; set aside.

3 For a charcoal grill, arrange medium-hot coals around a drip pan. Test for medium heat above the pan. Place chicken thighs, bone sides up, on grill rack over drip pan. Cover; grill for 50 to 60 minutes or until chicken is no longer pink (180°F), turning once halfway through grilling and brushing with sauce during the last 10 minutes of grilling. (For a gas grill, preheat grill. Reduce heat to medium. Adjust for indirect cooking. Grill as above.) Serve with mango wedges, lime slices, and/or sweet cherries.

Nutrition Facts per serving: 450 cal., 27 g total fat (8 g sat. fat), 157 mg chol., 442 mg sodium, 17 g carbo., 1 g fiber, 33 g pro. Daily Values: 45% vit. A, 33% vit. C, 3% calcium, 12% iron. Exchanges: 1/2 Fruit, 1/2 Other Carbo., 4 1/2 Medium-Fat Meat, 1 Fat

Mango-Lime-Sauced Chicken Thighs

CHICKEN THIGHS IN BUTTERMILK-CHIVE MARINADE

Buttermilk gives chicken thighs the same moistness and tang that make buttermilk fried chicken so delectable.

Prep: 15 minutes Marinate: 4 to 6 hours Grill: 50 minutes
Makes: 4 servings

   8 chicken thighs
 3/4 cup buttermilk
   3 tablespoons snipped fresh chives
   1 tablespoon finely shredded lemon peel
   3 tablespoons lemon juice
   3 cloves garlic, minced
      Lemon wedges
      Snipped fresh chives

1 If desired, remove skin from chicken. Place chicken in a self-sealing plastic bag set in a shallow dish. For marinade, in a medium bowl combine buttermilk, the 3 tablespoons chives, the lemon peel, lemon juice, and garlic. Pour marinade over chicken; seal bag. Marinate in refrigerator for 4 to 6 hours; turn bag occasionally. Drain chicken, discarding marinade.

2 For a charcoal grill, arrange medium-hot coals around a drip pan. Test for medium heat above the pan. Place chicken thighs, bone sides up, on grill rack over drip pan. Cover; grill for 50 to 60 minutes or until chicken is no longer pink (180°F), turning once halfway through grilling. (For a gas grill, preheat grill. Reduce heat to medium. Adjust for indirect cooking. Grill as above.) Serve with lemon wedges and sprinkle with additional chives.

Nutrition Facts per serving: 556 cal., 39 g total fat (11 g sat. fat), 224 mg chol., 180 mg sodium, 2 g carbo., 0 g fiber, 47 g pro. Daily Values: 7% vit. A, 20% vit. C, 5% calcium, 14% iron. Exchanges: 7 Medium-Fat Meat, 1 Fat

PAPAYA-STUFFED CHICKEN THIGHS

The shape of boneless chicken thighs makes them naturals for stuffing and forming into tidy rolls.

Prep: 30 minutes Grill: 20 minutes
Makes: 6 servings

   1 tablespoon toasted sesame oil
   1 teaspoon grated fresh ginger or 1/2 teaspoon ground ginger
 1/4 teaspoon salt
   6 skinless, boneless chicken thighs
      Salt and black pepper
 1/4 cup sliced green onions (2)
   6 2×1/2-inch pieces peeled, seeded papaya or mango (1/4 of a medium papaya or 1/2 of a medium mango)
   2 tablespoons chopped fresh cilantro

1 In a small bowl, combine sesame oil, ginger, and 1/4 teaspoon salt; set aside.

2 Place each chicken thigh, boned side up, on a flat surface, spreading thigh open. Season with salt and pepper and brush with some of the oil mixture. Sprinkle each thigh with some of the green onions. Place 1 papaya piece crosswise near a short side of each thigh. Roll up, starting from side with fruit; secure with a wooden toothpick. Brush with remaining oil mixture.

3 For a charcoal grill, arrange medium-hot coals around a drip pan. Test for medium heat above the pan. Place chicken thighs on grill rack above drip pan. Cover; grill for 20 to 25 minutes or until chicken is no longer pink (180°F), turning once halfway through grilling. (For a gas grill, preheat grill. Reduce heat to medium. Adjust for indirect cooking. Grill as above.) To serve, sprinkle chicken with cilantro.

Nutrition Facts per serving: 169 cal., 8 g total fat (1 g sat. fat), 86 mg chol., 366 mg sodium, 3 g carbo., 1 g fiber, 21 g pro. Daily Values: 6% vit. A, 25% vit. C, 2% calcium, 7% iron. Exchanges: 3 Lean Meat

TURKISH CHICKEN THIGHS

An intriguing combination of chutney, ginger, mustard, and five-spice powder reinvents these chicken thighs.

Prep: 20 minutes Grill: 12 minutes
Makes: 4 to 6 servings

⅓ cup chutney
1 tablespoon honey
1 tablespoon lime juice
2 teaspoons spicy brown mustard
1½ teaspoons grated fresh ginger
¼ teaspoon five-spice powder
8 skinless, boneless chicken thighs
1 tablespoon snipped fresh parsley
1 tablespoon sesame seeds, toasted
2 teaspoons finely shredded
    orange peel

1 Snip any large pieces of chutney. In a small bowl combine chutney, honey, lime juice, mustard, ginger, and five-spice powder; set aside.

2 For charcoal grill, grill chicken thighs on rack of an uncovered grill directly over medium coals for 12 to 15 minutes or until chicken is no longer pink (180°F), turning once halfway through grilling and brushing with chutney mixture during the last 4 minutes of grilling. (For a gas grill, preheat grill. Reduce heat to medium. Place chicken on grill rack. Cover; grill as above.) Discard any remaining chutney mixture.

3 Meanwhile, in a small bowl combine parsley, sesame seeds, and orange peel. To serve, place chicken on a serving platter. Sprinkle with parsley mixture.

Nutrition Facts per serving: 384 cal., 11 g total fat (3 g sat. fat), 181 mg chol., 213 mg sodium, 24 g carbo., 1 g fiber, 46 g pro. Daily Values: 33% vit. C, 4% calcium, 14% iron. Exchanges: 1½ Other Carbo., 6½ Very Lean Meat, 1½ Fat

ALL-AMERICAN BARBECUED CHICKEN

Prep: 30 minutes Marinate: 4 to 24 hours Grill: 50 minutes
Makes: 4 servings

1 2½- to 3-pound broiler-fryer
    chicken, quartered
3 tablespoons lemon juice
1 tablespoon cooking oil
½ teaspoon bottled minced garlic (1 clove)
1 cup All-American Barbecue Sauce

1 Place chicken in a self-sealing plastic bag set in a shallow dish. For marinade, stir together lemon juice, oil, 1 teaspoon salt, ½ teaspoon black pepper, and garlic. Pour marinade over chicken; seal bag. Marinate in the refrigerator for 4 to 24 hours, turning bag occasionally. Prepare All-American Barbecue Sauce. Drain chicken, discarding marinade.

2 For a charcoal grill, arrange medium-hot coals around a drip pan. Test for medium heat above the pan. Place chicken, bone sides up, on grill rack over drip pan. Cover; grill for 50 to 60 minutes or until chicken is no longer pink (170°F for breast portions; 180°F for drumstick portions), turning once halfway through grilling and brushing with some of the sauce during the last 15 minutes of grilling. (For a gas grill, preheat grill. Reduce heat to medium. Adjust for indirect cooking. Grill as above.) To serve, pass the remaining sauce with the chicken.

All-American Barbecue Sauce: For sauce, in a large saucepan combine 1¼ cups water, ½ cup coarsely chopped onion, ¼ to ⅓ cup sugar, ¼ cup butter or margarine, 3 tablespoons yellow mustard, 2 tablespoons cider vinegar, and ¼ teaspoon black pepper. Bring to boiling; reduce heat. Simmer, uncovered, for 20 minutes. Stir in 1¼ cups catsup, ¼ cup Worcestershire sauce, 3 to 4 tablespoons lemon juice, and ¼ teaspoon cayenne pepper. Return to boiling; reduce heat. Simmer, uncovered, for 50 to 60 minutes or until reduced to about 2 cups. Cover extra sauce; chill up to 1 week.

Nutrition Facts per serving: 571 cal., 38 g total fat (12 g sat. fat), 160 mg chol., 1,320 mg sodium, 21 g carbo., 1 g fiber, 37 g pro. Daily Values: 16% vit. A, 28% vit. C, 4% calcium, 14% iron. Exchanges: 1½ Other Carbo., 5½ Lean Meat, 4 Fat

SESAME GRILLED CHICKEN

Prep: 25 minutes Marinate: 3 to 4 hours Grill: 50 minutes
Makes: 8 servings

- **5 to 6 pounds meaty chicken pieces (breast halves, thighs, and drumsticks) or two 2½- to 3-pound broiler-fryer chickens, quartered**
- **½ cup olive oil**
- **½ cup dry white wine**
- **½ cup soy sauce**
- **½ cup chopped green onions (4)**
- **3 tablespoons sesame seeds**
- **4 cloves garlic, minced**
- **1 tablespoon grated fresh ginger**
- **1 teaspoon dry mustard**
- **1 teaspoon freshly ground black pepper**
- **Steamed baby bok choy (optional)**

1 If desired, remove skin from chicken. Place the chicken in self-sealing plastic bag(s) set in shallow dish(es).

2 For marinade, in a bowl combine oil, wine, soy sauce, green onions, sesame seeds, garlic, ginger, dry mustard, and pepper. Pour marinade over chicken; seal bag(s). Marinate in refrigerator for 3 to 4 hours, turning bag(s) occasionally. Drain chicken, reserving marinade.

3 For a charcoal grill, arrange medium-hot coals around a drip pan. Test for medium heat above the pan. Place chicken pieces, bone sides up, on grill rack over drip pan. Cover; grill for 50 to 60 minutes or until chicken is no longer pink (170°F for breasts; 180°F for thighs), turning once halfway through grilling and brushing frequently with about half of the reserved marinade during the first 35 minutes of grilling. (For a gas grill, preheat grill. Reduce heat to medium. Adjust for indirect cooking. Grill as above.) Discard any remaining marinade. If desired, serve chicken with baby bok choy.

Nutrition Facts per serving: 486 cal., 36 g total fat (9 g sat. fat), 144 mg chol., 570 mg sodium, 1 g carbo., 0 g fiber, 37 g pro. Daily Values: 5% vit. A, 6% vit. C, 3% calcium, 11% iron. Exchanges: 5½ Lean Meat, 4 Fat

Sesame Grilled Chicken

Honey-Dijon Barbecued Chicken

HONEY-DIJON BARBECUED CHICKEN

A combination of wine, honey, and Dijon-style mustard adds irresistible flavor to these grilled chicken quarters.

Prep: 15 minutes Marinate: 8 to 24 hours Grill: 50 minutes
Makes: 4 servings

- **1** **2½- to 3-pound broiler-fryer chicken, quartered**
- **½** **cup white Zinfandel wine, apple juice, or apple cider**
- **¼** **cup olive oil or cooking oil**
- **¼** **cup honey**
- **¼** **cup Dijon-style mustard**
- **4** **cloves garlic, minced**
- **½** **teaspoon black pepper**
- **¼** **teaspoon salt**
  Grilled vegetables (optional)

1 Place chicken in a self-sealing plastic bag set in a shallow dish. For marinade, in a medium bowl combine wine, oil, honey, mustard, garlic, pepper, and salt. Pour marinade over chicken; seal bag. Marinate in the refrigerator for 8 to 24 hours, turning bag occasionally. Drain chicken, reserving marinade.

2 For charcoal grill, arrange medium-hot coals around drip pan. Test for medium heat above pan. Place chicken pieces, bone sides up, on rack over drip pan. Cover; grill for 50 to 60 minutes or until chicken is no longer pink (170°F for breast portions; 180°F for thigh portions), turning once halfway through grilling and brushing once with reserved marinade after 30 minutes of grilling. (For a gas grill, preheat grill. Reduce heat to medium. Adjust for indirect cooking. Grill as above.) Discard any remaining marinade. If desired, serve with grilled vegetables.

Nutrition Facts per serving: 516 cal., 35 g total fat (9 g sat. fat), 144 mg chol., 362 mg sodium, 11 g carbo., 0 g fiber, 38 g pro. Daily Values: 4% vit. A, 5% vit. C, 4% calcium, 11% iron. Exchanges: ½ Other Carbo., 6½ Medium-Fat Meat, 1½ Fat

SMOKIN' BARBECUED CHICKEN

Build your next outdoor gathering around this saucy chicken. To round out the menu, add coleslaw, baked beans, and ice-cold watermelon for dessert.

Prep: 20 minutes Marinate: 2 to 4 hours Grill: 50 minutes
Makes: 4 servings

Hickory chips (optional)
1 3- to 3½-pound broiler-fryer chicken, quartered or cut into 8 pieces
1 cup red wine vinegar
½ cup Worcestershire sauce
½ cup packed brown sugar
2 tablespoons liquid smoke
1 teaspoon seasoned salt
½ teaspoon black pepper

1 If using chips, at least 1 hour before grilling, soak in enough water to cover.

2 Place chicken in a self-sealing plastic bag set in a shallow dish. For marinade, in a medium bowl combine vinegar, Worcestershire sauce, brown sugar, liquid smoke, seasoned salt, and pepper. Pour marinade over chicken; seal bag. Marinate in the refrigerator for 2 to 4 hours, turning the bag occasionally. Drain chicken, reserving marinade.

3 For a charcoal grill, arrange medium-hot coals around a drip pan. Test for medium heat above the pan. If using, drain wood chips and add to coals. Place chicken pieces, bone sides up, on grill rack over drip pan. Cover; grill for 50 to 60 minutes or until chicken is no longer pink (170°F for breast portions; 180°F for thigh portions), turning and brushing once with reserved marinade halfway through grilling. (For a gas grill, preheat grill. Reduce heat to medium. Adjust for indirect cooking. Grill as above.) Discard remaining marinade.

Nutrition Facts per serving: 521 cal., 33 g total fat (10 g sat. fat), 172 mg chol., 325 mg sodium, 9 g carbo., 0 g fiber, 43 g pro. Daily Values: 5% vit. A, 5% vit. C, 3% calcium, 14% iron. Exchanges: ½ Other Carbo., 6 Medium-Fat Meat, ½ Fat

CHICKEN WITH LEMON-THYME PESTO

This recipe makes twice as much pesto as you need for the chicken. Save the rest to toss with pasta or drizzle over sliced summer tomatoes.

Prep: 1 hour Grill: 50 minutes
Makes: 6 servings

3 to 3½ pounds meaty chicken pieces (breast halves, thighs, and drumsticks)
Salt and black pepper
1⅓ cups lemon thyme*
½ cup salted pistachio nuts
½ cup olive oil
¼ teaspoon freshly ground black pepper
Lemon wedges

1 If desired, remove skin from chicken. Season with salt and pepper.

2 For pesto, in a food processor or blender combine lemon thyme and pistachios. Cover and process or blend with several on/off turns until finely chopped. With processor or blender running, gradually drizzle in oil, stopping to scrape down sides as necessary. Stir in freshly ground pepper. Set aside.

3 For a charcoal grill, arrange medium-hot coals around a drip pan. Test for medium heat above the pan. Place chicken pieces, bone sides up, on grill rack over drip pan. Cover; grill for 50 to 60 minutes or until chicken is no longer pink (170°F for breasts; 180°F for thighs and drumsticks), turning once halfway through grilling and brushing with half of the pesto during the last 5 minutes of grilling. (For a gas grill, preheat grill. Reduce heat to medium. Adjust for indirect cooking. Grill as above.)

4 Cover and chill remaining pesto for another use. Serve chicken with lemon wedges.

*Note: If you don't have lemon thyme, substitute 1⅓ cups fresh thyme plus 2 teaspoons finely shredded lemon peel.

Nutrition Facts per serving: 371 cal., 24 g total fat (5 g sat. fat), 104 mg chol., 210 mg sodium, 3 g carbo., 1 g fiber, 35 g pro. Daily Values: 4% vit. A, 12% vit. C, 4% calcium, 14% iron. Exchanges: 6 Lean Meat, 2 Fat

CITRUS CHICKEN WITH HERBS AND SPICES

Toasting the coriander and fennel seeds takes only minutes and rewards your extra effort with a lovely toasted aroma and taste.

Prep: 25 minutes Marinate: 4 to 8 hours Grill: 50 minutes
Makes: 4 servings

- **1 teaspoon coriander seeds**
- **1 teaspoon fennel seeds**
- **2¹/₂ to 3 pounds meaty chicken pieces (breast halves, thighs, and drumsticks)**
- **¹/₂ cup orange juice**
- **¹/₄ cup thinly sliced green onions (2)**
- **3 tablespoons honey**
- **1 tablespoon snipped fresh thyme**
- **1 tablespoon snipped fresh sage**
- **1 tablespoon snipped fresh rosemary**
- **¹/₂ teaspoon cracked black pepper**

1 In a small skillet cook coriander seeds and fennel seeds over medium heat about 5 minutes or until seeds are fragrant and toasted, stirring constantly. Remove from heat; let cool. Grind spices with a mortar and pestle.

2 If desired, remove skin from chicken. Place chicken in a self-sealing plastic bag set in a shallow dish. For marinade, in a small bowl combine orange juice, green onions, honey, thyme, sage, rosemary, ¹/₂ teaspoon salt, and pepper. Stir in ground spices. Pour marinade over chicken; seal bag. Marinate in the refrigerator for 4 to 8 hours, turning bag occasionally. Drain chicken, discarding marinade.

3 For a charcoal grill, arrange medium-hot coals around a drip pan. Test for medium heat above the pan. Place chicken pieces, bone sides up, on grill rack over drip pan. Cover and grill for 50 to 60 minutes or until chicken is no longer pink (170°F for breasts; 180°F for thighs and drumsticks), turning once halfway through grilling. (For a gas grill, preheat grill. Reduce heat to medium. Adjust for indirect cooking. Grill as above.)

Nutrition Facts per serving: 357 cal., 16 g total fat (4 g sat. fat), 129 mg chol., 261 mg sodium, 9 g carbo., 1 g fiber, 42 g pro. Daily Values: 2% vit. A, 15% vit. C, 4% calcium, 12% iron. Exchanges: ¹/₂ Other Carbo., 5 Lean Meat

FINGER-LICKIN' BARBECUED CHICKEN

Prep: 45 minutes Marinate: 2 to 4 hours Grill: 50 minutes
Makes: 6 servings

- **3 to 4 pounds meaty chicken pieces (breast halves, thighs, and drumsticks)**
- **1¹/₂ cups dry sherry**
- **1 cup finely chopped onion (1 large)**
- **¹/₄ cup lemon juice**
- **2 bay leaves**
- **6 cloves garlic, minced**
- **1 15-ounce can tomato puree**
- **¹/₄ cup honey**
- **3 tablespoons mild-flavored molasses**
- **¹/₂ teaspoon dried thyme, crushed**
- **¹/₄ to ¹/₂ teaspoon cayenne pepper**
- **¹/₄ teaspoon black pepper**
- **2 tablespoons white vinegar**

1 Place chicken in a self-sealing plastic bag set in a shallow dish. For marinade, stir together sherry, onion, lemon juice, bay leaves, and garlic. Pour over chicken; seal bag. Marinate in the refrigerator for 2 to 4 hours, turning bag occasionally. Drain chicken, reserving marinade.

2 Meanwhile, for sauce, in a large saucepan combine reserved marinade, tomato puree, honey, molasses, thyme, cayenne pepper, black pepper, and 1 teaspoon salt. Bring to boiling; reduce heat. Simmer, uncovered, about 30 minutes or until reduced to 2 cups. Remove from heat; remove bay leaves. Stir in vinegar.

3 For a charcoal grill, arrange medium-hot coals around a drip pan. Test for medium heat above the pan. Place chicken pieces, bone sides up, on grill rack over drip pan. Cover; grill for 50 to 60 minutes or until chicken is no longer pink (170°F for breasts; 180°F for thighs and drumsticks), turning once halfway through grilling and brushing with some of the sauce during last 15 minutes of grilling. (For a gas grill, preheat grill. Reduce heat to medium. Adjust for indirect cooking. Grill as above.) To serve, reheat the remaining sauce; pass with chicken.

Nutrition Facts per serving: 503 cal., 18 g total fat (5 g sat. fat), 129 mg chol., 779 mg sodium, 35 g carbo., 2 g fiber, 35 g pro. Daily Values: 22% vit. A, 29% vit. C, 7% calcium, 18% iron. Exchanges: 1 Vegetable, 2 Other Carbo., 5 Lean Meat, 2 Fat

Finger-Lickin' Barbecued Chicken

FOOD FOR THOUGHT MOLASSES

A by-product of refining cane or beet sugar, thick, dark, syrupy molasses is often used in cakes, desserts, and other sweets, but it adds a unique flavor to savory dishes as well. Light, or mild-flavored, molasses comes from the first boiling of the refining process and is sweet in flavor. Dark molasses, from the second boiling, is not as sweet as light molasses but has distinctive, robust flavor that is ideal for cooking and baking. The final product, blackstrap molasses, is the darkest, has a slightly bitter taste, and is rarely used in cooking. Light and dark molasses are interchangeable in recipes. Sorghum molasses is similar in flavor and is used similarly to cane molasses but comes from the sap of sorghum, a cereal grain plant.

MOROCCAN CHICKEN WITH MELON-CUCUMBER RELISH

This well-seasoned chicken is well-suited for a crowd. Guests can choose their favorite pieces—light meat or dark.

Prep: 35 minutes Marinate: 4 to 24 hours Grill: 35 minutes
Makes: 12 servings

6 to 8 pounds meaty chicken pieces (breast halves, thighs, and drumsticks)
¹/₂ cup lemon juice
¹/₃ cup olive oil
4 cloves garlic, minced
3 tablespoons grated fresh ginger
2 tablespoons ground cumin
4 teaspoons ground coriander
1 tablespoon salt
1 tablespoon ground cinnamon
1 tablespoon paprika
2 teaspoons cayenne pepper
1¹/₂ teaspoons black pepper
1 recipe Melon-Cucumber Relish

1 If desired, remove skin from chicken. Divide chicken between 2 large self-sealing plastic bags set in 2 shallow dishes. For marinade, in a medium bowl stir together lemon juice, oil, garlic, ginger, cumin, coriander, salt, cinnamon, paprika, cayenne pepper, and black pepper. Pour half of the marinade over chicken in each bag; seal bags. Marinate in the refrigerator for 4 to 24 hours, turning bags occasionally. Drain chicken, discarding marinade.

2 For a charcoal grill, arrange medium-hot coals around a drip pan. Test for medium heat above the pan. Place chicken pieces, bone sides up, on grill rack over drip pan. Cover; grill for 50 to 60 minutes or until chicken is no longer pink (170°F for breasts; 180°F for thighs), turning once halfway through grilling. (For a gas grill, preheat grill. Reduce heat to medium. Adjust for indirect cooking Grill as above.) Serve chicken with Melon-Cucumber Relish.

Melon-Cucumber Relish: In a bowl combine 3 cups chopped cantaloupe, 1¹/₂ cups chopped honeydew melon, 1¹/₂ cups chopped cucumber, and ¹/₄ cup sliced green onions. In a small bowl combine 2 tablespoons lemon juice, 2 tablespoons snipped fresh mint, and 1 tablespoon honey. Pour honey mixture over melon mixture; toss gently to coat. Cover and chill for up to 8 hours. At serving time, stir relish. Using a slotted spoon, spoon relish into serving bowl.

Nutrition Facts per serving: 364 cal., 23 g total fat (6 g sat. fat), 113 mg chol., 243 mg sodium, 8 g carbo., 1 g fiber, 30 g pro. Daily Values: 33% vit. A, 38% vit. C, 3% calcium, 9% iron. Exchanges: ¹/₂ Other Carbo., 4 Medium-Fat Meat, ¹/₂ Fat

SWEET-AND-SMOKY CHICKEN

A favorite among basting sauces, this sweet-tart version boasts a hint of liquid smoke.

Prep: 25 minutes Grill: 50 minutes
Makes: 4 servings

2¹/₂ to 3 pounds chicken breasts and thighs
¹/₂ cup vinegar
¹/₃ cup packed brown sugar
2 tablespoons Worcestershire sauce
³/₄ teaspoon liquid smoke
¹/₂ teaspoon salt
¹/₄ teaspoon black pepper

1 If desired, remove skin from chicken. For sauce, in a small saucepan stir together vinegar, brown sugar, Worcestershire sauce, liquid smoke, salt, and pepper. Bring to boiling; reduce heat. Simmer, uncovered, for 5 to 8 minutes or until sauce is reduced to ²/₃ cup.

2 For a charcoal grill, arrange medium-hot coals around a drip pan. Test for medium heat above the pan. Place chicken pieces, bone sides up, on grill rack over drip pan. Cover; grill for 50 to 60 minutes or until chicken is no longer pink (170°F for breasts; 180°F for thighs), turning once and brushing occasionally with sauce during the first 35 minutes of grilling. (For a gas grill, preheat grill. Reduce heat to medium. Adjust for indirect cooking. Grill as above.) Discard any remaining sauce.

Nutrition Facts per serving: 486 cal., 27 g total fat (8 g sat. fat), 142 mg chol., 503 mg sodium, 22 g carbo., 0 g fiber, 36 g pro. Daily Values: 4% vit. A, 0% vit. C, 4% calcium, 15% iron. Exchanges: 1¹/₂ Other Carbo., 5 Medium-Fat Meat, ¹/₂ Fat

PESTO CHICKEN AND TOMATOES

This recipe employs a masterful French technique called *beurre composé,* or compound butter. A mixture of butter, pesto, and walnuts melts into the grilled chicken and tomatoes.

Prep: 10 minutes Grill: 50 minutes
Makes: 4 servings

- 1 **tablespoon olive oil**
- 4 **cloves garlic, minced**
- 6 **roma tomatoes, halved lengthwise**
- 2½ **to 3 pounds meaty chicken pieces (breast halves, thighs, and drumsticks)**
- 3 **tablespoons butter or margarine, softened**
- 3 **tablespoons purchased basil pesto**
- 2 **tablespoons chopped walnuts, toasted**
- 2 **tablespoons finely chopped kalamata olives (optional)**

1 In a small bowl combine oil and garlic. Lightly brush tomato halves and chicken pieces with oil mixture. Discard any remaining oil mixture.

2 For a charcoal grill, arrange medium-hot coals around a drip pan. Test for medium heat above the pan. Place chicken pieces, bone sides up, on grill rack over drip pan. Cover; grill for 50 to 60 minutes or until chicken is no longer pink (170°F for breasts; 180°F for thighs and drumsticks), turning once halfway through grilling. During the last 6 to 8 minutes of grilling, place the tomatoes, cut sides down, on grill rack directly over coals; turn once after 3 minutes of grilling. (For gas grill, preheat grill. Reduce heat to medium. Adjust for indirect cooking. Grill as above.)

3 Meanwhile, in a bowl combine butter, pesto, walnuts, and, if desired, olives. Cover and chill until serving time. To serve, remove chicken from grill. Immediately spread butter mixture over chicken pieces and cut sides of tomatoes.

Nutrition Facts per serving: 563 cal., 39 g total fat (10 g sat. fat), 155 mg chol., 272 mg sodium, 8 g carbo., 2 g fiber, 45 g pro. Daily Values: 25% vit. A, 26% vit. C, 4% calcium, 12% iron. Exchanges: ½ Vegetable, 4 Medium-Fat Meat, 2 Fat

SMOKIN' HOT TIP

Purchasing, storing, and handling poultry carries a risk for salmonella contamination. Here are some key precautions to remember:

● Purchase poultry by the sell–by date printed on the package. Be sure poultry feels cold to the touch when you buy it.

● Make the poultry case your last stop in the grocery store. Place poultry in a separate plastic bag to prevent juices from contaminating other grocery items.

● Refrigerate poultry immediately (at or below 40°F) when you get home because bacteria multiply rapidly at temperatures between 40°F and 140°F.

● Store poultry in its original packaging on a plate or tray to prevent juices from dripping onto other foods in the refrigerator.

● Use fresh poultry within 2 days. Otherwise freeze it in the original package for up to 2 months. For longer storage, wrap the package in heavy foil or place in a freezer bag. Freeze for up to 9 months for pieces or 1 year for whole birds.

● Defrost poultry in the refrigerator, allowing 1 day for every 5 pounds, not counting the day you'll be cooking it. Or place the chicken in an airtight plastic bag and submerge in cold water, changing the water every half hour. Allow 30 minutes of thawing time for every pound of poultry.

● Refrigerate cooked leftovers promptly. Use within 3 days.

● To avoid cross contamination, use warm, soapy water to thoroughly wash your hands, cutting surfaces, and utensils that have been in contact with raw poultry. Use clean kitchen towels and serving platters as necessary.

Orange-Coriander Glazed Chicken

ORANGE-CORIANDER GLAZED CHICKEN

The same plant yields two flavorings: cilantro is the parsleylike fresh leaves, coriander is ground from the seeds.

Prep: 30 minutes Grill: 50 minutes Makes: 4 servings

- ¹/₃ cup orange marmalade
- 1 tablespoon soy sauce
- 1 tablespoon Asian chili sauce
- 1¹/₂ teaspoons ground coriander

2¹/₂ to 3 pounds meaty chicken pieces (breast halves, thighs, and drumsticks)
Salt and black pepper
1 orange, cut into thin wedges
Snipped fresh cilantro (optional)

1 For glaze, in a saucepan combine marmalade, soy sauce, chili sauce, and coriander. Heat and stir over low heat until marmalade melts; set aside. If desired, remove skin from chicken. Sprinkle chicken with salt and pepper.

2 For a charcoal grill, arrange medium-hot coals around a drip pan. Test for medium heat above pan. Place chicken pieces, bone sides up, on grill rack over pan. Cover; grill for 50 to 60 minutes or until chicken is no longer pink (170°F for breasts; 180°F for thighs and drumsticks); turn once halfway through grilling and brush occasionally with glaze during the last 10 minutes of grilling. (For a gas grill, preheat grill. Reduce heat to medium. Adjust for indirect cooking. Grill as above.)

3 Serve with orange wedges. If desired, sprinkle chicken with cilantro.

Nutrition Facts per serving: 411 cal., 16 g total fat (4 g sat. fat), 130 mg chol., 700 mg sodium, 23 g carbo., 1 g fiber, 43 g pro. Daily Values: 2% vit. A, 32% vit. C, 5% calcium, 10% iron. Exchanges: 1½ Other Carbo., 6 Lean Meat

---

BEER CAN CHICKEN

Before you cook this succulent bird, be sure the grill cover is tall enough for the bird to stand upright.

Prep: 30 minutes Grill: 1¼ hours Stand: 10 minutes
Makes: 4 to 6 servings

- **2 teaspoons packed brown sugar**
- **2 teaspoons paprika**
- **2 teaspoons salt**
- **1 teaspoon dry mustard**
- **½ teaspoon black pepper**
- **½ teaspoon dried thyme, crushed**
- **¼ teaspoon garlic powder**
- **1 12-ounce can beer**
- **1 3½- to 4-pound whole broiler-fryer chicken**
- **2 tablespoons butter or margarine, softened**
- **1 lemon quarter**

1 In a small bowl combine brown sugar, paprika, salt, dry mustard, pepper, thyme, and garlic powder. Discard about half of the beer from the can. Add 1 teaspoon of the spice mixture to the half empty can (beer will foam up).

2 Remove neck and giblets from chicken. Sprinkle 1 teaspoon of the spice rub inside the body cavity. Rub the outside of the chicken with butter and sprinkle on the remaining spice rub.

3 Hold the chicken upright with the opening of the body cavity at the bottom; lower the chicken onto the beer can so the can fits into the cavity. Pull the chicken legs forward so the bird rests on its legs and the can. Twist wing tips behind back. Stuff the lemon quarter in the neck cavity to seal in steam.

4 For a charcoal grill, arrange medium-hot coals around a drip pan. Test for medium heat above pan. Stand chicken upright on grill rack over the drip pan. Cover; grill for 1¼ to 1¾ hours or until chicken is no longer pink (180°F in thigh muscle). If necessary, tent chicken with foil to prevent overbrowning. (For a gas grill, preheat grill. Reduce heat to medium. Adjust for indirect cooking. If necessary, remove upper grill racks so chicken will stand upright. Grill as above.) Remove chicken from grill, holding by the can. Cover with foil; let stand for 10 minutes before carving. Use a hot pad to grasp can and heavy tongs to carefully remove the chicken.

Nutrition Facts per serving: 635 cal., 45 g total fat (15 g sat. fat), 217 mg chol., 1,180 mg sodium, 3 g carbo., 0 g fiber, 51 g pro. Daily Values: 19% vit. A, 6% vit. C, 4% calcium, 14% iron. Exchanges: 7 Medium-Fat Meat, 2 Fat

FOOD FOR THOUGHT
BEER CAN CHICKEN

While its exact origin is unknown, beer can chicken began popping up at barbecue competitions around the country in the mid to late 1990s. This method, which positions a whole chicken vertically on top of an open can of beer or other beverage, creates a flavor-infused steam that penetrates the chicken and generates incredibly tender and juicy results. The upright position also allows the bird to cook evenly. The fat runs off and a crisp, golden skin results. Form a tripod with the legs and can of beer to provide stability; position the bird over indirect heat.

CURRY-ROASTED CHICKEN

The spice mixture gives the chicken an appetizing golden color as well as a warm taste.

Prep: 20 minutes Grill: 1¼ hours Stand: 10 minutes
Makes: 5 servings

- 1 **3- to 4-pound whole broiler-fryer chicken**
- 2 **tablespoons olive oil**
- 1 **teaspoon salt**
- 1 **teaspoon ground cumin**
- 1 **teaspoon ground turmeric**
- ½ **teaspoon ground mustard**
- ¼ **teaspoon ground cardamom**
- ¼ **teaspoon cayenne pepper**
   Salt and black pepper
- 1 **recipe Minted Cucumber Sauce**

1 Remove the neck and giblets from chicken. Twist wing tips under the back. In a small bowl combine oil, salt, cumin, turmeric, mustard, cardamom, and cayenne pepper. Brush over chicken. Season cavity with salt and black pepper.

2 For a charcoal grill, arrange medium-hot coals around a drip pan. Test for medium heat above the pan. Place chicken, breast side up, on grill rack over drip pan. Cover; grill for 1¼ to 1¾ hours or until chicken is no longer pink and drumsticks move easily (180°F in thigh muscle). (For gas grill, preheat grill. Reduce heat to medium. Adjust for indirect cooking. Grill as above, except place chicken on a rack in a roasting pan.)

3 Remove chicken from grill. Cover with foil; let stand for 10 minutes before carving. Serve with Minted Cucumber Sauce.

Minted Cucumber Sauce: Combine 1 cup chopped, seeded cucumber; one 8-ounce carton plain low-fat yogurt; 1 roma tomato, seeded and chopped; 2 tablespoons snipped fresh mint; 1 tablespoon olive oil; and ¼ teaspoon salt. Cover and chill for up to 2 hours. If desired, let stand at room temperature for 30 minutes before serving.

Nutrition Facts per serving: 504 cal., 36 g total fat (9 g sat. fat), 141 mg chol., 838 mg sodium, 6 g carbo., 1 g fiber, 37 g pro. Daily Values: 11% vit. A, 20% vit. C, 12% calcium, 13% iron. Exchanges: ½ Other Carbo., 5½ Medium-Fat Meat, 1½ Fat

GARLIC-GRILLED WHOLE CHICKEN

A mixture of garlic and basil is inserted under the skin, and a combination of lemon, sweet pepper, and more garlic cooks inside the cavity.

Prep: 20 minutes Grill: 1 hour Stand: 10 minutes
Makes: 5 servings

- 1 **2½- to 3-pound whole broiler-fryer chicken**
- 3 **cloves garlic, peeled**
- ½ **of a lemon, sliced**
- ½ **of a red sweet pepper, sliced**
- 2 **tablespoons snipped fresh basil**
- ⅛ **teaspoon salt**
- 1 **tablespoon olive oil or cooking oil**
- 1 **tablespoon lemon juice**

1 Remove the neck and giblets from chicken. Twist wing tips under the back. Cut 1 garlic clove in half lengthwise. Rub skin of chicken with cut edge of garlic. Place garlic halves, lemon slices, and sweet pepper slices in cavity of chicken. Mince remaining 2 cloves of garlic. Combine minced garlic, basil, and salt; set aside. Starting at the neck on one side of the breast, slip your fingers between skin and meat, loosening the skin as you work toward the tail end. Once your entire hand is under the skin, free the skin around the thigh and leg area up to, but not around, the tip of the drumstick. Repeat on the other side of the breast. Rub garlic mixture under skin over entire surface. Skewer the neck skin to the back. Stir together oil and lemon juice; brush over chicken.

2 For a charcoal grill, arrange preheated coals around a drip pan. Test for medium heat above the pan. Place chicken, breast side up, on grill over drip pan. Cover; grill for 1 to 1¼ hours or until chicken is no longer pink and drumsticks move easily (180°F in thigh muscle); brush occasionally with oil-lemon mixture. (For a gas grill, preheat grill. Reduce heat to medium. Adjust for indirect cooking. Grill as above.)

3 Remove chicken from grill. Cover with foil; let stand for 10 minutes before carving.

Nutrition Facts per serving: 245 cal., 15 g total fat (4 g sat. fat), 79 mg chol., 127 mg sodium, 2 g carbo., 0 g fiber, 25 g pro. Daily Values: 9% vit. A, 28% vit. C, 1% calcium, 8% iron. Exchanges: 3½ Lean Meat, 1 Fat

GREMOLATA ROTISSERIE CHICKEN

Prep: 40 minutes Grill: 1 hour Stand: 10 minutes
Makes: 8 to 10 servings

3 tablespoons finely chopped fresh parsley
1 tablespoon minced garlic
1 tablespoon finely shredded lemon peel
1 anchovy fillet, finely chopped (optional)
½ cup butter, softened
2 3- to 3½-pound whole broiler-fryer chickens
  Salt and black pepper
1 recipe Orzo Salad

1 For gremolata butter, in a small bowl stir together parsley, garlic, lemon peel, anchovy (if using), and butter; set aside.

2 Remove the neck and giblets from chickens. Starting at the neck on one side of the breast, slip your fingers between skin and meat, loosening skin as you work toward the tail end. Once your entire hand is under the skin, free the skin around the thigh and leg area up to, but not around, the tip of the drumstick. Repeat on the other side of the breast. Rub gremolata butter under the skin over entire surface. Skewer the neck skin to the back. Repeat with remaining chicken. Sprinkle surfaces and cavities of chickens with salt and pepper.

3 To secure chickens on a spit rod, place one holding fork on rod, tines toward point. Insert rod through one of the chickens, neck end first, pressing tines of holding fork firmly into breast meat. To tie wings, slip a 24-inch piece of 100-percent-cotton kitchen string under back of chicken; bring ends of string to front, looping around each wing tip. Tie in center of breast, leaving equal string ends. To tie legs, slip a 24-inch piece of string under tail. Loop string around tail, then around crossed legs. Tie very tightly to hold bird securely on spit, again leaving string ends. Pull together the strings attached to wings and legs; tie tightly. Trim any excess string. Place second holding fork on rod, tines toward the chicken; press tines of holding fork firmly into thigh meat. Adjust forks and tighten screws. Repeat with remaining chicken on the same rod. Test balance, making adjustments as necessary.

4 For a charcoal grill, arrange medium-hot coals around a drip pan. Test for medium heat above the pan. Attach spit; turn on the motor and lower the grill hood. Let the chickens rotate over drip pan for 1 to 1¼ hours or until chicken is no longer pink and drumsticks move easily (180°F in thigh muscle). (For a gas grill, preheat grill, reduce heat to medium. Adjust for indirect cooking. Grill as above.)

5 Remove chickens from spit. Cover with foil; let stand for 10 minutes before carving. Serve with Orzo Salad.

Orzo Salad: Cook 8 ounces of dried orzo (rosamarina) according to package directions. Drain. Rinse with cold water until cooled; drain. In a medium bowl combine cooked orzo; ½ cup bottled Italian salad dressing; ½ cup crumbled feta cheese or fresh mozzarella cheese cut into ½-inch cubes; ½ cup halved kalamata olives; 2 roma tomatoes, seeded and finely chopped; and 4 green onions, thinly sliced. Season to taste with salt and pepper. Cover; chill until ready to serve.

Nutrition Facts per serving: 526 cal., 36 g total fat (12 g sat. fat), 111 mg chol., 581 mg sodium, 26 g carbo., 2 g fiber, 23 g pro. Daily Values: 17% vit. A, 17% vit. C, 7% calcium, 13% iron. Exchanges: 1 Starch, ½ Other Carbo., 3 Medium-Fat Meat, 4 Fat

FOOD FOR THOUGHT
GREMOLATA

Classically served with osso buco, gremolata is an aromatic garnish that consists of finely chopped parsley, garlic, and lemon peel. While these ingredients form the basis of gremolata, today's chefs are adding their own creative touches such as olives, nuts, or other herbs and citrus. Whatever the combination, gremolata adds a fresh dimension as a rub or as a finishing touch to poultry, meat, fish, and pasta.

BAYOU ROTISSERIE CHICKEN

If you have yet to brine poultry, here's a great recipe to get you started. Brining is easy and produces a succulently moist, tender bird.

Prep: 30 minutes Marinate: 6 to 8 hours
Grill: 1 hour Stand: 10 minutes
Makes: 8 to 10 servings

 2 3- to 3¹/₂-pound whole broiler-fryer
     chickens
 8 cups water
¹/₂ cup kosher salt
¹/₂ cup bourbon
¹/₂ cup honey
 2 tablespoons finely shredded
     lemon peel
¹/₄ cup lemon juice
¹/₄ cup bottled hot pepper sauce
 6 cloves garlic, minced
 1 recipe Cajun Spice Rub
 1 recipe Cajun Broccoli Slaw

1 Remove the neck and giblets from chickens. Place chickens in a 2-gallon self-sealing plastic bag set in a large, deep bowl. For brine, in a large bowl combine water, salt, bourbon, honey, lemon peel, lemon juice, bottled hot pepper sauce, and garlic. Stir until salt and honey are dissolved. Pour brine over chickens; seal bag. Marinate in the refrigerator for 6 to 8 hours.

2 Remove chickens from brine, discarding brine. Pat chickens dry with paper towels. Sprinkle Cajun Spice Rub evenly onto chickens; rub in with your fingers.

3 To secure chickens on a spit rod, place one holding fork on rod, tines toward point. Insert rod through one of the chickens, neck end first, pressing tines of holding fork firmly into breast meat. To tie wings, slip a 24-inch piece of 100-percent-cotton kitchen string under back of chicken; bring ends of string to front, looping around each wing tip. Tie in center of breast, leaving equal string ends. To tie legs, slip a 24-inch piece of string under tail. Loop string around tail, then around crossed legs. Tie very tightly to hold bird securely on spit, again leaving string ends. Pull together the strings attached to wings and legs; tie tightly. Trim any excess string. Place second holding fork on rod, tines toward the chicken; press tines of holding fork firmly into thigh meat. Adjust forks and tighten screws. Repeat with remaining chicken. Test balance, making adjustments as necessary.

4 For a charcoal grill, arrange medium-hot coals around a drip pan. Test for medium heat above the pan. Attach spit; turn on the motor and lower the grill hood. Let the chickens rotate over the drip pan for 1 to 1¹/₄ hours or until chicken is no longer pink and drumsticks move easily (180°F in thigh muscle). (For a gas grill, preheat grill, reduce heat to medium. Adjust for indirect cooking. Grill as above.)

5 Remove chickens from spit. Cover with foil; let stand for 10 minutes before carving. Serve with Cajun Broccoli Slaw.

Cajun Spice Rub: In a small bowl combine 2 tablespoons brown sugar; 2 teaspoons paprika; 1 teaspoon garlic powder; 1 teaspoon onion powder; 1 teaspoon dried thyme, crushed; ¹/₂ teaspoon ground allspice; ¹/₄ teaspoon cayenne pepper; and ¹/₄ teaspoon black pepper.

Cajun Broccoli Slaw: For dressing, in a small bowl stir together ¹/₂ cup mayonnaise or salad dressing, 2 tablespoons snipped fresh parsley, 1 tablespoon white wine vinegar, 2 teaspoons brown sugar, 1 teaspoon snipped fresh thyme, ¹/₂ teaspoon salt, ¹/₄ teaspoon black pepper, and ¹/₄ teaspoon cayenne pepper; set aside. In a large bowl combine one 16-ounce package shredded broccoli (broccoli slaw mix); 3 green onions, sliced; and ³/₄ cup finely chopped red sweet pepper. Stir in dressing. Chill until ready to serve. Before serving, top slaw with ¹/₄ cup chopped toasted pecans.

Nutrition Facts per serving: 672 cal., 47 g total fat (11 g sat. fat), 182 mg chol., 1,113 mg sodium, 14 g carbo., 3 g fiber, 45 g pro. Daily Values: 31% vit. A, 139% vit. C, 7% calcium, 17% iron. Exchanges: ¹/₂ Vegetable, 1 Other Carbo., 6 Medium-Fat Meat, 3¹/₂ Fat

Bayou Rotisserie Chicken

FOOD FOR THOUGHT CHICKEN LINGO

Fresh or frozen, whole or in parts, chickens are classified into five categories:

● Game Hen: These small, very tender, and flavorful birds are about 1½ months old and weigh less than 2 pounds. Commonly stuffed and roasted, they are easy to prepare and make an impressive presentation.

● Broiler-Fryer: Also young and tender, broiler-fryers weigh an average of 3½ pounds and are well-suited to a variety of cooking methods.

● Roaster: While still relatively moist and tender, roasters have more meat per pound than broiler-fryers and weigh up to 5 pounds. They are best roasted whole but are suitable for any cooking method.

● Capon: This castrated rooster has been raised to produce tender, juicy, flavorful meat. It has a higher proportion of white to dark meat and weighs up to 10 pounds.

● Stewing Hen: These mature females have a lot of meat and are very flavorful but less tender. They are best cooked using moist heat.

GAME HENS WITH RHUBARB BARBECUE GLAZE

Prep: 30 minutes Cook: 20 minutes Grill: 40 minutes
Makes: 6 servings

3½ to 4 cups chopped fresh or
    frozen rhubarb
1 cup bottled tomato-based
    barbecue sauce
¼ cup water
3 1¼- to 1½-pound Cornish game hens
    Olive oil
    Salt and black pepper
8 ounces dried orzo (rosamarina)
1 cup packaged shredded carrots
¼ cup sliced green onions (2)

1 For sauce, in a medium saucepan combine rhubarb, barbecue sauce, and water; bring to boiling over medium-high heat. Reduce heat to medium-low and cook, covered, about 20 minutes or until the rhubarb loses its shape. Remove from the heat and coarsely mash the rhubarb in the pan. Remove and reserve 1 cup of the sauce.

2 Use a long, heavy knife or kitchen shears to halve Cornish hens lengthwise, cutting through the breast bone, just off-center, and through the center of the backbone. (Or ask the butcher to cut hens into halves.) Twist wing tips under back. Rub surface and cavity of each hen half with oil; sprinkle with salt and pepper.

3 For a charcoal grill, arrange medium-hot coals around a drip pan. Test for medium heat above pan. Place hens, bone sides down, on rack over drip pan. Cover; grill for 40 to 50 minutes or until no longer pink (180°F), brushing with some of the remaining sauce during the last 15 minutes of grilling. (For a gas grill, preheat grill. Reduce heat to medium. Adjust for indirect cooking. Grill as above.)

4 Meanwhile, cook orzo according to package directions; drain. In a large bowl stir together orzo, the 1 cup reserved sauce, carrots, and green onions. Season to taste with salt and pepper. Serve hens with orzo mixture and remaining sauce.

Nutrition Facts per serving: 375 cal., 10 g total fat (2 g sat. fat), 111 mg chol., 609 mg sodium, 39 g carbo., 4 g fiber, 31 g pro. Daily Values: 124% vit. A, 18% vit. C, 10% calcium, 17% iron. Exchanges: 1½ Starch, 1 Other Carbo., 4 Very Lean Meat, 1½ Fat

GREEK-STYLE TURKEY BURGERS

These lean, juicy burgers get mellow Greek flavor from feta cheese, olives, and cucumber.

Prep: 20 minutes Grill: 14 minutes
Makes: 4 servings

⅓ cup fine dry wheat bread crumbs
1 slightly beaten egg white
1 tablespoon milk
1 0.7-ounce envelope Italian salad
    dressing mix (5 teaspoons)
1 pound uncooked ground turkey
    or chicken
4 thick pita bread rounds, toasted,
    or 4 whole wheat hamburger
    buns, split and toasted
1 recipe Greek Salsa
¼ cup crumbled feta cheese

1 In a medium bowl combine bread crumbs, egg white, milk, and half of the salad dressing mix. (Reserve the remaining half of salad dressing mix for Greek Salsa.) Add turkey; mix well. Shape turkey mixture into four ¾-inch-thick patties.

2 For a charcoal grill, grill patties on the rack of an uncovered grill directly over medium coals for 14 to 18 minutes or until no longer pink (170°), turning once halfway through grilling. (For a gas grill, preheat grill. Reduce heat to medium. Place patties on grill rack over heat. Cover; grill as above.)

3 Serve burgers on pita bread rounds with Greek Salsa and feta cheese.

Greek Salsa: In a small bowl stir together 2 tablespoons white wine vinegar, 2 teaspoons olive oil, and the remaining half of the salad dressing mix. Stir in 1 cup finely chopped tomato, ¼ cup finely chopped cucumber, and ¼ cup finely chopped, pitted kalamata or ripe olives.

Nutrition Facts per serving: 403 cal., 18 g total fat (5 g sat. fat), 96 mg chol., 1,177 mg sodium, 32 g carbo., 3 g fiber, 28 g pro. Daily Values: 7% vit. A, 15% vit. C, 10% calcium, 20% iron. Exchanges: 2 Starch, 3 Medium-Fat Meat, ½ Fat

GLAZED TURKEY BURGERS

A glaze of mustard and fruit preserves lends these burgers a sweet-sour dimension.

Prep: 20 minutes Grill: 14 minutes
Makes: 4 servings

- **1 tablespoon yellow mustard**
- **1 tablespoon cherry, apricot, peach, or pineapple preserves**
- **1 beaten egg**
- **¼ cup quick-cooking rolled oats**
- **¼ cup finely chopped celery**
- **3 tablespoons snipped dried tart cherries or dried apricots**
- **¼ teaspoon salt**
- **⅛ teaspoon black pepper**
- **1 pound uncooked ground turkey**
- **4 kaiser rolls or hamburger buns, split and toasted**
  Mayonnaise or salad dressing, lettuce leaves, and/or tomato slices (optional)

1 For glaze, stir together mustard and preserves; set aside. In a medium bowl combine egg, rolled oats, celery, dried cherries, salt, and pepper. Add ground turkey; mix well. Shape turkey mixture into four ¾-inch-thick patties.

2 For a charcoal grill, grill patties on the rack of an uncovered grill directly over medium coals for 14 to 18 minutes or until no longer pink (170°F), turning once halfway through grilling and brushing with glaze during the last minute of grilling. (For a gas grill, preheat grill. Reduce heat to medium. Place burgers on grill rack over heat. Cover; grill as above.)

3 Serve burgers on buns. Brush any remaining glaze over burgers. If desired, serve burgers with mayonnaise, lettuce, and tomato.

Nutrition Facts per serving: 397 cal., 14 g total fat (3 g sat. fat), 143 mg chol., 599 mg sodium, 38 g carbo., 2 g fiber, 28 g pro. Daily Values: 2% vit. A, 2% vit. C, 9% calcium, 21% iron. Exchanges: 2½ Starch, 3 Lean Meat, ½ Fat

Glazed Turkey Burgers

GARLIC TURKEY SAUSAGE WITH GARLIC-CRANBERRY SAUCE

Prep: 20 minutes Grill: 15 minutes
Makes: 6 servings

1 16-ounce can whole berry
   cranberry sauce
1 tablespoon finely shredded
   orange peel
¼ cup orange juice
2 teaspoons bottled minced garlic
   (4 cloves)
1¼ pounds uncooked ground turkey
4 ounces bulk pork sausage
5 teaspoons bottled minced garlic
   (10 cloves)
1 tablespoon snipped fresh marjoram
   or 1 teaspoon dried marjoram,
   crushed
1 tablespoon snipped fresh oregano
   or 1 teaspoon dried oregano,
   crushed
1 tablespoon snipped fresh parsley
1 teaspoon salt
¼ teaspoon black pepper
   Dash cayenne pepper

1 For sauce, in a medium bowl combine cranberry sauce, orange peel, orange juice, and the 2 teaspoons garlic. Set aside ¼ cup of the sauce to brush on turkey sausage. Cover and chill the remaining sauce.

2 For sausage, in a large bowl combine the turkey, pork sausage, the 5 teaspoons garlic, marjoram, oregano, parsley, salt, black pepper, and cayenne pepper. Divide mixture into 6 portions. Shape each portion around a 10-inch metal skewer, forming a 5-inch log.

3 For a charcoal grill, grill skewers on the rack of an uncovered grill directly over medium coals for 15 to 18 minutes or until no longer pink (170°F), turning to brown evenly and brushing with the reserved ¼ cup sauce during the last 3 minutes of grilling. (For a gas grill, preheat grill. Reduce heat to medium. Place skewers on grill rack over heat. Cover; grill as above.) Serve with chilled sauce.

Nutrition Facts per serving: 321 cal., 12 g total fat (3 g sat. fat), 87 mg chol., 568 mg sodium, 33 g carbo., 1 g fiber, 20 g pro. Daily Values: 3% vit. A, 19% vit. C, 4% calcium, 10% iron. Exchanges: 2 Other Carbo., 3 Lean Meat, ½ Fat

CHILI-RUBBED BRATWURSTS WITH CHERRY PEPPER CATSUP

To warm tortillas, wrap them tightly in foil. Place on edge of grill rack and heat for 10 minutes, turning once.

Prep: 15 minutes Marinate: 2 hours or overnight
Grill: 12 minutes Makes: 6 servings

6 turkey bratwursts
1 tablespoon packaged ground chili
   seasoning blend or Mexican
   seasoning blend
6 10-inch corn or flour tortillas,
   warmed
1 recipe Cherry Pepper Catsup
   Shredded lettuce (optional)
   Pickled carrots and peppers
   (optional)

1 Pierce turkey bratwurst casings several times with tines of a fork; rub with seasoning blend. Cover and chill for 2 hours or overnight.

2 For a charcoal grill, grill bratwursts on the rack of an uncovered grill directly over medium-hot coals for 12 to 15 minutes or until done (170°F), turning once halfway through grilling. (For a gas grill, preheat grill. Reduce heat to medium-high. Place bratwursts on grill rack over heat. Cover; grill as above.) Serve in tortillas with Cherry Pepper Catsup and, if desired, shredded lettuce and/or pickled carrots and peppers.

Cherry Pepper Catsup: Remove stems and seeds from 4 or 5 canned red cherry peppers. In blender or food processor combine peppers, 1 cup catsup, 1 tablespoon red wine vinegar, ½ teaspoon white pepper or cayenne pepper, and ¼ teaspoon salt. Cover and blend or process until nearly smooth. Cover; chill until serving time.

Nutrition Facts per serving: 298 cal., 14 g total fat (3 g sat. fat), 71 mg chol., 1,660 mg sodium, 21 g carbo., 1 g fiber, 22 g pro. Daily Values: 5% vit. A, 6% vit. C, 4% calcium, 6% iron. Exchanges: 1½ Starch, 2½ Lean Meat, 1 Fat

TURKEY CAESAR SANDWICHES

If you can't find thick pita bread rounds, substitute toasted kaiser or other rolls.

Prep: 10 minutes Grill: 12 minutes
Makes: 4 servings

2 8-ounce turkey breast tenderloins
¹⁄₂ cup bottled Caesar salad dressing
4 teaspoons olive oil
1 clove garlic, minced
4 thick pita bread rounds, split
     horizontally
     Romaine lettuce leaves
2 medium tomatoes, sliced
1 medium avocado, peeled and sliced
     (optional)

1 Cut tenderloins in half horizontally to make 4 steaks. For a charcoal grill, grill turkey steaks on the rack of an uncovered grill directly over medium coals for 12 to 15 minutes or until turkey is no longer pink (170°F), turning once halfway through grilling and brushing with half of the salad dressing during the last 5 minutes of grilling. (For a gas grill, preheat grill. Reduce heat to medium. Place turkey on grill rack over heat. Cover; grill as above.)

2 Meanwhile, stir together oil and garlic. Using a pastry brush, brush oil mixture over cut sides of pita breads. Place pita breads, brushed sides down, on grill rack over medium heat. Grill for 2 to 3 minutes or until toasted.

3 To assemble, place lettuce leaves on grilled side of four pita bread halves. Top with turkey, tomatoes, and, if desired, avocado; drizzle with the remaining salad dressing. Top with remaining pita bread halves.

Nutrition Facts per serving: 370 cal., 14 g total fat (2 g sat. fat), 70 mg chol., 870 mg sodium, 27 g carbo., 2 g fiber, 32 g pro. Daily Values: 2% vit. A, 3% vit. C, 17% calcium, 14% iron. Exchanges: 2 Starch, 3½ Very Lean Meat, 2 Fat

BUFFALO-STYLE TURKEY WRAPS

Prep: 35 minutes Marinate: 2 to 3 hours Grill: 12 minutes
Makes: 6 servings

2 8-ounce turkey breast tenderloins
3 tablespoons bottled hot pepper sauce
2 tablespoons cooking oil
2 teaspoons paprika
¹⁄₄ teaspoon salt
¹⁄₄ teaspoon cayenne pepper
6 10-inch flour tortillas
1¹⁄₂ cups carrots cut into thin strips
1¹⁄₂ cups thinly bias-sliced celery
3 cups shredded lettuce
1 recipe Blue Cheese Dressing

1 Cut tenderloins in half horizontally to make 4 steaks. Place turkey steaks in a self-sealing plastic bag set in a shallow dish. For marinade, in a small bowl combine hot pepper sauce, oil, paprika, salt, and cayenne pepper. Pour marinade over turkey in bag; seal bag. Marinate in the refrigerator for 2 to 3 hours; turn occasionally. Drain turkey steaks, discarding marinade.

2 For a charcoal grill, grill turkey on the rack of an uncovered grill directly over medium coals for 12 to 15 minutes or until turkey is no longer pink (170°), turning once halfway through grilling. Wrap tortillas tightly in foil. Place on grill rack with turkey; heat for 10 minutes, turning once. (For a gas grill, preheat grill. Reduce heat to medium. Place turkey steaks and wrapped tortillas on grill rack over heat. Cover; grill as above.)

3 Thinly slice turkey across the grain. Divide turkey, carrot strips, celery, and lettuce among the warm tortillas. Top with Blue Cheese Dressing. Roll up tortillas tightly. Serve immediately.

Blue Cheese Dressing: In a blender or food processor combine ¹⁄₂ cup dairy sour cream; ¹⁄₄ cup mayonnaise; ¹⁄₄ cup crumbled blue cheese; 1 tablespoon lemon juice; 1 clove garlic, cut up; and ¹⁄₈ teaspoon salt. Cover and blend or process until nearly smooth.

Nutrition Facts per serving: 407 cal., 22 g total fat (6 g sat. fat), 60 mg chol., 584 mg sodium, 29 g carbo., 3 g fiber, 24 g pro. Daily Values: 199% vit. A, 23% vit. C, 14% calcium, 17% iron. Exchanges: 1 Vegetable, 1½ Starch, 2½ Very Lean Meat, 4 Fat

THAI CURRIED TURKEY WITH SCALLION SLAW

The sweet coconut here cools the spicy curry. Purchase the green curry paste and coconut milk from an Asian specialty store.

Prep: 15 minutes Cook: 2 minutes Grill: 12 minutes
Makes: 4 servings

- **6 scallions or green onions**
- **2 cups finely shredded savoy cabbage, napa cabbage, bok choy, or gai choy**
- **3 tablespoons dry-roasted cashew halves**
- **¼ cup rice vinegar**
- **½ teaspoon sugar**
- **2 8-ounce turkey breast tenderloins**
- **2 to 3 tablespoons Thai green curry paste**
- **¼ cup dry white wine**
- **½ cup purchased unsweetened coconut milk**

1 Using a sharp knife, cut scallions lengthwise into thin slivers. In a medium bowl toss together scallion slivers, cabbage, and cashews. In a small bowl stir together vinegar and sugar until sugar dissolves. Set aside.

2 Cut turkey breast tenderloins crosswise into 1-inch slices; place a slice between 2 sheets of plastic wrap. Using the flat side of a meat mallet, pound turkey lightly to ½-inch thickness. Repeat with remaining slices. Spread turkey with half of the green curry paste.

3 For a charcoal grill, grill turkey on the rack of an uncovered grill directly over medium coals for 12 to 15 minutes or until turkey is no longer pink (170°F), turning once halfway through grilling. (For a gas grill, preheat grill. Reduce heat to medium. Place turkey on grill rack over heat. Cover; grill as above.) Set aside; keep warm.

4 For sauce, in a small skillet stir together remaining green curry paste and the wine. Cook, uncovered, over medium-high heat for 1 to 2 minutes or until liquid is almost evaporated, stirring often. Carefully add coconut milk. Bring to boiling; reduce heat. Cook, uncovered, for 1 to 2 minutes or until thickened.

5 In a large bowl, toss cabbage mixture with vinegar mixture; divide among 4 dinner plates. Arrange turkey on plates; drizzle with sauce.

Nutrition Facts per serving: 297 cal., 14 g total fat (6 g sat. fat), 68 mg chol., 637 mg sodium, 10 g carbo., 2 g fiber, 29 g pro. Daily Values: 9% vit. A, 50% vit. C, 5% calcium, 15% iron. Exchanges: ½ Vegetable, ½ Other Carbo., 4 Very Lean Meat, 2½ Fat

Thai Curried Turkey with
Scallion Slaw

SAGE TURKEY KABOBS

Prep: 30 minutes Marinate: 2 to 8 hours Grill: 12 minutes
Makes: 4 servings

- **1 pound turkey breast tenderloins**
- **1 small red onion, cut into wedges**
- **½ cup cider vinegar**
- **¼ cup olive oil**
- **2 tablespoons sugar**
- **2 cloves garlic, minced**
- **1 teaspoon snipped fresh thyme or**
- **½ teaspoon dried thyme, crushed**
- **1 teaspoon salt**
- **20 fresh sage leaves**
- **Salt and black pepper**
- **2 medium sweet potatoes**

1 Cut turkey lengthwise into ½-inch slices. Place turkey strips and onion wedges in a self-sealing plastic bag set in a shallow dish.

2 For marinade, in a small bowl combine vinegar, oil, sugar, garlic, thyme, and salt. Snip 4 of the sage leaves; stir into marinade. Pour half of the marinade over turkey and onion; seal bag. Marinate in the refrigerator for 2 to 8 hours, turning bag occasionally. Cover remaining marinade and chill. Drain turkey and onion, discarding marinade.

3 On a flat surface spiral each turkey strip into an "S" shape. On 8 medium skewers alternately thread sage leaves, onion wedges, and turkey spirals, leaving a ¼-inch space between pieces. Sprinkle with salt and pepper.

4 Scrub sweet potatoes but do not peel. Cut potatoes diagonally into ½-inch slices. Brush with some of the reserved marinade.

5 For a charcoal grill, grill kabobs and sweet potatoes on the rack of an uncovered grill directly over medium coals for 12 to 14 minutes or until turkey is no longer pink (170°F) and potatoes are tender, turning once and brushing occasionally with marinade. (For a gas grill, preheat grill. Reduce heat to medium. Place turkey and potatoes on grill rack over heat. Cover and grill as above.)

Nutrition Facts per serving: 370 cal., 15 g total fat (2 g sat. fat), 70 mg chol., 780 mg sodium, 30 g carbo., 3 g fiber, 30 g pro. Daily Values: 312% vit. A, 26% vit. C, 5% calcium, 12% iron. Exchanges: 1½ Starch, ½ Other Carbo., 3½ Very Lean Meat, 2½ Fat

COCONUT TURKEY SPEARS

Skewered turkey tenderloin rubbed with five-spice powder is grilled to perfection and served with Thai-style coconut curry sauces.

Prep: 20 minutes Soak: 30 minutes Grill: 8 minutes
Makes: 4 servings

- **8 6-inch bamboo skewers**
- **½ cup purchased unsweetened coconut milk**
- **2 tablespoons toasted shredded coconut**
- **1 teaspoon packed brown sugar**
- **1 teaspoon green curry paste**
- **1 teaspoon red curry paste**
- **12 ounces turkey breast tenderloins, cut into 1-inch strips**
- **1 tablespoon five-spice powder**
- **¼ teaspoon salt**
- **1 tablespoon cooking oil**
- **2 Key limes, halved crosswise**

1 Soak skewers in water for 30 minutes. For sauces, in a small bowl combine coconut milk, coconut, and brown sugar. Divide mixture in half. Stir green curry paste into half of the mixture; cover and chill until serving time. Stir red curry paste into remaining coconut mixture; cover and chill until serving time.

2 Rub turkey strips with five-spice powder and salt. If desired, place a strip between 2 pieces of plastic wrap. Using the side of a meat mallet, pound turkey lightly to ¼-inch thickness. Repeat with remaining turkey strips.

3 Thread pounded strips lengthwise onto soaked skewers. Keep strips straight; do not weave. Brush turkey with oil.

4 For a charcoal grill, grill skewers on the rack of an uncovered grill directly over medium-hot coals for 8 to 10 minutes or until turkey is no longer pink (170°F), turning once halfway through grilling. (For a gas grill, preheat grill. Reduce heat to medium-high. Place chicken on grill rack over heat. Cover; grill as above.) Serve with sauces and lime halves.

Nutrition Facts per serving: 214 cal., 12 g total fat (7 g sat. fat), 51 mg chol., 382 mg sodium, 4 g carbo., 1 g fiber, 21 g pro. Daily Values: 10% vit. C, 3% calcium, 12% iron. Exchanges: 3 Very Lean Meat, 2½ Fat

TERIYAKI TURKEY TENDERLOINS

The crisp texture of the warm slaw is a pleasant surprise and an appealing contrast to the turkey.

Prep: 25 minutes Marinate: 1 to 2 hours Grill: 12 minutes
Makes: 4 servings

    2 8-ounce turkey breast tenderloins
  1/4 cup soy sauce
    2 tablespoons brown sugar
    2 tablespoons lemon juice
    1 tablespoon cooking oil
    1 teaspoon grated fresh ginger
    1 clove garlic, minced
    1 recipe Hot Pineapple Slaw

1 Cut turkey tenderloins in half horizontally to make 4 steaks. Place turkey steaks in a self-sealing plastic bag set in a shallow dish. For marinade, in a small bowl combine soy sauce, brown sugar, lemon juice, oil, ginger, and garlic. Pour marinade over turkey; seal bag. Marinate in the refrigerator for 1 to 2 hours, turning once. Drain turkey, reserving marinade.

2 For a charcoal grill, grill turkey on the rack of an uncovered grill directly over medium coals for 12 to 15 minutes or until turkey is no longer pink (170°F), turning once and brushing with marinade halfway through grilling. (For a gas grill, preheat grill. Reduce heat to medium. Place turkey on grill rack over heat. Cover; grill as above.) Serve turkey with Hot Pineapple Slaw.

Hot Pineapple Slaw: In a medium saucepan cook 1/4 cup thinly sliced green onions and 1/8 teaspoon crushed red pepper in 1 tablespoon cooking oil for 2 minutes. Stir in 2 cups shredded napa cabbage, 1 cup bite-size fresh pineapple pieces, 1/4 cup green sweet pepper cut into thin strips, 1 teaspoon toasted sesame oil, and dash salt. Heat and stir until cabbage is just wilted.

Nutrition Facts per serving: 239 cal., 8 g total fat (1 g sat. fat), 68 mg chol., 557 mg sodium, 12 g carbo., 2 g fiber, 29 g pro. Daily Values: 11% vit. A, 45% vit. C, 6% calcium, 9% iron. Exchanges: 1/2 Vegetable, 1/2 Other Carbo., 4 Very Lean Meat, 1 Fat

TURKEY PLATTER WITH ROASTED TOMATO SALSA

You can find crisp, sweet jicama in the produce section of most supermarkets. Purchase jicama that is very firm with a smooth, tan skin that has no wrinkles or deep pits.

Prep: 15 minutes Grill: 26 minutes
Makes: 6 servings

  12 roma tomatoes, halved lengthwise
    2 tablespoons olive oil
    2 tablespoons balsamic vinegar
    1 to 2 fresh jalapeño chile peppers, chopped (see tip, page 36)
    2 teaspoons snipped fresh rosemary or 1/2 teaspoon dried rosemary, crushed
    1 teaspoon ground cumin
  1/2 teaspoon salt
  1/2 teaspoon black pepper
    3 turkey breast tenderloins (about 1 1/2 pounds total)
    8 cups shredded fresh spinach
    1 small jicama, peeled and cut into matchstick pieces

1 For salsa, brush tomatoes with half of the oil. For a charcoal grill, grill tomatoes on the rack of an uncovered grill directly over medium coals about 10 minutes or until slightly charred, turning once. Cool tomatoes slightly; chop and combine with remaining oil, vinegar, jalapeño(s), and rosemary. Set aside. For rub, combine cumin, salt, and black pepper. Sprinkle over turkey tenderloins; rub in with your fingers.

2 For a charcoal grill, grill turkey on the rack of an uncovered grill directly over medium coals for 16 to 20 minutes or until turkey is no longer pink (170°F), turning once halfway through grilling. (For a gas grill, preheat grill. Reduce heat to medium. Place tomatoes and turkey on grill rack over heat. Cover; grill as above.)

3 Arrange spinach and jicama on a platter; top with salsa. Slice turkey and arrange on salsa.

Nutrition Facts per serving: 236 cal., 7 g total fat (1 g sat. fat), 68 mg chol., 14 g carbo., 3 g fiber, 30 g pro. Daily Values: 104% vit. A, 70% vit. C, 8% calcium, 18% iron. Exchanges: 2 Vegetable, 4 Very Lean Meat, 1 Fat

TURKEY WITH CRANBERRY-DRIED FRUIT CHUTNEY

Prep: 15 minutes Grill: 22 minutes
Makes: 4 servings

- **2 8-ounce turkey breast tenderloins**
- **2 tablespoons olive or cooking oil**
- **1 cup whole berry cranberry sauce**
- **4 teaspoons honey mustard**
- **¹/₂ teaspoon dried rosemary, finely crushed**
- **¹/₄ teaspoon salt**
- **¹/₄ teaspoon black pepper**
- **¹/₂ cup dried apricots, snipped**
- **¹/₂ cup dried Calimyrna figs, snipped**
- **2 tablespoons toasted slivered almonds**

1 Cut turkey tenderloins in half horizontally to make 4 steaks. Lightly brush turkey with oil; set aside.

2 For chutney, in a small bowl combine the cranberry sauce, mustard, rosemary, salt, and pepper. Set aside half of the mixture.

3 In a small bowl combine remaining chutney, apricots, and figs. Fold an 18-inch square of heavy foil in half to make an 18×9-inch rectangle. Mound chutney in center of foil. Bring up two opposite edges of foil and seal with a double fold. Fold remaining edges together to completely enclose fruit, leaving space for steam to build.

4 For a charcoal grill, grill foil packet on the rack of an uncovered grill directly over medium coals for 10 minutes. Remove from grill. Open packet and stir in almonds; cool. Grill turkey on rack for 12 to 15 minutes or until turkey is no longer pink, turning once halfway through grilling and brushing occasionally with the reserved chutney during the last 5 minutes of grilling. (For a gas grill, preheat grill. Reduce heat to medium. Place foil packet and turkey on grill rack over heat. Cover; grill as above.) Slice turkey and serve with chutney.

Nutrition Facts per serving: 422 cal., 11 g total fat (2 g sat. fat), 68 mg chol., 258 mg sodium, 55 g carbo., 6 g fiber, 29 g pro. Daily Values: 13% vit. A, 1% vit. C, 8% calcium, 14% iron. Exchanges: 1 Fruit, 2½ Other Carbo., 4 Very Lean Meat, 1½ Fat

Turkey with Cranberry-Dried Fruit Chutney

PESTO TURKEY PLATTER

Prep: 20 minutes Grill: 16 minutes
Makes: 6 servings

3 turkey breast tenderloins (about 1½ pounds total)
6 small tomatoes, halved lengthwise
Salt and black pepper
½ cup purchased pesto
1 tablespoon olive oil
3 Meyer lemons or lemons, halved
2 avocados, seeded, peeled, and sliced
Fresh basil leaves (optional)

1 Sprinkle turkey and tomatoes with salt and pepper. For a charcoal grill, grill turkey on the rack of an uncovered grill directly over medium coals for 16 to 20 minutes or until turkey is no longer pink (170°F), turning once halfway through grilling and brushing with pesto the last 5 minutes of grilling.

2 Meanwhile, in a large bowl toss tomatoes with oil. Grill, cut sides down, over medium coals about 5 minutes per side until slightly charred. Add lemons, cut sides down, for the last 5 minutes of grilling. (For a gas grill, preheat grill. Reduce heat to medium. Place turkey, tomatoes, and lemons on grill rack. Cover; grill as above.)

3 Slice turkey; arrange on platter with tomatoes, lemons, and avocado slices. Squeeze lemon halves over avocado and tomatoes. If desired, garnish platter with basil.

Nutrition Facts per serving: 401 cal., 25 g total fat (2 g sat. fat), 78 mg chol., 305 mg sodium, 13 g carbo., 5 g fiber, 32 g pro. Daily Values: 16% vit. A, 37% vit. C, 3% calcium, 11% iron. Exchanges: ½ Vegetable, ½ Other Carbo., 4½ Very Lean Meat, 4½ Fat

FOOD FOR THOUGHT
MEYER LEMONS

Frank Meyer first introduced Meyer lemon trees to the United States from China in 1908. Meyer worked for the United States Department of Agriculture. Initially the trees were primarily used for decoration, but in the 1980s, chefs took notice of the fruit's complex flavor and added it to both sweet and savory dishes. Considered a cross between an orange and a lemon, its flavor is sweeter than ordinary lemons, it's slightly less acidic, and both its peel and flesh are edible. Look for Meyer lemons that are firm with an even yellow-orange color.

Pesto Turkey Platter

TURKEY WITH PEPPER SAUCE

Prep: 20 minutes Cook: 10 minutes Grill: 16 minutes
Makes: 4 servings

**2 medium red or yellow sweet
      peppers, chopped**
1/2 cup finely chopped onion (1 medium)
2 tablespoons olive oil or cooking oil
3/4 cup chicken broth
1/4 teaspoon salt
1/4 teaspoon black pepper
2 cloves garlic, minced
**2 turkey breast tenderloins (about
      1 pound total)**
3 cups hot cooked mafalda or fettuccine
2 tablespoons finely shredded fresh basil

1 For sauce, in a large skillet cook sweet peppers and onion in 1 tablespoon of the oil over medium heat about 10 minutes or until vegetables are very tender, stirring occasionally. Transfer to a food processor or blender; add broth, salt, and black pepper. Cover and process or blend until mixture is smooth. Return to skillet; set aside.

2 In a small bowl combine remaining 1 tablespoon oil and garlic. Brush over turkey.

3 For a gas grill, grill turkey on the rack of an uncovered grill directly over medium coals for 16 to 20 minutes or until turkey is no longer pink (170°F). (For a gas grill, preheat grill. Reduce heat to medium. Place turkey on grill rack over heat. Cover; grill as above.)

4 Slice turkey. Reheat sauce. Serve turkey and sauce over pasta. Sprinkle with basil.

Nutrition Facts per serving: 380 cal., 9 g total fat (2 g sat. fat), 68 mg chol., 348 mg sodium, 38 g carbo., 3 g fiber, 34 g pro. Daily Values: 62% vit. A, 153% vit. C, 4% calcium, 17% iron. Exchanges: 1 Vegetable, 2 Starch, 4 Very Lean Meat, 1/2 Fat

TURKEY WITH LEMON-SAGE BUTTER SAUCE

Prep: 20 minutes Cook: 5 minutes Grill: 1 3/4 hours
Stand: 10 minutes Makes: 10 to 12 servings

1/2 cup butter, softened
**3 tablespoons snipped fresh sage or
      2 teaspoons dried sage, crushed**
2 teaspoons finely shredded lemon peel
2 cloves garlic, minced
**1 5- to 6-pound whole turkey breast
      with bone**
2 tablespoons cornstarch
1/4 teaspoon black pepper
**1 14-ounce can reduced-sodium
      chicken broth**
**2 tablespoons dry sherry or dry white
      wine or 1 tablespoon lemon juice**

1 In a food processor or mixer bowl combine butter, sage, lemon peel, and garlic. Process or beat with an electric mixer on medium speed until combined. Divide mixture in half; cover and chill half of the mixture.

2 Starting at the breast bone, slip your fingers between skin and meat to loosen skin, leaving skin attached at the sides to make a pocket. Lift skin and spread half of the butter mixture under skin of turkey. Place turkey on a rack in a shallow roasting pan. Insert a meat thermometer into the thickest part of the breast without touching bone.

3 For a charcoal grill, arrange medium-hot coals around edges of grill. Test for medium heat in center of grill. Place turkey in roasting pan on grill rack in center of grill. Cover; grill for 1 3/4 to 2 1/4 hours or until thermometer registers 170°F. (For a gas grill, preheat grill. Reduce heat to medium. Adjust for indirect cooking. Grill as above.) Remove turkey from grill. Cover with foil; let stand for 10 minutes before slicing.

4 Meanwhile, in a medium saucepan melt remaining butter mixture. Stir in cornstarch and pepper; add chicken broth. Cook and stir over medium-high heat until thickened and bubbly; cook and stir 2 minutes more. Stir in sherry. Serve sauce with sliced turkey.

Nutrition Facts per serving: 399 cal., 23 g total fat (10 g sat. fat), 151 mg chol., 287 mg sodium, 2 g carbo., 0 g fiber, 42 g pro. Daily Values: 8% vit. A, 1% vit. C, 4% calcium, 13% iron. Exchanges: 6 Lean Meat, 1 Fat

JERK-RUBBED TURKEY BREAST

Prep: 30 minutes Grill: 1¼ hours Stand: 10 minutes
Makes: 12 servings

- **1 large red onion, finely chopped (1 cup)**
- **3 cloves garlic, minced**
- **1 fresh jalapeño chile pepper, seeded and finely chopped (see tip, page 36)**
- **1 tablespoon cooking oil**
- **1 teaspoon snipped fresh thyme**
- **½ teaspoon salt**
- **½ teaspoon ground allspice**
- **¼ teaspoon ground nutmeg**
- **⅛ teaspoon ground cloves**
- **¼ cup dark rum**
- **2 tablespoons lime juice**
- **1 4- to 5-pound whole turkey breast with bone, split**
- **Salt and black pepper**

1 In a large skillet cook onion, garlic, and jalapeño pepper in hot oil over medium heat about 4 minutes or until tender. Add thyme, the ½ teaspoon salt, the allspice, nutmeg, and cloves. Cook and stir for 1 minute. Remove from heat; add rum and lime juice. Return to heat and bring to boiling; reduce heat. Simmer, uncovered, for 1 to 2 minutes or until liquid is evaporated. Remove from heat and cool.

2 Starting at the breast bone of each turkey half, slip your fingers between skin and meat to loosen skin, leaving skin attached at the sides to make a pocket. Lift skin and spread onion mixture evenly under skin. Sprinkle each turkey breast half with additional salt and pepper. Insert a meat thermometer into thickest part of a turkey breast half, without touching bone.

3 For a charcoal grill, arrange medium-hot coals around a drip pan. Test for medium heat above pan. Place turkey breast halves, bone sides down, on grill rack over drip pan. Cover; grill for 1¼ to 2 hours or until meat thermometer registers 170°F. (For a gas grill, preheat grill. Reduce heat to medium. Adjust for indirect cooking. Grill as above.) Remove turkey breast halves from grill. Cover with foil; let stand 10 minutes before slicing.

Nutrition Facts per serving: 236 cal., 11 g total fat (3 g sat. fat), 84 mg chol., 203 mg sodium, 2 g carbo., 0 g fiber, 28 g pro. Daily Values: 5% vit. C, 3% calcium, 9% iron. Exchanges: 4 Lean Meat

TURKEY WITH DRIED TOMATO PESTO

Prep: 15 minutes Grill: 1¼ hours Stand: 10 minutes
Makes: 8 servings

- **⅓ cup purchased basil pesto**
- **3 tablespoons chopped, drained oil-packed dried tomatoes**
- **1 2- to 2½-pound turkey breast half with bone**
- **Salt and black pepper**
- **12 ounces dried fettuccine, cooked and drained**

1 In a small bowl stir together pesto and dried tomatoes; set aside. Starting at the breast bone, slip your fingers between skin and meat to loosen skin, leaving skin attached at the side to make a pocket. Lift skin and spoon half the pesto mixture evenly over turkey meat; rub in with your fingers. Fold skin back over meat, covering as much as possible. Sprinkle breast with salt and pepper. Insert a meat thermometer into the thickest part of the turkey breast half, without touching bone.

2 For a charcoal grill, arrange medium-hot coals around a drip pan. Test for medium heat above the pan. Place turkey breast half, bone side down, on grill rack over drip pan. Cover; grill for 1¼ to 2 hours or until meat thermometer registers 170°F. (For a gas grill, preheat grill. Reduce heat to medium. Adjust for indirect cooking. Grill as above.) Remove turkey from grill. Cover with foil; let stand for 10 minutes before slicing.

3 Meanwhile, toss remaining pesto mixture with hot pasta. Slice turkey. Serve with pasta.

Nutrition Facts per serving: 328 cal., 9 g total fat (1 g sat. fat), 50 mg chol., 196 mg sodium, 34 g carbo., 1 g fiber, 26 g pro. Daily Values: 1% vit. A, 4% vit. C, 2% calcium, 12% iron. Exchanges: 2 Starch, 3 Lean Meat

HERBED TURKEY BREAST WITH SWEET ONION AND GARLIC

Quick to cook and easy to carve, a breast portion is the perfect way to enjoy turkey when the whole bird is too much. Thyme and sweet onions add memorable flavor.

Prep: 20 minutes Grill: 1 hour Stand: 10 minutes
Makes: 4 servings

- 1 1½- to 1¾-pound boneless turkey breast portion
- 2 tablespoons olive oil or cooking oil
- 2 tablespoons snipped fresh lemon thyme, or thyme plus 2 teaspoons finely shredded lemon peel
- ¾ teaspoon salt
- ¼ to ½ teaspoon black pepper
- 1 medium sweet onion, cut into thin wedges (1 cup)
- 1 medium red onion, cut into thin wedges (1 cup)
- 3 cloves garlic, cut into thin slivers
- 2 tablespoons white wine vinegar or white balsamic vinegar
- 1 tablespoon honey

1 Brush turkey with 1 tablespoon of the oil. Combine thyme, salt, and pepper. Sprinkle half of the mixture over the turkey breast portion; rub in with your fingers. Insert a meat thermometer into the thickest part of the turkey breast.

2 For a charcoal grill, arrange medium-hot coals around a drip pan. Test for medium heat above the pan. Place turkey on grill rack over drip pan. Cover; grill for 30 minutes. (For a gas grill, preheat grill. Reduce heat to medium. Adjust for indirect cooking. Grill as above.)

3 Meanwhile, fold a 36×18-inch piece of heavy foil in half to make an 18-inch square. In a bowl combine sweet onion, red onion, garlic, vinegar, honey, remaining oil, and remaining herb mixture. Mound vegetable mixture into center of foil. Bring up two opposite edges of foil and seal with a double fold. Fold remaining edges together to completely enclose mixture, leaving space for steam to build. Add to center of grill.

4 Continue to grill for 30 to 45 minutes or until meat thermometer registers 170°F, turning vegetable packet once. Remove turkey and vegetable packet from grill. Cover turkey with foil; let stand for 10 minutes before slicing. Serve turkey with vegetables.

Nutrition Facts per serving: 373 cal., 18 g total fat (4 g sat. fat), 110 mg chol., 515 mg sodium, 12 g carbo., 2 g fiber, 38 g pro. Daily Values: 1% vit. A, 13% vit. C, 6% calcium, 14% iron. Exchanges: ½ Vegetable, ½ Other Carbo., 5 Very Lean Meat, 3 Fat

Herbed Turkey Breast with
Sweet Onion and Garlic

Turkey Fajitas

TURKEY FAJITAS

Pile ingredients onto the tortillas and serve the fajitas ready–made or present the makings on a platter and let diners assemble their own.

Prep: 20 minutes Marinate: 1 hour Grill: 12 minutes
Makes: 4 servings

12 ounces boneless turkey breast
1 cup bottled green taco sauce or
    green salsa (salsa verde)
2 tablespoons olive oil
10 8-inch flour tortillas
1 medium red onion, cut into
    ¹/₂-inch slices
2 medium zucchini and/or yellow
    summer squash, cut lengthwise
    into ¹/₂-inch slices
1 medium red sweet pepper,
    quartered and seeded
    Bottled green taco sauce or green
    salsa (salsa verde)
    Snipped fresh cilantro

1 Cut turkey into ¹/₂-inch slices. Place turkey in a self-sealing plastic bag set in a shallow dish. For marinade, in a small bowl combine the 1 cup taco sauce and the oil. Pour ¹/₂ cup of marinade over turkey; seal bag. Marinate in the refrigerator for 1 hour, turning bag once. Reserve remaining marinade. Stack tortillas and wrap in foil.

2 Drain turkey, discarding marinade. Skewer onion slices with wooden toothpicks, inserting from one edge to the center. Brush onion, squash, and sweet pepper with reserved marinade.

3 For a charcoal grill, grill turkey and vegetables on the rack of an uncovered grill directly over medium coals for 12 to 14 minutes or until turkey is no longer pink (170°F) and vegetables are tender, turning once halfway through grilling. Place tortilla packet on grill for the last 5 minutes of grilling. (For a gas grill, preheat grill. Reduce heat to medium. Place turkey, vegetables, and tortillas on grill over heat. Cover; grill as above.)

4 Cut turkey and vegetables into bite-size strips. On each tortilla arrange turkey, onion, squash, and red pepper; drizzle with taco sauce, sprinkle with cilantro. Fold in sides; roll up tortillas.

Nutrition Facts per serving: 430 cal., 13 g total fat (3 g sat. fat), 53 mg chol., 573 mg sodium, 48 g carbo., 3 g fiber, 27 g pro. Daily Values: 40% vit. A, 108% vit. C, 11% calcium, 21% iron. Exchanges: 1 Vegetable, 2½ Starch, ½ Other Carbo., 2½ Very Lean Meat, 2 Fat

TURKEY WITH TOMATILLO GUACAMOLE

Prep: 15 minutes Grill: 1¼ hours Stand: 10 minutes
Makes: 8 servings

1 **2- to 2½-pound turkey breast
    portion**
2 **teaspoons ground coriander**
½ **teaspoon onion powder**
¼ **teaspoon chili powder**
   Dash cayenne pepper
1 **tablespoon butter or margarine**
1 **tablespoon lemon juice**
1 **recipe Tomatillo Guacamole**

1 Remove skin from turkey. In a small saucepan cook coriander, onion powder, chili powder, and cayenne pepper in hot butter for 1 minute. Remove from heat; stir in lemon juice. Brush over turkey. Insert a meat thermometer into the thickest part of turkey, without touching bone (if present).

2 For a charcoal grill, arrange medium-hot coals around a drip pan. Test for medium heat above the pan. Place turkey on the grill rack over drip pan. Cover; grill for 1¼ to 2 hours or until thermometer registers 170°F. (For a gas grill, preheat grill. Reduce heat to medium. Adjust for indirect cooking. Grill as above.)

3 Remove turkey from grill. Cover with foil; let stand for 10 minutes before slicing. Serve with Tomatillo Guacamole.

Tomatillo Guacamole: In a small bowl stir together ½ of a small avocado, seeded, peeled, and chopped (about ½ cup); 2 canned tomatillos, rinsed, drained, and finely chopped (about ¼ cup); 1 roma tomato, chopped; 1 tablespoon canned diced green chiles; 2 teaspoons lemon juice; and ⅛ teaspoon garlic salt.

Nutrition Facts per serving: 156 cal., 6 g total fat (1 g sat. fat), 50 mg chol., 157 mg sodium, 3 g carbo., 0 g fiber, 22 g pro. Daily Values: 34% vit. A, 5% vit. C, 27% calcium, 1% iron. Exchanges: ½ Vegetable, 3 Very Lean Meat, 1 Fat

SWEET-AND-SPICY TURKEY LEGS

Prep: 20 minutes Grill: 45 minutes
Makes: 6 servings

1 **teaspoon onion salt**
½ **teaspoon garlic salt**
½ **teaspoon black pepper**
¼ **teaspoon cayenne pepper**
¼ **teaspoon dry mustard**
¼ **teaspoon ground allspice**
⅛ **teaspoon ground cloves**
6 **turkey drumsticks (5½ to
    6 pounds total)**
2 **tablespoons olive oil**
½ **cup jalapeño pepper jelly**

1 For rub, in a small bowl combine onion salt, garlic salt, black pepper, cayenne pepper, mustard, allspice, and cloves. Brush drumsticks with oil. Sprinkle with rub; rub in with fingers. In a small saucepan, heat pepper jelly until melted.

2 For a charcoal grill, arrange medium-hot coals around a drip pan. Test for medium heat above the pan. Place drumsticks on grill rack over drip pan. Cover; grill for 45 minutes to 1¼ hours or until turkey is no longer pink (180°F), turning occasionally and brushing with pepper jelly during the last 10 minutes of grilling. (For a gas grill, preheat grill. Reduce heat to medium. Adjust for indirect cooking. Grill as above.)

Nutrition Facts per serving: 478 cal., 15 g total fat (4 g sat. fat), 277 mg chol., 520 mg sodium, 18 g carbo., 0 g fiber, 65 g pro. Daily Values: 1% vit. A, 1% vit. C, 5% calcium, 30% iron. Exchanges: 1 Other Carbo., 9 Very Lean Meat, 2 Fat

FOOD FOR THOUGHT TOMATILLO

Mexican for "little tomato," a tomatillo looks like a small green tomato in a light brown, parchmentlike husk. Cooked or uncooked, the tomatillo imparts a delicate, slightly tart flavor to sauces and salsas. Although yellow when ripe, the fruit is typically used when it's still green and slightly firm. Be sure to choose fruit with a tight-fitting husk and firm flesh. Remove the husk before using and wash the vegetable to remove any residue. Store tomatillos in a paper bag in the refrigerator for up to 1 month.

TAHINI TURKEY THIGHS

Prep: 45 minutes Grill: 50 minutes
Makes: 6 servings

- 4 **turkey thighs (3½ to 4 pounds total)**
- ½ **cup tahini (sesame seed paste)**
- ¼ **cup water**
- 2 **tablespoons soy sauce**
- 1 **tablespoon lemon juice**
- 1 **tablespoon honey**
- 1 **tablespoon Asian chili garlic sauce**
- 1 **teaspoon grated fresh ginger**
- 1 **recipe Chickpea Salad**

1 If desired, remove skin from turkey. For sauce, in a medium bowl whisk together tahini, water, soy sauce, lemon juice, honey, chili garlic sauce, and ginger until combined; set aside.

2 For a charcoal grill, arrange medium-hot coals around a drip pan. Test for medium heat above pan. Place turkey thighs, bone sides up, on grill rack over pan. Cover; grill for 50 to 60 minutes or until turkey is no longer pink (180°F), turning once halfway through grilling and brushing frequently with sauce during the last 20 minutes of grilling. (For a gas grill, preheat grill. Reduce heat to medium. Adjust for indirect cooking. Grill as above.) Discard remaining sauce.

3 Cut turkey meat from bones. Serve with Chickpea Salad.

Chickpea Salad: In a small screwtop jar combine 3 tablespoons olive oil, 3 tablespoons lemon juice, ¼ teaspoon salt, and ⅛ teaspoon black pepper. Cover and shake well. Rinse and drain two 15-ounce cans garbanzo beans (chickpeas). In a large bowl combine the beans; ¾ cup finely chopped yellow or red sweet pepper; ⅔ cup snipped fresh parsley; ½ cup finely chopped, seeded cucumber; ⅓ cup snipped fresh mint; 2 roma tomatoes, seeded and chopped; and ¼ cup finely chopped red onion. Add dressing; toss to combine. Cover and chill until ready to serve.

Nutrition Facts per serving: 600 cal., 32 g total fat (6 g sat. fat), 119 mg chol., 985 mg sodium, 34 g carbo., 8 g fiber, 44 g pro. Daily Values: 13% vit. A, 135% vit. C, 14% calcium, 36% iron. Exchanges: 1½ Starch, ½ Other Carbo., 6 Medium-Fat Meat

ALOHA TURKEY THIGHS

Prep: 30 minutes Grill: 50 minutes Makes: 4 servings

- ¾ **cup pineapple juice**
- 2 **tablespoons honey**
- 1 **tablespoon Dijon-style mustard**
- 1 **tablespoon soy sauce**
- 1½ **teaspoons cornstarch**
- 1 **clove garlic, minced**
- 2 **turkey thighs (about 2 pounds total)**
- 1 **recipe Hawaiian Noodles**

1 For sauce, in a small saucepan combine pineapple juice, honey, mustard, soy sauce, cornstarch, and garlic. Cook and stir over medium heat until thickened and bubbly. Cook and stir for 1 minute more. Remove from heat. Transfer half of the sauce to a bowl; cover and set aside. If desired, remove skin from turkey. Sprinkle turkey with salt and pepper.

2 For a charcoal grill, arrange medium-hot coals around a drip pan. Test for medium heat above the pan. Place turkey, bone sides down, on grill rack over drip pan. Cover; grill for 50 to 60 minutes or until turkey is no longer pink (180°F), brushing turkey frequently with sauce during the last 20 minutes of grilling. (For a gas grill, preheat grill. Reduce heat to medium. Adjust for indirect cooking. Grill as above.)

3 Cut meat from bones. Serve with reserved sauce and Hawaiian Noodles.

Hawaiian Noodles: Cook one 3-ounce package broken ramen noodles according to directions (omit spice packet). Rinse with cold water; drain. For dressing, in a screw-top jar combine 2 tablespoons lime juice; 1 tablespoon salad oil; 2 teaspoons toasted sesame oil; 1 fresh jalapeño chile pepper, seeded and finely chopped (see tip, page 36); 2 teaspoons finely chopped crystallized ginger; and ¼ teaspoon salt. Cover; shake well. Combine noodles; dressing; one 8-ounce can crushed pineapple, drained; ½ cup finely chopped red sweet pepper; 4 green onions, thinly sliced; and ¼ cup chopped toasted macadamia nuts. Toss.

Nutrition Facts per serving: 533 cal., 22 g total fat (4 g sat. fat), 151 mg chol., 584 mg sodium, 44 g carbo., 2 g fiber, 40 g pro. Daily Values: 23% vit. A, 89% vit. C, 7% calcium, 23% iron. Exchanges: 2 Starch, ½ Fruit, ½ Other Carbo., 4½ Lean Meat, 1 Fat

Tahini Turkey Thighs

FOOD FOR THOUGHT TAHINI

Tahini is a sesame seed paste that's similar to natural peanut butter. Nutritionally, it's high in fat, but it's also a good source of protein and calcium. It's traditionally used in Middle Eastern cuisine as a flavoring ingredient.

NEW ENGLAND GRILLED TURKEY

Due to the large amount of turkey drippings, you may prefer to omit the drip pan and place the turkey on a rack in a roasting pan.

Prep: 40 minutes Cook: 20 minutes
Marinate: 12 to 24 hours Grill: 2½ hours Stand: 15 minutes
Makes: 8 to 12 servings

- 1 8- to 10-pound whole turkey
- 4 cups hot water
- 1¼ cups kosher salt
- 1 cup pure maple syrup
- 1 6-ounce can apple juice concentrate, thawed
- 3 cloves garlic, crushed
- 4 whole cloves
- ¼ teaspoon whole black peppercorns
- 16 cups cold water
- ½ cup butter, softened
- 1 teaspoon ground sage
- 1 recipe Gingered Cranberry Sauce

1 Thaw turkey, if frozen. For brine, in a deep pot combine hot water, salt, maple syrup, and juice concentrate. Stir until salt dissolves. Add garlic, cloves, peppercorns, and cold water.

2 Remove the neck and giblets from turkey. Add turkey to brine; weight it to keep it covered. Cover and brine in the refrigerator overnight. Drain turkey and pat dry. In a small bowl combine butter and sage; set aside. Starting at the neck on one side of the breast, slip your fingers between skin and meat, loosening the skin as you work toward the tail end. Once your entire hand is under the skin, free the skin around thigh and leg area up to, but not around, the tip of the drumstick. Repeat on other side of the breast. Rub sage butter under the skin directly on meat. Skewer the neck skin to the back. Twist wing tips behind back. Sprinkle surface and cavity of turkey with salt and pepper. Tuck drumsticks under band of skin or tie to tail. If desired, insert a meat thermometer into the center of an inside thigh muscle.

3 For a charcoal grill, arrange medium-hot coals around a drip pan. Test for medium heat above the pan. Place turkey on grill rack over the drip pan. Cover; grill for 2½ to 3 hours or until thermometer registers 180°F and turkey is no longer pink, adding fresh coals every 45 to 60 minutes and cutting band of skin or string the last hour of grilling. (For a gas grill, preheat grill. Reduce heat to medium. Adjust for indirect cooking. Grill as above.)

4 Remove turkey from grill. Cover with foil; let stand for 15 minutes before carving. Serve with Gingered Cranberry Sauce.

Gingered Cranberry Sauce: In a medium saucepan combine 1 cup sugar and 1 cup water. Bring to boiling, stirring to dissolve sugar. Boil rapidly for 5 minutes. Add 2 cups fresh cranberries, ½ cup snipped dried apples, 1½ teaspoons grated fresh ginger, and 1 teaspoon finely shredded lemon peel. Return to boiling; reduce heat. Boil gently, uncovered, over medium heat for 3 to 4 minutes or until skins pop, stirring occasionally. Remove from heat. Serve warm or chilled.

Nutrition Facts per serving: 676 cal., 26 g total fat (11 g sat. fat), 308 mg chol., 1,223 mg sodium, 31 g carbo., 2 g fiber, 76 g pro. Daily Values: 10% vit. A, 7% vit. C, 7% calcium, 27% iron. Exchanges: 1 Fruit, 1 Other Carbo., 10 Lean Meat

SMOKIN' HOT TIP

Turkey is wonderful all year long, not only during the holiday season. For something new, follow these guidelines for turkey on the grill:

● **Grill only unstuffed birds. The center of a stuffing may not reach the safe temperature of 165°F by the time the bird is done.**

● **For best results, select a turkey that's less than 16 pounds; bigger birds may be too large for some grills and are difficult to remove from the grill.**

● **A turkey is done when a meat thermometer inserted in the center of an inside thigh muscle registers 180°F.**

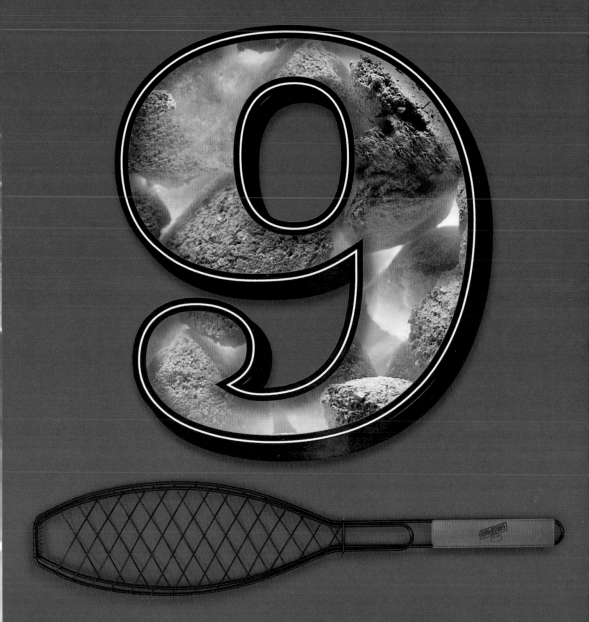

Fish
& Shellfish

Cajun Fish Soup

CAJUN FISH SOUP

This light soup is just right for a hot summer evening. Cool mango complements the soup.

Start to Finish: 35 minutes
Makes: 4 servings

- **12 ounces fresh or frozen skinless cod or haddock fillets**
- **8 ounces fresh or frozen peeled and deveined medium shrimp**
- **1 tablespoon Cajun seasoning**
- **3 14-ounce cans reduced-sodium chicken broth**
- **2 teaspoons finely shredded lime peel**
- **1 tablespoon lime juice**
- **1 tablespoon soy sauce**
- **Few dashes bottled hot pepper sauce (optional)**
- **½ cup thinly sliced green onions (4)**
- **¼ cup cilantro leaves, snipped**
- **1 medium fresh mango, chopped**
- **Cilantro leaves**

1 Thaw fish and shrimp, if frozen. Rinse; pat dry with paper towels. Place shrimp in a small bowl. Sprinkle half of the Cajun seasoning evenly over fish; rub in with your fingers. Sprinkle remaining seasoning over shrimp; toss to coat. Thread shrimp onto four 10- to 12-inch metal skewers, leaving a ¼-inch space between pieces.

2 Lightly grease or coat with nonstick cooking spray an unheated grill rack. For a charcoal grill, grill fish on the greased rack of an uncovered grill directly over medium coals for 4 to 6 minutes per ½-inch thickness of fish or until fish flakes easily when tested with a fork, turning once. Grill shrimp for 5 to 8 minutes or until shrimp turn opaque, turning once. (For a gas grill, preheat grill. Reduce heat to medium. Place fish and shrimp on greased grill rack over heat. Cover; grill as above.) When done, flake fish into bite-size pieces; remove shrimp from skewers.

3 Meanwhile, in a large saucepan stir together broth, lime peel, lime juice, soy sauce, and, if desired, hot pepper sauce. Bring to boiling; reduce heat. Stir in fish, shrimp, green onions, and cilantro; heat through.

4 To serve, ladle soup into bowls. Garnish each serving with mango and cilantro leaves.

Nutrition Facts per serving: 216 cal., 4 g total fat (1 g sat. fat), 122 mg chol., 1,744 mg sodium, 14 g carbo., 2 g fiber, 31 g pro. Daily Values: 50% vit. A, 39% vit. C, 8% calcium, 13% iron. Exchanges: ½ Fruit, ½ Other Carbo., 4½ Very Lean Meat

CATFISH IN CORN HUSKS

By sealing in moisture the corn husks keep the catfish juicy. They also impart a hint of toasted corn flavor.

Prep: 20 minutes Grill: 20 minutes
Makes: 4 servings

4 6-ounce fresh or frozen catfish fillets
4 ears corn with husks
Salt
Freshly ground black pepper
½ cup thinly sliced green onions (4)
¼ cup chopped red sweet pepper
4 teaspoons drained capers
4 tablespoons butter or margarine
4 sprigs fresh thyme
Fresh lime wedges (optional)

1 Thaw catfish, if frozen. rinse; pat dry with paper towels. Peel back the husks from the corn and remove the silks. Break off the cobs at the base, leaving husks attached to stem. Cut the kernels off two of the ears (should yield 1 cup); set aside remaining corn for another use.

2 Fold back part of each corn husk; place a catfish fillet in each. Season lightly with salt and black pepper. Top each fillet with one-fourth of the corn kernels, the green onions, sweet pepper, capers, and butter; top with a thyme sprig. Fold remaining husks over fish. Tie each husk together at the ends with 100-percent-cotton string.

3 For a charcoal grill, arrange medium-hot coals around the edges of grill. Test for medium heat in center of grill. Place fillets in corn husks on grill rack in center of grill. Cover; grill about 20 minutes or until fish flakes easily when tested with a fork.* (For a gas grill preheat grill. Reduce heat to medium. Adjust for indirect cooking. Grill as above.) To serve, remove string; fold back the corn husks. If desired, serve with lime wedges.

*Note: To test for doneness carefully push aside the husk of one of the catfish packages with a fork to test center of fish.

Nutrition Facts per serving: 422 cal., 26 g total fat (9 g sat. fat), 112 mg chol., 350 mg sodium, 19 g carbo., 3 g fiber, 30 g pro. Daily Values: 22% vit. A, 47% vit. C, 3% calcium, 9% iron. Exchanges: 1 Starch, 4 Lean Meat, 2½ Fat

CILANTRO-LIME TROUT

A fish that is "dressed" has had its gills, innards, and scales removed. A good fishmonger can prepare fish for any manner of cooking.

Prep: 10 minutes Grill: 6 minutes
Makes: 4 servings

4 8- to 10-ounce fresh or frozen
dressed trout, heads removed
3 tablespoons lime juice
2 tablespoons olive oil
2 tablespoons snipped fresh cilantro
or parsley
½ teaspoon salt
¼ teaspoon cracked black pepper
Lime wedges

1 Thaw trout, if frozen. Rinse trout; pat dry with paper towels. In a small bowl combine lime juice and oil. Brush the inside and outside of each trout with juice mixture. Sprinkle cilantro, salt, and pepper evenly inside the cavity of each fish.

2 Place trout in a well-greased grill basket. Place trout on the rack of the grill directly over medium coals. Grill for 6 to 9 minutes or until trout flakes easily when tested with a fork, turning basket once halfway through grilling. (For a gas grill, preheat grill. Reduce heat to medium. Place fish in a well-greased grill basket. Place grill basket on grill rack over heat. Cover; grill as above.) Serve trout with lime wedges.

Nutrition Facts per serving: 378 cal., 19 g total fat (4 g sat. fat), 133 mg chol., 372 mg sodium, 2 g carbo., 0 g fiber, 47 g pro. Daily Values: 15% vit. A, 20% vit. C, 16% calcium, 4% iron. Exchanges: 7 Very Lean Meat, 3 Fat

HERB-STUFFED TROUT WITH VEGETABLE KABOBS

When herbs are abundant in the summer months, who can resist using them on everything? Here you can take your pick of fresh rosemary, oregano, or sage to pair with basil.

Prep: 25 minutes Grill: 14 minutes
Makes: 4 servings

- **4 10- to 12-ounce fresh or frozen dressed trout, or coho salmon (scaled, with head and tail intact)**
- **$1/8$ teaspoon salt**
- **$1/8$ teaspoon ground black pepper**
- **1 small lemon or lime, halved and thinly sliced**
- **$1/4$ cup packed fresh basil leaves**
- **16 to 20 branches fresh rosemary, oregano, and/or sage**
- **2 zucchini and/or yellow summer squash, cut into $3/4$-inch pieces**
- **1 medium sweet onion, cut into 8 wedges**
- **8 large fresh mushrooms**
- **$1/4$ cup olive oil**
- **1 tablespoon snipped fresh rosemary**

1 Thaw fish, if frozen. Rinse fish; pat dry with paper towels. Sprinkle cavity and outside of each fish evenly with salt and pepper. Place one-fourth of the lemon slices and basil leaves in the cavity of each fish. Lay some herb branches over each fish; secure the branches to the fish in three places with 100-percent-cotton string.

2 Thread zucchini pieces and onion wedges onto four 8-inch metal skewers. Cook vegetable kabobs in a small amount of boiling water in a covered $4^{1}/_{2}$-quart Dutch oven for 5 minutes. With tongs, carefully remove the kabobs from the water; place on a platter. Add a mushroom to the end of each skewer.

3 In a small bowl combine oil and the 1 tablespoon snipped rosemary. Brush fish bundles and vegetables lightly with oil mixture.

4 For a charcoal grill, grill fish on the rack of an uncovered grill directly over medium coals about 14 minutes or until fish flakes easily when tested with a fork, turning halfway through grilling. Place vegetable kabobs on grill rack directly over coals for the last 6 minutes of grilling, turning kabobs once. (For a gas grill, preheat grill. Reduce heat to medium. Place fish and vegetable kabobs on grill rack over heat. Cover; grill as above.)

5 To serve, snip strings and discard herbs from fish. Serve whole or remove heads and tails. Serve with vegetable kabobs.

Nutrition Facts per serving: 555 cal., 30 g total fat (6 g sat. fat), 167 mg chol., 186 mg sodium, 11 g carbo., 3 g fiber, 62 g pro. Daily Values: 22% vit. A, 78% vit. C, 24% calcium, 10% iron. Exchanges: $1^{1}/_{2}$ Vegetable, $8^{1}/_{2}$ Very Lean Meat, 5 Fat

FOOD FOR THOUGHT
PAN-DRESSED FISH

A "dressed" fish is a whole fish that has been scaled, gutted, and has had its gills removed. A "pan-dressed" fish has been prepared in the same way and also has had its head, tail, and fins removed.

Trout with Mushroom Stuffing

1 At least 1 hour before grilling, soak wood chips or chunks and several wooden toothpicks in enough water to cover.

2 Thaw fish, if frozen. Rinse fish; pat dry with paper towels. Set fish aside. For stuffing, in a large skillet cook bacon over medium heat for 3 to 4 minutes or until softened and beginning to brown. Add mushrooms; cook for 5 to 8 minutes or until mushrooms are tender and most of liquid has evaporated, stirring occasionally. Set aside.

3 Meanwhile, brush the outside and cavity of each fish with melted butter. For each fish, sprinkle the cavity with salt, pepper, and garlic slices. Add one-fourth of the mushroom mixture and 2 thyme sprigs. Sprinkle stuffing with 1 tablespoon of the wine. Secure stuffing inside fish with 4 or 5 short metal skewers or soaked toothpicks. Place fish on a sheet of heavy-duty foil. Drain wood chips or chunks.

4 For a charcoal grill, arrange medium-hot coals around a drip pan. Test for medium heat above the drip pan. Add drained wood chips or chunks to coals. Place foil with fish on grill rack over drip pan. Cover; grill for 20 to 25 minutes or until fish flakes easily when tested with a fork. (For a gas grill, preheat grill. Reduce heat to medium. Adjust for indirect cooking. Add wood chips or chunks according to manufacturer's directions. Grill as above.) If desired, serve fish with Grilled Apple Slices.

TROUT WITH MUSHROOM STUFFING

Wild mushrooms and bacon create a savory stuffing. Grilled apples, although not a must, provide a sweet accompaniment.

Prep: 25 minutes Cook: 8 minutes Grill: 20 minutes
Makes: 4 servings

- **1 cup apple or alder wood chips or chunks**
- **4 10- to 12-ounce fresh or frozen dressed trout**
- **4 slices bacon, chopped**
- **2 cups sliced fresh assorted wild mushrooms (such as cremini, shiitake, chanterelle, oyster, porcini, and/or cèpes)**
- **3 tablespoons butter, melted**
- **1/2 teaspoon salt**
- **1/2 teaspoon coarsely ground black pepper**
- **3 large cloves garlic, thinly sliced**
- **8 sprigs fresh thyme**
- **1/4 cup dry white wine**
- **Grilled Apple Slices (optional)**

Nutrition Facts per serving: 316 cal., 19 g total fat (7 g sat. fat), 89 mg chol., 556 mg sodium, 12 g carbo., 2 g fiber, 24 g pro. Daily Values: 4% vit. A, 24% vit. C, 6% calcium, 12% iron. Exchanges: 1/2 Vegetable, 1/2 Other Carbo., 3 Very Lean Meat, 4 Fat

Grilled Apple Slices: Remove the core from 2 apples. Cut apples crosswise into 1/2-inch slices; brush with olive oil. Grill apple slices directly over medium heat for 5 to 6 minutes or until apples are tender, turning once. Serve warm apple slices with fish.

STACKED ASIAN-STYLE GROUPER

Egg roll wrappers are fried and layered with fish, tomatoes, and avocados. The finished dish is drizzled with wasabi-spiked mayonnaise.

Prep: 30 minutes Marinate: 30 to 60 minutes
Grill: 4 minutes per ½-inch thickness
Makes: 4 servings

4 4- to 6-ounce fresh or frozen grouper, red snapper, or orange roughy fillets, ½ to 1 inch thick
2 tablespoons rice vinegar
2 tablespoons soy sauce
1 tablespoon minced garlic
¼ teaspoon ground ginger
¼ cup mayonnaise
½ teaspoon wasabi paste
4 egg roll wrappers
   Cooking oil
2 medium tomatoes, sliced
1 medium avocado, peeled, seeded, and cut into ¼-inch slices
2 teaspoons toasted sesame oil
1 teaspoon toasted sesame seeds (optional)
   Sliced green onions (optional)

1 Thaw fish, if frozen. Rinse fish; pat dry with paper towels. Place fish in a self-sealing plastic bag set in a shallow dish. For marinade, in a small bowl combine vinegar, soy sauce, garlic, and ginger. Pour marinade over fish in bag. Seal bag. Marinate in refrigerator 30 minutes to 1 hour, turning bag occasionally.

2 In a small self-sealing plastic bag combine mayonnaise and wasabi paste. Seal bag and chill until ready to use.

3 Meanwhile, in a large skillet fry egg roll wrappers one at a time in ½ inch of hot oil for 30 to 45 seconds or until golden, turning once. Remove from oil. Drain on paper towels. Remove fish from marinade; discard marinade. Place fish fillets in a well-greased grill basket, tucking under any thin edges.

4 For a charcoal grill, grill fish on the rack of an uncovered grill directly over medium coals for 4 to 6 minutes per ½-inch thickness or until fish flakes easily when tested with a fork, turning basket once halfway through grilling. (For a gas grill, preheat grill. Reduce heat to medium. Place fish on grill rack over heat. Cover; grill as above.)

5 To assemble, for each serving, place an egg roll wrapper on a plate. Top with one-fourth of the tomato slices. Place a fish fillet on top of tomatoes. Top with one-fourth of the avocado slices. Cut a small hole in the corner of the plastic bag containing mayonnaise mixture; drizzle some over all. Drizzle with ½ teaspoon of the sesame oil. If desired, sprinkle with ¼ teaspoon sesame seeds and green onions. Repeat for each serving.

Nutrition Facts per serving: 448 cal., 26 g total fat (4 g sat. fat), 50 mg chol., 787 mg sodium, 25 g carbo., 3 g fiber, 28 g pro. Daily Values: 12% vit. A, 19% vit. C, 6% calcium, 16% iron. Exchanges: 1½ Other Carbo., 3½ Very Lean Meat, 4½ Fat

Stacked Asian-Style Grouper

TILAPIA WITH ORANGE-PECAN SAUCE

Pecans are pan-toasted in butter until golden and combined with oranges and orange juice for a delightfully crunchy sauce.

Prep: 25 minutes Cook: 3 minutes
Grill: 4 minutes per $\frac{1}{2}$-inch thickness
Makes: 4 servings

**4 4-ounce fresh or frozen tilapia
    or orange roughy fillets,
    $\frac{3}{4}$ inch thick
$\frac{1}{2}$ cup parsley, finely chopped
4 teaspoons finely shredded
    orange peel
1 clove garlic, minced
1 tablespoon vegetable oil
$\frac{1}{3}$ cup pecan pieces
2 tablespoons butter
2 medium oranges, peeled and sectioned
$\frac{1}{3}$ cup orange juice**

1 Thaw fish, if frozen. Rinse fish; pat dry with paper towels.

2 In a bowl stir together parsley, orange peel, garlic, and $\frac{1}{4}$ teaspoon salt. Divide parsley mixture in half. Set half of parsley mixture aside. To the remaining half, add the oil; spread mixture over fish fillets. Place fish, parsley side up, in a well-greased grill basket, tucking under any thin edges.

3 For a charcoal grill, grill fish on the rack of an uncovered grill directly over medium coals for 4 to 6 minutes per $\frac{1}{2}$-inch thickness of fish or until fish flakes easily when tested with a fork, turning basket once halfway through grilling. (For a gas grill, preheat grill. Reduce heat to medium. Place fish on grill rack over heat. Cover; grill as above.)

4 For sauce, in a medium skillet cook pecans in hot butter about 3 minutes or until golden; remove from heat. Stir in orange sections and orange juice; return to heat. Cook and gently stir until sauce is heated through. Gently stir in reserved parsley mixture.

5 To serve, place fish on a platter; spoon sauce over fish.

Nutrition Facts per serving: 281 cal., 19 g total fat (5 g sat. fat), 16 mg chol., 266 mg sodium, 9 g carbo., 2 g fiber, 20 g pro. Daily Values: 16% vit. A, 67% vit. C, 7% calcium, 11% iron. Exchanges: $\frac{1}{2}$ Fruit, 3 Very Lean Meat, 3 Fat

RED SNAPPER AND VEGETABLES

Cook the potatoes ahead of time, and this snappy fish packet comes together in minutes.

Prep: 20 minutes Cook: 5 minutes Grill: 20 minutes
Makes: 4 servings

**4 6-ounce fresh or frozen red
    snapper fillets (with skin),
    $\frac{1}{2}$ to $\frac{3}{4}$ inch thick
12 ounces whole tiny new potatoes,
    Yukon gold potatoes, or purple
    potatoes, quartered
2 cups broccoli florets
$\frac{1}{3}$ cup purchased pesto
    Additional pesto (optional)**

1 Thaw fish, if frozen. Rinse fish; pat dry with paper towels. If desired, remove and discard skin; set fish aside.

2 In a microwave-safe medium bowl cook potatoes, covered, on 100 percent power (high) for 5 to 7 minutes or until nearly tender, stirring once. Add broccoli and half of the pesto; toss to coat.

3 Tear off four 12-inch squares of heavy-duty foil. Divide vegetable mixture evenly among foil, placing in the center of each square. Top each with a fish fillet, tucking under any thin edges. Spoon remaining pesto over fish. Bring up two opposite edges of foil; seal with a double fold. Fold remaining edges together to enclose mixture, leaving space for steam to build.

4 For a charcoal grill, grill packets on the rack of an uncovered grill directly over medium coals for 20 to 25 minutes or until fish flakes easily when tested with a fork (carefully open one packet to check for fish doneness). (For a gas grill, preheat grill. Reduce heat to medium. Place packets on grill rack over heat. Cover; grill as above.) If desired, serve with additional pesto.

Nutrition Facts per serving: 375 cal., 16 g total fat (0 g sat. fat), 45 mg chol., 174 mg sodium, 21 g carbo., 3 g fiber, 40 g pro. Daily Values: 6% vit. A, 78% vit. C, 6% calcium, 14% iron. Exchanges: 1 Vegetable, 1 Starch, 5 Very Lean Meat, 2 Fat

BLACKENED SNAPPER WITH ROASTED POTATOES

Prep: 20 minutes Grill: 35 minutes
Makes: 4 servings

4 4- to 5-ounce fresh or frozen red
    snapper or catfish fillets, $\frac{1}{2}$ to
    1 inch thick
$\frac{1}{2}$ teaspoon Cajun seasoning
    Nonstick cooking spray
1 tablespoon olive oil
$\frac{1}{4}$ teaspoon salt
    Several dashes bottled hot pepper
    sauce
$1\frac{1}{2}$ pounds tiny new potatoes,
    thinly sliced
4 medium carrots, thinly sliced
1 medium green sweet pepper,
    cut into thin strips
1 medium onion, sliced
1 tablespoon snipped fresh chervil
    or parsley

1 Thaw fish, if frozen. Rinse fish; pat dry with paper towels. Measure thickness of fish. Sprinkle both sides of fish evenly with Cajun seasoning and lightly coat with nonstick cooking spray. Place fish in a well-greased wire grill basket. Cover and chill until needed.

2 Tear a 48×18-inch piece of heavy-duty foil; fold in half to make a 24×18-inch rectangle. In a large bowl combine oil, salt, and pepper sauce. Add the potatoes, carrots, sweet pepper, and onion; toss to coat. Place in the center of foil. Bring up two opposite edges of foil; seal with a double fold. Fold remaining edges to completely enclose the vegetables, leaving space for steam to build.

3 For a charcoal grill, grill packet on the rack of an uncovered grill directly over medium coals for 35 to 40 minutes or until potatoes and carrots are tender. (For a gas grill, preheat grill. Reduce heat to medium. Place vegetables on grill rack over heat. Cover; grill as above.)

4 For a charcoal grill, place grill basket on the grill rack next to the vegetables. Grill fish in basket on the rack of an uncovered grill directly over medium coals for 4 to 6 minutes per $\frac{1}{2}$-inch thickness or until fish flakes easily when tested with a fork, turning the basket once. (For a gas grill, preheat grill. Reduce heat to medium. Place grill basket on the grill rack next to vegetables. Cover; grill as above.) To serve, sprinkle fish and vegetables with snipped chervil.

Nutrition Facts per serving: 352 cal., 6 g total fat (1 g sat. fat), 42 mg chol., 266 mg sodium, 48 g carbo., 5 g fiber, 28 g pro. Daily Values: 173% vit. A, 63% vit. C, 7% calcium, 24% iron. Exchanges: 1 Vegetable, 2 Starch, $3\frac{1}{2}$ Lean Meat

SEA BASS WITH FENNEL SLAW

Fennel bulb is cut into strips to make a slaw and fennel seeds are used to season the fish.

Prep: 40 minutes Chill: 2 to 24 hours
Grill: 4 minutes per $\frac{1}{2}$-inch thickness Makes: 4 servings

3 tablespoons white wine vinegar
1 tablespoon olive oil
2 teaspoons snipped fresh tarragon
1 teaspoon Dijon-style mustard
3 fennel bulbs, thinly sliced and cut
    into thin strips (4 cups)
1 cup purchased shredded carrots
4 4- to 5-ounce fresh or frozen sea
    bass or grouper fillets,
    $\frac{3}{4}$ to 1 inch thick
1 teaspoon fennel seeds, crushed

1 For slaw, in a screw-top jar combine vinegar, oil, tarragon, mustard, $\frac{1}{8}$ teaspoon salt, and dash black pepper. Cover and shake well. Reserve 1 tablespoon of the vinaigrette; cover and chill until serving time. In a large bowl combine fennel strips and carrots. Pour remaining vinaigrette over fennel mixture. Toss lightly to coat. Cover and chill 2 to 24 hours.

2 Thaw fish, if frozen. Rinse fish, pat dry with paper towels. Measure thickness of fish. In a bowl stir together crushed fennel seeds, $\frac{1}{2}$ teaspoon salt, and $\frac{1}{4}$ teaspoon black pepper. Sprinkle evenly over both sides of fish. Place fish in a well-greased grill basket or in a greased grill wok.

3 For a charcoal grill, grill fish on the rack of an uncovered grill directly over medium coals for 4 to 6 minutes per $\frac{1}{2}$-inch thickness of fish or until fish flakes easily when tested with a fork, turning basket once or carefully turning fish once halfway through grilling. (For a gas grill, preheat grill.

Reduce heat to medium. Place basket or wok on grill rack over heat. Cover; grill as above.) Drizzle reserved 1 tablespoon vinaigrette over grilled fish. Serve fish with slaw.

Nutrition Facts per serving: 213 cal., 6 g total fat (1 g sat. fat), 58 mg chol., 557 mg sodium, 10 g carbo., 24 g fiber, 28 g pro. Daily Values: 78% vit. A, 21% vit. C, 8% calcium, 4% iron. Exchanges: 1½ Vegetable, 3½ Very Lean Meat, 1 Fat

PLANK-SMOKED SEA BASS

Prep: 30 minutes Grill: 15 minutes
Makes: 4 servings

- 1 12×6×¾-inch cedar or alder grill plank
- 1 19-ounce can cannellini beans, rinsed and drained
- 2 medium roma tomatoes, seeded and chopped
- 2 tablespoons white balsamic vinegar
- 2 tablespoons olive oil
- 4 6-ounce sea bass steaks, ¾ to 1 inch thick
- 1 tablespoon lemon juice
- 2 teaspoons ground coriander
- ¼ teaspoon salt
- ¼ teaspoon black pepper
- 1 cup fresh whole cremini mushrooms
- 1 medium shallot, halved

1 At least 1 hour before grilling, soak plank in enough water to cover, weighting it to keep it submerged.

2 Combine beans, tomatoes, vinegar, and 1 tablespoon of the olive oil; cover, set aside. Brush sea bass steaks with lemon juice. In a small bowl combine coriander, ¼ teaspoon salt, and ¼ teaspoon black pepper; sprinkle evenly over fish. Thread mushrooms and shallot halves on 2 long metal skewers. Brush with remaining 1 tablespoon oil.

3 For a charcoal grill, place plank on grill rack of an uncovered grill directly over medium coals about 5 minutes or until plank begins to crackle and smoke. Place sea bass on plank. Place skewers on grill rack over medium heat. Cover; grill sea bass for 15 minutes or until fish flakes easily when tested with a fork. Grill vegetables about 10 minutes or until tender, turning once during grilling. (For a gas grill, preheat grill. Reduce to medium. Grill as above.)

4 Transfer fish to serving platter; keep warm. Remove vegetables from grill. When cool enough to handle, chop mushrooms and shallot; stir into bean mixture. Season to taste with salt and pepper. Serve fish with bean mixture.

Nutrition Facts per serving: 317 cal., 11 g total fat (2 g sat. fat), 69 mg chol., 504 mg sodium, 21 g carbo., 6 g fiber, 39 g pro. Daily Values: 14% vit. A, 13% vit. C, 6% calcium, 12% iron. Exchanges: ½ Vegetable, 1 Starch, 5 Very Lean Meat, 1 Fat

SMOKIN' HOT TIP

It's hard to know just how fresh the fish at your supermarket is and how it has been handled since it was first caught. Here are a few things to look for when buying whole fish, fillets, and frozen fish:

Whole fish
- Bright, shiny skin with a slick, transparent film or mucus
- Scales that are intact and adhere tightly to the skin
- Firm flesh that doesn't leave an imprint when pressed with your finger
- Fins and a tail that aren't dry or damaged
- An aroma that smells of the sea, not fishy
- Cherry red gills and clear, protruding eyes

Fillets
- Firm, elastic flesh with no blemishes
- Fresh smell

Frozen fish
- Slightly shiny skin/flesh, not matte
- No white spots, a sign of freezer burn
- Even color and texture
- Packaging that is secure and undamaged

Sea Bass with Wilted Greens

grill, preheat grill. Reduce heat to medium. Place fish in basket on grill rack over heat. Cover; grill as above.)

4 In a large skillet heat remaining vinaigrette over medium heat. Add spinach, gently tossing to coat. Remove from heat. Stir in tomatoes. To serve, divide spinach mixture evenly among 4 dinner plates. Top with fish.

Nutrition Facts per serving: 201 cal., 10 g total fat (2 g sat. fat), 46 mg chol., 231 mg sodium, 5 g carbo., 1 g fiber, 23 g pro. Daily Values: 94% vit. A, 42% vit. C, 6% calcium, 10% iron. Exchanges: 1½ Vegetable, 3 Very Lean Meat, 1½ Fat

SEA BASS WITH WILTED GREENS

A refreshing citrus vinaigrette dresses the fish, spinach greens, and grape tomatoes.

Prep: 25 minutes Marinate: 30 minutes
Grill: 4 minutes per ½-inch thickness Makes: 4 servings

- **4 4- to 5-ounce fresh or frozen sea bass, tilapia, or catfish fillets**
- **1 teaspoon finely shredded orange peel**
- **⅓ cup orange juice**
- **3 tablespoons olive oil**
- **1 tablespoon snipped fresh chives**
- **2 cloves garlic, minced**
- **¼ teaspoon salt**
- **6 cups torn fresh spinach**
- **⅔ cup red grape tomatoes or red teardrop tomatoes, halved**

1 Thaw fish, if frozen. Rinse fish; pat dry with paper towels. For vinaigrette, in a screw-top jar combine orange peel, orange juice, oil, chives, garlic, and salt. Cover and shake well.

2 Place fish in a shallow dish. Pour half of the vinaigrette over fish; turn fish to coat. Cover and marinate in the refrigerator for 30 minutes. Drain fish; discard marinade.

3 Place fish in a well-greased grill basket, tucking under any thin edges. For a charcoal grill, grill fish on the rack of an uncovered grill directly over medium coals for 4 to 6 minutes per ½-inch thickness of fish or until fish flakes easily when tested with a fork, turning basket once. Remove fish from basket; keep warm. (For a gas

ORANGE AND DILL SEA BASS

Prep: 15 minutes Grill: 4 to 6 minutes per ½-inch thickness
Makes: 4 servings

- **4 5- to 6-ounce fresh or frozen sea bass or orange roughy fillets, ¾ inch thick**
- **2 tablespoons snipped fresh dill**
- **2 tablespoons olive oil**
- **4 large oranges, cut into ¼-inch slices**
- **1 orange, cut into wedges**

1 Thaw fish, if frozen. Rinse fish; pat dry with paper towels. In a small bowl stir together dill, oil, ¼ teaspoon salt, and ¼ teaspoon white pepper. Brush both sides of fish fillets with dill mixture.

2 Lightly grease or coat with nonstick cooking spray an unheated grill rack. For a charcoal grill, arrange a bed of orange slices on greased grill rack. Arrange fish on orange slices. Grill orange slices and fish on the rack of an uncovered grill directly over medium coals for 4 to 6 minutes per ½-inch thickness or until fish flakes easily when tested with a fork. (For a gas grill, preheat grill. Reduce heat to medium. Arrange orange slices and fish on greased grill rack over heat. Cover; grill as above.)

3 To serve, use a spatula to transfer fish and grilled orange slices to a serving platter. Squeeze the juice from orange wedges over fish.

Nutrition Facts per serving: 268 cal., 10 g total fat (2 g sat. fat), 58 mg chol., 242 mg sodium, 18 g carbo., 3 g fiber, 28 g pro. Daily Values: 11% vit. A, 133% vit. C, 7% calcium, 4% iron. Exchanges: 1 Fruit, 4 Very Lean Meat, 1½ Fat

CAMPING-OUT CITRUS SALMON

This recipe is great for camping out because it requires foil in place of pots or pans.

Prep: 20 minutes Cook: 2 minutes Grill: 15 minutes
Makes: 4 servings

**4 4-ounce fresh or frozen skinless
   salmon fillets, ³/₄ inch thick
2 cups thinly bias-sliced carrots
2 cups sliced fresh mushrooms
¹/₂ cup sliced green onions (4)
2 teaspoons finely shredded
   orange peel
2 teaspoons snipped fresh oregano
   or ¹/₂ teaspoon dried oregano,
   crushed
4 cloves garlic, thinly sliced
¹/₄ teaspoon salt
¹/₄ teaspoon black pepper
2 tablespoons olive oil
   Salt
   Black pepper
1 medium orange, thinly sliced**

1 Thaw salmon, if frozen. Rinse salmon; pat dry with paper towels. Set aside. In a saucepan cook carrots in a small amount of boiling water for 2 minutes. Drain and set aside. Tear four 24×18-inch pieces of heavy-duty foil; fold each in half to make 12×18-inch pieces.

2 In a large bowl combine carrots, mushrooms, onions, orange peel, oregano, garlic, the ¹/₄ teaspoon salt, and the ¹/₄ teaspoon pepper; toss gently.

3 Divide vegetables among the four pieces of heavy-duty foil, placing in center. Top each with a salmon fillet; drizzle with 1¹/₂ teaspoons oil. Sprinkle each lightly with additional salt and pepper; top with orange slices. Bring together two opposite edges of foil; seal with a double fold. Fold remaining edges to enclose the fish and vegetable mixture; leave space for steam to build.

4 For a charcoal grill, grill the foil packet on the rack of an uncovered grill directly over medium heat for 15 to 20 minutes or until carrots are tender and fish flakes easily when tested with a fork. (For a gas grill, preheat grill. Reduce heat to medium. Place foil packet on grill rack over heat. Cover; grill as above.)

Nutrition Facts per serving: 283 cal., 15 g total fat (3 g sat. fat), 60 mg chol., 342 mg sodium, 13 g carbo., 3 g fiber, 26 g pro. Daily Values: 144% vit. A, 40% vit. C, 8% calcium, 9% iron. Exchanges: 1 Vegetable, ¹/₂ Other Carbo., 3¹/₂ Lean Meat, 1 Fat

FOOD FOR THOUGHT
FISH FINDER

Occasionally the market may not have the fish you're looking for, or the fish you want may not be the freshest catch of the day. That's why it's good to go to the market with ideas of fish you can substitute, keeping in mind whether you want one that is mild or strong in flavor and/or firm or delicate in texture. Below are suggestions.

● Catfish: **Cod, Grouper, Haddock, Ocean Perch, Red Snapper, Whiting**
● Cod: **Grouper, Haddock, Halibut, Monkfish, Red Snapper, Turbot, Whiting**
● Grouper: **Cod, Haddock, Monkfish, Sea Bass, Red Snapper, Striped Bass**
● Haddock: **Cod, Grouper, Sea Bass, Red Snapper, Turbot**
● Halibut: **Cod, Haddock, Turbot**
● Mahi Mahi: **Swordfish**
● Orange Roughy: **Sole, Flounder**
● Red Snapper: **Grouper, Haddock, Monkfish, Ocean Perch, Turbot, Whiting**
● Sea Bass: **Cod, Grouper, Haddock, Ocean Perch, Red Snapper, Striped Bass**
● Swordfish: **Grouper, Halibut, Mahi Mahi, Red Snapper, Tuna**
● Tilapia: **Sea Bass, Red Snapper**
● Tuna: **Mackerel, Salmon**

PLANKED SALMON WITH CUCUMBER-DILL SAUCE

Prep: 10 minutes Chill: 8 to 24 hours Grill: 18 minutes
Makes: 4 to 6 servings

- 1 1½-pound fresh or frozen salmon fillet, 1 inch thick
- 1 tablespoon brown sugar
- 1 teaspoon salt
- ¼ teaspoon black pepper
- 1 12×6×¾-inch cedar grill plank
- 1 recipe Cucumber-Dill Sauce

1 Thaw salmon, if frozen. Rinse salmon; pat dry with paper towels. Place salmon, skin side down, in a shallow dish. For rub, in a small bowl stir together brown sugar, salt, and pepper. Sprinkle rub evenly over salmon (not on skin side); rub in with your fingers. Cover and chill in the refrigerator for 8 to 24 hours.

2 At least 1 hour before grilling, soak plank in enough water to cover, weighting it to keep it submerged.

3 For a charcoal grill, arrange medium-hot coals around edge of grill. Place salmon, skin side down, on grill plank. Place plank in center of grill rack. Cover; grill for 18 to 22 minutes or until fish flakes easily when tested with a fork. (For a gas grill, preheat grill. Reduce heat to medium. Adjust heat for indirect cooking. Grill as above.)

4 To serve, cut salmon into four to six pieces. Slide a spatula between the fish and skin to release pieces from plank. Serve with Cucumber-Dill Sauce.

Cucumber-Dill Sauce: In a small bowl combine ⅓ cup finely chopped cucumber, 3 tablespoons plain yogurt, 2 tablespoons mayonnaise or salad dressing, 2 teaspoons snipped fresh dill, and 2 teaspoons prepared horseradish. Cover and chill until serving time or for up to 4 hours.

Nutrition Facts per serving: 314 cal., 17 g total fat (4 g sat. fat), 96 mg chol., 757 mg sodium, 5 g carbo., 0 g fiber, 35 g pro. Daily Values: 2% vit. A, 2% vit. C, 8% calcium, 8% iron. Exchanges: 5 Lean Meat, ½ Fat

SMOKIN' HOT TIP

Overcooked fish is tough and dry. Follow these tips for grilling fish that's moist and tender:

● If grilling with the skin on, let the skin become crisp and brown and allow it to pull away from the grill before turning.

● Check the flesh at the thickest part of a fillet. When cooked, it will be opaque, moist, and will begin to pull apart easily into large flakes when tested with a fork.

● Cooked whole fish has opaque flesh that's moist and begins to pull away from the bones.

● For thicker, denser fish steaks where the flake test is difficult, insert an instant-read thermometer horizontally and stop grilling when the steaks reach an internal temperature of 140°F.

SALMON WITH ASIAN GLAZE

The Pineapple Rice with green soybeans is a side dish your family will ask for again and again.

Prep: 20 minutes Grill: 4 to 6 minutes per ½-inch thickness
Makes: 4 servings

> **4** 4-ounce fresh or frozen skinless
>   salmon fillets, 1 inch thick
> **1** recipe Pineapple Rice
> **2** tablespoons hoisin sauce
> **1** tablespoon soy sauce
> **1½** teaspoons peanut oil
> **1** teaspoon grated fresh ginger
> **1** clove garlic, minced

1 Thaw salmon, if frozen. Rinse salmon; pat dry with paper towels. Cover and chill until needed.

2 Prepare Pineapple Rice; cover and keep warm. Meanwhile, for glaze, in a small bowl stir together hoisin sauce, soy sauce, peanut oil, ginger, and garlic; set glaze aside.

3 For a charcoal grill, grill fish on a greased rack of an uncovered grill directly over medium coals for 4 to 6 minutes per ½-inch thickness or until fish flakes easily with a fork, turning once halfway through grilling and brushing with glaze during the last 2 minutes of grilling. (For a gas grill, preheat grill. Reduce heat to medium. Place fish on greased grill rack over heat. Cover; grill as above.) Serve salmon with Pineapple Rice.

Pineapple Rice: In a medium saucepan combine 1 cup chicken broth, ¾ cup jasmine or long grain rice, and ½ cup pineapple juice. Bring to boiling; reduce heat. Simmer, covered, for 15 minutes. Stir in 1 cup frozen shelled green or sweet soybeans (edamame) and ½ cup sliced green onions. Cook about 3 minutes more or until rice is tender. Stir in 1 cup bite-size pieces fresh pineapple.

Nutrition Facts per serving: 502 cal., 19 g total fat (3 g sat. fat), 67 mg chol., 711 mg sodium, 50 g carbo., 4 g fiber, 34 g pro. Daily Values: 4% vit. A, 71% vit. C, 17% calcium, 26% iron. Exchanges: ½ Fruit, 2½ Starch, ½ Other Carbo., 3½ Lean Meat, 1 Fat

CARAMELIZED SALMON WITH MANGO SALSA

Prep: 15 minutes Chill: 4 to 24 hours Grill: 20 minutes
Makes: 4 servings

> **4** 6- to 8-ounce fresh or frozen
>   salmon fillets (with skin),
>   1 inch thick
> **2** tablespoons sugar
> **1½** teaspoons finely shredded lime peel
> **¼** teaspoon cayenne pepper
> **1** large ripe mango, peeled, seeded,
>   and cut into thin bite-size strips
> **½** of a medium cucumber, seeded and
>   cut into thin bite-size strips
> **¼** cup sliced green onions (2)
> **3** tablespoons lime juice
> **1** tablespoon snipped fresh cilantro or
>   2 teaspoons snipped fresh mint
> **1** small fresh jalapeño chile pepper,
>   seeded and chopped (see tip,
>   page 36)
> **1** clove garlic, minced

1 Thaw fish, if frozen. Rinse fish; pat dry. Place fish, skin sides down, in a shallow dish. For rub, in a bowl stir together sugar, lime peel, ½ teaspoon salt, and the cayenne pepper. Sprinkle rub evenly over fish; rub in with your fingers. Cover and chill fish in the refrigerator for 4 to 24 hours.

2 Meanwhile, for salsa, in a medium bowl combine mango, cucumber, green onions, lime juice, cilantro, jalapeño pepper, garlic, and ¼ teaspoon salt. Cover and chill until ready to serve.

3 For a charcoal grill, arrange medium-hot coals around a drip pan. Test for medium heat above the pan. Place fish, skin side down, on a greased grill rack over drip pan, tucking under any thin edges. Cover; grill for 20 to 25 minutes or until fish flakes easily when tested with a fork. (For a gas grill, preheat grill. Reduce heat to medium. Adjust heat for indirect cooking. Grill as above.)

4 To serve, if desired, remove skin from fish. Serve salsa with fish.

Nutrition Facts per serving: 352 cal., 15 g total fat (3 g sat. fat), 105 mg chol., 520 mg sodium, 18 g carbo., 2 g fiber, 37 g pro. Daily Values: 50% vit. A, 38% vit. C, 3% calcium, 6% iron. Exchanges: ½ Fruit, ½ Other Carbo., 5 Lean Meat

SALMON AND VEGETABLE PACKETS

The majority of this meal is cooked on the grill in a foil packet. Served in its foil pouch, it makes a great-tasting dinner with few dishes to wash.

Prep: 40 minutes Grill: 12 minutes per ½-inch thickness
Makes: 4 servings

1 pound fresh or frozen skinless salmon, orange roughy, cod, or tilapia fillets, ½ to ¾ inch thick
2 cups thin bite-size strips carrots
2 cups bite-size strips red sweet peppers
12 fresh asparagus spears (about 12 ounces), trimmed
4 small yellow summer squash (about 1 pound), cut into ¼-inch slices
½ cup dry white wine or chicken broth
2 teaspoons snipped fresh rosemary or ½ teaspoon dried rosemary, crushed
2 cloves garlic, minced
¼ teaspoon salt
¼ teaspoon black pepper
2 tablespoons butter or margarine, cut up
Hot cooked white or brown rice (optional)

1 Thaw fish, if frozen. Rinse fish; pat dry with paper towels. Measure thickness of fish. Cut into 4 serving-size pieces. Set aside.

2 Tear off eight 18-inch squares heavy-duty foil. Layer two squares together to form four separate layers. Coat one side of each layer with nonstick cooking spray. Divide carrots, sweet peppers, and asparagus among coated foil layers. Top vegetables with the fish and squash.

3 For seasoning, in a small bowl combine wine, rosemary, garlic, salt, and black pepper. Drizzle over fish and vegetables; top with butter. Bring up two opposite edges of each foil stack; seal with a double fold. Fold remaining ends to completely enclose the fish and vegetables, leaving space for steam to build.

4 For a charcoal grill, grill foil packets on a grill rack of an uncovered grill directly over medium coals for 12 to 14 minutes per ½-inch thickness of fish or until fish flakes easily when tested with a fork and vegetables are tender, carefully opening packets to check doneness. (For a gas grill, preheat grill. Reduce heat to medium. Place foil packets on grill rack over heat. Cover; grill as above.) If desired, serve with hot rice.

Nutrition Facts per serving: 308 cal., 14 g total fat (5 g sat. fat), 76 mg chol., 320 mg sodium, 15 g carbo., 5 g fiber, 27 g pro. Daily Values: 177% vit. A, 212% vit. C, 9% calcium, 12% iron. Exchanges: 2½ Vegetable, 3 Very Lean Meat, 3 Fat

FOOD FOR THOUGHT SALMON

Farm-raised salmon and wild salmon differ in appearance, flavor, and texture. They both, however, serve as excellent sources of omega-3 fatty acids. These acids help reduce the risk of heart attack, stroke, and cancer as well as lower blood pressure, reduce depression, and relieve the pain of rheumatoid arthritis.

Salmon with Jicama Slaw

SALMON WITH JICAMA SLAW

Prep: 25 minutes Chill: 30 to 60 minutes
Grill: 4 to 6 minutes per ½-inch thickness
Makes: 4 servings

- **1 cup jicama cut into matchstick-size pieces**
- **1 cup shredded cabbage**
- **1 small tomato, seeded and chopped (¹/₃ cup)**
- **2 tablespoons thinly sliced green onion (1)**
- **1 tablespoon snipped fresh cilantro**
- **1 to 2 serrano chile peppers, seeded and finely chopped (see tip, page 36)**
- **¹/₄ cup apple juice**
- **1¹/₂ teaspoons finely shredded lime peel**
- **2 tablespoons lime juice**
- **1 tablespoon salad oil**
- **¹/₈ teaspoon salt**
- **¹/₄ teaspoon salt**
- **¹/₄ teaspoon black pepper**
- **¹/₄ teaspoon dried oregano, crushed**
- **1 1-pound skinless salmon fillet**
- **4 10-inch flour tortillas**
- **1 tablespoon salad oil**

1 For slaw, in a large bowl combine jicama, cabbage, tomato, green onion, cilantro, and serrano pepper(s). In a small bowl combine the apple juice, ½ teaspoon of the lime peel, the lime juice, 1 tablespoon oil, and the ¹/₈ teaspoon salt. Add to the jicama mixture; toss to combine. Cover and chill in the refrigerator for 30 minutes to 1 hour, stirring once or twice.

2 Combine the remaining 1 teaspoon lime peel, the ¹/₄ teaspoon salt, pepper, and oregano. Sprinkle over surface of salmon fillet; rub in with your fingers. Lightly grease or coat with nonstick cooking spray an unheated grill rack.

3 For a charcoal grill, grill fish on the greased grill rack of an uncovered grill directly over medium coals for 4 to 6 minutes per ½-inch thickness or until fish flakes easily when tested with a fork, turning once halfway through grilling. (For a gas grill, preheat grill. Reduce heat to medium. Place fish on greased grill rack over heat. Cover; grill as above.) Break salmon into pieces.

4 To serve, divide salmon and slaw among tortillas; fold over. Or, to serve wrap-style, place one-fourth of the salmon just below the center of each tortilla. Using a slotted spoon, top each salmon portion with one-fourth of the slaw. Fold bottom edge of tortilla up over filling. Fold in opposite sides; roll up from the bottom. Secure with a wooden toothpick, if necessary. Brush filled tortillas lightly with remaining oil; place on grill rack directly over medium heat. Grill 3 to 4 minutes or until heated through, turning once.

Nutrition Facts per serving: 419 cal., 21 g total fat (4 g sat. fat), 70 mg chol., 457 mg sodium, 31 g carbo., 2 g fiber, 28 g pro. Daily Values: 36% vit. C, 15% iron. Exchanges: ½ Vegetable, 2 Starch, 3 Lean Meat, 2 Fat

SALMON TACOS

Prep: 1 hour Cook: 15 minutes
Grill: 4 minutes per $\frac{1}{2}$-inch thickness
Makes: 24 to 32 tortillas

- **2 pounds fresh or frozen skinless salmon fillets**
- **1 pound medium round red or white potatoes**
- **1 tablespoon ground chipotle chile pepper**
- **1½ teaspoons sugar**
- **1½ teaspoons salt**
- **2 cups green salsa**
- **⅓ cup lime juice**
- **1½ cups thinly sliced green onions (12 onions)**
- **1 cup snipped fresh cilantro**
- **32 4-inch corn tortillas or twenty-four 6-inch corn tortillas, warmed**
- **1 cup crème fraîche**
  Lime wedges

1 Thaw fish, if frozen. Rinse fish; pat dry with paper towels. Measure thickness of fish. Peel and cube potatoes. Cook, covered, in enough boiling salted water to cover about 15 minutes or until tender. Drain and cool.

2 In a small bowl combine chipotle chile pepper, sugar, and ¾ teaspoon of the salt. Rub onto both sides of fish. Lightly grease or coat with nonstick cooking spray an unheated grill rack.

3 For a charcoal grill, grill fish on greased grill rack of an uncovered grill directly over medium coals for 4 to 6 minutes per ½-inch thickness or until fish flakes easily when tested with a fork. (For a gas grill, preheat grill. Reduce heat to medium. Place fish on grill rack over heat. Cover; grill as above.) Cool slightly; break into chunks.

4 In a large bowl stir together salsa, lime juice, and remaining ¾ teaspoon salt. Gently stir in salmon, potatoes, green onions, and cilantro. Divide salmon mixture among tortillas. Top each with a spoonful of crème fraîche. Serve immediately with lime wedges.

Nutrition Facts per serving: 161 cal., 5 g total fat (2 g sat. fat), 29 mg chol., 316 mg sodium, 19 g carbo., 2 g fiber, 10 g pro. Daily Values: 12% vit. A, 28% vit. C, 8% calcium, 7% iron. Exchanges: 1 Starch, 1 Lean Meat, ½ Fat

SALMON WITH CITRUS SAUCE

To make the orange and lemon peel strips for the sauce, use a vegetable peeler to peel orange and lemon. Use a sharp knife to cut peels into thin strips.

Prep: 15 minutes Marinate: 1 hour
Grill: 4 minutes per $\frac{1}{2}$-inch thickness
Makes: 6 servings

- **1 1½-pound fresh or frozen salmon fillet (with skin)**
- **1 tablespoon finely shredded orange peel**
- **¼ cup orange juice**
- **1 tablespoon finely shredded lemon peel**
- **2 tablespoons lemon juice**
- **2 tablespoons snipped fresh basil**
- **1 tablespoon snipped fresh lemon thyme**
- **1 tablespoon snipped fresh chives**
- **½ teaspoon salt**
- **⅛ teaspoon black pepper**
- **1 tablespoon olive oil**
- **1 recipe Citrus Sauce**
  Snipped fresh chives or basil (optional)

1 Thaw salmon, if frozen. Rinse fish; pat dry with paper towels. Measure thickness of fish. Place fish in a self-sealing plastic bag set in a shallow dish. Set fish aside.

2 For marinade, in a bowl combine orange peel, the ¼ cup orange juice, shredded lemon peel, lemon juice, basil, lemon thyme, the 1 tablespoon chives, salt, and pepper. Pour marinade over fish in bag. Seal bag. Marinate in refrigerator for 1 hour, turning bag occasionally. Remove fish from marinade, reserving marinade. Pat fish dry; brush with oil. Lightly grease or coat with nonstick cooking spray an unheated grill rack.

3 For a charcoal grill, grill fish, skin side up, on the greased rack of an uncovered grill directly over medium coals for 4 to 6 minutes per ½-inch thickness or until fish flakes easily when tested with a fork, brushing with reserved marinade and gently turning halfway through grilling. Discard any remaining marinade. Use a large spatula to remove fish from grill, leaving skin behind; discard skin. Transfer fish to a serving platter. (For a gas grill, preheat grill. Reduce heat to medium. Place fish on greased grill rack over heat. Cover; grill as at left.)

4 To serve, reheat Citrus Sauce, if necessary. Pour sauce over fish. If desired, sprinkle with additional snipped fresh herbs.

Citrus Sauce: In a small saucepan combine 1 tablespoon thin strips orange peel, 1 tablespoon thin strips lemon peel, ½ cup orange juice, and 3 tablespoons lemon juice. Bring to boiling; reduce heat to medium. Simmer, uncovered, about 10 minutes or until mixture is reduced by half and slightly syrupy. (Sauce can be made up to 1 hour ahead. Cover and chill; reheat before serving.)

Nutrition Facts per serving: 172 cal., 6 g total fat (1 g sat. fat), 59 mg chol., 270 mg sodium, 5 g carbo., 1 g fiber, 23 g pro. Daily Values: 5% vit. A, 46% vit. C, 3% calcium, 6% iron. Exchanges: ½ Other Carbo., 3 Very Lean Meat, 1 Fat

MAHI MAHI WITH TROPICAL FRUIT SALSA

Prep: 10 minutes Marinate: 30 minutes
Grill: 4 minutes per ½-inch thickness
Makes: 4 servings

- **4** 5- to 6-ounce fresh or frozen skinless mahi mahi or grouper fillets
- **½** cup reduced-sodium soy sauce
- **2** tablespoons honey
- **2** teaspoons toasted sesame oil or olive oil
- **1** teaspoon grated fresh ginger
- **1** cup peeled, seeded, and chopped mango
- **1** large firm, ripe banana, chopped (1 cup), or 1 cup sliced star fruit (carambola), quartered
- **⅓** cup chopped macadamia nuts
- **2** tablespoons lime juice
- **2** tablespoons toasted coconut

1 Thaw fish, if frozen. Rinse fish; pat dry with paper towels. Place fish in a shallow dish. Combine soy sauce, honey, oil, and ginger. Pour over fish; turn fish to coat. Cover; marinate in the refrigerator 30 minutes, turning once.

2 For salsa, in a medium bowl stir together mango, banana, macadamia nuts, and lime juice. Cover and chill until ready to serve.

3 Drain fish, discarding marinade. Lightly grease or lightly coat with nonstick cooking spray a grill basket. Place fish in greased grill basket, tucking under any thin edges.

4 For a charcoal grill, grill fish in basket on the rack of an uncovered grill directly over medium coals for 4 to 6 minutes per ½ inch of thickness or until fish flakes easily when tested with a fork, turning basket once halfway through grilling. (For a gas grill, preheat grill. Reduce heat to medium. Place basket on grill rack over medium heat. Cover; grill as above.) Serve fish with salsa. Sprinkle each serving with coconut.

Nutrition Facts per serving: 336 cal., 13 g total fat (3 g sat. fat), 103 mg chol., 1327 mg sodium, 28 g carbo., 3 g fiber, 30 g pro. Daily Values: 11% vit. A, 28% vit. C, 4% calcium, 17% iron. Exchanges: 1 Fruit, 1 Other Carbo., 4 Very Lean Meat, 1½ Fat

FOOD FOR THOUGHT
STAR FRUIT

The star fruit thrives in tropical climates and has been cultivated in Asia since ancient times. This golden yellow fruit grows 2 to 5 inches long and has five distinct ribs that run the length of the fruit. When sliced crosswise, the resulting slices look like stars, thus the name star fruit. Its tender, waxy skin is edible, and its translucent flesh is juicy and mildly flavored. A handful of tiny black seeds is interspersed throughout. Look for star fruit that is bright, firm, unblemished, and aromatic. Store it at room temperature to ripen or in the refrigerator for 1 to 2 weeks. Raw or cooked for short periods, star fruit is a nice addition to salads and stir-fries and makes an eye-catching garnish for drinks.

Blackened Swordfish with Hominy
Dirty Rice

BLACKENED SWORDFISH WITH HOMINY DIRTY RICE

Dirty rice is a Cajun specialty that gets its name from ground giblets that give the rice a "dirty" appearance. Here, sausage takes the place of ground giblets.

Prep: 30 minutes Cook: 15 minutes
Grill: 4 to 6 minutes per ½-inch thickness Makes: 4 servings

- **4 4- to 5-ounce fresh or frozen swordfish or tuna steaks, 1 inch thick**
- **2 teaspoons minced garlic**
- **1 teaspoon black pepper**
- **1 teaspoon paprika**
- **½ teaspoon cayenne pepper**
- **½ teaspoon ground white pepper**
- **½ teaspoon dried thyme, crushed**
- **½ teaspoon salt**
- **3 tablespoons butter, melted**
- **1 recipe Hominy Dirty Rice**

1 Thaw fish, if frozen. Rinse fish; pat dry with paper towels. In a small bowl combine garlic, black pepper, paprika, cayenne pepper, white pepper, thyme, and salt. Stir in melted butter. Brush both sides of fish with melted butter mixture.

2 Lightly grease or coat with nonstick cooking spray an unheated grill rack. For a charcoal grill, grill fish on the greased rack of an uncovered grill directly over medium coals for 4 to 6 minutes per ½-inch thickness or until fish flakes easily when tested with a fork, turning once halfway through grilling. (For a gas grill, preheat grill. Reduce heat to medium. Place fish on greased grill rack over heat. Cover; grill as above.) Serve with Hominy Dirty Rice.

Hominy Dirty Rice: In a large skillet place 8 ounces bulk pork sausage, ¼ cup finely chopped onion, 3 tablespoons finely chopped celery, 3 tablespoons finely chopped green sweet pepper, 3 tablespoons finely chopped red sweet pepper, and 2 tablespoons minced garlic. Cook over medium heat for 4 to 5 minutes or until sausage is no longer pink and vegetables are tender. Drain off fat, if necessary. Stir in 1½ cups cooked, chilled white rice; ⅔ cup chicken broth; ⅓ cup hominy; ¼ teaspoon black pepper; and ⅛ to ¼ teaspoon cayenne pepper. Bring mixture to boiling; reduce heat. Simmer, uncovered, about 5 minutes or until rice is heated through and most of the liquid has been absorbed, stirring occasionally. Serve immediately with Blackened Swordfish.

Nutrition Facts per serving: 504 cal., 27 g total fat (12 g sat. fat), 106 mg chol., 1,001 mg sodium, 26 g carbo., 2 g fiber, 34 g pro. Daily Values: 26% vit. A, 44% vit. C, 6% calcium, 16% iron. Exchanges: 1½ Other Carbo., 2 Very Lean Meat, 2 High-Fat Meat, 2 Fat

SWORDFISH STEAKS WITH TANGERINE SAUCE

Prep: 15 minutes Marinate: 30 minutes
Grill: 4 to 6 minutes per ½-inch thickness Makes: 4 servings

- **4 6- to 8-ounce fresh or frozen swordfish or tuna steaks, 1 inch thick**
- **1 teaspoon finely shredded fresh tangerine peel**
- **¼ cup fresh-squeezed tangerine juice**
- **3 tablespoons olive oil**
- **6 cloves garlic, minced**
- **1 recipe Tangerine Sauce**

1 Thaw fish, if frozen. Rinse fish; pat dry with paper towels. Measure thickness of fish. Place fish in a self-sealing plastic bag set in a shallow dish. For marinade, in a bowl combine tangerine peel, tangerine juice, olive oil, garlic, ¼ teaspoon salt, and ¼ teaspoon white pepper. Pour over fish; seal bag. Marinate in the refrigerator for 30 minutes, turning bag once.

2 Drain fish, discarding marinade. Lightly grease or coat with nonstick cooking spray an unheated grill rack. For a charcoal grill, grill fish on a greased rack of an uncovered grill directly over medium coals for 4 to 6 minutes per ½-inch thickness or until fish flakes easily when tested with a fork, gently turning once halfway through grilling. (For a gas grill, preheat grill. Reduce heat to medium. Place fish on greased grill rack over heat. Cover; grill as above.) Serve fish with Tangerine Sauce.

Tangerine Sauce: Finely shred 1 teaspoon tangerine peel; set aside. Cut ¼ cup butter into four pieces; bring to room temperature. In a saucepan, combine 3 tablespoons dry white wine, 3 tablespoons fresh-squeezed tangerine juice, 2 teaspoons finely chopped shallot, 2 teaspoons snipped fresh tarragon, and 5 whole black peppercorns. Bring to boiling. Boil, uncovered, over medium-high heat for 3 to 4 minutes or until liquid is reduced to 2 tablespoons; strain into top of a double boiler. (Water should not touch upper pan.) Add 2 beaten egg yolks, 2 teaspoons warm water, and a piece of the butter. Cook over gently simmering water, stirring rapidly with a whisk, until butter melts and sauce begins to thicken.

Add remaining butter, one piece at a time, stirring constantly until melted. Continue to cook and stir until sauce is thickened (1 to 2 minutes more). Immediately remove pan from heat. Stir in tangerine peel.

Nutrition Facts per serving: 402 cal., 26 g total fat (9 g sat. fat), 199 mg chol., 318 mg sodium, 4 g carbo., 0 g fiber, 35 g pro. Daily Values: 15% vit. A, 16% vit. C, 3% calcium, 10% iron. Exchanges: 5 Very Lean Meat, 5 Fat

HALIBUT VERACRUZ

Prep: 20 minutes Grill: 4 to 6 minutes per ½-inch thickness
Makes: 4 servings

- **4 6-ounce fresh or frozen halibut or tuna steaks**
- **1 14½-ounce can chopped tomatoes with green chiles, drained**
- **¼ cup sliced green onions (2)**
- **1 tablespoon olive oil**
- **1 teaspoon minced garlic**
- **1 teaspoon drained capers**
- **1 teaspoon snipped fresh oregano or ½ teaspoon dried oregano, crushed**
- **½ teaspoon snipped fresh thyme or ¼ teaspoon dried thyme, crushed**

1 Thaw fish, if frozen. Rinse fish; pat dry with paper towels. Measure fish thickness. Sprinkle fish with salt and pepper. In a bowl combine drained tomatoes with green chiles, green onions, oil, garlic, capers, oregano, and thyme.

2 Fold a 36×18-inch piece of heavy-duty foil in half to make an 18-inch square. Place fish steaks in center of foil. Top with tomato mixture. Bring up two opposite edges of foil; seal with a double-fold. Fold remaining edges together to completely enclose fish, leaving space for steam to build.

3 For a charcoal grill, grill foil packet on the rack of an uncovered grill directly over medium coals for 4 to 6 minutes per ½-inch thickness of fish or until fish flakes easily when tested with a fork. (For a gas grill, preheat grill. Reduce heat to medium. Place foil packet on grill rack over heat. Cover; grill as above.)

Nutrition Facts per serving: 254 cal., 7 g total fat (1 g sat. fat), 54 mg chol., 651 mg sodium, 8 g carbo., 2 g fiber, 36 g pro. Daily Values: 5% vit. A, 15% vit. C, 10% calcium, 10% iron. Exchanges: 1 Vegetable, 5 Very Lean Meat, 1 Fat

HALIBUT WITH CHUTNEY CREAM SAUCE

This velvety rich sauce makes a perfect partner to any type of white-fleshed fish.

Prep: 20 minutes Grill: 4 minutes per ½-inch thickness
Makes: 4 servings

- **4 5- to 6-ounce fresh or frozen halibut steaks, about 1 inch thick**
- **1 tablespoon lime juice**
- **Salt**
- **Black pepper**
- **1 tablespoon finely chopped shallot**
- **½ cup mango chutney**
- **⅓ cup dry white wine**
- **2 tablespoons whipping cream**
- **½ cup butter, cut into 8 slices**
- **Shredded lettuce (optional)**
- **1 mango, peeled, seeded, and sliced**
- **Sliced green onions**

1 Thaw halibut, if frozen. Rinse fish; pat dry with paper towels. Measure thickness of fish. Brush fish with the lime juice and sprinkle with salt and black pepper.

2 Lightly grease or coat with nonstick cooking spray an unheated grill rack. For a charcoal grill, grill fish on the greased rack of an uncovered grill directly over medium coals for 4 to 6 minutes per ½-inch thickness or until fish flakes easily when tested with a fork, turning once. (For a gas grill, preheat grill. Reduce heat to medium. Place fish on greased grill rack over heat. Cover; grill as above.)

3 Meanwhile, for sauce, in a small saucepan stir together the shallot, chutney, and wine. Bring to boiling; reduce heat. Boil gently, uncovered, about 5 minutes or until thickened, stirring occasionally. Add cream; heat through. Whisk in butter, one piece at a time, until melted. Serve fish on a bed of lettuce, if desired. Top with sauce and mango slices; sprinkle with green onions.

Nutrition Facts per serving: 563 cal., 31 g total fat (15 g sat. fat), 138 mg chol., 515 mg sodium, 24 g carbo., 2 g fiber, 43 g pro. Daily Values: 37% vit. A, 41% vit. C, 13% calcium, 13% iron. Exchanges: ½ Fruit, 1 Other Carbo., 6 Very Lean Meat, 6 Fat

Halibut with Chutney Cream Sauce

HALIBUT WITH BLUEBERRY-BLACK PEPPER JAM

Prep: 25 minutes Grill: 12 minutes Makes: 4 servings

4 **5- to 6-ounce fresh or frozen halibut steaks or fillets or salmon fillets, about 1 inch thick**
1 **cup garlic croutons, coarsely crushed**
¼ **cup snipped fresh sage**
1 **teaspoon finely shredded orange peel**
2 **tablespoons orange juice**
1 **tablespoon olive oil**
1 **recipe Blueberry-Black Pepper Jam**

1 Thaw fish, if frozen. Rinse fish; pat dry with paper towels. In a small bowl combine crushed croutons, sage, orange peel, and ¼ teaspoon black pepper. Stir in orange juice and the 1 tablespoon olive oil until lightly moistened; set aside.

2 Lightly grease or coat an unheated grill rack with nonstick cooking spray. For a charcoal grill, grill fish, skin side up if using fillets, on the greased grill rack of an uncovered grill directly over medium coals for 5 minutes. Turn fish; top evenly with the crouton mixture, gently pressing onto fish. Grill fish for 7 to 10 minutes more or until fish flakes easily when tested with a fork. (For a gas grill, preheat grill. Reduce heat to medium. Place fish on greased grill rack over heat. Cover; grill as above.)

3 To serve, place fish on a serving platter. Serve with Blueberry-Pepper Jam. If desired, drizzle additional olive oil over crouton topping.

Blueberry-Black Pepper Jam: In a medium bowl mash ¾ cup fresh rinsed and drained blueberries with a potato masher or fork. Stir in ¼ cup blueberries, 1 teaspoon snipped fresh sage, and ½ teaspoon freshly ground black pepper. Cover and chill until ready to serve.

Nutrition Facts per serving: 222 cal., 7 g total fat (1 g sat. fat), 45 mg chol., 101 mg sodium, 8 g carbo., 1 g fiber, 30 g pro. Daily Values: 6% vit. A, 16% vit. C, 4% calcium, 20% iron. Exchanges: ½ Fruit, 4 Very Lean Meat, 1 Fat

FISH BURGERS WITH DILLED SLAW

Prep: 45 minutes Grill: 10 minutes Makes: 6 burgers

1 **pound fresh tuna fillet**
8 **ounces fresh salmon fillet**
¼ **cup snipped fresh cilantro**
2 **tablespoons fresh lime juice**
2 **cloves garlic, minced**
2 **tablespoons olive oil**
1 **tablespoon purchased pickled ginger, finely chopped**
1 **tablespoon chili sauce**
1 to 2 **teaspoons wasabi paste**
¼ **teaspoon sea salt**
6 **soft flatbreads, such as Afghan bread, naan, or lefsa, or split rolls**
1 **recipe Dilled Slaw**

1 Rinse fish; pat dry. Finely chop tuna and salmon. Combine tuna, salmon, cilantro, lime juice, garlic, 4 teaspoons of the olive oil, the ginger, chili sauce, wasabi, salt, and ¼ teaspoon black pepper. Shape into six ¾-inch-thick patties.

2 For a charcoal grill, grill patties on the rack of an uncovered grill directly over medium coals for 10 to 12 minutes or until 160°F, turning burgers once halfway through grilling. Brush flatbread with remaining oil. Grill on grill rack for 1 to 2 minutes or until toasted. (For a gas grill, preheat grill. Reduce heat to medium. Place patties, then flatbread, on grill rack over heat. Cover; grill as above.) To serve, place burgers on flatbread; top with Dilled Slaw.

Dilled Slaw: For dressing, in a food processor or blender combine ½ cup plain low-fat yogurt; 1 to 2 cloves garlic, minced; 2 tablespoons snipped fresh parsley; 2 tablespoons snipped fresh dill; 2 tablespoons lime juice; ⅛ teaspoon sea salt; and ⅛ teaspoon black pepper. Cover and process or blend until smooth. Combine dressing and 3 cups finely shredded napa cabbage; toss well to coat. Cover and chill until serving time or overnight.

Nutrition Facts per serving: 344 cal., 12 g total fat (2 g sat. fat), 57 mg chol., 413 mg sodium, 28 g carbo., 2 g fiber, 31 g pro. Daily Values: 10% vit. A, 34% vit. C, 15% calcium, 14% iron. Exchanges: ½ Vegetable, 2 Starch, 3½ Very Lean Meat, 1½ Fat

TERIYAKI TUNA WRAPS

Prep: 25 minutes Marinate: 1 to 2 hours Grill: 8 minutes
Makes: 8 wraps

 3 8-ounce fresh or frozen tuna steaks,
    1 inch thick
 1/3 cup soy sauce
 2 cloves garlic, minced
 1 1/2 teaspoons packed brown sugar
 1 1/2 teaspoons finely shredded fresh ginger
 8 10-inch flour tortillas
 1 tablespoon cooking oil
 3/4 cup fat-free dairy sour cream
 3/4 cup bottled honey-mustard
    salad dressing
 2 cups lightly packed arugula or
    spinach leaves
 1 large red onion, sliced
 1 medium tomato, chopped

1 Thaw tuna, if frozen. Rinse fish; pat dry with paper towels. Place fish in a self-sealing plastic bag set in a shallow dish. In a small bowl stir together soy sauce, garlic, brown sugar, and ginger. Pour over fish; seal bag. Marinate in refrigerator for 1 to 2 hours, turning bag occasionally. Drain, discarding marinade. Lightly grease or coat with nonstick cooking spray an unheated grill rack.

2 For charcoal grill, grill fish on greased rack of uncovered grill directly over medium coals for 8 to 12 minutes or until fish flakes easily when tested with a fork and center of fish is slightly pink, turning once. (For gas grill, preheat grill. Reduce heat to medium. Place fish on greased grill rack over heat. Cover; grill as above.) Cut tuna into 1/2-inch chunks. Brush both sides of tortillas lightly with oil; place, two at a time, on grill rack for 30 to 45 seconds or just until warm.

3 Stir together sour cream and salad dressing. For each wrap, spread 3 tablespoons of the sour cream mixture on a tortilla. Place one-eighth of the tuna near an edge of tortilla. Top with some of the arugula, onion, and tomato. Fold edge over filling; fold in the sides and roll up.

Nutrition Facts per wrap: 384 cal., 15 g total fat (3 g sat. fat), 42 mg chol., 610 mg sodium, 35 g carbo., 2 g fiber, 25 g pro. Daily Values: 46% vit. A, 11% vit. C, 10% calcium, 14% iron. Exchanges: 1/2 Vegetable, 2 Starch, 2 1/2 Very Lean Meat, 3 Fat

GINGERED TUNA KABOBS

Tuna steaks benefit from a tasty marinade. Be sure to reserve the marinade, which combines with a touch of honey for a splendid serve-along sauce.

Prep: 20 minutes Marinate: 20 minutes Grill: 6 minutes
Makes: 4 servings

 12 ounces fresh or frozen tuna steaks
 3 tablespoons soy sauce
 1 tablespoon toasted sesame oil
 1 tablespoon chopped green onion
 2 teaspoons grated fresh ginger
 1 mango, peeled, seeded, and cut into
    1 1/2-inch cubes
 1 medium green sweet pepper, cut
    into 1 1/2-inch pieces
 6 green onions, cut into 2-inch pieces
 1/4 cup honey

1 Thaw tuna, if frozen. Rinse fish; pat fish dry with paper towels. Cut into 1 1/2-inch cubes. Place fish cubes in a self-sealing plastic bag. Add soy sauce, sesame oil, chopped green onion, and ginger. Seal bag; gently turn to coat tuna. Marinate in the refrigerator for 20 minutes. Drain, reserving marinade.

2 On four 8-inch skewers thread tuna, mango, sweet pepper, and green onion pieces. For a charcoal grill, grill fish kabobs on the rack of an uncovered grill directly over medium-hot coals for 6 to 9 minutes or until desired doneness, turning several times and brushing with some of the reserved marinade during the last 5 minutes of grilling. (For a gas grill, preheat grill. Reduce heat to medium-high heat. Place kabobs on grill rack over heat. Cover; grill as above.)

3 In a small saucepan bring remaining marinade just to boiling. Remove from heat; stir in honey. Brush skewers with heated marinade before serving. Pass remaining heated marinade.

Nutrition Facts per serving: 274 cal., 8 g total fat (2 g sat. fat), 32 mg chol., 730 mg sodium, 30 g carbo., 2 g fiber, 22 g pro. Daily Values: 79% vit. A, 67% vit. C, 3% calcium, 8% iron. Exchanges: 1/2 Fruit, 1 1/2 Other Carbo., 3 Very Lean Meat, 1 Fat

TUNA STEAKS WITH CUMIN TARTAR SAUCE

To toast cumin seeds for the tartar sauce, place seeds in a small, nonstick skillet. Heat over medium heat for several minutes until fragrant, stirring occasionally.

Prep: 25 minutes Marinate: 30 minutes to 60 minutes
Grill: 8 to 12 minutes Makes: 4 servings

**4 6-ounce fresh or frozen tuna steaks,
   1 inch thick
¼ cup cooking oil
3 tablespoons lemon juice
2 cloves garlic, minced
1 teaspoon cumin seeds, toasted
¼ teaspoon black pepper
1 recipe Cumin Tartar Sauce**

1 Thaw fish, if frozen. Rinse fish; pat dry with paper towels. Place fish in a self-sealing plastic bag set in a shallow dish. For marinade, in a small bowl stir together oil, lemon juice, garlic, cumin seeds, and pepper. Pour over fish; seal bag and turn to coat fish. Marinate in the refrigerator for 30 to 60 minutes, turning fish once. Remove fish from marinade, reserving marinade.

2 Lightly grease or coat with nonstick cooking spray an unheated grill rack. For a charcoal grill, grill fish on the greased rack of an uncovered grill directly over medium coals for 8 to 12 minutes, or until fish flakes when tested with a fork and center of fish is still slightly pink, gently turning and brushing once with remaining marinade halfway through grilling. Discard any remaining marinade. (For a gas grill, preheat grill. Reduce heat to medium. Place fish on greased grill rack directly over heat. Cover; grill as above.) Serve fish with sauce.

Cumin Tartar Sauce: Finely chop any large fruit pieces in 2 tablespoons mango chutney. In a small bowl combine chutney, ⅓ cup mayonnaise or salad dressing, 1 teaspoon Dijon-style mustard, 1 teaspoon lemon juice, and 1 teaspoon cumin seeds, toasted. Cover and chill until serving time.

Nutrition Facts per serving: 520 cal., 37 g total fat (6 g sat. fat), 77 mg chol., 231 mg sodium, 6 g carbo., 0 g fiber, 40 g pro. Daily Values: 68% vit. A, 14% vit. C, 3% calcium, 14% iron. Exchanges: ½ Other Carbo., 6 Very Lean Meat, 6 Fat

TUNA STEAKS WITH HOT-AND-SOUR RELISH

Prep: 25 minutes Grill: 8 minutes
Makes: 6 servings

**6 6-ounce fresh or frozen tuna steaks,
   1 inch thick
¼ cup finely chopped green onions (2)
¼ cup pimiento-stuffed green olives,
   finely chopped
¼ cup finely chopped red sweet pepper
1 tablespoon hot chile oil
1 recipe Hot-and-Sour Relish**

1 Thaw fish, if frozen. Rinse fish; pat dry with paper towels. For stuffing, in a bowl stir together onions, olives, and sweet pepper.

2 Cut a horizontal pocket in each steak by cutting from one side to, but not through, the other side. Spoon 2 tablespoons stuffing into each pocket. If necessary, secure with short metal skewers. Brush half the oil over both sides of fish.

3 Lightly grease or coat with nonstick cooking spray an unheated grill rack. For a charcoal grill, grill fish on the greased rack of an uncovered grill directly over medium coals for 8 to 12 minutes or until fish flakes easily when tested with a fork and center of fish is still slightly pink, gently turning and brushing once with remaining oil halfway through grilling. (For a gas grill, preheat grill. Reduce heat to medium. Place fish on greased grill rack over heat. Cover; grill as above.) To serve, spoon Hot-and-Sour Relish over fish.

Hot-and-Sour Relish: In a large skillet cook 2 large onions, sliced and separated into rings; 1 red sweet pepper, sliced into 2-inch strips; 2 cloves minced garlic; and 1 fresh jalapeño chile pepper, seeded and chopped (see tip, page 36), in 2 tablespoons hot olive oil until tender. Stir in ¾ cup sliced pimiento-stuffed green olives, ½ cup red wine vinegar, and 1 teaspoon dried thyme, crushed. Bring to boiling; reduce heat. Simmer, uncovered, until almost all of liquid has evaporated.

Nutrition Facts per serving: 358 cal., 17 g total fat (3 g sat. fat), 64 mg chol., 450 mg sodium, 8 g carbo., 2 g fiber, 41 g pro. Daily Values: 104% vit. A, 103% vit. C, 4% calcium, 15% iron. Exchanges: 1 Vegetable, 5½ Very Lean Meat, 3 Fat

THAI-STYLE SEAFOOD KABOBS

While the coconut milk-and-lime marinade is doing its magic, you have time to make a simple peanut sauce. Just minutes on the grill and the kabobs are ready to enjoy.

Prep: 20 minutes Marinate: 30 minutes Grill: 5 minutes
Makes: 4 to 6 servings

8 ounces fresh or frozen peeled and deveined medium shrimp
8 ounces fresh or frozen sea scallops
¼ cup purchased unsweetened coconut milk
2 tablespoons lime juice
1 tablespoon soy sauce
⅓ cup purchased unsweetened coconut milk
¼ cup peanut butter
2 tablespoons snipped fresh cilantro
1 tablespoon thinly sliced green onion
1 tablespoon lime juice
½ teaspoon chile paste or ⅛ teaspoon crushed red pepper

1 Thaw shrimp and scallops, if frozen. Rinse and pat dry. Place in a medium bowl.

2 For marinade, in a small bowl combine the ¼ cup coconut milk, the 2 tablespoons lime juice, and the soy sauce. Pour marinade over shrimp and scallops; stir to coat. Cover; marinate in the refrigerator for 30 minutes, stirring once.

3 Meanwhile, for sauce, in a small bowl whisk together the ⅓ cup coconut milk, the peanut butter, cilantro, green onion, the 1 tablespoon lime juice, and the chile paste. Cover and let stand at room temperature for 30 minutes.

4 Drain shrimp and scallops; discard marinade. On long metal skewers, alternately thread shrimp and scallops, leaving a ¼-inch space between pieces.

5 Lightly grease or coat with nonstick cooking spray an unheated grill rack. For a charcoal grill, grill kabobs on the greased rack of an uncovered grill directly over medium coals for 5 to 8 minutes or until shrimp and scallops are opaque, turning once halfway through grilling. (For a gas grill, preheat grill. Reduce to medium. Place skewers on greased grill rack over heat. Cover; grill as above.) Serve seafood with sauce.

Nutrition Facts per serving: 247 cal., 15 g total fat (6 g sat. fat), 84 mg chol., 350 mg sodium, 7 g carbo., 1 g fiber, 23 g pro. Daily Values: 5% vit. A, 9% vit. C, 5% calcium, 10% iron. Exchanges: ½ Other Carbo., 3 Very Lean Meat, 2½ Fat

FOOD FOR THOUGHT SCALLOPS

Scallops tend to deteriorate quickly once removed from the water. They're usually shucked when harvested and sold with or without the edible orange roe attached. They may be pale beige to creamy pink in color—avoid those that are stark white, a coloring that indicates they have been soaked in water to plump them up. Three types of scallops are available.

● Sea Scallops: Harvested from North Atlantic waters, sea scallops are widely available. They average 1½ inches in diameter, making them easy to grill, and weigh in at 12 to 15 scallops per pound.

● Bay Scallops: Bay scallops are smaller than sea scallops, with a diameter of about ½ inch and weighing in at 100 scallops per pound. They're more tender and sweeter than sea scallops but also more expensive because they're less plentiful.

● Calico Scallops: Gathered from warmer waters off the Atlantic and Gulf Coasts, as well as Central and South America, these scallops are smaller than bay scallops and require steaming to remove the shells. Because they are so small, they are prone to overcooking.

Soy-Lime Scallops with Leeks

SOY-LIME SCALLOPS WITH LEEKS

Prep: 10 minutes Marinate: 30 minutes Grill: 8 minutes
Makes: 4 servings

- **1 pound fresh or frozen sea scallops**
- **¼ cup soy sauce**
- **¼ cup rice vinegar**
- **8 baby leeks or 2 small leeks**
- **12 medium green or red scallions, or green onions**
- **1 medium lime, halved**
  - **Black and/or white sesame seeds (optional)**
- **¼ cup butter, melted**

1 Thaw scallops, if frozen. Rinse scallops; pat dry with paper towels. For marinade, in a bowl combine soy sauce and rice vinegar; set aside.

2 Trim root ends and green tops of leeks. Rinse leeks thoroughly to remove any grit. If using, cut the small leeks lengthwise into quarters; insert a wooden pick crosswise through each leek quarter to hold layers together when grilling.

3 Place scallops, leeks, and scallions in a self-sealing plastic bag set in a shallow dish. Pour in marinade; seal the bag, turning to coat scallops and vegetables. Marinate in refrigerator for 30 minutes. Remove scallops, leeks, and scallions from bag. Discard marinade.

4 For a charcoal grill, place scallops, leeks, scallions, and lime halves (cut sides down) on the rack of an uncovered grill directly over medium coals. Grill for 8 to 10 minutes or until scallops are opaque, turning scallops and vegetables occasionally. Remove any scallions from grill rack before they overbrown. (For a gas grill, preheat grill. Reduce heat to medium. Place scallops, leeks and scallions on grill rack over heat. Cover; grill as above.)

5 To serve, transfer leeks and scallions to serving plates. Top with scallops. Using grilling tongs, remove limes from grill and squeeze over scallops. If desired, sprinkle with sesame seeds. Serve with melted butter.

Nutrition Facts per serving: 229 cal., 13 g total fat (8 g sat. fat), 70 mg chol., 467 mg sodium, 8 g carbo., 1 g fiber, 20 g pro. Daily Values: 24% vit. C, 6% calcium, 6% iron. Exchanges: ½ Other Carbo., 2½ Very Lean Meat, 2½ Fat

SEAFOOD PAELLA

This recipe is a twist on the Spanish classic. Fish, sausage, and vegetables are grilled on skewers and served with saffron-infused rice.

Prep: 30 minutes Cook: 18 minutes Grill: 9 minutes
Makes: 4 servings

- **8 ounces fresh or frozen tuna, mahi mahi, grouper, and/or sea bass fillets**
- **8 fresh or frozen sea scallops (about 12 ounces)**
- **½ cup chopped onion (1 medium)**
- **2 cloves garlic, minced**
- **2 teaspoons olive oil**
- **1 cup long grain rice**
- **⅓ cup water**
- **1 14-ounce can chicken broth**
- **¼ teaspoon saffron threads, crushed**
- **½ cup frozen peas**
- **8 ounces cooked chicken sausage or smoked turkey sausage, cut into 1-inch pieces**
- **2 red, yellow, and/or green sweet peppers, cut into 1-inch pieces**
- **2 tablespoons olive oil**
- **1 clove garlic, minced**
- **¼ teaspoon salt**
- **⅛ teaspoon cayenne pepper**

1 Thaw fish and scallops, if frozen. Rinse fish and scallops; pat dry with paper towels. Cut fish into 1-inch cubes. Set aside.

2 In a medium saucepan cook the onion and garlic in the 2 teaspoons olive oil over medium heat until tender. Stir in uncooked rice; cook for 1 minute. Carefully add ⅓ cup water, the broth, and saffron to saucepan. Bring to boiling; reduce heat to low. Cook, covered, for 18 to 20 minutes or until all the liquid is absorbed and rice is tender. Remove from heat. Stir in peas; cover and let stand for 5 minutes.

3 Meanwhile, on 8 long metal skewers, alternately thread fish, sausage, and sweet peppers, leaving a ¼-inch space between pieces. Add a scallop to the end of each skewer. In a small bowl combine the 2 tablespoons olive oil, garlic, salt, and cayenne pepper; brush on kabobs.

4 Lightly grease or coat with nonstick cooking spray an unheated grill rack. For a charcoal grill, grill kabobs on the greased rack of an uncovered grill directly over medium coals for 9 to 11 minutes or until fish flakes easily when tested with a fork and scallops turn opaque, turning occasionally. (For a gas grill, preheat grill. Reduce heat to medium. Place kabobs on greased grill rack over heat. Cover; grill as at left.) Serve kabobs with the rice.

Nutrition Facts per serving: 533 cal., 19 g total fat (4 g sat. fat), 70 mg chol., 1,087 mg sodium, 48 g carbo., 3 g fiber, 42 g pro. Daily Values: 47% vit. A, 201% vit. C, 6% calcium, 20% iron. Exchanges: ½ Vegetable, 3 Starch, 4½ Very Lean Meat, 3 Fat

FOOD FOR THOUGHT
SAFFRON

Saffron is a delicate yet conspicuous spice that is derived from the tiny purple flowers of the crocus. Within each flower are three bright orange threads or stigmas, which are a mere ½ to ⅔ inch long. These threads are picked by hand over a 3-week period each year in a highly labor-intensive process and are then dried. It takes about 100,000 flowers to produce 1 pound of dried saffron, so it's no wonder saffron is the world's most expensive spice. Valued as a spice, a dye, and medicine in ancient times, today saffron is widely used in Indian rice dishes, Italian risotto, and Spanish paella. Its strength in flavor and color vary depending on its origin and variety.

Shrimp Po'Boy with Dried Tomato Aïoli

SHRIMP PO' BOY WITH DRIED TOMATO AÏOLI

Prep: 30 minutes Marinate: 1 hour
Grill: 7 minutes plus 12 minutes Makes: 4 servings

- **1 pound fresh or frozen jumbo shrimp in shells**
- **2 tablespoons lemon juice**
- **2 tablespoons olive oil**
- **1 teaspoon seafood seasoning (such as Old Bay)**
- **1 8-ounce loaf or ¹/₂ of a 16-ounce loaf unsliced French bread**
- **¹/₂ cup mayonnaise**
- **¹/₄ cup chopped dried tomatoes (oil pack), drained**
- **2 tablespoons dairy sour cream**
- **2 cloves garlic, minced**
- **¹/₂ of a medium red onion, thinly sliced**
- **Shredded lettuce (optional)**

1 Thaw shrimp, if frozen. Peel and devein shrimp, removing tails. Rinse shrimp; pat dry. Place shrimp in a self-sealing plastic bag set in a shallow dish. Stir together 1 tablespoon of the lemon juice, 1 tablespoon of the olive oil, and the seafood seasoning. Pour the marinade over shrimp; seal bag. Marinate shrimp in refrigerator for 1 hour, turning bag occasionally. On 4 long metal skewers thread shrimp, leaving a ¹/₄-inch space between pieces.

2 Halve bread horizontally. Lightly brush cut bread surface with remaining 1 tablespoon olive oil.

3 For a charcoal grill, grill shrimp on a grill rack directly over medium coals for 7 to 9 minutes or until shrimp are opaque, turning once halfway through grilling. Meanwhile, add bread to grill. Grill about 2 minutes or until bread is lightly toasted. Remove bread from grill. (For a gas grill, preheat grill. Reduce heat to medium. Place shrimp and bread on grill rack over heat. Cover; grill as above.)

4 Meanwhile, in a small bowl stir together the remaining 1 tablespoon lemon juice, mayonnaise, dried tomatoes, sour cream, and garlic. Spread on toasted bread. Place bottom, spread side up, in the center of an 18-inch square of heavy-duty foil. Arrange shrimp and red onion slices on bread bottom; add bread top. Bring up two opposite edges of foil and seal with a double fold. Fold remaining edges together to completely enclose. Return to grill; grill for 12 to 15 minutes or until heated through, turning once.

5 To serve, remove foil from po' boy. Remove top and, if desired, add lettuce. Replace top; cut into 4 equal pieces.

Nutrition Facts per serving: 545 cal., 34 g total fat (5 g sat. fat), 152 mg chol., 831 mg sodium, 35 g carbo., 3 g fiber, 23 g pro. Daily Values: 7% vit. A, 24% vit. C, 11% calcium, 20% iron. Exchanges: ¹/₂ Vegetable, 2 Starch, 2¹/₂ Very Lean Meat, 6 Fat

CURRIED COCONUT SHRIMP AND RICE IN BANANA LEAVES

Use banana leaves if you want to impress your guests. Otherwise heavy-duty foil will suffice.

Prep: 30 minutes Soak: 1 hour Marinate: 30 minutes
Grill: 20 minutes Makes: 4 servings

  4 6- to 8-inch wooden skewers
1½ pounds fresh or frozen peeled and
      deveined medium shrimp
1½ teaspoons curry powder
 ¾ teaspoon garam masala
 ½ teaspoon salt
 ¼ teaspoon ground cardamom
 ¼ teaspoon cayenne pepper
 ½ cup purchased unsweetened
      coconut milk (no substitutes)
  6 cloves garlic, minced garlic
  1 firm, ripe banana, cut into
      ¼-inch slices
  2 to 3 large fresh or frozen banana
      leaves,* thawed and cut into four
      9-inch and four 10-inch squares
  1 recipe Spiced Basmati Rice

1 Soak skewers in water for 1 hour; drain. Meanwhile, thaw shrimp, if frozen; set aside. In a large bowl stir together the curry powder, garam masala, salt, cardamom, and cayenne pepper. Reserve 2 teaspoons of the curry mixture for the Spiced Basmati Rice; set aside. For marinade, stir coconut milk and garlic into remaining curry mixture. Add shrimp and banana slices; toss gently to coat. Cover and marinate in the refrigerator for 30 minutes.

2 Rinse banana leaves; pat dry with paper towels. To assemble, spoon one-fourth of the shrimp mixture (about 1 cup) onto the center of a 9-inch square banana leaf. Fold two opposite sides of the leaf pieces over the center, then fold over the remaining sides. Place package seam side down in the center of a 10-inch square banana leaf. Wrap as directed above to form an outer package. Secure the package with soaked skewers. Repeat for remaining 3 banana leaf packets.

3 For a charcoal grill, arrange medium-hot coals around the edge of the grill. Test for medium heat in the center of the grill. Place packets on grill rack in the center of the grill. Cover; grill for

20 to 25 minutes or until shrimp turn opaque. (For a gas grill, preheat grill. Reduce heat to medium. Adjust for indirect cooking. Grill as above.)

4 To serve, remove wooden skewers. Unfold outside leaf layer of packets. Cut open inside leaf layer to expose filling. Serve immediately with Spiced Basmati Rice.

Spiced Basmati Rice: In a medium saucepan heat 3 tablespoons cooking oil over medium heat. Add the reserved spice mixture. With a wooden spoon, stir for 10 to 15 seconds. Add ½ cup chopped onion, ¼ cup finely chopped carrot, and one 2-inch piece stick cinnamon. Reduce heat to medium-low. Cook, covered, stirring occasionally, for 8 to 10 minutes or until onions are soft and translucent. Remove from heat. Carefully add 1¼ cups water. Return to heat; bring just to boiling. Stir in ½ cup uncooked basmati rice. Reduce heat to low. Simmer, covered, about 20 minutes or until rice is tender. Discard cinnamon stick. Fluff rice with a fork. Makes about 2½ cups.

*Note: If banana leaves are unavailable, cut four 10-inch squares of heavy-duty foil. Place one-fourth of the shrimp mixture in the center of each square. For each packet, bring up two opposite edges of foil; seal with a double fold. Fold remaining ends to completely enclose the filling, leaving space for steam to build.

Nutrition Facts per serving: 464 cal., 19 g total fat (7 g sat. fat), 259 mg chol., 413 mg sodium, 34 g carbo., 2 g fiber, 38 g pro. Daily Values: 46% vit. A, 14% vit. C, 12% calcium, 33% iron. Exchanges: 1 Starch, 5 Very Lean Meat, 4 Fat

LINGUINE AND CLAMS IN HERBED WINE SAUCE

If you don't have a foil pan, cover the outside of a 13×9×2-inch baking pan with foil.

Prep: 30 minutes Stand: 45 minutes Grill: 10 minutes
Makes: 4 servings

  2 dozen fresh clams in shells
  1 cup salt
  5 tablespoons olive oil
  6 cloves garlic, minced
  2 medium onions, sliced
  4 anchovy fillets, finely chopped, or
      ¼ teaspoon anchovy paste

½ cup dry white wine

¼ teaspoon sea salt

¼ teaspoon coarsely ground black pepper

⅛ to ¼ teaspoon crushed red pepper

6 medium roma tomatoes, seeded and finely chopped

¼ cup snipped fresh basil

1 tablespoon snipped fresh oregano

2 tablespoons olive oil

8 ounces dried linguine or spaghetti

8 sprigs fresh thyme

2 bay leaves

4 slices French bread

1 Scrub clams in shells under cold running water. In an 8-quart Dutch oven combine 4 quarts cold water and ⅓ cup of the salt; add clams. Let stand for 15 minutes; drain and rinse. Using fresh water and salt, repeat two more times.

2 For sauce, in a large skillet heat 3 tablespoons of the olive oil over medium heat. Cook garlic in the hot oil about 30 seconds. Add onions and anchovies; cook for 4 to 5 minutes or until onions are tender, stirring occasionally. Add wine, sea salt, black pepper, and crushed red pepper; continue cooking for 2 minutes more. Remove from heat. Stir in tomatoes, 2 tablespoons of the basil, and the oregano. Set aside.

3 Meanwhile, prepare linguine according to package directions. Toss pasta with remaining 2 tablespoons olive oil; cover and keep warm.

4 Place the clams in a 13×9×2-inch disposable foil pan. Tie thyme sprigs and bay leaves together in a bundle with 100-percent-cotton string. Add thyme and bay leaves to pan. Add sauce. Cover pan with foil, sealing tightly.

5 For a charcoal grill, grill clams in foil pan on a grill rack directly over medium-hot coals for 10 to 12 minutes or until shells open and sauce is hot. (For a gas grill, preheat grill. Reduce heat to medium-high. Place pan on a grill rack. Cover; grill as above.) Discard clams that do not open. Discard thyme sprigs and bay leaves. Sprinkle with remaining 2 tablespoons basil. Serve immediately with linguine and French bread.

Nutrition Facts per serving: 551 cal., 20 g total fat (3 g sat. fat), 23 mg chol., 448 mg sodium, 69 g carbo., 5 g fiber, 20 g pro. Daily Values: 22% vit. A, 59% vit. C, 10% calcium, 60% iron. Exchanges: ½ Vegetable, 4 Starch, ½ Other Carbo., 1 Lean Meat, 3½ Fat

Linguine and Clams in Herbed Wine Sauce

FOOD FOR THOUGHT
CLAMS

Clams are a tasty treat, especially when cooked on the grill. Cultivated on both East and West Coasts, three basic categories of hard-shell clams (also called quahogs) are based on size. In general, the smaller the variety, the more tender the clam.

● Littleneck Clams: These are the smallest, ranging from about 1½ to 2½ inches in diameter. They are the most common variety available and also the most expensive. Tender and sweet, these clams are commonly eaten grilled or steamed.

● Japanese or Manila Clams: A popular variety of littleneck, these thin-shelled clams are cultivated on the Pacific Coast.

● Cherrystone Clams: Slightly less expensive than littlenecks, cherrystones are approximately 2½ to 3 inches in diameter.

● Chowder Clams: More than 3 inches in diameter, these are best used to make chowders and fritters.

Clam Bake

CLAM BAKE

Although traditional clam bakes are cooked in a pit on the beach, you can enjoy this version in your backyard.

Prep: 20 minutes Soak: 45 minutes Grill: 20 minutes
Makes: 4 servings

- **1 pound fresh littleneck clams in shells**
- **1 pound fresh mussels in shells**
- **1 pound cooked smoked chorizo sausage, sliced ½ inch thick (optional)**
- **1 pound small round red potatoes, cut into 1-inch pieces**
- **4 ears fresh corn, husks and silks removed**
- **4 6- to 8-ounce lobster tails**
- **½ cup butter, melted**

1 Scrub clams and mussels in shells under cold running water. Remove beards from mussels, if present. Place clams and mussels in a large bowl; add ⅓ cup salt and enough cold water to cover. Soak for 15 minutes; drain and rinse. Using fresh water and salt repeat two more times.

2 Place clams and mussels in the bottom of a 13×9×3-inch disposable foil pan. Place chorizo (if desired), potatoes, and corn on top of shellfish. Place lobster tails on top. Cover pan with foil, sealing tightly.

3 For a charcoal grill, grill foil pan on the rack of an uncovered grill directly over medium coals for 20 to 30 minutes or until potatoes are tender. (For a gas grill, preheat grill. Reduce heat to medium. Place foil pan on the grill rack over heat. Cover; grill as above.)

4 Transfer clam mixture to a serving platter, reserving cooking liquid. Discard clams and mussels that don't open. Serve seafood and vegetables with butter and cooking liquid.

Nutrition Facts per serving: 564 cal., 34 g total fat (17 g sat. fat), 166 mg chol., 647 mg sodium, 44 g carbo., 4 g fiber, 25 g pro. Daily Values: 31% vit. A, 56% vit. C, 10% calcium, 78% iron. Exchanges: 3 Starch, 2½ Very Lean Meat, 5½ Fat

MUSSELS IN ANISE-SAFFRON BROTH

Although fennel has a lighter, sweeter flavor than anise, either will add the coveted licorice-like flavor.

Prep: 15 minutes Soak: 45 minutes Grill: 6 minutes
Makes: 4 servings

2 pounds fresh mussels
1 cup salt
¹⁄₂ cup finely chopped fennel bulb or
**   3 tablespoons anise liqueur (such**
**   as Pernod or Pastis)**
2 tablespoons shallot, finely chopped
1 tablespoon minced garlic
¹⁄₄ cup butter
¹⁄₄ cup dry white wine
¹⁄₈ teaspoon saffron threads, crushed
1 medium tomato, peeled, seeded,
**   and finely chopped**
2 tablespoons snipped fresh chives
1 recipe Grilled Garlic Toast

1 Scrub mussels in shells under cold running water. Remove beards, if present. Place mussels in a large bowl; add ¹⁄₃ cup salt and enough cold water to cover. Let stand for 15 minutes; drain and rinse. Using fresh water and salt, repeat two more times; set aside.

2 For sauce, cook fennel (if using), shallot, and garlic in hot butter over medium heat until tender. Add wine, anise liqueur (if using), and saffron. Stir in tomato; remove from heat.

3 Place mussels in a 13×9×3-inch disposable foil pan; add sauce. Cover pan with foil; seal tightly. For a charcoal grill, grill pan on a grill rack directly over medium-hot coals for 6 to 8 minutes or until shells open. (For a gas grill, preheat grill. Reduce heat to medium-high. Place pan on a grill rack. Cover; grill as above.) Discard any empty shells and mussels that do not open.

4 To serve, transfer mussels to large bowls; ladle sauce over each serving. Garnish with snipped chives. Serve with Grilled Garlic Toast.

Grilled Garlic Toast: In a small bowl combine 3 tablespoons olive oil, ¹⁄₄ teaspoon garlic salt, and ¹⁄₄ teaspoon ground white pepper. Brush mixture evenly onto eight ¹⁄₂-inch slices French bread. Grill bread slices directly over medium-high heat about 2 minutes or until bread slices are toasted, turning once halfway through grilling.

Nutrition Facts per serving: 490 cal., 26 g total fat (10 g sat. fat), 65 mg chol., 818 mg sodium, 37 g carbo., 2 g fiber, 19 g pro. Daily Values: 19% vit. A, 26% vit. C, 9% calcium, 32% iron. Exchanges: 2 Starch, ¹⁄₂ Other Carbo., 2 Very Lean Meat, 5 Fat

SMOKIN' HOT TIP

Clams, scallops, mussels, and oysters are best enjoyed when they are fresh. Keep these important guidelines in mind when you shop for them:
● Purchase shellfish from a reputable supplier who can provide certification showing when and where the shellfish were harvested.
● Shells that are slightly opened when purchased should close when gently tapped. Discard any clams, mussels, or scallops whose shells don't close tightly and also those with broken shells.
● Fresh shellfish smell sweet or like the sea.
● Refrigerate shellfish within 1 hour after purchase or keep in an ice chest until refrigeration is possible.
● Eat fresh shellfish as soon as possible. If necessary, store in the refrigerator in a container covered with a damp towel for 1 to 2 days. Don't store shellfish in a plastic bag or in fresh water as this will kill them.
● Rinse or scrub shellfish under running water before cooking.
● Shellfish are cooked and ready to eat when the shells open and the flesh inside appears plump and opaque.

ZUCCHINI CRAB CAKES

Prep: 20 minutes Grill: 8 minutes
Makes: 8 crab cakes (4 servings)

1 cup coarsely shredded zucchini
¼ cup thinly sliced green onions (2)
2 teaspoons cooking oil
1 egg, beaten
⅔ cup seasoned fine dry bread crumbs
1 tablespoon Dijon-style mustard
1 teaspoon snipped fresh thyme or
½ teaspoon dried thyme, crushed
⅛ to ¼ teaspoon cayenne pepper
8 ounces fresh lump crabmeat
(1½ cups) or two 6-ounce cans
crabmeat, drained, flaked, and
cartilage removed
2 large red and/or yellow tomatoes,
sliced ¼ inch thick
1 recipe Tomato-Sour Cream Sauce
Lemon wedges (optional)

1 In a medium skillet cook zucchini and green onion in hot oil over medium-high heat for 3 to 5 minutes or until vegetables are just tender and liquid is evaporated. Cool slightly.

2 In a large bowl combine egg, bread crumbs, mustard, thyme, and cayenne pepper. Add crabmeat and the zucchini mixture; mix well. Using about ¼ cup mixture per crab cake, shape into eight ½-inch-thick patties.

3 Lightly grease or coat with nonstick cooking spray an unheated grill rack. For a charcoal grill, grill crab cakes on the greased rack of an uncovered grill directly over medium coals for 8 to 10 minutes or until golden, turning once. For a gas grill, preheat grill. Reduce heat to medium. Place crab cakes on greased grill rack over heat. Cover; grill as above.

4 To serve, arrange tomato slices and crab cakes on plates. Serve with Tomato-Sour Cream Sauce and, if desired, lemon wedges.

Tomato-Sour Cream Sauce: In a small bowl stir together ½ cup dairy sour cream, ¼ cup finely chopped yellow or red tomato, 1 tablespoon lemon or lime juice, and ⅛ teaspoon seasoned salt. Cover and chill until serving time.

Nutrition Facts per serving: 232 cal., 10 g total fat (4 g sat. fat), 131 mg chol., 917 mg sodium, 20 g carbo., 2 g fiber, 17 g pro. Daily Values: 20% vit. A, 29% vit. C, 12% calcium, 8% iron. Exchanges: 1 Vegetable, 1 Other Carbo., 2 Very Lean Meat, 1½ Fat

ROCK LOBSTER TAILS

Prep: 15 minutes Grill: 11 minutes
Makes: 4 servings

4 6-ounces fresh or frozen rock
lobster tails
2 tablespoons olive oil
½ teaspoon finely shredded lemon or
lime peel (set aside)
4 teaspoons lemon or lime juice
2 cloves garlic, minced
1 teaspoon chili powder
½ cup mayonnaise or salad dressing
1 teaspoon snipped fresh dill or
¼ teaspoon dried dill
Lemon or lime wedges (optional)

1 Thaw rock lobster tails, if frozen. Rinse lobster; pat dry with paper towels. Using kitchen shears or a large sharp knife, cut each lobster tail in half through center of hard top shell, meat of lobster tail, and undershells. Set lobster tails aside.

2 In a small bowl combine oil, 2 teaspoons of the lemon juice, the garlic, and chili powder; brush on exposed lobster meat, reserving some of the lemon juice mixture.

3 For a charcoal grill, grill lobster tails, cut sides down, on the rack of an uncovered grill directly over medium heat for 6 minutes. Turn lobster tails; brush with reserved lemon juice mixture. Grill for 5 to 8 minutes more or until meat is opaque in the center. Do not overcook. (For a gas grill, preheat grill. Reduce heat to medium. Place lobster tails on grill rack over heat. Cover; grill as above.)

4 Meanwhile, for sauce, combine mayonnaise, dill, lemon peel, and remaining 2 teaspoons lemon juice. Serve lobster with sauce and, if desired, lemon wedges.

Nutrition Facts per serving: 367 cal., 30 g total fat (4 g sat. fat), 128 mg chol., 462 mg sodium, 2 g carbo., 0 g fiber, 22 g pro. Daily Values: 6% vit. A, 6% vit. C, 6% calcium, 3% iron. Exchanges: 3 Very Lean Meat, 6 Fat.

10

Game
& Fowl

BISON

BBQ Bison Ribs with Sorghum-Bourbon Sauce, 347
Bison Cheeseburgers, 345
Bison-Romano Burgers with Pimiento Catsup, 345
Bison Steaks with White Wine-Shallot Sauce, 346
Marinated Bison London Broil, 346

CONDIMENTS & SAUCES

Armagnac-Mushroom Cream, 353
Basil Mayonnaise, 352
Currant-Balsamic Sauce, 358
Fig Chutney, 350
Garlic-Mustard Mayonnaise, 345
Mediterranean Olive Relish, 348
Orange-Balsamic Vinaigrette, 357
Pimiento Catsup, 345
Porcini-Garlic Butter, 346
Sorghum-Bourbon Sauce, 347
White Wine-Shallot Sauce, 346

DUCK

Duck Breasts with Arugula and Orange-Balsamic Vinaigrette, 357
Duck Breasts with Currant-Balsamic Sauce, 358
Rosemary Duck Breasts with Marinated Pears, 356
Smoked Duck with Honey-Thyme Sauce, 358

ELK

Elk Steaks with Mediterranean Olive Relish, 348
Ground Elk Kabobs with Currant-Pine Nut Couscous, 348

OSTRICH

Ostrich Burgers à la Mediterranea, 352
Ostrich Fan Roast with Aromatic Spices, 351

PHEASANT

Grilled Pheasant with Armagnac-Mushroom Cream, 353
Juniper-Scented Pheasant with Caramelized Apples, 353

SIDE DISHES

Caramelized Apples, 353
Currant-Pine Nut Couscous, 348

SMALL GAME BIRDS

Maple-Glazed Quail, 355
Quail in Grape Leaves, 355
Smoked Guinea Hen, 354

VENISON

Spicy-Sweet Venison Tenderloins with Fig Chutney, 350
Venison Tenderloins Wrapped in Bacon, 350

BISON CHEESEBURGERS

Prep: 10 minutes Grill: 20 minutes
Makes: 4 servings

1 **large sweet onion, cut into
¹/₂-inch slices**
2 **teaspoons olive oil**
1 **pound ground bison**
4 **1-ounce slices smoked Swiss cheese**
4 **kaiser rolls, split and toasted**
1 **recipe Garlic-Mustard Mayonnaise**
4 **lettuce leaves**

1 Brush onion slices with oil; set aside. Shape ground bison into four ³/₄-inch-thick patties.

2 For a charcoal grill, grill onion slices on the rack of an uncovered grill directly over medium coals for 5 minutes. Add patties to grill. Grill for 14 to 18 minutes more or until onion is tender and meat is done (160°F), turning onion slices and patties once halfway through grilling. Top burgers with cheese. Grill about 1 minute more or until cheese is melted. (For a gas grill, preheat grill. Reduce heat to medium. Place onion slices, then patties on grill rack over heat. Cover; grill as above.)

3 Serve burgers on rolls with grilled onion slices, Garlic-Mustard Mayonnaise, and lettuce.

Garlic-Mustard Mayonnaise: In a small bowl combine ¹/₃ cup mayonnaise or salad dressing, 1 tablespoon country-style Dijon mustard, and 2 cloves garlic, minced.

Nutrition Facts per serving: 570 cal., 29 g total fat (9 g sat. fat), 107 mg chol., 642 mg sodium, 36 g carbo., 1 g fiber, 39 g pro. Daily Values: 9% vit. A, 4% vit. C, 29% calcium, 34% iron. Exchanges: ½ Vegetable, 2 Starch, 3½ Very Lean Meat, 1 High-Fat Meat, 4 Fat

FOOD FOR THOUGHT BUFFALO

Bison and buffalo meat are one and the same. Its flavor is similar to lean beef but slightly sweeter. Moreover, it's high in iron and low in cholesterol and fat, making it a good alternative for the beef in most recipes. Buffalo is available fresh or frozen year-round. Look for it in gourmet and specialty foods sections at the supermarket or butcher shop.

BISON-ROMANO BURGERS WITH PIMIENTO CATSUP

As with other ground meat burgers, bison burgers must be cooked to an internal temperature of 160°F.

Prep: 20 minutes Grill: 14 minutes
Makes: 6 servings

1 **slightly beaten egg**
1 **cup grated Romano cheese**
¹/₂ **cup finely chopped red onion**
¹/₄ **cup fine dry bread crumbs**
2 **teaspoons dried Italian
seasoning, crushed**
¹/₂ **teaspoon salt**
¹/₄ **teaspoon crushed red pepper
(optional)**
2 **pounds ground bison**
6 **kaiser rolls, split and toasted**
1 **recipe Pimiento Catsup
Tomato slices, red onion slices,
and/or dill pickle slices (optional)**

1 In a large bowl combine egg, Romano cheese, onion, bread crumbs, Italian seasoning, salt, and, if desired, crushed red pepper. Add ground bison; mix well. Shape meat mixture into six ³/₄-inch-thick patties.

2 For a charcoal grill, grill patties on the rack of an uncovered grill directly over medium coals for 14 to 18 minutes or until meat is done (160°F); turn once halfway through grilling. (For a gas grill, preheat grill. Reduce heat to medium. Place patties on grill rack over heat. Cover; grill as above.)

3 Serve burgers on rolls with Pimiento Catsup. If desired, serve burgers with tomato, onion, and/or pickles.

Pimiento Catsup: In a food processor or blender combine ¹/₂ cup catsup, ¹/₄ cup diced pimientos, 4 teaspoons bottled minced roasted garlic, 1 tablespoon mild-flavored molasses, 1 teaspoon cider vinegar, and ¹/₈ teaspoon crushed red pepper. Cover and process or blend until smooth. Cover and chill until serving time.

Nutrition Facts per serving: 452 cal., 10 g total fat (4 g sat. fat), 143 mg chol., 1,085 mg sodium, 44 g carbo., 2 g fiber, 45 g pro. Daily Values: 11% vit. A, 20% vit. C, 24% calcium, 39% iron. Exchanges: 3 Starch, 5 Very Lean Meat, 1 Fat

BISON STEAKS WITH WHITE WINE-SHALLOT SAUCE

Prep: 25 minutes Grill: 16 minutes
Makes: 4 servings

  4 **10-ounce bison top loin steaks, cut 1 inch thick**
  1 **tablespoon coarsely cracked black pepper**
  ¾ **teaspoon kosher salt**
  1 **recipe White Wine-Shallot Sauce**

1 Trim fat from steaks. For rub, combine pepper and salt. Sprinkle rub evenly over both sides of steaks; rub in with your fingers.

2 For a charcoal grill, grill steaks on the rack of an uncovered grill directly over medium coals until desired doneness, turning once halfway through grilling. Allow 16 to 19 minutes for medium-rare (145°F) or 19 to 22 minutes for medium (160°F). (For a gas grill, preheat grill. Reduce heat to medium. Place steaks on grill rack over heat. Cover; grill as above.) Serve with White Wine-Shallot Sauce.

White Wine-Shallot Sauce: In a medium saucepan combine ½ cup dry white wine, ⅓ cup finely chopped shallots, and ¼ cup beef broth. Bring to boiling; reduce heat to medium. Simmer, uncovered, for 12 to 14 minutes or until liquid is reduced to 1 to 2 tablespoons. Reduce heat to low. Using a wire whisk, stir in 2 tablespoons whipping cream. Add 6 tablespoons softened butter, 1 tablespoon at a time, allowing each tablespoon to melt before adding the next. Season to taste with salt and pepper. Serve immediately.

Nutrition Facts per serving: 542 cal., 28 g total fat (13 g sat. fat), 260 mg chol., 771 mg sodium, 4 g carbo., 0 g fiber, 62 g pro. Daily Values: 17% vit. A, 2% vit. C, 4% calcium, 51% iron. Exchanges: 9 Very Lean Meat, 5 Fat

MARINATED BISON LONDON BROIL

Prep: 20 minutes Marinate: 2 to 8 hours Grill: 12 minutes
Makes: 8 servings

  1 **2-pound bison flank steak**
  ¾ **cup dry red wine**
  ¼ **cup water**
  2 **tablespoons finely chopped shallots**
  2 **tablespoons olive oil**
  1 **tablespoon snipped fresh oregano, thyme, or basil, or ¼ teaspoon dried oregano, thyme, or basil, crushed**
  ¼ **teaspoon salt**
  ⅛ **teaspoon black pepper**
  1 **recipe Porcini-Garlic Butter**

1 Score steak on both sides by making shallow cuts at 1-inch intervals in a diamond pattern. Place steak in a self-sealing plastic bag set in a shallow dish. For marinade, in a small bowl stir together wine, water, shallots, oil, oregano, salt, and pepper. Pour over steak; seal bag. Marinate in refrigerator for 2 to 8 hours; turn bag occasionally. Drain steak, discarding marinade.

2 For a charcoal grill, grill steak on the rack of an uncovered grill directly over medium coals for 12 to 14 minutes for medium (160°F), turning once halfway through grilling. (For a gas grill, preheat grill. Reduce heat to medium. Place steak on grill rack over heat. Cover; grill as above.)

3 To serve, thinly slice steak diagonally across the grain. Spoon melted Porcini-Garlic Butter over steak slices.

Porcini-Garlic Butter: In a small bowl cover ½ ounce dried porcini mushrooms with 1 cup boiling water. Let stand for 15 minutes. Drain mushrooms; finely chop. In a small bowl combine chopped mushrooms, ½ cup softened butter, 1 teaspoon snipped fresh parsley, ⅛ teaspoon salt, and 2 cloves garlic, minced. Cover and chill for up to 8 hours. Just before serving, in a small saucepan melt butter mixture over low heat.

Nutrition Facts per serving: 262 cal., 15 g total fat (8 g sat. fat), 101 mg chol., 238 mg sodium, 6 g carbo., 1 g fiber, 25 g pro. Daily Values: 12% vit. A, 3% vit. C, 1% calcium, 21% iron. Exchanges: ½ Other Carbo., 3½ Very Lean Meat, 2½ Fat

BBQ Bison Ribs with Sorghum-Bourbon Sauce

BBQ BISON RIBS WITH SORGHUM-BOURBON SAUCE

You'll be pleasantly surprised by how well the bison meat soaks up the smoke flavor. The sauce has just the right amount of bourbon to marry well with the smoky ribs.

Prep: 20 minutes Chill: 8 to 24 hours Grill: 1¼ hours
Makes: 4 to 5 servings

- **4 to 5 pounds bison ribs**
- **1 tablespoon salt**
- **1 tablespoon black pepper**
- **2 teaspoons garlic powder**
- **4 to 6 cups hickory wood chips**
- **1 recipe Sorghum-Bourbon Sauce**

1 Trim fat from ribs. For rub, in a small bowl combine salt, pepper, and garlic powder. Sprinkle rub evenly over both sides of ribs; rub in with your fingers. Cover; chill for 8 to 24 hours.

2 At least 1 hour before grilling, soak wood chips in enough water to cover. Drain wood chips.

3 For a charcoal grill, arrange medium-hot coals around a drip pan. Test for medium heat above pan. Sprinkle drained wood chips over coals. Place ribs, bone sides down, on grill rack over drip pan. (Or place ribs in a rib rack; place on grill rack.) Cover; grill for 1¼ to 1½ hours or until ribs are tender, brushing twice with ½ cup of the Sorghum-Bourbon Sauce during the last 30 minutes of grilling. (For a gas grill, preheat grill. Reduce heat to medium. Adjust for indirect cooking. Grill as above, except place ribs in a roasting pan.)

4 To serve, reheat remaining Sorghum-Bourbon Sauce until bubbly; pass with ribs.

Sorghum-Bourbon Sauce: In a medium saucepan stir together ⅓ cup sorghum, ¼ cup strong coffee, ¼ cup bourbon, 2 tablespoons white wine Worcestershire sauce, 2 teaspoons dry mustard, 1 teaspoon onion powder, and ¼ teaspoon bottled hot pepper sauce. Bring to boiling, stirring frequently. Stir in 1½ cups catsup. Return to boiling; remove from heat.

Nutrition Facts per serving: 436 cal., 6 g total fat (2 g sat. fat), 141 mg chol., 2,935 mg sodium, 38 g carbo., 2 g fiber, 53 g pro. Daily Values: 17% vit. A, 24% vit. C, 5% calcium, 43% iron. Exchanges: 2½ Other Carbo., 7½ Very Lean Meat, ½ Fat

GROUND ELK KABOBS WITH CURRANT-PINE NUT COUSCOUS

Shop the Internet to find suppliers of everything from ground elk to elk jerky and elk brats.

Prep: 45 minutes Grill: 8 minutes
Makes: 6 servings

$1/3$ **cup finely chopped peeled Granny Smith apple**
$1/4$ **cup finely chopped pine nuts, toasted**
$1/4$ **cup snipped fresh parsley**
  1 **tablespoon bottled minced garlic**
$1/2$ **teaspoon ground cumin**
$1/4$ **teaspoon cayenne pepper**
$1/4$ **teaspoon ground cinnamon**
$1/4$ **teaspoon ground coriander**
$1 1/2$ **pounds ground elk or lean ground beef**
  2 **small Granny Smith apples, cored and cut into $1/2$-inch-thick wedges**
  2 **medium red sweet peppers, cut into 1-inch pieces**
$1/2$ **cup apple jelly**
  1 **recipe Currant-Pine Nut Couscous**

1 In a large bowl combine the chopped apple, pine nuts, parsley, garlic, cumin, cayenne pepper, cinnamon, coriander, 1 teaspoon salt, and $1/2$ teaspoon black pepper. Add ground elk; mix well. Shape meat mixture into twenty-four 2-inch meatballs.

2 On 6 long metal skewers, alternately thread meatballs, apple wedges, and sweet pepper pieces, leaving a $1/4$-inch space between pieces.

3 For a charcoal grill, grill kabobs on the rack of an uncovered grill directly over medium coals for 8 to 10 minutes or until meat is done (160°F), turning occasionally. (For a gas grill, preheat grill. Reduce heat to medium. Place kabobs on grill rack over heat. Cover; grill as above.)

4 Meanwhile, in a small saucepan heat apple jelly over low heat until melted.

5 To serve, spread Currant-Pine Nut Couscous on a large serving platter; top with kabobs. Drizzle melted jelly over all.

Currant-Pine Nut Couscous: In a medium saucepan bring $1 1/2$ cups chicken broth to boiling. Stir in 1 cup quick-cooking couscous and $1/4$ cup currants. Remove saucepan from heat. Cover and let stand for 5 minutes. Stir in $1/3$ cup chopped pine nuts, toasted.

Nutrition Facts per serving: 454 cal., 10 g total fat (2 g sat. fat), 63 mg chol., 703 mg sodium, 60 g carbo., 5 g fiber, 35 g pro. Daily Values: 31% vit. A, 138% vit. C, 4% calcium, 31% iron. Exchanges: $1/2$ Fruit, 2 Starch, $1 1/2$ Other Carbo., 4 Very Lean Meat, 1 Fat

ELK WITH MEDITERRANEAN OLIVE RELISH

Individual cuts of elk look a lot like beef except for their color. Prior to cooking, the meat is darker because it's not marbled with fat.

Prep: 30 minutes Chill: 2 to 4 hours Grill: 14 minutes
Makes: 4 servings

  3 **tablespoons olive oil**
  2 **tablespoons minced garlic (12 cloves)**
  4 **6- to 8-ounce elk top loin steaks**
  1 **recipe Mediterranean Olive Relish**

1 In a small bowl combine the oil, garlic, $1/2$ teaspoon salt, and $1/4$ teaspoon black pepper. Brush garlic mixture over both sides of steaks. Cover and chill for 2 to 4 hours.

2 For a charcoal grill, grill steaks on the rack of an uncovered grill directly over medium-hot coals until desired doneness, turning once halfway through grilling. Allow 14 to 16 minutes for medium-rare (145°F) or 16 to 18 minutes for medium (160°F). (For a gas grill, preheat grill. Reduce heat to medium-hot. Place steaks on grill rack over heat. Cover; grill as above.) Serve steaks with Mediterranean Olive Relish.

Mediterranean Olive Relish: In a small bowl combine $1/4$ cup chopped pitted oil-cured Greek olives or kalamata olives; 3 tablespoons roasted red sweet peppers, drained and chopped; 2 tablespoons capers, drained; 1 tablespoon olive oil; 1 tablespoon lemon juice; and $1/8$ teaspoon anise seeds, crushed. Cover and chill for up to 24 hours.

Nutrition Facts per serving: 337 cal., 17 g total fat (3 g sat. fat), 93 mg chol., 598 mg sodium, 5 g carbo., 1 g fiber, 40 g pro. Daily Values: 40% vit. C, 3% calcium, 29% iron. Exchanges: 6 Very Lean Meat, 3 Fat

VENISON TENDERLOINS WITH FIG CHUTNEY

If fig preserves are unavailable for the chutney, make with ½ cup blackberry preserves plus ½ cup snipped dried figs.

Prep: 15 minutes Chill: 2 to 24 hours
Grill: 25 minutes Stand: 10 minutes
Makes: 6 to 8 servings

- ½ **teaspoon cumin seeds**
- 1 **tablespoon paprika**
- 1 **tablespoon brown sugar**
- ½ **teaspoon dried thyme, crushed**
- ¼ **teaspoon cayenne pepper**
- 1 **tablespoon cooking oil**
- 2 **12- to 16-ounce venison tenderloins**
- 1 **recipe Fig Chutney**

1 To toast cumin seeds, place seeds in a small skillet. Heat over medium-high heat for 2 to 3 minutes or until toasted, shaking skillet occasionally. For rub, in a small bowl combine toasted cumin seeds, paprika, brown sugar, thyme, cayenne pepper, ½ teaspoon salt, and ½ teaspoon black pepper. Brush oil over meat. Sprinkle rub evenly over meat; rub in with your fingers. Cover and chill for 2 to 24 hours.

2 For a charcoal grill, arrange medium-hot coals around a drip pan. Test for medium heat above pan. Place meat on grill rack over drip pan. Cover; grill for 25 to 30 minutes or until a meat thermometer registers 150°F. (For a gas grill, preheat grill. Reduce heat to medium. Adjust for indirect cooking. Grill as above, except place meat on a rack in a roasting pan.) Remove meat from grill. Cover with foil and let stand 10 minutes. (The meat's temperature will rise 5°F during standing.) Serve with Fig Chutney.

Fig Chutney: In a small saucepan combine ½ cup fig preserves, ¼ cup thinly sliced green onions, 3 tablespoons cider vinegar, 1 tablespoon brown sugar, 1 teaspoon Dijon-style mustard, ¼ teaspoon ground ginger, ⅛ teaspoon salt, and ⅛ teaspoon cayenne pepper. Bring to boiling; reduce heat. Simmer, covered, for 5 minutes. Serve warm or cold.

Nutrition Facts per serving: 257 cal., 5 g total fat (1 g sat. fat), 96 mg chol., 324 mg sodium, 25 g carbo., 1 g fiber, 27 g pro. Daily Values: 12% vit. A, 6% vit. C, 3% calcium, 26% iron. Exchanges: 1½ Other Carbo., 4 Very Lean Meat, ½ Fat

FOOD FOR THOUGHT VENISON

In general, venison refers to meat taken from deer and elk. Though both resemble lean beef, elk has a slightly coarser texture. Venison is available either farm-raised from the United States or imported from New Zealand, where the animals are raised free-range without hormones or steroids. High in protein and low in fat, venison is flavorful and goes well with full-bodied red wine.

VENISON TENDERLOINS WRAPPED IN BACON

Blue-purple juniper berries have a bitter-sweet taste and aroma which go particularly well with game.

Prep: 15 minutes Marinate: 4 to 24 hours
Grill: 25 minutes Stand: 10 minutes
Makes: 6 to 8 servings

- 2 **12- to 16-ounce venison tenderloins**
- ¾ **cup dry red wine**
- 1 **tablespoon olive oil**
- 10 **juniper berries, slightly crushed**
- 2 **bay leaves**
- ½ **teaspoon dried thyme, crushed**
- 6 **cloves garlic, minced**
- 6 **to 8 slices bacon, partially cooked and drained**

1 Place meat in a self-sealing plastic bag set in a shallow dish. For marinade, combine wine, oil, juniper berries, bay leaves, thyme, and garlic. Pour over meat; seal bag. Marinate in refrigerator for 4 to 24 hours, turning bag occasionally.

2 Drain meat, reserving marinade. Wrap 3 or 4 slices of the partially cooked bacon around each tenderloin; secure with wooden toothpicks.

3 For a charcoal grill, arrange medium-hot coals around a drip pan. Test for medium heat above pan. Place meat on grill rack over drip pan. Cover; grill for 25 to 30 minutes or until a meat thermometer registers 150°F, brushing with reserved marinade during the first 15 minutes of grilling. (For a gas grill, preheat grill. Reduce heat to medium. Adjust for indirect cooking. Grill as above, except place meat on a rack in a roasting pan.) Remove meat from grill. Cover with foil and let stand 10 minutes. (The meat's temperature will rise 5°F during standing.)

Nutrition Facts per serving: 230 cal., 9 g total fat (3 g sat. fat), 103 mg chol., 180 mg sodium, 2 g carbo., 0 g fiber, 29 g pro. Daily Values: 1% vit. A, 2% vit. C, 2% calcium, 24% iron. Exchanges: 4 Very Lean Meat, 2 Fat

---

OSTRICH FAN ROAST WITH AROMATIC SPICES

Beef eaters in the United States are finding that ostrich meat is a satisfying alternative. The color, flavor, and texture are very similar.

Prep: 15 minutes Marinate: 12 to 24 hours
Grill: 45 minutes Stand: 5 minutes
Makes: 10 to 12 servings

1   2¹/₂- to 3-pound ostrich thigh
     fan roast
1   teaspoon cumin seeds
¹/₃ cup plain yogurt
3   tablespoons minced garlic (18 cloves)
1¹/₂ teaspoons paprika
1   teaspoon garam masala
³/₄ teaspoon salt
¹/₂ teaspoon cardamom seeds, crushed
¹/₄ teaspoon ground cinnamon
¹/₄ teaspoon ground ginger
¹/₈ teaspoon ground cloves
¹/₈ teaspoon cayenne pepper

1 Place ostrich roast in a self-sealing plastic bag set in a shallow dish; set aside. To toast cumin seeds, place seeds in a small skillet. Heat over medium-high heat for 2 to 3 minutes or until toasted, shaking skillet occasionally. For marinade, in a small bowl stir together the toasted cumin seeds, yogurt, garlic, paprika, garam masala, salt, cardamom seeds, cinnamon, ginger, cloves, and cayenne pepper. Pour over roast; seal bag. Marinate in refrigerator for 12 to 24 hours, turning bag occasionally.

2 Drain roast, discarding marinade. Insert a meat thermometer into center of roast.

3 For a charcoal grill, arrange medium-hot coals around a drip pan. Test for medium heat above pan. Place roast on grill rack over drip pan. Cover; grill for 45 to 60 minutes or until thermometer registers 140°F. (For a gas grill, preheat grill. Reduce heat to medium. Adjust for indirect cooking. Grill as above.)

4 Remove meat from grill. Cover with foil and let stand for 10 minutes before slicing. (The meat's temperature will rise 5°F during standing.) Slice roast diagonally across the grain.

Nutrition Facts per serving: 149 cal., 3 g total fat (0 g sat. fat), 0 mg chol., 267 mg sodium, 3 g carbo., 0 g fiber, 26 g pro. Daily Values: 3% vit. A, 3% vit. C, 4% calcium, 30% iron. Exchanges: 4 Very Lean Meat

SMOKIN' HOT TIP

What's the No. 1 rule for grilling game? Do not overcook. Because game has minimal fat running through it, it's not naturally moist and juicy. Aside from paying careful attention to timing and doneness tests, you can retain moisture by marinating first. Game is sold at specialty markets, butcher shops, and on the Internet. Leading suppliers are www.dartagnan.com, www.brokenarrowranch.com, and www.atlanticgamemeats.com.

Ostrich Burgers à la Mediterranean

OSTRICH BURGERS À LA MEDITERRANEAN

Ostrich is farm-raised in the United States and is available fresh or frozen year-round. Ground ostrich meat usually comes from the leg.

Prep: 10 minutes Grill: 15 minutes
Makes: 4 servings

- 1 **slightly beaten egg**
- ¼ **cup fine dry bread crumbs**
- ¼ **cup chopped pitted green olives**
- ¼ **cup chopped roasted red sweet peppers, drained**
- 3 **tablespoons snipped fresh basil**
- 1 **tablespoon capers, drained**
- ½ **teaspoon salt**
- ¼ **teaspoon black pepper**
- 1 **pound ground ostrich meat or lean ground beef**
- 1 **tablespoon cooking oil**
- 4 **1-ounce slices provolone cheese**
- 4 **egg buns, split and toasted**
- 1 **recipe Basil Mayonnaise**
- 4 **thin slices tomato**

1 In a large bowl combine egg, bread crumbs, olives, sweet peppers, basil, capers, salt, and black pepper. Add ostrich meat; mix well. Shape meat mixture into four ¾-inch-thick patties. Brush both sides of patties with oil.

2 For a charcoal grill, grill patties on the rack of an uncovered grill directly over medium coals for 14 to 18 minutes or until meat is done (160°F); turn once halfway through grilling. (For a gas grill, preheat grill. Reduce heat to medium. Place patties on grill rack over heat. Cover; grill as above.)

3 Top burgers with provolone cheese. Grill about 1 minute more or until cheese is melted. Serve burgers on rolls with Basil Mayonnaise and a slice of tomato.

Basil Mayonnaise: In a small bowl stir together ¼ cup mayonnaise or salad dressing, 1½ tablespoons snipped fresh basil, and, if desired, ¼ teaspoon crushed red pepper.

Nutrition Facts per serving: 651 cal., 33 g total fat (9 g sat. fat), 123 mg chol., 1,565 mg sodium, 45 g carbo., 3 g fiber, 42 g pro. Daily Values: 16% vit. A, 47% vit. C, 33% calcium, 47% iron. Exchanges: 2½ Starch, ½ Other Carbo., 4 Very Lean Meat, 1 High-Fat Meat, 4 Fat

JUNIPER-SCENTED PHEASANT WITH CARAMELIZED APPLES

You'll find domestic pheasant near the frozen turkeys in large supermarkets or specialty stores.

Prep: 30 minutes Marinate: 4 to 12 hours Grill: 50 minutes
Makes: 4 servings

> 1 **2- to 2¹/₂-pound pheasant**
> ¹/₄ **cup olive oil**
> 3 **tablespoons apple brandy**
> 2 **tablespoons juniper berries, crushed**
> ¹/₂ **teaspoon sea salt**
> ¹/₂ **teaspoon ground white pepper**
> ¹/₂ **teaspoon ground cinnamon**
> 1 **recipe Caramelized Apples**

1 Using poultry shears, cut closely along one side of backbone the entire length of pheasant. Repeat on other side. Discard backbone. Cut pheasant in quarters. Place quarters in a self-sealing plastic bag set in a shallow dish. For marinade, in a small bowl combine oil, apple brandy, juniper berries, salt, white pepper, and cinnamon. Pour over pheasant; seal bag. Marinate in refrigerator for 4 to 12 hours, turning bag occasionally. Drain pheasant, discarding marinade.

2 For a charcoal grill, arrange medium-hot coals around a drip pan. Test for medium heat above pan. Place pheasant quarters on grill rack over drip pan. Cover; grill for 50 to 60 minutes or until a meat thermometer inserted in breast portion registers 180°F. (For gas grill, preheat grill. Reduce heat to medium. Adjust for indirect cooking. Grill as above.) Serve with Caramelized Apples.

Caramelized Apples: In a large skillet melt 3 tablespoons butter or margarine. Add 2 medium cooking apples, peeled and thickly sliced, and 1 tablespoon sugar. Cook over medium heat for 8 to 10 minutes or until apples are tender and golden, stirring occasionally.

Nutrition Facts per serving: 549 cal., 33 g total fat (11 g sat. fat), 162 mg chol., 228 mg sodium, 13 g carbo., 2 g fiber, 45 g pro. Daily Values: 12% vit. A, 19% vit. C, 3% calcium, 12% iron. Exchanges: ¹/₂ Fruit, ¹/₂ Other Carbo., 6¹/₂ Lean Meat, 3 Fat

GRILLED PHEASANT WITH ARMAGNAC-MUSHROOM CREAM

Armagnac (ar-mahn-YAK) is a fine dry brandy distilled in the Armagnac district of France.

Prep: 30 minutes Chill: 4 hours Grill: 50 minutes
Makes: 4 servings

> 1 **2- to 2¹/₂-pound pheasant**
> 3 **tablespoons olive oil**
> 2 **tablespoons snipped fresh thyme**
> 2 **tablespoons coarsely cracked**
>   **mixed peppercorns**
> 1¹/₂ **teaspoons kosher salt**
> 1 **recipe Armagnac-Mushroom Cream**

1 Using poultry shears, cut closely along one side of backbone the entire length of pheasant. Repeat on other side. Discard backbone. Cut pheasant into quarters. In a small bowl combine oil, thyme, peppercorns, and salt. Rub oil mixture evenly over pheasant quarters. Cover and chill for 4 hours.

2 For a charcoal grill, arrange medium-hot coals around a drip pan. Test for medium heat above pan. Place pheasant quarters on grill rack over drip pan. Cover; grill for 50 to 60 minutes or until a meat thermometer inserted into breast portion registers 180°F. (For a gas grill, preheat grill. Reduce heat to medium. Adjust for indirect cooking. Grill as above.) Serve with Armagnac-Mushroom Cream.

Armagnac-Mushroom Cream: In a large skillet cook 1¹/₂ cups sliced fresh mushrooms (such as cremini, shiitake, chanterelle, oyster, and/or porcini) in 3 tablespoons hot butter or margarine for 5 to 8 minutes or until tender. Stir in 2 tablespoons Armagnac or Cognac. Cook and stir for 1 minute. Stir in ³/₄ cup whipping cream. Cook and stir for 2 to 3 minutes more or until sauce is slightly thickened. Serve immediately.

Nutrition Facts per serving: 705 cal., 54 g total fat (21 g sat. fat), 224 mg chol., 870 mg sodium, 4 g carbo., 1 g fiber, 47 g pro. Daily Values: 25% vit. A, 18% vit. C, 7% calcium, 17% iron. Exchanges: 7 Lean Meat, 6¹/₂ Fat

FOOD FOR THOUGHT SMALL GAME BIRDS

Small game birds, such as guinea fowl, pheasant, and quail, are delicious treats. Each bird has its own distinct qualities, making them unique alternatives to serving grilled chicken.

● Guinea Fowl/Hen: **Common on dining tables in Europe, guinea fowl or hen has tender white meat that's similar to chicken but much more flavorful and lower in fat. Weighing 2 to 4 pounds, these birds have a higher meat-to-bone ratio, and unlike some other game birds, their leg meat has no tendons and is therefore very tender.**

● Pheasant: **Another lean alternative to chicken, pheasant has a firm texture and full flavor. Younger pheasant is prepared similarly to chicken, but meat from older birds is less tender and therefore best braised or wrapped in some type of fat (such as bacon or pancetta) to retain moisture.**

● Quail: **Quail are also very lean with a mild game flavor. Due to their small size, they are best cooked quickly with the high heat of grilling, broiling, or sautéing.**

SMOKED GUINEA HEN

Prep: 25 minutes Chill: 3 to 6 hours Grill: 1 hour
Stand: 10 minutes Makes: 4 servings

 2 **slices pancetta or bacon, finely chopped**
 2 **tablespoons olive oil**
 1 **tablespoon snipped fresh oregano**
 1 **tablespoon snipped fresh rosemary**
 1 **teaspoon finely shredded lemon peel**
 1 **teaspoon lemon juice**
 ³⁄₄ **teaspoon salt**
 ¹⁄₂ **teaspoon black pepper**
 4 **cloves garlic, minced**
 1 **2¹⁄₂- to 3-pound guinea hen**
 2 **cups alder or pecan wood chips**

1 For rub, in a small bowl stir together pancetta, oil, oregano, rosemary, lemon peel, lemon juice, salt, pepper, and garlic. Slip your fingers between skin and meat of hen to loosen the skin over the breast and leg areas. Lift skin and spread some of the rub directly over breast, thigh, and drumstick meat. Tie legs to tail with 100-percent-cotton string. Twist wing tips behind back. Cover and chill for 3 to 6 hours.

2 At least 1 hour before grilling, soak wood chips in enough water to cover. Drain wood chips.

3 For a charcoal grill arrange medium-hot coals around a drip pan. Test for medium heat above drip pan. Sprinkle drained wood chips over coals. Place hen, breast side up, on grill rack over drip pan. Cover; grill for 1 to 1¹⁄₄ hours or until drumsticks move easily in their sockets and a meat thermometer inserted into the inner part of the thigh registers 180°F. (For a gas grill, preheat grill. Reduce heat to medium. Adjust grill for indirect cooking. Add wood chips according to manufacturer's directions. Grill as above.)

4 Remove hen from grill. Cover and let stand 10 minutes.

Nutrition Facts per serving: 467 cal., 25 g total fat (6 g sat. fat), 181 mg chol., 735 mg sodium, 1 g carbo., 0 g fiber, 57 g pro. Daily Values: 4% vit. A, 7% vit. C, 3% calcium, 11% iron. Exchanges: 8 Very Lean Meat, 4 Fat

Quail in Grape Leaves

3 For a charcoal grill, arrange medium-hot coals around a drip pan. Test for medium heat above pan. Place quail, breast side down, on grill rack over drip pan. Cover; grill for 25 to 30 minutes or until a meat thermometer inserted into the breast portion registers 170°F. (For a gas grill, preheat grill. Reduce heat to medium. Adjust heat for indirect cooking. Grill as above.) To serve, remove strings and discard grape leaves.

Nutrition Facts per serving: 270 cal., 19 g total fat (4 g sat. fat), 81 mg chol., 388 mg sodium, 2 g carbo., 0 g fiber, 22 g pro. Daily Values: 5% vit. A, 11% vit. C, 3% calcium, 23% iron. Exchanges: 3 Lean Meat, 2 Fat

QUAIL IN GRAPE LEAVES

For a semiboneless quail, check a good butcher shop. They can provide you with a whole quail prepared for cooking in the "European style." This means the bird is split open, rib cages removed, with the wing and leg bones left intact.

Prep: 40 minutes Soak: 2 hours Grill: 25 minutes
Makes: 8 servings

- **¹/₂ of a 16-ounce jar (16 leaves) brine-packed grape leaves**
- **¹/₄ cup olive oil**
- **2 tablespoons bottled minced garlic**
- **4 teaspoons dried herbes de Provence, crushed**
- **1 tablespoon coarsely cracked black pepper**
- **1 teaspoon sea salt or ³/₄ teaspoon salt**
- **8 4- to 4¹/₂-ounce semiboneless quail**
- **4 thin slices prosciutto, halved**

1 Gently rinse grape leaves in cold water. Place leaves in a medium bowl; add fresh cold water to cover. Soak for 1 hour; drain. Add fresh cold water to cover. Soak for 1 hour more. Gently rinse grape leaves; pat dry.

2 In a small bowl combine oil, garlic, herbes de Provence, pepper, and salt. Brush half of the oil mixture over quail. Place 1 slice of prosciutto over the breast of each quail. Brush the prosciutto with some of the remaining oil mixture. Place two grape leaves on top of the prosciutto on each quail, with the stem ends of the grape leaves at the tail end of each quail. Wrap leaves around each quail. Tie each quail lengthwise and crosswise with 100-percent-cotton string. Brush each quail with the remaining oil mixture.

MAPLE-GLAZED QUAIL

Prep: 10 minutes Chill: 2 to 24 hours Grill: 15 minutes
Makes: 8 servings

- **2 teaspoons hot chili powder**
- **1 teaspoon dried thyme, crushed**
- **³/₄ teaspoon salt**
- **8 4- to 4¹/₂-ounce semiboneless quail**
- **¹/₂ cup pure maple syrup**
- **2 tablespoons peanut oil or cooking oil**
- **Fresh pineapple wedges (optional)**
- **Torn mixed salad greens (optional)**

1 For rub, in a small bowl combine chili powder, thyme, and salt. Sprinkle rub evenly over quail; rub in with your fingers. Place quail in a shallow dish. Combine ¹/₄ cup of the maple syrup and the oil; spoon over quail, turning to coat. Cover and chill for 2 to 24 hours.

2 For a charcoal grill, arrange medium-hot coals around a drip pan. Test for medium heat above pan. Place quail, breast side down, on the lightly oiled rack over drip pan. Cover; grill for 15 to 20 minutes or until a meat thermometer inserted into the breast portion registers 180°F, turning and brushing once halfway through grilling with the remaining ¹/₄ cup maple syrup. (For a gas grill, preheat grill. Reduce heat to medium. Adjust for indirect cooking. Grill as above.)

3 If desired, serve with pineapple wedges and salad greens.

Nutrition Facts per serving: 299 cal., 17 g total fat (4 g sat. fat), 86 mg chol., 275 mg sodium, 14 g carbo., 0 g fiber, 22 g pro. Daily Values: 9% vit. A, 10% vit. C, 3% calcium, 25% iron. Exchanges: 1 Other Carbo., 3 Lean Meat, 1¹/₂ Fat

Rosemary Duck Breasts with Marinated Pears

ROSEMARY DUCK BREASTS WITH MARINATED PEARS

Prep: 30 minutes Chill: 12 to 24 hours Grill: 23 minutes
Makes: 4 servings

2 tablespoons snipped fresh rosemary
1½ teaspoons kosher salt
2 cloves garlic, minced
4 boneless duck breasts with skin
  (about 1¾ pounds)
2 large ripe pears
1 cup dry red wine
¼ cup sugar
¼ teaspoon ground cloves
¼ teaspoon ground ginger
1 cup oak wood chips
1 tablespoon cracked green
  peppercorns (optional)

1 For rub, combine rosemary, salt, garlic, and ½ teaspoon black pepper. Sprinkle evenly over the meat side of each duck breast; rub in with your fingers. Cover and chill for 12 to 24 hours.

2 Cut pears in half lengthwise, leaving stems intact. Remove core and peel pear halves. Place pear halves in a self-sealing plastic bag set in a shallow dish. For marinade, combine wine, sugar, cloves, and ginger. Pour over pears; seal bag. Marinate in refrigerator for 12 to 24 hours.

3 At least 1 hour before grilling, soak wood chips in enough water to cover. Meanwhile, using a sharp knife, score skin sides of duck breasts diagonally to create a ½-inch-wide diamond pattern, making cuts about ¼ inch deep. Drain pears, discarding marinade.

4 For a charcoal grill, arrange medium-hot coals around a drip pan. Test for medium heat above pan. Place pear halves, cut sides down, on grill rack over drip pan. Cover; grill for 8 to 10 minutes or until tender. (For a gas grill, preheat grill. Reduce heat to medium. Adjust for indirect cooking. Grill as above.) Remove from grill; set aside.

5 Drain wood chips. Sprinkle wood chips over coals. Place duck breasts on grill rack over drip pan. Cover; grill for 15 to 18 minutes or until a meat thermometer registers 155°F. (For a gas grill, add wood chips according to manufacturer's directions. Grill as above.)

6 Cut each pear half in half to form eight quarters. To make pear fans, use a sharp knife to make a series of ⅛-inch lengthwise slices in each pear quarter, starting from stem end and cutting to bottom (leave stem ends intact). Gently push down on each pear quarter to fan the slices. Serve pears alongside duck. If desired, garnish with green peppercorns.

Nutrition Facts per serving: 787 cal., 68 g total fat (23 g sat. fat), 141 mg chol., 826 mg sodium, 17 g carbo., 3 g fiber, 23 g pro. Daily Values: 18% vit. A, 14% vit. C, 4% calcium, 26% iron. Exchanges: 1 Fruit, 3½ Medium-Fat Meat, 10 Fat

DUCK BREASTS WITH ARUGULA AND ORANGE-BALSAMIC VINAIGRETTE

Most domestic duck breasts are sold with the skin on.

Prep: 25 minutes Chill: 2 to 24 hours Grill: 10 minutes
Makes: 4 servings

4 boneless duck breasts with skin (about 1¾ pounds)

¼ cup finely chopped shallots

2 tablespoons snipped fresh thyme

2 teaspoons finely shredded orange peel

1½ teaspoons kosher salt

1 teaspoon black pepper

6 cups arugula or mixed baby salad greens

1 recipe Orange-Balsamic Vinaigrette

1 Remove skin from duck breasts. For rub, in a small bowl stir together shallots, thyme, orange peel, salt, and pepper. Sprinkle evenly over both sides of duck breasts; rub in with your fingers. Cover and chill for 2 to 24 hours.

2 For a charcoal grill, grill duck on the rack of an uncovered grill directly over medium coals for 10 to 12 minutes or until a meat thermometer registers 155°F, turning once halfway through grilling. (For gas grill, preheat grill. Reduce heat to medium. Place duck breasts on grill rack over heat. Cover; grill as above.)

3 To serve, arrange arugula on individual plates. Slice duck breasts diagonally; arrange on top of arugula. Drizzle with some of the Orange-Balsamic Vinaigrette. If desired, pass additional vinaigrette.

Orange-Balsamic Vinaigrette: In a blender container combine ¼ cup white balsamic vinegar, 1 teaspoon finely shredded orange peel, 2 tablespoons orange juice, 2 tablespoons honey, 2 teaspoons Dijon-style mustard, ¼ teaspoon kosher salt, ⅛ teaspoon black pepper, and 2 cloves garlic, minced. Cover and blend until combined. With blender running, slowly add ¼ cup olive oil in a thin, steady stream until mixture is slightly thickened. Serve immediately or cover and chill for up to 1 week. Makes about ¾ cup.

Nutrition Facts per serving: 910 cal., 82 g total fat (25 g sat. fat), 141 mg chol., 1,018 mg sodium, 19 g carbo., 1 g fiber, 25 g pro. Daily Values: 35% vit. A, 30% vit. C, 9% calcium, 31% iron. Exchanges: 1½ Vegetable, 1 Other Carbo., 3 Medium-Fat Meat, 13 Fat

FOOD FOR THOUGHT DUCK

Both wild and domestic ducks are known for their distinct taste and moist, dark meat. The flavor of duck is affected by the diet of the bird as well as its age and weight. Generally, older and heavier birds are more flavorful and less tender. Domestic ducks have a layer of fat under their skins that wild ducks don't have.

DUCK BREASTS WITH CURRANT-BALSAMIC SAUCE

Order duck breasts from the butcher at your local supermarket or purchase online.

Prep: 30 minutes Grill: 10 minutes
Makes: 4 servings

2 teaspoons walnut oil
**4 4- to 6-ounce skinless, boneless
    duck breasts**
1/2 teaspoon salt
1/2 teaspoon black pepper
1 recipe Currant-Balsamic Sauce

1 Brush oil over both sides of duck breasts; sprinkle with salt and pepper. For a charcoal grill, grill duck on the rack of an uncovered grill directly over medium coals for 10 to 12 minutes or until a meat thermometer registers 155°F; turn once halfway through grilling and brushing with a few tablespoons of the sauce during the last 3 minutes of grilling. (For a gas grill, preheat grill. Reduce heat to medium. Place duck breasts on grill rack over heat. Cover; grill as above.)

2 Slice duck breasts diagonally into 1/2-inch slices. Arrange slices on individual plates; drizzle with 2 to 3 tablespoons Currant-Balsamic Sauce. Pass remaining sauce.

Currant-Balsamic Sauce: In a small saucepan combine 1/2 cup currant, lingonberry, or seedless raspberry jam or preserves; 1/4 cup port wine; and 3 tablespoons balsamic vinegar. Bring just to boiling over medium heat, stirring frequently; reduce heat to medium-low. Simmer, uncovered, about 15 minutes or until slightly thickened and reduced to 1/2 cup, stirring occasionally. Remove saucepan from heat; stir in 1 teaspoon butter (no substitutes). Keep sauce warm.

Nutrition Facts per serving: 299 cal., 5 g total fat (1 g sat. fat), 124 mg chol., 406 mg sodium, 33 g carbo., 1 g fiber, 24 g pro. Daily Values: 2% vit. A, 11% vit. C, 2% calcium, 24% iron. Exchanges: 2 Other Carbo., 3½ Very Lean Meat, 1 Fat

SMOKED DUCK WITH HONEY-THYME SAUCE

The dark, moist flesh of duck lends itself beautifully to smoking.

Prep: 15 minutes Marinate: 2 to 24 hours Grill: 15 minutes
Makes: 4 servings

**4 4- to 6-ounce skinless, boneless
    duck breasts**
2/3 cup chicken broth
1/3 cup honey
1 shallot, finely chopped
**1 tablespoon snipped fresh lemon
    thyme or thyme**
1 teaspoon bottled minced garlic
1 teaspoon white wine vinegar
1/4 teaspoon salt
1/8 teaspoon black pepper
4 cups orange or apple wood chips

1 Place duck in self-sealing plastic bag set in a shallow dish. For marinade, in a small bowl combine chicken broth, honey, shallot, thyme, garlic, vinegar, salt, and pepper. Pour half of the marinade over duck; seal bag. Marinate in refrigerator for 2 to 24 hours; turn bag occasionally. Cover and chill the remaining marinade to use as sauce.

2 At least 1 hour before grilling, soak wood chips in enough water to cover.

3 Drain duck, reserving marinade. Drain wood chips. For a charcoal grill, arrange medium-hot coals around a drip pan. Test for medium heat above pan. Sprinkle drained wood chips and thyme sprigs over coals. Place duck on grill rack over drip pan. Cover; grill for 15 to 18 minutes or until a meat thermometer registers 155°F; brush once with reserved marinade halfway through grilling. (For a gas grill, preheat grill. Reduce heat to medium. Adjust for indirect cooking. Add wood chips according to manufacturer's directions. Grill as above.)

4 Meanwhile, for sauce, in a small saucepan bring the chilled marinade to boiling; reduce heat. Simmer, uncovered, about 5 minutes or until reduced to 1/3 cup. Serve duck with sauce.

Nutrition Facts per serving: 360 cal., 5 g total fat (1 g sat. fat), 272 mg chol., 512 mg sodium, 25 g carbo., 0 g fiber, 53 g pro. Daily Values: 2% vit. A, 13% vit. C, 3% calcium, 49% iron. Exchanges: 1½ Other Carbo., 7½ Very Lean Meat

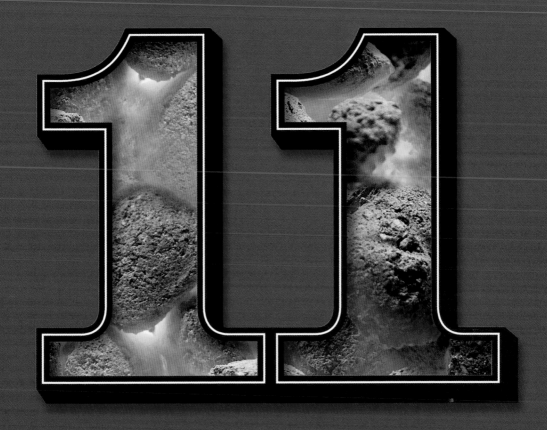

Smoke
Cooking

BEEF

CHICKEN & TURKEY

FISH

LAMB

PORK

SAUCES

SMOKE COOKING

At least 1 hour before smoke cooking, soak wood chunks (for smoker) in enough water to cover. Drain before using.

 Trim fat from meat. Rinse fish; pat dry with paper towels. If smoking fish, lightly grease or coat with nonstick cooking spray the rack of a smoker. Prepare smoker as directed. Place meat, poultry, or fish on the grill rack. For fish fillets, tuck under any thin edges. Cover and smoke for the time given below or until done. After smoking, cover roasts, turkeys, and larger chickens with foil; let stand for 15 minutes before carving.

CUT OR TYPE	THICKNESS, WEIGHT, OR SIZE	DONENESS	SMOKER TIME
BEEF			
Boneless steak (ribeye or top loin)	1 inch	Medium-rare Medium	40 to 50 minutes 50 to 60 minutes
Brisket (fresh)	3 to 4 pounds	Tender	5 to 6 hours
Ribeye roast	4 pounds	Medium-rare	3 to 3½ hours
Ribs (back)	3 to 4 pounds	Tender	2½ to 3 hours
LAMB			
Boneless leg (rolled and tied)	3 pounds	Medium-rare Medium	2½ to 3 hours 3¼ to 3¾ hours
Boneless sirloin roast	1½ to 2 pounds	Medium-rare Medium	1¾ to 2 hours 2¼ to 2½ hours
Chop	1¼ to 1½ inches	Medium-rare Medium	55 to 65 minutes 65 to 75 minutes
PORK			
Boneless top loin roast (single loin)	2 to 3 pounds	160°F	1¾ to 2 hours
Chop	1¼ to 1½ inches	Juices run clear	1¾ to 2¼ hours
Ribs (loin back or spareribs)	2 to 4 pounds	Tender	3 to 4 hours
POULTRY			
Meaty chicken pieces	2 to 3 pounds	Juices run clear	1½ to 2 hours
Chicken, whole	3 to 3½ pounds 6 to 7 pounds	180°F 180°F	2½ to 3 hours 3¼ to 4 hours
Turkey, whole	8 to 10 pounds	180°F	4½ to 5 hours
Turkey breast, half	2 to 2½ pounds	170°F	2 to 2½ hours
Turkey drumstick	8 to 12 ounces	Juices run clear	2½ to 3 hours
Turkey tenderloin	8 to 10 ounces	Juices run clear	1¼ to 1½ hours
FISH			
Fish, dressed	8 to 10 ounces 3 pounds	Flakes Flakes	1½ to 2 hours 2½ to 3 hours
Fish fillet or steak	1 inch	Flakes	45 to 60 minutes

All cooking times are based on meat removed directly from refrigerator.

LEMON-BASIL STEAKS

Balsamic vinegar is responsible for the glaze's rich mahogany color and malty sweetness. Serve the steaks with potato salad and crusty sourdough bread.

Prep: 5 minutes Soak: 1 hour Smoke: 40 minutes
Makes: 4 servings

- 4 **hickory, pecan, or oak wood chunks**
- 2 **teaspoons country-style Dijon mustard**
- 2 **teaspoons balsamic vinegar**
- 1½ **teaspoons lemon-pepper seasoning**
- 2 **cloves garlic, minced**
- 1 **teaspoon dried basil, crushed**
- ⅛ **teaspoon salt**
- 4 **boneless beef ribeye steaks, cut 1 inch thick (1¾ to 2 pounds)**

1 At least 1 hour before smoke cooking, soak wood chunks in enough water to cover. Drain before using.

2 For glaze, in a small bowl stir together the mustard, vinegar, lemon-pepper seasoning, garlic, basil, and salt. Trim fat from steaks. Brush glaze onto both sides of steaks.

3 In a smoker arrange preheated coals, drained wood chunks, and water pan according to the manufacturer's directions. Pour water into pan. Place steaks on the grill rack over water pan. Cover; smoke until steaks are desired doneness. Allow 40 to 50 minutes for medium-rare (145°F) or 50 to 60 minutes for medium (160°F).

Nutrition Facts per serving: 307 cal., 12 g total fat (5 g sat. fat), 94 mg chol., 599 mg sodium, 2 g carbo., 0 g fiber, 44 g pro. Daily Values: 1% vit. C, 3% calcium, 22% iron. Exchanges: 6 Very Lean Meat, 2 Fat

MESQUITE-SMOKED BEEF ROAST

Prep: 10 minutes Soak: 1 hour
Smoke: 3 hours Stand: 15 minutes Makes: 12 servings

- 6 to 8 **mesquite or hickory wood chunks**
- 1 **4-pound boneless beef ribeye roast Whole black peppercorns**
- 1½ **teaspoons Worcestershire sauce**
- ½ **teaspoon seasoned salt**
- ½ **teaspoon celery salt**

1 At least 1 hour before smoke cooking, soak wood chunks in enough water to cover. Drain before using.

2 Trim fat from meat. Using a long-tined fork, make holes about ¾ inch apart and 1 inch deep on top side of meat; insert a whole peppercorn into each hole. Close holes by rubbing the surface of the meat with the smooth edge of the fork.

3 For rub, in a small bowl combine Worcestershire sauce, seasoned salt, and celery salt. Drizzle mixture evenly over meat; rub in with your fingers. Insert meat thermometer into center of meat.

4 In a smoker arrange preheated coals, drained wood chunks, and water pan according to the manufacturer's directions. Pour water into pan. Place meat on the grill rack over water pan. Cover; smoke until meat thermometer registers 140°F for medium-rare (3 to 3½ hours). Add additional coals and water as needed to maintain temperature and moisture.

5 Remove meat from smoker. Cover the meat with foil; let stand for 15 minutes before carving. (The meat's temperature will rise 5°F during standing.)

Nutrition Facts per serving: 226 cal., 9 g total fat (4 g sat. fat), 71 mg chol., 216 mg sodium, 0 g carbo., 0 g fiber, 33 g pro. Daily Values: 1% calcium, 16% iron. Exchanges: 5 Very Lean Meat, 1 Fat

TEXANS' BEEF BRISKET

Texans have a particular way of eating their barbecue. This brisket—with a mopping sauce, dry rub, and passing sauce—covers all the bases.

Prep: 30 minutes Soak: 1 hour Smoke: 5 hours
Makes: 12 servings

- 6 to 8 **mesquite, hickory, or pecan wood chunks**
- 1 **recipe Vinegar Mop Sauce**
- 1 **3- to 3½-pound fresh beef brisket**
- 2 **teaspoons seasoned salt**
- 1 **teaspoon paprika**
- 1 **teaspoon chili powder**
- 1 **teaspoon garlic pepper**
- ½ **teaspoon ground cumin**
- 1 **recipe Spicy Beer Sauce**
- 12 **kaiser rolls, split and toasted (optional)**

1 At least 1 hour before smoke cooking, soak wood chunks in enough water to cover. Drain before using.

2 Prepare Vinegar Mop Sauce; set aside. Trim fat from meat. For rub, in a small bowl combine seasoned salt, paprika, chili powder, garlic pepper, and cumin. Sprinkle mixture evenly over meat; rub in with your fingers.

3 In a smoker arrange preheated coals, drained wood chunks, and water pan according to the manufacturer's directions. Pour water into pan. Place meat on grill rack over water pan. Cover; smoke for 5 to 6 hours or until meat is tender, brushing occasionally with Vinegar Mop Sauce during the last hour of smoking. Add additional coals and water as needed to maintain temperature and moisture.

4 To serve, thinly slice meat across the grain. Serve meat with Spicy Beer Sauce. If desired, serve meat and sauce in kaiser rolls.

Vinegar Mop Sauce: In a small bowl stir together ¼ cup beer, 4 teaspoons Worcestershire sauce, 1 tablespoon cooking oil, 1 tablespoon vinegar, ½ teaspoon jalapeño mustard or other hot-style mustard, and a few dashes bottled hot pepper sauce.

Spicy Beer Sauce: In a medium saucepan melt 2 tablespoons butter or margarine. Add ¾ cup chopped, seeded, peeled tomato; ½ cup chopped onion; and ½ cup chopped green sweet pepper. Cook about 5 minutes or until onion is tender, stirring occasionally. Stir in 1 cup bottled chili sauce, ½ cup beer, ½ cup cider vinegar, 2 tablespoons brown sugar, 1 to 2 tablespoons chopped canned chipotle peppers in adobo sauce, 1¼ teaspoons black pepper, and ½ teaspoon salt. Bring to boiling; reduce heat. Boil gently, uncovered, about 10 minutes or until reduced to about 2¼ cups.

Nutrition Facts per serving: 253 cal., 12 g total fat (4 g sat. fat), 77 mg chol., 770 mg sodium, 11 g carbo., 2 g fiber, 24 g pro. Daily Values: 10% vit. A, 16% vit. C, 2% calcium, 16% iron. Exchanges: 1 Other Carbo., 3½ Lean Meat

Texans' Beef Brisket

FOOD FOR THOUGHT MOPS

A mop is a thin solution of liquid and seasonings used to baste meats with flavor while helping retain moisture. Most mops include a blend of water and vinegar to tenderize, plus any combination of seasonings, beer, juices, or other liquids to develop the flavor of the meat. The solution is applied generously using a cooking tool that looks like a miniature mop. For best results, apply the mop at regular intervals throughout cooking.

GINGER-ORANGE BEEF RIBS

Soy sauce and fresh ginger give these meaty ribs Pacific Rim flair. Asian cooks have been smoking ribs in a kamado (an egg-shape ceramic oven) for centuries.

Prep: 10 minutes Soak: 1 hour Smoke: 2½ hours
Makes: 4 servings

6 to 8 hickory or oak wood chunks
2 teaspoons paprika
½ to 1 teaspoon salt
½ teaspoon black pepper
3 to 4 pounds beef back ribs
    (about 8 ribs)
½ cup bottled barbecue sauce
¼ cup frozen orange juice concentrate,
    thawed
2 tablespoons soy sauce
1 tablespoon grated fresh ginger

1 At least 1 hour before smoke cooking, soak wood chunks in enough water to cover. Drain before using.

2 For rub, in a small bowl combine paprika, salt, and pepper. Trim fat from ribs. Sprinkle rub evenly over ribs; rub in with your fingers.

3 For sauce, in a small bowl stir together barbecue sauce, orange juice concentrate, soy sauce, and ginger.

4 In a smoker arrange preheated coals, drained wood chunks, and water pan according to the manufacturer's directions. Pour water into pan. Place ribs, bone sides down, on the grill rack over water pan. (Or place ribs in a rib rack; place on grill rack.) Cover; smoke for 2½ to 3 hours or until ribs are tender, brushing once with sauce during the last 15 minutes of cooking. Add additional coals and water as needed to maintain temperature and moisture. Pass any remaining sauce with ribs.

Nutrition Facts per serving: 277 cal., 12 g total fat (5 g sat. fat), 79 mg chol., 897 mg sodium, 13 g carbo., 1 g fiber, 28 g pro. Daily Values: 19% vit. A, 46% vit. C, 3% calcium, 20% iron. Exchanges: 1 Other Carbo., 4 Lean Meat

MOROCCAN-STYLE LAMB CHOPS

Prep: 15 minutes Chill: 6 to 24 hours
Soak: 1 hour Smoke: 55 minutes
Makes: 4 servings

8 lamb loin chops, cut 1¼ to
    1½ inches thick
2 tablespoons sliced green onion (1)
1½ teaspoons ground coriander
½ teaspoon ground cumin
½ teaspoon ground cardamom
¼ teaspoon ground cinnamon
¼ teaspoon ground cloves
¼ teaspoon ground ginger
4 cherry or alder wood chunks
1 recipe Cucumber-Yogurt Sauce
Hot cooked couscous or rice (optional)

1 Trim fat from chops. Place chops in a single layer in a shallow dish. For rub, in a small bowl combine the green onion, coriander, cumin, cardamom, cinnamon, cloves, ginger, and ½ teaspoon salt. Sprinkle mixture evenly over chops; rub in with your fingers. Cover and chill for 6 to 24 hours.

2 At least 1 hour before smoke cooking, soak wood chunks in enough water to cover. Drain before using.

3 In a smoker arrange preheated coals, drained wood chunks, and water pan according to the manufacturer's directions. Pour water into pan. Place chops on the grill rack over water pan. Cover; smoke until chops are desired doneness. Allow 55 to 65 minutes for medium-rare (145°F) or 65 to 75 minutes for medium (160°F).

4 About 30 minutes before serving, prepare Cucumber-Yogurt Sauce. If desired, serve chops with couscous. Pass the Cucumber-Yogurt Sauce with chops.

Cucumber-Yogurt Sauce: Combine 1¼ cups chopped, seeded cucumber; ½ cup chopped, seeded tomato; ½ cup plain low-fat yogurt; ⅓ cup chopped onion; and ⅛ teaspoon salt. Cover and chill until ready to serve.

Nutrition Facts per serving: 466 cal., 30 g total fat (13 g sat. fat), 142 mg chol., 501 mg sodium, 7 g carbo., 2 g fiber, 40 g pro. Daily Values: 7% vit. A, 18% vit. C, 11% calcium, 17% iron. Exchanges: ½ Vegetable, 5½ Lean Meat, 3 Fat

LAMB ROAST WITH MINT

Prep: 20 minutes   Marinate: 4 to 24 hours   Soak: 1 hour
Smoke: 1¾ hours   Stand: 10 minutes
Makes: 6 to 8 servings

**½ cup mint jelly or ½ cup apple
   jelly plus 2 tablespoons snipped
   fresh mint**
¼ cup white wine vinegar
2 tablespoons olive oil or cooking oil
1 tablespoon grated onion
¼ teaspoon salt
¼ teaspoon black pepper
**1 1½- to 2-pound boneless lamb
   sirloin roast or leg of lamb,
   rolled and tied**
6 to 8 pecan or oak wood chunks

1 For marinade, in a small saucepan combine jelly, vinegar, oil, onion, salt, and pepper. Cook and stir over low heat until jelly is melted. Cool.

2 Trim fat from meat. On top side of meat, cut slits about 1½ inches apart and ½ inch deep. Place meat in a plastic bag set in a deep, large bowl. Pour marinade over meat; seal bag. Marinate in the refrigerator for 4 to 24 hours, turning bag occasionally.

3 At least 1 hour before smoke cooking, soak wood chunks in enough water to cover. Drain before using. Drain meat, reserving marinade. Insert a meat thermometer into thickest part of meat.

4 In a smoker arrange preheated coals, drained wood chunks, and water pan according to the manufacturer's directions. Pour water into pan. Place meat on the grill rack over water pan. Cover; smoke until roast is desired doneness, brushing once with marinade halfway through cooking. Allow 1¾ to 2 hours for medium-rare (140°F) or 2¼ to 2½ hours for medium (150°F). Add additional coals and water as needed to maintain temperature and moisture. Discard the remaining marinade.

5 Remove meat from smoker. Cover the meat with foil; let stand for 10 minutes before carving. (The meat's temperature will rise 5°F during standing.)

Nutrition Facts per serving: 297 cal., 22 g total fat (9 g sat. fat), 77 mg chol., 73 mg sodium, 5 g carbo., 0 g fiber, 20 g pro. Daily Values: 1% calcium, 10% iron. Exchanges: ½ Other Carbo., 3 Lean Meat, 2½ Fat

MUSTARD-RUBBED PORK CHOPS

Smoking is an ideal way to cook thick cuts like these super-size chops. Long, slow cooking ensures moist and tender meat.

Prep: 10 minutes   Soak: 1 hour   Smoke: 1¾ hours
Makes: 4 servings

6 to 8 oak or pecan wood chunks
1 tablespoon dry mustard
1½ teaspoons salt
1½ teaspoons paprika
1½ teaspoons dried basil, crushed
1 to 1½ teaspoons black pepper
½ teaspoon garlic powder
**4 bone-in pork loin or rib chops,
   cut 1¼ inches thick
   (about 3 pounds total)**

1 At least 1 hour before grilling, soak wood chunks in enough water to cover. Drain wood chunks before using.

2 For rub, in a small bowl stir together dry mustard, salt, paprika, basil, pepper, and garlic powder. Sprinkle rub evenly over the chops; rub in with your fingers.

3 In a smoker arrange preheated coals, drained wood chunks, and water pan according to manufacturer's directions. Pour water into the pan. Place chops on the grill rack over the water pan. Cover; smoke for 1¾ to 2¼ hours or until the juices run clear (160°F). Add additional coals and water as needed to maintain temperature and moisture.

Nutrition Facts per serving: 318 cal., 11 g total fat (4 g sat. fat), 138 mg chol., 990 mg sodium, 1 g carbo., 1 g fiber, 50 g pro. Daily Values: 8% vit. A, 4% vit. C, 6% calcium, 13% iron. Exchanges: 7 Very Lean Meat, 1½ Fat

CHOPS WITH CHERRY SALSA

The salsa here features the refreshing combo of sweet and hot. The sweet comes from dried cherries; the heat from chili sauce.

Prep: 15 minutes Soak: 1 hour Smoke: 1¾ hours
Makes: 4 servings

**6 to 8 cherry, orange, or apple
  wood chunks
½ cup dried tart or sweet cherries,
  snipped
½ cup bottled chili sauce
½ teaspoon finely shredded
  orange peel
¼ cup orange juice
2 tablespoons thinly sliced
  green onion (1)
4 pork loin chops, cut
  1½ inches thick
Salt
Black pepper**

1 At least 1 hour before smoke cooking, soak wood chunks in enough water to cover. Drain before using.

2 For salsa, in a small saucepan combine the cherries, chili sauce, orange peel, orange juice, and green onion. Bring just to boiling; remove from heat. Cool to room temperature.

3 Trim fat from chops. Sprinkle both sides of chops with salt and pepper.

4 In a smoker arrange preheated coals, drained wood chunks, and water pan according to the manufacturer's directions. Pour water into the pan. Place chops on the grill rack over water pan. Cover; smoke for 1¾ to 2¼ hours or until juices run clear (160°F). Add additional coals and water as needed to maintain temperature and moisture. Serve the chops with salsa.

Nutrition Facts per serving: 394 cal., 10 g total fat (4 g sat. fat), 138 mg chol., 519 mg sodium, 21 g carbo., 3 g fiber, 50 g pro. Daily Values: 6% vit. A, 26% vit. C, 5% calcium, 12% iron. Exchanges: 1 Fruit, ½ Other Carbo., 7 Very Lean Meat, 1½ Fat

CARIBBEAN SMOKED CHOPS

When buying mangoes, look for fruit that has smooth, unblemished skins and flesh that yields to gentle pressure. If a mango is too firm, ripen it in a paper bag at room temperature for a few days.

Prep: 20 minutes Soak: 1 hour
Smoke: 1¾ hours Stand: 15 minutes Makes: 4 servings

**6 to 8 pecan or cherry wood chunks
4 pork loin chops, cut
  1½ inches thick
2 to 3 teaspoons Jamaican jerk
  seasoning
1 medium mango, peeled, seeded, and
  finely chopped (about 1 cup)
¼ cup sliced green onions (2)
2 tablespoons snipped fresh cilantro
  or parsley
½ teaspoon finely shredded
  orange peel
2 teaspoons orange juice
¼ teaspoon Jamaican jerk seasoning
  Fresh cilantro or parsley sprigs
  (optional)**

1 At least 1 hour before smoke cooking, soak the wood chunks in enough water to cover. Drain before using.

2 Trim fat from chops. Sprinkle the 2 to 3 teaspoons jerk seasoning evenly over chops; rub in with your fingers.

3 In a smoker arrange preheated coals, drained wood chunks, and water pan according to the manufacturer's directions. Pour water into pan. Place chops on the grill rack over water pan. Cover; smoke for 1¾ to 2¼ hours or until the juices run clear (160°F). Add additional coals and water as needed to maintain temperature and moisture.

4 Meanwhile, for sauce, in a medium bowl stir together mango, green onions, cilantro, orange peel, orange juice, and the ¼ teaspoon jerk seasoning. Let stand at room temperature for 15 to 20 minutes to blend flavors. Serve the sauce over chops. If desired, garnish with cilantro sprigs.

Nutrition Facts per serving: 347 cal., 11 g total fat (4 g sat. fat), 138 mg chol., 224 mg sodium, 11 g carbo., 1 g fiber, 49 g pro. Daily Values: 13% vit. A, 37% vit. C, 7% calcium, 14% iron. Exchanges: ½ Fruit, 7 Very Lean Meat, 1½ Fat

Prosciutto-Stuffed Pork

PROSCIUTTO-STUFFED PORK

Prep: 10 minutes Soak: 1 hour
Smoke: 1¾ hours Stand: 10 minutes
Makes: 6 to 8 servings

6 to 8 hickory or oak wood chunks
1 2- to 2½-pound boneless pork top
 loin roast (single loin)
2 tablespoons olive oil
1 to 2 tablespoons snipped fresh
 rosemary or 1 to 2 teaspoons
 dried rosemary, crushed
3 ounces thinly sliced prosciutto or
 dried beef
3 cups fresh spinach leaves,
 stems removed
2 teaspoons crushed peppercorns
 (optional)
 Peach wedges, fresh Italian parsley
 sprigs, and fresh rosemary sprigs
 (optional)

1 At least 1 hour before smoke cooking, soak wood chunks in enough water to cover. Drain before using.

2 Trim fat from meat. To butterfly meat, make a lengthwise cut down center of meat, cutting to within ½ inch of the other side but not through it. Starting at the center of the meat, make one horizontal slit to the right, cutting to within ½ inch of the other side. Repeat on the left side of center.

3 Brush the surface of meat with oil; sprinkle with rosemary. Cover with prosciutto and spinach. Starting from a short side, roll up into a spiral. Tie with 100-percent-cotton kitchen string. If desired, brush meat with additional oil and sprinkle with peppercorns. Insert a meat thermometer into center of meat.

4 In a smoker arrange preheated coals, drained wood chunks, and water pan according to the manufacturer's directions. Pour water into pan. Place meat on the grill rack over water pan. Cover; smoke for 1¾ to 2 hours or until the meat thermometer registers 150°F. Add additional coals and water as needed to maintain temperature and moisture. Remove meat from smoker. Cover meat with foil and let stand for 10 minutes before slicing. (The meat temperature will rise 10°F during standing.)

5 To serve, transfer meat to serving platter; remove strings from meat. If desired, garnish with peach wedges, Italian parsley, and rosemary. Carve meat into ¼- to ½-inch slices, being careful to keep the spiral intact.

Nutrition Facts per serving: 209 cal., 10 g total fat (3 g sat. fat), 69 mg chol., 342 mg sodium, 1 g carbo., 1 g fiber, 28 g pro. Daily Values: 13% vit. A, 5% vit. C, 3% calcium, 10% iron. Exchanges: ½ Vegetable, 4 Very Lean Meat, 1 Fat

MEMPHIS-STYLE SMOKED PORK WITH BOURBON SAUCE

Prep: 25 minutes Marinate: 24 hours Soak: 1 hour
Smoke: 4 hours Stand: 15 minutes
Makes: 12 servings

  1 **8-ounce can tomato sauce**
  1 **cup chopped onion (1 large)**
  1 **cup vinegar**
  ½ **cup bourbon or beef broth**
  ¼ **cup Worcestershire sauce**
  2 **tablespoons brown sugar**
    Dash bottled hot pepper sauce
  1 **4½- to 5-pound boneless pork shoulder roast**
  6 to 8 **hickory wood chunks**

1 For sauce, in a medium saucepan combine tomato sauce, onion, ½ cup of the vinegar, the bourbon, Worcestershire sauce, brown sugar, hot pepper sauce, and ¼ teaspoon black pepper. Bring to boiling; reduce heat. Simmer, covered, for 15 minutes; cool. Reserve 1 cup of sauce; cover reserved sauce and chill until ready to serve.

2 Trim fat from meat. Place meat in self-sealing plastic bag set in a shallow dish. For marinade, combine the remaining sauce and the remaining vinegar. Pour over meat; seal bag. Marinate in the refrigerator for 24 hours; turn bag occasionally. Drain meat, reserving marinade.

3 At least 1 hour before smoke cooking, soak wood chunks in enough water to cover. Drain before using.

4 In a smoker arrange preheated coals, drained wood chunks, and water pan according to the manufacturer's directions. Pour water into pan. Place meat in grill rack over water pan. Cover; smoke for 4 to 5 hours or until meat is very tender, basting occasionally with marinade during the first 3 hours of smoking. Add additional coals and water as needed to maintain temperature and moisture. Remove meat from smoker.

5 Cover meat with foil; let stand for 15 minutes. Meanwhile, in a saucepan cook reserved 1 cup sauce over medium heat until heated through. Serve meat with sauce.

Nutrition Facts per serving: 354 cal., 17 g total fat (6 g sat. fat), 112 mg chol., 253 mg sodium, 6 g carbo., 0 g fiber, 30 g pro. Daily Values: 2% vit. A, 18% vit. C, 1% calcium, 16% iron. Exchanges: ½ Other Carbo., 4 Medium-Fat Meat

COASTAL CAROLINA PULLED PORK BBQ

When the meat is done smoking, it's pulled apart into shreds and mixed with sauce before being served on toasted buns and topped with slaw.

Prep: 15 minutes Soak: 1 hour
Smoke: 4 hours Stand: 15 minutes
Makes: 12 servings

  6 to 8 **chicory wood chunks**
  1½ **teaspoons salt**
  1½ **teaspoons black pepper**
  1 **4½- to 5-pound boneless pork shoulder roast**
  2 **cups cider vinegar**
  3 **tablespoons brown sugar (optional)**
  1 **tablespoon salt**
  1 **tablespoon crushed red pepper**
 12 **hamburger buns, split and toasted**
    Coleslaw (optional)

1 At least 1 hour before smoke cooking, soak wood chunks in enough water to cover. Drain before using.

2 For rub, in a bowl combine the 1½ teaspoons salt and the black pepper. Trim fat from meat. Sprinkle rub evenly over meat; rub in with your fingers. For sauce, in a medium bowl combine vinegar, brown sugar (if desired), the 1 tablespoon salt, and the crushed red pepper. Set aside.

3 In a smoker arrange preheated coals, drained wood chunks, and water pan according to the manufacturer's directions. Pour water into pan. Place meat on the grill rack over water pan. Cover; smoke for 4 to 5 hours or until meat is very tender. Add additional coals and water as needed to maintain temperature and moisture.

4 Remove meat from smoker. Cover meat with foil; let stand for 15 minutes. Using two forks, gently shred the meat into long, thin strands. Add enough of the sauce to moisten the meat. Serve shredded meat on toasted buns. If desired, top meat with coleslaw. Pass the remaining sauce and, if desired, bottled hot pepper sauce.

Nutrition Facts per serving: 314 cal., 11 g total fat (3 g sat. fat), 64 mg chol., 1,096 mg sodium, 24 g carbo., 1 g fiber, 31 g pro. Daily Values: 3% vit. A, 1% vit. C, 4% calcium, 17% iron. Exchanges: 2 Starch, 3 Lean Meat

MEMPHIS-STYLE RIBS

Dry rubs star in Memphis-style barbecue, and
the flavorful brown sugar rub that coats these
ribs proves that even ribs without sauce
are finger-licking good.

Prep: 5 minutes Marinate: 4 to 24 hours Soak: 1 hour
Smoke: 3 hours Makes: 4 servings

4 pounds pork loin back ribs or
    meaty spareribs
3 tablespoons brown sugar
3 tablespoons paprika
2 tablespoons chili powder
1 tablespoon ground cumin
1 tablespoon garlic pepper
1 teaspoon seasoned salt
1/2 to 1 teaspoon cayenne pepper
6 to 8 hickory wood chunks

1 Trim fat from ribs. Place ribs in a shallow dish.
For rub, in a small bowl combine the brown
sugar, paprika, chili powder, cumin, garlic pepper,
seasoned salt, and cayenne pepper. If desired,
reserve 2 tablespoons of the rub to sprinkle on ribs
near the end of smoking. Sprinkle remaining rub
evenly over ribs; rub in with your fingers. Cover
and marinate in the refrigerator for 4 to 24 hours.

2 At least 1 hour before smoke cooking, soak
wood chunks in enough water to cover. Drain
before using.

3 In a smoker arrange preheated coals, drained
wood chunks, and water pan according to the
manufacturer's directions. Pour water into pan.
Place ribs on grill rack over water pan. (Or place
ribs in a rib rack; place on grill rack.) Cover;
smoke for 3 to 4 hours or until ribs are tender. Add
additional coals and water as needed to maintain
the temperature and moisture. If desired, sprinkle
ribs with the reserved rub during the last 15 minutes of smoking.

Nutrition Facts per serving: 509 cal., 27 g total fat
(9 g sat. fat), 118 mg chol., 163 mg sodium, 15 g carbo.,
1 g fiber, 51 g pro. Daily Values: 43% vit. A, 11% vit. C,
6% calcium, 36% iron. Exchanges: 1 Other Carbo.,
7 Lean Meat, 1 Fat

FOOD FOR THOUGHT REGIONAL BARBECUE

Across the United States, you can find as many styles of barbecue as there are
backyards. Needless to say, it's difficult to pin down a "best" one, but here are some
of the more fierce competitors:

● Carolinas: In the Carolinas, it's all about hickory smoked pork, with whole
barbecued pig in the east and pork shoulder in the west. Whether the meat's
pulled or chopped, sauce adds the perfect finishing touch. Vinegar-based sauces
rule in the east, tomato-based in the west, and mustard-based in South Carolina.

● Kansas City: With more barbecue restaurants than any other kind, Kansas City
is considered the barbecue capital by many. All different styles merge here and
they're all slow cooked—ribs, brisket, pork shoulder, and chicken. Dry or wet,
sauce or no sauce, smoky or sweet, anything goes.

● Memphis: In Memphis, grillers have gone back to basics. Traditionalists use
charcoal and a minimal amount of seasoning to let the natural flavors shine. Pork
ribs, either dry or wet, and pork shoulder sandwiches with slaw are the local
favorites. When sauce is used, it's spicy, sweet, and tomato-based.

● Texas: When it comes to beef, Texans stake their claim. They are especially
proud of their barbecued beef brisket, which boasts simple dry rubs in lieu of
heavy sauces.

Spicy Hoisin-Honey Ribs

Sprinkle the rub evenly over ribs; rub in with your fingers. Cover and chill for 1 to 4 hours.

2 At least 1 hour before smoke cooking, soak wood chunks in enough water to cover. Drain before using.

3 In a smoker arrange preheated coals, drained wood chunks, and water pan according to the manufacturer's directions. Pour water into pan. Place ribs, bone sides down, on the grill rack over water pan. (Or place ribs in a rib rack; place on grill rack.) Cover; smoke for 3 to 4 hours or until ribs are tender. Add additional coals and water as needed to maintain temperature and moisture.

4 Meanwhile, for sauce, if using dried chipotle peppers, soak them in warm water for 30 minutes; drain well and finely chop. In a small saucepan stir together the dried chipotle peppers or the chipotle peppers in sauce, hoisin sauce, honey, vinegar, mustard, and garlic. Cook and stir over low heat until heated through.

5 Before serving, brush ribs with some of the sauce. Pass the remaining sauce.

SPICY HOISIN-HONEY RIBS

Thick and reddish brown in color, hoisin sauce is a sweet and spicy medley of soybeans, garlic, chile peppers, and spices.

Prep: 15 minutes Chill: 1 to 4 hours
Soak: 1 hour Smoke: 3 hours
Makes: 4 servings

- **1 tablespoon paprika**
- **$1/2$ teaspoon coarsely ground black pepper**
- **$1/4$ teaspoon onion salt**
- **4 pounds pork loin back ribs**
- **1 lime, halved**
- **6 to 8 oak or hickory wood chunks**
- **2 dried chipotle peppers or 1 to 2 tablespoons finely chopped canned chipotle peppers in adobo sauce**
- **$1/2$ cup bottled hoisin sauce**
- **$1/4$ cup honey**
- **2 tablespoons cider vinegar**
- **2 tablespoons Dijon-style mustard**
- **2 cloves garlic, minced**

1 For rub, in a small bowl combine paprika, black pepper, and onion salt. Trim fat from ribs. Place ribs in a shallow dish. Squeeze and rub the cut surfaces of the lime halves over ribs.

Nutrition Facts per serving: 509 cal., 25 g total fat (8 g sat. fat), 110 mg chol., 898 mg sodium, 40 g carbo., 1 g fiber, 28 g pro. Daily Values: 19% vit. A, 8% vit. C, 4% calcium, 11% iron. Exchanges: $2^1/2$ Other Carbo., 4 Medium-Fat Meat, 1 Fat

TEXAS BEER-SMOKED RIBS

The ancho peppers give these Lone Star ribs border flair. Choose a deep-flavored beer for the marinade.

Prep: 10 minutes Marinate: 24 hours
Soak: 1 hour Smoke: 3 hours
Makes: 6 servings

- **6 pounds meaty pork spareribs or loin back ribs**
- **1 12-ounce bottle beer**
- **2 tablespoons chili powder**
- **2 tablespoons lime juice**
- **1 teaspoon ground cumin**
- **3 cloves garlic, minced**
- **$3/4$ teaspoon salt**
- **4 to 6 mesquite or hickory wood chunks**
- **3 dried ancho or other dried large chile peppers (optional)**

1 Trim fat from ribs. Cut ribs into 8-rib portions. Place ribs in an extra-large self-sealing plastic bag set in a large shallow dish. For marinade, in a medium bowl combine beer, chili powder, lime juice, cumin, garlic, and salt. Pour over ribs; seal bag. Marinate ribs in the refrigerator for 24 hours, turning the bag occasionally. Drain ribs, reserving the marinade.

2 At least 1 hour before smoke cooking, soak wood chunks in enough water to cover. Drain before using. Line water pan with heavy-duty foil.

3 In the smoker arrange preheated coals, drained wood chunks, and the lined water pan according to the manufacturer's directions. Pour the marinade into pan. If desired, add the dried peppers to the marinade. Place ribs on grill rack over pan. Cover; smoke for 3 to 4 hours or until ribs are tender. Add additional coals and water as needed to maintain temperature and moisture.

Nutrition Facts per serving: 580 cal., 43 g total fat (17 g sat. fat), 133 mg chol., 232 mg sodium, 1 g carbo., 0 g fiber, 43 g pro. Daily Values: 2% vit. A, 1% vit. C, 7% calcium, 22% iron. Exchanges: 6 High-Fat Meat

---

SMOKED PINEAPPLE-SOY CHICKEN

Prep: 15 minutes Marinate: 4 hours
Soak: 1 hour Smoke: 1½ hours
Makes: 4 servings

  1 3-pound whole broiler-fryer chicken, quartered
½ cup unsweetened pineapple juice
¼ cup vinegar
  2 tablespoons cooking oil
  1 tablespoon soy sauce
  6 to 8 apple or hickory wood chunks
1½ teaspoons sugar

¾ teaspoon salt
¾ teaspoon paprika
¾ teaspoon ground sage
¼ to ½ teaspoon black pepper
¼ teaspoon chili powder
⅛ teaspoon onion powder

1 Place chicken in a self-sealing plastic bag set in a shallow dish. For marinade, in a small bowl combine pineapple juice, vinegar, oil, and soy sauce. Pour over chicken; seal bag. Marinate chicken in the refrigerator for 4 hours, turning the bag occasionally.

2 At least 1 hour before smoke cooking, soak wood chunks in enough water to cover. Drain before using.

3 For rub, in a small bowl stir together sugar, salt, paprika, sage, pepper, chili powder, and onion powder; set aside. Drain chicken; discard marinade. Pat dry with paper towels. Sprinkle rub evenly over chicken; rub in with your fingers.

4 In a smoker arrange preheated coals, drained wood chunks, and water pan according to manufacturer's directions. Pour water into pan. Place chicken, bone sides down, on the grill rack over the water pan. Cover; smoke for 1½ to 2 hours or until chicken is tender and juices run clear (170°F for breasts; 180°F for thighs and drumsticks). Add additional coals and water as needed to maintain temperature and moisture.

Nutrition Facts per serving: 548 cal., 38 g total fat (10 g sat. fat), 174 mg chol., 715 mg sodium, 5 g carbo., 0 g fiber, 43 g pro. Daily Values: 11% vit. A, 9% vit. C, 3% calcium, 13% iron. Exchanges: ½ Other Carbo., 6 Medium-Fat Meat, 1½ Fat

SMOKIN' HOT TIP

A rack of beef or pork ribs has a thick membrane that stretches across the underside of the bones and is best removed prior to cooking. This tough layer makes for a difficult time eating and also inhibits smoke and flavor from penetrating the meat. To remove, loosen the membrane from the large end of the rack using the tip of a small knife until you are able to get two fingers underneath it. Then, using paper towels to secure your grip, pull the membrane off at an angle, working your way over each rib toward the smaller end of the rack. Be careful not to remove the thinner underlying membrane, which holds the meat and bones together.

Sweet 'n' Sticky Chicken

SWEET 'N' STICKY CHICKEN

Tie a napkin around your neck and dig into this American barbecue classic served with potato salad, sliced fresh tomatoes, and fresh berries for dessert.

Prep: 30 minutes Soak: 1 hour Smoke: 1½ hours
Makes: 6 servings

- **6 to 8 maple or hickory wood chunks**
- **6 whole chicken legs (drumstick and thigh)**
- **1½ teaspoons dried oregano, crushed**
- **1½ teaspoons dried thyme, crushed**
- **½ teaspoon garlic salt**
- **¼ teaspoon onion powder**
- **¼ teaspoon black pepper**
- **1 recipe Sweet 'n' Sticky Barbecue Sauce**

1 At least 1 hour before smoke cooking, soak wood chunks in enough water to cover. Drain before using.

2 If desired, remove skin from chicken. For rub, in a small bowl stir together oregano, thyme, garlic salt, onion powder, and pepper. Sprinkle evenly over chicken; rub in with your fingers.

3 In a smoker, arrange preheated coals, drained wood chunks, and water pan according to the manufacturer's directions. Pour water into pan. Place chicken, bone sides down, on the grill rack over water pan. Cover; smoke for 1½ to 2 hours or until chicken is tender and juices run clear (180°F). Add additional coals and water as needed to maintain temperature and moisture. Remove chicken from smoker.

4 Meanwhile, prepare Sweet 'n' Sticky Barbecue Sauce. Generously brush some of the sauce over chicken; pass remaining sauce.

Sweet 'n' Sticky Barbecue Sauce: In a saucepan cook ½ cup finely chopped onion and 2 cloves garlic, minced, in 1 tablespoon hot olive oil until onion is tender. Stir in ¾ cup bottled chili sauce, ½ cup unsweetened pineapple juice, ¼ cup honey, 2 tablespoons Worcestershire sauce, and ½ teaspoon dry mustard. Bring to boiling; reduce heat. Simmer, uncovered, for 20 to 25 minutes or until desired consistency.

Nutrition Facts per serving: 535 cal., 29 g total fat (8 g sat. fat), 186 mg chol., 725 mg sodium, 25 g carbo., 2 g fiber, 43 g pro. Daily Values: 10% vit. A, 22% vit. C, 6% calcium, 18% iron. Exchanges: 1½ Other Carbo., 6 Medium-Fat Meat

SMOKIN' JERK CHICKEN

Prep: 15 minutes Marinate: 1 to 4 hours
Soak: 1 hour Smoke: 1½ hours
Makes: 6 servings

3 **pounds meaty chicken pieces**
  (breasts, thighs, and drumsticks)
½ **cup tomato juice**
⅓ **cup finely chopped onion (1 small)**
2 **tablespoons water**
2 **tablespoons lime juice**
1 **tablespoon cooking oil**
1 **tablespoon Pickapeppa sauce**
  (optional)
4 **cloves garlic, minced**
½ **teaspoon salt**
6 **to 8 fruit wood chunks**
1 **to 2 tablespoons Jamaican jerk**
  seasoning
  Lime wedges

1 If desired, remove skin from chicken. Place chicken in a self-sealing plastic bag set in a deep dish. For marinade, in a small bowl combine tomato juice, onion, water, lime juice, oil, Pickapeppa sauce (if desired), garlic, and salt. Pour over chicken; seal bag. Marinate in refrigerator for 1 to 4 hours, turning bag occasionally.

2 At least 1 hour before smoke cooking, soak wood chunks in enough water to cover. Drain before using. Drain chicken, discarding marinade. Sprinkle jerk seasoning evenly over chicken; rub in with your fingers.

3 In a smoker arrange preheated coals, drained wood chunks, and water pan according to the manufacturer's directions. Pour water into pan. Place chicken, bone sides down, on the grill rack over water pan. Cover; smoke for 1½ to 2 hours or until chicken is tender and juices run clear (170°F for breasts; 180°F for thighs and drumsticks). Add additional coals and water as needed to maintain temperature and moisture. Serve chicken with lime wedges.

Nutrition Facts per serving: 283 cal., 14 g total fat (4 g sat. fat), 104 mg chol., 331 mg sodium, 3 g carbo., 0 g fiber, 34 g pro. Daily Values: 2% vit. A, 8% vit. C, 3% calcium, 10% iron. Exchanges: 5 Very Lean Meat

BARBECUED TURKEY TENDERLOINS

Prep: 15 minutes Soak: 1 hour Smoke: 1¼ hours
Makes: 4 servings

6 **to 8 hickory or oak wood chunks**
½ **cup bottled hickory barbecue sauce**
1 **small fresh jalapeño chile pepper,**
  seeded and finely chopped
  (see tip, page 36)
1 **tablespoon tahini (sesame butter)**
4 **tomatillos, husked and halved**
  lengthwise, or ½ cup salsa verde
2 **turkey breast tenderloins**
  (about 1 pound)
4 **French-style rolls, split and toasted**
  Spinach leaves

1 At least 1 hour before smoke cooking, soak wood chunks in enough water to cover. Drain before using.

2 For sauce, in a small bowl combine barbecue sauce, jalapeño pepper, and tahini. Transfer half of the sauce to another bowl and reserve until ready to serve. If using tomatillos, thread them onto metal skewers. Set aside.

3 In a smoker arrange preheated coals, drained wood chunks, and water pan according to the manufacturer's directions. Pour water into pan. Brush both sides of turkey with the remaining sauce. Place turkey on the grill rack over water pan. Cover; smoke for 1¼ to 1½ hours or until turkey is tender and juices run clear (170°F). Place tomatillos next to turkey on grill rack directly over coals during the last 20 minutes of smoking. Add additional coals and water as needed to maintain temperature and moisture. Remove turkey and tomatillos from smoker. Thinly slice the turkey and chop the tomatillos.

4 To serve, in a small saucepan cook and stir the reserved sauce over low heat until heated through. Remove from heat. Fill the toasted rolls with a few spinach leaves, the smoked turkey, and tomatillos or salsa verde. Top with the reserved sauce.

Nutrition Facts per serving: 303 cal., 5 g total fat (1 g sat. fat), 68 mg chol., 695 mg sodium, 32 g carbo., 1 g fiber, 31 g pro. Daily Values: 2% vit. A, 15% vit. C, 6% calcium, 14% iron. Exchanges: ½ Vegetable, 1 Starch, 1 Other Carbo., 4 Very Lean Meat

Chili-Rubbed Drumsticks

Cover; smoke for 2½ to 3 hours or until turkey is tender and juices run clear (180°F). Add coals and water as needed to maintain temperature and moisture. If desired, serve the turkey with salsa.

Nutrition Facts per serving: 178 cal., 9 g total fat (3 g sat. fat), 80 mg chol., 269 mg sodium, 1 g carbo., 1 g fiber, 22 g pro. Daily Values: 9% vit. A, 4% vit. C, 4% calcium, 11% iron. Exchanges: 3 Lean Meat

DOUBLE-SMOKED SALMON WITH HORSERADISH CREAM

This salmon dish is twice as nice because it's fresh salmon stuffed with smoked salmon and then smoked in a smoker.

Prep: 15 minutes Soak: 1 hour Smoke: 45 minutes
Makes: 4 servings

    4 hickory or apple wood chunks
    4 6-ounce fresh or frozen salmon
         fillets (with skin), about
         1 inch thick
    4 slices smoked salmon (lox-style)
         (about 3 ounces)
    4 teaspoons snipped fresh dill
    1 tablespoon lemon juice
       Salt
       Black pepper
    1 recipe Horseradish Cream

1 At least 1 hour before smoke cooking, soak wood chunks in enough water to cover. Drain before using.

2 Thaw salmon fillets, if frozen. Rinse fillets; pat dry with paper towels. Make a pocket in each fish fillet by cutting horizontally from one side almost to, but not through, the other side. Fill with smoked salmon slices and 2 teaspoons of the dill, folding salmon slices as necessary to fit. Brush fish with lemon juice and top with the remaining 2 teaspoons of the dill. Sprinkle with salt and pepper.

3 In a smoker arrange preheated coals, drained wood chunks, and water pan according to the manufacturer's directions. Pour water into pan. Place fish, skin side down, on grill rack over water pan. Cover; smoke for 45 to 60 minutes or until fish flakes easily when tested with a fork. Serve fish with Horseradish Cream.

CHILI-RUBBED DRUMSTICKS

Prep: 5 minutes Soak: 1 hour Smoke: 2½ hours
Makes: 6 servings

    6 to 8 hickory wood chunks
    1 tablespoon chili powder
    1 tablespoon finely shredded lime peel
 1½ teaspoons ground cumin
    ½ teaspoon salt
    6 turkey drumsticks (about 3 to
         4½ pounds)
       Bottled salsa or barbecue sauce
       (optional)

1 At least 1 hour before smoke cooking, soak wood chunks in enough water to cover. Drain before using.

2 For rub, in a small bowl combine chili powder, lime peel, cumin, and salt. Sprinkle mixture evenly over turkey; rub in with your fingers.

3 In a smoker arrange preheated coals, drained wood chunks, and water pan according to the manufacturer's directions. Pour water into pan. Place drumsticks on grill rack over water pan.

Horseradish Cream: In a small bowl stir together ½ cup dairy sour cream, 2 tablespoons thinly sliced green onion, 4 teaspoons prepared horseradish, and 2 teaspoons snipped fresh dill.

Nutrition Facts per serving: 245 cal., 13 g total fat (5 g sat. fat), 48 mg chol., 337 mg sodium, 2 g carbo., 0 g fiber, 29 g pro. Daily Values: 11% vit. A, 6% vit. C, 4% calcium, 9% iron. Exchanges: 4 Lean Meat, ½ Fat

FENNEL-STUFFED TROUT

Perhaps because trout evokes images of fishing in pristine freshwater streams, it is especially appealing cooked over a smoky fire. Serve this delicate fish with a mixture of new potatoes, zucchini, and red peppers.

Prep: 10 minutes Soak: 1 hour Smoke: 1½ hours
Makes: 4 servings

- **6 to 8 alder or pecan wood chunks**
- **4 8- to 10-ounce fresh or frozen dressed trout or other fish**
- **2 fennel bulbs**
- **1 clove garlic, minced**
- **¼ teaspoon salt**
- **⅛ teaspoon black pepper**
- **2 tablespoons butter or margarine**
- **1 tablespoon snipped fresh parsley**
- **3 tablespoons butter or margarine**
- **1 tablespoon lemon juice**
- **½ teaspoon dried rosemary, crushed**
- **Dash black pepper**
- **Lemon wedges (optional)**

1 At least 1 hour before smoke cooking, soak wood chunks in enough water to cover. Drain before using.

2 Thaw fish, if frozen. For stuffing, cut off and discard upper stalks of fennel. Remove any wilted outer layers; cut off a thin slice from bases. Chop fennel bulbs (should have about 2½ cups). In a medium saucepan cook and stir fennel, garlic, salt, and the ⅛ teaspoon pepper in the 2 tablespoons butter about 10 minutes or until fennel is tender. Stir in parsley; set aside.

3 For sauce, in a small saucepan combine the 3 tablespoons butter, the lemon juice, rosemary, and dash pepper. Heat through.

4 Rinse fish; pat dry with paper towels. Spoon the stuffing into the fish cavities. Skewer the cavities closed with wooden toothpicks. Brush fish with some of the sauce.

5 In a smoker arrange preheated coals, drained wood chunks, and water pan according to the manufacturer's directions. Pour water into pan. Place fish on the greased grill rack over water pan. Cover; smoke for 1½ to 2 hours or until fish flakes easily when tested with a fork, brushing once with sauce halfway through cooking. Add additional coals and water as needed to maintain the temperature and moisture. Discard any remaining sauce.

6 Remove the toothpicks from fish. If desired, serve fish with lemon wedges.

Nutrition Facts per serving: 486 cal., 28 g total fat (11 g sat. fat), 174 mg chol., 394 mg sodium, 9 g carbo., 4 g fiber, 49 g pro. Daily Values: 26% vit. A, 38% vit. C, 22% calcium, 9% iron. Exchanges: 2 Vegetable, 6 Very Lean Meat, 5 Fat

SMOKIN' HOT TIP

Supermarkets that stock charcoal usually carry wood chips and chunks as well. The following companies will ship them right to your front door:

● Woodbridge Vintage Barrel Chips: **Made from oak wine barrels. Call 888-982-2447 or visit www.woodbridgechips.com**

● Blanton Mesquite Wood: **Carries pecan and mesquite woods. Call 877-891-3597 or visit www.bbqblanton.com**

● The Barbecue Store: **Offers mesquite, alder apple, or hickory woods, and Cabernet and Chardonnay wine-soaked oak woods. Call 888-789-0650 or visit www.barbecue-store.com**

Tropical Halibut Steaks

TROPICAL HALIBUT STEAKS

Toasting the coconut for this tropically inclined
entrée heightens its sweet nuttiness. Simply
bake the coconut in a 350°F oven about
10 minutes, stirring once, until it's golden.

Prep: 15 minutes Marinate: 1 hour
Soak: 1 hour Smoke: 45 minutes
Makes: 4 servings

4 apple or orange wood chunks
4 6-ounce fresh or frozen halibut
   steaks, cut 1 inch thick
¹/₃ cup pineapple-orange juice
¹/₃ cup soy sauce
¹/₄ teaspoon curry powder
1 recipe Chunky Pineapple Sauce
2 tablespoons coconut, toasted

1 At least 1 hour before smoke cooking, soak
wood chunks in enough water to cover. Drain
before using.

2 Thaw fish, if frozen. Rinse fish; pat dry with
paper towels. Place fish in a self-sealing
plastic bag set in a shallow dish. For marinade, in
a small bowl combine pineapple-orange juice, soy
sauce, and curry powder. Pour marinade over fish;
seal bag. Marinate in the refrigerator for 1 hour,
turning bag occasionally. Drain the fish, reserving
the marinade.

3 In a smoker arrange preheated coals, drained
wood chunks, and water pan according to the
manufacturer's directions. Pour water into pan.
Place fish on the greased grill rack over water pan.
Cover; smoke for 45 to 60 minutes or until fish
flakes easily when tested with a fork, brushing
once with marinade halfway through cooking.
Discard the remaining marinade.

4 To serve, if necessary, reheat the Chunky
Pineapple Sauce and spoon over fish. Sprinkle
the fish with toasted coconut.

Chunky Pineapple Sauce: Drain one 8-ounce
can pineapple chunks (juice pack), reserving juice.
Peel and seed one-fourth a medium cantaloupe or
half of one papaya. Finely chop pineapple and
cantaloupe or papaya. In a saucepan combine the
chopped fruit and a dash curry powder. Add
enough water to the reserved pineapple juice to
make ¹/₂ cup liquid. Stir in 2 teaspoons cornstarch;
add to the fruit mixture. Cook and stir over
medium heat until thickened and bubbly. Cook
and stir for 2 minutes more. Remove from heat.

Nutrition Facts per serving: 262 cal., 5 g total fat
(1 g sat. fat), 54 mg chol., 740 mg sodium, 16 g carbo.,
1 g fiber, 38 g pro. Daily Values: 26% vit. A, 35% vit. C,
9% calcium, 10% iron. Exchanges: 1 Fruit, 5 Very Lean
Meat, ¹/₂ Fat

12

Indoor
Grilling

BEEF & VEAL

Adobo Steaks, 384
Beef Kabobs with Blue Cheese Dipping Sauce, 381
Garlic Veal Chops, 384
Garlicky Steak and Asparagus, 383
Herb-Pepper Sirloin Steak, 382
Indian-Style Beef with Cucumber Sauce, 382
Jalapeño-Glazed Ribeyes, 380
Porcini Mushroom Burgers, 380
Southwest Steak, 383

BURGERS

Cantonese Chicken Burgers, 390
Currant-Glazed Pork Burgers, 386
Lamb Burgers with Feta and Mint, 385
Porcini Mushroom Burgers, 380
Smoked Gouda and Caramelized Onions Turkey Burgers, 394
Teriyaki Turkey Patties, 393

CHICKEN & TURKEY

Apple-Glazed Chicken Kabobs, 391
Cantonese Chicken Burgers, 390
Chicken and Roasted Pepper Sandwich, 390
Chicken Fajitas with Guacamole, 392
Chicken with Mango Chutney, 393
Smoked Gouda and Caramelized Onions Turkey Burgers, 394
Tangy Lemon Chicken, 392
Teriyaki Turkey Patties, 393
Turkey and Vegetables, 395

DIPS & SAUCES

Blue Cheese Dipping Sauce, 381
Guacamole, 392

FISH

Mango-Topped Salmon, 397
Swordfish with Tomato Relish, 397
Tuna Steaks with Jalapeño Mayo, 395

LAMB

Lamb Burgers with Feta and Mint, 385
Lamb Chops with Cranberry-Port Sauce, 385
Lamb with Sweet Potato Chutney, 386

PORK

Apple-Sauced Chops, 387
Currant-Glazed Pork Burgers, 386
Jerk Pork and Pineapple Salsa Sandwiches, 388
Spicy Chipotle Pork Soft Tacos, 388

SANDWICHES, TACOS & FAJITAS

Chicken and Roasted Pepper Sandwich, 390
Chicken Fajitas with Guacamole, 392
Jerk Pork and Pineapple Salsa Sandwiches, 388
Spicy Chipotle Pork Soft Tacos, 388

SIDE DISHES

Grilled Plantains, 388
Herbed Ratatouille and Polenta, 398
Marinated Tomatoes and Onions, 380

INDOOR ELECTRIC GRILLS

If grilling poultry, fish, or seafood, lightly grease the rack of an indoor electric grill or lightly coat with cooking spray. Preheat grill. Place meat, poultry, fish, or seafood on grill rack. (For fish fillets, tuck under any thin edges.) If using a grill with a cover, close the lid. Grill for the time given below or until done. If using a grill without a cover, turn food once halfway through grilling. The following times should be used as general guidelines. Test for doneness using a meat thermometer. Refer to your owner's manual for preheating directions, suggested cuts, and recommended grilling times.

CUT OR TYPE	THICKNESS, WEIGHT, OR SIZE	COVERED GRILLING TIME	UNCOVERED GRILLING TIME	DONENESS
BEEF				
Boneless steak (ribeye, tenderloin, top loin)	1 inch	4 to 6 minutes 6 to 8 minutes	8 to 12 minutes 12 to 15 minutes	145°F medium-rare 160°F medium
Boneless top sirloin steak	1 inch	5 to 7 minutes 7 to 9 minutes	12 to 15 minutes 15 to 18 minutes	145°F medium-rare 160°F medium
Flank steak		7 to 9 minutes	12 to 14 minutes	160°F medium
Ground meat patties	½ to ¾ inch	5 to 7 minutes	14 to 18 minutes	160°F medium
Sausages, cooked through (frankfurters, smoked bratwurst, etc.)	6 per pound	2½ to 3 minutes	5 to 6 minutes	140°F heated
Steak with bone (porterhouse, rib, T-bone)	1 inch	Not recommended Not recommended	8 to 12 minutes 12 to 15 minutes	145°F medium-rare 160°F medium
LAMB				
Chop (loin or rib)	1 inch	6 to 8 minutes	12 to 15 minutes	160°F medium
VEAL				
Chop (boneless loin)	¾ inch	4 to 5 minutes	7 to 9 minutes	160°F medium
PORK				
Chop (boneless top loin)	¾ inch	6 to 8 minutes	12 to 15 minutes	160°F medium
POULTRY				
Chicken breast half, skinned and boned	4 to 5 ounces	4 to 6 minutes	12 to 15 minutes	170°F
FISH AND SEAFOOD				
Fillets or steaks	½ to 1 inch	2 to 3 minutes per ½-inch thickness	4 to 6 minutes per ½-inch thickness	Flakes
Sea scallops	15 to 20 per pound	2½ to 4 minutes	6 to 8 minutes	Opaque
Shrimp	Medium (41 to 50 per pound)	2½ to 4 minutes	6 to 8 minutes	Opaque

All cooking times are based on meat removed directly from refrigerator.

PORCINI MUSHROOM BURGERS

If dried porcini mushrooms aren't available, substitute ½ cup thinly sliced cooked button mushrooms.

Prep: 30 minutes
Grill: 9 minutes (covered) or 22 minutes (uncovered)
Makes: 6 burgers

- **1 ounce dried porcini mushrooms**
- **2 pounds ground beef**
- **¼ cup snipped fresh basil**
- **1 teaspoon snipped fresh thyme**
- **1½ teaspoons kosher salt**
- **1 teaspoon freshly ground black pepper**
- **1 to 2 tablespoons garlic-flavored olive oil**
- **6 olive focaccia bread wedges, sliced horizontally**
- **½ cup shredded Asiago or mozzarella cheese (2 ounces)**
- **1 recipe Marinated Tomatoes and Onions**

1 Place mushrooms in a small bowl; cover with boiling water. Let soak for 10 minutes. Drain, rinse well, and chop. Set aside.

2 Lightly grease or coat with nonstick cooking spray the rack of an indoor electric grill. Preheat grill.

3 In a large bowl combine drained mushrooms, beef, basil, thyme, salt, and pepper. Mix well. Shape into six ¾-inch-thick patties. Brush each with garlic oil; set aside.

4 Place focaccia wedges on the grill rack. If using a covered grill, close lid. Grill until toasted. For a covered grill, allow 4 to 6 minutes. For an uncovered grill, allow 8 to 10 minutes, turning once. Remove focaccia from grill.

5 Place patties on grill. If using a covered grill, close lid. Grill patties until meat is no longer pink and an instant-read thermometer inserted in centers registers 160°F. For a covered grill, allow 5 to 7 minutes. For an uncovered grill, allow 14 to 18 minutes, turning once halfway through grilling.

6 Place each patty on a bottom half of a wedge of focaccia; sprinkle immediately with Asiago cheese. Top each with some of the Marinated Tomatoes and Onions and a top half of focaccia.

Marinated Tomatoes and Onions: In a medium bowl combine 1 medium yellow or red tomato, thinly sliced; ½ of a thinly sliced sweet onion; 1 tablespoon olive oil; 1 tablespoon white balsamic vinegar; ¼ teaspoon salt; and ¼ teaspoon freshly ground black pepper. Cover and chill until serving time.

Nutrition Facts per burger: 534 cal., 29 g total fat (10 g sat. fat), 110 mg chol., 1,001 mg sodium, 32 g carbo., 2 g fiber, 37 g pro. Daily Values: 2% vit. A, 8% vit. C, 17% calcium, 20% iron. Exchanges: 2 Starch, 4½ Medium-Fat Meat, 1 Fat

JALAPEÑO-GLAZED RIBEYES

These hot southwestern steaks are sizzling with corn relish made from pepper jelly. If that's not hot enough for you, add a chopped jalapeño.

Prep: 20 minutes
Grill: 4 minutes (covered) or 8 minutes (uncovered)
Makes: 4 servings

- **¼ cup jalapeño pepper jelly**
- **¼ cup catsup**
- **4 boneless beef ribeye steaks, 1 inch thick (1¾ to 2 pounds total)**
- **2 tablespoons jalapeño pepper jelly**
- **1 tablespoon lime juice**
- **½ teaspoon chili powder**
- **¼ teaspoon ground cumin**
- **1 10-ounce package frozen whole kernel corn, thawed**
- **¾ cup chopped red sweet pepper**
- **¼ cup finely chopped green onions (2)**
- **1 fresh jalapeño chile pepper, seeded and finely chopped (optional) (see tip, page 36)**

1 Preheat indoor electric grill. For glaze, in a small saucepan melt the ¼ cup jelly. Stir in catsup; set aside.

2 Trim fat from steaks. Place steaks on the grill rack. If using a covered grill, close lid. Grill until steaks are desired doneness. For a covered grill, allow 4 to 6 minutes for medium-rare or 6 to 8 minutes for medium, brushing once with glaze the last 1 to 2 minutes of grilling. For an uncovered grill, allow 8 to 12 minutes for medium-rare or 12 to 15 minutes for medium, turning once halfway through grilling time and brushing with glaze the last 5 minutes of grilling.

3 Meanwhile, for relish, in another small saucepan stir together the 2 tablespoons jelly, the lime juice, chili powder, and cumin. Cook and stir until jelly is melted and mixture is bubbly. Stir in corn, sweet pepper, green onions, and, if desired, jalapeño pepper. Cook and stir until just heated through. Season to taste with salt. Serve the steaks with corn relish.

Nutrition Facts per serving: 474 cal., 16 g total fat (6 g sat. fat), 116 mg chol., 434 mg sodium, 41 g carbo., 3 g fiber, 43 g pro. Daily Values: 23% vit. A, 89% vit. C, 4% calcium, 27% iron. Exchanges: 1 Starch, 1½ Other Carbo., 5½ Lean Meat

BEEF KABOBS WITH BLUE CHEESE DIPPING SAUCE

This blue cheese dipping sauce takes kabobs to a new level of sophistication. If you're in a hurry, substitute a purchased blue cheese dressing.

Prep: 25 minutes
Grill: 3 minutes (covered) or 6 minutes (uncovered)
Makes: 4 servings

- **1 pound beef top sirloin, cut into 1-inch cubes**
- **2 teaspoons steak seasoning**
- **12 cremini mushrooms, halved**
- **6 green onions, cut into 2-inch pieces**
- **1 recipe Blue Cheese Dipping Sauce**

1 Preheat indoor electric grill. In a medium bowl combine beef and steak seasoning; toss to coat beef. On eight 8-inch metal skewers alternately thread beef, mushrooms, and onions, leaving a ¼-inch space between pieces.

2 Place kabobs on the grill rack. If using a covered grill, close lid. Grill until beef is cooked to desired doneness. For a covered grill allow, 3 to 4 minutes for medium. For uncovered grill, allow 6 to 8 minutes for medium, turning kabobs occasionally to brown evenly. Serve kabobs with Blue Cheese Dipping Sauce.

Blue Cheese Dipping Sauce: In a small bowl combine 2 ounces crumbled blue cheese, ⅔ cup mayonnaise, 2 tablespoons dairy sour cream, 1 teaspoon lemon juice, ½ teaspoon Worcestershire sauce, and ¼ teaspoon black pepper. Cover and chill sauce until serving time.

Nutrition Facts per serving: 484 cal., 39 g total fat (9 g sat. fat), 104 mg chol., 641 mg sodium, 5 g carbo., 1 g fiber, 29 g pro. Daily Values: 7% vit. A, 8% vit. C, 12% calcium, 21% iron. Exchanges: ½ Vegetable, 4 Medium-Fat Meat, 4 Fat

Jalapeño-Glazed Ribeyes

HERB-PEPPER SIRLOIN STEAK

A mixture of catsup, herbs, and black pepper draws out the hearty beef flavor of sirloin steak.

Prep: 10 minutes
Grill: 5 minutes (covered) or 12 minutes (uncovered)
Makes: 4 servings

1 tablespoon catsup
1 teaspoon snipped fresh rosemary
    or 1/4 teaspoon dried rosemary,
    crushed
1 teaspoon snipped fresh basil or
    1/4 teaspoon dried basil, crushed
1/4 teaspoon coarsely ground
    black pepper
    Dash garlic powder
    Dash ground cardamom (optional)
1 1-pound boneless beef sirloin steak,
    1 inch thick

1 Preheat indoor electric grill. In a small bowl stir together catsup, rosemary, basil, pepper, garlic powder, and, if desired, cardamom. Trim fat from steak. Coat both sides of steak evenly with catsup mixture.

2 Place steak on grill rack. If using a covered grill, close lid. Grill until steak is desired doneness. For a covered grill, allow 5 to 7 minutes for medium-rare or 7 to 9 minutes for medium. For an uncovered grill, allow 12 to 15 minutes for medium-rare or 15 to 18 minutes for medium, turning once halfway through grilling. To serve, cut steak into four equal pieces.

Nutrition Facts per serving: 144 cal., 4 g total fat (1 g sat. fat), 53 mg chol., 105 mg sodium, 1 g carbo., 0 g fiber, 24 g pro. Daily Values: 1% vit. A, 1% vit. C, 2% calcium, 14% iron. Exchanges: 3½ Very Lean Meat, ½ Fat

INDIAN-STYLE BEEF WITH CUCUMBER SAUCE

Prep: 15 minutes
Grill: 5 minutes (covered) or 12 minutes (uncovered)
Makes: 4 servings

1 8-ounce carton plain fat-free or
    low-fat yogurt
1/4 cup coarsely shredded unpeeled
    cucumber
1 tablespoon finely chopped red or
    yellow onion
1 tablespoon snipped fresh mint
1/4 teaspoon sugar
1 pound boneless beef sirloin steak,
    1 inch thick
1/2 teaspoon lemon-pepper seasoning
    Fresh mint leaves (optional)

1 Preheat indoor electric grill. For the sauce, in a small bowl combine yogurt, cucumber, onion, snipped mint, and sugar. Season with salt and black pepper; set aside.

2 Trim fat from steak. Sprinkle steak with lemon-pepper seasoning. Place steak on the grill rack. If using a covered grill, close lid. Grill until steak is desired doneness. For a covered grill, allow 5 to 7 minutes for medium-rare or 7 to 9 minutes for medium. For an uncovered grill, allow 12 to 15 minutes for medium-rare or 15 to 18 minutes for medium, turning once halfway through grilling.

3 Thinly slice steak across the grain. If desired, arrange slices on mint leaves. Top with sauce.

Nutrition Facts per serving: 237 cal., 10 g total fat (4 g sat. fat), 77 mg chol., 235 mg sodium, 5 g carbo., 0 g fiber, 29 g pro. Daily Values: 1% vit. A, 3% vit. C, 10% calcium, 21% iron. Exchanges: ½ Other Carbo., 4 Very Lean Meat, 1 Fat

SMOKIN' HOT TIP

Despite the many styles and sizes, there are only two types of indoor grills: covered and uncovered. Covered grills typically have a hinged lid, and foods are cooked with the lid closed. Because foods are heated from both the top and bottom, they cook more quickly than they would on an uncovered grill. Uncovered grills are open, and foods are heated from the bottom only, so foods cook more slowly. Grills that are sold as part of ranges with special grates and exhaust fans also fit into this category. The recipes in this chapter will work for both types of grills. Simply follow the directions and timings according to your appliance. Your grill may take a bit more or less time to cook, so use the timings as guidelines.

SOUTHWEST STEAK

The mild, medium, or hot salsa you choose sets the heat index here.

Prep: 20 minutes Marinate: 8 to 24 hours
Grill: 5 minutes (covered) or 12 minutes (uncovered) for medium
Makes: 4 to 6 servings

- **¼ cup lime juice**
- **¼ cup bottled steak sauce**
- **¼ cup bottled salsa**
- **1 tablespoon cooking oil**
- **1 clove garlic, minced**
- **½ teaspoon coarsely ground black pepper**
- **1 pound boneless beef top sirloin steak, 1 inch thick**
  Flour tortillas, warmed
  Bottled salsa

1 For marinade, in a small saucepan combine lime juice, steak sauce, the ¼ cup salsa, oil, garlic, and pepper. Bring to boiling; reduce heat. Simmer, uncovered, for 5 minutes, stirring occasionally; cool.

2 Place steak in a self-sealing plastic bag set in a shallow dish. Pour marinade over steak; seal bag. Marinate in the refrigerator for 8 to 24 hours, turning bag occasionally.

3 Preheat indoor electric grill. Drain steak, discarding the marinade. Place steak on the grill rack. If using a covered grill, close lid. Grill steak until desired doneness. For a covered grill, allow 5 to 7 minutes for medium-rare or 7 to 9 minutes for medium. For an uncovered grill, allow 12 to 15 minutes for medium-rare or 15 to 18 minutes for medium, turning steak once halfway through grilling.

4 To serve, thinly slice meat across grain. Serve with warmed tortillas and additional salsa.

Nutrition Facts per serving: 265 cal., 9 g total fat (3 g sat. fat), 69 mg chol., 345 mg sodium, 18 g carbo., 1 g fiber, 26 g pro. Daily Values: 3% vit. A, 9% vit. C, 5% calcium, 23% iron. Exchanges: 1 Starch, 3½ Lean Meat

GARLICKY STEAK AND ASPARAGUS

Prep: 15 minutes Cook: 4 minutes
Grill: 3 minutes (covered) or 6 minutes (uncovered)
Makes: 2 servings

- **1 or 2 large cloves garlic, coarsely chopped**
- **½ teaspoon cracked or coarsely ground black pepper**
- **¼ teaspoon salt**
- **1 12- to 14-ounce boneless beef top loin (strip) steak, about ¾ inch thick**
- **8 to 10 thin fresh asparagus spears, trimmed (6 ounces)**
- **2 teaspoons garlic-flavored olive oil or olive oil**
- **½ cup beef broth**
- **1 tablespoon dry white wine**
- **¼ teaspoon Dijon-style mustard**

1 For rub, in a bowl combine garlic, pepper, and salt. Sprinkle rub evenly over both sides of steak; rub in and press onto steak. Place asparagus in a shallow dish and drizzle with oil. Set aside.

2 For sauce, in a medium skillet stir together the broth and wine. Cook over high heat for 4 to 5 minutes or until broth mixture is reduced to ¼ cup. Whisk in mustard; keep warm.

3 Preheat indoor electric grill. Place steak on the grill rack. If using a covered grill, close lid. Grill until steak is desired doneness. For a covered grill, allow 3 to 4 minutes for medium-rare or 5 to 7 minutes for medium. For an uncovered grill, allow 6 to 8 minutes for medium-rare or 8 to 12 minutes for medium, turning steak once. If space allows, add asparagus to a covered grill for the last 2 to 4 minutes of grilling or to uncovered grill the last 3 to 5 minutes of grilling. Cook until asparagus is crisp-tender, turning occasionally to cook evenly.

4 Divide sauce between 2 serving plates. Cut steak in half crosswise. Place a steak on top of sauce; top steaks with asparagus.

Nutrition Facts per serving: 319 cal., 15 g total fat (4 g sat. fat), 100 mg chol., 626 mg sodium, 3 g carbo., 1 g fiber, 40 g pro. Daily Values: 2% vit. A, 37% vit. C, 3% calcium, 21% iron. Exchanges: ½ Vegetable, 5½ Lean Meat

ADOBO STEAKS

Mexican adobo sauce is a potent red sauce made from ground chiles, vinegar, and herbs. This homemade version makes a great marinade. To crank up the heat, add the optional cayenne pepper.

Prep: 15 minutes Marinate: 2 to 24 hours
Grill: 3 minutes (covered) or 6 minutes (uncovered)
Makes: 4 servings

2 tablespoons packed brown sugar
2 tablespoons snipped fresh cilantro
2 tablespoons olive oil
2 tablespoons orange juice
1 tablespoon red wine vinegar or
     cider vinegar
2 teaspoons hot chili powder
1 teaspoon ground cumin
1 teaspoon dried oregano, crushed
½ teaspoon salt
¼ teaspoon cayenne pepper (optional)
¼ teaspoon ground cinnamon
3 cloves garlic, minced
4 6- to 8-ounce boneless beef top loin
     (strip) steaks, ¾ inch thick

1 For marinade, in a small bowl combine brown sugar, cilantro, oil, orange juice, vinegar, chili powder, cumin, oregano, salt, cayenne pepper (if desired), cinnamon, and garlic. Trim fat from steaks. Place steaks in a self-sealing plastic bag set in a shallow dish. Pour marinade over steaks; seal bag. Marinate in the refrigerator 2 to 24 hours, turning bag occasionally.

2 Preheat indoor electric grill. Drain steaks, discarding marinade. Place steaks on the grill rack. (If grill is too small to hold all of the steaks at once, grill in two batches.) If using a covered grill, close lid. Grill until desired doneness. For a covered grill, allow 3 to 4 minutes for medium-rare or 5 to 7 minutes for medium. For uncovered grill, allow 6 to 8 minutes for medium-rare or 8 to 12 minutes for medium, turning once halfway through grilling.

Nutrition Facts per serving: 336 cal., 19 g total fat (7 g sat. fat), 99 mg chol., 163 mg sodium, 3 g carbo., 0 g fiber, 37 g pro. Daily Values: 3% vit. A, 3% vit. C, 2% calcium, 17% iron. Exchanges: 5 Lean Meat, 1 Fat

GARLIC VEAL CHOPS

If veal chops are unavailable, use pork loin chops.

Prep: 15 minutes Marinate: 30 minutes
Grill: 6 minutes (covered) or 10 minutes (uncovered)
Makes: 4 servings

1 pound asparagus spears
2 tablespoons dry sherry
2 tablespoons olive oil
1 clove garlic, minced
4 boneless veal top loin chops,
     ¾ inch thick
3 or 4 cloves garlic, cut into thin slivers
1 tablespoon snipped fresh thyme or
     1 teaspoon dried thyme, crushed
⅛ teaspoon salt
⅛ teaspoon black pepper

1 Snap off and discard woody stems from asparagus spears. In a medium skillet bring a small amount of water to boiling; add asparagus. Simmer, covered, for 3 minutes; drain. Place asparagus in a self-sealing plastic bag. Add sherry, 1 tablespoon of the olive oil, and the minced garlic; seal bag. Marinate at room temperature for 30 minutes, turning bag occasionally.

2 Preheat indoor electric grill. Trim fat from chops. With the tip of a paring knife, make small slits in chops; insert garlic slivers into slits. Combine remaining olive oil, the thyme, salt, and pepper; brush over chops.

3 Place chops on the grill rack. If using a covered grill, close lid. Grill until chops are desired doneness. For a covered grill, allow 4 to 5 minutes for medium. For an uncovered grill, allow 7 to 9 minutes for medium, turning once halfway through grilling. Remove from grill; cover and keep warm.

4 Add asparagus to the grill rack. If using a covered grill, close lid. Grill until asparagus is crisp-tender and lightly browned. For a covered grill, allow 2 to 4 minutes. For an uncovered grill, allow 3 to 5 minutes, turning occasionally to cook evenly. Serve the chops with asparagus.

Nutrition Facts per serving: 237 cal., 11 g total fat (3 g sat. fat), 92 mg chol., 131 mg sodium, 5 g carbo., 2 g fiber, 27 g pro. Daily Values: 6% vit. A, 37% vit. C, 2% calcium, 9% iron. Exchanges: 1 Vegetable, 3½ Very Lean Meat, 2 Fat

LAMB BURGERS WITH FETA AND MINT

For an extra flavor boost, use feta cheese that's seasoned with herbs or vegetables.

Prep: 15 minutes
Grill: 5 minutes (covered) or 14 minutes (uncovered)
Makes: 4 burgers

1½ **pounds lean ground lamb or beef**
  2 **teaspoons black pepper**
  4 **kaiser rolls, split**
  4 **lettuce leaves**
½ **cup crumbled feta cheese**
    (2 ounces)
  4 **tomato slices**
  1 **tablespoon snipped fresh mint**

1 Lightly grease or coat with nonstick cooking spray the rack of an indoor electric grill. Preheat grill.

2 Shape lamb into four ¾-inch-thick patties. Sprinkle pepper evenly onto patties. Place patties on grill rack. If using a covered grill, close lid. Grill patties until meat is no longer pink and an instant-read thermometer inserted in centers registers 160°F. For a covered grill, allow 5 to 7 minutes. For an uncovered grill, allow 14 to 18 minutes, turning once halfway through grilling.

3 Serve patties on kaiser rolls; top each with a lettuce leaf, feta cheese, a tomato slice, and fresh mint.

Nutrition Facts per burger: 544 cal., 29 g total fat (12 g sat. fat), 126 mg chol., 564 mg sodium, 32 g carbo., 2 g fiber, 37 g pro. Daily Values: 5% vit. A, 6% vit. C, 16% calcium, 26% iron. Exchanges: ½ Vegetable, 2 Starch, 4½ Medium-Fat Meat, ½ Fat

LAMB CHOPS WITH CRANBERRY-PORT SAUCE

Lamb chops rise to the occasion when partnered with a port (sweet fortified wine) and cranberry sauce. Your guests don't need to know how easy they are to make.

Prep: 15 minutes Marinate: 4 to 24 hours
Grill: 6 minutes (covered) or 12 minutes (uncovered)
Cook: 8 minutes Makes: 4 servings

  8 **lamb rib or loin chops, 1 inch thick**
    (about 2 pounds)
½ **teaspoon salt**
¼ **teaspoon coarsely ground black pepper**
  1 **cup cranberry juice cocktail**
  1 **cup tawny port**
  2 **tablespoons packed brown sugar**
  4 **cloves garlic, minced**
½ **cup dried cranberries**

1 Trim fat from chops. Sprinkle both sides of chops evenly with salt and pepper. Place chops in a self-sealing plastic bag set in a shallow dish. For marinade, in a medium bowl combine cranberry juice, tawny port, brown sugar, and garlic. Pour half of the juice mixture over chops. Seal bag and marinate in the refrigerator for 4 to 24 hours. Add cranberries to remaining juice mixture; cover and chill.

2 Preheat indoor electric grill. Drain chops, discarding marinade. Place chops on the grill rack. If using a covered grill, close lid. Grill until lamb is desired doneness. For a covered grill, allow 6 to 8 minutes for medium. For uncovered grill, allow 12 to 15 minutes for medium, turning once halfway through grilling.

3 Meanwhile, for sauce, place reserved juice mixture in a small saucepan. Bring to boiling; reduce heat. Boil gently, uncovered, for 8 to 10 minutes or until reduced to ¾ cup, stirring occasionally. Serve lamb with sauce.

Nutrition Facts per serving: 368 cal., 8 g total fat (3 g sat. fat), 64 mg chol., 310 mg sodium, 38 g carbo., 1 g fiber, 20 g pro. Daily Values: 39% vit. C, 3% calcium, 17% iron. Exchanges: 1 Fruit, 1½ Other Carbo., 3 Lean Meat

LAMB WITH SWEET POTATO CHUTNEY

Petite lamb chops make a simple but special dinner—especially when crowned with a colorful homemade chutney.

Prep: 20 minutes
Grill: 6 minutes (covered) or 12 minutes (uncovered)
Cook: 12 minutes Makes: 4 servings

    8 lamb rib or loin chops, 1 inch thick
  1/3 cup finely chopped shallots
  1/4 teaspoon crushed red pepper
  1/4 cup packed brown sugar
  1/4 cup vinegar
    2 tablespoons dried cranberries
        or currants
  1/2 teaspoon grated fresh ginger
    1 medium sweet potato, peeled
        and cubed

1 Preheat indoor electric grill. Trim fat from chops. In a bowl combine shallots and crushed red pepper. Reserve 2 tablespoons shallot mixture for chutney. Sprinkle remaining shallot mixture evenly over chops; rub in with your fingers.

2 Place chops on the grill rack. If using a covered grill, close lid.* Grill until chops are desired doneness. For a covered grill, allow 6 to 8 minutes for medium. For an uncovered grill, allow 12 to 15 minutes for medium, turning once halfway through grilling.

3 Meanwhile, for chutney, in a medium saucepan combine the reserved shallot mixture, brown sugar, vinegar, dried cranberries, and ginger. Stir in sweet potato. Bring to boiling; reduce heat. Simmer, covered, for 10 minutes; stir occasionally. Serve the chops with chutney.

*Note: When cooking in a covered grill, it is important that the chops are the same thickness so the grill lid sits evenly and closes completely. If the lid does not fit tightly over the chops, turn the chops once halfway through grilling.

Nutrition Facts per serving: 317 cal., 11 g total fat (4 g sat. fat), 97 mg chol., 83 mg sodium, 24 g carbo., 1 g fiber, 30 g pro. Daily Values: 81% vit. A, 13% vit. C, 3% calcium, 22% iron. Exchanges: 1/2 Starch, 1 Other Carbo., 4 Lean Meat

CURRANT-GLAZED PORK BURGERS

Currant jelly and cloves—famous for their holiday appearances—are everyday winners in these savory pork burgers.

Prep: 15 minutes
Grill: 5 minutes (covered) or 14 minutes (uncovered)
Makes: 4 servings

  1/4 cup currant jelly
    3 tablespoons catsup
    1 tablespoon white wine vinegar
  1/8 teaspoon ground cinnamon
        Dash ground cloves
    1 slightly beaten egg
    3 tablespoons fine dry bread crumbs
    2 tablespoons chopped onion
    2 tablespoons milk
  1/4 teaspoon salt
  1/4 teaspoon dried thyme, crushed
  1/8 teaspoon black pepper
    1 pound lean ground pork
    4 lettuce leaves
    4 whole wheat hamburger buns,
        split and toasted

1 For sauce, in a small saucepan combine currant jelly, catsup, vinegar, cinnamon, and cloves. Cook and stir just until boiling. Remove from heat and keep warm.

2 Preheat indoor electric grill. In a medium bowl combine egg, bread crumbs, onion, milk, salt, thyme, and pepper. Add ground pork; mix lightly but thoroughly. Shape pork mixture into four 3/4-inch-thick patties.

3 Place patties on the grill rack. If using a covered grill, close lid. Grill patties until meat is no longer pink and an instant-read thermometer inserted in centers registers 160°F. For a covered grill, allow 5 to 7 minutes. For an uncovered grill, allow 14 to 18 minutes, turning once halfway through grilling.

4 For each burger, place a lettuce leaf on bottom half of bun. Top each with a burger, sauce, and top half of bun.

Nutrition Facts per serving: 347 cal., 11 g total fat (4 g sat. fat), 107 mg chol., 612 mg sodium, 43 g carbo., 3 g fiber, 21 g pro. Daily Values: 5% vit. A, 6% vit. C, 6% calcium, 18% iron. Exchanges: 2 Starch, 1 Other Carbo., 2 Medium-Fat Meat

Apple-Sauced Chops

APPLE-SAUCED CHOPS

Prep: 10 minutes Cook: 20 minutes
Grill: 6 minutes (covered) or 12 minutes (uncovered)
Makes: 4 servings

- **1 teaspoon ground cinnamon**
- **1/2 teaspoon dried thyme, crushed**
- **1/4 teaspoon onion salt**
- **1/4 teaspoon dry mustard**
- **4 boneless pork loin chops, 3/4 inch thick**
- **1 medium onion, cut into thin wedges**
- **2 tablespoons butter or margarine**
- **1 large cooking apple (such as Rome Beauty), cored and thinly sliced**
- **1 tablespoon brown sugar**
- **1/2 cup whipping cream**

1 In a small bowl stir together cinnamon, thyme, onion salt, and dry mustard. Trim fat from chops. Sprinkle cinnamon mixture evenly over chops; rub in with your fingers. Set aside.

2 For sauce, in a medium skillet cook onion, covered, in hot butter over medium-low heat for 13 to 15 minutes or until onion is tender. Uncover; add apple slices and brown sugar. Cook and stir over medium-high heat about 5 minutes or until onion is golden and apple is tender. Carefully stir in whipping cream. Bring just to boiling; reduce heat. Boil gently, uncovered, for 2 to 3 minutes or until sauce is slightly thickened.

3 Meanwhile, preheat indoor electric grill. Place chops on the grill rack. If using a covered grill, close lid. Grill until an instant-read thermometer inserted in the center of pork registers 160°F. For a covered grill, allow 6 to 8 minutes. For an uncovered grill, allow 12 to 15 minutes, turning once halfway through grilling. Serve the chops with sauce.

Nutrition Facts per serving: 357 cal., 23 g total fat (10 g sat. fat), 107 mg chol., 233 mg sodium, 12 g carbo., 2 g fiber, 25 g pro. Daily Values: 19% vit. A, 7% vit. C, 6% calcium, 7% iron. Exchanges: 1/2 Fruit, 3 1/2 Lean Meat, 2 1/2 Fat

SPICY CHIPOTLE PORK SOFT TACOS

Prep: 15 minutes Marinate: 2 to 4 hours
Grill: 6 minutes (covered) or 12 minutes (uncovered)
Makes: 4 servings

4 **boneless pork loin chops,**
   ³/₄ inch thick
¼ **cup sherry vinegar**
2 **tablespoons finely chopped canned**
   chipotle chile peppers in adobo
   sauce (see tip, page 36)
1 **tablespoon packed brown sugar**
1 **teaspoon dried thyme, crushed**
½ **teaspoon salt**
½ **teaspoon ground cumin**
¼ **teaspoon black pepper**
   Dash ground cloves
4 **cloves garlic, minced**
8 **(6-inch) flour tortillas**
   Shredded lettuce
   Chopped tomatoes
   Shredded Monterey Jack cheese
      with jalapeño peppers
   Dairy sour cream

1 Place chops in a self-sealing plastic bag set in a large bowl; set aside. For marinade, in a bowl stir together vinegar, chipotle peppers, brown sugar, thyme, salt, cumin, black pepper, cloves, and garlic. Pour marinade over chops in bag; seal bag. Marinate in refrigerator for 2 to 4 hours; turn bag occasionally. Drain, discarding marinade.

2 Preheat indoor electric grill. Place chops on the grill rack. If using a covered grill, close lid. Grill until an instant-read thermometer inserted in the center of pork registers 160°F. For a covered grill, allow 6 to 8 minutes. For an uncovered grill, allow 12 to 15 minutes, turning once halfway through grilling. Slice pork against the grain into bite-size strips.

3 Place tortillas on grill rack. Grill for 20 to 30 seconds or until warm, turning once if using uncovered grill. Serve pork on tortillas with lettuce, tomato, cheese, and sour cream.

Nutrition Facts per serving: 534 cal., 24 g total fat (11 g sat. fat), 107 mg chol., 540 mg sodium, 34 g carbo., 2 g fiber, 43 g pro. Daily Values: 15% vit. A, 12% vit. C, 30% calcium, 18% iron. Exchanges: 2 Starch, 5 Lean Meat, 2 Fat

JERK PORK AND PINEAPPLE SALSA SANDWICHES

Prep: 10 minutes Marinate: 4 to 24 hours
Grill: 3 minutes (covered) or 7 minutes (uncovered)
Makes: 4 servings

1 **pound pork tenderloin**
³/₄ **cup purchased Caribbean jerk**
   marinade with papaya juice
1 **cup chopped fresh pineapple**
¼ **cup finely chopped red sweet pepper**
1 **tablespoon finely chopped shallot**
1 **tablespoon snipped fresh cilantro**
1 **tablespoon lime juice**
1 **teaspoon finely chopped and seeded**
   jalapeño pepper (see tip, page 36)
8 **slices Italian bread, toasted**
1 **recipe Grilled Plantains (optional)**

1 Trim fat from meat. Cut the pork crosswise into four equal pieces. Place each piece between 2 pieces of plastic wrap. Using the flat side of a meat mallet, pound the meat to ¼-inch thickness. Remove plastic wrap. Place meat in a self-sealing plastic bag set in a shallow dish. Pour marinade over meat; seal bag. Marinate in the refrigerator for 4 to 24 hours, turning bag occasionally. Drain meat, discarding marinade.

2 Meanwhile, for salsa, in a small bowl stir together pineapple, sweet pepper, shallot, cilantro, lime juice, jalapeño pepper, salt, and black pepper. Cover and chill for 4 to 24 hours.

3 Preheat indoor electric grill. Place pork on the grill rack. If using a covered grill, close lid. Grill until still slightly pink in center. For covered grill, allow 3 to 5 minutes. For uncovered grill, allow 7 to 8 minutes, turning once halfway through grilling. Serve pork on bread slices with salsa. If desired, serve with Grilled Plantains.

Nutrition Facts per serving: 375 cal., 6 g total fat (2 g sat. fat), 73 mg chol., 1,368 mg sodium, 48 g carbo., 2 g fiber, 30 g pro. Daily Values: 13% vit. A, 44% vit. C, 6% calcium, 18% iron. Exchanges: 2½ Starch, ½ Other Carbo., 3 Very Lean Meat, 1 Fat

Grilled Plantains: Bias-slice peeled plantains ½ inch thick. Brush with peanut oil. Place on the grill rack. If using a covered grill, close lid. Grill until centers are just soft. For an uncovered grill, grill until centers are just soft, turning once.

Jerk Pork and Pineapple Salsa Sandwiches

SMOKIN' HOT TIP

Love to grill but hate to clean up? Well, here's some good news: Indoor grills are designed to keep dishwashing chores to a minimum.

● Start by reading and following the manufacturer's directions for your grill.

● After grilling, unplug grill and let it cool to the point that you can touch it safely. To loosen stubborn food, lay wet paper towels over grill rack and let it soak.

To clean a covered grill:

● Never immerse covered grill in water. Some grills have a removable grill rack and drip pan. Wash in hot, soapy water, then rinse and dry.

● Wipe a nonremovable grill rack with a warm, damp paper towel or sponge. A bit of dishwashing detergent helps get the job done.

To clean an uncovered grill:

● For easier cleanup, line the drip pan or base with foil or coat with cooking spray before grilling.

● Remove the power cord or heat control (if removable). Wash the grill rack and drip pan in hot, soapy water; rinse and dry. Or wash the rack and pan in the dishwasher, if recommended.

CANTONESE CHICKEN BURGERS

Prep: 15 minutes
Grill: 5 minutes (covered) or 14 minutes (uncovered)
Makes: 4 servings

  1 **slightly beaten egg**
  1 **teaspoon toasted sesame oil**
  1 **teaspoon soy sauce**
  $^1/_3$ **cup fine dry bread crumbs**
  $^1/_4$ **cup chopped peanuts**
  2 **tablespoons shredded carrot**
  1 **green onion, thinly sliced**
  $^1/_8$ **teaspoon garlic powder**
  1 **pound uncooked ground chicken
       or turkey**
  4 **sesame hamburger buns, split and
       toasted**
  8 **spinach leaves, shredded**
  $^1/_4$ **cup plum sauce**

1 Lightly grease or coat with nonstick cooking spray the rack of an indoor electric grill. Preheat grill.

2 In a medium bowl combine egg, sesame oil, and soy sauce. Stir in bread crumbs, peanuts, carrot, green onion, and garlic powder. Add ground chicken; mix lightly but thoroughly. Shape into four $^3/_4$-inch-thick patties.

3 Place patties on the grill rack. If using covered grill, close lid. Grill patties until chicken is no longer pink and an instant-read thermometer inserted in centers registers 170°F. For a covered grill, allow 5 to 7 minutes. For an uncovered grill, allow 14 to 18 minutes, turning once halfway through grilling. Serve burgers on buns with shredded spinach and plum sauce.

Nutrition Facts per serving: 377 cal., 15 g total fat (3 g sat. fat), 108 mg chol., 429 mg sodium, 35 g carbo., 2 g fiber, 25 g pro. Daily Values: 17% vit. A, 4% vit. C, 5% calcium, 17% iron. Exchanges: 2 Starch, ½ Other Carbo., 2½ Medium-Fat Meat

CHICKEN AND ROASTED PEPPER SANDWICH

Prep: 15 minutes Marinate: 15 minutes
Grill: 4 minutes (covered) or 10 minutes (uncovered)
Makes: 4 servings

  $^1/_4$ **cup olive oil**
  4 **teaspoons red wine vinegar**
  1 **tablespoon snipped fresh thyme**
  $^1/_2$ **teaspoon salt**
  $^1/_4$ **teaspoon crushed red pepper**
  4 **skinless, boneless chicken breast
       halves (about 1$^1/_4$ pounds total)**
  4 **1-inch bias-cut slices Italian bread**
  $^1/_4$ **cup semisoft cheese with herbs or
       semisoft goat cheese (chèvre)**
  1 **cup roasted red sweet peppers (one
       7-ounce jar), cut into strips**
  $^1/_2$ **cup fresh basil, watercress, or baby
       spinach leaves**

1 For marinade, whisk together oil, vinegar, thyme, salt, and crushed red pepper. Reserve 2 tablespoons; set aside.

2 Place each chicken breast between 2 pieces of plastic wrap; pound lightly with a meat mallet to about ½-inch thickness. Place chicken in a self-sealing plastic bag; add the remaining marinade. Seal bag; marinate for 15 minutes or up to 1 hour in the refrigerator.

3 Lightly grease or coat with nonstick cooking spray the rack of an indoor electric grill. Preheat grill. Drain chicken; discard marinade. Place chicken on the grill rack. If using a covered grill, close the lid. Grill until chicken is tender and no longer pink (170°F). For a covered grill, allow 3 to 4 minutes. For an uncovered grill, allow 8 to 10 minutes, turning chicken once halfway through grilling.

4 Brush cut sides of bread with reserved marinade. Place bread, cut sides down, on grill rack. If using a covered grill, close the lid. Grill until lightly toasted. For a covered grill, allow 1 to 2 minutes. For an uncovered grill, allow 2 to 4 minutes, turning once halfway through grilling. Remove bread from grill.

5 To serve, place a chicken breast on each grilled bread slice. Spread with cheese. Top each sandwich with sweet pepper strips and basil.

Nutrition Facts per serving: 418 cal., 20 g total fat (5 g sat. fat), 82 mg chol., 629 mg sodium, 21 g carbo., 2 g fiber, 37 g pro. Daily Values: 5% vit. A, 177% vit. C, 5% calcium, 14% iron. Exchanges: ½ Vegetable, 1 Starch, 4½ Very Lean Meat, 3½ Fat

APPLE-GLAZED CHICKEN KABOBS

Prep: 30 minutes
Grill: 4 minutes (covered) or 10 minutes (uncovered)
Makes: 4 servings

- **1 cup apple jelly**
- **2 tablespoons honey**
- **2 tablespoons lemon juice**
- **2 tablespoons butter or margarine**
- **1 teaspoon ground cinnamon**
- **¼ teaspoon ground cloves**
- **1 pound skinless, boneless chicken breasts, cut into 1-inch cubes**
- **1 teaspoon garlic powder**
- **½ teaspoon celery salt**
- **½ to 1 teaspoon ground black pepper**
- **1 large onion, cut into 8 wedges**
- **1 large green sweet pepper, cut into 1-inch pieces**
- **1 large red apple, cut into 8 wedges**
- **1 tablespoon olive oil**

1 For glaze, in a medium saucepan combine jelly, honey, lemon juice, butter, cinnamon, and cloves. Bring to boiling; reduce heat. Simmer, uncovered, for 6 to 8 minutes or until reduced to 1⅓ cups, whisking frequently. Set aside.

2 Lightly grease or coat with nonstick cooking spray the rack of an indoor electric grill. Preheat grill. Sprinkle chicken with garlic powder, celery salt, and black pepper. On eight medium metal skewers alternately thread chicken, onion, sweet pepper, and apple, leaving a ¼-inch space between pieces. Drizzle with oil.

3 Place kabobs on the grill rack. (If grill is too small to hold all of the kabobs at once, grill in two batches.) If using a covered grill, close lid. Grill until chicken is no longer pink and vegetables are crisp-tender. For a covered grill, allow 4 to 6 minutes. For an uncovered grill, allow 10 to 14 minutes, turning frequently.

4 To serve, reheat glaze. Brush kabobs with glaze; pass remaining glaze with kabobs.

Nutrition Facts per serving: 494 cal., 12 g total fat (4 g sat. fat), 82 mg chol., 330 mg sodium, 75 g carbo., 3 g fiber, 27 g pro. Daily Values: 7% vit. A, 56% vit. C, 5% calcium, 9% iron. Exchanges: ½ Vegetable, ½ Fruit, 4½ Other Carbo., 4 Very Lean Meat, 1½ Fat

Apple-Glazed Chicken Kabobs

CHICKEN FAJITAS WITH GUACAMOLE

Fresh homemade guacamole is unsurpassable, but if you're short on time, purchased guacamole will do.

Prep: 25 minutes Marinate: 1 hour
Grill: 4 minutes (covered) or 12 minutes (uncovered)
Makes: 4 servings

3 medium skinless, boneless chicken breast halves (about 14 ounces total)
¼ cup snipped fresh cilantro or parsley
¼ cup olive oil or cooking oil
1 teaspoon finely shredded lemon peel
2 tablespoons lemon juice
1 teaspoon chili powder
½ teaspoon ground cumin
½ teaspoon black pepper
8 8-inch flour tortillas
2 cups shredded lettuce
1 cup shredded cheddar cheese (4 ounces)
1 large tomato, chopped
½ cup sliced pitted ripe olives
1 recipe Guacamole

1 Place chicken in a self-sealing plastic bag set in a shallow dish. For marinade, in a small bowl combine cilantro, oil, lemon peel, lemon juice, chili powder, cumin, and black pepper. Pour over chicken. Seal bag; turn to coat chicken. Marinate in the refrigerator for 1 hour, turning once.

2 Lightly grease or coat with nonstick cooking spray the rack of an indoor electric grill. Preheat grill. Drain chicken, discarding the marinade. Place chicken on the grill rack. If using a covered grill, close lid. Grill until chicken is tender and no longer pink (170°F). For a covered grill, allow 4 to 6 minutes. For an uncovered grill, allow 12 to 15 minutes, turning once halfway through grilling.

3 Stack tortillas; wrap in microwave-safe paper towels. Microwave tortillas on 100 percent power (high) 30 to 45 seconds or until warm.

4 Meanwhile, slice chicken diagonally into bite-size strips. To serve, arrange chicken, lettuce, cheese, tomato, and olives on each tortilla. Fold in sides; roll up tortilla. Serve with Guacamole.

Guacamole: Seed and peel 1 ripe avocado. In a small bowl coarsely mash avocado. Stir in 1 medium tomato, seeded, chopped, and drained; 2 tablespoons finely chopped onion; 1 tablespoon lemon juice; and ¼ teaspoon salt. Cover and chill for up to 4 hours..

Nutrition Facts per serving: 576 cal., 32 g total fat (10 g sat. fat), 74 mg chol., 745 mg sodium, 45 g carbo., 5 g fiber, 30 g pro. Daily Values: 19% vit. A, 39% vit. C, 28% calcium, 31% iron. Exchanges: 1 Vegetable, 2½ Starch, 2 Very Lean Meat, 1 High-Fat Meat, 4 Fat

TANGY LEMON CHICKEN

A simple marinade of store-bought dressing, lemon peel, and lemon juice keeps prep time to a minimum.

Prep: 10 minutes Marinate: 2 to 4 hours
Grill: 4 minutes (covered) or 12 minutes (uncovered)
Makes: 4 servings

4 skinless, boneless chicken breast halves (about 1¼ pounds total)
½ cup bottled creamy Italian salad dressing
1 tablespoon finely shredded lemon peel
¼ cup lemon juice
Dash black pepper

1 Place chicken in a self-sealing plastic bag set in a shallow dish. For marinade, in a small bowl stir together salad dressing, lemon peel, lemon juice, and pepper. Pour marinade over chicken. Seal bag; turn to coat chicken. Marinate chicken in the refrigerator for 2 to 4 hours, turning the bag occasionally.

2 Lightly grease or coat with nonstick cooking spray the rack of an indoor electric grill. Preheat grill. Drain chicken, discarding marinade. Place chicken on the grill rack. If using a covered grill, close the lid. Grill until chicken is tender and no longer pink (170°F). For a covered grill, allow 4 to 6 minutes. For an uncovered grill, allow 12 to 15 minutes, turning once halfway through grilling.

Nutrition Facts per serving: 187 cal., 5 g total fat (1 g sat. fat), 82 mg chol., 137 mg sodium, 1 g carbo., 0 g fiber, 33 g pro. Daily Values: 1% vit. A, 4% vit. C, 2% calcium, 5% iron. Exchanges: 5 Very Lean Meat

CHICKEN WITH MANGO CHUTNEY

Prep: 20 minutes
Grill: 4 minutes (covered) or 12 minutes (uncovered)
Makes: 4 servings

1 **ripe mango, seeded, peeled, and sliced**
1/4 **cup dried currants or raisins**
1/4 **cup thinly sliced green onions (2)**
2 to 3 **tablespoons cider vinegar**
2 **tablespoons brown sugar**
1/2 **teaspoon mustard seeds, crushed**
1/8 **teaspoon salt**
1 **teaspoon five-spice powder**
1 **pound skinless, boneless chicken thighs**

1 In a medium saucepan combine half of the mango slices, the currants, green onions, vinegar, brown sugar, mustard seeds, and salt. Bring to boiling; reduce heat. Simmer, covered, for 5 minutes. Remove from heat.

2 Lightly grease or coat with nonstick cooking spray a rack of an indoor electric grill. Preheat grill. Meanwhile, chop the remaining mango slices; set aside. Sprinkle five-spice powder evenly over chicken; rub in with your fingers.

3 Place chicken on the grill rack. If using a covered grill, close lid. Grill until chicken is tender and no longer pink (180°F). For a covered grill, allow 4 to 6 minutes. For an uncovered grill, allow 12 to 15 minutes, turning chicken once halfway through grilling.

4 To serve, stir chopped mango into cooked mango mixture. Serve with the chicken.

Nutrition Facts per serving: 205 cal., 6 g total fat (2 g sat. fat), 54 mg chol., 125 mg sodium, 22 g carbo., 2 g fiber, 17 g pro. Daily Values: 22% vit. A, 26% vit. C, 3% calcium, 10% iron. Exchanges: 1 Fruit, 1/2 Other Carbo., 2 1/2 Lean Meat

TERIYAKI TURKEY PATTIES

If you want to make sandwiches, toast some buns and top the patties with shredded Chinese cabbage and mayonnaise.

Prep: 15 minutes
Grill: 5 minutes (covered) or 14 minutes (uncovered)
Makes: 4 servings

1 **beaten egg**
1/2 **cup soft bread crumbs**
1/4 **cup chopped water chestnuts**
2 **tablespoons chopped onion**
2 **tablespoons teriyaki sauce**
1 **pound uncooked ground turkey**
1/4 **cup orange marmalade**
1/2 **teaspoon sesame seeds**

1 Lightly grease or coat with nonstick cooking spray the rack of an indoor electric grill. Preheat grill.

2 In a medium bowl combine egg, bread crumbs, water chestnuts, onion, and 1 tablespoon of the teriyaki sauce. Add ground turkey; mix well. Shape turkey mixture into four 3/4-inch-thick patties (mixture will be soft).

3 Place patties on grill rack. If using a covered grill, close lid. Grill patties until turkey is no longer pink and an instant-read thermometer inserted in centers registers 170°F. For a covered grill, allow 5 to 7 minutes. For an uncovered grill, allow 14 to 18 minutes, turning once halfway through grilling.

4 For sauce, in a small saucepan combine the remaining teriyaki sauce, orange marmalade, and sesame seeds. Cook over low heat until marmalade melts, stirring occasionally. To serve, spoon sauce over patties.

Nutrition Facts per serving: 266 cal., 11 g total fat (3 g sat. fat), 143 mg chol., 453 mg sodium, 19 g carbo., 0 g fiber, 23 g pro. Daily Values: 2% vit. A, 3% vit. C, 5% calcium, 12% iron. Exchanges: 1 Other Carbo., 3 Medium-Fat Meat

SMOKIN' HOT TIP

When cooking with a contact or covered indoor grill, it's important to use meat of equal thickness so the lid sits evenly on top and closes completely. Whether you're grilling chops, chicken breasts, or burgers, the lid must fit tightly over the meat. Otherwise, you'll have to turn the meat once halfway through grilling.

Smoked Gouda and Caramelized
Onions Turkey Burgers

SMOKED GOUDA AND CARAMELIZED ONIONS TURKEY BURGERS

With luscious smoked Gouda and caramelized onions, this burger will undoubtedly be one of the best you've ever eaten!

Prep: 15 minutes Cook: 16 minutes
Grill: 6 minutes (covered) or 13 minutes (uncovered)
Makes: 4 servings

- **2 cups thinly sliced onions**
- **½ teaspoon sugar**
- **1 tablespoon butter or margarine**
- **1 slightly beaten egg**
- **3 tablespoons fine dry bread crumbs**
- **1 tablespoon fresh parsley
  or 1 teaspoon dried parsley**
- **1 tablespoon Worcestershire sauce**
- **¼ teaspoon garlic salt**
- **¼ teaspoon black pepper**
- **1 pound uncooked ground turkey**
- **4 ounces smoked Gouda cheese, shredded**
- **4 hamburger buns or kaiser rolls, split**

1 In a large skillet cook onions and sugar, covered, in hot butter over medium-low heat for 13 to 15 minutes or until onions are tender, stirring occasionally. Uncover; cook and stir over medium-high heat for 3 to 5 minutes more or until onions are golden.

2 In a medium bowl combine egg, bread crumbs, parsley, Worcestershire sauce, garlic salt, and pepper. Add ground turkey; mix well. Shape turkey mixture into four ¾-inch-thick patties.

3 Preheat indoor electric grill. Place patties on the grill rack. If using a covered grill, close lid. Grill patties until turkey is no longer pink and an instant-read thermometer inserted in centers registers 170°F. For a covered grill, allow 5 to 7 minutes. For an uncovered grill, allow 12 to 14 minutes, turning halfway through grilling.

4 Top burgers with cheese and onions. Grill, uncovered, for 1 to 2 minutes more or until cheese is melted. Serve burgers on buns.

Nutrition Facts per serving: 480 cal., 23 g total fat (10 g sat. fat), 174 mg chol., 962 mg sodium, 35 g carbo., 3 g fiber, 32 g pro. Daily Values: 5% vit. A, 11% vit. C, 29% calcium, 21% iron. Exchanges: ½ Vegetable, 2 Starch, 3½ Medium-Fat Meat, 1 Fat

TURKEY AND VEGETABLES

Prep: 6 minutes
Grill: 5 minutes (covered) or 9 minutes (uncovered)
Makes: 4 servings

2 tablespoons vegetable juice
2 tablespoons mayonnaise or
salad dressing
1½ teaspoons snipped fresh chives or
green onion tops
1 teaspoon snipped fresh thyme or
½ teaspoon dried thyme, crushed
¼ teaspoon minced garlic
1 1-inch-thick turkey breast tenderloin
(about 8 ounces)
Salt
Black pepper
1 small zucchini, halved lengthwise
2 medium plum tomatoes, halved
lengthwise

1 For sauce, in a small bowl gradually stir vegetable juice into mayonnaise; stir in chives, thyme, and garlic. Set aside.

2 Lightly grease or coat with nonstick cooking spray the rack of an indoor electric grill. Preheat grill. Cut tenderloin in half horizontally to make 2 steaks. Sprinkle turkey with salt and black pepper. Place turkey and zucchini, cut sides down, on the grill rack. If using a covered grill, close lid. Grill until turkey is tender and no longer pink (170°F) and zucchini is crisp-tender. For a covered grill, allow 4 to 6 minutes, brushing once with sauce the last 1 minute of grilling. For an uncovered grill, allow 8 to 12 minutes, turning once halfway through and brushing turkey and zucchini occasionally with sauce the last 4 minutes of grilling. Remove turkey and zucchini from grill; cover and keep warm.

3 Add tomatoes, cut sides down, to the grill rack. If using a covered grill, close lid. For a covered or uncovered grill, grill for 1 to 2 minutes or until tomatoes are heated through. Serve the turkey with zucchini and tomatoes.

Nutrition Facts per serving: 187 cal., 6 g total fat (1 g sat. fat), 50 mg chol., 91 mg sodium, 3 g carbo., 1 g fiber, 18 g pro. Daily Values: 4% vit. A, 18% vit. C, 2% calcium, 7% iron. Exchanges: ½ Vegetable, 2½ Very Lean Meat, 1½ Fat

TUNA STEAKS WITH JALAPEÑO MAYO

Spiked mayo gives these tuna steaks some heat. Try it with other fish as well.

Prep: 20 minutes
Grill: 4 minutes (covered) or 8 minutes (uncovered)
Makes: 4 servings

4 6-ounce fresh or frozen tuna or
halibut steaks, 1 inch thick
1 tablespoon olive oil or cooking oil
Dash cayenne pepper
Salt
Black pepper
⅓ cup mayonnaise or salad dressing
1 fresh jalapeño chile pepper, finely
chopped (see tip, page 36)
1 tablespoon Dijon-style mustard
1 teaspoon lemon juice

1 Thaw fish, if frozen. Rinse fish; pat dry with paper towels. In a small bowl combine oil and cayenne pepper; brush over both sides of fish. Sprinkle both sides of fish with salt and black pepper. Set aside.

2 For sauce, in a small bowl stir together mayonnaise, jalapeño pepper, mustard, and lemon juice. Cover and chill until serving time.

3 Lightly grease or coat with nonstick cooking spray the rack of an indoor electric grill. Preheat grill. Place fish on grill rack. If using a covered grill, close lid. Grill until fish flakes easily when tested with a fork. For a covered grill, allow 4 to 6 minutes. For an uncovered grill, allow 8 to 12 minutes, gently turning fish once. Serve fish with sauce.

Nutrition Facts per serving: 350 cal., 19 g total fat (3 g sat. fat), 89 mg chol., 300 mg sodium, 1 g carbo., 0 g fiber, 41 g pro. Daily Values: 3% vit. A, 6% vit. C, 3% calcium, 8% iron. Exchanges: 6 Very Lean Meat, 3 Fat

Mango-Topped Salmon

SMOKIN' HOT TIP

Because most indoor grills have grill racks with nonstick surfaces, you should not need to grease the rack unless you're cooking poultry, fish, seafood, or vegetables. For these foods, lightly brush cooking oil over the rack, or lightly coat the rack with nonstick cooking spray before preheating. To protect the nonstick surface of the grill rack, use only plastic or wooden utensils so you don't scratch the surface. When the food is cooked, transfer it to a plate or cutting board before cutting it into serving-size portions.

MANGO-TOPPED SALMON

Prep: 20 minutes
Grill: 4 minutes (covered) or 8 minutes (uncovered)
Makes: 4 servings

- ¼ **cup snipped fresh cilantro**
- ¼ **cup orange juice**
- 3 **tablespoons lime juice**
- 2 **tablespoons dry sherry**
- 1 **tablespoon honey**
- 2 **teaspoons finely chopped canned chipotle peppers in adobo sauce (see tip, page 36)**
- ¼ **teaspoon salt**
- ¼ **teaspoon black pepper**
- ¼ **cup cooking oil**
- 4 **6-ounce salmon fillets, about 1 inch thick**
- 1 **small red onion**
- 2 **medium mangoes, seeded, peeled, and chopped**
- 1 **red sweet pepper, chopped**
- 4 **cups torn mixed salad greens**

1 For dressing, in a small bowl combine cilantro, orange juice, lime juice, sherry, honey, chipotle peppers, ⅛ teaspoon of the salt, and ⅛ teaspoon of the pepper. Whisk in oil; set aside. Sprinkle fish with remaining salt and pepper.

2 Lightly grease or coat with nonstick cooking spray the rack of an indoor electric grill. Preheat grill. Place fish on grill rack, tucking under any thin edges. If using a covered grill, close lid. Grill until fish flakes easily when tested with a fork. For a covered grill, allow 4 to 6 minutes. For uncovered grill, allow 8 to 12 minutes; carefully turn once halfway through grilling.

3 Meanwhile, chop 2 tablespoons of the red onion; cut remaining red onion into thin bite-size strips. In a bowl combine chopped red onion, mangoes, and sweet pepper; drizzle with half of the dressing. In a medium bowl combine red onion strips and salad greens. Drizzle with remaining dressing; toss to coat. To serve, spoon mango mixture over salmon. Serve with greens mixture.

Nutrition Facts per serving: 488 cal., 25 g total fat (5 g sat. fat), 90 mg chol., 284 mg sodium, 30 g carbo., 4 g fiber, 37 g pro. Daily Values: 47% vit. A, 169% vit. C, 8% calcium, 11% iron. Exchanges: 1½ Vegetable, 1 Fruit, ½ Other Carbo., 5 Lean Meat, 2 Fat

SWORDFISH WITH TOMATO RELISH

Also try this warm fresh tomato and basil relish on grilled chicken breast halves.

Prep: 20 minutes
Grill: 4 minutes (covered) or 8 minutes (uncovered)
Makes: 4 servings

- 2 **6-ounce fresh or frozen swordfish or halibut steaks, 1 inch thick**
- 2 **teaspoons olive oil**
- 1 **small leek or 2 green onions, chopped**
- 1 **cup chopped, seeded tomato**
- ¼ **cup snipped fresh basil**
- 1 **tablespoon drained capers**
- ¼ **teaspoon black pepper**
- ⅛ **teaspoon salt**
- 2 **teaspoons olive oil**

1 Thaw fish, if frozen. Rinse fish; pat dry with paper towels. Lightly grease or coat with nonstick cooking spray the rack of an indoor electric grill. Preheat grill.

2 For tomato relish, in a small saucepan heat 2 teaspoons oil over medium heat. Add leek; cook and stir for 2 to 3 minutes or just until tender. Remove from heat. Stir in tomato, basil, capers, pepper, and salt. Set aside.

3 Brush 2 teaspoons oil over fish steaks. Place fish on grill rack. If using a covered grill, close lid. Grill until fish flakes easily when tested with a fork. For a covered grill, allow 4 to 6 minutes. For an uncovered grill, allow 8 to 12 minutes; carefully turn once halfway through grilling. To serve, cut each fish steak into 2 serving pieces. Top each serving with relish.

Nutrition Facts per serving: 154 cal., 8 g total fat (2 g sat. fat), 32 mg chol., 217 mg sodium, 3 g carbo., 1 g fiber, 17 g pro. Daily Values: 14% vit. A, 13% vit. C, 2% calcium, 6% iron. Exchanges: 2½ Very Lean Meat, 1½ Fat

Herbed Ratatouille and Polenta

HERBED RATATOUILLE AND POLENTA

Ratatouille—a chunky Italian mix of vegetables—
becomes a meal when spooned over
grilled polenta slices.

Prep: 25 minutes
Grill: 7 minutes (covered) or 14 minutes (uncovered)
Cook: 5 minutes Makes: 4 servings

¹/₂ of a small eggplant (about 6 ounces)
**1 medium zucchini or yellow summer
squash (about 5 ounces)**
¹/₄ cup olive oil
2 teaspoons snipped fresh rosemary
¹/₂ teaspoon salt
¹/₂ teaspoon black pepper
**1 16-ounce tube plain refrigerated
cooked polenta, cut into 12 slices**
**1 14¹/₂-ounce can diced tomatoes
with garlic and onion**

1 If desired, peel the eggplant. Cut eggplant and
zucchini crosswise into ¹/₄-inch slices. In a
small bowl combine oil, rosemary, salt, and
pepper. Brush vegetables with half of the oil
mixture; set remaining mixture aside.

2 Preheat an indoor electric grill. Arrange half of
the vegetables on the grill rack. If using a
covered grill, close lid. Grill until vegetables are
crisp-tender. For a covered grill, allow 3 to
4 minutes. For an uncovered grill, allow 6 to
8 minutes, turning once halfway through grilling.
Remove vegetables from grill; set aside. Repeat
with remaining vegetables.

3 Brush polenta slices with reserved oil mixture.
Place polenta on grill rack. If using a covered
grill, close lid. Grill polenta until heated through
and lightly browned. For a covered grill, allow 4 to
5 minutes. For an uncovered grill, allow 8 to
10 minutes, turning once halfway through grilling.

4 Meanwhile, in a medium saucepan bring
undrained tomatoes to boiling. If desired, cut
grilled vegetable slices in half. Stir grilled
vegetables into tomatoes. Simmer, uncovered,
about 5 minutes or to desired consistency, stirring
occasionally. To serve, place 3 polenta slices on
each plate. Spoon vegetable mixture over polenta.

Nutrition Facts per serving: 269 cal., 14 g total fat
(2 g sat. fat), 0 mg chol., 1,233 mg sodium, 31 g carbo.,
5 g fiber, 6 g pro. Daily Values: 2% vit. A, 21% vit. C,
2% calcium, 9% iron. Exchanges: 1 Vegetable, 1¹/₂ Starch,
2¹/₂ Fat

Turkey Fryer
Cooking

BEEF & PORK

BUTTERS & GLAZES

CHICKEN & TURKEY

FISH & SHELLFISH

SAUCES & SPREADS

USING A TURKEY FRYER SAFELY

Whether you're using a turkey fryer to fry turkey, steaks, or fish, there are no shortcuts when it comes to safety and setting up.

Set Up and Take Down

● Carefully read and follow the manufacturer's instructions that come with the fryer and propane tank.

● NEVER operate a turkey fryer indoors or in a garage or other attached structure. Avoid cooking on wooden decks, which can catch fire.

● Position the fryer on a level dirt or grassy area. You also can place the fryer on a concrete surface. To avoid grease stains, put a layer of sand under and around the fryer. The sand will absorb any oil that spills and easily cleans up when finished.

● Check the level of fuel in your propane tank. You will need about 1½ hours of fuel for deep-frying a turkey—half for bringing the oil up to temperature and half for the actual cooking.

● NEVER leave hot oil unattended. The oil stays hot for hours after you turn off the burner, so allow it to cool in a safe place.

● Keep children and pets away from cooking area.

Equipment—Bigger Is Better!

● Use a pot, basket, and burner designed for deep-frying.

● Wear heat-resistant gloves, long sleeves, and an apron to protect yourself from heat and splattering oil.

● Use long-handled tongs, meat forks, slotted fry spoons, and/or a fry basket.

● Have plates, platters, and paper towels handy.

● Keep a fire extinguisher close at hand for emergencies.

Working with Oil

● Use one of the oils listed on the chart below. They are great for deep-frying because of their high smoking points.

● Do not cover the pot when deep-frying.

● Do not overfill the fryer with oil.

● Make sure there is 5 to 6 inches from the top of the oil to the top of the pot for the oil to bubble up when cooking.

● Once the oil reaches the appropriate temperature, turn off the burner before SLOWLY lowering the food into the hot oil. Relight the burner after the food is in the pot and turn it off again when you're ready to remove the food.

● Monitor the oil temperature using a deep-fry thermometer.

● Allow the oil to cool completely after use. To discard, ladle or use a funnel to pour the oil back into the original container.

● If you plan to reuse the oil, strain it through 100-percent-cotton cheesecloth and store in a covered container in the refrigerator. You can reuse the oil once or twice within one month only if the food cooked in the oil didn't burn.

CALCULATING FRY TIME

FOOD	MINUTES PER POUND	OIL TEMPERATURE*
Turkey, whole	3	350°F
Turkey breast with bone	8	350°F
Turkey legs	8	350°F
Chicken, whole	7	350°F
Cornish hens	8	350°F
Duck, whole	10	350°F

*To maintain recommended temperatures, oil must be 10°F hotter before food is added.

COOKING OIL SMOKING POINTS

COMMON OIL	OIL TEMPERATURE
Safflower oil	450°F
Cottonseed oil	450°F
Canola oil	437°F
Soybean oil	410°F
Peanut oil	410°F
Corn oil	410°F

Chicken Fried Steak For-a-Crowd

golden. Do not crowd. Be cautious of splattering oil. Maintain oil temperature around 360°F. Remove steaks from hot oil; drain on wire racks. Keep warm in a 300°F oven while frying remaining steaks. If desired, serve with mashed potatoes and gravy.

Nutrition Facts per serving: 360 cal., 11 g total fat (2 g sat. fat), 86 mg chol., 376 mg sodium, 31 g carbo., 1 g fiber, 32 g pro. Daily Values: 2% vit. A, 4% calcium, 24% iron. Exchanges: 2 Starch, 3½ Very Lean Meat, 1½ Fat

CHICKEN FRIED STEAK FOR-A-CROWD

Prep: 20 minutes Fry: 4 minutes per batch Oven: 300°F
Makes: 12 servings

> 2 cups all-purpose flour
> 2 teaspoons black pepper
> 1½ teaspoons salt
> 1 teaspoon dried thyme, crushed
> ½ teaspoon cayenne pepper (optional)
> 2 beaten eggs
> 1 egg white
> 1 cup milk
> 2 cups cracker meal
> 12 4- to 6-ounce beef cubed steaks
>   Peanut oil
>   Prepared mashed potatoes and gravy (optional)

1 In a large shallow dish combine flour, black pepper, salt, thyme, and, if desired, cayenne pepper. In another shallow dish combine whole eggs, egg white, and milk. Place cracker meal in another shallow dish.

2 Dip each steak in flour mixture. Dip each steak in egg mixture, then coat with the cracker meal. Place coated steaks on wire racks; let stand for 10 minutes.

3 Meanwhile, preheat oil to 360°F. Fry steaks, three or four at a time, about 4 minutes or until

PITCHFORK STEAKS AND COWBOY FRIES

To prevent oil from splattering bare arms, long oven mitts are necessities.

Start to Finish: 1¼ hours Oven: 300°F
Makes: 6 servings

> Peanut oil
> 6 medium baking potatoes (2 pounds)
> 6 beef ribeye or top loin steaks, cut 1 inch thick (about 4 pounds)
> 1½ to 2 teaspoons Key West seasoning, Cajun seasoning, or lemon-pepper seasoning
> 1 recipe Tangy Barbecue Sauce (page 34)

1 Preheat oil to 350°F. Peel potatoes. Cut potatoes lengthwise into ¼-inch-wide sticks. Place in a large bowl of ice water; soak for 10 minutes. Drain potatoes; pat dry with paper towels. Fry potatoes, one-third at a time, in a basket for 5 to 6 minutes or until crisp and golden. Be cautious of splattering oil. Maintain oil temperature around 350°F. Remove potatoes from hot oil; drain on wire racks. Keep warm in 300°F oven while frying remaining potatoes and steaks.

2 Place each steak on a clean, heavy-duty, long-handled barbecue fork. Fry steaks, two or three at a time, for 4 to 6 minutes or to desired doneness. Remove steaks from hot oil; drain on wire racks.

3 Sprinkle fries with seasoning blend. Serve steaks with Tangy Barbecue Sauce.

Nutrition Facts per serving: 705 cal., 31 g total fat (9 g sat. fat), 144 mg chol., 291 mg sodium, 33 g carbo., 3 g fiber, 70 g pro. Daily Values: 6% vit. A, 53% vit. C, 4% calcium, 37% iron. Exchanges: 1 Starch, 1 Other Carbo., 9 Very Lean Meat, 1 Fat

Italian-Style Corn Dogs

ITALIAN-STYLE CORN DOGS

Make cornmeal fritters out of the remaining batter by spooning rounded tablespoons into the hot oil. Fry 2 to 3 minutes or until golden, turning once.

Prep: 30 minutes Fry: 3 minutes per batch
Makes: 12 servings

12 uncooked Italian sausage links
¹/₂ cup water
  Peanut oil
1¹/₂ cups yellow cornmeal
  1 cup all-purpose flour
¹/₂ cup grated Romano or Parmesan cheese
  2 teaspoons baking powder
  1 teaspoon salt
  2 beaten eggs
1¹/₄ cups half-and-half or light cream
12 10×¹/₄-inch-thick wooden skewers or dowels
  Warm marinara sauce (optional)

1 To cook Italian sausages, use the tines of a fork to prick several holes in each sausage link. In a large skillet cook sausage links over medium heat about 5 minutes or until brown, turning frequently. Carefully add water. Bring to boiling; reduce heat. Simmer, covered, for 5 minutes. Uncover and cook, turning frequently, until liquid evaporates and sausages are done (160°F). Drain on paper towels.

2 Preheat oil to 375°F. For batter, in a large bowl combine cornmeal, flour, Romano cheese, baking powder, and salt. Make a well in center of cornmeal mixture. In a medium bowl combine eggs and half-and-half. Add egg mixture to cornmeal mixture. Stir just until moistened.

3 Insert one wooden skewer into one end of each sausage link. Dip sausage links into batter, using a spoon to coat all sides evenly.

4 Fry corn dogs, three at a time, about 3 minutes or until golden. Do not crowd. Be cautious of splattering oil. Maintain oil temperature around 375°F. Remove corn dogs from hot oil; drain on wire racks. If desired, serve with marinara sauce.

Nutrition Facts per serving: 539 cal., 36 g total fat (14 g sat. fat), 125 mg chol., 928 mg sodium, 23 g carbo., 2 g fiber, 22 g pro. Daily Values: 4% vit. A, 2% vit. C, 11% calcium, 9% iron. Exchanges: 1½ Starch, 2½ High-Fat Meat, 3½ Fat

BUFFALO-STYLE HOT WINGS

You can easily double this recipe to
serve a crowd.

Prep: 30 minutes Fry: 10 minutes per batch
Makes: 15 appetizer servings

 Peanut oil
15 **chicken wings or 30 chicken wing**
 drumettes (3 to 3½ pounds)
⅓ **cup all-purpose flour**
 1 **teaspoon salt**
 1 **teaspoon black pepper**
¼ **cup butter or margarine**
 2 **to 4 tablespoons bottled hot**
 pepper sauce
 1 **tablespoon red wine vinegar**
 1 **cup bottled blue cheese salad**
 dressing
 Celery sticks (optional)

1 Preheat oil to 350°F. Cut off and discard tips of
chicken wings. Cut wings at joints to form
30 pieces. In a self-sealing plastic bag combine
flour, salt, and pepper. Add chicken wing pieces, a
few at a time, shaking to coat.

2 Fry chicken wing pieces, half at a time, for
10 to 12 minutes or until golden. Do not
crowd. Be cautious of splattering oil. Maintain oil
temperature around 350°F. Remove chicken wing
pieces from hot oil; drain on wire racks.

3 Meanwhile, in a small saucepan melt the
butter; remove from heat. Stir in the hot
pepper sauce and vinegar.

4 To serve, place chicken wing pieces in a large
shallow serving dish. Drizzle with butter
mixture; toss to coat. Drizzle with some of the
salad dressing. Serve with remaining salad
dressing and, if desired, celery sticks.

Nutrition Facts per serving: 289 cal., 25 g total fat
(6 g sat. fat), 51 mg chol., 408 mg sodium, 3 g carbo.,
0 g fiber, 14 g pro. Daily Values: 5% vit. A, 1% vit. C,
2% calcium, 5% iron. Exchanges: 2 Lean Meat, 4 Fat

MAPLE-MUSTARD GLAZED CHICKEN

A sweet-and-salty, thick-and-syrupy
glaze results in the chicken's tempting
golden brown color.

Prep: 30 minutes Fry: 35 minutes Stand: 15 minutes
Makes: 6 to 8 servings

 Peanut oil
 1 **5- to 6-pound whole roasting**
 chicken
 1 **recipe Maple-Mustard Glaze**
 Mashed cooked sweet potatoes
 (optional)

1 Preheat oil to 350°F. Remove neck and giblets
from chicken. Rinse inside of chicken; pat dry
with paper towels. Skewer neck skin to back. Tie
legs to tail with 100-percent-cotton string. Twist
wing tips under back.

2 Place chicken, breast side up, in basket. Slowly
lower basket into hot oil, being cautious of
splattering oil. Maintain oil temperature around
350°F. Fry chicken for 35 to 42 minutes (about
7 minutes per pound).

3 Remove chicken from hot oil to check
doneness. Insert a meat thermometer into the
meaty part of the thigh. Chicken is done when
thermometer reads 180°F. Remove chicken from
hot oil; drain on wire rack. Spoon Maple-Mustard
Glaze over hot chicken. Let stand for 15 minutes
before carving.

4 If desired, serve chicken with hot mashed
sweet potatoes.

Maple-Mustard Glaze: In a small saucepan
combine ¼ cup pure maple syrup, 3 tablespoons
butter or margarine, 2 tablespoons frozen orange
juice concentrate, 2 tablespoons coarse-grain
brown mustard, and ¼ to ½ teaspoon cayenne
pepper. Bring to boiling; reduce heat. Simmer,
uncovered, for 2 to 3 minutes. Remove saucepan
from heat; stir in ¼ cup finely chopped pecans,
toasted, and 1 to 1½ teaspoons finely shredded
orange peel.

Nutrition Facts per serving: 719 cal., 55 g total fat
(15 g sat. fat), 205 mg chol., 230 mg sodium, 6 g carbo.,
0 g fiber, 47 g pro. Daily Values: 8% vit. A, 8% vit. C,
3% calcium, 15% iron. Exchanges: ½ Other Carbo.,
6½ Medium-Fat Meat, 4½ Fat

Maple-Mustard Glazed Chicken

SOUTHERN-STYLE BUTTERMILK FRIED CHICKEN

This chicken becomes "southern" when you soak it in buttermilk before coating it with flour.

Prep: 30 minutes Chill: 2 to 8 hours
Fry: 15 minutes per batch Oven: 300°F Makes: 12 servings

  8 pounds meaty chicken pieces
      (breast halves, thighs, and
      drumsticks)
  3 cups buttermilk
  2 teaspoons salt
2¼ teaspoons black pepper
      Peanut oil
  5 cups all-purpose flour
  4 teaspoons salt
  4 teaspoons paprika
  3 beaten eggs
  1 cup milk

1 If desired, skin chicken. In a very large bowl combine buttermilk, the 2 teaspoons salt, and 1 teaspoon of the pepper. Add chicken pieces to bowl, turning to coat. Cover; chill for 2 to 8 hours.

2 Preheat oil to 350°F. In a large shallow dish combine flour, the 4 teaspoons salt, paprika, and the remaining 1¼ teaspoons pepper. In another large dish combine eggs and milk. Remove chicken from buttermilk mixture, allowing excess to drip off. Coat chicken with flour mixture. Dip chicken in egg mixture; coat again with flour mixture.

3 Fry chicken thigh and drumstick pieces, four or five at a time, about 15 minutes or until crust is golden and chicken is no longer pink (180°F). Do not crowd. Be cautious of splattering oil. Maintain oil temperature around 350°F. Remove chicken pieces from hot oil; drain on wire racks. Keep warm in a 300°F oven while frying remaining chicken.

4 Fry chicken breast halves, four or five at a time, for 12 to 15 minutes or until crust is golden and chicken is no longer pink (170°F). Season chicken pieces to taste with additional salt and pepper.

Nutrition Facts per serving: 717 cal., 40 g total fat (11 g sat. fat), 207 mg chol., 1,123 mg sodium, 39 g carbo., 2 g fiber, 46 g pro. Daily Values: 12% vit. A, 3% vit. C, 7% calcium, 24% iron. Exchanges: 2½ Starch, 5½ Medium-Fat Meat, 2½ Fat

CAJUN DEEP-FRIED TURKEY

If the turkey has not reached 180°F when you check for doneness, remove the thermometer and slowly lower the turkey back into the oil. Fry 3 to 5 minutes more and check temperature again.

Prep: 30 minutes Fry: 24 minutes Stand: 15 minutes
Makes: 10 to 12 servings

  1 8- to 10-pound turkey
      Peanut oil
1½ teaspoons salt
1½ teaspoons sweet paprika
  ¾ teaspoon dried thyme, crushed
  ¾ teaspoon black pepper
  ½ teaspoon garlic powder
  ½ teaspoon onion powder
  ¼ teaspoon cayenne pepper

1 Remove neck and giblets from turkey. Rinse inside of turkey; pat dry with paper towels. If present, remove and discard plastic leg holder and pop-up timer.

2 Preheat oil to 350°F. For rub, in a small bowl combine salt, paprika, thyme, black pepper, garlic powder, onion powder, and cayenne pepper. Slip your fingers between skin and meat to loosen the skin over the breast and leg areas. Lift turkey skin and spread some of the rub directly over breast, thigh, and drumstick meat. Season body cavity with any remaining rub. Tuck the ends of the drumsticks under the band of skin across the tail or tie legs to tail with 100-percent-cotton string. Twist wing tips under back.

3 Place turkey, breast side up, in basket. Slowly lower basket into hot oil being cautious of splattering oil. Maintain oil temperature around 350°F. Fry turkey for 24 to 30 minutes (3 minutes per pound). Remove turkey from hot oil to check doneness. Insert a meat thermometer into the meaty part of the thigh. Turkey is done when the thermometer reads 180°F.

4 Remove turkey from hot oil; drain on wire rack. Let stand 15 minutes before carving.

Nutrition Facts per serving: 553 cal., 33 g total fat (7 g sat. fat), 220 mg chol., 468 mg sodium, 1 g carbo., 0 g fiber, 61 g pro. Daily Values: 4% vit. A, 5% calcium, 21% iron. Exchanges: 8½ Lean Meat, 2 Fat

THANKSGIVING-STYLE TURKEY SANDWICHES

Layer by layer, these superb sandwiches meld into one decadent whole.

Prep: 45 minutes Fry: 48 minutes Stand: 15 minutes
Makes: 12 servings

  1 6- to 8-pound turkey breast
    with bone
   Peanut oil
   Salt
   Black pepper
  1 recipe Orange-Walnut Cream
    Cheese Spread
 24 sweet Hawaiian or egg bread
    rolls, split
 24 lettuce leaves
  1 16-ounce can whole cranberry
    sauce, drained

1 Rinse inside of turkey breast; pat dry with paper towels. If present, remove and discard pop-up timer.

2 Preheat oil to 350°F. Place turkey breast, breast side up, in a basket; slowly lower basket into hot oil. Be cautious of splattering oil. Maintain oil temperature around 350°F. Fry turkey breast for 48 to 64 minutes (8 minutes per pound). Remove turkey from hot oil to check doneness. Insert a meat thermometer into the thickest part of the breast without touching bone. Turkey is done when thermometer reads 170°F. Remove turkey breast from hot oil; drain on a wire rack. Let stand 15 minutes before carving.

3 To serve, thinly slice turkey breast. Season to taste with salt and pepper. Spread Orange-Walnut Cream Cheese Spread on bottoms of rolls. Top each with lettuce, turkey, and a spoonful of cranberry sauce. Top with roll tops.

Orange-Walnut Cream Cheese Spread: In a small bowl stir together one 8-ounce package cream cheese, softened; 2 tablespoons chopped walnuts; 1 tablespoon honey; and ½ teaspoon finely shredded orange peel.

Nutrition Facts per serving: 962 cal., 49 g total fat (14 g sat. fat), 186 mg chol., 450 mg sodium, 75 g carbo., 5 g fiber, 54 g pro. Daily Values: 15% vit. A, 2% vit. C, 9% calcium, 34% iron. Exchanges: 3 Starch, 2 Other Carbo., 6½ Lean Meat, 5½ Fat

SMOKIN' HOT TIP

For a turkey that's tasty and tender, follow these tips:

● Select turkeys that are 12 pounds or less.

● NEVER fry a turkey that's too big for the pot. The pot must be big enough to hold the turkey and enough oil to completely cover the turkey (up to 5 gallons).

● To determine the amount of oil needed, place the unwrapped, frozen turkey in an empty pot and fill with water to cover the bird by 1 to 2 inches. Remove the bird and mark the waterline. This is the level of oil you'll need. Then, remember to dry the pot thoroughly before adding the oil.

● Water and oil don't mix! After the turkey is thawed completely, rinse it, then dry thoroughly inside and out with paper towels. Also make sure the equipment is clean and dry. All food that goes into the fryer must be blotted dry with paper towels to remove any moisture.

● Do not stuff the bird.

● Any plastic pieces left on the turkey will melt. Remove all the plastic parts, including the tie that holds the legs together and the pop-up timer.

● Check the internal temperature of the bird for doneness with an instant-read thermometer.

FISH 'N' CHIPS

Without a doubt, this is the United Kingdom's
most famous dish. Liberally salted, the fish and
chips are traditionally doused with malt
vinegar and served on newspaper.

Start to Finish: 50 minutes Oven: 300°F
Makes: 6 servings

 2 pounds fresh or frozen skinless cod
   or haddock fillets, 1/2 inch thick
 2 cups all-purpose flour
1/2 teaspoon baking powder
1/2 teaspoon salt
 1 cup milk
 1 cup beer
 6 medium baking potatoes (2 pounds)
   Peanut oil
1/4 teaspoon coarse salt
 2 tablespoons malt vinegar or
   cider vinegar

1 Thaw fish, if frozen. Cut fish into 4×2-inch
pieces. Rinse fish; pat dry. Cover and chill fish
pieces until needed.

2 For batter, in a large bowl combine flour,
baking powder, and the 1/2 teaspoon salt. Add
milk and beer; beat with a rotary beater or wire
whisk until smooth. Let batter stand, covered, at
room temperature until needed.

3 For chips, peel potatoes. Cut potatoes lengthwise into 1/2-inch-wide sticks. Place potatoes
in a large bowl of ice water; soak for 10 minutes.

4 Meanwhile, preheat oil to 350°F. Drain
potatoes; pat dry with paper towels. Fry
potatoes, one-third at a time, in a basket about
10 minutes or until crisp and golden. Be cautious
of splattering oil. Maintain oil temperature around
350°F. Remove potatoes from hot oil; drain on
wire racks. Keep warm in a 300°F oven while
frying remaining potatoes.

5 To fry fish, gently stir batter. Dip fish in batter,
allowing excess to drip off. Fry fish pieces,
half at a time, 3 to 4 minutes or until golden brown
and fish flakes easily when tested with a fork,
carefully turning once or twice to prevent sticking.
Do not crowd. Be cautious of splattering oil.
Maintain oil temperature around 350°F. Remove
fish from hot oil; drain on wire racks. Keep warm
in oven with potatoes while frying remaining fish.

6 To serve, sprinkle salt over fish and chips.
Sprinkle with vinegar.

Nutrition Facts per serving: 663 cal., 29 g total fat
(5 g sat. fat), 89 mg chol., 445 mg sodium, 59 g carbo.,
3 g fiber, 37 g pro. Daily Values: 3% vit. A, 37% vit. C,
12% calcium, 25% iron. Exchanges: 4 Starch,
3½ Very Lean Meat, 5 Fat

CORNMEAL CATFISH AND HUSH PUPPIES

Hush puppies are deep-fried cornmeal dumplings
that are traditionally served with catfish.

Start to Finish: 50 minutes Oven: 300°F
Makes: 8 servings

 8 fresh or frozen skinless catfish
   fillets (about 3 to 3½ pounds)
   Peanut oil
 3 cups cornmeal
1/2 cup all-purpose flour
 2 teaspoons baking powder
1¾ teaspoons salt
1/8 teaspoon cayenne pepper (optional)
 2 beaten eggs
3/4 to 1 cup buttermilk
 2 tablespoons finely chopped onion
 1 teaspoon bottled minced garlic
   (optional)
 1 teaspoon paprika or chili powder
   (optional)
   Salt
   Prepared coleslaw (optional)

1 Thaw fish, if frozen. Rinse fish; pat dry. Cover
and chill fish until needed.

2 Preheat oil to 350°F. For hush puppies, in a
large bowl combine 1½ cups of the cornmeal,
flour, baking powder, 3/4 teaspoon of the salt, and,
if desired, cayenne pepper. Make a well in center
of cornmeal mixture. In a medium bowl combine
eggs, 3/4 cup of the buttermilk, onion, and, if
desired, garlic. Add buttermilk mixture all at once
to cornmeal mixture. Stir just until moistened. (If
batter seems stiff, gradually add as much of the
remaining buttermilk as needed.)

3 Drop batter by rounded tablespoons into hot oil. Fry hush puppies, eight to ten at a time, for 2 to 3 minutes or until golden brown on both sides, turning once. Do not crowd. Be cautious of splattering oil. Maintain oil temperature around 350°F. Remove hush puppies from hot oil; drain on wire racks. Keep warm in a 300°F oven while frying fish.

4 In a shallow dish combine the remaining 1½ cups cornmeal, the remaining 1 teaspoon salt, and, if desired, paprika. Coat fish fillets with cornmeal mixture.

5 Fry fish fillets, two or three at a time, for 4 to 6 minutes or until golden and fish flakes easily when tested with a fork, carefully turning once or twice to prevent sticking; do not crowd. Be cautious of splattering oil. Maintain oil temperature around 350°F. Remove fish from the hot oil; drain on wire racks. Season to taste with salt. Serve fish with hush puppies and, if desired, coleslaw.

Nutrition Facts per serving: 551 cal., 24 g total fat (5 g sat. fat), 133 mg chol., 702 mg sodium, 47 g carbo., 4 g fiber, 34 g pro. Daily Values: 5% vit. A, 2% vit. C, 7% calcium, 11% iron. Exchanges: 3 Starch, 3½ Very Lean Meat, 4 Fat

---

WISCONSIN FISH BOIL

Prep: 20 minutes Boil: 26 minutes
Makes: 16 servings

**6 pounds fresh or frozen whitefish
   or halibut steaks, 1 inch thick
4 gallons water
1 cup salt
4 pounds small red potatoes
2 1-pound packages peeled baby
   carrots
2 pounds boiling onions (32)
1 recipe Butter Sauce
   Freshly ground black pepper
   (optional)**

1 Thaw fish, if frozen. Place water and salt in pot of 30- to 34-quart turkey fryer. Bring to boiling. Meanwhile, place potatoes, carrots, and onions in basket. Carefully lower basket into boiling water. Cover and boil for 18 minutes.

2 Carefully add fish steaks to basket. Cover and boil for 8 to 11 minutes more or until fish flakes easily when tested with a fork and the vegetables are tender.

3 Carefully lift basket from turkey fryer; remove fish and vegetables. Serve with Butter Sauce. If desired, season to taste with pepper.

Butter Sauce: In a small saucepan heat ¾ cup butter, ⅓ cup Dijon-style mustard, and ¼ cup snipped fresh dill or flat-leaf parsley, whisking together until butter is melted.

Nutrition Facts per serving: 445 cal., 20 g total fat (7 g sat. fat), 117 mg chol., 464 mg sodium, 30 g carbo., 4 g fiber, 37 g pro. Daily Values: 145% vit. A, 36% vit. C, 10% calcium, 13% iron. Exchanges: 1½ Vegetable, 1½ Starch, 4 Very Lean Meat, 3 Fat

FOOD FOR THOUGHT
WISCONSIN FISH BOIL

Scandinavian immigrants who settled on the shores of Lake Michigan more than 100 years ago brought with them the concept of the fish boil. It was an efficient way to cook large quantities of fish and potatoes to feed the fishermen and lumberjacks. Today fish boils are a popular dining experience for tourists who visit Door County, Wisconsin. Whitefish is harvested from Lake Michigan, cut into chunks, and boiled in a large pot along with potatoes over an open flame.

Lobster-and-Corn Boil
with Lemon Butter

LOBSTER-AND-CORN BOIL
WITH LEMON BUTTER

Allow at least 1 hour for the water to come
to boiling in the fryer.

Prep: 20 minutes Boil: 20 minutes
Makes: 6 servings

4 gallons water
³/₄ cup salt
6 1- to 1¹/₂-pound live lobsters
6 fresh ears corn
1 recipe Lemon Butter

1 Place water and salt in boiling pot of a 30- to 34-quart turkey fryer. Bring to boiling.

2 Carefully lower basket into boiling water. Grasp lobsters just behind the eyes; rinse under cold running water. Quickly plunge lobsters, one at a time, headfirst into boiling water. Return water to boiling. Boil for 15 minutes (start timing when water returns to boil). Carefully lift basket from turkey fryer; remove lobsters.

3 Return water to boiling. Place corn in basket. Carefully lower basket into boiling water. Cover and boil for 5 to 7 minutes or until tender. Carefully lift basket from turkey fryer; remove corn. Serve lobster and corn with Lemon Butter.

Lemon Butter: In a small saucepan melt ³/₄ cup butter; remove from heat. Stir in 3 tablespoons snipped fresh chives, ¹/₂ to 1 teaspoon finely shredded lemon peel, 1 tablespoon lemon juice, and ¹/₂ teaspoon black pepper.

Nutrition Facts per serving: 384 cal., 26 g total fat (13 g sat. fat), 159 mg chol., 824 mg sodium, 18 g carbo., 3 g fiber, 22 g pro. Daily Values: 21% vit. A, 11% vit. C, 6% calcium, 4% iron. Exchanges: 1 Starch, 3 Very Lean Meat, 4¹/₂ Fat

14

Desserts

✪ **Highlighted recipes are grilled**

Rum Raisin and Chocolate
Bread Pudding

RUM RAISIN AND CHOCOLATE BREAD PUDDING

You'll need about 12 ounces of bread to yield 16 cups of bread cubes. To dry, place cubes, half at a time, in a large, shallow baking pan; bake in a 350°F oven about 10 minutes, stirring twice.

Prep: 30 minutes Stand: 8 to 12 hours Chill: 1 to 12 hours
Grill: 40 minutes Cool: 30 minutes
Makes: 10 servings

½ **cup raisins**
¼ **cup dark rum or apple juice**
16 **cups dry 1-inch French bread cubes**
2 **ounces bittersweet chocolate, coarsely chopped**
½ **cup coarsely chopped pecans, toasted**
5 **beaten eggs**
3 **cups milk**
1 **cup whipping cream, half-and-half, or light cream**
¾ **cup granulated sugar**
1 **teaspoon vanilla**
¼ **cup packed brown sugar**
Ice cream or whipped cream (optional)

1 In a small bowl combine raisins and rum. Cover and let stand for 8 to 12 hours. Drain, discarding liquid.

2 Grease a 13×9×2-inch disposable foil pan. Arrange half of the bread cubes in a single layer in pan. Sprinkle with half of the raisins, half of the chocolate, and half of the pecans. Top with remaining bread cubes. Sprinkle with remaining raisins, chocolate, and pecans.

3 In a large bowl whisk together eggs, milk, cream, granulated sugar, and vanilla. Pour egg mixture evenly over bread. Using the back of a large spoon, lightly press bread down into egg mixture. Sprinkle with brown sugar. Cover and chill for 1 to 12 hours. Cover pan with foil, leaving one corner slightly open to vent.

4 For a charcoal grill, arrange medium-hot coals around edge of grill. Test for medium heat above center of grill rack. Place foil pan in the center of rack. Cover; grill for 40 to 50 minutes or until a knife inserted near center in a portion without chocolate comes out clean (temperature will be about 170°F). (For a gas grill, preheat grill. Reduce heat to medium-high. Adjust for indirect cooking. Grill as above.)

5 Transfer pan to a wire rack; cool, uncovered, for 30 minutes. Serve warm. If desired, serve with ice cream or whipped cream.

Nutrition Facts per serving: 461 cal., 20 g total fat (9 g sat. fat), 145 mg chol., 357 mg sodium, 58 g carbo., 3 g fiber, 11 g pro. Daily Values: 13% vit. A, 2% vit. C, 17% calcium, 12% iron. Exchanges: 4 Other Carbo., 3 Fat

STRAWBERRY CROQUE MONSIEUR

Croque monsieur (KROHK-m'-SUR), a
French-style grilled sandwich, usually has a
savory filling, but here it's stuffed with
strawberries, nuts, and mascarpone for dessert.

Prep: 40 minutes Chill: 1 hour Grill: 4 minutes
Makes: 8 servings

 1 **12-ounce loaf unsliced French or
     Italian bread**
 1 **8-ounce carton mascarpone cheese**
¼ **cup sugar**
½ **teaspoon ground cinnamon**
½ **cup chopped fresh strawberries**
⅓ **cup chopped pecans, toasted**
 2 **slightly beaten eggs**
½ **cup milk**
½ **teaspoon vanilla**
 1 **recipe Vanilla Custard
     Strawberry fans and/or whole fresh
     strawberries (optional)**

1 Cut bread crosswise into 8 slices. Make a
4-inch-long slit in the center of the top crust of
each bread slice, cutting to but not through the
other side. Set aside. In a medium bowl stir
together the mascarpone cheese, sugar, and
cinnamon. Fold in chopped berries and pecans.

2 Spread filling into pockets of bread slices. In a
shallow dish beat together eggs, milk, and
vanilla. Quickly dip both sides of bread into egg
mixture, allowing excess to drip off.

3 For a charcoal grill, grill bread slices on the
lightly oiled rack of an uncovered grill
directly over medium coals for 2 minutes on each
side or until golden brown. (For a gas grill,
preheat grill. Reduce heat to medium. Place bread
on grill rack over heat. Cover; grill as above.)

4 To serve, spoon several tablespoons Vanilla
Custard onto individual warm dessert plates.
Arrange grilled bread slices on each plate. If
desired, garnish with strawberry fans and/or
whole strawberries.

Vanilla Custard: In a medium saucepan
combine 1⅓ cups whole milk and 1 vanilla bean,
split lengthwise. Bring just to simmering, stirring
often with a wooden spoon. Remove from heat. In
a small mixing bowl beat 2 egg yolks. Gradually
stir ½ cup of the milk mixture, 2 tablespoons at a
time, into the beaten yolks. Gradually stir egg and
milk mixture back into hot milk mixture in
saucepan. Stir in ⅓ cup sugar. Return mixture to
heat. Cook and stir over low heat for 10 minutes or
until mixture coats the back of a metal spoon.
Remove from heat. Transfer to another container;
discard vanilla bean. Cover and chill for 1 hour.

Nutrition Facts per serving: 398 cal., 22 g total fat
(10 g sat. fat), 150 mg chol., 320 mg sodium,
42 g carbo., 2 g fiber, 14 g pro. Daily Values: 5% vit. A,
10% vit. C, 12% calcium, 9% iron. Exchanges: 1½ Starch,
1½ Other Carbo., 1 Medium-Fat Meat, 2½ Fat

FOOD FOR THOUGHT
S'MORES

S'mores put the final
touch on barbeques all
across the country.
To make them, follow
these directions: Butter a 10-inch
square of foil. Arrange four graham
cracker squares on the foil. Top
each square with half of a milk
chocolate bar, then a marshmallow,
and finish off with a second graham
cracker square. Grill the s'mores on
the foil on the grill rack directly
over low heat until the chocolate is
melted and the marshmallows are
lightly puffed and toasted. For new
twists on this old favorite, try the
following:
● Use dark chocolate instead of
milk chocolate and add a teaspoon
of your favorite jam.
● Substitute 2 teaspoons of
chocolate-hazelnut spread (such as
Nutella) for the milk chocolate bar.
● Spread 2 teaspoons of peanut
butter on the square before topping
with chocolate and marshmallows.

TROPI-KABOBS

Sweet fruits become even sweeter when kissed
by the heat of your grill.

Prep: 15 minutes Stand: 15 minutes Grill: 10 minutes
Makes: 6 servings

**2 medium bananas, peeled and cut
into 1- to 1¹/₂-inch pieces**
**¹/₄ of a small fresh pineapple, cut into
1- to 1¹/₂-inch pieces**
**1 small papaya, peeled, seeded, and
cut into 2-inch pieces**
3 tablespoons orange juice
2 teaspoons ground cinnamon
2 teaspoons cooking oil
3 tablespoons honey
**1 recipe Coconut Frozen Yogurt
Toasted coconut (optional)**

1 Soak twelve 6-inch bamboo skewers in water
for 30 minutes. On skewers, alternately thread
bananas, pineapple, and papaya. Brush fruits with
orange juice and sprinkle with cinnamon. Cover
and let stand for 15 minutes. Brush fruit with oil.

2 For a charcoal grill, grill kabobs on the rack of
an uncovered grill directly over medium-hot
coals about 10 minutes or until fruit is sizzling and
edges are slightly golden, turning kabobs once and
brushing with honey the last 1 minute of grilling.
(For a gas grill, preheat grill. Reduce heat to
medium-high. Place kabobs on grill rack over heat.
Cover; grill as above.)

3 To serve, place a scoop of Coconut Frozen
Yogurt in each of 6 serving bowls. Arrange
2 kabobs in each bowl. If desired, sprinkle with
toasted coconut.

Coconut Frozen Yogurt: Let 1¹/₂ cups vanilla
frozen yogurt soften slightly. Stir in ¹/₄ cup
toasted shredded coconut and ¹/₂ teaspoon
coconut-flavor extract. Cover and freeze about
1 hour or until serving time.

Nutrition Facts per serving: 181 cal., 4 g total fat
(2 g sat. fat), 4 mg chol., 46 mg sodium, 36 g carbo.,
2 g fiber, 4 g pro. Daily Values: 4% vit. A, 45% vit. C,
13% calcium, 4% iron. Exchanges: 1 Fruit, 1 Other Carbo.

GRILL-ROASTED FRESH FIGS

Golden syrup soaks into the halved figs as they
cook. They're best served warm.

Prep: 15 minutes Grill: 20 minutes
Makes: 4 servings

**6 large fresh figs, halved; 6 medium
fresh plums, pitted and halved;
or 3 small fresh peaches, pitted
and quartered**
2 tablespoons honey
**1 tablespoon butter or margarine,
melted**
1 tablespoon water
1 tablespoon sugar
**2 tablespoons blanched slivered
almonds, toasted**
1 tablespoon lemon juice (optional)
¹/₂ cup mascarpone cheese

1 Place figs in a 12×8-inch disposable foil pan.
Drizzle with honey, melted butter, and water.
Cover pan tightly with foil.

2 For a charcoal grill, arrange medium-hot coals
around edge of grill. Test for medium heat
above center of grill rack. Place foil pan in the
center of rack. Cover; grill about 15 minutes or
until figs are heated through. Remove foil cover
from pan. Brush figs with any juices that have
collected in the bottom of pan. Sprinkle sugar and
almonds evenly over figs in pan. Cover pan with
foil. Return pan to grill. Cover; grill 5 minutes
more. (For a gas grill, preheat grill. Reduce heat to
medium. Adjust for indirect cooking. Place pan on
grill rack. Grill as above.)

3 Carefully remove figs and liquid to a serving
dish. If desired, sprinkle with lemon juice.
Serve warm with mascarpone cheese.

Nutrition Facts per serving: 253 cal., 18 g total fat
(9 g sat. fat), 44 mg chol., 39 mg sodium, 23 g carbo.,
3 g fiber, 7 g pro. Daily Values: 4% vit. A, 3% vit. C,
4% calcium, 3% iron. Exchanges: 1 Fruit, ¹/₂ Other Carbo.,
¹/₂ High-Fat Meat, 2¹/₂ Fat

Gorgonzola-and-Walnut-Stuffed Apples

FILL-THE-GRILL NECTARINE TOSS

For all the parents who beg their children to eat fresh fruit, serve this with a big bowl of ice cream.

Prep: 15 minutes Grill: 8 minutes
Makes: 6 servings

6 ripe medium nectarines, halved and pitted
2 tablespoons olive oil
 Ground cinnamon or nutmeg (optional)
3 cups vanilla ice cream
 Coarsely chopped chocolate chunks

1 Brush nectarines with olive oil. If desired, sprinkle with cinnamon. For a charcoal grill, place a grill wok or grill basket on the rack of an uncovered grill directly over medium coals; heat for 5 minutes. Place nectarine halves in the wok or basket. Grill for 8 to 10 minutes or until heated through, turning gently halfway through cooking time. (For gas grill, preheat grill. Reduce heat to medium. Place grill wok or grill basket on grill rack over heat. Cover; grill as above.)

2 To serve, place ice cream in a large serving bowl. Top with grilled nectarine halves. Sprinkle with chocolate chunks.

Nutrition Facts per serving: 312 cal., 19 g total fat (9 g sat. fat), 46 mg chol., 46 mg sodium, 36 g carbo., 2 g fiber, 4 g pro. Daily Values: 13% vit. C, 10% calcium, 1% iron. Exchanges: 1 Fruit, 1½ Other Carbo., 3 Fat

GORGONZOLA-AND-WALNUT-STUFFED APPLES

These stuffed apples ooze with melted cheese. Honey is the natural choice for a sweetener.

Prep: 20 minutes Grill: 30 minutes
Makes: 4 servings

4 medium cooking apples, such as Granny Smith or Jonathan
¼ cup crumbled Gorgonzola, Stilton, or Roquefort cheese (1 ounce)
¼ cup chopped walnuts
2 tablespoons butter or margarine, melted
4 teaspoons honey
 Honey

1 Core apples almost to the bottom, leaving about ½ inch. Remove 1 inch of peel from the top of each apple.

2 In a small bowl stir together Gorgonzola, walnuts, and melted butter. Fill each cored apple three-fourths full with cheese mixture. Drizzle 1 teaspoon honey into each. Add the remaining filling to apples. Place apples in a disposable foil pan.

3 For a charcoal grill, arrange medium-hot coals around edge of grill. Test for medium heat over center of grill. Place foil pan in the center of the rack. Cover; grill for 30 to 40 minutes or until tender. (For a gas grill, preheat grill. Reduce heat to medium. Adjust for indirect cooking. Place foil pan on grill rack. Grill as above.)

4 Drizzle each serving with additional honey; serve warm.

Nutrition Facts per serving: 226 cal., 14 g total fat (5 g sat. fat), 22 mg chol., 163 mg sodium, 26 g carbo., 4 g fiber, 3 g pro. Daily Values: 6% vit. A, 9% vit. C, 6% calcium, 2% iron. Exchanges: 1 Fruit, ½ Other Carbo., ½ High-Fat Meat, 2 Fat

RHUBARB-RASPBERRY CRISP

Prep: 25 minutes Grill: 40 minutes Cool: 20 minutes
Makes: 6 to 8 servings

**5 cups fresh or frozen unsweetened
  sliced rhubarb**
2 cups fresh raspberries
½ cup granulated sugar
2 tablespoons brown sugar
2 teaspoons quick-cooking tapioca
½ cup regular rolled oats
⅓ cup packed brown sugar
¼ cup all-purpose flour
¼ cup granulated sugar
½ teaspoon cinnamon
¼ teaspoon ground ginger
¼ cup butter, cut up
1 recipe Honey-Ginger Yogurt

1 Thaw rhubarb, if frozen. In a 2- to 3-quart disposable foil pan stir together rhubarb, berries, the ½ cup granulated sugar, the 2 tablespoons brown sugar, and the tapioca. Set aside.

2 For topping, combine oats, the ⅓ cup brown sugar, flour, the ¼ cup granulated sugar, the cinnamon, and ground ginger. Using a pastry blender, cut in butter until mixture resembles coarse crumbs. Sprinkle oat mixture evenly over rhubarb mixture in foil pan. Cover pan tightly with foil.

3 For a charcoal grill, arrange medium-hot coals around edge of grill. Test for medium heat over center of grill. Place foil pan on rack in the center of grill. Cover; grill for 30 minutes. Uncover pan. Cover grill; cook for 10 to 15 minutes more or until mixture is bubbly and fruit has thickened. (For a gas grill, preheat grill. Reduce heat to medium. Adjust for indirect cooking. Place foil pan on grill rack. Grill as above.) Cool on wire rack for 20 minutes. Serve warn with Honey-Ginger Yogurt.

Honey-Ginger Yogurt: In a small bowl combine one 8-ounce container plain low-fat yogurt, 2 to 3 tablespoons honey, and 1 tablespoon finely chopped crystallized ginger.

Nutrition Facts per serving: 378 cal., 10 g total fat (6 g sat. fat), 24 mg chol., 121 mg sodium, 71 g carbo., 5 g fiber, 5 g pro. Daily Values: 10% vit. A, 29% vit. C, 19% calcium, 9% iron. Exchanges: 1 Fruit, ½ Starch, 3 Other Carbo., 2 Fat

PEAR TART WITH CARDAMOM WHIPPED CREAM

A covered grill acts as a surprisingly effective oven, cooking both pastry and fruit filling to perfection.

Prep: 20 minutes Grill: 35 minutes Stand: 20 minutes
Makes: 6 to 8 servings

**½ of a 15-ounce package folded
  refrigerated unbaked piecrust
  (1 crust)**
**2 large ripe pears, peeled, cored, and
  very thinly sliced (3½ cups)**
2 tablespoons sugar
1 tablespoon cornstarch
¼ teaspoon ground cardamom
1 recipe Cardamom Whipped Cream

1 Let piecrust stand according to package directions. Meanwhile, in a medium bowl toss pear slices with sugar, cornstarch, and cardamom. Wrap a 10- to 12-inch pizza pan with heavy foil.

2 Unroll piecrust on the pizza pan. Mound pear slices in center of piecrust in a single layer, leaving a 2-inch border. Fold border up over the pears, pleating as necessary to fit.

3 For a charcoal grill, arrange medium-hot coals around edge of grill. Test for medium heat over center of grill. Place pizza pan on rack in the center of grill. Cover; grill for 35 to 45 minutes or until pears are tender and pastry is golden brown. (For a gas grill, preheat grill. Reduce heat to medium. Adjust for indirect cooking. Place pizza pan on grill rack. Grill as above.) Cool on wire rack for 20 to 30 minutes before serving. Serve with Cardamom Whipped Cream.

Cardamom Whipped Cream: In a chilled mixing bowl combine ⅔ cup whipping cream, 1 tablespoon sifted powdered sugar, 1 tablespoon pear brandy or pear liqueur (if desired), and ⅛ teaspoon ground cardamom. Beat with an electric mixer on medium speed until soft peaks form (tips curl).

Nutrition Facts per serving: 307 cal., 19 g total fat (10 g sat. fat), 43 mg chol., 142 mg sodium, 33 g carbo., 2 g fiber, 1 g pro. Daily Values: 8% vit. A, 4% vit. C, 2% calcium, 1% iron. Exchanges: ½ Fruit, 1½ Other Carbo., 4 Fat

DESSERT POLENTA WITH GRILLED BALSAMIC PLUMS

Prep: 30 minutes Stand: 1 hour Chill: at least 4 hours
Grill: 8 minutes Makes: 8 servings

2¼ cups water
¾ cup yellow cornmeal
¾ cup cold water
¼ cup packed brown sugar
½ teaspoon salt
¼ teaspoon ground allspice or ground
   cardamom
1 teaspoon finely shredded orange
   peel
3 tablespoons butter, melted
8 small fresh plums, pitted and halved
¼ cup balsamic vinegar
   Sifted powdered sugar

1 In a medium saucepan, bring 2¼ cups water to boiling. Meanwhile, in a small bowl combine cornmeal, ¾ cup cold water, brown sugar, salt, and allspice. Slowly add cornmeal mixture to boiling water, stirring constantly. Cook and stir until mixture returns to boiling. Reduce heat to low. Cover and simmer for 10 to 15 minutes or until mixture is thick, stirring occasionally. Stir in orange peel. Pour the polenta into a buttered 8×8×2-inch baking pan. Let stand for 1 hour. Cover and chill at least 4 hours or until firm.

2 Remove polenta from pan. Cut into quarters. Brush both sides of polenta quarters with melted butter.

3 For a charcoal grill, grill plum halves, cut sides down, on the rack of an uncovered grill directly over medium coals for 4 to 5 minutes or until tender and heated through, turning once. Grill polenta squares directly over medium coals for 8 to 10 minutes, turning once, or until light brown on both sides. (For a gas grill, preheat grill. Reduce heat to medium. Place plums and polenta on grill rack over heat. Cover; grill as above.) Remove from grill and cut each polenta square in half diagonally, forming 8 triangles.

4 For each serving, place a polenta triangle and 2 plum halves on a serving dish. Drizzle plum halves with balsamic vinegar. Just before serving, sprinkle with powdered sugar.

Nutrition Facts per serving: 160 cal., 5 g total fat (2 g sat. fat), 12 mg chol., 184 mg sodium, 28 g carbo., 2 g fiber, 2 g pro. Daily Values: 8% vit. A, 11% vit. C, 2% calcium, 2% iron. Exchanges: ½ Fruit, ½ Starch, 1 Other Carbo., 1 Fat

DESSERT BURRITOS

Place the makings for one or more fillings on separate trays and let your guests prepare their own for the grill.

Prep: 10 minutes Grill: 13 minutes Cool: 5 minutes
Makes: 4 servings

4 9- to 10-inch flour tortillas
¼ cup caramel ice cream topping
1 medium ripe banana, sliced
½ cup crushed chocolate sandwich
   cookies with white filling
2 tablespoons butter, melted
   Whipped cream, desired jam, or
   chopped fresh strawberries
   (optional)

1 Wrap tortillas in foil. For a charcoal grill, grill tortilla packet on the rack of an uncovered grill directly over medium coals about 10 minutes or until warm, turning once. Working with one tortilla at a time, spread 1 tablespoon ice cream topping down the center of each tortilla. Top with 3 or 4 banana slices and 2 tablespoons crushed cookies. Fold one-third of the tortilla over filling. Fold in ends and roll up, forming a burrito. Secure with wooden toothpicks. Brush with melted butter.

2 Grill burritos directly over medium coals for 3 to 4 minutes, turning once, or until tortillas are lightly browned. Let cool 5 minutes before serving. (For a gas grill, preheat grill. Reduce heat to medium. Place tortilla packet and burritos on grill rack over heat. Cover; grill as above.)

3 If desired, serve with whipped cream, desired jam, or chopped fresh strawberries.

Nutrition Facts per serving: 358 cal., 13 g total fat (5 g sat. fat), 16 mg chol., 382 mg sodium, 56 g carbo., 3 g fiber, 4 g pro. Daily Values: 4% vit. A, 4% vit. C, 6% calcium, 12% iron Exchanges: 3½ Other Carbo., 2½ Fat

Dessert Burritos

Apple-Brown Sugar Burritos: Prepare and grill as directed, except slice 1 medium apple and arrange down the center of tortillas. Sprinkle apple slices with ¼ cup chopped pecans, ¼ cup packed brown sugar, and 1 teaspoon ground cinnamon. Drizzle with ¼ cup melted butter.

Nutrition Facts per serving: 362 cal., 21 g fat (7 g sat. fat), 32 mg chol., 272 mg sodium, 43 g carbo., 3 g dietary fiber, 4 g pro. Daily Values: 8% vit. A, 3% vit. C, 8% calcium, 12% iron. Exchanges: 3 Other Carbo., 5 Fat

Cherry-Mascarpone Burritos: Prepare and grill as directed, except spread ½ cup mascarpone cheese down the center of tortillas. Sprinkle with ½ cup crushed amaretti cookies and ½ cup snipped dried cherries or apricots. Drizzle with ¼ cup honey.

Nutrition Facts per serving: 406 cal., 17 g fat (8 g sat. fat), 36 mg chol., 200 mg sodium, 59 g carbo., 2 g dietary fiber, 10 g pro. Daily Values: 5% calcium, 8% iron. Exchanges: 4 Other Carbo., 3½ Fat

Chocolate-Marshmallow Burritos: Prepare and grill as directed, except spread ¼ cup marshmallow creme down the center of tortillas.

Sprinkle with ¼ cup chopped peanuts. Drizzle with ¼ cup chocolate-flavored syrup.

Nutrition Facts per serving: 234 cal., 8 g fat (2 g sat. fat), 0 mg chol., 227 mg sodium, 36 g carbo., 2 g dietary fiber, 6 g pro. Daily Values: 3% vit. C, 6% calcium, 11% iron. Exchanges: 2½ Other Carbo., 2 Fat

Lemon-Raspberry Burritos: Prepare and grill as directed, except spread ½ cup purchased lemon curd down the center of tortillas. Sprinkle with ⅔ cup fresh raspberries.

Nutrition Facts per serving: 273 cal., 6 g fat (2 g sat. fat), 30 mg chol., 209 mg sodium, 27 g carbo., 6 g dietary fiber, 3 g pro. Daily Values: 1% vit. A, 9% vit. C, 5% calcium, 8% iron. Exchanges: ½ Other Carbo., 2 Fat

Peanut Butter-Banana Burritos: Prepare and grill as directed, except spread ½ cup peanut butter down the center of tortillas. Top with 1 banana, sliced; ½ cup tiny marshmallows; and ¼ cup candy-coated milk chocolate pieces.

Nutrition Facts per serving: 427 cal., 23 g fat (5 g sat. fat), 1 mg chol., 352 mg sodium, 48 g carbo., 4 g dietary fiber, 12 g pro. Daily Values: 1% vit. A, 4% vit. C, 7% calcium, 12% iron. Exchanges: 3 Other Carbo., 1 High-Fat Meat, 3½ Fat

MANGO BLOSSOMS

Prep: 30 minutes Grill: 6 minutes
Makes: 8 servings

4 mangoes
4 kiwifruits, peeled
½ of a 15-ounce purchased angel
    food cake
¼ cup butter or margarine, melted
3 tablespoons mild-flavor molasses or
    honey

1 Using a sharp knife, cut each mango length-wise down both flat sides, keeping the blade about ¼ inch from the seed. Set seeds aside. Score mango pieces, making cuts through fruit but not through peel in a crosshatch fashion. Set aside.

2 Carefully remove and discard peel remaining around mango seeds. Cut away as much of the fruit remaining around the mango seeds as you can; discard seeds. Place removed fruit portion in a food processor or blender. Cover and process or blend until smooth. Transfer pureed fruit to a small covered container or a clean squeeze bottle. Chill until ready to use.

3 Rinse the food processor or blender. Place peeled kiwifruits in processor or blender. Cover and process or blend until smooth. If desired, strain kiwifruit puree through a sieve to remove seeds. Transfer to a covered container or squeeze bottle. Chill until ready to use.

4 Cut angel food cake in half horizontally (forming 2 half-rings). Brush all sides of cake with half of the melted butter. For a charcoal grill, grill cake on rack of an uncovered grill directly over medium coals for 2 to 3 minutes or until lightly browned, turning once. Cut angel food cake into large croutons.

5 Brush fruit side of reserved mango pieces with molasses and remaining melted butter. Grill mangoes, cut sides down, over medium coals for 4 to 6 minutes or until brown around the edges and heated through. (For a gas grill, preheat grill. Reduce heat to medium. Place cake and mangoes on grill rack over heat. Cover; grill as above.)

6 To serve, spoon or drizzle mango and kiwifruit sauces on the bottom of 8 chilled, shallow dessert bowls. Carefully bend the peel back on each mango half, pushing the inside up and out until the mango cubes pop up and separate. Place each mango "blossom" on sauces in a dessert bowl. Surround with several cake croutons.

Nutrition Facts per serving: 215 cal., 4 g total fat (3 g sat. fat), 15 mg chol., 249 mg sodium, 45 g carbo., 2 g fiber, 3 g pro. Daily Values: 44% vit. A, 119% vit. C, 6% calcium, 5% iron. Exchanges: 1½ Fruit, 1½ Other Carbo., 1 Fat

GRILLED PEARS WITH HAZELNUTS

Serve this elegant dessert with purchased lemon shortbread cookies.

Prep: 15 minutes Grill: 10 minutes
Makes: 8 servings

1 tablespoon lemon juice
4 teaspoons butter, melted
¼ teaspoon vanilla
4 medium pears, halved lengthwise
    and cored
2 tablespoons sugar
½ cup chocolate-hazelnut spread
    (such as Nutella)
2 tablespoons hazelnut liqueur (optional)
¼ cup chopped hazelnuts (filberts),
    toasted

1 In a small bowl combine lemon juice, melted butter, and vanilla; brush over pear halves. Sprinkle with sugar. If desired, place pears on a greased grilling tray. For a charcoal grill, grill pears, cut sides down, on the rack of an uncovered grill directly over medium coals (or place grilling tray on rack directly over medium coals) for 10 to 15 minutes or until pears are tender and very lightly golden, turning occasionally. (For a gas grill, preheat grill. Reduce heat to medium. Place pears or grilling tray on grill rack over heat. Cover; grill as above.) Place pears on dessert plates.

2 Meanwhile, in a small saucepan heat chocolate-hazelnut spread over low heat just until warm. If desired, drizzle liqueur over warm pears. Drizzle warmed chocolate-hazelnut spread over pears; sprinkle with hazelnuts.

Nutrition Facts per serving: 185 cal., 9 g total fat (1 g sat. fat), 6 mg chol., 30 mg sodium, 26 g carbo., 3 g fiber, 2 g pro. Daily Values: 2% vit. A, 8% vit. C, 1% calcium, 2% iron. Exchanges: 1 Fruit, 1 Other Carbo., 1 Fat

APPLES WITH CARAMEL CRÈME FRAÎCHE

On a chilly evening this elegant take on the caramel apple will warm you from the inside out.

Prep: 15 minutes Grill: 8 minutes
Makes: 6 servings

4 Granny Smith apples, cored
4 cups water
3 tablespoons lemon juice
3 tablespoons butter, melted
1 recipe Caramel Crème Fraîche

1 Cut apples crosswise into ½-inch slices. In a large bowl combine water and lemon juice. Let apple slices stand in water mixture to prevent browning.

2 Drain apple slices; pat dry with paper towels. Brush both sides of each apple slice with melted butter.

3 For a charcoal grill, place apple slices on the grill rack directly over medium-hot coals. Cover; grill for 2 minutes. Rotate apple slices a half-turn to create a checkerboard grill pattern. Cover and grill for 2 minutes more. Turn apples over and repeat on other side. (For a gas grill, preheat grill. Reduce heat to medium-hot. Place apples on grill rack over heat. Grill as above.) To serve, arrange 3 or 4 apple slices on each dessert plate. Top with Caramel Crème Fraîche.

Caramel Crème Fraîche: In a food processor or blender combine ½ cup whipping cream, ½ cup dairy sour cream, and ⅓ cup caramel ice cream topping. Cover and process or blend for 1 to 2 minutes or until slightly thickened. (Or beat with an electric mixer on high speed about 2 minutes or until slightly thickened.)

Nutrition Facts per serving: 265 cal., 17 g total fat (11 g sat. fat), 51 mg chol., 118 mg sodium, 28 g carbo., 2 g fiber, 2 g pro. Daily Values: 14% vit. A, 9% vit. C, 7% calcium, 1% iron. Exchanges: ½ Fruit, 1½ Other Carbo., 3½ Fat

GRILLED-PEACH ICE CREAM

Prep: 20 minutes Grill: 8 minutes Chill: 4 hours or overnight
Freeze: according to manufacturer's directions
Ripen: 4 hours Makes: 10 servings (about 5 cups)

1 pound fresh peaches, peeled, halved, and pitted
¾ cup half-and-half or whole milk
½ cup packed brown sugar
1½ cups whipping cream
2 teaspoons vanilla
1 cup Candied Pecans (about ½ recipe)

1 For a charcoal grill, grill peach halves on the rack of an uncovered grill directly over medium coals for 8 to 10 minutes or until peaches are tender and lightly browned, turning once. (For a gas grill, preheat grill. Reduce heat to medium. Place peach halves on grill rack over heat. Cover; grill as above.) Remove from grill. Cool slightly; chop peaches.

2 Meanwhile, in a medium saucepan heat and stir the half-and-half and brown sugar over medium heat just until sugar dissolves. Remove from heat; transfer mixture to a large bowl. Cool to room temperature; stir in whipping cream, chopped peaches, and vanilla. Cover and chill for 4 hours or overnight.

3 Freeze cream mixture in a 1½-quart ice cream freezer according to manufacturer's directions. Transfer to a freezer container; stir in Candied Pecans. Cover; freeze at least 4 hours.

Nutrition Facts per serving: 302 cal., 22 g total fat (11 g sat. fat), 59 mg chol., 34 mg sodium, 25 g carbo., 2 g fiber, 2 g pro. Daily Values: 18% vit. A, 6% vit. C, 6% calcium, 3% iron. Exchanges: 1½ Other Carbo., 4½ Fat

Candied Pecans: Line a baking sheet with foil. Butter foil; set aside. In a heavy 10-inch skillet combine 1½ cups pecan halves, ½ cup sugar, 2 tablespoons butter, and ½ teaspoon vanilla. Spread evenly in skillet. Cook over medium-high heat until butter melts; stir and continue cooking until sugar begins to melt, shaking skillet occasionally to heat evenly. Reduce heat to low. Continue cooking, stirring occasionally, until sugar is golden brown. Remove from heat. Spread nut mixture on prepared baking sheet. Cool completely. Break into small clusters. Store covered in the refrigerator for up to 3 weeks.

Butter Pecan Ice Cream

BUTTER PECAN ICE CREAM

Homemade ice cream like this beats even
the fanciest gourmet brands.

Prep: 20 minutes
Freeze: according to manufacturer's directions
Ripen: 4 hours **Makes:** 16 servings (about 2 quarts)

- **1 cup coarsely chopped pecans**
- **¹/₂ cup granulated sugar**
- **2 tablespoons butter**
- **4 cups half-and-half or light cream**
- **2 cups packed brown sugar**
- **1 tablespoon vanilla**
- **4 cups whipping cream**

1 Line a baking sheet with foil. Butter foil; set aside. In a heavy 8-inch skillet combine pecans, granulated sugar, and butter. Heat mixture over medium heat, stirring constantly, for 6 to 8 minutes or until sugar melts and turns a rich brown color.

2 Remove from heat. Spread nut mixture on parepared baking sheet; separate into clusters and cool. Break clusters into small chunks.

3 In a large bowl combine half-and-half, brown sugar, and vanilla; stir until sugar is dissolved. Stir in whipping cream.

4 Freeze cream mixture in a 4- to 5-quart ice cream freezer according to the manufacturer's directions, using crushed ice and rock salt. Stir in pecan mixture. Ripen for 4 hours.

Nutrition Facts per serving: 354 cal., 16 g total fat (10 g sat. fat), 52 mg chol., 49 mg sodium, 51 g carbo., 1 g fiber, 3 g pro. Daily Values: 15% vit. A, 10% vit. C, 9% calcium, 2% iron. Exchanges: 3½ Other Carbo., 2½ Fat

CREAM CHEESE ICE CREAM

Prep: 20 minutes Chill: 4 hours or overnight
Freeze: according to manufacturer's directions
Ripen: 4 hours Makes: 24 servings (about 3 quarts)

5 cups half-and-half or light cream
2½ cups sugar
4 beaten eggs
**3 8-ounce packages cream cheese or
  reduced-fat cream cheese
  (Neufchâtel), softened**
1 teaspoon finely shredded lemon peel
2 tablespoons lemon juice
2 teaspoons vanilla
  **Fresh blueberries, nectarines,
  and/or dark cherries (optional)**

1 In a medium saucepan combine 3 cups of the half-and-half, the sugar, and eggs. Cook and stir over medium heat just until boiling. In a large mixing bowl beat cream cheese with an electric mixer on low speed until smooth; gradually beat in hot mixture. Cover and chill 4 hours or overnight.

2 Stir in remaining half-and-half, lemon peel, lemon juice, and vanilla. Freeze in a 4- or 5-quart ice cream freezer according to the manufacturer's directions, using crushed ice and rock salt. Ripen for 4 hours. If desired, top each serving with fresh fruit.

Nutrition Facts per serving: 255 cal., 16 g total fat (10 g sat. fat), 85 mg chol., 116 mg sodium, 23 g carbo., 0 g fiber, 5 g pro. Daily Values: 12% vit. A, 2% vit. C, 8% calcium, 3% iron. Exchanges: 1½ Other Carbo., 3 Fat

TAFFY APPLE ICE CREAM

Combine two favorite summer treats to make yet a third. This ice cream tastes like a taffy apple.

Prep: 20 minutes Chill: 4 hours or overnight
Freeze: according to manufacturer's directions
Ripen: 4 hours Makes: 16 servings (about 2 quarts)

1 cup granulated sugar
½ cup packed brown sugar
**2 12-ounce cans (3 cups total)
  evaporated milk**
1 tablespoon molasses
4 beaten eggs
2 cups whipping cream
**3 cups peeled, cored, and finely
  chopped apple**
1 teaspoon vanilla

1 In a medium saucepan combine granulated sugar, brown sugar, milk, and molasses. Cook and stir over medium heat until sugar dissolves; remove from heat. Slowly stir 1 cup of hot milk mixture into beaten eggs; return egg mixture to hot mixture in saucepan. Cook and stir over low heat just until bubbling; do not boil. Remove from heat. Cover and chill 4 hours or overnight.

2 Stir in whipping cream, apple, and vanilla. Freeze in a 4- or 5-quart ice cream freezer according to manufacturer's directions, using crushed ice and rock salt. Ripen for 4 hours.

Nutrition Facts per serving: 271 cal., 16 g total fat (9 g sat. fat), 106 mg chol., 78 mg sodium, 29 g carbo., 1 g fiber, 5 g pro. Daily Values: 12% vit. A, 4% vit. C, 15% calcium, 3% iron. Exchanges: 2 Other Carbo., 3 Fat

SMOKIN' HOT TIP

Letting homemade ice creams rest after freezing is called ripening. Although it isn't absolutely necessary, ripening improves the ice cream's texture and helps keep it from melting too quickly.

● To ripen in a traditional-style ice cream freezer, after churning, remove the lid and dasher and cover the top of the freezer can with waxed paper or foil. Plug the hole in the lid with a small piece of cloth; replace the lid. Pack the outer freezer bucket with enough ice and rock salt to cover the top of the freezer can (use 1 cup salt for each 4 cups ice). Ripen about 4 hours.

● When using an ice cream freezer with an insulated freezer bowl, transfer the ice cream to a covered freezer container and ripen by freezing in your regular freezer about 4 hours (or check the manufacturer's recommendations).

TROPICAL SORBET

Sultry evenings and hearty meals call for a cool, refreshing dessert like this one.

Prep: 30 minutes Freeze: 6 hours Stand: 10 minutes
Makes: 8 servings

$\frac{1}{2}$ **cup water**
$\frac{1}{3}$ **cup sugar**
$\frac{1}{4}$ **cup light-colored corn syrup**
$\frac{1}{2}$ **of a small fresh pineapple, peeled, cored, and chopped ($1\frac{1}{2}$ cups)**
1 **medium mango, seeded, peeled, and chopped (1 cup)**
1 **medium papaya, peeled, seeded, and chopped ($1\frac{1}{2}$ cups)**
1 **cup unsweetened pineapple juice**
2 **tablespoons lemon juice**

1 In a small saucepan combine water, sugar, and corn syrup. Bring just to boiling, stirring to dissolve sugar; remove from heat. Cool mixture to room temperature.

2 In a food processor or blender combine half of the fruits and half of the pineapple juice; cover and process or blend until smooth. Transfer to a shallow 3-quart freezer-safe container or dish. Repeat with remaining fruit and juice; add to dish. Stir in cooled syrup and lemon juice.

3 Cover and freeze for 4 to 5 hours or until just firm. Break up mixture and transfer to a chilled large mixing bowl; beat with an electric mixer until fluffy but not melted. Return to freezer container; spread evenly. Freeze until firm.

4 Let stand for 10 minutes at room temperature before scooping to serve.

Nutrition Facts per serving: 131 cal., 0 g total fat (0 g sat. fat), 0 mg chol., 17 mg sodium, 34 g carbo., 2 g fiber, 1 g pro. Daily Values: 22% vit. A, 70% vit. C, 2% calcium, 2% iron. Exchanges: 1 Fruit, 1 Other Carbo.

PEACHES AND ICE CREAM SANDWICH BARS

Purchased ice cream sandwiches are great on their own, but they also make a superb base for this frozen dessert.

Prep: 25 minutes Freeze: $4\frac{1}{4}$ hours Stand: 10 minutes
Makes: 12 servings

10 to 14 **rectangular ice cream sandwiches, unwrapped**
2 **pints peach or mango sorbet, softened**
1 **8-ounce carton dairy sour cream**
1 **cup whipping cream**
$\frac{3}{4}$ **cup sifted powdered sugar**
2 **cups fresh blueberries or raspberries**

1 Place ice cream sandwiches in the bottom of a 13×9×2-inch baking pan or a 3-quart rectangular baking dish, cutting to fit as necessary. Spread sorbet on top of ice cream sandwiches. Freeze for 15 minutes or until sorbet is firm.

2 In a medium bowl combine sour cream, whipping cream, and powdered sugar. Beat with an electric mixer on medium speed until mixture thickens and holds soft peaks (tips curl). Spread cream mixture on top of sorbet.

3 Cover and freeze for 4 to 24 hours or until firm. Let stand at room temperature for 10 minutes before serving. Top with fresh berries.

Nutrition Facts per serving: 354 cal., 16 g total fat (10 g sat. fat), 52 mg chol., 49 mg sodium, 51 g carbo., 1 g fiber, 3 g pro. Daily Values: 15% vit. A, 10% vit. C, 9% calcium, 2% iron. Exchanges: $3\frac{1}{2}$ Other Carbo., $2\frac{1}{2}$ Fat

EASY LEMON SUGAR SNAPS

Buy the kind of cake mix that boasts "pudding in the mix." Otherwise, the mixture will be too dry to shape.

Prep: 25 minutes Bake: 9 minutes per batch Oven: 375°F
Makes: about 42 cookies

   ³/₄ **cup butter, softened**
   1 **egg**
   1 **2-layer-size package lemon cake mix (with pudding in the mix)**
   1 **cup yellow cornmeal**
   2 **tablespoons finely shredded lemon peel**
      Coarse sugar or granulated sugar

1 In a large mixing bowl beat butter and egg with an electric mixer on medium to high speed for 30 seconds. Gradually beat in cake mix until combined; stir in cornmeal and lemon peel. If necessary, use your hands to knead in cornmeal until well combined.

2 Using 1 tablespoon of dough for each cookie, roll into 1-inch balls. Roll in sugar. Place balls 2 inches apart on ungreased cookie sheets.

3 Bake in a 375°F oven for 9 to 10 minutes or until bottoms are lightly browned. Cool on cookie sheet for 1 minute. Transfer cookies to wire rack and cool.

Nutrition Facts per cookie: 99 cal., 5 g total fat (2 g sat. fat), 14 mg chol., 114 mg sodium, 14 g carbo., 0 g fiber, 1 g pro. Daily Values: 3% vit. A, 1% vit. C, 3% calcium, 2% iron. Exchanges: 1 Other Carbo., ½ Fat

CHOCOLATE CHOCOLATE-CHUNK COOKIES

Simply drop this dough onto a cookie sheet and watch it spread into a chocolate lover's dream.

Prep: 30 minutes Bake: 9 minutes per batch Oven: 375°F
Makes: about 45 cookies

   2 **ounces unsweetened chocolate, chopped**
   1 **cup butter, softened**
   ³/₄ **cup granulated sugar**
   ³/₄ **cup packed brown sugar**
   1 **teaspoon baking soda**
   2 **eggs**
   1 **teaspoon vanilla**
   2 **cups all-purpose flour**
   6 **ounces white baking bar, cut into chunks**
   6 **ounces semisweet or bittersweet chocolate, cut into chunks**
   1 **cup chopped walnuts or pecans (optional)**

1 Place unsweetened chocolate in a heavy small saucepan. Cook and stir over very low heat until chocolate melts. Set aside to cool.

2 In a large mixing bowl beat butter with an electric mixer on medium to high speed for 30 seconds. Add cooled chocolate, granulated sugar, brown sugar, and baking soda. Beat until combined, scraping sides of bowl. Beat in eggs and vanilla until combined. Gradually beat in flour. Stir in the white baking bar and semisweet chocolate chunks and, if desired, nuts.

3 Drop by rounded tablespoons 3 inches apart onto an ungreased cookie sheet. Bake in a 375°F oven for 9 to 11 minutes or until edges are firm. Cool on cookie sheet for 1 minute. Transfer cookies to a wire rack and cool.

Nutrition Facts per cookie: 134 cal., 8 g total fat (4 g sat. fat), 22 mg chol., 68 mg sodium, 16 g carbo., 1 g fiber, 2 g pro. Daily Values: 3% vit. A, 1% calcium, 4% iron. Exchanges: 1 Other Carbo., 1 Fat

DOUBLE-CHERRY STREUSEL BARS

Prep: 20 minutes Bake: 32 minutes Oven: 350°F
Cool: 2 hours Makes: 48 bars

- **2 cups water**
- **1 cup dried tart cherries or dried cranberries, snipped**
- **2 cups quick-cooking rolled oats**
- **1½ cups all-purpose flour**
- **1½ cups packed brown sugar**
- **1 teaspoon baking powder**
- **½ teaspoon baking soda**
- **1 cup butter**
- **½ cup coarsely chopped slivered almonds**
- **2 12-ounce jars cherry preserves**
- **1 teaspoon finely shredded lemon peel**
- **½ cup semisweet chocolate pieces**
- **1 teaspoon shortening**

1 In a small saucepan bring water to boiling; remove from heat. Add dried cherries and let stand about 10 minutes or until softened. Drain and set aside.

2 For crust, in a large bowl combine oats, flour, brown sugar, baking powder, and baking soda. Using a pastry blender, cut in butter until mixture resembles coarse crumbs. Reserve 1 cup of the crumb mixture. Stir almonds into the reserved crumb mixture; set aside. Press remaining crumb mixture into the bottom of an ungreased 15×10×1-inch baking pan. Bake for 12 minutes.

3 Meanwhile, for filling, stir together drained cherries, cherry preserves, and lemon peel. Spread filling evenly over hot crust; sprinkle with reserved crumb mixture. Bake in a 350°F oven for 20 to 25 minutes more or until top is golden brown. Cool in pan on a wire rack for 2 hours.

4 In a small saucepan combine chocolate pieces and shortening. Heat and stir over medium-low heat until chocolate melts; drizzle over top. Cut into bars.

Nutrition Facts per bar: 157 cal., 6 g total fat (3 g sat. fat), 11 mg chol., 70 mg sodium, 26 g carbo., 1 g fiber, 2 g pro. Daily Values: 3% vit. A, 2% vit. C, 2% calcium, 4% iron. Exchanges: 2 Other Carbo., 1 Fat

COCONUT PINEAPPLE BARS

No mixer needed! Just stir, spread, and bake to golden perfection.

Prep: 20 minutes Bake: 35 minutes Oven: 325°F
Makes: 24 bars

- **1½ cups all-purpose flour**
- **1½ cups sugar**
- **½ teaspoon baking soda**
- **4 beaten eggs**
- **1 20-ounce can crushed pineapple, drained**
- **½ cup butter, melted**
- **½ cup chopped nuts**
- **½ cup shredded coconut**

1 Grease a 3-quart rectangular baking dish; set aside.

2 In a large bowl stir together flour, sugar, and baking soda. Stir in eggs, pineapple, and melted butter until combined. Fold in nuts and coconut. Spread mixture in prepared baking dish.

3 Bake in a 325°F oven about 35 minutes or until a wooden toothpick inserted near center comes out clean. Cool in the dish on a wire rack. Cut into bars.

Nutrition Facts per bar: 157 cal., 7 g total fat (3 g sat. fat), 46 mg chol., 67 mg sodium, 22 g carbo., 1 g fiber, 2 g pro. Daily Values: 3% vit. A, 4% vit. C, 1% calcium, 4% iron. Exchanges: 1½ Other Carbo., 1 Fat

SMOKIN' HOT TIP

Make bar cookies look even more appealing by cutting them into triangles or diamonds.

● **For triangles, cut the pan of cookies into 2- or 2½-inch squares. Then cut each square in half diagonally to serve.**

● **For diamonds, first make straight parallel cuts 1 to 1½ inches apart down the length of the pan. Then make diagonal cuts 1 to 1½ inches apart across the straight cuts.**

Tri-Level Brownies

TRI-LEVEL BROWNIES

As the name implies, these scrumptious bars boast three sweet layers: a chewy oatmeal cookie crust, a fudgy center, and a creamy frosting.

Prep: 15 minutes Bake: 35 minutes Oven: 350°F
Makes: 24 bars

- **1 cup quick-cooking rolled oats**
- **¹/₂ cup all-purpose flour**
- **¹/₂ cup packed brown sugar**
- **¹/₄ teaspoon baking soda**
- **¹/₂ cup butter, melted**
- **1 egg**
- **³/₄ cup granulated sugar**
- **²/₃ cup all-purpose flour**
- **¹/₄ cup milk**
- **¹/₄ cup butter, melted**
- **1 ounce unsweetened chocolate, melted and cooled**
- **1 teaspoon vanilla**
- **¹/₄ teaspoon baking powder**
- **¹/₂ cup chopped walnuts**
- **1 ounce unsweetened chocolate**
- **2 tablespoons butter**
- **1¹/₂ cups sifted powdered sugar**
- **¹/₂ teaspoon vanilla**
- **Walnut halves (optional)**

1 For bottom layer, stir together oats, ¹/₂ cup flour, the brown sugar, and baking soda. Stir in ¹/₂ cup melted butter. Pat mixture into the bottom of an ungreased 11×7×1¹/₂-inch baking pan. Bake in a 350°F oven for 10 minutes.

2 Meanwhile, for middle layer, stir together egg, granulated sugar, ²/₃ cup flour, milk, ¹/₄ cup melted butter, 1 ounce melted chocolate, 1 teaspoon vanilla, and baking powder until smooth. Stir in chopped walnuts. Spread batter evenly over baked layer in pan. Bake for 25 minutes more. Place on a wire rack while preparing top layer.

3 For top layer, in a medium saucepan heat and stir 1 ounce chocolate and 2 tablespoons butter until melted. Stir in powdered sugar and ¹/₂ teaspoon vanilla. Stir in enough hot water (1 to 2 tablespoons) to make a mixture that is almost pourable. Spread over brownies. If desired, garnish with walnut halves. Cool in pan on wire rack. Cut into bars.

Nutrition Facts per bar: 199 cal., 11 g total fat (6 g sat. fat), 28 mg chol., 96 mg sodium, 25 g carbo., 1 g fiber, 2 g pro. Daily Values: 6% vit. A, 2% calcium, 4% iron. Exchanges: 1¹/₂ Other Carbo., 2 Fat

STRAWBERRIES WITH LEMON CREAM

A few snips of lemon basil top this simple dessert.

Start to Finish: 10 minutes
Makes: 6 servings

3 cups halved fresh strawberries
1 cup whipping cream
2 tablespoons sifted powdered sugar
⅛ teaspoon ground cardamom
¼ teaspoon finely shredded lemon peel
1 tablespoon snipped fresh
    lemon basil or basil

1 Divide berries among 6 dessert dishes; set aside. In a chilled medium mixing bowl beat cream, sugar, and cardamom with an electric mixer on medium speed until soft peaks form (tips curl). Fold in lemon peel. Spoon cream onto berries in dishes. Sprinkle each serving with lemon basil.

Nutrition Facts per serving: 168 cal., 15 g total fat (9 g sat. fat), 55 mg chol., 16 mg sodium, 8 g carbo., 2 g fiber, 1 g pro. Daily Values: 12% vit. A, 69% vit. C, 4% calcium, 2% iron. Exchanges: ½ Fruit, 3 Fat

MANGO WHIP

Dress up juicy golden mangoes with a fluffy topping and a sprinkling of pistachio nuts.

Start to Finish: 20 minutes
Makes: 4 servings

4 mangoes or peaches
½ of an 8-ounce package reduced-fat
    cream cheese (Neufchâtel),
    softened
¼ cup white grape or orange juice
1 tablespoon chopped pistachio nuts

1 Seed and peel mangoes. Cut fruit into wedges. Divide fruit among 4 chilled dessert bowls.
2 In a small mixing bowl beat together cream cheese and grape juice. Spoon over mangoes. Top with chopped pistachios.

Nutrition Facts per serving: 229 cal., 8 g total fat (4 g sat. fat), 21 mg chol., 117 mg sodium, 39 g carbo., 4 g fiber, 4 g pro. Daily Values: 38% vit. A, 103% vit. C, 4% calcium, 2% iron. Exchanges: 2½ Fruit, 1½ Fat

KEEN NECTARINES

To ripen nectarines, let them stand at room temperature for a couple of days. Then store in the refrigerator and use within 3 days.

Start to Finish: 10 minutes
Makes: 4 servings

1½ cups vanilla- or peach-flavor frozen
    yogurt or ice cream
2 nectarines, halved and pitted
8 amaretti cookies or 4 gingersnaps,
    crumbled

1 Scoop frozen yogurt into 4 chilled dessert bowls. Add half of a nectarine to each bowl. Sprinkle with crumbled cookies.

Nutrition Facts per serving: 140 cal., 3 g total fat (1 g sat. fat), 8 mg chol., 26 mg sodium, 26 g carbo., 1 g fiber, 3 g pro. Daily Values: 8% vit. A, 6% vit. C, 23% calcium, 1% iron Exchanges: ½ Fruit, 1 Other Carbo., ½ Fat

CHERRY DREAM

The season for sweet cherries is short. Use this super-simple dessert to show them off.

Prep: 15 minutes Chill: 4 hours
Makes: 6 servings

1 4-serving-size package cook-and-
    serve vanilla pudding
3 cups halved pitted dark sweet cherries
6 tablespoons kirsch or cherry liqueur

1 Prepare pudding according to package directions. Cover and chill for 4 hours.
2 Spoon pudding into 6 dessert bowls. Spoon cherries over pudding. Drizzle 1 tablespoon kirsch over each dessert.

Nutrition Facts per serving: 186 cal., 2 g total fat (1 g sat. fat), 7 mg chol., 113 mg sodium, 35 g carbo., 2 g fiber, 4 g pro. Daily Values: 4% vit. A, 8% vit. C, 11% calcium, 4% iron. Exchanges: ½ Milk, 1 Fruit, 1 Other Carbo., ½ Fat

SWEET LAYERS OF RED, WHITE, AND BLUE

Proudly show your patriotic colors! Lemon peel and rosemary flavor the creamy white layers that separate red strawberries and blueberries.

Prep: 20 minutes Chill: up to 24 hours
Makes: 12 servings

1 ⅓ cups whipping cream
  5 4-inch sprigs fresh rosemary or
    ¼ cup torn basil leaves
  1 2×1-inch piece lemon peel
  1 8-ounce carton dairy sour cream
  ⅓ cup sifted powdered sugar
  6 cups cut-up fresh strawberries or
    raspberries
  6 cups fresh blueberries
  1 5.1-ounce container vanilla-flavored
    bite-size meringue cookies

1 In a 2-cup glass measuring cup combine whipping cream, rosemary, and lemon peel. Cover with plastic wrap and chill for up to 24 hours. Strain whipping cream to remove herb and lemon peel; discard herb and peel.

2 In a large mixing bowl combine whipping cream, sour cream, and sifted powdered sugar. Beat with an electric mixer on medium speed until mixture thickens and holds soft peaks (tips curl). Use immediately or cover and chill for up to 24 hours. (Cream may thicken upon chilling. Stir before serving.)

3 In twelve 16-ounce glasses or bowls alternate layers of berries with layers of meringue cookies and whipped cream mixture. (The cream helps soften the crunch of the cookies.)

Nutrition Facts per serving: 232 cal., 14 g total fat (9 g sat. fat), 45 mg chol., 28 mg sodium, 25 g carbo., 5 g fiber, 3 g pro. Daily Values: 12% vit. A, 81% vit. C, 6% calcium, 3% iron. Exchanges: 1 Fruit, ½ Other Carbo., 3 Fat

BERRY CLAFOUTI

The French clafouti puffs up during baking and deflates as it cools.

Prep: 15 minutes Bake: 30 minutes
Stand: 20 minutes Oven: 350°F
Makes: 8 servings

  ½ cup all-purpose flour
  ½ cup sugar
  ½ teaspoon salt
  5 beaten eggs
  1 cup milk
  3 tablespoons butter, melted
  2 cups fresh blueberries
    Powdered sugar
    Sweetened whipped cream (optional)

1 Generously grease a 2-quart square baking dish; set aside.

2 In a medium bowl stir together flour, sugar, and salt. Whisk in eggs, milk, and melted butter. Pour batter into the prepared dish. Sprinkle blueberries evenly over batter.

3 Bake in a 350°F oven for 30 to 35 minutes or until puffed and light brown. Let stand 20 minutes before serving. To serve, dust with powdered sugar. If desired, serve with sweetened whipped cream.

Nutrition Facts per serving: 202 cal., 9 g total fat (4 g sat. fat), 148 mg chol., 242 mg sodium, 25 g carbo., 1 g fiber, 6 g pro. Daily Values: 8% vit. A, 8% vit. C, 6% calcium, 6% iron. Exchanges: 1½ Other Carbo., ½ Medium-Fat Meat, 1 Fat

FOOD FOR THOUGHT CLAFOUTI

Clafouti is a rustic country French dessert similar to a fruit tart, though it has no crust. Fruit is placed on top of a thick, custardlike batter. Once baked, the batter puffs up and becomes light, golden, and cakey. Although it's traditionally made with dark cherries, you can use any fruit to make clafouti. It's delicious dusted with powdered sugar and served with ice cream or whipped cream.

Mixed Berry Shortcake

MIXED BERRY SHORTCAKE

Prep: 25 minutes Bake: 15 minutes
Cool: 10 minutes Oven: 450°F
Makes: 8 servings

**6 cups sliced fresh strawberries,
     raspberries, blueberries, and/or
     blackberries**
¹/₂ cup sugar
2 cups all-purpose flour
2 teaspoons baking powder
¹/₂ cup butter
1 beaten egg
²/₃ cup milk
1 cup whipping cream, whipped

1 Grease an 8×1¹/₂-inch round baking pan. In a
small bowl stir together berries and ¹/₄ cup of
the sugar; set aside. Stir together remaining sugar,
flour, and baking powder. Cut in butter until
mixture resembles coarse crumbs. Combine egg
and milk; add to flour mixture. Stir just to moisten. Spread dough into prepared pan.

2 Bake in a 450°F oven for 15 to 18 minutes or
until a wooden toothpick inserted near center
comes out clean. Cool in pan for 10 minutes.
Remove from pan. Split into two layers. Spoon half
of the berries and half of the whipped cream over the
bottom layer. Replace top layer. Top with remaining
whipped cream and remaining berries. Cut into
wedges and serve immediately.

Individual Shortcakes: Drop dough into
8 mounds on an ungreased baking sheet; flatten
each mound with the back of a spoon until
about ³/₄ inch thick. Bake in a 450°F oven about
10 minutes or until golden. Cool on a wire rack
about 10 minutes. Cut shortcakes in half
horizontally. Spoon half of the berries and half of
the whipped cream over bottom layers. Replace
top layers. Top with remaining whipped cream
and remaining berries.

Nutrition Facts per serving: 423 cal., 25 g total fat
(15 g sat. fat), 102 mg chol., 255 mg sodium,
45 g carbo., 3 g fiber, 6 g pro. Daily Values: 20% vit. A,
103% vit. C, 13% calcium, 11% iron. Exchanges: 1 Fruit,
2 Other Carbo., 4¹/₂ Fat

BANANA CHEESECAKE

Cooking for a crowd? For convenient serving, this rich coconut-topped cheesecake is baked in a rectangular baking pan.

Prep: 30 minutes Bake: 35 minutes
Chill: 4 to 24 hours Oven: 350°F
Makes: 16 servings

2 cups crushed graham crackers
1/4 cup sugar
1/2 cup finely chopped pecans
1/2 cup butter, melted
3 8-ounce packages cream cheese, softened
3/4 cup sugar
1 teaspoon vanilla
3 eggs
1 cup mashed banana (about 2 medium)
1 8-ounce carton dairy sour cream
2 tablespoons white crème de cacao
2 tablespoons rum
1 1/2 cups flaked coconut, toasted

1 For the crust, combine crushed graham crackers, 1/4 cup sugar, and pecans. Stir in melted butter. Press crumb mixture onto the bottom of a 13×9×2-inch baking pan. Set aside.

2 For the filling, in a large mixing bowl beat cream cheese, 3/4 cup sugar, and vanilla with an electric mixer on low speed until combined. Add eggs, beating on low speed until just combined. Stir in mashed banana.

3 Pour filling into crust-lined pan. Bake in a 350°F oven for 30 minutes or until center is set. Meanwhile, in a small bowl stir together sour cream, crème de cacao, and rum. Spoon sour cream mixture over filling, spreading evenly, and bake for 5 minutes more (sour cream layer may crack slightly).

4 Cool in pan on a wire rack. Cover and chill for 4 to 24 hours. To serve, sprinkle with toasted coconut.

Nutrition Facts per serving: 472 cal., 35 g total fat (22 g sat. fat), 109 mg chol., 270 mg sodium, 33 g carbo., 1 g fiber, 7 g pro. Daily Values: 20% vit. A, 3% vit. C, 7% calcium, 10% iron. Exchanges: 2 Other Carbo., 6 1/2 Fat

POLKA-DOT CUPCAKES

The berries are unexpected bursts of jamlike flavor. Use whatever fruit suits the season.

Prep: 1 hour Bake: 15 minutes Oven: 350°F
Cool: 1 hour Makes: 12 cupcakes

1 1/2 cups egg whites (10 to 12)
1 cup sifted cake flour
1/2 cup sugar
1 1/2 teaspoons cream of tartar
1 teaspoon vanilla
1/2 teaspoon almond extract
1/2 teaspoon salt
3/4 cup sugar
1 cup fresh blueberries, raspberries, and/or diced strawberries (1/4 inch)

1 In a very large mixing bowl allow egg whites to stand at room temperature for 30 minutes. Meanwhile, sift cake flour and 1/2 cup sugar together three times; set aside. Line twelve 3 1/4-inch muffin cups with large paper bake cups.

2 Add cream of tartar, vanilla, almond extract, and salt to egg whites. Beat with an electric mixer on medium speed until soft peaks form (tips curl). Gradually add 3/4 cup sugar, about 2 tablespoons at a time, beating until stiff peaks form (tips stand straight).

3 Sift one-fourth of the cake flour mixture over beaten egg whites; fold in gently. Repeat, folding in the remaining flour mixture by fourths.

4 Spoon batter into muffin cups, filling about half full. Sprinkle a few berry pieces on top of each, then top with another large dollop of batter and remaining berries. Mound remaining batter over fruit pieces (cups will be very full).

5 Bake in a 350°F oven for 15 to 18 minutes or until tops are light golden brown and spring back when lightly touched with a finger. Cool cakes in pan on a wire rack.

Nutrition Facts per cupcake: 134 cal., 0 g total fat (0 g sat. fat), 0 mg chol., 143 mg sodium, 29 g carbo., 1 g fiber, 4 g pro. Daily Values: 2% vit. C, 4% iron. Exchanges: 2 Other Carbo.

OATMEAL CAKE

This old-fashioned favorite with a caramel-nut topping totes well to potlucks and picnics.

Prep: 45 minutes Bake: 40 minutes Broil: 2 minutes
Cool: 1 hour 40 minutes Oven: 350°F
Makes: 12 servings

- ½ **cup butter**
- 2 **eggs**
- 1¼ **cups boiling water**
- 1 **cup rolled oats**
- 2 **cups all-purpose flour**
- 2 **teaspoons baking powder**
- ¾ **teaspoon ground cinnamon**
- ½ **teaspoon baking soda**
- ½ **teaspoon salt**
- ¼ **teaspoon ground nutmeg**
- ¾ **cup granulated sugar**
- ½ **cup packed brown sugar**
- 1 **teaspoon vanilla**
- 1 **recipe Broiled Nut Topping**

1 Allow butter and eggs to stand at room temperature for 30 minutes. Meanwhile, grease and lightly flour a 9-inch springform pan; set pan aside. Pour boiling water over oats. Stir until combined; let stand for 20 minutes. Stir together flour, baking powder, cinnamon, baking soda, salt, and nutmeg; set aside.

2 In a large mixing bowl beat butter with an electric mixer on medium to high speed for 30 seconds. Add granulated sugar, brown sugar, and vanilla; beat until well combined. Add eggs, one at a time, beating well after each. Alternately add flour mixture and oatmeal mixture to beaten mixture, beating on low speed after each addition just until combined. Pour batter into prepared pan.

3 Bake in a 350°F oven for 40 to 45 minutes or until a wooden toothpick inserted near center comes out clean. Cool cake in pan on a wire rack for 20 minutes. Remove sides of pan; cool on wire rack at least 1 hour more.

4 Transfer cake to a baking sheet. Spread Broiled Nut Topping over warm cake. Broil about 4 inches from heat for 2 to 3 minutes or until topping is bubbly and golden. Cool on a wire rack about 20 minutes before serving.

Broiled Nut Topping: In a medium saucepan combine ¼ cup butter and 2 tablespoons half-and-half, light cream, or milk. Cook and stir until butter melts. Add ½ cup packed brown sugar; stir until sugar dissolves. Remove from heat. Stir in ¾ cup chopped pecans or walnuts and ⅓ cup flaked coconut.

Nutrition Facts per serving: 410 cal., 20 g total fat (10 g sat. fat), 70 mg chol., 273 mg sodium, 54 g carbo., 2 g fiber, 5 g pro. Daily Values: 11% vit. A, 8% calcium, 11% iron. Exchanges: 3½ Other Carbo., 3 Fat

CHOCOLATE-BUTTERMILK SHEET CAKE

Known to some as Texas Sheet Cake, this sinfully rich dessert is a cousin to the brownie.

Prep: 30 minutes Bake: 25 minutes Oven: 350°F
Cool: 1 hour Makes: 24 servings

- 2 **cups all-purpose flour**
- 2 **cups sugar**
- 1 **teaspoon baking soda**
- ¼ **teaspoon salt**
- 1 **cup butter**
- ⅓ **cup unsweetened cocoa powder**
- 1 **cup water**
- 2 **eggs**
- ½ **cup buttermilk or sour milk***
- 1½ **teaspoons vanilla**
- 1 **recipe Chocolate-Buttermilk Frosting**

1 Grease a 15×10×1- or a 13×9×2-inch baking pan; set aside. Combine flour, sugar, baking soda, and salt; set aside.

2 In a medium saucepan combine butter, cocoa powder, and water. Bring mixture just to boiling, stirring constantly. Remove from heat. Add the cocoa mixture to flour mixture and beat with an electric mixer on medium to high speed until thoroughly combined. Add eggs, buttermilk, and vanilla. Beat for 1 minute (batter will be thin). Pour batter into the prepared pan.

3 Bake in a 350°F oven about 25 minutes for 15×10×1-inch pan, 35 minutes for 13×9×2-inch pan, or until a wooden toothpick inserted near center comes out clean.

4 Pour warm Chocolate-Buttermilk Frosting over the warm cake, spreading evenly. Place cake in pan on a wire rack; cool thoroughly.

Chocolate-Buttermilk Frosting: In a medium saucepan combine ¼ cup butter or margarine, 3 tablespoons unsweetened cocoa powder, and 3 tablespoons buttermilk. Bring to boiling. Remove from heat. Add 2¼ cups sifted powdered sugar and ½ teaspoon vanilla. Beat until smooth. If desired, stir in ¾ cup coarsely chopped pecans.

Chocolate-Cinnamon Sheet Cake: Prepare as above, except add 1 teaspoon ground cinnamon to the flour mixture.

*Note: To make sour milk, place 1½ teaspoons lemon juice or vinegar in a glass measuring cup. Add enough milk to make ½ cup; stir. Let stand for 5 minutes before using.

Nutrition Facts per serving: 244 cal., 11 g total fat (6 g sat. fat), 45 mg chol., 193 mg sodium, 35 g carbo., 0 g fiber, 2 g pro. Daily Values: 8% vit. A, 4% calcium, 5% iron. Exchanges: 2½ Other Carbo., 2 Fat

---

BEST-EVER CHOCOLATE CAKE

Super moist and equally as rich, this cake will find a place high on your list of favorites. Chocolate Butter Frosting is the classic finishing touch.

Prep: 30 minutes Bake: 35 minutes Oven: 350°F
Cool: 1 hour Makes: 12 to 16 servings

¾ **cup butter**
3 **eggs**
2 **cups all-purpose flour**
¾ **cup unsweetened cocoa powder**
1 **teaspoon baking soda**
¾ **teaspoon baking powder**
½ **teaspoon salt**
2 **cups sugar**
2 **teaspoons vanilla**
1½ **cups milk**
   Chocolate Butter Frosting

1 Allow butter and eggs to stand at room temperature for 30 minutes. Lightly grease bottoms of two 8×8×2-inch square or 9×1½-inch round cake pans. Line bottoms of pans with waxed paper. Grease and lightly flour waxed paper and sides of pans. Or grease one 13×9×2-inch baking pan. Set pan(s) aside.

2 In a medium bowl stir together flour, cocoa powder, baking soda, baking powder, and salt; set aside.

3 In a large mixing bowl beat butter with an electric mixer on medium to high speed for 30 seconds. Gradually add sugar, about ¼ cup at a time, beating on medium speed for 3 to 4 minutes or until well combined. Scrape sides of bowl; continue beating on medium speed for 2 minutes. Add eggs, one at a time, beating after each addition (about 1 minute total). Beat in vanilla.

4 Alternately add flour mixture and milk to beaten mixture, beating on low speed just until combined after each addition. Beat on medium to high speed for 20 seconds more. Spread batter evenly into the prepared pan(s).

5 Bake in a 350°F oven for 35 to 40 minutes for 8-inch pans and the 13×9×2-inch pan, 30 to 35 minutes for 9-inch pans, or until a wooden toothpick inserted in center(s) comes out clean. Cool cake layers in pans for 10 minutes. Remove from pans. Peel off waxed paper. Cool thoroughly on wire racks. Or place 13×9×2-inch cake in pan on a wire rack; cool thoroughly. Frost cake(s) with Chocolate Butter Frosting.

Chocolate Butter Frosting: In a very large mixing bowl combine ¾ cup butter, softened, and ½ cup unsweetened cocoa powder; beat with an electric mixer on low speed until smooth. Gradually add 2 cups sifted powdered sugar, beating well. Slowly beat in ¼ cup milk and 2 teaspoons vanilla. Gradually beat in 6½ cups sifted powdered sugar. Beat in enough additional milk to reach spreading consistency. Makes enough to frost the tops and sides of two or three 8- or 9-inch cake layers. (Halve the recipe to frost the top of a 13×9×2-inch cake.)

Nutrition Facts per serving: 767 cal., 27 g total fat (16 g sat. fat), 121 mg chol., 509 mg sodium, 127 g carbo., 1 g fiber, 6 g pro. Daily Values: 21% vit. A, 13% calcium, 10% iron. Exchanges: 38 Other Carbo., 4 Fat

Apple-Spice Cake

high speed for 30 seconds. Add sugar and vanilla; beat until well combined. Add eggs, one at a time, beating well after each. Stir together applesauce and buttermilk. Alternately add flour mixture and applesauce mixture to beaten mixture, beating on low speed after each addition just until combined. Pour into prepared pans.

3 Bake in a 350°F oven about 35 minutes or until a wooden toothpick inserted near centers comes out clean. Cool cakes in pans on wire racks for 10 minutes. Remove cakes from pans. Cool thoroughly. Frost tops of cakes with Butter Frosting; stack cakes. If desired, garnish cake with apple slices and pecans.

Butter Frosting: In a large mixing bowl beat ⅓ cup butter with an electric mixer on medium speed until fluffy. Gradually add 2 cups sifted powdered sugar, beating well. Slowly beat in 2 tablespoons milk and 1 teaspoon vanilla. Slowly beat in 2½ cups additional sifted powdered sugar. Beat in additional milk, if necessary, until frosting is of spreading consistency.

Nutrition Facts per serving: 740 cal., 28 g total fat (12 g sat. fat), 107 mg chol., 297 mg sodium, 119 g carbo., 1 g fiber, 5 g pro. Daily Values: 14% vit. A, 1% vit. C, 5% calcium, 10% iron. Exchanges: 8 Other Carbo., 4 Fat

APPLE-SPICE CAKE

Prep: 30 minutes Bake: 35 minutes
Cool: 1 hour Oven: 350°F
Makes: 8 to 10 servings

¼ cup butter
2 eggs
2 cups all-purpose flour
1½ teaspoons baking powder
1 teaspoon ground cinnamon
½ teaspoon baking soda
¼ teaspoon ground nutmeg
¼ teaspoon ground cloves
¼ teaspoon ground ginger
¼ cup shortening
1½ cups sugar
½ teaspoon vanilla
1 cup applesauce
¼ cup buttermilk or sour milk
1 recipe Butter Frosting
Dried apple slices (optional)
Coarsely chopped pecans (optional)

1 Allow butter and eggs to stand at room temperature for 30 minutes. Grease and lightly flour two 8×1½-inch round baking pans; set aside. Stir together flour, baking powder, cinnamon, baking soda, nutmeg, cloves, and ginger; set aside.

2 In a large mixing bowl beat butter and shortening with an electric mixer on medium to

CHEERY CHERRY-LEMON CAKE

Prep: 40 minutes Bake: 30 minutes Oven: 375°F
Cool: 1 hour Makes: 12 servings

1½ cups coarsely chopped pitted sweet cherries
2½ cups all-purpose flour
2½ teaspoons baking powder
½ teaspoon salt
¾ cup butter, softened
1¾ cups sugar
1½ teaspoons vanilla
3 eggs
1¼ cups milk
2 teaspoons finely shredded lemon peel
1 recipe Cream Cheese Frosting
Pitted red sweet cherries with stems (optional)
Fresh mint leaves (optional)

1 Grease a 13×9×2-inch baking pan; set aside. Pat the chopped cherries as dry as possible with paper towels to prevent bleeding. In a medium bowl combine flour, baking powder, and salt; set aside.

2 In a large mixing bowl beat butter with an electric mixer on medium to high speed for 30 seconds. Add sugar and vanilla; beat until well combined. Add eggs one at a time, beating for 1 minute after each. Alternately add flour mixture and milk to beaten mixture, beating on low speed after each addition just until combined. Stir lemon peel into batter. Pour batter into prepared pan. Sprinkle chopped cherries evenly over batter (the cherries will sink during baking).

3 Bake in a 375°F oven for 30 to 35 minutes or until a wooden toothpick inserted near center comes out clean. Cool cake in pan on a wire rack.

4 To serve, cut cake into 12 pieces. Top each piece with a dollop of Cream Cheese Frosting and, if desired, a pitted cherry and a mint leaf.

Cream Cheese Frosting: In a large mixing bowl beat together one 8-ounce package cream cheese, softened; ⅔ cup butter, softened; 2 teaspoons finely shredded lemon peel; and 2 tablespoons lemon juice until fluffy. Gradually add 3 cups sifted powdered sugar, beating well. Gradually beat in about 1½ cups additional sifted powdered sugar to reach desired consistency.

Nutrition Facts per serving: 676 cal., 32 g total fat (20 g sat. fat), 138 mg chol., 498 mg sodium, 94 g carbo., 1 g fiber, 8 g pro. Daily Values: 26% vit. A, 8% vit. C, 12% calcium, 10% iron. Exchanges: 6½ Other Carbo., 5 Fat

---

BANANA SPLIT CAKE

Prep: 30 minutes Bake: 55 minutes Oven: 350°F
Cool: 1 hour Makes: 12 servings

1 cup butter
4 eggs
3 cups all-purpose flour
2 teaspoons baking powder
1 teaspoon salt
¼ teaspoon baking soda
1½ cups sugar
½ cup mashed ripe banana (1 large)
½ cup dairy sour cream

½ cup milk
1 teaspoon vanilla
½ cup strawberry preserves
    Few drops red food coloring
½ cup presweetened cocoa powder
    (not low-calorie)
1 12-ounce jar chocolate fudge
    ice cream topping
    Vanilla ice cream

1 Allow butter and eggs to stand at room temperature for 30 minutes. Grease and flour a 10-inch fluted tube pan. In a medium bowl stir together flour, baking powder, salt, and baking soda; set aside.

2 In a large mixing bowl beat butter with an electric mixer on low to medium speed about 30 seconds. Add sugar; beat until fluffy. Add eggs, one at a time, beating well after each addition. In a small bowl combine banana, sour cream, milk, and vanilla. Alternately add flour mixture and banana mixture to butter mixture, beating on low speed after each addition just until combined.

3 Stir strawberry preserves and red food coloring into 1 cup of the batter. Stir cocoa powder into another 1 cup of the batter. Spoon half of the remaining plain batter into the prepared pan. Spoon strawberry batter over. Top with remaining plain batter, then chocolate batter.

4 Bake in a 350°F oven for 55 to 65 minutes or until a wooden toothpick inserted near center comes out clean. Cool in pan on a wire rack for 10 minutes; remove from pan. Cool completely on wire rack. In a small saucepan heat ice cream topping until warm. Drizzle over cake. Serve cake with ice cream topped with additional chocolate fudge topping.

Nutrition Facts per serving: 561 cal., 24 g total fat (12 g sat. fat), 120 mg chol., 560 mg sodium, 79 g carbo., 2 g fiber, 8 g pro. Daily Values: 13% vit. A, 3% vit. C, 9% calcium, 10% iron. Exchanges: 5½ Other Carbo., 4 Fat

Apricot-Cherry Slab Pie

3 In a large bowl combine sugar and cornstarch. Stir in apricots and cherries. Spoon into prepared crust.

4 Roll remaining dough into a 16×11-inch rectangle; place over fruit. Bring bottom pastry up and over top pastry. Seal edges by pressing with the tines of a fork. Prick top pastry over entire surface with the tines of a fork.

5 Bake in a 375°F oven about 40 minutes or until crust is golden brown. Drizzle with Vanilla Glaze. Cool in pan on a wire rack. Serve warm or cool. Cut into 3×2-inch pieces.

Vanilla Glaze: In a small bowl combine 1¼ cups sifted powdered sugar, ½ teaspoon vanilla, and enough milk (5 to 6 teaspoons) to make of drizzling consistency.

Nutrition Facts per serving: 230 cal., 8 g total fat (2 g sat. fat), 9 mg chol., 104 mg sodium, 37 g carbo., 1 g fiber, 2 g pro. Daily Values: 16% vit. A, 3% vit. C, 2% calcium, 8% iron. Exchanges: 2½ Other Carbo., 1½ Fat

APRICOT-CHERRY SLAB PIE

A bit sturdier than typical pies, this oversize version made on a baking sheet is good for eating out of hand.

Prep: 30 minutes Bake: 40 minutes Oven: 375°F
Makes: 25 servings

3¼ **cups all-purpose flour**
1 **teaspoon salt**
1 **cup shortening**
1 **egg yolk**
  Milk
½ **cup sugar**
3 **tablespoons cornstarch**
3 **15¼-ounce cans apricot halves, drained and cut into quarters**
1 **16-ounce can pitted tart red cherries, drained**
1 **recipe Vanilla Glaze**

1 For pastry, in a large bowl stir together flour and salt. Using a pastry blender, cut in shortening until mixture resembles coarse crumbs. Lightly beat egg yolk in a glass measuring cup. Add enough milk to egg yolk to make ¾ cup total liquid; mix well. Stir egg yolk mixture into flour mixture; mix well. Divide dough into two-thirds and one-third portions.

2 On a lightly floured surface, roll two-thirds of dough into an 18×12-inch rectangle. To transfer pastry, wrap it around the rolling pin; unroll into a 15×10×1-inch baking pan (pastry will hang over edges of pan).

IT'S-THE-BERRIES PIE

Put a spin on traditional lattice-top pie by twisting pastry strips into a pinwheel.

Prep: 30 minutes Bake: 50 minutes
Cool: 3 hours Oven: 375°F
Makes: 8 servings

1 **recipe Pastry for Double-Crust Pie**
½ **to ⅔ cup sugar**
⅓ **cup all-purpose flour**
2 **cups halved fresh strawberries**
2 **cups fresh blueberries**
1 **cup fresh blackberries or raspberries**
2 **teaspoons finely shredded lemon peel**
  Milk
  Sugar

1 Prepare and roll out half of the pastry. Line a 9-inch pie plate with pastry; set aside.

2 In a large bowl stir together sugar and flour. Stir in berries and lemon peel; gently toss until berries are coated. Transfer berry mixture to the pastry-lined pie plate. Trim bottom pastry to ½ inch beyond edge of pie plate; fold the extra pastry under, even with the plate's rim, to build up the edge.

3 On a lightly floured surface roll remaining pastry into a 12-inch circle. Cut into ¾-inch strips. Place strips on top of pie, twisting them so the ends form a pinwheel in the center. Trim strips to about ½ inch beyond the edge of the plate, turn them under the bottom crust, and pinch at the edge to form a seal. Crimp edge as desired.

4 Brush pastry strips with milk; sprinkle with sugar. To prevent overbrowning, cover edge of pie with foil. Bake in a 375°F oven for 25 minutes. Remove foil. Bake 25 to 30 minutes more or until top is golden. Cool on a wire rack for 3 hours.

Pastry for Double-Crust Pie: In a large bowl stir together 2¼ cups all-purpose flour and ¾ teaspoon salt. Using a pastry blender, cut in ⅔ cup shortening until the pieces are the size of small peas. Sprinkle 1 tablespoon water over part of the mixture; gently toss with a fork. Push moistened dough to the side of the bowl. Repeat with 5 to 7 tablespoons water, using 1 tablespoon at a time, until all the dough is moistened. Divide dough in half. Form each half into a ball. Use your hands to slightly flatten one ball of dough on a lightly floured surface. Roll dough from the center to the edge into a 12-inch circle. To transfer pastry, wrap it around the rolling pin. Unroll into a 9-inch pie plate. Ease pastry into pie plate, being careful not to stretch pastry. Do not trim edge.

Nutrition Facts per serving: 385 cal., 18 g total fat (4 g sat. fat), 0 mg chol., 222 mg sodium, 53 g carbo., 4 g fiber, 5 g pro. Daily Values: 2% vit. A, 51% vit. C, 2% calcium, 11% iron. Exchanges: ½ Fruit, 3 Other Carbo., 2½ Fat

PEACH CROSTADA

The essence of summer lingers in this rustic pie. Super-fresh peaches need little embellishment beyond some sugar and a buttery pastry.

Prep: 1 hour Chill: 1 to 24 hours
Bake: 35 minutes Oven: 425°F
Makes: 6 servings

2 cups all-purpose flour
¼ teaspoon salt
¾ cup cold butter, cut into small cubes
6 to 7 tablespoons cold water
6 ripe medium peaches (about 2 pounds)

¼ cup packed brown sugar
1 tablespoon all-purpose flour
½ teaspoon vanilla
1 tablespoon packed brown sugar
¼ cup orange blossom honey or ¼ cup honey plus ¼ teaspoon finely shredded orange peel

1 In a medium bowl combine flour and salt. Using a pastry blender, cut in butter until pieces are the size of small peas. Sprinkle water, 1 tablespoon at a time, over flour mixture, tossing with a fork, until all the flour mixture is moistened. Gently knead the dough just until it forms a ball. If necessary, wrap dough in plastic wrap; chill for 1 to 24 hours.

2 To peel peaches, bring a medium saucepan of water to boiling. Add peaches, one at a time, for 20 seconds. Remove from boiling water and immediately place in a bowl of ice water. Peel, pit, and slice peaches (should have about 6 cups).

3 For filling, in a large bowl combine peach slices, ¼ cup brown sugar, 1 tablespoon flour, and vanilla; toss gently to coat. Set aside.

4 On a lightly floured surface, roll pastry from center to edges into a 16×12-inch oval. (If chilled pastry is too firm, let stand at room temperature for 10 to 15 minutes before rolling.) Transfer to a very large ungreased baking sheet. Mound the peach filling in the center of the dough, leaving a 2-inch border. Fold border up and over peach mixture, pleating edges as necessary (the dough won't cover the filling completely). Sprinkle filling with 1 tablespoon brown sugar.

5 Bake in a 425°F oven for 35 to 40 minutes or until filling is bubbly, covering loosely with foil, if necessary, to prevent overbrowning. Remove from oven and drizzle fruit with honey. Let cool on a wire rack. Serve warm or at room temperature.

Nutrition Facts per serving: 386 cal., 19 g total fat (11 g sat. fat), 50 mg chol., 267 mg sodium, 52 g carbo., 3 g fiber, 5 g pro. Daily Values: 24% vit. A, 11% vit. C, 2% calcium, 10% iron. Exchanges: 1 Fruit, 2½ Other Carbo., 3 Fat

APPLE BISTRO TART

Prep: 30 minutes Bake: 20 minutes Oven: 425°F
Makes: 8 servings

1/2 of a 15-ounce package folded
    refrigerated unbaked piecrust
    (1 crust)
3 tablespoons granulated sugar
1 teaspoon ground cinnamon
1 teaspoon finely shredded lemon peel
2 medium tart green apples, peeled,
    cored, and cut into 1/2-inch slices
1/2 cup chopped pecans
1/2 cup caramel apple dip
    Sifted powdered sugar

1 Let piecrust stand according to package directions. In a bowl combine granulated sugar, cinnamon, and lemon peel. Add apple slices and pecans; toss to coat.

2 Place piecrust on a large baking sheet. Spread the caramel apple dip over crust to within 2 inches of edge. Place apple mixture over caramel. Fold edges of crust 2 inches up and over apple mixture, pleating edges as necessary.

3 Bake in a 425°F oven about 20 minutes or until crust is golden brown and apples are just tender. Cool slightly on a wire rack. To serve, sprinkle with powdered sugar. Serve warm.

Nutrition Facts per serving: 273 cal., 12 g total fat (3 g sat. fat), 5 mg chol., 174 mg sodium, 41 g carbo., 2 g fiber, 2 g pro. Daily Values: 1% vit. A, 4% vit. C, 2% calcium, 2% iron Exchanges: 2½ Other Carbo., 2½ Fat

FOOD FOR THOUGHT
MERINGUE POWDER

Meringue powder is a convenient alternative to using fresh egg whites when making meringue or icing. Made from dried egg whites, sugar, and edible gums, the powder combines with water to form icing that's equal in quality to icings made with fresh eggs. It is great for making soft meringue toppings for pies or crisp, delicate dessert meringues.

FUDGE RIBBON PIE

If making a meringue is too fussy, you can top the pie with whipped cream instead.

Prep: 50 minutes Freeze: several hours or overnight
Bake: 3 minutes Oven: 475°F
Makes: 8 servings

1 cup sugar
1 5-ounce can evaporated milk (2/3 cup)
2 tablespoons butter
2 ounces unsweetened chocolate, cut up
1 teaspoon vanilla
2 pints (4 cups) peppermint ice cream
1 9-inch baked pastry shell, cooled
3/4 cup sugar
1/2 cup boiling water
1/4 cup meringue powder
1/4 cup crushed peppermint-stick candy

1 For fudge sauce, in a small saucepan combine 1 cup sugar, evaporated milk, butter, and chocolate. Cook and stir over medium heat until bubbly. Reduce heat and boil gently for 4 to 5 minutes, stirring occasionally, until mixture is thickened and reduced to 1½ cups. Remove from heat; stir in vanilla. If necessary, beat until smooth with wire whisk or rotary beater. Set aside to cool completely.

2 In a chilled bowl stir 1 pint of the ice cream until softened. Spread into cooled pastry shell. Cover with half of the fudge sauce. Freeze until nearly firm. Repeat with remaining ice cream and fudge sauce. Return to freezer while preparing meringue.

3 For meringue, in a medium mixing bowl dissolve 3/4 cup sugar in the boiling water. Cool to room temperature. Add meringue powder. Beat on low speed until combined; beat on high speed until stiff peaks form (tips stand straight). By hand, fold 3 tablespoons of the crushed candy into the meringue. Spread meringue over chocolate sauce layer, sealing to edge. Sprinkle top with remaining crushed candy. Freeze for several hours or overnight or until firm.

4 Bake frozen pie in a 475°F oven for 3 to 4 minutes or just until meringue is golden. Cover loosely; freeze for several hours or overnight before serving.

Nutrition Facts per serving: 567 cal., 24 g total fat (11 g sat. fat), 43 mg chol., 198 mg sodium, 85 g carbo., 1 g fiber, 6 g pro. Daily Values: 3% vit. A, 1% vit. C, 10% calcium, 7% iron. Exchanges: 5½ Other Carbo., 5 Fat

Index

FOOD SAFETY AT THE GRILL

Cooking and keeping foods safe is easy if you follow a few guidelines.

- Use an oven/grill-safe meat thermometer when cooking large cuts of meat or poultry. Be sure to place the thermometer deep into the center of the meat. Smaller cuts, such as hamburgers, boneless chicken breasts, or pork chops, don't lend themselves to the use of an oven/grill-safe meat thermometer but can be checked with an instant-read thermometer as well as following the doneness descriptions.
- Cook roasts and steaks to a temperature of at least 145°F. Whole chicken or turkey should reach 180° F. The center of the stuffing should reach 165°F.
- Cook ground beef to at least 160°F and ground chicken or turkey to 170°F because bacteria can spread during processing. The Centers for Disease Control and Prevention believes there is a connection between eating undercooked, pink ground beef and a higher risk of illness. To keep from becoming ill, it's best to avoid eating ground beef that is still pink.
- Fish that is cooked properly should be opaque and flake easily when tested with a fork.
- After marinating, if using the marinade to serve with the meat, heat the marinade to a full rolling boil, stirring often during heating. Leftover sauces should also be heated to a full rolling boil. The temperature should reach at least 165°F.

RECOMMENDED DEGREE OF DONENESS

FOOD	MEDIUM-RARE	MEDIUM	WELL DONE
Beef	145°F	160°F	170°F
Veal	*	160°F	170°F
Lamb	145°F	160°F	170°F
Pork	*	160°F	170°F
Ground Meats	*	160°F	170°F

*Not recommended for less than medium degree of doneness.

IN A PINCH: HOW HOT IS HOT?

Unless you have a thermometer built into your grill, you'll need a good way to measure the approximate temperature of the coals. This simple test will help: Hold your hand at the level the food will cook for as long as it's comfortable. The number of seconds you can hold it there will give you an estimate for the heat of the fire.

TEMPERATURE	NUMBER OF SECONDS
High	2
Medium-high	3
Medium	4
Medium-low	5
Low	6

For More Information

If you would like to know more or have questions about meat or poultry, contact the USDA Meat and Poultry Hotline

800-535-4555

The National Cattlemen's Beef Association

312-467-5520

or National Pork Board

515-223-2600

For grilling tips and recipes, visit

www.bhg.com/bkgrilling

METRIC INFORMATION

The charts on this page provide a guide for converting measurements from the U.S. customary system, which is used throughout this book, to the metric system.

PRODUCT DIFFERENCES

Most of the ingredients called for in the recipes in this book are available in most countries. However, some are known by different names. Here are some common American ingredients and their possible counterparts:

● Sugar (white) is granulated, fine granulated, or castor sugar.

● Powdered sugar is icing sugar.

● All-purpose flour is enriched, bleached or unbleached white household flour. When self-rising flour is used in place of all-purpose flour in a recipe that calls for leavening, omit the leavening agent (baking soda or baking powder) and salt.

● Light-colored corn syrup is golden syrup.

● Cornstarch is cornflour.

● Baking soda is bicarbonate of soda.

● Vanilla or vanilla extract is vanilla essence.

● Green, red, or yellow sweet peppers are capsicums or bell peppers.

● Golden raisins are sultanas.

VOLUME AND WEIGHT

The United States traditionally uses cup measures for liquid and solid ingredients. The chart below shows the approximate imperial and metric equivalents. If you are accustomed to weighing solid ingredients, the following approximate equivalents will be helpful.

● 1 cup butter, castor sugar, or rice = 8 ounces = $\frac{1}{2}$ pound = 250 grams

● 1 cup flour = 4 ounces = $\frac{1}{4}$ pound = 125 grams

● 1 cup icing sugar = 5 ounces = 150 grams

Canadian and U.S. volume for a cup measure is 8 fluid ounces (237 ml), but the standard metric equivalent is 250 ml.

1 British imperial cup is 10 fluid ounces.

In Australia, 1 tablespoon equals 20 ml, and there are 4 teaspoons in the Australian tablespoon.

Spoon measures are used for smaller amounts of ingredients. Although the size of the tablespoon varies slightly in different countries, for practical purposes and for recipes in this book, a straight substitution is all that's necessary. Measurements made using cups or spoons always should be level unless stated otherwise.

Common Weight Range Replacements

IMPERIAL / U.S.	METRIC
$\frac{1}{2}$ ounce	15 g
1 ounce	25 g or 30 g
4 ounces ($\frac{1}{4}$ pound)	115 g or 125 g
8 ounces ($\frac{1}{2}$ pound)	225 g or 250 g
16 ounces (1 pound)	450 g or 500 g
1$\frac{1}{4}$ pounds	625 g
1$\frac{1}{2}$ pounds	750 g
2 pounds or 2$\frac{1}{4}$ pounds	1,000 g or 1 Kg

Oven Temperature Equivalents

FAHRENHEIT SETTING	CELSIUS SETTING*	GAS SETTING
300°F	150°C	Gas Mark 2 (very low)
325°F	160°C	Gas Mark 3 (low)
350°F	180°C	Gas Mark 4 (moderate)
375°F	190°C	Gas Mark 5 (moderate)
400°F	200°C	Gas Mark 6 (hot)
425°F	220°C	Gas Mark 7 (hot)
450°F	230°C	Gas Mark 8 (very hot)
475°F	240°C	Gas Mark 9 (very hot)
500°F	260°C	Gas Mark 10 (extremely hot)
Broil	Broil	Grill

*Electric and gas ovens may be calibrated using celsius. However, for an electric oven, increase celsius setting 10 to 20 degrees when cooking above 160°C. For convection or forced air ovens (gas or electric) lower the temperature setting 25°F/10°C when cooking at all heat levels.

Baking Pan Sizes

IMPERIAL / U.S.	METRIC
9×1$\frac{1}{2}$-inch round cake pan	22- or 23×4-cm (1.5 L)
9×1$\frac{1}{2}$-inch pie plate	22- or 23×4-cm (1 L)
8×8×2-inch square cake pan	20×5-cm (2 L)
9×9×2-inch square cake pan	22- or 23×4.5-cm (2.5 L)
11×7×1$\frac{1}{2}$-inch baking pan	28×17×4-cm (2 L)
2-quart rectangular baking pan	30×19×4.5-cm (3 L)
13×9×2-inch baking pan	34×22×4.5-cm (3.5 L)
15×10×1-inch jelly roll pan	40×25×2-cm
9×5×3-inch loaf pan	23×13×8-cm (2 L)
2-quart casserole	2 L

U.S. / Standard Metric Equivalents

$\frac{1}{8}$ teaspoon = 0.5 ml	
$\frac{1}{4}$ teaspoon = 1 ml	
$\frac{1}{2}$ teaspoon = 2 ml	
1 teaspoon = 5 ml	
1 tablespoon = 15 ml	
2 tablespoons = 25 ml	
$\frac{1}{4}$ cup = 2 fluid ounces = 50 ml	
$\frac{1}{3}$ cup = 3 fluid ounces = 75 ml	
$\frac{1}{2}$ cup = 4 fluid ounces = 125 ml	
$\frac{2}{3}$ cup = 5 fluid ounces = 150 ml	
$\frac{3}{4}$ cup = 6 fluid ounces = 175 ml	
1 cup = 8 fluid ounces = 250 ml	
2 cups = 1 pint = 500 ml	
1 quart = 1 litre	